Middle East Terrorism

The International Library of Terrorism

Series Editors:
Yonah Alexander and Alan O'Day

Titles in the Series:

Terrorism: British Perspectives
Paul Wilkinson

Dimensions of Irish Terrorism
Alan O'Day

European Terrorism
Edward Moxon-Browne

Terrorism in Africa
Martha Crenshaw

Middle East Terrorism: Current Threats and Future Prospects
Yonah Alexander

Middle East Terrorism:
Current Threats and Future Prospects

Edited by

Yonah Alexander

The George Washington University

G.K. Hall & Co.
An Imprint of Macmillan Publishing Company
New York

Maxwell Macmillan Canada
Toronto

This American edition published in 1994 by G.K. Hall & Co.,
An Imprint of Macmillan Publishing Company

G.K. Hall & Co.
An Imprint of Macmillan Publishing Company
866 Third Avenue
New York, NY 10022

Maxwell Macmillan Canada, Inc.
1200 Eglinton Avenue East, Suite 200
Don Mills, Ontario M3C 3N1

First published in Great Britain by
Dartmouth Publishing Company Limited
Gower House
Croft Road
Aldershot
Hampshire GU11 3HR
England

Macmillan Publishing Company is part of the Maxwell Communication Group of Companies.

Library of Congress Catalog Card Number: 93-33931

PRINTED IN GREAT BRITAIN

printing number
1 2 3 4 5 6 7 8 9 10

Library of Congress Cataloging-in-Publication Data
Middle East terrorism : current threats and future prospects / edited by Yonah Alexander.
        p.   cm. -- (International library of terrorism : 5)
    Includes index.
    ISBN 0-8161-7337-0 (alk. paper)
    1. Terrorism--Middle East. I. Alexander, Yonah. II. Series.
    HV6431.I546   1994 vol. 5
    [HV6433.M5]
    303.6'25 s--dc20
    [303.6'25'0956]
                                                                93-33931
                                                                CIP

The paper used in this publication meets the minimum requirements of American National Standard for Information Sciences—Permanence of Paper for Printed Library Materials. ANSI Z39.48—194.∞TM

ISBN 0-8161-7337-0

Contents

PART V CHRISTIAN TERRORIST GROUPS

PART VI JEWISH TERRORIST GROUPS

PART VII STATE SPONSORS OF TERRORISM

PART VIII MIDDLE EAST TERRORISM SPILL-OVER INTO OTHER REGIONS

PART IX REGIONAL RESPONSES TO MIDDLE EAST TERRORISM

PART X   INTERNATIONAL RESPONSES TO MIDDLE EAST TERRORISM

Acknowledgements

The editor and publishers wish to thank the following for permission to use copyright material.

The American Academy of Political and Social Science for the essay: Sepehr Zabih (1982), 'Aspects of Terrorism in Iran', *The Annals of the American Academy of Political and Social Science*, **463**, pp. 84–94. Reprinted from *The Annals of The American Academy of Political and Social Science*. Copyright © The American Academy of Political and Social Science.

Center for the Study of the Presidency for the essay: Eytan Gilboa (1990), 'Effects of Televised Presidential Addresses on Public Opinion: President Reagan and Terrorism in the Middle East', *Presidential Studies Quarterly*, **20**, pp. 43–53. Permission granted by the Center for the Study of the Presidency, publisher of *Presidential Studies Quarterly*.

Centre for Conflict Studies for essays: Dennis Pluchinsky (1986), 'Middle Eastern Terrorist Activity in Western Europe: A Diagnosis and Prognosis', *Conflict Quarterly*, **6**, pp. 5–25, and Diane Tueller Pritchett (1988), 'The Syrian Strategy on Terrorism: 1971–1977', *Conflict Quarterly*, **8**, pp. 27–48. Copyright © Centre for Conflict Studies.

Contemporary Review Company Limited for the essay: Robin E. Hill (1990), 'Terrorist Hijackings and the Inadequacies of International Law: A Case Study of the Kuwait Airways Flight 422 Incident', *Contemporary Review*, **257**, pp. 308–16.

Foreign Policy Research Institute for the essay: Daniel Pipes (1989), 'Why Asad's Terror Works and Qadhdhafi's Does Not', *Orbis*, **33**, pp. 501–8. This article originally appeared in the Spring 1984 and Autumn 1989 issues, respectively, of *Orbis: A Journal of World Affairs*, published by the Foreign Policy Research Institute.

Islamic Quarterly for the essay: William C. Chittick (1990), 'The Theological Roots of Peace and War According to Islam', *Islamic Quarterly*, pp. 145–63.

Journal of International Affairs for the essay: Nazih N.M. Ayubi (1982), 'The Politics of Militant Islamic Movements in the Middle East', *Journal of International Affairs*, **36**, pp. 271–83. Published by permission of the *Journal of International Affairs* and the Trustees of Columbia University in the City of New York.

Journal of Palestine Studies for the essay: Rex Brynen (1989), 'PLO Policy in Lebanon: Legacies and Lessons', *Journal of Palestine Studies*, **18**, pp. 48–70.

The Mackenzie Institute for the essay: Evelyn le Chêne (1989), 'Chemical and Biological Warfare – Threat of the Future', *Mackenzie Paper*, pp. 7–29.

Series Preface

The International Library of Terrorism puts into book form a wide range of important and influential academic articles on contemporary terrorist political violence. The articles were initially published in English-language journals or have previously appeared in English. Each volume in the Library is devoted to a specific geographical region which has been afflicted by political terrorism during the past two decades.

Political terrorism has been a concern of national policy in numerous states and received the attention of international bodies including the United Nations. At the same time it has gripped public imagination, on occasion causing disruption in patterns of transnational tourism or influencing international investment decisions. Not surprisingly, political terrorism has found a place in the academic programmes of universities and other educational establishments. In the present series no line of inquiry or ideological outlook is deliberately favoured or excluded - the aim of the Library is to constitute a useful and representative sampling of quality work on terrorism. As the contributions are drawn from previously published studies in periodicals, this imposes perimeters on the sorts of material included. Thus, all volumes reflect an incompleteness resulting from lacuna in the literature. Nevertheless, the series aims to bring into wider accessibility materials scattered throughout many periodicals, some having only limited circulations. Indeed, in no volume can all of the articles selected be located in a single repository, including even the great national and famous university libraries of Great Britain and North America.

Each volume's articles have been chosen by a recognized authority on the political terrorism of the region. In no instance does the omission of a specific article or category of material imply a value judgement, for the selection process has been governed by relevance to a theme, space, and similar considerations. The general editors are grateful to the individuals who compiled each book and prepared the introductions. Their efforts and scholarly judgement are the cornerstone of the series. We wish to express our thanks to John Irwin of Dartmouth Publishing Company, from whom the idea of the Library originally sprang, and who brought the project through some dark hours to fruition. Also, we have appreciated, notably, the kindly efforts of Sonia Hubbard.

YONAH ALEXANDER
The George Washington University
Washington DC

ALAN O'DAY
University of North London, England
and Concordia University, Montreal, Canada

Introduction

Terrorism is as old as history itself. A classic example is the martyrdom missions of the Hashashin (Assassins), an offspring of the Ismailis, targeting the Crusaders and Sunni adversaries in Persia, Syria, and elsewhere in the Middle East from the eleventh to the thirteenth centuries. Their experience has proven that terrorism is attractive, effective, and durable, even if its tools are rather primitive.

In the twentieth century, during the period between the world wars, nationalist groups fought for their liberation from colonial rule, some utilizing terrorist tactics. But it was not until the post-World War II period that Middle East terrorism became institutional, brutal, and global. Several factors have contributed to the escalation of terrorism, including pronounced ethnic and national fragmentation; intensification of religious fundamentalism; and rapid developments in modern technology, communication facilities, and inexpensive and convenient travel.

Another contributing factor to the expansion of contemporary Middle East terrorism is the role of certain states, such as Iran, Iraq, Libya, Sudan and Syria. Because modern weapons and all-out wars are so expensive and destructive, these states restrict themselves systematically to secret low-intensity conflict, well away from the high intensity of open, organized military hostilities. Since state sponsors of terrorism are engaged in operations without having to be held accountable for their actions, they are not usually subject to reprisals by the target states.

It is these political circumstances and technological and military realities that guided both sub-national groups and state actors to employ terrorism as a cost-effective, extra-legal tool in the struggle for power domestically and internationally. Although they are nourished by various political and social roots and sustained by wide-ranging ideologies, sub-state terrorist groups have, nevertheless, a common disposition, namely, contempt and hostility towards the moral and legal norms of the domestic and international order and glorification of violent deeds for the sake of the causes they seek to advance. Terrorists regard themselves as beyond the limit of any society and system of government and, consequently, not bound by any obligations and constraints, except those they have imposed on themselves for purposes of sub-revolutionary and revolutionary success.

These indigenous organizations, mostly acting independently and sometimes as proxies of foreign governments, have proliferated throughout the Middle East. Seeking to achieve ideological, fundamentalist, nationalist, or other goals, these groups have varying objectives. Thus the Kurdish Workers' Party (PKK) is dedicated to establishing a Marxist-Leninist state in southeastern Turkey; the Hizballah aims to form an Iranian-style Shiite Islamic Republic in Lebanon and bring about the elimination of non-Islamic presence and influences from the Middle East; the objective of the Popular Front for the Liberation of Palestine–General Command is to destroy Israel and establish an independent Palestine in its place; the Hamas, a radical Islamic movement in the Gaza Strip and the West Bank, seeks to establish a Palestinian state through the destruction of Israel, to be ruled by the 'Shariah' (Islamic Holy Law); El-Gama'a el-Islamyia (Islamic Grouping) is determined to overthrow the Egyptian government and replace it by an Islamic state; and the Islamic Salvation Front (FIS) in Algeria aims to eliminate the ruling National Liberation Front and establish an Islamic government.

Despite the historic Israeli-Palestinian Peace Agreement signed in Washington, D.C. on 13 September, 1993, Middle East terrorism is alive and well. Radical groups such as the Popular Front for the Liberation of Palestine–General Command and Hamas, with the encouragement of Iran, asserted that they will continue their 'armed struggle'. Terrorist attacks are escalating in Gaza, the West Bank, Israel, and Lebanon. Elsewhere in the Middle East, such as in Egypt and Turkey, the Arab-Israeli peace process is a factor contributing to the expansion of political violence.

Moreover, because the new world order in the post-Cold War era is characterized by numerous political conflicts and arms races, terrorism will inevitably continue to plague the Middle East in the future. What raises the stakes of terrorism in the 1990s and beyond is the danger that the coming years are likely to see probable escalation to biological, chemical, and nuclear violence. A number of state sponsors of terrorism such as Iran, Iraq, and Libya have already undertaken considerable research and development efforts in these fields. If these nations be successful in their efforts, they might provide weapons of mass destruction to proxy terrorist groups in the region.

If a Middle East terrorist group succeeds in achieving its goals through super-terrorism, the temptation for other perpetrators to escalate their operations may become irresistible. The human, physical, psychological and political consequences for regional and global security will be devastating.

The purpose of this volume is to provide a wide range of perspectives on contemporary Middle East terrorism in terms of the nature of the threats and various national, regional, and global responses. To be sure, any serious student of the region will consider this collection as a beginning of a learning process of terrorism as a permanent fixture of international life. Special thanks are due to my research assistants James T. Kirkhope and Ayal Frank in preparing the manuscript for publication.

Yonah Alexander

Part I
Middle East Terrorism:
Past Experiences

[1]

Terrorism in the Middle East:
The Diffusion of Violence

John W. Amos II

The 23 October 1983 bombings of the U.S. Marine and French headquarters in Beirut, with resulting large numbers of casualties, focused world attention on the ability of small groups with limited technological resources to inflict major damage. The use of truck bombs driven by suicidal volunteers seemed to hark back to earlier patterns of terrorism in the Middle East wherein extremist Shiite assassins fanned out from mountain hideouts to strike their victims. Although it may be true in a romantic sense that some Shiite terrorist groups do in fact use traditional organizational and ideological techniques, this obscures a larger pattern of violence that has emerged in the Middle East in the last decade.

EVOLUTION: FROM PROFESSIONALS TO AMATEURS

Modern international terrorism dates from the 1968 hijacking of a Tel Aviv–bound airliner by the Popular Front for the Liberation of Palestine (PFLP). This was the first such attack on an aircraft and represented the introduction of a strategy of conflict designed to exploit both the destructive power and the vulnerabilities of Western technology. In the 1960s and 1970s, Middle Eastern terrorists (principally Palestinian in origin) sought to exploit a number of political and technological trends: (1) the development of air transport systems, which offered easy targets for spectacular terrorist attacks; (2) the emergence of global communication facilities, which facilitated the transmission of terrorist demands; (3) the creation of sophisticated weaponry, which gave small groups the ability to inflict enormous destruction; and (4) the appearance of multiple sources of political and financial support (Beres 1974; Weisband and Roguly 1976).

The original Middle Eastern terrorist organizations were largely secular (e.g., nationalist or Marxist) in organization and orientation and Westernized in terms of education and training. Most of the terrorists were pragmatic professionals in the sense that they had discernible career patterns and a commonality of outlook, and were careful to provide for their own safety. Carlos was the prototype of the Middle Eastern terrorist of the 1960s and 1970s (Dobson and Payne 1977).

In the 1970s, Sunni-Muslim terrorism emerged and nationalistic violence was paralleled by religious violence. In the 1980s, terrorism has become a minority (either ethnic or religious) phenomenon. Existing terrorist groups are now complemented by Christian and Shiite groups. The professional terrorist has given way to the amateur: Terrorists of the 1980s are less well trained (with the exceptions of the Armenians and the Abu Nidal group members) and more extreme in their willingness to risk their own lives. Suicide volunteers now compete for headlines.

The willingness and means to resort to terrorist violence have become more diffuse. Existing Middle East conflicts—for example between the Lebanese, between Iraq and Iran, and between the Palestinians and Israelis—have been increasingly metasticized in scope and impact. The transnational quality of Middle Eastern violence has been accentuated, as has its unfocused quality in the sense that much contemporary terrorist targeting appears randomly directed.

This diffuse and unfocused nature is reflected in the common practice of referring to all of it as "terrorism." In a technical sense, terrorism is any act that in itself is a crime, specifically a violent crime, and that is conducted for psychological purposes. External terrorism, or transnational terror, is terrorism conducted across national boundaries or against citizens of another state. Beyond these generalized observations, there is no agreement on what constitutes terrorism. For example, Israeli spokesmen routinely refer to any Palestinian activity as "terrorism"; similarly, the term *terrorist* has been used by opponents to describe a number of governments in the Middle East and it has been used also to identify combatants in the Lebanese conflict.

Part of the difficulty in defining a person or an act as "terrorist" (aside from propagandistic differences) has to do with the motives, political or otherwise that are associated with the violence. (See Murphy 1975; Jenkins 1981; and Hacker 1976 for attempts to distinguish among the sorts of violence perpetrated by terrorists, criminals, and psychopaths.)

Given the already complex pattern of political and sectarian conflicts within the Middle East, the added problem of distinguishing terrorist from nonterrorist violence becomes almost impossible. But for our purposes here, this article utilizes the following working definition: a terrorist act is an act that is perpetrated for discernible political purposes and that employs more or less identifiable terrorist techniques—assassination, bombing, kidnapping, hijacking, and hostage-taking.

CONFLICT PATTERNS: THE SOURCES AND LINKAGES OF VIOLENCE

Contemporary Middle Eastern terrorism (including even random interpersonal violence) has its roots in the multiplicity of conflicts that characterize the Middle East as a system of politics. At least three sources or levels of conflict are discernible: (1) intracommunal conflicts, that is to say, conflicts between individual cliques, factions, or parties, conflicts that grow out of small groups or organizational structure (an example would be the conflict among factions in the PLO); (2) intercommunal conflicts, which are larger and more inclusive conflicts between ethnic and sectarian groups, conflicts that originate in the relations between these communities (the Lebanese war is an example of a series of these conflicts); and (3) intracultural conflicts, which are more pervasive conflicts between value systems (for example, conflicts that occur between religiously defined communities—Christians and Muslims, or Sunnis and Shi'as) (LeVine 1961; Snyder 1979). Each of these three levels is worked into a fourth level, that of interstate conflict—conflict among the Middle Eastern states themselves or between these states and non–Middle Eastern states: Arab-Israeli, Iraq and Iran, Libya and the United States.

These various levels of conflict are linked by a complex web of shared interests and strategies. The result is a series of cross-cutting coalitions on the part of governments and communal and organizational leaders, which leads to a pattern of violence that not only cross-cuts existing conflicts, but ties in previously unrelated conflicts. For example, Shiite militants in southern Lebanon receive aid from the Iranian government. Aid to these militants, in turn, is a function of conflicts within the Iranian elite. Aid also comes from Syria and Libya. Similarly, Armenian militancy is tied into the Iraq-Iran war by Iranian and Syrian contacts and into European politics by European contacts.

Terrorist linkage politics is not new. Palestinian groups in the early 1970s created linkages with a variety of non–Middle Eastern groups (Sterling 1981). Given the emergence of successive waves of terrorist groups, however, the linkage phenomenon has taken on added dimensions as a device for surrogate conflict: the use of terrorist groups by Middle Eastern governments as an adjunct to regular intelligence and clandestine activities. This use is the product of a realization that conventional violence is far too dangerous; in a sense, it also represents a realization on the part of certain governments that their conventional military capabilities are clearly no match for those of their neighbors. Terrorism, if the responsibility can be mediated through other groups, is a cost-effective way of engaging in violence against both domestic and foreign opponents. Libya and Iran have become the major transnational terror brokers of the early 1980s. The Syrians train (or permit training on Syrian-controlled territories) a number of groups. However, Syrian sponsorship of terrorist groups appears to be limited to groups operating in Lebanon or in countries immediately adjacent to Syria. Iraq, which used to be a major source of support for terrorism, has sharply reduced this activity. Since 1980, Iraqi support appears limited to groups operating against Iran, Syria, and Kurdish nationalists.

VIOLENCE BY SUBMERGED MINORITIES: SHI'A AND ARMENIANS

In contrast to earlier decades when violence was the prerogative mainly of regular governments and/or predominantly Sunni groups, violence in 1984 was mostly a minority phenomenon. Both Shi'a violence and Armenian violence are responses, albeit in a different manner, to the Muslim trend, which accelerated after the 1967 war and brought in its train an intensification of the sectarian aspect of Middle Eastern politics. (On the Muslim trend. see. for example. Lewis 1976; Dekmejian 1980; Dessouki 1973; Ajami 1981; Cudsi and Dessouki 1981; and Esposito 1983.)

Shiite communities were mobilized by the twin impact of the Lebanese conflict and of Khomeini's call for a revolution among the oppressed. meaning a revolution among Shiite populations. This heightened sense of identity has occurred throughout the Gulf region but it is particularly intense in Lebanon where Shiite communities in the south have suffered enormous casualties and destruction of property as a consequence of Israeli-Palestinian military activities in that area. The result on the part of Shiite communities has been to organize in their own defense and articulate their own specifically Shiite interests.

Armenian violence is part of a larger trend of Christian militancy in the Middle East. Heretofore submerged Christian communities have become politically mobilized as a consequence of the Islamic resurgence. The conflict in Lebanon again has accelerated this trend. For a number of Christians. the issue presented by Lebanon is that of the survival of a distinct Christian identity.

Like the Shiites. the position of Christians in the Middle East has been anomalous. The Islamic trend. however. with its emphasis on Muslim-ness. has made the situation of non-Muslims much more visible and much more uncomfortable. Christian communities are progressively more alienated and are suffering their own identity crisis. The rise of nongovernmental Islamic militancy. along with regular governmental repression. have forced Christians into an agonizing reappraisal of their situation. The choice seems to be one of submerging themselves as Christians and losing their identity or seeking a new identity through some form of nationalism. Those Christians who choose the nationalist route have become increasingly more militant in response to the rising tide of violence around them. (For an overview. see Joseph 1983. especially 129ff; Hovannisian 1974; and Joseph and Pillsbury 1978.)

SHIITE ORGANIZATIONS: OLD STRUCTURE. NEW TECHNIQUE

Geographically. Shiite communities stretch in a belt from the east coast of the Gulf through southern Iraq into Iran. parts of northern Syria and southern Lebanon. and up into Azerbaijan. Historically. these communities were religiously distinct from the dominant Sunni communities. relatively isolated both sociologically and geographically from the intellectual and political mainstreams of the area. and relatively disadvantaged in economic terms (Mortimer 1982. 360ff). But even though their religion. sociology, and standard of living would have predisposed them toward revolutionary violence. Shiite communities by and large remained quiescent. (Some Shiite militancy was expressed by young political parties opposed to Sunni establishment.) Shiite quietism took the form of an inward-turning practice of religious study and meditation. *al-taqiyah.* a system of religious study engaged in by Shiite youth in private. The essence of this training was development of an inward sense of identity hidden from public view. Over the years Shiite communities had developed an organizational structure that would support the Shiite religious identity. The basic unit of this structure was the *husayniyah*, a cadre of Shiites concerned with religious and educational activities. By the 1970s, hundreds of husayniyahs were in operation in Iraq and the Gulf area (*Arab Press Service*, 19–26 Sept. 1979); *Arab Press Service*, 28 Dec. 1983). Thus, Shiite communities were, in a structural sense, capable of organized militancy, and in an ideological sense, the tenets of Shiism contained a messianic element that could provide a possible ideological justification for violence (Sachedina 1981). In spite of this, however, Shiite communities remained relatively quiescent until the events in Lebanon and Iran mobilized them.

The emerging Shiite sense of identity (and alienation) was intensified by the Iraq-Iran war, which accentuated Shiite-Sunni tensions throughout the Middle East. In Iraq, the extensive internal security apparatus was particularly concerned to suppress any potential Shiite uprising; in Syria, the minority Shiite elite found itself targeted by Sunni Islamic fundmentalists (in turn, partly organized by the Iraqis). In the Gulf region, both Iranian and Iraqi organizational activities contributed to the mobilization of these populations.

The impulse to convert traditional Shiite social organizations into political organizations with terrorist potential came from both within and without the Syrian community. In Lebanon, the original impetus came from the Amal (hope) movement. Amal was founded by Imam Musa al-Sadr in the middle 1970s. The movement provided military training in Lebanon for Shiites, its main thrust being to organize a force capable of protecting Shiite communities. As such, it became the mainstream movement among Shiites in Lebanon (*al-Watan*, 20 June 1980). (Musa al-Sadr disappeared in 1978 while visiting Libya.)

The Amal maintained its own militia, which participated in the Lebanese National Resistance Front, along with other groups. The Amal militia has carried out a number of attacks against Israeli troops in southern Lebanon. Its members operate in three-man cells using light weapons, basically Kalashnikov rifles, Soviet RPG launchers, and German submachine guns (*Borneo Post*, 9 Sept. 1984). In 1984 these attacks escalated and became a major factor in the Israeli decision to withdraw their forces from southern Lebanon.

However, a number of splinter and more radical Shiite groups rapidly emerged, many of them under the aegis of Iran and Syria. Radical groups within the Amal umbrella now include the Islamic Jihad organization, the Islamic Amal, and the Hizb Allah (Party of God). The Islamic Jihad organization originally had both Syrian and Libyan support, but Libyan links were severed in early 1984 because of a conflict between Qaddafi and the Islamic leadership of the Jihad over Libyan aid to Lebanese Sunni militant groups. The Islamic Amal and Hizb Allah are said to be sponsored by the Iranians, more specifically the radical faction within the Iranian elite headed by the speaker of the Iranian parliament, Hashemi Rafsanjani. Both also have Syrian backing (*Arab Press Service*, 20–27 Aug. 1984; *Arab Press Service*, 26 Nov. 1984).

In Lebanon, Shiite volunteers for the more radical groups are trained at husayniyahs in Shiite-inhabited suburbs in the Beirut area, and in military bases in the Shiite-inhabited parts of the Bekaa Valley. The training centers recruit young volunteers between the ages of seventeen and twenty and put them through a course that is a variation on the traditional taqiyah training. The curriculum is said to take between six and eight weeks to complete. Trained militants are sent to other military camps for training in explosives and other specifically military weaponry and are then assigned targets (*Arab Press Service*. 28 Dec. 1983).

Of the Lebanese Shiite groups, the Islamic Jihad party is the most aggressive in its terrorist activities. It was responsible for the truck bombing of the U.S. embassy in West Beirut in April 1983 (*Washington Post*, 25 Oct. 1983), the bombing of the U.S. and French military headquarters in October 1983, a bombing of a hotel and French military court command post in West Beirut in December 1983, and the bombing of the U.S. embassy in East Beirut in September 1984. The 1983 bombings were one of the major factors in influencing the United States to pull its Marine contingent out of Lebanon (*New York Times*, 24 Oct. 1983: *New York Times*, 22 Dec. 1983). In August 1984, the Islamic Jihad group threatened to "purify" Lebanese territory of American presence and indicated that the July 1984 attack on the Soviet embassy in Beirut was also carried out by it. In December 1984, Jihad gunmen hijacked a Kuwaiti airliner to Tehran. Three passengers were killed before Iranian security forces stormed the plane.

Shiite militancy outside of Lebanon was promoted by Iranians and Syrians. In Iraq, for example, al-Hizb al-Da'wah al-Islamiyah (Party of the Islamic Call) was founded in 1968–69 under the leadership of Imam Muhammad al-Sadr (who was executed by the Iraqi government in 1980.) Hizb al-Da'wah is currently headquartered in Tehran: it has Syrian as well as Iranian support. This was the group responsible for blowing up the Iraqi embassy in Beirut in December 1981, and it has claimed responsiblity for a number of attacks on Iraqi officials both before and after the embassy bombing. Hizb al-Da'wah also claims it made an unsuccessful attempt to assassinate Saddam Hussein himself (*al-Nashrah*. Dec. 1983, 23–25: Batatu 1981).

The group currently is said to be active in Iran, Iraq, Syria, Kuwait, and other Gulf countries. According to its spokesman, its goal is to change the ruling regimes in these countries and set up Islamic republics along the lines advocated by the Khomeini regime (*al-Watan al-'Arabi*, 17–23 Feb. 1984). In this regard, its most spectacular attack was the bombing in December 1983 of the American embassy along with other American, French, and Kuwaiti buildings in Kuwait. At that time, some six bombs were detonated. Twenty-five people were apparently involved, and the weapons and explosives were smuggled into Kuwait from Iran. The personnel themselves moved into Kuwait from Iran via Syria, where they were trained in the use of weapons and explosives.

ARMENIAN TERRORISM: ASSERTION OF A CHRISTIAN IDENTITY

Contemporary Armenian militancy is part of a long tradition of Armenian concern with ethnocultural survival. Historically Armenian communities were both closely integrated internally and isolated from surrounding Muslim society externally. Armenians as a rule did not share the customs or language of majority populations. (The same is true of Assyrian communities in the area.) Armenian nationalist organizations, the Hunchak and Dashnak parties, were founded as early as the 1880s and were concerned with defending the Armenian identity. In this sense, contemporary Armenian terrorist groups are the heirs of these earlier parties.

Armenian militancy today is a specific reaction to the massacre of Armenians carried out by the Young Turks in 1915. The Armenian populations were dramatically and brutally mobilized by the violence. At that time, most of the Armenian community in Turkey was either killed or deported, and survivors were relocated in camps. As a consequence, the Armenian community as a whole became even more alienated from its surrounding populations. (For detailed accounts, see Toynbee 1916; Morgenthau 1918.)

The Armenian Secret Army for the Liberation of Armenia (ASALA) and the Justice Commandos of the Armenian Genocide were formed in 1975. The Armenian Revolutionary Army (ARA) began operations in 1983. Some sources indicate as many as ten to twelve Armenian terrorist organizations may have been active at one time. All these groups share a similar goal of avenging the Turkish genocide of the Armenians. In their formative stages, many of these groups had linkages with Palestine organizations: Armenians received training in PLO camps in Lebanon until 1982. According to some sources, ASALA split with the PLO, specifically Fatah, in the 1980s but remained in contact with Abu Nidal's faction (*al-Nashrah*, 31 Oct. 1983). After the Israeli invasion of 1982, ASALA moved its training camps to Cyprus and Syria (Perera 1984; *Marmara*, 24 Apr. 1984). Apparently some ASALA camps remain in Syrian-controlled areas of the Bekaa Valley.

ASALA is organized in a cell structure along the lines of the Irish Republican Army. The apex of this structure is the General Command of the People of Armenia (VAN). Specifically military policy is drawn up by a political bureau. Each cell is self-sufficient and its members are given only enough information to attack their targets: cell members ordinarily do not know even who their leaders are. This cell structure parallels that of the old Palestinian Black September organization (*ALIK*, 24 Oct. 1983).

ASALA claims to have cadres in a number of countries, including Switzerland, France, West Germany, Italy, the United States, Cyprus, Greece, Australia, Spain, Portugal, and Iran. In addition, the group has had contacts for some time with Kurdish insurgents (*Arab Press Service*, 30 Apr.–7 May 1980), specifically the Kurdish Workers party (PKK) of Turkey, a contact probably mediated by the Palestinians who also trained Kurdish groups (Van Bruinessen 1984). In Lebanon, ASALA was said to have five bases and to be headquartered in Beirut. After 1982, it was headquartered in Paris, and Turkish sources claim that ASALA is now in the process in moving its headquarters to either Spain or Italy (*Marmara*, 25 Sept. 1984).

ASALA is alleged to have a number of ties with other groups—Abu Nidal's Palestinians and the Red Brigades, for example, and through them to still others (*Marmara*, 17 Sept. 1984). The group appears to receive some Syrian training, Greek support via Cyprus, and Iranian assistance (*Marmara*, 31 Mar. 1984). Armenian communities in Iran have been subject to governmental surveillance, and pressure has been put on Armenian schools to teach their curricula in Farsi (*ALIK*, 23 Oct. 1983). Iranian support is said to include target selection: the threat of increased harassment of Armenian communities in Iran is cited probably as an inducement to secure Armenian cooperation.

In 1982, following the loss of its Lebanese base. ASALA is said to have split into two wings, a military and nationalist wing, which stresses terrorism, and a more political wing known as ASALA– Revolutionary Movement, which stresses political action (Perera 1984).

Unlike their Shiite counterparts who employ techniques designed to kill as many as possible, members of ASALA (along with other Armenian organizations) operate in a more classic terrorist tradition. Their main tactics have been the assassination of Turkish diplomatic personnel and the occupation of Turkish embassies. Accordingly, ASALA has been implicated in approximately fifty murders, including twenty-nine Turkish diplomats or their dependents. ASALA in all organized some one hundred attacks on Turkish targets in over fifteen countries. (Again unlike Shiite counterparts. ASALA operates on an international rather than a Middle Eastern scale.)

Extremely sophisticated weapons are used, including antitank rockets, Soviet-made guns, grenades, and other explosives. Also in the classic Western terrorist tradition. ASALA uses a series of safe houses in major cities (Wilkinson 1983).

Not all ASALA attacks have been limited to single individuals. In August 1982, members machine-gunned passengers at the Ankara airport: in June 1983, ASALA terrorists killed two and injured twenty-three people in a bazaar in Istanbul: the next month, a suitcase bomb was exploded at the Orly airport (*New York Times*, 18 July 1983). In 1984, ASALA attacked two Turkish diplomats in Tehran (*Marmara*, 29 Mar. 1984) and claimed responsibility for the shooting of a Turkish businessman in the same city in May (*Tehran Times*, 1 May 1984).

Two other Armenian organizations are also active. The Justice Commandos of the Armenian Genocide is apparently headquartered in California and employs the same tactics as ASALA. In March 1983, the Justice Commandos assasinated the Turkish ambassador in Belgrade. Yugoslavia (*Aztag*, 23 Apr. 1983). The group's first attack occurred in 1975 when it assassinated Turkish ambassadors in Vienna and Paris.

The Armenian Revolutionary Army (ARA) is the newest group. Its first known attacks were the assassination of a Turkish diplomat in Brussels and the occupation of the Turkish embassy in Lisbon. Both of these events took place in July 1983 (*ALIK*, 30 June 1984). Since then it has been extremely active in attacking Turkish officials. In 1984, ARA assassinated two Turkish diplomats in Vienna (*Marmara*, 20 Nov. 1984).

Armenian activities have occasioned great concern in the United States, where it was felt that Armenians might attempt to attack Turkish team members during the 1984 Olympic Games, much as the Black September organization attacked the Israeli team in Munich in 1972. Planning for Olympic security was said to have started as early as 1979, some five years before the games were held (*Los Angeles Times*, 19 Oct. 1983; Charters 1983). Elsewhere, governments have cracked down on Armenian activities, notably Spain, France, and Iran. In Turkey. Armenian communities have been subjected to official surveillance and governmental harassment. Authorities there arrested a group of Armenian goldsmiths: accusations were made under the pretext that they were financially supporting ASALA (*Zartonk*, 7 Dec. 1984).

In addition, it appears that some counterterror operations have been organized allegedly by Turkish intelligence. In 1983 a bomb exploded in the Armenian Cultural Center at Alfortville. France. and in March 1984 a second bomb exploded in the Marseilles Cultural Center (*Le Monde*. 5 May 1984). Other bombs were exploded at Alfortville in May of 1984 and in Paris in November 1984 (*Le Monde*. 5 May 1984: 27 Nov. 1984).

PALESTINIAN TERRORISM: FACTIONALISM AND PROFESSIONALISM

Palestinian terrorist activities in 1983–84 were dominated by the Abu Nidal group. Abu Nidal (code name of Sabri al-Banna) broke with the Fatah establishment in 1972 and formed Fatah–The Revolutionary Command. From the beginning. the Abu Nidal group opposed any diplomatic solution of the Arab-Israeli conflict and accused Yasir Arafat of being too soft on the Israelis. It followed up these accusations with the assassination of PLO moderates. This, in turn. provoked a Fatah riposte in the form of a special counterinsurgency squad organized by Fatah's Salah Khalaf. Both sides train and operate in the old Black September tradition. The Abu Nidal group is relatively small. with about two hundred to five hundred members. and is organized in cells. Most of these cells are in Kuwait and the Gulf states. although there are a number in European cities as well.

Originally the Abu Nidal group was supplied by the Iraqis: since 1980 it has received Libyan and Syrian aid. After 1982. the group joined the Syrian-sponsored anti-Arafat rebellion. Most of the group's training bases currently are located in Libya (*Arab Press Service*. 16–23 Jan. 1984).

Organizationally. the Abu Nidal group is said to be one of the most professional of all terrorist groups. It presently recruits from Arab students studying in Europe. Tactically. terrorist operations are normally carried out by three-man assassination squads. These squads spend some time in advance of the planned attack familiarizing themselves with the city in which the attack is to take place and acquiring weapons. Most of the attacks are aimed at pro-Arafat Palestinians. but the group has carried out a number of attacks on Jordanian officials as well (*Arab Press Service*. 16–23 Nov. 1983: *Arab Press Service*. 3 Sept. 1984: see also a series by Nadim Nasir in *al-Majallah*. 24–30 Mar. through 28 Apr.–4 May 1984). In 1984 the attacks continued in the form of bombings. and Arab sources indicated that the group had received Syrian as well as Libyan support in carrying them out (*Arab Press Service*. 3 Sept. 1984).

In January 1984. Libyan. Iranian. and Abu Nidal representatives met in Tripoli to coordinate a strategy designed to "punish all those regimes which have backed Egypt's return to the Arab fold and the union plans between Jordan and the PLO." According to Arab sources. the punishment objectives were set by the Libyans and Abu Nidal's representatives. while Iran insisted on the inclusion of those regimes supporting Iraq in the war (*Arab Press Service*. 16–23 Jan. 1984).

Abu Nidal himself is said to have died in November 1984 of a heart attack (*al-Watan al-'Arabi* 1984): thus the group's future is uncertain. Arab sources indicate that the group had planned (with Syrian and Libyan encouragement) to infiltrate Palestinian communities throughout the Gulf area and create a broad-based anti-Arafat movement there. The Abu Nidal group also planned to infiltrate pro-Arafat guerrillas who are currently languishing in camps throughout North Africa and the Middle East.

SURROGATE TERRORISM: LIBYA AND IRAN

The major terrorist brokers in the Middle East are Libya and Iran. (Iraq, a strong supporter of terrorism in the 1960s and 1970s, sharply reduced its support for such groups as part of a major policy shift prior to the 1980 war.) Both Libya and Iran support terrorist groups as part of their overall foreign policy objectives of exporting revolution and eliminating expatriate sources of opposition (*Arab Press Service*, 20–27 Aug. 1984).

In line with these general foreign policy objectives, both Iran and Libya have sponsored a number of groups and provided training facilities for others. Although their overall outlines of strategies are the same, their operationalization is different. Libya, for example, is said to maintain thirty-four camps for the training of various revolutionaries. The camps are specialized in terms both of personnel (e.g., special camps set aside for North Africans, as against Palestinians, as against Africans), and of military training techniques. Some camps are devoted to training for desert warfare, others are for training frogmen, and still others teach demolition techniques (*Arab Press Service*, 30 Apr. 1984, contains a list of these camps). Frogmen trained in Libyan camps were thought to be the men who placed mines in the Red Sea; the Islamic Jihad claimed responsibility for the operation (*Kayhan*, 23 Aug. 1984). According to Egyptian sources, training is given to Egyptians, Tunisians, Sudanese, Yemenese, Palestinians, Iraqis, Algerians, Moroccans, Omanis, Iranians, Italians, Japanese, Latin Americans, and others. Instructors come from the U.S.S.R., East Germany, Cuba, and other Communist bloc states (*Arab Press Service*, 7 May 1984; see also Weber 1978).

The Libyan terrorist infrastructure relies heavily on the People's Bureaus. These bureaus function as centers for purchasing arms (particularly in London, Brussels, Paris, Berne, Istanbul, Athens, and Rabat) and for coordinating terrorist activities. According to *Africa Confidential* (1984), key terrorist coordinating centers are the bureaus in Berne, Switzerland, and Madrid, Spain. They apparently coordinate, supply, and dispatch Libyan hit teams, six-member squads whose chief function is the assassination of Libyan expatriates.

In 1983, these teams conducted assassinations in the United States, Italy, France, and West Germany. In April 1984, a series of incidents involving Libyan personnel—a gunman firing from the Libyan embassy in London; a bomb exploding at Heathrow airport; the British embassy besieged in Tripoli—led to a break in relations between Libya and Britain (*Washington Post*, 18 Apr. 1984; New York Times, 22 Apr. 1984). Both sides began deporting the other's nationals. Libyan hit team activities were also directed against members of the National Front for the Salvation of Libya (NFSL) after they attempted a coup against Qaddafi in May of 1984. The NFSL itself was made up of members of the Muslim Brethren and received support from the Sudan (al-Mukhtar 1984). People's Bureaus' activities are supplemented by a series of front groups and private individuals who operate in Europe, the Middle East, Asia, Africa, and Latin America (Tariq 1984).

Whereas Libyan activities are more or less standard terrorism, the Iranians have opted for a much more exotic symbiosis of modern and traditional forms of violence. On the one hand. Iranian embassy personnel throughout Europe. and particularly in Spain, have been accused of sponsoring terrorist cadres in several countries. In late 1983. Spanish police arrested a number of Iranians who confessed that they were planning to attack expatriate Iranian opponents of the Khomeini regime (*Arab Times*. 13 Oct. 1984, 5).

In December 1983. the French government expelled several Iranian diplomats. According to French sources. the Iranian embassy in Paris served as a center for the organization of cadres of terrorists. whose main function was the listing. location. and assassination of anti-Khomeini Iranians. Regular embassy resources were supplemented by cultural and student organizations.

The Iranian strategy here was to train terrorists in Syrian and Libyan camps and then send them abroad with diplomatic cover. In France. 150 to 300 such "students" were said to be supervised by embassy personnel (*Liberation*. 30 Dec. 1983). Iranian liquidation squads are suspected to be operating as far afield as the Philippines (*Bulletin Today*. 3 Dec. 1983. 6) and Indonesia (*Asiaweek*. 4 Nov. 1983).

Iranian-conducted terrorism. however. has been directed at other targets as well. In August 1984. Spanish police arrested four Iranians, members of the Martyrs of the Iranian Revolution. in connection with a plot to hijack a Saudi airliner. The Iranian press attaché was said to be in contact with the Martyrs. In the same month. a French airliner was hijacked to Tehran. The hijackers demanded the release of Iranians jailed in France following an attempt to assassinate Shapur Bakhtiari in 1980 (*Washington Post*, 2 Aug. 1984). Following the hijacking. Iranian spokesman described it as a "lesson for France" because of French policies toward both Iraq and Iranian expatriates living in France (*Le Quotidien*. 6 Aug. 1984).

On the other hand. Iranian activities in the Middle East have also utilized Shiite husayniyahs and other traditional Shiite organizations. In Lebanon. for example. Iranian volunteers began training with the Amal movement as early as 1979. These volunteers later returned to Iran to become part of the Pasdaran (Mortimer 1982. 372).

The introduction in 1982 of Iranian Revolutionary Guard units in Lebanon enabled the Iranians to penetrate the Shiite community. Iranians helped organize Amal splinter groups, the Islamic Amal. the Hizbullah (Partisans of God). and the Islamic Jihad. The Guards. the Hizbullah. and Syrian intelligence all cooperate in organizing terrorism (*Newsweek*. 7 Nov. 1983. 90: *Arab Press Service*. 26 Nov. 1984: *al-Majallah* 1983).

Terrorist training in both Iran and Syria began in early 1983 (*Arab Press Service 3*. 20–27 Aug. 1984). In Iran. two camps are maintained for the training of "suicide" volunteers. According to Arab sources. the number being trained in these camps rose sharply following the attack on the U.S. embassy in April 1983. The largest camp, outside of Qum. is said to have about two thousand personnel (*Liberation*. 30 Dec. 1983). Volunteers for the training are selected by Iranian embassy officials in the Middle East and Europe. The programs, which last approximately three weeks. involve training in truck bombing and the use of weapons and explosives. and attendance at ideological indoctrination sessions. Palestinian. Cuban. Syrian. and Polisario personnel are said to serve as instructors. After graduation. the trainees are then given

their assignments (Nurizadah 1983). Some of them go into the Basij forces,
which are used in suicidal attacks against the Iraqis (*Arab Press Service*, 27
Feb. 1984).

CONCLUSION: THE SYMBIOTIC USE OF VIOLENCE

Violence in the Middle East in the middle of the 1980s has taken on a new
dimension. The old pattern of conventional warfare is being increasingly replaced by violence predicated upon small-scale operations involving small
numbers of individuals using sophisticated weaponry. Violence, which used to
be the prerogative of governments or majority populations, is now increasingly
filtering down to minorities. The use of terrorism as a political technique for
inducing governmental change and/or symbolically expressing minority grievances has become more and more widespread. Professional terrorism is being
augmented by suicidal amateur terrorism. Random violence has increased; any
limitation that pragmatism may have placed on terrorist violence is rapidly
eroding.

In addition, however, a more profound trend is occurring: that is the
amalgam between traditional social structure and twentieth-century weapons
technology. This trend started in the 1960s and 1970s when Palestinian groups
utilized traditional social organization and kinship structure as the basis for a
sophisticated terrorist organizational format. Similarly, Sunni fundamentalist
organizations in the 1970s, or more specifically, offshoots of the Muslim Brethren made use of existing kinship linkages as a basis for organized revolutionary
violence. What is new is that this particular symbiosis has been adopted by a
succession of groups, predominantly the Shiites and, to a lesser extent, the
Armenians. As a long-term trend in the region, the diffusion of the technology
of violence will produce long-term instability.

REFERENCES

Africa Confidential 1984. No. 9 (Apr.): 1–4.

Ajami, Fouad. 1981. *The Arab predicament: Arab political thought and practice
since 1967.* Cambridge: Cambridge University Press.

Batatu, Hanna. 1981. Iraq's underground Shi'a movement: Characteristics, causes,
and prospects. *Middle East Journal.* Autumn.

Beres, Louis Rene. 1974. Guerrillas, terrorists, and polarity: New structural models
of world politics. *Western Political Science Quarterly* 27 (Dec.): 624–36.

Charters, David A. 1983. Terrorism and the 1984 Olympics. *Conflict Quarterly.*
Summer. 37–47.

Cudsi, Alexander S., and Ali E. Hillal Dessouki, eds. 1981. *Islam and power.*
Baltimore, Md.: Johns Hopkins University Press.

Dekmejian. R. Hrair. 1980. The anatomy of the Islamic revival: Legitimacy crisis. ethnic conflict, and the search of Islamic alternatives. *Middle East Journal* 34, no. 1 (Winter): 1–12.

Dessouki. Ali E. Hillal. 1973. Arab intellectuals and al-Nakba: The search for fundamentalism. *Middle Eastern Studies* 9, no. 2 (May): 187–96.

Dobson. Christopher. and Ronald Payne. 1977. *The Carlos complex: A study in terror.* New York: C. Putnam & Sons.

Esposito. John L., ed. 1983. *Voices of resurgent Islam.* New York: Oxford University Press.

Hacker. Frederick J. 1976. *Crusaders. criminals. crazies: Terror and terrorism in our time.* New York: W.W. Norton & Co.

Hovannisian. Richard G. 1974. Ebb and flow of the Armenian minority in the Arab Middle East. *Middle East Journal* 28 (Winter): 19–32.

Jenkins. Brian M. 1981. The study of terrorism: Definitional problems. In *Behavioral and quantitative perspectives on terrorism.* edited by Yonah Alexander and John M. Gleason. 3–10. New York: Pergamon Press.

Joseph. John. 1983. *Muslim-Christian relations and inter-Christian rivalries in the Middle East: The case of the Jacobites in an age of transition.* Albany: State University of New York Press.

Joseph. Suad. and Barbara L.K. Pillsbury. eds. 1978. *Muslim Christian conflicts: Economic. political and social origins.* Boulder. Colo.: Westview Press.

LeVine. Robert A. 1961. Anthropology and the study of conflict: Introduction. *Journal of Conflict Resolution* 5:3–15.

Lewis. Bernard. 1976. The return of Islam. *Commentary* 61. no. 1 (January): 39–49.

al-Majallah. 1983. No. 195 (5–11 Nov.): 10–12.

Morgenthau. Henry. 1918. *Ambassador Morgenthau's story.* New York: Doubleday.

Mortimer. Edward. 1982. *Faith and power: The Politics of Islam.* New York: Random House.

al-Mukhtar. Omar. 1984. The struggle for Libya. *Arabia. the Islamic World Review.* no. 34 (June): 6–13.

Murphy. John F. 1975. International legal controls of international terrorism: Performance and prospects. *Illinois Bar Journal.* Apr. 444–52.

Nurizadah. 'Ali. 1983. The Gulf: An exciting investigation of a 'base' for launching terrorists. *al-Dustur.* nos. 318–19 (26 Sept.): 14–15.

Perera. Judith. 1984. Who can heal Armenian wounds? *Middle East Magazine.* no. 116 (June): 29–30.

Sachedina. Abdulaziz Abdulhussein. 1981. *Islamic messianism: The idea of the Mahdi in twelver Shiism*. Albany: State University of New York Press.

Snyder. Lewis W. 1979. Minorities and political power in the Middle East. In *The political role of minority groups in the Middle East*. edited by R.D. McLaurin. 240–65. New York: Praeger Publications.

Sterling. Claire. 1981. *The terrorist network*. New York: Readers Digest Publications.

Tariq. Abi. 1984. The terrorists' intelligence agencies and the policy of fronts. *al-Inqadh*. no. 8 (Apr.): 37–39.

Toynbee. Arnold. 1916. *The treatment of Armenians in the Ottoman Empire. 1850–1860*. London: His Majesty's Stationery Office.

Van Bruinessen. Martin. 1984. The Kurds in Turkey. *MERIP Reports*. 6–12 Feb.. 14.

al-Watan al-'Arabi. 1984. No. 405 (16–23 Nov.): 26–30.

Weber. Tom. 1978. The strange capital of world terrorism. *San Francisco Chronicle*. 9. 11. 19 Oct.

Weisband. Edward. and Damir Roguly. 1976. Palestinian terrorism: Violence. verbal strategy and legitimacy. In *International terrorism: National regional and global perspectives*. edited by Yonah Alexander. 258–319. New York: Praeger Publishers.

Wilkinson. Paul. 1983. Armenian terrorism. *World Today*. Sept. 344–50.

[2]

Conflict Quarterly

The Syrian Strategy on Terrorism:

1971 - 1977

by
Diane Tueller-Pritchett

INTRODUCTION

In October 1986, Nizar Hindawi, a Palestinian of Jordanian extraction, was found guilty by the British courts of concealing explosives in a secret compartment of his pregnant girlfriend's suitcase with the intent of blowing up an El-Al flight on its way from London to Israel. During an internationally publicized trial, the British government had alleged that Hindawi had acted under instructions from the Syrian intelligence service, traveled to London under a false name on a Syrian diplomatic passport and had received active cooperation and encouragement from the Syrian embassy staff. As a result, two days after the trial the United Kingdom announced the severance of diplomatic relations with Syria. The United States, Canada and Austria, supporting Britain, withdrew their ambassadors from Damascus in protest of the Syrian government's involvement in terrorism.

The Hindawi trial and the subsequent "punishment" of Syria was the culmination of increasing frustration among Western states, and the United States in particular, with terrorism in the Middle East. During 1985 and 1986 the United States led efforts to punish states which supported or approved of the use of terrorism. In various speeches and publications, the American administrators singled out Iran, Libya and Syria as the main "criminals" behind terrorism and advocated a tough policy of fighting terrorists through diplomatic isolation, intelligence gathering, economic pressures, strong condemnations and, as a last resort, military reprisals to punish "these perpetrators of violence."[1]

Any policy to combat the use of terrorism in the Middle East cannot ignore the fact that there has been a continual state of war in the region for forty years. Every state and every group in the Middle East has committed an act of terror as part of a larger strategy towards the war. Solutions to the problem of terrorism will come only with an understanding of the various strategies towards the larger conflict. This is particularly true of Syria which is an important front-line state in the Arab-Israeli conflict.

To understand the Syrian use of terrorism, it is necessary to examine Syrian strategy within the context of its policy towards the Arab-Israel conflict. This research attempts to deepen this understanding by addressing three main questions: when does Syria use terrorism and against whom; what is Syria trying to accomplish when it does use terrorism; and is Syrian terrorism related to the Arab-Israeli conflict? The patterns that emerge from an exhaustive study of terrorist events suggest that during the period studied, Syria used terrorism in four instances: 1) to create

pressure in specific situations of negotiation; 2) to express adamant rejection of policy which would leave Syria regionally isolated; 3) to alleviate
strain caused by internal disagreement over the regime's Arab-Israeli
policy; and 4) to keep the Arab-Israeli conflict simmering when there are
no international or regional plans for war or peace. Conversely, Syria cut
back on terrorism under three circumstances: 1) to comply with a specific
agreement such as the Golan I agreement; 2) when the regime is feeling
strong internally and not isolated externally; and 3) when it needs to
avoid the rish of premature war. The strongest conclusion of this study is
that Syria's use of terrorism is related to the Arab-Israeli conflict and
that Syria can, does and has controlled the use of terrorism when other
viable options towards its conflict with Israel are presented.

METHODOLOGY

The conclusions about Syrian terrorism were reached through a
detailed analysis of Syrian policy and action from 1971 to 1977. There
were several reasons for choosing this six year period. It was necessary to
limit the range of years studied because no work has been done
specifically on Syrian terrorism and therefore no public data bank exists.
Limiting the time-span allowed for detailed examination of each terrorist
incident. Secondly, 1971 was chosen as a good starting point because it
marks the beginning of the Asad regime and thus conclusions would still
have relevance as long as Asad maintains power. Finally, the period from
1971 to 1977 is a fruitful time to study Syrian policy towards the Arab-
Israeli conflict because it was a period of great activity and allows for a
look at Syrian action both under conditions of conflict and negotiation.

Once the time period was established, information was gathered.
Hard evidence of Syrian involvement in terrorism is fragmentary and difficult to come by both because of the professionalism of the operations
and the intelligence nature of the information.[2] The only way to gather
information is to comb through newspapers and terrorism chronologies
with a list of assumptions about acts that were either Syrian sponsored
or, at the minimum, Syrian approved. Information was collected from
FBIS, *Arab Report and Record, New York Times, an-Nahar Arab
Report* and Mickolus' *Transnational Terrorism: A Chronology of
Events, 1968-1979.*

The assumptions determining Syrian acts were developed through a
survey of the literature on Syrian-Palestinian relations, analysis of Syrian
press commentaries and official speeches, and a survey of official visits
and military maneuvers. During his sixteen years in power, Asad has
built up an enormously complex intelligence network with several secret
services and agencies assigned to work with various Palestinian terrorist
organizations. Syria has generally carried out terrorism in three ways: 1)
through Saiqa, the Syrian/Palestinian group which is virtually an integrated part of the Syrian army; 2) in collaboration with and giving
logistical support to Palestinian groups which remain largely their own
masters when outside of Syria;[3] and 3) using 'cutouts' or lone terrorists
to accomplish a specific action. The list of specific assumptions guiding

this research and derived from the above information is included in the appendix.

Over 200 separate incidents were gathered and organized into a monthly chronology briefly describing each event. (See attached appendix.) The amount of activity was totaled by month to give a general indicator of an increase or decrease in activity.[4] The chronology of Syrian terrorism was then analyzed by comparing the monthly terrorist activities to other political activities and to the foreign policy goals being pursued at that time. What follows is a yearly summary from 1971 to 1977 of Syrian policy towards the Israeli dispute, highlighting the use of terrorism in order to ascertain when and why Syria uses terrorism as a tactic.

SYRIAN STRATEGY UNDER HAFIZ AL-ASAD

The challenge of Syrian foreign policy under Hafiz al-Asad has been to end the costly conflict with Israel while guaranteeing domestic stability and regime survival. The recovery of the Golan Heights has always been the main priority because the Baath Party's and the military's domestic prestige is perceived by Syrian policy-makers as being tied up in the Golan. As a military regime, Asad and his advisors are conscious of the defense posture of Syria.[5] Asad's legitimacy is also linked, via the Baathi heritage of his regime, to Arab nationalism. All Syrian actions must therefore, at the minimum, be rhetorically rooted in Arab unity.[6]

Syria, under Hafiz al-Asad, has cautiously accepted the principle of negotiation to resolve the conflict with Israel.[7] It has always insisted, however, that this be conducted in an international arena and in partnership with others. Syria is a small country (a population of approximately 9.5 million) and a poor country (per capita income is below $2000). It is easily dwarfed by the size of Egypt, the wealth of Saudi Arabia, and the development of Israel and has always feared being ignored because of that. The only card Syria has felt it holds in bargaining is the ability to insure nothing succeeds without its participation. Syria's strategic position, its military strength, and the territory from which that strength can be directly deployed (Lebanon, Golan) allows it to influence decisively any option against Israel. However, alone, it cannot defeat Israel nor can it hope to persuade Israel to bargain. Syria therefore seeks partners.[8] Operating in partnership with other Arabs also allows Syria to bolster its Arab legitimacy.

A negotiated solution to the conflict with Israel is not an easy option for Syria because of the nature of its political system. It is much more difficult for Damascus to think of contracting out of the conflict than it was for Cairo. Syria has no reason to believe the Israelis can easily be persuaded into returning the Golan and Syria has not yet had the desperate economic problems which would force the regime to choose butter over guns. Syria is also more geographically enmeshed in the conflict and the Palestinian ties are stronger because of the "Greater Syria" idea left over from colonial days and revived in the late 70s. Most importantly, the legacy of radical nationalism and a strong party system which curtails the president's freedom of action in foreign policy, coupled with a regime dependent on a minority and iron-fisted rule, has made reaching a negotiation consensus difficult.[9]

Embedded in the recent history of the Baath Party in Syria is a division over the means of resolving the conflict with Israel.[10] Ideological orthodoxy, represented prior to Asad in Salah Jadid and his radical civilian supporters, calls for a people's war of liberation against Israel in association with the Palestinians. The more pragmatic Asad and his military supporters argue for a strengthened army and a conventional battle against Israel in alliance with other Arabs.[11] Although Asad preempted the debate through a coup, ideological purity remains in the Baath Party and in the Palestinian alliance to continually pressure moves towards a negotiating stance. The challenge of Syrian foreign policy towards the conflict with Israel is to develop a negotiating position that will not only yield results (regain the Golan), but that will insure the security of Syria and of the regime while maintaining credible radical ideological orthodoxy. A year by year analysis of Syrian policy from 1971 to 1977 will demonstrate some of the tactics used to further these goals.

1971: Hafiz al-Asad did three things upon coming to power in November 1970. He sought to end Syria's isolation by joining the Tripoli Charter, an alliance between Egypt, Sudan and Libya, which signalled his intention to wage a conventional battle against Israel. Secondly, he subtly accepted the principal of a negotiated solution by turning to the Soviet Union for arms.[12] Finally, he ordered the reorganization and control of the fedayeen groups. The year of 1971 was spent implementing these actions. In January, the presidents of the Tripoli Charter states met and agreed "to mobilize their various resources and capabilities in order to eliminate the effects of the aggressor [and] liberate Arab territory."[13] Preparations for battle included military union with Egypt, putting all forces under one command in March, visiting the Soviet Union for arms in February and a series of crack-downs on the Palestinians in January, at the end of June, early July and October.[14] Sadat later revealed that war was intended for the end of November or December.

The terrorist activity during 1971, when Syria was planning the battle with Egypt and when, for a short period of time in November and December, the battle was imminent, was lower than the previous three years (not included in this study). In November and December, when war was expected, the activity was at its lowest of the year. The highest months of activity, January, July and October are all followed by months of dramatic decreases in activity and coincide with the crack-downs on fedayeen freedom. It suggests that the Asad regime, as it was increasing controls on fedayeen, allowed a brief increase in action to defray internal opposition to such a policy. There is also a slight increase in action at the end of March when the Baath Congress and general elections were being held. From 1971 it can be concluded that terrorism increased for internal reasons and decreased when conventional battle plans emerged.

1972: This was a year of frustration for Syrian strategy. The 1971 war plans had fallen apart because of lack of supplies and organization and, according to Sadat, because superpower attention had been diverted by the Indian-Pakistani war. In February, Asad met with Sadat and Qaddafi to discuss options towards Israel. Libya and the Palestinians were pressuring Asad to "take a true stand on the battle . . . every state has the duty to let Palestinians operate from its territory . . . escalation of the fedayeen is an essential step so long as we cannot wage a decisive battle."[15] Syria was also having problems with Egypt because of Sadat's Soviet dispute. Lacking the cohesive alliance needed to wage a conventional battle, Syria renewed the non-conventional warfare option. In June, *al-Ahram* reported secret resolutions between the three federated states "providing support for the fedayeen action and approving its operations from all fronts."[16] Although Syria accepted the short-term strategy of terrorism until conventional battle plans could be arranged, it changed the nature of the attacks so as to avoid triggering a surprise retaliatory attack on the Golan. Lt. Colonel Izz ad-Din Idris, Assistant Director of the Political Bureau of the Syrian Army (the branch in charge of supervising Palestinians), called upon the fedayeen to "adopt the principle of mobile bases instead of fixed bases . . . [noting] maneuverability, flexibility and initiative are among the most important tactical qualities of guerrilla warfare."[17] Many of the restrictions imposed on the guerrillas in 1971 were temporarily lifted during this period.

March 1972 was an important month for policy because it was the first time Asad publicly stated his regime's cautious commitment to a negotiated or "political" solution to the conflict. While at the same time searching for a battle alliance and while still determined to fight, the Asad regime was also introducing the negotiating option.

The highest amount of terrorist activity of the six years studied was in 1972. The activity in the second half of the year is notable because it reflects the tactic of mobile bases. In August the first sign of Syrian involvement outside the immediate war region is seen. September, a month of intense activity, mostly because of the flagrance of the acts (Munich and the letter bombs),[18] was the lowest point in Syrian-Egyptian relations because Sadat had expelled the Soviets and thus erased any chance of acquiring sufficient arms for war. The Asad regime was caught during 1972 in the difficult position of trying, but failing, to maintain a semi-moderate position towards the Arab-Israeli conflict. As long as there was no positive action towards a conventional battle in alliance with Egypt, to maintain internal stability and credibility, non-conventional tactics were used. The only two months of low activity were March and May during which time Syria was talking to Egypt and the Soviet Union about renewing battle plans.

1973: The year of the battle was the high point of the early Asad strategy. At the beginning of 1973, Syria was in the difficult position of having allowed fedayeen action escalate to the point of subjecting civilians to retaliatory IDF bombing. There were reports of open tension between local residents and fedayeen because of civilian deaths and property damage.[19] In response, Syria attacked Egypt and Libya for failing to support it in 'the battle' and threatened to withdraw from the alliance unless conventional war plans were put into motion. The Syrian army once more imposed controls over fedayeen activity and ordered the evacuation of the Golan area.[20] On April 22, 1973, Asad and Sadat secretly agreed to launch a surprise attack against Israel across the Golan and Sinai cease-fire lines in the coming fall. The attack was launched in October. Although Syria lost rather than gained territory, the success involved in the surprise and in achieving international attention placed Syria in a relatively strong bargaining position but only for as long as the partnership with Egypt could be maintained. Syria accepted the UN-sponsored cease-fire and November and December were dedicated to working out the Syrian position towards an international conference.

The pattern of Syrian terrorism in 1973 is simple. It abated from 1972 levels in January because the cost of Israeli reprisals was threatening the regime. Once a war decision was made in April, terrorism practically disappeared except for two outrageous acts in July and September which were clearly meant to goad Israel and distract attention away from the Golan as war preparations were being put into place. During November and December, while the decision about Geneva was being made, there were continual cease-fire violations but these were all carefully controlled conventional violations. The terrorist activity in 1973 demonstrates that when civilians were threatened or when conventional war plans were in place, Syria lowered and carefully controlled fedayeen action.

1974: January through May of 1974 was a time of intense consultation and negotiation for Syria, the purpose of which was to solidify Syria's position with regards to negotiation. There was strong internal disagreement over the position Syria should take in the Kissinger peace efforts. One approach insisted on coordinating policy with Egypt, accepting a disengagement agreement, and attending Geneva without demanding prior Israeli withdrawal from the Golan. The second group argued for a policy independent of Egypt, coordination with the Palestinians, and a continuation of the boycott of Geneva until Israel withdrew from the Golan. Syrian generals were said to be particularly suspicious of talks at a time when Israel was reasserting that its forces would never withdraw from the Golan.[21] These differences were eventually overcome; on April 9, a Syrian delegation left for Washington to begin negotiations with Kissinger on the Golan. It took two months of arduous diplomacy but on May 29, 1974, the Golan I agreement was signed which included a tacit Syrian promise (via a note from the United States to Israel) not to allow further fedayeen action from the Golan.

The remainder of 1974 was spent trying to move towards a Geneva conference by first settling the Palestinian issue. Syria's policy was to insure control over any Palestinian delegation to Geneva. In the latter part of the year a serious rift developed between Syria and Egypt as it became clear Sadat meant to go ahead with the second stage of disengagement without a concomitant agreement on the Golan. Syrian strategy then turned from alliance with Egypt to the international front where it began a European diplomatic offensive emphasizing Syria's negotiating stance.

Arafat's address before the United Nations was seen by Syrian policy-makers as a victory for this strategy.

Terrorist activity during 1974 is closely related to the negotiating position and internal politics. During the entire five month negotiation period, Syria and Israel carried on high level artillery and air battles. Although terrorist forces may have participated in this activity, it was all waged on a conventional level. Syria's tactic of fighting while talking is a product of its political system designed to reduce the strength of domestic groups opposed to negotiation while simultaneously pressuring Israel and demonstrating the unacceptability of the status quo. In April, two days after the Syrian delegation arrived in Washington to open negotiations, there was a flagrant terrorist attack on Qiryat Shemona[22] which was clearly meant to pressure Israel and to relieve inner hostility against negotiation. The same is true of the dramatic Maalot attack in May. By allowing these attacks Syria could send a dual message—one to Israel and one to its radical critics. The other attention getting attack on a Beit Shean apartment house in November, a few days before the UNDOF six-month mandate was about to expire, served the same emphatic purpose. Terrorist action increased in August and September but it no longer came from the Golan. The data shows that except in two instances, one in 1975 and one in 1976, Syria held to the Golan agreement on terrorism. The activity in August and September came from Jordan and was meant to pressure Jordan, in addition to Israel, because at the end of July Jordan had signed an agreement with Egypt concerning the status of the PLO which excluded Syria. Terrorism decreased again in November and December when there was a serious threat of war with Israel. (Kissinger warned Syria of a possible Israeli attack during his November visit.)

1975: During the first half of 1975, Syria continued attempts to negotiate a resolution by going along with Kissinger's efforts in January and February and, when those broke apart, by asking the Soviets to reconvene Geneva. Syria also continued its public relations offensive in the Western press as a way of seeking alternatives to superpower mediation. In March, Asad gave an interview and declared that Syria was "seriously and explicitly interested in reaching a final peace settlement with Israel provided that it included the creation of a Palestinian state."[23] Syrian policy in the latter half of the year began to change as it became clear that the alliance with Egypt was not going to settle the conflict in Syria's best interests. Increased involvement in Lebanon led to a more ambitious strategy designed to gain hegemony over the immediate Arab environment in competition with Egypt rather than cooperation. As relations with Egypt worsened, due to Egypt's separate negotiations with Kissinger, Syria began to seek other partners in the Palestinians and King Hussein. This would lead to the Lebanese invasion in 1976.

Terrorism in 1975 agrees with previously observed patterns. In January and February, as Kissinger was renewing his efforts and while Syria still had hopes of being included in the negotiation process, terrorist action was low. In March, when Egypt decided to go ahead with

Kissinger without Syria an emphatic act was committed clearly designed to embarrass Egypt and remind the United States and Israel that Syria, via the Palestinians, could not be ignored. In April, May, June, and July, terrorist activity was low as Syrian hopes for an international conference grew. However, in September, when Sinai II was signed and Syria was left isolated without legitimate alternatives, action increased. In November another outrageous act occurred in time for the UNDOF expiration as a reminder that Syria still considered itself to be at war.

1976: This was a year of inactivity on the Arab-Israeli front but of great activity for Syrian policy as it attempted to settle the Lebanese problem in a way that would benefit its position *vis-à-vis* Israel. The invasion of Lebanon was, in part, designed to further the Eastern Front strategy where Palestinian leadership would be "restructured to accommodate Syrian policy [so that Syria would] emerge as a dominant factor in the Middle East settlement because it was able to deliver Syrians, Jordanians, Lebanese and Palestinians to a settlement."[24]

Relations with Egypt continued to be strained in the first half of 1976 as did relations with Saudi Arabia and the Soviet Union who both objected to Syrian interference in Lebanon. However, in October, once its position in Lebanon had been established, Syria acknowledged Arab pressure and reconciled with Sadat. Sadat agreed not to push for Syrian withdrawal from Lebanon and Asad agreed to end criticism of Sinai II and resume diplomatic relations and cooperation with Egypt. Syria had, in a sense, reached a position of equality with Egypt and that, combined with the newly established control over the Palestinians, gave Syria the needed strength to proceed with a bargaining process. With the election of Jimmy Carter, the future for a negotiated solution to the conflict with Israel looked bright.

Terrorist activity in 1976 related to domestic concerns. Heavily involved in Lebanon, Syria and its Palestinian allies could not afford to wage a battle of subterfuge with Israel. The only two months of significant activity are April and July. In April, one of the two acts committed was undertaken against a Palestinian group thus pressuring it to conform to Syrian peace-making efforts. The other brief action on the Golan could be related to the need to divert domestic and Palestinian attention away from Syrian collusion with the United States and rightist elements in Lebanon. The series of explosions in July was designed to defray the growing opposition within Syria to the Lebanese invasion. That the terrorist activity was low is consistent with the observation that when engaged in conventional warfare, Syrian terrorist activity decreases.

1977: January 1977 was a time of optimism for the Arabs and particularly for Syria. The Arab coalition, on the surface, was strong: the Palestinians were chastened and under control; Syrian relations with Jordan and Egypt were good; Israel had indicated a willingness to negotiate (September 1976); and Carter was anxious to try his hand at resolving the conflict.

On March 9, 1977, Carter issued a statement which appeared to

34

support the Israeli policy of not returning all the land acquired in 1967. This was a change from previous American policy. In reaction, the Syrian government newspaper *al-Thawrah* responded with the strong statement that the only "just solution to the Middle East conflict lay in total Israeli withdrawal."[25] This represented a hardening of the Syrian position. However, *Tishrin,* a better indicator of Asad's mood, adopted a more conciliatory tone indicating that the regime, while still probably divided, was willing to give Carter a chance. The Asad government continued efforts towards reconvening a Geneva conference which led to a successful meeting between Carter and Asad in May. However, before the good will of that meeting could be translated into policy, Israeli elections produced a more militant line from Israel which changed the Syrian mood dramatically. Syrian suspicions about a separate peace approach were seemingly confirmed in the summer when, during Vance's tour of the Middle East, Egypt and the United States proposed the idea of a 'working group' of foreign ministers to meet before Geneva as a way of circumventing the Palestinian issue. Syria saw the proposal as an attempt to split the Arab bargaining position. During this period Syria was also facing internal opposition to the Lebanese occupation as well as increased Israeli involvement in Lebanon and therefore did not have the strength to accept change in the negotiation process. As a result, the Syrian line hardened. In November, Sadat made his historic decision to go to Jerusalem.

According to Syrian policy-makers, Sadat's action destroyed everything Syria had been working for. The only cards Syria felt it had in bargaining were the threat of activating the war option, kept believable through Arab unity, Soviet backing in negotiation, and the withholding of the recognition of Israel until Arab demands were met. Sadat erased all three Syrian strengths by going to Jerusalem. Given the nature of its domestic political arrangements and the increasing Israeli challenge in Lebanon, Syria was not capable of following Sadat's initiative. The momentum moved away from an international conference towards a separate Egyptian-Israeli settlement leaving Syria isolated and immobilized. In a sense, Syria was back to the stalemated position of 1972 with no hopes for peace and no potential for war.

Terrorist patterns were consistent with previous years. In January and February, while embarking on a new plan for negotiation, there was no terrorist activity. In March there was a brief flurry of activity in response to Carter's statement which was most likely meant to quell internal disagreement about trusting Carter. Terrorism disappeared again until June and then rapidly escalated in July and August in reaction to rising Israeli militancy and American/Egyptian agreements. The attacks stopped in September and October when Israeli aircraft and tanks entered Southern Lebanon thus directly threatening Syrian conventional forces. Terrorism predictably rose again to high levels in November and December in reaction to the isolation and frustration caused by Sadat's Jerusalem visit and was directed against Egypt as well as Israel.

CONCLUSIONS

The Syrian use of terrorism from 1971 to 1977 can be explained in terms of Syrian strategy towards the Arab-Israeli conflict. Several patterns emerge. The most consistent pattern was an increase in terrorism when the failure of Syrian efforts to stir the conflict, either towards war or negotiation, resulted in a period with no coherent alternative being actively pursued. Another discernible pattern is perceptible between domestic disagreements over policy towards the conflict and brief increases in terrorism. A third characteristic of the Syrian use of terrorism was the use of provocative actions to apply pressure on friend or foe in order to achieve a specific negotiating purpose. Such acts can be called 'emphatic' terrorism because they are deliberately dramatic and are designed to focus attention on Syrian purpose. A fourth pattern in Syrian terrorism was the decrease in action when conventional war was planned or on-going. Decreases in action are also seen when negotiation was proceeding to Syria's benefit and when agreement had been reached. A final pattern observed is the temporary decrease in activity, or a change in the pattern of activity, when Israeli retaliation escalated to threatening levels.

From the patterns observed from 1971 to 1977, a tentative conclusion about Syrian use of terrorism can be reached. Syria uses terrorism as a tactic when it lacks viable alternatives either for war or peace. As a result, two policy options to curb Syrian use of terrorism are available. The first option is intensive retaliation which threatens regime stability. Israeli retaliation against civilians and conventional forces has worked to inhibit Syrian terrorism temporarily because the Asad regime cannot afford a war it has not started itself on its own terms. However, the patterns of this research suggest retaliation is only a transient solution. It is also not an appropriate response for non-Middle Eastern states whose roles in the Middle East have been, and should be, that of mediators in the Arab-Israeli conflict rather than combatants. The premise of mediation is that "sufficient respect and good-will exist toward the mediator for the antagonist to be amenable to his interpretations of their differences . . . ."[26] Western retaliation against Syria as a solution to the Syrian use of terrorism, although temporarily effective, will only serve to destroy what little good-will there is towards the West and will promulgate the very conflict which needs to be resolved.

A second, but more difficult, policy option remains. The patterns of this research project suggest that Syrian terrorism declines when negotiation is ongoing or when a satisfying agreement has been reached. Any negotiated solution of the Arab-Israeli conflict which involves Syria will be an arduous and lengthy process. The emphatic use of terrorism can be expected to continue up to the last minute; however, if an acceptable settlement is reached, Syria can be expected to abide by it. The Asad regime has very carefully outlined its position on negotiation; the flexibility of that position has never been tested and, in the last ten years, the possibility of a negotiated solution involving Syria has been ignored. By emphasizing Syria's terrorism and ignoring the larger context of the Arab-

Israeli conflict, the Western world is losing the opportunity to resolve one of the world's most troubling conflicts. Although it may seem a circuitous solution to the problem of terrorism, re-opening negotiation on the problem of the Palestinians and the Golan Heights in an international conference will be more effective in stopping Syrian terrorism than any threat or punishment.

Endnotes

1. An address by Caspar Weinberger to the International Conference on Terrorism, January 21, 1987, is a concise statement of the Reagan administration's policy towards terrorism. A copy is available through the author.

2. There is a large body of literature discussing the semantics of terrorism. See, for instance, Paul Wilkinson, *Terrorism and the Liberal State* (New York: New York University Press, 1986), especially pp. 23-68; Walter Laqueur, *Terrorism* (London: Weidenfeld and Nicolson, 1977); and A.P. Schmid, *Political Terrorism: A Research Guide to Concepts, Theories, Data Bases and Literature* (Amsterdam: North-Holland Publishing Co., 1983). Most definitions distinguish between guerrilla warfare [tactics involving conventions of war but with small numbers and inadequate weaponry (see Wilkinson, p. 53)] and terrorism ["a special mode of violence which . . . involves the threat of murder, injury or destruction to terrorize a given target into conceding . . . " (Wilkinson, p. 53)]. Terrorism in this research paper is meant to include both the guerrilla and psychological aspects of terrorism. It is defined very loosely as the use, or threat of use, of violence, against civilian and military targets for political purposes which does not involve the conventional Syrian forces.

3. Syrians work with these groups by setting down guidelines and delineating objectives of what to attack and what to avoid and approving or disapproving autonomously planned attacks.

4. Included in the chronology are several incidents which do not fit the definitional criteria. They are marked with two stars ** to indicate that they have not been counted as terrorist activity. They are included only to demonstrate how the terrorist activity can escalate activity involving the conventional Syrian forces.

5. Vulnerability to Israel results from the fact that there are not one, but three plausible land invasion routes Israel could use. The Golan is the most obvious route but, from the Israeli point of view, the most costly. One route could proceed past Irbid in Jordan and strike north of the Dera-Damascus access road. The other invasion route could proceed north from Galilee through the Bekaa Valley.

6. For an excellent discussion of the roots of Syrian Arab nationalism and Arab nationalism in general see Tawfic Farah, *Pan-Arabism and Arab Nationalism: The Continuing Debate* (Boulder, Colorado: Westview Press, 1987).

7. There is, admittedly, a debate about how committed Asad's acceptance of the principle of negotiation is. For a good review of the ambiguity of Syrian policy see footnote #24 in Raymond A. Hinnebusch, "Revisionist Dreams, Realist Strategies: The Foreign Policy of Syria," in *The Foreign Policies of Arab States,* edited by Bahgat Korany and Ali E. Dessouki (Boulder, Colorado: Westview Press, 1984), p. 319.

8. Syria's relationship with the Soviet Union has been cultivated for just this purpose. For a discussion of the Syrian-Soviet relation see Galia Golan, "Syria and the Soviet Union Since the Yom Kippur War," *Orbis,* 21, 4 (1978), pp. 777-802.

9. For a thorough analysis of Syrian foreign policy from a decision-making perspective seen Raymond A. Hinnebusch, "Revisionist Dreams, Realist Strategies: The Foreign Policy of Syria," in *The Foreign Policies of Arab States*, edited by Bahgat Korany and Ali E. Hillal Dessouki (Boulder, Colorado: Westview Press, 1984), pp. 283-322.

10. As Adeed Dawisha has carefully shown (*Syria and the Lebanese Crisis* [New York: St. Martin's Press, 1980]), Syria's presidential system includes a powerful sub-system in

the form of the Baath Party within which the remnants of the debate over the battle with Israel still exist.

11. In the words of Moshe Ma'oz, the Asad wing "conceived the war against Israel as a classical, ordinary, military campaign to be launched at the right moment by all Arab confrontation states." See Moshe Ma'oz, "Syria Under Hafiz al-Asad: New Domestic and Foreign Policies," Jerusalem Papers on Peace Problems (Jerusalem: Leonard Davis Institute for International Relations, 1975), p. 21.

12. Asad took power after a Baath National Conference where civilian and military factions clashed angrily over the policy of accepting the principal of peaceful resolution which the Soviet Union was calling for (see Paris AFP report, FBIS, November 10, 1970, p. F1). The military and Asad were in favor of responding to Moscow's call in order to gain weapons for a conventional battle.

13. MENA, FBIS, January 25, 1971, p. A1.

14. Crack-downs consisted of forbidding shipments of arms to Fateh (Jerusalem Domestic, FBIS, July 6, 1971, p. A3), banning operations against Jordan (Reuter, FBIS, July 16, 1971, p. F1), and issuing travel documents, censoring publications and supervising training bases and refugee camps (Cairo DPA, FBIS, October 22, 1971, p. F3).

15. Tripoli Domestic, FBIS, March 10, 1972, p. H2.

16. Tripoli Domestic, FBIS, June 26, 1972, p. F2.

17. Damascus MENA to Cairo, FBIS, June 29, 1972, p. F1.

18. Although there is no direct proof of Syrian collusion in the Munich Act, it is clear that Syria was at least aware of the plans in advance. Syrian intelligence closely monitored Black September as it did all Palestinian groups at that time and communications with Libya (heavily implicated in the attack) were extensive.

19. Tel Aviv Davar, FBIS, January 10, 1973, p. I6.

20. Paris AFP, January 23, 1973, p. F1.

21. *New York Times*, January 6, 1974, p. 10:1.

22. Although this attack may not have been Syrian planned, it counts as a Syrian act because it was carried out from Syrian controlled territory at a time when fedayeen groups were under very close supervision. Iraq claimed 30 such attacks were planned by the fedayeen during this period and yet only two were carried through, thus demonstrating the Syrian ability to control the fedayeen.

23. *Arab Report and Record*, February 15-29, 1975, p. 72.

24. Ronald McLaurin, Mohammen Mughisuddin and Abraham R. Wagner, *Foreign Policy-Making in the Middle East* (New York: Praeger, 1977), p. 241.

25. *Arab Report and Record*, March 15-30, 1977, p. 183.

26. William R. Brown, *The Last Crusade: A Negotiator's Middle East Handbook* (Chicago: Nelson-Hall, 1980), p. 143.

APPENDIX

The assumptions guiding the collection of information in the chronology are as follows:

1.   Fedayeen action carried out in the Golan after Asad's rise to power is assumed to be Syrian-approved because the Asad regime made it a clear policy as of February 1970 that there was to be no fedayeen action from Syrian-controlled territory without prior Syrian approval. This is true of attacks carried out from Mt. Hermon and the Arquob region of Lebanon which was dominated by Syrian-backed PLA after September 1970.

2.   All acts carried out from Jordan after the summer of 1971 are assumed to be Syrian-approved because all the fedayeen were expelled from Jordan in September. To infiltrate Jordan it was necessary to come from Syria. Because of an agreement with King Hussein, the Syrian authorities carefully controlled the border with Jordan to prevent infiltration. Any fedayeen operating from Jordan did so with Syrian approval or suffered punishment.

3.   Actions claimed by Damascus Radio are assumed to be Syrian-approved.

4.   Actions carried out and claimed by Syrian-supported groups such as Saiqa, PLA and ALF are always included in the chronology.

5.   Actions carried out by other Palestinian groups such as the PFLP-GC, the PDFLP and the PFLP are assumed to be Syrian-approved when those groups are in harmony with Syria. The relationship between these groups and Syria fluctuates back and forth. It was therefore necessary to determine whether they were in favor with Syria by monitoring whether their communiqués and publications were censored or not, whether their spoken goals conflicted with Syria's and whether they were included in Syrian-sponsored Palestinian meetings or not.

CHRONOLOGY OF SYRIAN INCIDENTS

DATE(S)	ACTION	MONTHLY TOTAL
1971		
January		
1,2,6,10	Guerrilla attacks on Israeli posts in Golan.	8
2	Guerrilla attack on UN Observer post.	
25	Guerrillas and Israeli soldiers clash on Golan.	
28, 30	Exchange of fire involving guerrillas.	
February		
5, 9,	Seven fedayeen infiltrating Golan captured and killed.	4
21, 22	Clashes with infiltrators on Golan.	
March		
3, 4, 8, 9	Rocket and other attacks on Golan.	5
22	Four captured, four killed in largest of recent attacks on Golan.	
April		
24	Outbreak of firing on Golan.	1
May		
9	Three infiltrators killed in Golan clash.	2
18	Two killed, one wounded in Golan clash.	
June		
22	Guerrilla firing in Golan.	2
25	Eight fedayeen, one Syrian officer killed in clash on Golan.	
July		
8	Exchange of fire on Golan.	8
20, 22-24	Highest number of fedayeen incidents in Golan	
26, 27,	in recent months including mortar fire.	
28		
August		0
September		
1, 10, 12	Border action in Golan.	6
9	Three separate infiltration attempts.	
9	Fedayeen from Syria damage Trans-Arabian pipe-line.	
15	More damage to pipe-line on Syrian border.	
October		
6	Assassination attempt on Arafat while visiting Golan.	9
7	Exchange of fire on Mt. Hermon.	
16, 19		
21-23	Fedayeen incidents reported on Golan.	
29, 30		
November		
27	Clash in Golan.	1
December		0

DATE(S)	ACTION	MONTHLY TOTAL
1972		
January		
1, 3, 6, 11	Mine and rocket attacks in Golan reported by Damascus Radio.	15
6, 11, 12	Rockets fired from Lebanese border at Kfar Blum and Qiryat Shemona reported by Damascus Radio.	
16	Damascus Radio reports fedayeen attack on camp in Golan with rockets.	
19, 20	More rocket attacks near Qunaitra.	
23	Clash of fedayeen and Israeli patrol.	
26	Fedayeen rocket attack on Tal Abu Qithat.	
28	Israeli patrol ambushed.	
30	Katyusha rockets fired at Israeli positions.	
31	Fedayeen lay and detonate minefield in Golan.	
February		
2	Damascus communiqué announces fedayeen attack on camp in Firdawi area.	12
4	Rocket attack in Khushniya area.	
11	Shells fired at Israeli positions in Golan.	
21	Mortar fire from Kfar Shuba (SW Lebanon)	
15	Fedayeen attack post near Qunaitra.	
19	Fedayeen attack observation post in Golan.	
20	Attack on Israeli position near Jukhdar in Golan.	
22	Firing in Nahal Golan region.	
24	Fedayeen clash with patrols after setting fire to Israeli plants in Yaqouta area.	
27	Fighters of Abu Ali Iya (Damascus) attack El-Al settlement in Golan. Later undertook rocket attack.	
28, 19	Damascus communiqués on mortar and rocket attacks near Qunaitra.	
March		
2, 3,	Heavy rockets and shells fired at camps in Qunaitra.	4
26, 27	Fedayeen attack posts in Golan.	
April		
7	Firing reported from Syrian territory in Golan.	8
10	Clash in Dubbasiya in Golan with machine guns and rockets.	
18, 19	Fedayeen attack Israeli positions in Golan.	
26-30	More attacks in Golan including destruction of electronic fortifications at Qunaitra.	
May		
9	Attacks on pipeline and reports of fighting between PFLP and PFLP-GC.	3
16	Firing south-west of Sea of Galilee.	
17	Fedayeen shell machine-gun emplacements in Golan.	

Summer 1988

DATE(S)	ACTION	MONTHLY TOTAL
1972		
June		
5	Bazooka attack from Syrian territory in Golan.	8
8	Israeli truck blown up near Qunaitra.	
15	Four infiltrators killed in Golan.	
20	Two Israeli soldiers killed by mine in Golan.	
20	PFLP-GC fire rockets at Israeli bus in Golan.	
22	Settlements in Golan attacked with rockets and mortar.	
24	Shelling of Qunaitra.	
26	Shelling of Khushniya.	
July		
3	Guerrillas rocketed village of Banias.	6
7, 10	Bazooka attacks in Golan.	
18	Israeli engineering patrol ambushed in Golan.	
19	Jibbin settlement in Golan rocketed and mortared.	
27	Bridge destroyed in Saluqiya region.	
August		
1, 4, 8	Bazooka attacks and shelling on Golan from Syria.	9
16	Bomb placed in portable record player stored in baggage on El-Al flight from Rome to Tel Aviv. Record player given to British girl by Syrian boyfriend.	
20	Settlements in Golan attacked by guerrillas.	
21, 22, 29, 30	Rocket and mortar attacks on Nahal Golan.	
September		
7	Munich Olympic attack on Israeli athletes.	8
13	Shelling, small-arms fire in Mt. Hermon area.	
15	Two Israeli soldiers ambushed in Mt. Hermon.	
16	Fedayeen shell Qunaitra and Nahal Golan.	
18	Jibbin settlement in Golan attacked with rockets and bridge blown up.	
20	Israeli positions shelled in Golan.	
19-20	PFLP-GC letter-bombs to various Zionist organizations in Europe, Israel and US.	
October		
24-30	More letter-bombs throughout Middle East.	7
24	PFLP planted network of rockets and bombs in Golan.	
November		
6	Nahal Golan under mortar fire from Syria.	5
11	Israeli patrol ambushed in Golan.	
21	Fierce fighting lasting more than eight hours in Golan.	
17	Two Israeli vehicles hit mine in Nahal Golan.	
18	Israeli soldiers killed by mine in Jordan Valley. Voice of Palestine (Syria) report.	

DATE(S)	ACTION	MONTHLY TOTAL
1972		
December		
3	Two Israeli military vehicles destroyed by mine in Golan.	5
7	Guerrillas attack Israeli position near Dabusiya.	
15	Firing from Syrian territory reported.	
22	Fedayeen attack Israeli troops and vehicles in Golan.	
26	Shells fired at Israeli positions in Golan.	
1973		
January		
7, 8	Fedayeen attack on Golan.	4
20, 27	Three Black September arrested in Vienna with sketches of Schonau camp. One admitted to casing it. Carrying Syrian passports.	
February		
7, 8	Israeli patrols attacked by fedayeen in Golan.	3
15	Clash of forces in Golan.	
March		0
April		
10	Three fedayeen infiltrating from Golan killed.	6
11	Fedayeen attack Israeli positions in Golan.	
21	Fedayeen attack patrol in Debusiya.	
25	Rockets fired from Syrian territory at Qunaitra.	
26	Fedayeen/Israeli patrol clash. Fedayeen admit Syrian approval of raid.	
16	PFLP-GC attempt to blow up pipeline in Zahrani.	
May		0
June		
16, 20	Clashes in Lebanon between Saiqa and Fateh.	2
July		
1	PFLP-GC kill Colonel Yosef Alon, one of Israel's most famous pilots, in Rome.	1
August		
27	Israeli patrol stumbles into guerrilla ambush in Golan.	2
30	Heavy mortar attack by fedayeen in Golan.	
September		
28	Eagles of Revolution (Saiqa) take five hostages on passenger train from Czechoslovakia to Austria demanding the closure of Austrian Soviet Jew emigration center.	1
October		
6-24	War.**	0
November		
7, 15	Artillery battles in north Golan.	0
6, 8	Air clashes over Golan.**	

43

Summer 1988

DATE(S)	ACTION	MONTHLY TOTAL
1973		
December		
2, 3	Artillery and tank battles in Golan.**	1
10, 11	More clashes in Golan.**	
28	Fedayeen attack Israeli positions in Mt. Hermon.	
1974		
January		
26, 27	Ceasefire violations along Syrian front.**	0
February		
1-14	Tank and artillery battles on front.**	0
15-30	Clashes continue but lessen in intensity.**	
March		
8	Forces clash in Golan.**	0
12-15	More clashes.**	
26	Syrian artillery shell Golan settlements.**	
April		
	Fighting over Mt. Hermon continues through month.	1
11	PFLP-GC enter Qiryat Shemona via SW Lebanese border attacking apartment complex. Saiqa spokesman says "We promise to undertake more such operations."	
May		
	Golan fighting with ground and air forces continue.**	0
15	PDFLP attack on Maalot.	
23	Fedayeen infiltrating from Golan captured with plans for second Maalot-like attack.	
24	Attacks on post on eastern shore of Galilee.	
31	Fighting in Golan ends.**	
June		0
July		0
August		
24	Three Fateh fedayeen captured infiltrating from Syria near Jordan River carrying six bazookas and machine-guns	3
25, 26	More fedayeen infiltrators from Syria via Jordan captured.	
September		
2-4	PDFLP Damascus communiqué claims attempts to enter Hanita from Western end of Lebanese border killed by Israeli troops—intended to seize hostages.	3
27	Two fedayeen infiltrating from Jordan captured with sabotage equipment and leaflets.	
October		0

DATE(S)	ACTION	MONTHLY TOTAL
1974		
November		
15-17	Israeli and Syrian forces in Golan on alert but no outbreak.**	1
19	PDFLP enter Beit Shean apartment house killing four civilians. (Announced in Damascus.)	
December		0
1975		
January		
11	Fedayeen ambush Israeli patrol on Mt. Hermon.	2
17	Units of PLA, usually stationed in Syria, arrive in South Lebanon to help guerrillas resist Israeli attack.	
February		0
March		
5	Fateh fedayeen used rubber dinghies to land in Tel Aviv took hostages at Hotel Savoy. Asked to fly to Damascus. Said trained in Damascus. Were told to say from Port Said, Egypt. Slogan: "Kissinger's efforts will fail."	1
April		
4	Three Israelis wounded in clash with fedayeen on Mt. Hermon.	1
May		0
June		
24	Israel reports hundreds of fedayeen crossed into Lebanon from Syria.	0
July		0
August		
5	Rockets fired at Qiryat Shemona from SW Lebanon.	2
11	Fedayeen rocket firing from Jordanian territory.	
September		
5	Four Saiqa members arrested in Amsterdam planning to hijack Warsaw-Amsterdam express to stop Soviet emigration to Israel.	2
15	Four fedayeen (1 Syrian) take Egyptian embassy hostage denouncing Sinai.	
October		
20	Forces clash in Golan.	3
24	Fedayeen cross into Israel via Jordan captured with mortar shells, explosives and small arms. Intended to shell Neo Hakikar and sabotage installations in area.	
28	Fedayeen crossed from Syria into Golan—brief fight.	

45

Summer 1988

DATE(S)	ACTION	MONTHLY TOTAL
1975		
November		
13	23 pounds explosives inside luggage near coffeehouse in Jerusalem. Damascus Radio claims for Fateh.	2
19	PDFLP attacked Israeli yeshiva farm in Golan at Ramit Magashimim.	
December		
13	Saiqa attacks on Israeli army patrols in N. Galilee. Damascus Radio reports. Also attacks on Qiryat Shemona.	1
1976		
January		
1	Katyusha rockets fired at northern Galilee from SW Lebanon.	1
16-31	Israel reports fewest incidents of fedayeen action since 1966.**	
February		0
March		
8	First attack on Israeli patrols since November '75 from Syrian borders; fedayeen fired rockets at patrols.	1
April		
8	PFLP and Saiqa forces clash in Beirut.	2
?	One fedayeen operation reported in Golan sometime in April.	
May		
18	PDFLP (currently friendly with Syria) attack Israeli bridges, infiltrated from Jordan, said to be in retaliation for shooting relative of former Jordanian Premier during riots in Nablus.	1
June		0
July		
18	Saiqa claims responsibility for bus explosion in West Bank. There has been continuous light explosion activity in West Bank rumored engineered by Saiqa cell.	1
August		
early	Fedayeen crossing Dead Sea from Jordan clash with patrol.	1
September		
16	Shimon Peres disclosed Israeli and Syrian officers met in presence of UN to discuss reunion of Druze families.	0
October		
26	Syria agrees to help fedayeen return to military bases in South Lebanon. PLA moves into Arqoub region.	0

46

DATE(S)	ACTION	MONTHLY TOTAL
1976		
November		0
December		
24	Fedayeen successfully launched rocket attack from Jordan on Neve Ur, important Israeli target.	1
1977		
January		0
February		0
March		0
April		0
May		0
June		0
July		
6	Explosion in Tel Aviv market place claimed by Fateh, PDFLP, Saiqa and ALF.	17
16-31	Bombs daily in public places claimed by above mentioned groups.	
August		
4	Israeli forces report killing two fedayeen, injuring third, crossing border and planning attack three miles south of Sea of Galilee.	8
9, 10, 12	Nablus explosions claimed by PLO or Saiga.	
16	Qiryat Shemona bus explosion (planted from Arqoub region.)	
27, 29, 30	More Nablus explosions.	
September		
16	Israeli aircraft and tanks enter South Lebanon on side of rightist. Syrian army positions shelled but did not take up challenge.	0
October		0
November		
?	Seven bomb explosions in public places in West Bank, Jerusalem and Tel Aviv similar to previous explosions.	8
17	Two bombs exploded in Egyptian embassy in Damascus; no injuries; slight damage; came after Sadat's departure from Syria.	
December		
13	Reports that Syrian authorities plotting to assassinate Egyptian embassy staff in Beirut.	6
18	Explosive-laden suitcase removed from Beirut residence of Egyptian diplomat.	
19	Thirteen pounds of explosives in suitcase found in Egyptian embassy in Beirut.	

Summer 1988

DATE(S)	ACTION	MONTHLY TOTAL
1977		
December		
20	Two rockets, dynamite found in vegetable cart near Egyptian embassy in Beirut.	
22	Bomb damaged three Egyptian organization buildings in Beirut.	
31	Bomb exploded in car belonging to Syrian embassy in front of Egyptian embassy in London.	
1978		
January		
2	Egyptian security official defused four pound bomb hidden in shopping bag by Egyptian embassy in West Germany.	4
10	Intelligence office in Jerusalem blown up.	
13	Explosion in office in Jaffa.	
26	Jerusalem office explosion (all three claimed by SANA 5 Feb. 1978).	
February		
14	Saiqa claims explosion of bus in Jerusalem killing forty.	1
March		
11	PLO attack in Israel announced over Damascus Radio.	1
April		
5	Damascus Radio reported fedayeen operation against soldiers in Jerusalem.	1
May		0
June		0
July		
31	Two PLO members, in coordination with Syrian intelligence, seize hostages in Iraqi embassy in Libya.	1
August		
2	Attack on Iraqi officials in Pakistan.	3
13	PFLP-GC blow up headquarters of Iraqi-backed Palestinian group in Beirut.	
17	Fateh fedayeen traveling from Damascus shoots Iraqi embassy employee.	
September		0
October		0
November		0
December		0

Part II
Current and Future Threats:
A Regional Overview

[3]

Recent Trends and Future Prospects of Iranian Sponsored International Terrorism

Bruce Hoffman

I. INTRODUCTION

International terrorism has been a prominent feature of Iran's foreign policy since the revolution in 1979 that brought Ayatollah Khomeini to power. At the root of this policy is a desire to extend the fundamentalist interpretation of Islamic law by exporting the Islamic revolution in Iran to other Muslim countries and cleansing the Middle East of all Western influence. Iran has sought to overthrow not only the ruling regime of its arch-enemy Iraq, but also the regimes of the conservative Arab monarchies of Saudi Arabia, Kuwait, Bahrain, and Jordan; it has also attempted to establish an Islamic Republic along the Iranian model in Lebanon. An ancillary, but no less consequential motivation of this policy has been the Iranian regime's enmity toward the West. This enmity has inevitably brought Iran into conflict with the United States, Israel, and France, along with a number of other European countries.

This report examines the basic *raison d'etre* of Iran's international terrorist campaign, its trends and patterns of activity over the past six years, and the Iranian personalities behind the policy. It seeks to assess the future course of Iran's policy of supporting terrorism and, accordingly, focuses on the ongoing power struggles within the Iranian regime that are likely to determine the country's foreign policy now that Khomeini has died. Four key issues are discussed:

- Why has Iran supported international terrorism as an instrument of the regime's foreign policy?
- What ties exist between Iran and extremist Shia organizations elsewhere?
- What have been the trends in international Shia terrorist activity and what explanations account for these patterns?
- How have these trends been affected or influenced by internal rivalries within the Iranian ruling elite?

1

II. IRAN'S REVOLUTIONARY GOALS AND SUPPORT OF INTERNATIONAL TERRORISM

On the occasion of the Iranian New Year in March 1980—just over a year after the establishment of the Islamic Republic of Iran— Ayatollah Khomeini laid out the purpose of both the Islamic fundamentalist revolution that brought him to power and the foreign policy that the new regime would pursue:

> We must strive to export our Revolution throughout the world, and must abandon all idea of not doing so, for not only does Islam refuse to recognize any difference between Muslim countries, it is the champion of all oppressed people. Moreover, all the powers are intent on destroying us, and if we remain surrounded in a closed circle, we shall certainly be defeated. We must make plain our stance toward the powers and superpowers and demonstrate to them that despite the arduous problems that burden us. Our attitude to the world is dictated by our beliefs.[1]

Khomeini's proclamation became a clarion call for a global Islamic revolution based on his fundamentalist interpretation of Islamic tenets. Thus, much as the fledgling Soviet Union had embarked on a dual campaign to consolidate the revolution in Russia and export it to other countries nearly sixty years earlier, Khomeini defined a similar purpose for Iran. As a report in *The Economist* noted,

> The Iranian revolution changed the political landscape for Shias in two ways. First, it inspired Moslem—Sunni, as well as Shia— fundamentalists to take a stand against governments they regarded as immorally secular. Second, it brought into being in Iran a government which wants to export the Islamic revolution, and which has the resources to try it.[2]

The revolution in Iran, accordingly, was held up as an example to Muslims throughout the world to reassert the fundamental teachings of the Koran and at the same time resist the intrusion of Western—and, particularly U.S.—influence in the Middle East. This policy was, in fact, a reflection of the beliefs and history of Shia Islam as interpreted by Khomeini and pursued by his followers both in Iran and elsewhere.

---

[1]Imam Khomeini, *Islam and Revolution* (translated by Hamid Algar), London: KPI, Ltd., 1981, pp. 286–287.

[2]*The Economist* (London), July 13, 1985.

"The world as it is today is how others shaped it," Ayatollah Mohammed Baqer al-Sadr, a prominent Shia cleric, has written. "We have
two choices: either to accept it with submission, which means letting
Islam die, or to destroy it, so that we can construct the world as Islam
requires."[3] Indeed, three ineluctable desiderata form the basis of this
ideology:

> First, Shiites do not believe in the legitimate authority of secular
> governments. The 12th and last of the Shiite Imams, or successors
> to the Prophet Mohammed, is expected to reappear eventually to
> institute the rule of God's law on earth. Until then, all states are, on
> some level, inalienably illegitimate. Since Iran is the only state to
> have begun to implement "true" Islam, however, it is thought to be
> the world's only legitimate state with a unique obligation of facilitat-
> ing the worldwide implementation of Islamic law. Force and violence
> are not only acceptable but necessary means of doing so.
>
> . . .
>
> Second, the Shiites see themselves as a persecuted minority. They
> believe that through their special knowledge of the Koran . . . passed
> on to them by the Prophet Mohammed and the 12 Imams, they are
> the righteous few dominated by an innately wrongful majority.
>
> . . .
>
> Third, the Shiites view themselves as victims of injustice and oppres-
> sion. Ayatollah Khomeini has interpreted this theme to make the
> Shiites the representatives, even vanguard, of the "oppressed and
> innocent masses crushed under foot all over the world."[4]

In this respect, the necessity for continuous and intensive struggle
against Western influence and domination was embraced as one of the
primary aims of Iranian foreign policy. Indeed, as Marvin Zonis has
stated, "Islam is being used as a vehicle for striking back at the West,
in the sense of people trying to reclaim a very greatly damaged sense of
self-esteem. They feel that for the past 150 years the West has totally
overpowered them culturally, and in the process their own institutions
and way of life have become second rate."[5]

The first tangible manifestation of this resentment toward the West
in general and the United States in particular appeared in November
1979, when militant religious students seized the U.S. Embassy in
Teheran and held 52 American diplomats hostage for 444 days. As

---

[3]Quoted in Amir Taheri, *Holy Terror: The Inside Story of Islamic Terrorism*, London:
Sphere Books, 1987, pp. 7–8.

[4]Marvin Zonis and Daniel Brumberg, "Behind Beirut Terrorism," *New York Times*,
October 8, 1984.

[5]Quoted in Robin Wright, *Sacred Rage: The Crusade of Modern Islam*, New York:
Linden Press/Simon and Schuster, 1985, p. 252.

4   RECENT TRENDS AND FUTURE PROSPECTS OF IRANIAN-SPONSORED TERRORISM

events would later show, this incident was only the beginning of an increasingly serious and extensive international terrorist campaign directed against the United States and other Western countries.

The reverberations of this policy, however, were felt almost immediately throughout the Middle East and in other regions with considerable Muslim populations. Inspired by the Islamic revolution in Iran—though perhaps not directly ordered to action by Iran—Sunni fundamentalists seized the Grand Mosque in Mecca in November 1979 and staged a bloody uprising that, although quickly and viciously suppressed, proved to be a harbinger of similar religiously motivated disturbances elsewhere. Soon Shia workers rioted in the oil-rich eastern provinces of Saudi Arabia. In Bahrain, mass demonstrations by Shias (who comprise over 60 percent of the country's population) erupted in protest against alleged discrimination by the minority Bahraini Sunnis. Later on, violence broke out in Turkey, when protests by the Shia minority there provoked bloody clashes with government troops. In the early 1980s, more serious disturbances occurred in Iraq during the annual march between the Shia holy cities of Karbala and Najaf commemorating the death of the Shia martyr Hussein. As a result of the disturbances, many leading Shia clerics were arrested and later executed, and thousands of Iraqi Shias (who form a majority of the population in that country) were forcibly deported to Iran.[6]

These heady currents soon erupted into terrorist violence. Throughout 1979 and 1980, militant followers of a prominent Shia cleric in Lebanon, the Imam Musa al-Sadr, who had mysteriously disappeared while on a visit to Libya in August 1979, pursued a campaign of aircraft hijackings and bombings to pressure the Qaddafi regime to release the Imam. In March 1981, a group of Indonesian Muslim extremists dedicated to implementing an Islamic revolution based on the Iranian model seized a passenger jet in Indonesia and hijacked it to Thailand.

Isolated and uncoordinated as these events were, they represented the beginning of an international terrorist campaign by Shia extremists throughout the Middle East and in Europe. Iraq's invasion of Iran in September 1980 proved to be the catalyst for a more intense and wide-ranging onslaught of Shia terrorism. The new regime was now provided with a visible and immediate external threat to the revolution. In this respect, the use of violence against several of the Gulf countries—particularly Saudi Arabia, Kuwait, and Bahrain—occurred within the context of the war with Iraq (and countries that the Iranians regarded as virtual belligerents on the side of Iraq), alongside the

---

[6]Ibid.

regime's wider regional and revolutionary objectives. Thus, although local Shias in these countries clearly had their own agendas, Iranian support was a critical element in their actions.

In December 1981, the first of many international terrorist attacks in Beirut occurred when a terrorist organization composed of Iraqi Shia—backed by Iran and calling itself *al-Dawa* ("The Call," as in "the call for Holy War")—bombed the Iraqi Embassy in Beirut.

During the months following the Beirut attack, Iran established an organizational framework for exploiting the revolutionary fervor of external Shia extremist groups and providing the financing needed to support their activities. At the vortex of this policy was Khomeini's dictum that "boundaries should not be considered as the means of separation. . . . Not only does Islam refuse to recognize any difference between Muslim countries, it is the champion of the oppressed people."[7]

At about this time, Ayatollah Hussein Ali Montazeri emerged as the regime's key "front man" in these efforts.[8] The regime's strategy was based on the principle that "religion and politics are indivisible." Mosques, Montazeri declared, "should not only be places of prayer but, as in the Prophet Mohammed's time, should be centres of political, cultural and military activities."[9] Islam was to function "not just as a religion but [as] a religious polity."[10]

The foundation of this campaign was laid at a conference to promote the creation of the "Ideal Islamic Government," held in Teheran during March 1982. Under the aegis of the Association of Combatant Clerics and the Islamic Revolution Guard Corps (IRGC), representatives from two dozen Arab and Islamic countries met with Iranian officials to discuss the means required to achieve this goal. The participants discussed three primary objectives:

1. To unite "true Islam" against imperialism.
2. To raise the flag of "authentic Islam" against its usurpers, principally seen as the rulers of Saudi Arabia and their agents.
3. To promote the aims of the Iranian revolution throughout the Moslem world.[11]

---

[7]Ibid., p. 42.

[8]Colin Legum, "Iran's Role in World Terrorism Depicted," *The Age* (Melbourne), January 5, 1984.

[9]Ibid.

[10]Robin Wright, "Quiet Revolution: The Islamic Movement's New Phase," *Christian Science Monitor*, November 6, 1987.

[11]Legum, "Iran's Role in World Terrorism Depicted," 1984.

6   RECENT TRENDS AND FUTURE PROSPECTS OF IRANIAN-SPONSORED TERRORISM

The conference reportedly represented the heart of a movement advocating worldwide Islamic revolution. The attendees embraced Islam as "a weapon in revolutionary wars against the rich and corrupt ... [aiming to awaken Muslims] from the sleep of centuries, putting a sword in their hands and sending them into battle against the forces of Satan."[12] To this end, a special training program was established for Muslims throughout the Islamic world as "messengers of true Islam." After receiving instruction in Iran, these militants were to return to their home countries to popularize and advance the regime's revolutionary goals, foment unrest, and generally create a climate favorable to the adoption of fundamentalist Islamic precepts.[13]

Iran's clerical rulers were to pursue a two-pronged strategy. On the one hand, the regime would use international terrorist activities as a planned and deliberate instrument of Iranian foreign policy; on the other, it would exploit and co-opt the spontaneous support for its revolutionary goals among radical Muslims throughout the world. The necessity for continuous struggle against Iran's enemies consequently became inextricably intertwined with the broader struggle against Islam's enemies as well—and terrorism became the essential cornerstone of this campaign. An ideal opportunity for Teheran to implement the revolutionary strategy and exert its influence in another part of the Middle East arose within months of the March conference, when Israel invaded Lebanon.

IRAN'S INTERVENTION IN LEBANON

Although the Israeli invasion facilitated Iran's involvement in Lebanese affairs, a number of other factors made Lebanon susceptible to foreign intervention in general and Iranian exploitation in particular.

In June 1982, Israeli forces stormed across the border into Lebanon in a massive attack on the military and political infrastructure of the Palestine Liberation Organization (PLO) in that country. Since its expulsion from Jordan over a decade before, the PLO had sought to transform Lebanon into a base from which to attack Israel and a training site from which to dispatch its fighters to assault Israeli targets throughout the world. The historically fragile foundations of the Lebanese state had enabled the PLO to operate from that country with virtual impunity, flouting the authority of the government and

---

[12]Quoted in Wright, *Sacred Rage: The Crusade of Modern Islam*, pp. 27–28.

[13]Thomas L. Friedman, "Some Detect Master Plan," *New York Times,* December 13, 1983.

establishing within part of Lebanon literally a state within a state. The inability to constrain the growth of the PLO's power in Lebanon and prevent it from carrying out operations from Lebanese soil further weakened the ability of the Lebanese government to prevent Israeli reprisal attacks, much less repel the more serious invasions that occurred in 1978 and 1982.

The chronic weakness of the Lebanese state stemmed from the imbalance of political power among its many sectarian groups. The Maronite Christians and the Sunni Muslims had shared power uneasily since Lebanon was granted its independence in 1946; the Shia community, meanwhile, was all but ignored. Although this system may have been appropriate to the population divisions that existed in the 1940s, less than 30 years later it had become outmoded. The higher Shia birthrate had transformed a minority group into the majority, yet the Lebanese political system was never altered to compensate for this change. The poor, less-educated, and politically disorganized Shia were powerless to redress the imbalance. Residing in the underdeveloped southern half of Lebanon, they suffered discrimination from their Sunni co-religionists and the Christians for years. Consequently, the Shia felt disenfranchised and alienated from the mainstream of Lebanese politics, commerce, and society.

This situation began to change in 1968, after Imam Musa al-Sadr returned to his native country from the Iranian holy city of Qom. In 1974, al-Sadr organized the Movement of the Underprivileged to advance Shia interests and improve the community's lowly socioeconomic condition. This movement was subsequently reorganized as the principal Shia political party in Lebanon, *Amal*, which formed its own militia during the civil war that wracked Lebanon a year later.

In 1979, as previously noted, al-Sadr vanished during a visit to Libya. The disappearance of the Imam created a vacuum within *Amal* that made the party fertile ground for Iranian influence and rendered the movement susceptible to the fundamentalist call of the revolution that had brought Khomeini to power earlier that year. Nabih Berri, a lawyer, was appointed head of *Amal* in 1980. Hussein Musavi, the alleged mastermind behind the terrorist campaign against Libya to recover the Imam, was named as Berri's deputy and commander of the militia. A fanatical supporter of Khomeini, Musavi sought to place *Amal* in the vanguard of a regional revolution based on the new Iranian Islamic Republic. Berri, on the other hand, clung to a moderate line and advocated a new deal for the Shia community within the confines of the existing Lebanese state structure.

By this time, the radicalization of the Shia in Lebanon had gone far beyond the narrow nationalist and social aims of *Amal.* In 1981, Musavi broke with Berri and founded his own organization, *Islamic Amal.* Shortly thereafter, another faction split from *Amal,* and under the leadership of Abbas Musavi (a nephew of Hussein Musavi) and the "spiritual guidance" of Mohammed Hussein Fadlallah, it soon came to be known as the *Hezbollah,* or the Party of God. Like *Islamic Amal, Hezbollah* embraced Khomeini's summons for a pan-Islamic revolt designed to turn Lebanon into an Iranian-style Islamic Republic.

Although these developments made Lebanon the immediate cynosure of Iranian revolutionary efforts, Iran was not accorded the crucial opening needed to consolidate and expand its influence in that country until Israel invaded Lebanon in 1982. Within months of the invasion, the first IRGC cadres were dispatched to Lebanon, ostensibly in support of the beleaguered PLO forces. As Iran's Foreign Minister, Ali Akbar Velayati, later explained, "If our friends anywhere in the world ask us, of course we will help them." Thus, Velayati described the deployment of the Revolutionary Guard units to Lebanon as "a symbol of help . . . in the confrontation with Israel."[14]

Iran's motives in aiding the PLO, however, went far beyond the simple altruistic missions to which Velayati alluded. They were part and parcel of the two-pronged international terrorist strategy the regime had formulated earlier that year. The IRGC, for example, quickly established a forward headquarters at Baalbek in the predominantly Shia Bekaa Valley and a general headquarters just over the border in the Syrian village of Zebdani.[15] The Zebdani headquarters, in fact, was transformed by the Revolutionary Guards into their largest single base of operations outside Iran.[16] With the IRGC firmly entrenched in Lebanon, direct and immediate contact had been established between Teheran and sympathetic Shia extremist groups in that country. Iran's ruling clerics, in pursuit of their original goals, could now take advantage simultaneously of the revolutionary ferment among Lebanon's Shia and the massive disruption caused by the Israeli invasion in the already fragile Lebanese state.

---

[14]Quoted in Elaine Sciolino, "Iranian Promises Help to World's Oppressed," *New York Times,* October 4, 1984.

[15]Friedman, "Some Detect Master Plan"; and David B. Ottaway, "Baalbek Seen as Staging Area for Terrorism," *Washington Post,* January 19, 1984.

[16]Wright, *Sacred Rage: The Crusade of Modern Islam,* pp. 80–81, 84.

THE ESCALATION OF SHIA TERRORISM IN LEBANON

The establishment of Iran's policies in Lebanon depended largely on the latter's continued instability. Only as long as the fighting between the myriad indigenous factions and external forces continued unabated and the Lebanese government remained incapable of asserting its authority would Iran be able to fill this vacuum. The deployment of a Multi-National Peacekeeping Force (MNF) comprising military units from the United States, Great Britain, France, and Italy to Lebanon in August 1982 thus posed a serious threat to Iranian aims. Although the MNF had been dispatched to Lebanon following the massacre of Palestinian civilians by Maronite militiamen that month in order to protect the Palestinians from further attack, its broader objective was to restore some semblance of order to the country and stabilize the worsening situation there. Hence, it was not surprising that the targets of Shia terrorist activity in Lebanon soon expanded to include the diplomatic and military facilities, attendant personnel, and private citizens of the MNF member nations as well as the Israeli forces occupying the southern part of the country.

On March 15, 1983, the first of a series of terrorist operations against the MNF occurred when a detachment of Italian soldiers was attacked by Shia operatives. The following day, a group of U.S. Marines was fired upon, and three days later a French paratroop unit was targeted. Another attack was carried out against the French on April 9. But these incidents paled in comparison with the April 18 suicide car bombing that destroyed the U.S. Embassy in West Beirut and killed 69 persons.

This new and more wide-ranging terrorist campaign was probably the result of another conference chaired by Montazeri in Teheran in February 1983. Some 400 persons attended this co-called "First Conference on Islamic Thought." After the meeting, another special training center for foreign Muslims was reportedly established in Qom, where sponsored students pursued both religious studies and methods of armed insurrection.[17] In addition, responsibility for channeling Iranian volunteers to Lebanon was assigned to Fazollah Mahalati, who acted as Khomeini's "special representative" to the Lebanese Shia organizations. Under a banner proclaiming "The path to Jerusalem passes through Beirut," which hung on the wall of his Teheran office, Mahalati oversaw the dispatch of volunteers to Lebanon to fight against Iran's three principal enemies there: the United States, Israel,

---

[17]Legum, "Iran's Role in World Terrorism Depicted."

and France.[18] By the end of 1983, the number of Revolutionary
Guards deployed in Lebanon had grown to between 2,000 and 3,000.[19]
As Mahalati explained in an interview broadcast by Teheran radio in
late 1983, "There is no other country in the world where Muslims find
such joy in fighting." Lumping Lebanon and Syria together in a single
entity, he went on to state, "We find in Syria the three main enemies
of Islam at the same time."[20]

The basic underpinnings of the Iranian strategy were subsequently
elucidated by Mohammed Hussein Fadlallah, one of the leaders of the
principal Shia terrorist group in Lebanon, *Hezbollah,* and a key figure
in the terrorist campaign unleashed against the United States in that
country:

> We do not hold in our Islamic belief that violence is the solution to
> all types of problems; rather, we always see violence as a kind of
> surgical operation that a person should use only after trying all other
> means, and only when he finds his life imperiled. . . . The violence
> began as the people, feeling themselves bound by impotence, stirred
> to shatter some of that enveloping powerlessness for the sake of
> liberty.

In this context, Fadlallah pointed out, Israel's invasion of Lebanon in
1982 was the embodiment of the United States' hostility to revolutionary Islam:

> This invasion was confronted by the Islamic factor, which had its
> roots in the Islamic Revolution in Iran. And throughout these
> affairs, America was the common denominator. America was gen-
> erally perceived as the great nemesis behind the problems of the
> region, due to its support for Israel and many local reactionary
> regimes, and because it distanced itself from all causes of liberty and
> freedom in the area.[21]

Thus, according to this analysis, the Israeli invasion indirectly
brought Iran into renewed conflict with the United States. As Fadlallah explained,

> Confronting the question of America, which was itself exerting politi-
> cal, military, economic and intelligence pressure on the area in order
> to deliver it to Israel's grip, the people felt they had to do something.

---

[18]"Extent of Iranian Involvement in Lebanon Is Discussed," *al-Majallah* (London),
November 5–11, 1983.

[19]Unidentified Lebanese intelligence sources cited in Friedman, "Some Detect Master
Plan."

[20]Quoted in "Extent of Iranian Involvement in Lebanon Is Discussed."

[21]Ayatollah Muhammad Hussein Fadl Allah [sic], "Islam and Violence in Political
Reality," *Middle East Insight,* Vol. 4, Nos. 4–5, 1986, pp. 4–13.

It's only to be expected that any situation of despair can impel one to suicide, when it is a personal matter involved. When a person owns nothing, or has nothing to lose, he will resort to any means, ordinary and extraordinary, even those which would destroy both his adversary and himself. . . . Islam takes to war . . . [not] to bring people to Islam, but only when others try to limit its freedom of movement.[22]

Velayati made the identical point in a 1984 newspaper interview. "The United States intervention in Lebanon," he stated, "is the main cause of developments that followed. When the United States intervenes in another country it should expect certain reactions from people."[23]

The intervention to which Velayati referred was the increasing assistance U.S. military forces were providing to the Lebanese Army in its offensive against Shia militiamen and their Druse allies during September 1983. On September 8, the U.S. Navy battleship *New Jersey* had shelled Druse positions in the mountains around Beirut. Targeting instructions were relayed to the gunners aboard the *New Jersey* by the U.S. Marine contingent in the MNF from its headquarters and observation post at the Beirut International Airport. This provision of support profoundly changed the Marines' role—no longer an impartial peacekeeping force, the Marines had become active participants in the fighting. By this time, moreover, their mission in Lebanon had become to support U.S. Secretary of State George Schulz's unrealistic and doomed effort to force Lebanon into a peace treaty with Israel against the inclinations of numerous Lebanese internal elements and in the face of Syria's total hostility. Thus the Marines were militarily supporting one faction in Lebanon and pursuing Israel's goals there. In turn, the United States was brought into direct conflict with the Shia and Druse militias, and with their Iranian patrons as well.

In response to this situation, Iran—with Syrian backing—unleashed an intensified campaign of terrorist suicide car and truck bombings in October and November designed to drive the U.S. forces from Lebanon and destroy the MNF arrangement. On October 23, simultaneous suicide truck bombings rocked the U.S. Marine Headquarters at Beirut International Airport (killing 241 Marines) and the French paratroop headquarters in that city (killing 58 persons). A similar attack was staged on the Israeli military government building in Sidon on November 4, resulting in 67 deaths.

The uproar generated in the United States over the attacks played right into Iran's hands. One of the main aims of a terrorist act is to

---

[22]Ibid. See also, "Muhammad Husayn Fadlallah: The Palestinians, the Shia, and South Lebanon," Interview on November 21, 1986, *Journal of Palestine Studies*, pp. 3–10.

[23]Quoted in Sciolino, "Iranian Promises Help to World's Oppressed."

produce far-reaching psychological repercussions, and the American reaction to the suicide bombings of the Marine Headquarters and the U.S. Embassy in Kuwait (described below) provides a textbook case of how this objective was achieved.[24] For example, U.S. naval vessels stationed off the coast of Lebanon were immediately placed on alert because of fears that Islamic terrorists were planning to make "kamikaze-type" attacks in airplanes loaded with explosives. The concern over suicidal attacks by Islamic fanatics, moreover, was not confined to the Middle East: Concrete barriers were hastily erected outside the White House, the Department of State, the Pentagon, and other government and military facilities in the United States.

In addition, the decision to deploy the Marines to Lebanon as part of the MNF was criticized with increasing fervor in the United States. The Reagan Administration was faulted both for putting the Marines at risk and for inadequately considering the implications of their active involvement in support of the Lebanese Army. When the Marine contingent sustained further casualties after heavy fighting erupted between Lebanese Army units and Shia militiamen in February 1984 (bringing the number of U.S. servicemen killed in Lebanon to 264),[25] the United States bowed to public pressure and ordered the withdrawal of its troops from Lebanon. With the departure of the U.S. forces, the MNF arrangement crumbled. Iran had achieved an important objective, and a major obstacle to its designs in Lebanon was removed.

IRAN'S TERRORIST SPEARHEAD: ISLAMIC JIHAD

At the end of 1983, the geographical scope of Iranian-backed Shia terrorist operations broadened as six bombing attacks rocked Kuwait. A suicide truck bomb exploded at the U.S. Embassy and nonsuicide vehicular bombings occurred at the French Embassy, the Kuwaiti Water and Electricity Ministries, the Kuwait airport, an American diplomatic residential compound, and a Kuwaiti petrochemical factory. Another car bomb was discovered and defused near the Kuwaiti government passport office. Nine days later, bombs exploded near the Iraqi Embassy in Istanbul and in Ankara; and on the same day, car bombs were set off near a French military post and a hotel in Beirut.

The extension of the Iranian-backed terrorist campaign to Kuwait brought into sharp focus one of Teheran's principal foreign policy

---

[24]Bonnie Cordes et al., *Trends in International Terrorism, 1982 and 1983*, The RAND Corporation, R-3183-SL, August 1984, p. 1.

[25]Lou Cannon and Michael Getler, "Reagan's Decision: A Political Gamble," *Washington Post*, February 8, 1984.

objectives: the export of the Islamic revolution to other Muslim countries. Notwithstanding Kuwait's geostrategic position astride the Persian Gulf, it is a small, relatively defenseless, and thus vulnerable target. But more important, like Lebanon, Kuwait has a sizable Shia community, and consequently, Iran viewed it as fertile ground for subversive revolutionary activity. Finally, the generally pro-Western policies of Kuwait, coupled with its unstinting support of Iraq in the war with Iran, inevitably incurred the enmity of the Iranian regime. The terrorist attacks thus had a dual motivation: to advance Iran's regional, revolutionary ambitions and to punish the conservative Kuwaiti rulers for their support of Iraq.

The violent onslaught directed against the United States, France, Israel, Kuwait, and Iraq provided the first indication of the political consciousness and tactical sophistication of the Iranian regime's two-track strategy and the internal dynamics of its international terrorist campaign. All of these attacks were carried out by Arabs—either Lebanese or Iraqi Shia—not Iranians. Although the operations were staged at the behest of Iran, and the attacks in Lebanon doubtlessly were facilitated by the logistical support and guidance of the Revolutionary Guardsmen stationed in that country, Iran was able to preserve at least a veneer of deniability of the attacks and thereby avoid possible retaliation.[26]

Indeed, all of the 1983 attacks—in Lebanon, Kuwait, and Turkey—were claimed in the name of "Islamic Jihad." This term had first appeared in May 1982. Although it was initially suspected that Islamic Jihad was a previously unknown Lebanese Shia terrorist organization, the 1983 operations—in particular, the bombings in Kuwait and Turkey—suggested that Islamic Jihad was not in fact a single terrorist entity, but a front or coalition of individual Shia groups operating at the behest of Iran under a common framework. Islamic Jihad is in fact now known to be a cover name for operations carried out by Hezbollah, sponsored by Iran, with additional support provided by other Middle Eastern countries such as Libya and Syria.[27] The individual terrorist

---

[26]For example, retaliatory airstrikes were carried out by both France and Israel against Lebanese Shia terrorist concentrations in the Bekaa Valley in November 1983 and by the United States, through the guns on the USS *New Jersey*, in the same area the following month. Despite suspicion of Iranian complicity in the terrorist bombings, no military action whatsoever was carried out directly against Iran. (See Shahram Chubin, "Iran and Its Neighbors: The Impact of the Gulf War," *Conflict Studies* (London), No. 204, October 1987, pp. 4–5.)

[27]As many as 25 separate terrorist groups are believed to operate under the aegis of Islamic Jihad (*The Economist, Foreign Report*, No. 1841, September 27, 1984). However, Taheri notes that "a study of some of the most important terrorist attacks against Western interests since 1983 shows that at least eight different groups have been involved, most of which do not seem to have any structured and regular relationship with

14   RECENT TRENDS AND FUTURE PROSPECTS OF IRANIAN-SPONSORED TERRORISM

organizations that are believed to have carried out operations under the banner of Islamic Jihad include *Hezbollah, al-Dawa,* and *Jundollah* (Soldiers of God). At the same time, these organizations often carry out their own operations entirely separate from Islamic Jihad.

Although the inherent secrecy of this arrangement makes any definitive analysis of Islamic Jihad's organizational structure based on open, unclassified sources difficult, its operations are thought to be directed by a secret council with four regional and several local commands. Its controlling body, which is known as The Supreme Coordinating Council between the Iranian Islamic Revolution and Islamic Revolutionary Organizations in the World, is believed to be directed from Iran by Ayatollahs Montazeri and Musavi Khoeyniha. Members of the council reportedly include Mohsen Rafighdust, Iran's former Minister for the Revolutionary Guards; Mohammed Mir-Salim, adviser to the Iranian Defense Ministry; Zabih Zanganeh, a representative of the Iranian secret police; Hussein Musavi of *Islamic Amal*; and Ahmad Nahaullah, a leader of underground Shia cells in Saudi Arabia. The council also allegedly directs terrorist operations in Egypt.[28]

There is reason to believe that the nerve center of Islamic Jihad operations in the Middle East in the early 1980s was Iran's Embassy in Damascus. With an operational budget in 1983 of some $400 million—the largest of any Iranian legation—the embassy also had a staff of over 200 persons. The Ambassador, Ayatollah Ali-Akbar Mohtashami, reportedly enjoyed direct access to Khomeini in his role as coordinator of Islamic Jihad activities.[29] Mohtashami chaired an informal working group whose members included Hussein Musavi, Abbas Musavi, Ayatollah Fadlallah, and Mohammed Khansari (described as Khomeini's permanent link with Libyan leader Mu'ammar Qaddafi), together with several high-ranking Syrian intelligence officers, including Colonel Ghazi Kenaan, the head of Syrian military intelligence and the former military commander of Syria's armed forces in Lebanon. Acting on instructions from Teheran, this working group allegedly commissioned and paid for the terrorist attacks carried out by Islamic Jihad.[30]

---

one another beyond a deep ideological affinity." (Taheri, *Holy Terror: The Inside Story of Islamic Terrorism*, p. 125; see also Brian Michael Jenkins and Robin Wright, "The Kidnappings in Lebanon," *TVI Report*, Vol. 7, No. 4, 1987, p. 4.)

[28]*The Economist, Foreign Report*, No. 1841, September 27, 1984.

[29]Taheri, *Holy Terror: The Inside Story of Islamic Terrorism*, p. 126.

[30]See *The Economist, Foreign Report*, No. 1841, September 27, 1984; "Extent of Iranian Involvement in Lebanon Is Discussed"; and Taheri, *Holy Terror: The Inside Story of Islamic Terrorism*, p. 126.

III. TRENDS IN INTERNATIONAL SHIA TERRORISM

The clerics' involvement in Shia international terrorism has ebbed and flowed several times. Unlike most areas of Iranian foreign policy, the support for execution of terrorist operations has been related to both factional disputes in Teheran and tactical shifts in clerics' foreign policy calculations. This section examines patterns in international Shia terrorism since 1983 and attempts to explain these trends and place them within the context of developments in Teheran among the Iranian ruling elite.

1983: THE WAVE OF BOMBINGS

The establishment of Islamic Jihad and the attacks carried out under its aegis in 1983 were a watershed in the pattern of Shia terrorism. Whereas throughout the preceding four years the level of Shia terrorism had remained fairly low and constant (four incidents in 1979, three in 1980, five in 1981, and six in 1982), in 1983, Shia extremists staged 19 attacks (see Fig. 1).[1] Eleven of these attacks—more than half the total—occurred in Lebanon. Indeed, from this time onward, that country would be the primary locale of Shia terrorism. Similarly, Islamic Jihad was responsible for the majority of terrorist incidents that year, as it would be in succeeding years, carrying out eight of the attacks. At the same time, the proliferation of individual Shia terrorist groups in Lebanon also accounted for the increase recorded during 1983. *Al-Dawa* claimed responsibility for four incidents, and a variety of other Shia extremists groups such as the Black Berets, *al-Sadr* Brigades, and *Hezbollah* took credit for the remaining seven.

1984: THE EMERGENCE OF KIDNAPPING

In 1984, the number of terrorist operations carried out by Shia extremists again increased, to 31. Although a majority of the incidents occurred in Lebanon, others were carried out, or attempted, in France,

---

[1]Unless otherwise noted, the data and statistics on Shia terrorist incidents presented in this analysis are based upon information from the RAND Chronology of International Terrorism.

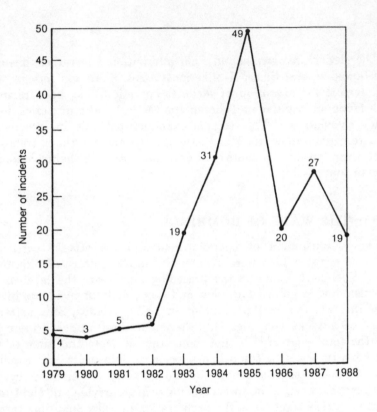

Fig. 1—International terrorist acts committed by Shia extremists

Spain, West Germany, Italy, Greece, Iraq, Kuwait, and Indonesia.[2]
The three most significant of these were an attempt by Islamic Jihad
to hijack a Saudi airliner and shoot down another in Spain in July, a
planned suicide truck bombing of the U.S. Embassy in Rome (which
was foiled when Italian police arrested seven Lebanese Shia members
of Islamic Jihad on November 27), and the hijacking in December of a
Kuwaiti airliner by five Iraqi Shia terrorists belonging to *al-Dawa*, in
which two American passengers were murdered. The bombing plot

---

[2]This list does not include the 19 ships that struck mines in the Suez Canal between
July 9 and September 20, 1984. Although Islamic Jihad released a communique on July
31 claiming that it had laid 190 acoustic mines in the Gulf of Suez and the southern
entrance to the Red Sea to punish "imperialists" for encouraging an expansion of the
Iran-Iraq war, the minings are believed to have been done by Libya. (Data from the
RAND Chronology of International Terrorism.)

against the U.S. Embassy and the hijacking of the Kuwaiti airliner were undertaken in a bid to obtain the release of 17 Islamic Jihad members who had been arrested and imprisoned in Kuwait following a series of bombings that rocked that country in December 1983; as noted above, those involving Saudi Arabia were intended to punish that country for its support of Iraq.

However, Shia terrorist tactics changed significantly at this time (see Table 1). Where bombings had previously been by far the preferred tactic (between 1979 and 1983, 56 percent of all Shia terrorist attacks involved bombing),[3] the 11 bombings in 1984 accounted for only 35 percent of Shia terrorist operations—a decline of 12 percent compared with the previous year (bombings accounted for 47 percent of all operations in 1983). In what was to become a pattern of Shia terrorist activity, kidnappings in 1984 accounted for 41 percent of all Shia terrorist incidents. There were 13 kidnappings that year and 23 in 1985. The number declined to 11 in 1986 (55 percent of all incidents) and to only 5 in 1987 (18 percent of the incidents that year).

The change in tactics from bombing to kidnapping appears to have been influenced by a number of factors. First, the increased security measures taken by foreign governments at their embassies and other diplomatic facilities in Lebanon had made bombing attacks more difficult to execute. The attackers were thus forced to shift their attention to less protected targets, such as foreign nationals, who became the victims of the new campaign. Indeed, analyses of terrorist tactics in

Table 1

SHIA TERRORIST TACTICS, 1979–1988

Year	Kidnapping	Attack	Hijacking	Bombing	Assassination	Threat
1979	—	1	2	1	—	—
1980	—	—	1	2	—	—
1981	—	—	2	3	—	—
1982	1	1	1	3	—	—
1983	1	6	1	9	2	—
1984	13	1	2	11	3	1
1985	23	2	2	17	5	—
1986	11	3	1	3	2	—
1987	5	3	1	14	3	1
1988	4	2	1	9	3	—

[3]During this four-year period, a total of 41 incidents occurred: 23 bombings, 7 aircraft hijackings, 7 armed assaults, 3 assassinations, and 1 kidnapping.

general have shown that increasing security at certain targets does not necessarily neutralize the terrorist threat, but merely shifts attention to "softer," more vulnerable targets. In Lebanon, foreign diplomats, businessmen, academicians, journalists, and clergymen became targets of tactical convenience for the Shia terrorist organizations.

Second, the seizure of foreigners provided the terrorists and their Iranian patrons with a sustained means of applying pressure to the victims' governments. Unlike the evanescent pressure created by bombings or other forms of immediate attack, the prolonged holding of hostages provided a festering reminder of the terrorists' demands. Islamic Jihad abducted five Americans in 1984 to coerce the United States into pressuring Kuwait to release the aforementioned 17 Islamic Jihad prisoners in that country. To pressure Saudi Arabia to end its support of Iraq, Islamic Jihad kidnapped a Saudi Arabian diplomat. Islamic Jihad abducted the Spanish Ambassador to Lebanon in an attempt to secure the release of four Iranian terrorists who had been arrested in Spain in July.[4] By the same token, the seizure of a French engineer in Beirut was most likely intended to exert pressure on France to end its arms sales to Iraq.

Islamic Jihad was responsible for 12 terrorist incidents in 1984—more than any other Shia extremist group. However, in contrast to the previous year, the number of incidents attributed to other groups declined slightly (from 11 to 9).[5] This decrease is probably attributable

---

[4]The Saudi Arabian consul in Beirut, Hussein Farrash, was the first person seized by the terrorists that year, on January 17. The following month, Frank Reiger, a U.S. citizen working as a professor at the American University of Beirut, was kidnapped; in March, Jeremy Levin, the Beirut bureau chief of Cable News Network, and William Buckley, the CIA station chief in Lebanon, were seized; the Rev. Benjamin Weir was kidnapped in May; and an American student was abducted in November. Of the nine hostages taken by Shia terrorists, only the American student and Weir were released voluntarily by their captors. Although the student was freed 48 hours after he was abducted, Weir was in captivity for 16 months before he was released in September 1985. In what his captors described as an "act of good faith," Weir was allowed to go free after being instructed to inform the U.S. government that more Americans would be kidnapped and possibly executed if the 17 Islamic Jihad terrorists in Kuwait were not released from prison and allowed to leave that country. Reiger, the French engineer, and the Spanish and Libyan diplomats were freed in three separate rescue operations staged by the mainstream Shia *Amal* militia. Buckley, however, was murdered by his captors after being tortured by them to obtain information on U.S. intelligence operations in Lebanon. Of the original kidnap victims, Levin escaped, or was released by his captors, in February 1985, and the Saudi consul, Farrash, was released in May 1985. At least eight different terrorist groups have claimed credit for the eight Americans and 12 other foreign nationals (including the British Anglican Church envoy, Terry Waite) who are currently held hostage in Lebanon.

[5]For example, the *al-Sadr* Brigades claimed responsibility for both the kidnapping of a Libyan diplomat in June and the attack on the Libyan Embassy in Beirut in July to protest the disappearance of Imam Musa al-Sadr; *al-Dawa* took credit for the bombing of the Kuwaiti Embassy in Beirut in November and for the hijacking of a Kuwaiti airliner

to the efforts reportedly undertaken by the Shia extremist groups in Lebanon to consolidate their forces and coordinate their varied operations. Indeed, all of the major Shia groups active in that country—including *Islamic Amal, al-Dawa, Jundallah*, the Hussein Suicide Squad, and the Islamic Students Union—apparently were absorbed by *Hezbollah*.[6] Hence, an array of terrorist operations under the catch-all banner of Islamic Jihad were carried out by a strengthened, internal Shia terrorist infrastructure in Lebanon.[7]

1985: FACTIONAL RIVALRY AMONG THE IRANIAN RULING ELITE

More significant than the developments in Lebanon were the reports that surfaced near the end of the year of internal disagreements within the ruling clerical elite over Iran's involvement in and support of international Shia terrorism. The main point of contention concerned the efforts of the government in Teheran to restrain Shia terrorist activities somewhat in order to improve Iran's relations with the West and the Persian Gulf states and to curtail their support of Iraq. A number of extremist clerics entrenched in several revolutionary organizations insisted on the continuation of the existing policy.

The dispute, it should be emphasized, was not over the use of international terrorism as a means of achieving Iran's foreign policy objectives, but rather over the emphasis, timing, and targets of such operations. The so-called revisionist politicians within the ruling elite—including Khamenei, Rafsanjani, and Velayati—apparently stressed the need to encourage like-minded revolutionaries abroad through example, notably by educating the oppressed in Islamic countries about how the Iranian people rose up against the Imperial regime and tyranny. To opponents of this approach, such measures were not enough. The extremists contended that revolutionary movements had to be supported through arms, funding, and training, and that Iran as a revolutionary country was obligated to actively encourage and be intimately

---

the following month; members of *Hezbollah* were responsible for the attack on the Saudi Embassy in Beirut in August; and two hitherto unknown groups, the Guardsmen of Islam and Islamic Action in Iraq, respectively, claimed credit for the hijacking of an Air France jet to Teheran in July and the three bombings of Iraqi targets in Greece in December.

[6]Wright, *Sacred Rage: The Crusade of Modern Islam,* p. 95.

[7]See "I Have Met the 'Suicide Men,'" *Jeune Afrique,* January 25, 1984; Richard Harwood, "The Riddle of Islamic Jihad," *Washington Post,* September 21, 1984; David B. Ottaway, "Fixing Responsibility in a Vacuum of Power," *Washington Post,* June 21, 1985; Peyman Pejman, "Hezbollah: Iran's Splintered Ally," *Washington Post,* August 1, 1985; and Glenn Frankel, "Hezbollah Threatens Precarious Balance in S. Lebanon," *Washington Post,* September 28, 1986.

involved in the conduct of these activities.[8] The revolutionary politicians apparently sought to check the ascendance of their rivals by backing an intensified and more geographically wide-ranging terrorist campaign to sabotage the government's new initiative. It was reported, for example, that on November 23, 1984, a meeting was held in Teheran between representatives of *al-Dawa* and *Islamic Amal* and Ayatollah Montazeri, the nominal head of a number of revolutionary organizations.[9] The meeting occurred just four days before the Islamic Jihad plot to bomb the U.S. Embassy in Rome was foiled and 11 days before the *al-Dawa* hijacking of the Kuwaiti airliner. According to some reports, the meeting resulted in a decision to launch more "armed resistance" actions against Saddam Hussein's helpers in the Gulf War, such as Kuwait, Saudi Arabia, and Jordan, and to shift the anti-American campaign to western Europe.[10]

The repercussions of this decision were evident in the dramatic escalation of Shia terrorist activity during 1985. A record 49 terrorist incidents were recorded—18 more than the previous year. Although there was no significant deviation from the 1984 pattern of operations—Lebanon again being the main site of Shia terrorism, Islamic Jihad claiming responsibility for the most incidents, and kidnapping accounting for the largest share of operations—each of these categories showed a percentage increase.

The escalation of terrorist incidents in Lebanon was largely a product of the consolidation of the Lebanese Shia terrorist forces and the support received from revolutionary clerics in Teheran. The latter also accounts for the succession of terrorist incidents that occurred during 1985 in Western Europe and the Persian Gulf region. In March 1985, a cinema in Paris at which a Jewish film festival was being held was bombed; in April, a car bomb exploded outside of a restaurant in Madrid frequented by U.S. servicemen; that same month, a branch of an Israeli bank in Paris was bombed. Two bombings (one near a U.S. military compound) occurred in Riyadh, Saudi Arabia, on May 19, and six days later, an attempt was made on the life of the Emir of Kuwait by a terrorist driving a car packed with explosives. Four simultaneous bombings were carried out in Copenhagen against two Jewish targets and two American airline offices, followed by the bombing of the Istan-

---

[8]Kambiz Foroohar, "The Post-Khomeini Era Begins," *The Middle East*, January 1988, pp. 12–13.

[9]These included the Office of Islamic Revolutionary Movements, a semi-independent structure which maintained close ties with a host of revolutionary and Islamic underground organizations throughout the world.

[10]See, for example, *The Economist, Foreign Report*, No. 1852, December 13, 1984.

bul offices of the Israeli airline, El Al, and several Paris department stores. All of these operations were claimed by Islamic Jihad.

The increasing incidence of kidnapping was also reflected in the diversity of the nationalities of the victims. In 1984, five U.S. citizens, four Lebanese, one Saudi, one French, one Spanish, and one Libyan national were kidnapped. In 1985, five Americans, five Britons, four Soviets, three Frenchmen, one Lebanese, one Kuwaiti, one Swiss, one Dutch, one Canadian, and one Austrian national were seized. With American targets in Lebanon in scarce supply as a result of repeated warnings by the U.S. State Department concerning the safety of U.S. citizens there, the Shia terrorist groups turned to nationals of other Western countries who remained in Lebanon.

Accordingly, a sort of competition was generated among the Shia groups, all of whom regarded the seizure of foreign nationals as a means to either enhance their own stature or better serve—and impress—their Iranian patrons. Although Islamic Jihad claimed credit for ten of the abductions, *Amal* and *Hezbollah* were each responsible for two more, and two hitherto unknown groups, the Khaibar Brigade and the Islamic Liberation Organization, respectively, kidnapped two Britons and four Soviets.

1986: THE STRUGGLE OVER THE DIRECTION OF IRAN'S FOREIGN POLICY

The dramatic escalation of Shia terrorism in 1985 was followed by an equally dramatic decline in 1986. For the first time since 1980, the level of Shia terrorist activity decreased. Only 20 incidents occurred— less than half the number of the previous year. This decline was partly the result of the Iranian factional disputes that had begun the year before. In June 1985, Iranian foreign policy behavior shifted after Khomeini endorsed the curtailment of international terrorist activity in order to mitigate Iran's diplomatic isolation. By improving relations with the West and Persian Gulf states, Iranian leaders, including Rafsanjani, apparently hoped that Iran would be able to acquire much-needed military hardware for use in the war with Iraq, and that such a policy would also reduce outside support for the Iraqi war effort.[11] As a result, the geographical scope of terrorist activity narrowed considerably in 1986. Whereas nine countries had been the sites of Shia terror-

---

[11]Robin Wright, "Iranian Power Plays Reflected in Terrorist Moves?" *Christian Science Monitor*, November 5, 1986.

ist incidents in 1985, attacks occurred in only four countries in 1986, and no operations at all were carried out in Western Europe.[12]

The first tangible manifestation of this change occurred in June 1985, when a TWA flight was hijacked and its 41 American passengers were taken hostage by terrorists belonging to *Hezbollah*. With Khomeini's backing, the Iranian regime played an active part in resolving the nearly month-long crisis, applying pressure on the terrorists to release their captives. In a stunning reversal of his earlier position, Speaker Rafsanjani emerged as a pivotal figure in the negotiations with *Hezbollah* to free the hostages, a role that the United States acknowledged promptly.[13] Iran's intervention also proved to be the catalyst behind subsequent efforts by the Reagan Administration to obtain the release of the ten Americans then being held by Shia terrorists in Lebanon and to improve U.S.-Iranian relations in general.

As part of the so-called "arms for hostages" deal the United States pursued, several shipments of weapons were delivered to Iran, and two of the American captives (Father Lawrence Jenco and David Jacobsen) were freed. More than any other development, the decline in the number of terrorist incidents that occurred while these negotiations proceeded underscored Iran's involvement in and support of international terrorism. Islamic Jihad, the terrorist entity most closely associated with Teheran, was responsible for only 13 incidents in 1986, compared with 23 in 1985. Moreover, whereas 10 of the kidnappings in 1985 were attributed to Islamic Jihad, only 3 of the 11 abductions in 1986 were claimed in its name.

This shift in Iranian policy, however, did not go uncontested by the Iranian factional leaders who were opposed to the pragmatist camp. Working through their minions in Lebanon, they attempted to thwart the negotiations with the United States through an independent terrorist campaign, hoping to thereby undermine the credibility of their rivals. The percentage increases recorded in 1986 in both kidnapping and terrorist attacks in Lebanon were a direct result of this campaign.

Although fewer persons were abducted in 1986 than in 1985, kidnappings nevertheless accounted for 55 percent of all terrorist incidents, an increase of 6 percent over the previous year. This increase was largely due to the activity of extremist Lebanese Shia groups other than Islamic Jihad and was reflected in the escalation of the percentage of operations in Lebanon.

---

[12]Kuwait, Egypt, and Israel accounted for one bombing each, and an Iraqi aircraft was hijacked en route from Baghdad to Saudi Arabia.

[13]Wright, "Iranian Power Plays Reflected in Terrorist Moves?"

A particularly significant aspect of the 1986 kidnappings was the predominance of French victims, especially early in the year. All but one of the *Hezbollah* kidnappings involved French nationals. This selective kidnapping appears to reflect some apprehension on the part of the Iranian clerics who exercised influence with the Lebanese extremist groups. They may have been wary of using anti-American actions to discredit their pragmatist rivals at a time when the "arms for hostages" deal was being negotiated. Anti-American actions were perhaps thought to be overly bold: They could backfire and turn the Teheran regime against its sponsors, rather than convincing the regime to reverse its "moderate" foreign policy tilt. Therefore, to test the reaction in Teheran to the continuation of its anti-Western terrorist campaign, the hardline faction at first focused exclusively on French targets. Only later, after the new round of abductions was not significantly opposed, did Americans again become the targets of the Shia extremists. Thus, in 1986, Lebanon simply became the battleground of a bitter power struggle within the Iranian ruling elite. And, as events progressed, two figures in particular emerged as the principal actors: Rafsanjani and Montazeri.

In a bid to strengthen his own position, Rafsanjani had almost abandoned the hardline position he previously shared with Montazeri and others. In addition to the prominent role he played in ending the TWA hostage incident, Rafsanjani also appeared to moderate his position on a number of key domestic policy issues. He began to "cultivate the image of the statesman, trying to reassure the middle classes that the days when patrols of zealots raided their homes with impunity in search of such emblems of the counter-revolution as a chess board or a cassette of music, [were] over."[14] In addition, he made increasingly reassuring public statements regarding Iran's intentions should it win the war with Iraq (e.g., that Iraq's territorial integrity would not be violated, nor would the country be dismembered), indicating a willingness to negotiate with a new government in Baghdad ("even if it were pro-American") and taking a less strident position on the extension of the Islamic revolution to the Gulf states.[15]

By contrast, following his reaffirmation in November 1985 as Khomeini's heir-designate, Montazeri seemed to gravitate further toward the factions opposing Rafsanjani's initiatives. In particular, Montazeri took a harder line against anything less than complete vic-

---

[14]Hazhir Teimourian, "Succession Struggle Gathers Pace," *The Middle East*, April 1987, p. 17.

[15]Jean Gueyras, "No-Holds-Barred as the Mullahs Struggle for Succession," *Le Monde* (Paris), October 25, 1986.

tory in the war with Iraq.[16] In the meantime, many of the most extremist Iranian clerics, including Medi Hashemi, the alleged mastermind behind many of the kidnappings in Lebanon, continued their close association with Montazeri.[17]

Events came to a head during October 1986—in the midst of what was to be the final round of U.S.-Iranian negotiations for the release of the hostages—when members of the Office of Islamic Liberation Movements (ILM), allegedly acting on Hashemi's orders, kidnapped Mahmud Ayat, the Syrian charge d'affairs in Teheran.[18] The abduction of Ayat was widely seen as an attack on Rafsanjani's policies.[19] It apparently was calculated both to embarrass Rafsanjani and his allies and to warn Syria about its support for and encouragement of Iran's "moderate" foreign policy tilt.[20] Although Ayat was freed by the government 24 hours later, it took the personal intervention of Ahmad Khomeini, the Imam's son, to secure his release.

The kidnappers were immediately denounced by Prime Minister Musavi as "agents of World arrogance," and within days, Hojatoleslam Reyshahri, the Minister of Intelligence, had issued a warrant for Hashemi's arrest.[21] Additional arrests followed, including those of Hashemi's brother, Hadi (Montazeri's son-in-law), a number of ILM officials, and several members of the *Majlis* (the Iranian Parliament). Hashemi was accused in the state-run press of a variety of serious crimes, committed both before and after the 1979 revolution and involving murder and cooperation with SAVAK (the Shah's secret police). The gravity of the charges brought against Hashemi—who, in addition to being a relative of Montazeri's by marriage, had been described as Montazeri's "right-hand man"—thus constituted a serious blow to Montazeri's political prestige.

Indeed, Rafsanjani himself is believed to have played a key role in orchestrating the arrests. As Khomeini's personal representative on the Supreme Defense Council, vice-chairman of the Assembly of Experts, and serving *Majlis* Speaker, Rafsanjani had both the influence

---

[16]Foroohar, "The Post-Khomeini Era Begins," p. 12.

[17]Teimourian, "Succession Struggle Gathers Pace," p. 17; see also Gueyras, "No-Holds-Barred," and Ihsan A. Hijazi, "Rift Among Iran's Leaders Appears to Widen," *New York Times,* November 6, 1986.

[18]Teimourian, "Succession Struggle Gathers Pace," p. 15.

[19]Loren Jenkins, "Iranian Power Struggle Said to Be Escalating," *Washington Post,* February 4, 1987.

[20]Ayat had reportedly been "accused by his kidnappers of meddling in the succession and plotting against Montazeri." It was later determined that the kidnapping had been undertaken in order "to teach him a lesson" and "teach him not to meddle in Iran's internal affairs." (See Gueyras, "No-Holds-Barred.")

[21]Teimourian, "Succession Struggle Gathers Pace."

to order Reyshahri to take Hashemi and his cohorts into custody and the access to Khomeini necessary to secure the Imam's consent in advance of the roundup. Moreover, by exploiting his reportedly close relationship with Ahmad Khomeini, the Imam's son, Rafsanjani was able to initiate a whispering campaign in the Iranian capital that Khomeini was considering reconvening the "Assembly of Experts" to review Montazeri's selection and possibly elect a council of leaders in his place.[22]

It appeared that Montazeri's fortunes had been dealt a devastating blow. On November 1, however, details of secret negotiations between the United States and Iran were leaked to a Beirut news magazine by supporters of both Montazeri and Hashemi.[23] They apparently hoped that disclosure of the deal would simultaneously embarrass Rafsanjani and undermine his personal base of support, as well as that of the pragmatist allies, and would thereby prompt the government to drop the charges against Hashemi and his associates.

At least initially, the revelations knocked Rafsanjani off balance. He was forced to confirm publicly that the magazine account was correct and later to defend his role in the affair before the *Majlis*. Efforts were mounted to remove him as *Majlis* Speaker, and demands were voiced for the convening of a special parliamentary committee to investigate everyone involved in the negotiations.[24] Radical "student" supporters of Montazeri circulated leaflets in Teheran denouncing Rafsanjani's "betrayal of the Islamic revolution,"[25] while senior Iranian officials condemned his willingness to deal with the United States. Prime Minister Musavi, for example, castigated Rafsanjani, declaring that "Iran could have no relations with the 'criminal' United States, because the resumption of ties would be contrary to the Islamic principles of the revolution."[26]

But as events continued to unfold in Teheran, it became obvious that the calumny and vituperation directed against Rafsanjani had little effect on his position. Rafsanjani was neither removed from any of

---

[22]Teimourian, "Succession Struggle Gathers Pace"; Foroohar, "The Post-Khomeini Era Begins," p. 13.

[23]Eric Hooglund, "The Islamic Republic at War and Peace," *Middle East Report*, January-February 1987, p. 6; Jenkins, "Iranian Power Struggle Said to Be Escalating"; Robin Wright, "Iran Looks Beyond Khomeini," *The Nation*, February 7, 1987, p. 147; and Foroohar, "The Post-Khomeini Era Begins."

[24]Wright, "Iran Looks Beyond Khomeini," p. 146.

[25]Quoted in Jenkins, "Iranian Power Struggle Said to Be Escalating"; see also "Iran's Hardliners Gain," *Foreign Report* (London), No. 1946, November 27, 1986; and Wright, "Iran Looks Beyond Khomeini," p. 146.

[26]Quoted in Elaine Sciolino, "Iranian Officials Portrayed as United in Their Effort to Exploit U.S. Arms Furor," *New York Times*, November 17, 1986.

the offices he held nor made the subject of a threatened parliamentary investigation. His survival was in large measure the result of the support he continued to receive from Khomeini. Indeed, the Imam acted quickly to silence the squabbling between the Montazeri and Rafsanjani factions and ordered the Parliament not to investigate the U.S. arms deal, thereby protecting Rafsanjani and his co-conspirators.[27]

At the same time, Khomeini continued to back Montazeri, who retained his role as the Imam's successor-designate. A less charitable fate, however, awaited Hashemi. After being forced to appear twice on Iranian television confessing to his crimes, Hashemi was convicted on charges of "waging war against Islam" and being "corrupt on earth"— the most serious offenses under Iranian law—and was executed in September 1987.[28]

More significant and far-reaching was the government's decision in December to disband the ILM and transfer responsibility for supervising the activities of all external revolutionary groups to the Foreign Ministry.[29] Control of Iran's foreign Shia allies was the key to understanding the factional disputes plaguing Iranian foreign policy. Earlier attempts by pragmatist politicians in and out of the government to centralize these activities in the Foreign Ministry had been rebuffed by powerful figures outside of the government, such as Montazeri and Hashemi, who sought to maintain their independent connections with foreign extremist groups. Indeed, the struggle for control over the extremist Shia groups abroad had set in motion the chain of events that began with Hashemi's arrest and led to the revelations of the secret negotiations with the United States. In the end, therefore, it was Rafsanjani and the pragmatist camp who gained the most from this internecine power struggle.

1987: A NEW TURNING POINT

Much as events during 1983 marked a watershed in Shia terrorist activity, heralding an intensified campaign of violence, trends in Shia terrorism during 1987 also proved to be a turning point. It is especially noteworthy that the disbanding of the ILM and reassignment of

---

[27]Wright, "Iran Looks Beyond Khomeini," p. 147.

[28]Roger East (ed.), *Keesing's Record of World Events*, Vol. 33, Nos. 5 and 11, Harlow, England: Longman, 1987, pp. 35541–35542; see also "Inside Iran," *Foreign Report* (London), No. 1949, December 18, 1986; Jenkins, "Iranian Power Struggle Said to Be Escalating"; Wright, "Iran Looks Beyond Khomeini," p. 147; and Foroohar, "The Post-Khomeini Era Begins," p. 13.

[29]For details see "Inside Iran," *Foreign Report* (London), No. 1949, December 18, 1986.

responsibility for the direction of external revolutionary activities did not result in a decline of Shia terrorist activity but, instead, brought changes in the geographical focus of these operations and in the terrorists' tactics.

For the first time since 1983, the majority of incidents did not occur in Lebanon. Only five terrorist operations (18 percent of the total) took place in that country, a particularly dramatic decline in contrast to the 16 operations (80 percent) that occurred there the previous year. Also, for the first time since 1983, there were more bombings than kidnappings. Fourteen bombings were recorded in 1987 (11 more than the previous year), a 36 percent increase over the 1986 total (15 percent in 1986, 51 percent in 1987). But only five kidnappings were carried out in 1987 (18 percent of all incidents), whereas 11 were carried out in 1986 (55 percent). Kidnappings probably declined because there were few operations in Lebanon, where, for logistical reasons, all of the abductions have occurred. Less dramatic, but nonetheless significant, was the increase in the total number of incidents that occurred in 1987 (26, in contrast to the 20 in 1986).

Trends in Shia terrorism continued to demonstrate the intimate connection between disputes in Teheran and terrorist operations elsewhere. The principal issue affecting both the constellation of factions within the Iranian ruling elite and the conduct of the regime's international terrorist campaign was the dispute over control of the foreign Shia extremist groups, in the context of the war with Iraq. At the heart of this power struggle was the pragmatist camp's contention that the United States and conservative Arab monarchies in the Gulf would never permit an outright Iranian victory. Accordingly, this faction often emphasized the need to end Iran's diplomatic isolation, which, they argued, could be achieved only by improving Iran's external relations through curtailing its support for international terrorism. However, after their efforts throughout 1986 failed to bear fruit, agitation for a resumption of the international terrorist campaign increased among those who opposed the pragmatist approach. Even more ominous were indications that this campaign was to be waged in Western Europe to further alienate the West and embarrass the pragmatist wing, thereby undermining its overall domestic position.

Evidence that the hardline faction had been planning for a renewal of Iranian-backed terrorist operations in Western Europe surfaced on January 12, 1987, when Bashir al-Khodur, a Lebanese national, was apprehended at an airport in Milan carrying 20 pounds of plastic explosives with detonators. The following day, Mohammed Ali Hamadi—one of the *Hezbollah* terrorists wanted for the June 1985 hijacking of a TWA aircraft—was arrested at the Frankfurt airport

when explosives were discovered in his suitcase. Hamadi's apprehension subsequently led to the arrest of his brother, Abbas Hamadi, on
January 26. According to some reports, the Hamadis and al-Khodur
were part of a new deployment of Shia extremists sent to Italy, West
Germany, and France either as active terrorists or as "sleepers."[30]

More successful were efforts to project the terrorist campaign in the
lower Persian Gulf region. On January 19, 1987, simultaneous explosions rocked three oil installations in Kuwait. Responsibility for the
bombings was claimed from Beirut by the Revolutionary Organization
Forces of the Prophet Mohammed in Kuwait, a terrorist group composed primarily of Kuwaiti Shias. Iranian complicity was suggested by
the fact that the bombings were timed to coincide with a meeting of
the 46-member Islamic Conference Organization in Kuwait three days
later, which Iran had refused to attend in protest of Kuwait's support
of Iraq in the Gulf War.[31] Six days earlier, a new round of kidnappings
had begun in Beirut, when a French journalist was seized by members
of the Revolutionary Justice Organization.[32] Then, on January 17,
West German businessman Rudolf Cordes was kidnapped by the Organization of the Oppressed of the Earth, in retaliation for the arrests of
the Hamadi brothers by West Germany the previous week. On
January 24, three American citizens and one person with a U.S.

---

[30]"Iran's New Terror Plan," *Foreign Report* (London), No. 1952, January 22, 1987.
As a result of information gleaned from the arrests of the two Hamadi brothers, eight
persons suspected of planning terrorist bombings in France were arrested by French
authorities on March 26. They admitted to having ties with both Iran's secret service
and *Hezbollah* and are suspected of having been involved in the series of bombings that
shook Paris in September 1986, designed to force France to release a Lebanese Christian
terrorist, Georges Ibrahim Abdullah, an imprisoned Armenian terrorist, and an Iranian
terrorist serving a prison sentence for an assassination attempt on former Iranian Prime
Minister Shahpur Baktiar in 1980. (See Richard Bernstein, "French Terror Suspects
Report Link to Iranians," *New York Times,* March 27, 1987.)

[31]On January 31, Kuwaiti authorities announced that 11 persons had been arrested
and five others were being sought for the attacks. The surnames of two of those
arrested, Behbahani and Dashti, "suggested that they were Shiite Moslem Kuwaitis of
Iranian origin." Both families are among "two of the half-dozen leading Shiite families
of Iranian origin who came here around the turn of the century. Those families are
regarded as the peers of the network of influential, largely merchant, Kuwaiti families at
the pinnacle of influence." Although Iranian expatriates working in Kuwait had been
regarded as the principal source of trouble, the involvement of members of these old,
established families, whose loyalty had not in the past been doubted, came as a shock.
An estimated 60,000 to 90,000 Iranians presently reside in Kuwait, despite the fact that
"tens of thousands . . . [of Iranian nationals] have been deported in the last two years as
part of a security crackdown, and because of cutbacks in the economy due to falling oil
prices" (John Kifner, "Kuwait Arrests 11 in Oilfield Blasts," *New York Times,* February
1, 1987).

[32]The victim, a French television reporter named Roger Auque, was later released
after France allowed Walid Gordji, an Iranian official suspected of involvement in a
series of bombing attacks in Paris in September 1986, to return to Iran.

residency permit were abducted by a previously unknown group calling itself the Islamic Jihad for the Liberation of Palestine.[33]

Meanwhile, Iran launched a major military offensive against Iraq in early January 1987, apparently hoping to deliver the decisive blow needed to improve Iran's bargaining position in any future negotiations and thereby bring about an acceptable settlement. The importance the regime placed on achieving this objective was evident in the assignment of responsibility for the offensive to Rafsanjani. Iraqi resistance, however, was stronger than expected, and six weeks later, the offensive ground to a halt; on February 26, it was suspended.[34]

The failure of the operation weighed most heavily on the person responsible for its direction, Rafsanjani. The massive battlefield casualties sustained by the Revolutionary Guards, one of Rafsanjani's most important domestic constituencies, undermined the confidence of even his closest supporters.[35] But apart from the blow dealt to Rafsanjani's position within the regime, the failed offensive represented a major, if temporary, setback to the pragmatists.

Within weeks of the suspension of the offensive, a series of terrorist attacks were executed throughout the Middle East. In April, a plot to bomb an American airbase and Israeli diplomatic offices in Turkey was uncovered when Turkish police arrested four members of Islamic Jihad. That same month, an individual claiming to be a member of *Hezbollah* was arrested in Egypt after a bombing attack at the American University in Cairo. In May, three American diplomats escaped injury when the car they were driving was raked with machinegun fire. The attack was claimed by the Islamic Jihad of Egypt, an Egyptian group of Islamic extremists who are believed to be funded and directed by Iran.[36] A few days later, the same group claimed credit for the attempted assassination of two prominent Egyptians, a former Minister of the Interior and a well-known newsmagazine editor. In the wake of these shootings, the police carried out a massive roundup of Muslim

---

[33]All four of the victims—Alan Steen, Robert Polhill, Jesse Turner, and an Indian national, Mithileshwar Singh, who holds an American residency permit—worked at the American University of Beirut. Although the group's name and its demand that 400 Palestinians being held by Israel be released in exchange for the four hostages suggest that it is a Palestinian terrorist organization, in recent years, particularly close ties have been established between the PLO and Iranian-backed Shia groups in Lebanon. Moreover, this particular organization is thought to include both radical Shia and Palestinian guerrillas and to be loosely tied to *Hezbollah*. (See Jenkins and Wright, "The Kidnappings in Lebanon," p. 5.)

[34]East, *Keesing's Record of World Events*, pp. 35158–35159.

[35]Ali Behrooz, "Iran Ponders Next Move," *Middle East*, August 1987, p. 6.

[36]Tom Porteous, "Cairo Breaks Ties with Tehran as Muslims Held," *The Guardian* (London and Manchester), May 15, 1987. In addition, this group had taken credit for the assassination of Egyptian President Anwar Sadat in 1981.

fundamentalists.[37] Information gleaned from the arrests led to the apprehension of 37 members of the group who were charged with planning and executing the attacks. They were also accused of plotting to overthrow the government of Egyptian President Hosni Mubarak through a campaign of selective assassination of Egyptian officials, military leaders, journalists, and foreign diplomats. Citing evidence of Iranian involvement in the plot, Egypt announced on May 14 that it was severing diplomatic relations with Iran.[38]

More terrorist incidents occurred in Lebanon during the summer. American journalist Charles Glass was kidnapped in June by a previously unknown Shia terrorist organization, calling itself The Organization for the Defense of Free People,[39] and in August, the Tunisian branch of Islamic Jihad claimed responsibility for a series of bombings in Tunis, while the Saudi Arabian arm of *Hezbollah* took credit for blowing up a natural-gas pipeline in that country.

Shortly afterward, the locus of Shia terrorist activity again shifted to Europe. During September and October, six terrorist incidents, all aimed at Arab or Iranian targets, occurred in France and one occurred in England. Islamic Jihad claimed responsibility for the bombings of branches of a Saudi and a Kuwaiti bank; the hitherto unknown Islamic Resistance Front took credit for the bombing of the Tunisian Consulate in Paris (in retaliation for the arrests of Muslim fundamentalists in Tunisia following the bombings in that country), as well as for the three other incidents directed against Arab nationals in France; and the Guardians of the Islamic Revolution and Soldiers of Khomeini claimed responsibility for the assassination of two Iranian dissidents in London. At the end of October, the Pan Am offices in Kuwait were bombed by a pro-Iranian Kuwaiti Shia group calling itself the Organization for the Liberation of Muslims in Kuwait. Finally, in late December, another pro-Iranian group, the Sons of Allah, claimed credit for the attempted assassination of an Iraqi diplomat in Cyprus.

This escalation of Shia terrorist activity was particularly significant because of the geographical diversity of the operations. In previous years, the vast majority of incidents had occurred in Lebanon, but in 1987, eight countries became the sites of terrorist activity and ten attacks were carried out in Europe.

---

[37]Risks International, Inc., *Weekly Risk Assessment,* Vol. 4, No. 24, June 12, 1987.

[38]Porteous, "Cairo Breaks Ties with Tehran as Muslims Held."

[39]On July 1, NBC news reported that U.S. intelligence agencies had intercepted messages between the Iranian Embassy in Damascus and *Hezbollah* operatives in Lebanon that provided "conclusive evidence that Iran had ordered the kidnapping" of Glass. (Data from the RAND Chronology of International Terrorism.)

This change of geographical focus may have been related to the earlier decision to reassign responsibility for the direction of foreign Shia extremist groups to the Foreign Ministry. The officials now responsible for external terrorist activities may have been hesitant to continue to rely on Lebanese groups who were closely linked to their longstanding rivals in the disbanded ILM. The Foreign Ministry officials may have feared that their instructions would be disregarded or that effective control had not been established over these organizations. The decision to use operatives outside of Lebanon also meant that the extensive terrorist infrastructure in Lebanon which had facilitated the execution of complex operations, such as kidnappings, which required sophisticated logistical support to maintain secure safehouses and move hostages at will, could not be used. As a result, simple bombing and assassination became the most commonly used tactics of Shia terrorists during 1987.

In sum, the shift of responsibility for international Shia extremist groups from the ILM to the Foreign Ministry did not appear to significantly moderate Teheran's commitment to the use of terrorism as an instrument of foreign policy, but simply changed the terrorists' geographical focus and tactics.

1988: A CONSOLIDATION OF POWER

Fewer Shia terrorist incidents were recorded during 1988 than in any year since 1983. This decrease appears to have been a product of Iran's waning fortunes in the war with Iraq coupled with the pragmatist camp's continued efforts to assert its authority over foreign extremist groups and consolidate its position within the Iranian ruling elite. The ascendancy of the pragmatists—and of Rafsanjani in particular—was evidenced not only by this decline in terrorism but also by Iran's unconditional acceptance of United Nations Security Council Resolution 598, calling for a ceasefire in the Gulf War.

At first, the pattern of Shia terrorist activity in 1988 was remarkably similar to that of past years, involving kidnappings in Lebanon and an international airline hijacking. In January, the Revolutionary Justice Organization claimed responsibility for abducting a West German citizen, Rudolf Schray. The following month, an American Marine officer serving with the U.N. truce monitoring group, Lieutenant-Colonel William Higgins, was seized by a group calling itself the Islamic Revolutionary Brigades.[40] Both organizations are believed to

[40]Although Schray was released by his captors in March, Higgins was executed, and a videotape of his death was made public in July 1989.

be closely connected to, or affiliated with, *Hezbollah*. Other terrorists suspected of having ties to *Hezbollah* attempted to hijack two Kuwaiti airliners en route from Thailand in April. Although Thai police arrested one of the hijack teams at the Bangkok airport before they could board the targeted flight, the other team was able to commandeer a plane and divert it to Iran. In the course of the 16-day ordeal that followed, the terrorists murdered two passengers. Eventually, a deal was made whereby the hijackers agreed to free their captives in return for their own safe passage to Beirut and Thailand's release of the second hijacking team.

The motive for all of these incidents appears to have been to obtain hostages to trade for the release of imprisoned pro-Iranian terrorists. The Schray abduction was undoubtedly linked to the Hamadi arrest and trial in West Germany, while the Higgins abduction and the Kuwaiti airlines incident were related to the 17 Iraqi and Lebanese Shia terrorists imprisoned in Kuwait. An ancillary motivation may once again have been the desire to embarrass the pragmatist faction and thereby undermine its overtures to Western countries. If that were the case, the incidents might have been isolated, independent actions or part of a more concerted, though inchoate, effort orchestrated by the pragmatists' rivals from Teheran.

The pattern of international Shia terrorism during the first six months of 1988 closely mirrored developments in the Iran-Iraq War.[41] As they had in 1987, Iranian battlefield reversals initially provoked an intensification of international terrorist activity, particularly against Iraq's two principal Gulf allies, Saudi Arabia and Kuwait. Bombing attacks were carried out against two Saudi targets in West Germany and one in Kuwait during April and against Kuwaiti and U.S. targets in that country in May.[42] This campaign, however, was cut short by Iran's agreement in July to the U.N.-brokered ceasefire.

By the summer, it had become impossible for Iran's leaders to ignore the toll that more than eight years of unrelenting—and mostly inconsequential—warfare had taken on the Iranian people and economy. Their conviction that Iran could no longer prosecute the war and hope to survive as a nation had gained greater urgency as a result of a series of defeats suffered by Iranian forces during April and May.

---

[41]See David B. Ottaway, "Iran Not Expected to Hit Back Quickly," *Washington Post*, July 7, 1988.

[42]Additional incidents recorded between January and June involved the kidnapping of a Belgian national, Jan Cools, in Lebanon; the attempted assassination of four Syrian generals in Beirut; a bombing claimed by Islamic Jihad in Jerusalem; and the bombing of a shop in West Germany belonging to Iranian dissidents. Cools was released by his captors in June 1989, following the intervention of Libyan leader Mu'ammar Qaddafi. Fourteen Western hostages, including nine Americans, are still being held in Lebanon.

On April 17, Iraqi forces dislodged some 50,000 Iranian troops from the Faw Peninsula. The military's failure to either muster enough volunteers to stem the Iraqi onslaught or marshal sufficient supplies and war materiel for a counterattack signaled that Iran had reached the limit of its warmaking capacity. The setback to Iran was all the more profound in view of the fact that this strategically important territory had been conquered by the Iranians at the cost of great loss of life only two years before.

The following day brought still more bad news for Iran: the loss of an estimated 20 percent of its already reduced operational naval forces. In retaliation for damage to a U.S. Navy frigate by an Iranian mine on April 14, President Reagan authorized the destruction of three Iranian oil platforms (that incidentally had also served as observation posts for Revolutionary Guards' attacks on passing commercial ships). Combined Navy and Marine units attacked the two platforms during the early hours of April 18. However, before the third platform could be destroyed, Iranian naval vessels appeared on the scene to challenge the Americans. In the brief encounter that followed, Iran's only two frigates were knocked out of action, a high-speed patrol boat was destroyed, and three smaller launches were sunk by the U.S. forces. American loses were confined to one Marine helicopter and its two-man crew (at least 44 Iranians are thought to have been killed).[43]

The following month, Iraq was able to parlay its victory at Faw into a general rout of Iranian forces from Iraqi soil. On May 25, Basra, Iran's last remaining stronghold on the Iraqi side of the strategic Shatt al-Arab waterway, fell to Saddam Hussein's forces. The war, for all intents and purposes, was over. Indeed, within weeks, Rafsanjani, Khamenei, and Hashemi had agreed to a cessation of hostilities with Iraq.[44] The accidental shooting down of an Iranian airliner by the USS *Vincennes* in July, which resulted in the deaths of all 290 persons on board, may have been the last straw in cementing the Iranian decision to sue for peace.[45] So determined was the ruling elite to end the war that Montazeri's calls for revenge attacks on American targets were immediately and completely stifled—with Khomeini's consent—by Rafsanjani.[46] Fifteen days later, Teheran officially informed U.N. Secretary-General Perez de Cuellar of Iran's unconditional acceptance of the ceasefire terms.

---

[43]"What Khomeini Will Do Next," *U.S. News & World Report*, May 2, 1988.

[44]Eric Hooglund, "The Islamic Republic at War and Peace," pp. 7–8.

[45]Ibid.

[46]Youssef M. Ibrahim, "A Key Iranian Leader Mutes Calls for Revenge Against U.S. Interests," *New York Times*, July 9, 1988.

Although a petulant spasm of terrorist incidents by foreign Shia extremists followed, Rafsanjani and his allies were successful in curtailing any sustained, independent campaign by the external groups. In fact, only 6 terrorist incidents occurred between July and December, compared with the 13 that were recorded during the first six months of the year.[47] Notably, only one of these attacks was directed against U.S. or Western targets. The one exception was the midair bombing of a Pan Am flight over Lockerbie, Scotland, in December, which killed all 259 passengers aboard. Although responsibility for the incident has yet to be definitely attributed to a specific terrorist group, Western intelligence experts have voiced suspicions that the bombing was carried out by Iranian elements—perhaps acting independently of Teheran—to extract revenge for the downing of the Iran Air plane by the USS *Vincennes*.

By the end of the year, the pragmatist camp appeared to have secured its power base and consolidated support for its policy of increased trade and diplomatic relations with the West. Given the resulting overall decline of Shia terrorist incidents, the Pan Am bombing could be dismissed as an aberration, an isolated instance of calculated vengeance, rather than the beginning of a renewed tilt toward anti-Western extremism. Such a dismissal, however, may have been too hasty, in light of the series of events that unfolded during the first half of 1989. These developments not only disrupted the pragmatists' efforts to push Iran further along the path of international moderation, but thrust the country into a new period of uncertainty.

1989: KHOMEINI'S DEATH AND THE SUCCESSION QUESTION

As the new year began, the pragmatist faction seemed solidly in control of Iran's foreign policy. But in February the pragmatists' ascendant position over their anti-Western, hardline rivals was suddenly undercut by no less an eminence than Khomeini himself. The catalyst behind the ayatollah's intervention was the U.S. publication of a novel that Muslims considered blasphemous. On February 12, 2,000 Muslim fundamentalists in Islamabad, Pakistan, staged a violent protest against Pakistani-born British writer Salman Rushdie's book, *The*

---

[47]Two incidents in Turkey involved Saudi targets (an attempted bombing of the cultural mission in Ankara in July and the assassination three months later of a Saudi diplomat stationed in Turkey); bombing attacks were carried out against Syrian and Israeli military targets in Lebanon during October; and in December, three Irish soldiers serving with UNIFIL were kidnapped by an offshoot of *Hezbollah* (they were later rescued by *Amal* forces).

Satanic Verses. The demonstration quickly degenerated into a riot; several protestors were killed and hundreds were wounded when Pakistani security forces opened fire on the crowd. Thus, the publication of a book that would normally have passed unnoticed outside of literary circles was suddenly transformed into an international phenomenon as agitated Muslims throughout the world staged their own protests. In this febrile atmosphere, Iranian hardline elements quickly exploited the furor over *The Satanic Verses* as a vehicle to gain ground on their pragmatist opponents.

The affair assumed a new and more sinister character two days later when Khomeini publicly passed a death sentence on Rushdie and his publishers, and some Iranian clerics promptly announced rewards of millions of dollars to whomever fulfilled the ayatollah's decree. Khomeini's pronouncement was a green light to aggrieved Muslims everywhere. Nine of the twelve international terrorist incidents attributed to Shia extremists in the succeeding two months were directly linked to the Rushdie novel and occurred in countries such as Britain, the United States, Italy, Belgium, and Turkey.[48] To many observers, Khomeini's action suggested a repudiation of the pragmatists' attempts to improve relations with the West and an endorsement of the hardline faction's views.[49] At the very least, the uproar over *The Satanic Verses*—like the Pan Am bombing the previous December—demonstrated the pragmatists' incomplete control of Iranian foreign policy and tenuous authority over foreign Shia extremists.

In March, however, the pragmatist faction appeared to have regained lost ground when Khomeini demanded—and received—the resignation of his designated heir, Montazeri. Although the ostensible reason for Montazeri's dismissal was his increasingly strident criticism of the country's political leadership,[50] his past association with radical hotheads like Hashemi and more recent relations with discredited liberals, such as former Prime Minister Mehdi Bazargan, had prompted Khomeini to reconsider his choice of heir. Montazeri's greatest sin,

---

[48]Based on a preliminary review of incidents recorded in the RAND Chronology of International Terrorism.

[49]Nick B. Williams, "Iranian Urges Palestinians to Kill Americans," *Los Angeles Times*, May 6, 1989.

[50]Montazeri reportedly sent a letter to Khomeini that stated, "I dissociate myself from the mass killings going on in our prisons. . . . The world thinks of us as a nation of killers. . . . This is not in the interest of Islam or of the state Your Excellency is leading." He also declared in a public broadcast on the tenth anniversary of the revolution, "We are being led by an unrepresentative clique. . . . We have failed the people [and] have not lived up to our promises. . . . The young are right to be alienated." Quoted in Hazhir Teimourian, "The Mullah Goes Back to the Mosque," *The Middle East*, May 1989, pp. 20–21.

however, probably was running afoul of the ayatollah's son, Ahmad Khomeini. It was Ahmad who—in concert with Rafsanjani, Ayatollah Ali Meshkini (the chairman of the Assembly of Experts), and his son-in-law Mohammed Reyshari (the Minister of Intelligence)—orchestrated Montazeri's fall from grace. The younger Khomeini's intent was most likely to guarantee himself a role in choosing his father's successor and perhaps even become a member of the three- or five-man collective religious leadership that the Assembly of Experts was considering to replace a single heir-designate.[51]

With his long-time rival Montazeri out of the way, Rafsanjani moved to strengthen his own position by reaching beyond his usual constituency. During April, his public statements assumed a distinctly anti-Western tone in a bid to appeal to hardline elements and thereby enhance his candidacy in the Iranian presidential elections scheduled for July 1989. He used one Friday sermon as an opportunity to announce a purge of high-ranking military officers who were arrested on charges of being part of "a big American spy ring."[52] Rafsanjani's cultivation of this hardline image continued into early May when, during another Friday prayer service, he called on Palestinians to avenge the deaths of their brethren in the Occupied Territories by killing five Americans, Britons, or Frenchmen for every Palestinian killed by the Israelis. The *Majlis* Speaker explained his offer of "serious advice" by stating that U.S., British, and French targets were more plentiful than Israeli ones.[53] Rafsanjani, however, later insisted that he had been misquoted.[54]

Nearly five months of enigmatic change and upheaval climaxed in June with Khomeini's death. In retrospect, the timing of Montazeri's removal as heir had been critical, given Khomeini's deteriorating health. But when the ayatollah finally died on June 4, he had named no new successor. Although the Assembly of Experts selected Iranian President Khamenei to fill this position, Khamenei's clerical status— he is a hojatolislam—is beneath that of Khomeini. Moreover, none of the other potential candidates has the religious stature that Khomeini, as an ayatollah and "supreme leader," possessed.[55] This implies that, in the absence of a successor who should have been designated before Khomeini died, the person (or persons) ultimately appointed will be vulnerable to charges of illegitimacy. In this situation, factional

---

[51]Ibid.

[52]Quoted in Williams, "Iranian Urges Palestinians to Kill Americans."

[53]Ibid.

[54]John Kifner, "Iran Now Seen as Free to Pursue a Softer Line," *New York Times*, June 13, 1989.

[55]Khamenei's title, for instance, is that of "leader of the revolution."

rivalries could intensify as contending groups vie for power. Given past instances of clerical infighting, the contending. factions' use of international terrorism either to advance their own claims or to undermine their opponents would not be unprecedented.

Iran's use of international terrorism and support of foreign Shia terrorist activities may also be determined by the way those in power interpret Khomeini's last will and testament. The will, which was made public two days after the ayatollah's death, denounced the United States and the Soviet Union, as well as Saudi Arabia, Iraq, Egypt, Jordan, and Morocco, before concluding, "May the curse of God and that of his angels be upon them all."[56]

---

[56]Quoted in "One Last Thing . . . ," *The Economist,* June 10, 1989.

IV. CONCLUSION: FUTURE PROSPECTS OF CLERICAL SUPPORT FOR INTERNATIONAL TERRORISM IN THE POST-KHOMEINI ERA

It appears that, in the short term at least, little change can be expected in Iran's use of international terrorism as an instrument of foreign policy. At the heart of this policy is the regime's avowed commitment to export the Islamic revolution to other Muslim countries—a commitment that has been neither tempered nor altered in the years since Khomeini came to power. As Iranian President Ali Khamenei once explained, "We have aided the liberation movements in the best possible manner, and no government has the right or power to tell us that we have intervened in their internal affairs. . . . No one can tell us to stop publicizing our version of Islam or stop us from describing our revolution to the people of the world."[1]

Terrorism, accordingly, has thus far remained a state policy, one agreed upon by most Iranian clerics because it has been sanctioned by Khomeini himself. But, even this salient consideration apart, terrorism has emerged as an especially useful tool for the contending factions within the Iranian ruling elite to gain leverage against their rivals. These factions have manipulated foreign Shia extremist groups to embarrass or undermine the power and prestige of domestic opponents, as well as to sabotage any improvement of Iran's relations with other Middle Eastern or Western states. Changes in the fortunes of individual factions are therefore unlikely to have much impact on the regime's overall commitment to the use of terrorism *except* when it can be exploited by one faction to weaken another. Consequently, international Shia terrorist activity may well increase following Khomeini's death and the ascendance to power of a new Iranian ruler or collective leadership. Since the authority of the successor (or successors) will certainly be unequal to that of Khomeini, his (their) rivals may have more freedom to mount independent terrorist campaigns in the service of personal or factional ambitions.

The possible escalation of international terrorism may include intensified operations against the United States and various regional adversaries if the current ceasefire between Iran and Iraq is broken by the Iraqis. In that case, the terrorist activities may also become far less discriminate. To date, Shia terrorist actions have been selective and

---

[1]Quoted in Wright, *Sacred Rage: The Crusade of Modern Islam*, pp. 33–34.

CONCLUSION: FUTURE PROSPECTS   39

cautious; their targets have been restricted to the United States, Israel, France, Kuwait, Saudi Arabia, and other countries that have incurred Iran's enmity either by supplying weapons to Iraq or by imprisoning Shia terrorists. Similarly, if the current Gulf ceasefire holds and is followed by an acceptable political resolution of the conflict, Iran's sponsorship of international terrorist activities can be expected to be greatly reduced.

In the future, however, if factional disputes in Teheran over the succession issue become sufficiently acute and persistent to supersede concern over foreign policy, terrorist activities could proliferate as a result of various factions' preoccupation with efforts to embarrass or undermine the power of other factions. It is important to note that the Iranian-sponsored terrorists have great potential for growth, since they have not developed particularly close ties with radical, left-wing, or anti-Western *non-Shia* terrorist groups in Europe or elsewhere. Alliances with these groups could be exploited if factional infighting were to increase radically now that Khomeini has died.

BIBLIOGRAPHY

Behrooz, Ali, "Iran Ponders Next Move," *Middle East*, August 1987, pp. 5–6.

Bernstein, Richard, "French Terror Suspects Report Link to Iranians," *New York Times*, March 27, 1987.

Cannon, Lou, and Michael Getler, "Reagan's Decision: A Political Gamble," *Washington Post*, February 8, 1984.

Chubin, Shahram, "Iran and Its Neighbors: The Impact of the Gulf War," *Conflict Studies* (London), No. 204, October 1987, pp. 1–23.

Cordes, Bonnie, et al., *Trends in International Terrorism, 1982 and 1983*, The RAND Corporation, R-3183-SL, August 1984.

East, Roger (ed.), *Keesing's Record of World Events*, Vol. 33, Nos. 5 and 11, Longman, Harlow, England, 1987.

Fadl Allah, Ayatollah Muhammed Hussein, "Islam and Violence in Political Reality," *Middle East Insight*, Vol. 4, Nos. 4–5, 1986, pp. 4–13.

Fadlallah, Muhammad Husayn, "Muhammad Husayn Fadlallah: The Palestinians, the Shia, and South Lebanon," Interview on November 21, 1986, *Journal of Palestine Studies*, pp. 3–10.

Foroohar, Kambiz, "The Post-Khomeini Era Begins," *The Middle East*, January 1988, pp. 11–13.

Frankel, Glenn, "Hezbollah Threatens Precarious Balance in S. Lebanon," *Washington Post*, September 28, 1986.

Friedman, Thomas L., "Some Detect Master Plan," *New York Times*, December 13, 1983.

Gueyras, Jean, "No-Holds-Barred as the Mullahs Struggle for Succession," *Le Monde* (Paris), October 25, 1986.

Harwood, Richard, "The Riddle of Islamic Jihad," *Washington Post*, September 21, 1984.

Hijazi, Ishan A., "Rift Among Iran's Leaders Appears to Widen," *New York Times*, November 6, 1986.

Hooglund, Eric, "The Islamic Republic at War and Peace," *Middle East Report*, January-February 1987, pp. 7–8.

———, "The Search for Iran's Moderates," *Middle East Report*, Vol. 17, No. 144, January-February 1987, pp. 5–6.

"I Have Met The 'Suicide Men'," *Jeune Afrique*, January 25, 1984.

Ibrahim, Youssef M., "A Key Iranian Leader Mutes Calls for Revenge Against U.S. Interests," *New York Times*, July 9, 1988.

Jenkins, Brian Michael, and Robin Wright, "The Kidnappings in Lebanon," *TVI Report*, Vol. 7, No. 4, 1987, pp. 2–11.

Jenkins, Loren, "Iranian Power Struggle Said to Be Escalating," *Washington Post*, February 4, 1987.

Khomeini, Imam, *Islam and Revolution* (translated by Hamid Algar), KPI, Ltd., London, 1981.

Kifner, John, "Iran Now Seen as Free to Pursue a Softer Line," *New York Times*, June 13, 1989.

———, "Kuwait Arrests 11 in Oilfield Blasts," *New York Times*, February 1, 1987.

Legum, Colin, "Iran's Role in World Terrorism Depicted," *The Age* (Melbourne), January 5, 1984.

Ottaway, David B., "Iran Not Expected to Hit Back Quickly," *Washington Post*, July 7, 1988.

———, "Fixing Responsibility in a Vacuum of Power," *Washington Post*, June 21, 1985.

———, "Baalbek Seen as Staging Area for Terrorism," *Washington Post*, January 19, 1984.

———, "Hijack Called Part of Plot to End Support for Iraq," *Washington Post*, January 15, 1984.

Pejman, Peyman, "Hezbollah: Iran's Splintered Ally," *Washington Post*, August 1, 1985.

Porteous, Tom, "Cairo Breaks Ties with Tehran as Muslims Held," *The Guardian* (London and Manchester), May 15, 1987.

Sciolino, Elaine, "Iranian Officials Portrayed as United in Their Effort to Exploit U.S. Arms Furor," *New York Times*, November 17, 1986.

———, "Iranian Promises Help to World's Oppressed," *New York Times*, October 4, 1984.

Shapira, Shimon, "The Origins of Hizballah," *The Jerusalem Quarterly*, No. 46, Spring 1988, pp. 115–130.

Taheri, Amir, *Holy Terror: The Inside Story of Islamic Terrorism*, Sphere Books, London, 1987.

Teimourian, Hazhir, "The Mullah Goes Back to the Mosque," *The Middle East*, May 1989.

———, "Succession Struggle Gathers Pace," *The Middle East*, April 1987, pp. 15–17.

Williams, Nick B., "Iranian Urges Palestinians to Kill Americans, *Los Angeles Times*, May 6, 1989.

Wright, Robin, "Quiet Revolution: The Islamic Movement's New Phase," *Christian Science Monitor*, November 6, 1987.

———, "Iran Looks Beyond Khomeini," *The Nation*, February 7, 1987.

BIBLIOGRAPHY   43

——, "Iranian Power Plays Reflected in Terrorist Moves?" *Christian
    Science Monitor*, November 5, 1986.
——, *Sacred Rage: The Crusade of Modern Islam*, Linden
    Press/Simon and Schuster, New York, 1985.
Zonis, Marvin, and Daniel Brumberg, *Khomeini, the Islamic Republic of
    Iran, and the Arab World*, Harvard Middle East Papers, Modern
    Series, No. 5, 1987.
——, "Behind Beirut Terrorism," *New York Times*, October 8, 1984.

Newspapers and Periodicals

The Age
al-Majallah
Christian Science Monitor
Conflict Studies
The Economist
Foreign Report
Guardian
Jeune Afrique
Journal of Palestine Studies
Los Angeles Times
The Middle East
Middle East Insight
Middle East Journal
Middle East Report
New York Times
The Nation
Risks International, Inc., *Weekly Risk Assessment*
TVI Report
U.S. News & World Report
Wall Street Journal
Washington Post

[4]

CHEMICAL AND BIOLOGICAL WARFARE – THREAT OF THE FUTURE

by Evelyn le Chêne

Introduction

There is little doubt that the signing of the INF Agreement between the superpowers elicited renewed anxiety in NATO regarding the Soviet Union's overwhelming superiority in chemical and biological weaponry (CBW), their means of delivery, and on-going research into "genetic engineering".[1] Of particular concern is Soviet development of a range of hallucinogens and psychochemical agents for application against civilian targets. Soviet Foreign Minister Eduard Shevardnadze's conditional offer in January 1989 that the Soviet Union "will begin in 1989 the elimination of its chemical weapon stockpiles" introduced a new dimension. Verification problems remain to be overcome, and so do the dangers of proliferation.

The recent United States and British intelligence reports that Libya has constructed a new facility to produce CBW brings into sharp focus the proliferation of these weapons within the developing world and the awesome possibility of terrorist acquisition. CBW is viewed as "the poor man's atomic bomb". It is currently possessed by fifteen countries – some say it could be as many as twenty-four – among which are nations the West has little or no cause to trust: Libya, Syria, Iraq and Iran.

Since the end of the Second World War, it has been the norm for the West to believe that CBW is so abhorrent that it constitutes its own deterrent. As a result, we have been slow to react to new developments. Part of the reason was our fixation with the "nuclear arms race", which tended to obscure developments in the East Bloc of a different nature. Irrefutable evidence of the use of chemical warfare agents in Afghanistan, Angola, the Iraq-Iran conflict and more recently against Iraqi Kurds has slowly forced a change of attitude, and there are now signs of serious reappraisals of the situation within the Western Alliance. The news media have also pushed for action.

In August 1988, Britain sponsored a UN Resolution threatening action against any nation using chemical weapons. One month later the United States Congress voted for an unprecedented range of sanctions against Iraq for its "genocide against the Kurdish population".

In Geneva the forty-nation Conference on Disarmament is locked in one of the most intractable problems in the history of arms control: defining what constitutes chemical warfare agents in order to formulate a policy and treaty for their banning. Any agreements that may emerge will be constrained by two major impediments – the problem of verification; and the difficulty of mobilizing the political will to take effective measures against treaty violators. The Meeting in Paris at which Shevardnadze spoke was intended to accelerate the work at Geneva. Unless and until a fully effective control regime comes into being, covering the Third World as well as industrialized powers, the threat can only be countered effectively if governments in the North Atlantic Alliance:

- Recognize the political and strategic implications of doing nothing;

- Provide increased resources to the military and other agencies;

- Institute educational programs for the civilian population and create a separate division within Civil Defence structures;

- Plan and provide communal shelters for the civilian population including provision of protective clothing; and

- Find the courage to do what must be done.

Failure could undermine NATO's credibility and lead to the further destabilization of the developing world.

Some of these ideas were presumably in British Prime Minister Margaret Thatcher's mind when, immediately after the signing of the INF Agreement in November 1987, she addressed a plea to Soviet leader Mikhail Gorbachev. In this she said:

> remember, we too have fears… so show your good faith by withdrawing and destroying your massive stockpile of chemical weapons along NATO's borders.

8

Presumably, Mr. Shevardnadze's initiative is an answer to this plea. Like so much else in the current phase of East-West relations, it is impossible to know whether it can be taken at face value as evidence of a sudden reversal of Soviet military (and, indeed, political and ideological) policy, or if it is a manoeuvre to disarm Western fears and make it impossible for Western governments to take the measures listed above. We are entitled to be hopeful; we are obliged to be cautious.

Historical Background

Paradoxically, the threat the West is just waking up to, CBW, is one of the oldest weapons in the history of mankind. Its use goes back as far as 2,000 BC when the Indian epic *Ramayana* tells of the 'Sammahonastra' – projectiles producing stupor or hypnosis, and arsenical and alkaloidal 'smokes' were understood during the Sung dynasty. At least one of the chemical tactics propounded in Leonardo da Vinci's 15th century *Notebooks* is copied from the *Histories* of Polybius. Chinese scientists wrote of toxic projectiles in the 11th century and the Moors used poisoned arrows in Spain in 1483. Sulphur was resorted to at Sevastopol during the Crimean war. Biological warfare is just as ancient, dating back to 600 BC when the spreading of disease and pollution of water sources under siege conditions led to surrender.

We tend, however, to think of Chemical Warfare in the context of the First World War.[2] It was first used on April 22, 1915, by the Imperial German Army against French forces at Ypres. It was a crude mustard gas (vesicant) that left approximately 5,000 dead and 10,000 injured. Before the global conflict ceased, all nationalities were to suffer the effects of diverse chemical warfare agents: Russia losing almost 100,000 with a further million and a quarter injured. Gas was used between the world wars: in Ethiopia by the Italians and in China by the Japanese. At the onset of the Second World War, Germany had developed a new and highly toxic nerve gas, TABUN, at its research and development plant at Dynerforth, Silesia. By the end of the war, another nerve agent even more lethal had been developed, SARIN. All CW agents, complete with research information, were removed from Germany by Soviet occupation forces and transferred to the USSR where they

9

formed, and still form, the basis of Soviet Chemical Warfare potential and knowledge.

The Soviet Concept of Chemical Warfare

U ntil the late 1970s the West tended to associate Soviet chemical warfare and weaponry with their nuclear war-fighting doctrine. From 1980, however, it became clear that chemical and biological agents within the Soviet arsenal had applications under conditions short of nuclear conflict. A leading Soviet authority remarked that:

> According to experience of a number of exercises, chemical weapons were adopted from the very beginning of combat operations in combination with conventional weapons.[3]

Since that time, CBW has been fully incorporated within the spectrum of Soviet "conventional" armaments.

Soviet attitudes to CBW were probably influenced by the obvious "flexibility" of the weapons due "not only to their high toxicity but also to the relative ease with which they can be synthesized, their low cost, and the possibility of obtaining them in a large quantity and using them in delivery means of all types, such as aerial sprays, cluster bombs, missile warheads, artillery rounds, chemical mines and so on".[4]

This was a theme taken up by Marshal Ogarkov who saw CW as "a means of armed struggle... capable even in non-nuclear war of rapidly destroying all life over an enormous area".[5] Soviet strategy in using CBW would be to accelerate an offensive in its initial stages or to regain the momentum in the event of stalled progress.[6] In the first wave it would be used to neutralize NATO's airfields, naval bases and seaports, command and control facilities, and storage depots. Being an "area cover" weapon, CW is seen as useful in depriving NATO of a timely response to aggression:

> under these circumstances, he (NATO) will have difficulty in setting up and preparing for use, nuclear and chemical weapons.[7]

The psychological impact on defending forces is also seen as a pertinent factor, as would be the choice of agent – the persistent or non-persistent varieties – to be used depending upon battlefield requirements.

The central role of CW in recent Soviet strategic planning for achieving a quick victory in a non-nuclear assault on Western Europe was indicated during the DRUZHBA '84 Warsaw Pact exercises in Czechoslovakia. In these exercises, CW attacks were simulated against NATO's anti-tank defences. Once breached, elite formations – "Operational Manoeuvre Groups" (OMG's) and helicopter forces, would be committed to operations in the NATO rear. A massive "conventional" wave would then follow through.

There have been similar exercises since that time with simulated CW attacks incorporated in the program. More pertinently perhaps, there is increasing evidence that the Soviet Union has resorted to chemical weaponry in regional conflicts in which it is either directly or indirectly involved. Brigadier Watay, former Chief of the Chemical Department of the 99th Rocket Regiment stationed in Afghanistan stated after his defection to the West:

> The Russians used chemical weapons at a time when their strategic tactics and the operations of their air and ground forces did not bear fruit and they failed to beat back the Mujahideen and break through their defences.[8]

Spetsnaz troops – the USSR's elite special forces – have received training in chemical/biological warfare for sabotage purposes, especially when "intentional, covert contamination of specific objectives is required".[9] Nor is the idea of CBW use for covert operations (sabotage) new. As far back as 1971 at a Warsaw Pact meeting in East Germany – more than two years after President Nixon's halting of US CW production – it was established that "under combat conditions they (CBW agents) can be used as an aerosol or in a solid or liquid state in mixed elements of ammunition: *they can also be used for sabotage purposes*".[10]

One analyst has concluded that Soviet CBW strategy towards the United Kingdom might "create maximum problems for the population, initially through blackmail and then by causing dislocation to public services, rail, port facilities, communications and power".[11]

11

The agents to be used for this purpose could include hallucinogens and psychochemical agents developed in the Soviet Union specifically for application against civilian populations. As the analyst points out:

> The USSR has shown great interest in the use of hallucinogens and other anti-personnel agents against populations, therefore we may expect to see a very selective and clinical employment of CBW using the latest technology in this area, particularly psychochemical agents to cause civilian panic.[12]

Spetsnaz training has included application of low level hallucinogens and high-level bio-contaminants for creation of this civilian panic.

The psychological reaction of the target population (military or civilian) to a CW attack is the key issue in this Soviet CBW strategy. Militarily, the defender's ability to fulfill his task and counter an offensive would be greatly reduced given the cumbersome protective clothing they would be obliged to wear. The heat factor, awkwardness of movement, diminution of flexibility with weapon and tool operation and reduced communication factors, all have their role in establishing a feeling of "isolation" and vulnerability. Combat effectiveness of military personnel under these conditions rapidly deteriorates and between 30 and 50 percent of their battle readiness would be forfeit after approximately two hours.

The effectiveness of CBW in an initial phase of conflict is dependent to a large degree on the psychological and physical resilience of the defending forces. Soviet thinking appears to be that general public opinion in the West will succumb to the intimidatory nature of such an attack on NATO forces with a subsequent collapse of morale among the military.

As for our civilian populations, the Soviets "are well aware of the total lack of any credible civil defence measures or precautions, not just in the United Kingdom, but across the whole of NATO".[13]

It was against a background of a virtual Soviet monopoly of modern CBW capability that Mikhail Gorbachev's "New Thinking" came on the scene. The excitement and hopes raised by Glasnost and Perestroika, the INF Agreement, and the general easing of East-West tensions have created a cli-

12

mate of opinion in NATO countries where military threats are simply not taken seriously by electorates. Consequently, the fact that the Soviet Union continued to develop, manufacture and deploy its CBW, unattached to any "linking" Treaty within ongoing disarmament talks, was a point that few governments in the West had the political will to acknowledge and confront. Now that the USSR has conditionally committed itself to destroying CB stocks, will Western leaders be content with reassuring statements, or will they push for the severe verification regime necessary to ensure that, after destroying quantities of older stocks, the Soviets do not conceal a war-winning quantity of the most modern concoctions? In short, will the Paris Meeting of January 1989 prove to have been a breakthrough for international security, or for the unilateral disarmament of the West?

Soviet Organization and Potential

C *hemical Troops – KvH.* There are currently 100,000 fully trained KvH of which 45,000 are attached to regular Soviet and Warsaw Pact units. Training takes place in more than 200 facilities and includes protection techniques and decontamination. Officers receive a four to five year instruction period in either the Timoshenko Military Academy for Chemical Defence or Higher Military Engineering School of Chemical Defence. "Realistic" field training includes simulated offensives using mustard gas substitutes.[14] All Soviet chemical detection kits captured in the Middle East and Afghanistan were equipped to detect gases known to be in Soviet and Warsaw Pact arsenals only, as are the medical antidotes carried by their troops. General V.K. Pilalov was head of all CBW activity when he described these forces as "special troops designated for chemical warfare support of armed forces combat formations".[15]

Soviet CBW Potential. The Soviet Union has ten CW agent production centres, all in the west of its territory, and nine chemical weapons depots more widely dispersed west-east. Storage sites for operational areas face NATO positions and are in Czechoslovakia (with nine), East Germany (nine also) and Poland with four sites, three of which are seaward oriented. Further south, to complete the cordon, there are five sites in

13

Hungary, four in Rumania and one in Bulgaria. The depots are organized for sophisticated distribution.

Chemical agents, stored in drums, are delivered by rail, tracks for which run into the depots from production centres. In the same complex chemical support vehicles assume liaison with KvHs, the Soviet chemical formations. Storage sites themselves are juxtaposed delivery systems and most CW agents are destined for incorporation into a delivery system "on the spot". Delivery is possible in any artillery weapon of 100 mm calibre or greater, from missiles and rockets, mortars and mines to bombs, spraying from the air and shelling from sea. The advent of the Soviet Typhoon class submarine and the military build-up in the Kola Peninsula bring the United States and Canada within range of chemical and biological attack from submarine-launched cruise missiles.

A statement made by the US Department of Defence in 1985 had this to say:

> The USSR is better prepared to conduct operations in a chemical environment than any other force in the world. Soldiers receive extensive chemical defence training. Most combat vehicles are equipped with a chemical protection system and a chemical detection alarm system. Chemical defence troops with specialized detection and decontamination equipment are found throughout the ground forces...Their continued testing of chemical weapons, the enlarged storage capacity of chemical agents and weapons, and the existence of active production facilities are indicators of a serious weapons program.[16]

Chemical Agents. There are eight basic categories of chemical warfare agents, namely:

- Choking agents such as Phosgene and Diphosgene;

- Nerve agents, Tabun, Sarin, Soman and VX;

- Blood agents, Cyanogen chloride and Hydrogen cyanide;

- Blister agents, also known as Vesicants. These include all the "mustard" range, and Lewisite;

14

- Respiratory irritants (persistent) such as Diaryl-chloroarsine;

- Vomiting agents, Adamsite, Diphenychloroarsine and Diphenylcyanoarsine;

- Lacrymatory agents such as Chloroacetophene and O-Chlorobenzylmalonotrile – CS;

- Incapacitating agents.

There are an estimated 300,000-400,000 tons of CW agents stockpiled, particularly within the range of the four most toxic – vesicants, nerve, blood and choking gases.

Biological Agents. The Soviet Union has a biological warfare test and evaluation centre on Vozrozhdeneniya Island in the Aral Sea and at least three Research and Development Institutes for biological warfare of which the Institute of Molecular Biology, some thirty km southeast of Novosibirsk, is largest, employing up to 2,000 scientists and technicians. It was from the Microbiological Research Institute in Sverdlovsk that a major leakage of anthrax dry spores occurred in 1979. As much as 22 lbs. (10 kg.) were released contaminating an area four or five kilometres in radius and reportedly leading to the deaths of approximately two thousand local inhabitants.

There are three categories of biological weapons. The first group are those organisms found in nature, alive and capable of reproducing themselves. Living viruses found in nature include yellow fever, smallpox, typhoid, plague, diphtheria, cholera, dysentery and anthrax. Of these, Soviet research appears to be concentrating on anthrax as it exists in active phase and in dry spore form, can be absorbed through the skin or by inhalation, and is as lethal to man as to livestock. The second category is the toxin range produced by bacteria and directed toward a specific human target. Thirdly, there are the microbiological organisms produced by *genetic engineering*. This latter group provides "model" agents to produce predetermined effects, be it to kill or temporarily incapacitate. It is also within this range that hallucinogens and psychochemical agents are to be found.

Of all the ranges mentioned, by far the most to be feared is the development in genetic engineering. By splicing DNA from an organism into another of grown controllable bacteria,

15

the new bacteria can be "programmed". The result is the spectre of "an organism owned by one aggressor nation which can produce it and its protective antiserum for its troops and population in large quantities at relatively small cost"[17]

It has taken decades of research for Soviet scientists to arrive at the level they have in all three biological ranges. As far back as 1971, the *role* that the State saw for such weapons within the future arsenal, was discussed during a Warsaw Pact scientific conference in East Germany. There it was reported

> The rapid development of biological engineering will make it possible in just a few years to produce synthetic or partially synthetic toxins on a large scale. Such toxin agents represent a combination of the hitherto chemical and biological weapons.

Five years later the development had taken place and was already incorporated in Soviet Military Technology published in the Military encyclopedia. Other points from the Conference were:

> Achievements in biology and related sciences (biochemistry, biophysics, molecular biology, genetics, microbiology and experimental aerobiology) have led to an increase in the effectiveness of biological agents as a means of conducting warfare. Improved methods of obtaining and using them have resulted in a qualitative reexamination of the very concept of "biological weapons", and

> Neurotropic toxins are toxic proteins which are primarily of the life cycle of micro-organisms. The neurotropic toxins are the most toxic chemical susbstances... Under combat conditions they can be used as an aerosol or in a solid or liquid state in mixed elements of ammunition; they can also be used for sabotage purposes.

Protection of civilians in the USSR. Protection of the civilian population in the USSR against chemical warfare attack is a longstanding commitment. From the age of eight years, all

16

children are trained in "what to do", i.e. to mask up and seek shelter in communal centres.

If the Soviet Union is serious about abandoning CBW, a weapon system in which she has invested so heavily and in which she enjoys so commanding a lead, she will presumably dismantle the entire research and development, production, storage and supply apparatus, the civil defence program, as well as the KvH specialist troops.

The Vulnerability of NATO

President Reagan's decision to authorize the development and production of the Binary System in 1986 resulted from the evidence of Soviet build-up in CBW capability. The timing of this decision was crucial given that stockpiled chemical weapons have a shelf-life of only twenty years. With President Nixon halting all production in 1968, unless Reagan had made his decision, no nation within the military structure of NATO would have had a deterrent in kind. Nonetheless, even were the Soviet Union to forego further development and production, it would take the United States twenty years at current rate to lift its stocks to parity with the Soviet Union.

US stocks rapidly becoming obsolete are mainly at the Toole Army Depot in Utah. There is a small amount under US control in West Germany. This supply is due to be destroyed and there are no plans to stockpile new sources in Germany. Indeed, due to the hesitancy of all European NATO partners, the United States will not be deploying the Binary System in Europe at all, even if there is no treaty.

Great Britain abolished production of chemical warfare in 1948 and two decades later the Labour Party Prime Minister, Harold Wilson, underlined the fact by dumping Britain's remaining stock of 20,000 gas masks in the North Sea.

France, the only other independent nuclear nation in Western Europe, does produce a small amount of chemical warfare agent but is not in the integrated NATO structure and would not be obliged to react were any of its EEC or NATO partners so attacked.

Great strides have however been made in prophylaxis: the development of antidotes has gone ahead, and NATO's protective clothing is certainly superior to anything to be found

17

within the Warsaw Pact. This consists of protective jacket and trousers, overboots, gloves and mask. The British S.10, developed at Porton Down, is perhaps the best of its kind and includes communication and drinking attachment. NATO's ability to detect the presence of toxic agents is advanced, as is the medical care of those affected by CBW. Yet none of these undeniable "good points" suffice to protect either our forces from threat or actual use of CW against them, or our civilian population.

There is no nation within NATO that has its civilian population protected against the effects of CBW. There is no provision for funding of clothing or medical care and, importantly, no structure per se within Civil Defence Organizations for this explicit purpose. Therefore there is a lack of training, understanding, and of course, facilities.

There are only two countries in Europe possessing what is required. Both are so-called "neutral nations": Sweden and Switzerland.

NATO's military ability to withstand CW attacks and to pursue a counter-offensive is impressive and sufficient to force hesitation on the part of the potential enemy. The vulnerability lies much more with the total lack of protection of the civilian populations. This fact diminishes NATO's ability to "protect" and could be a key consideration in any Soviet strategic planning.

Proliferation

Of no less concern to the West must be the proliferation of chemical and biological warfare agents within the developing world and the risk of such falling into the hands of terrorists and nations over whom we have little or no control. In this context, the United States submitted two reports providing details of Soviet provision of CBW agents to developing nations which were known to have been used in conflict.[18] There have been other reports of CBW use, some confirmed, all with at least circumstantial evidence:

- Iraq's use of Tabun confirmed by Sweden;[19]
- Thailand's complaint against Vietnam in 1985;[20]
- Libyan use in Chad;

- Libyan use in Northern Uganda in support of the pro-Moscow government; and

- Cuban use against Jonas Savimbi's UNITA forces in Angola.[21]

The most recent evidence of chemical weapon usage against civilian populations is that of Iraq against the Kurdish minority.

Egypt has a potential as does North (and possibly South) Korea. But of all the nations acquiring or having access to CBW within the developing world, the most alarming for the West must be Iraq, Iran, Syria and Libya.

Iraq has its own production centre some forty miles outside Samarra and its own "test grids". According to the influential RUSI *Newsbrief*, the installation extends over a surface of 25 sq km and has the ability to produce 1,000 tons of poison gas per year.[22]

Iran has had access to chemical weapons for some time and avowed publicly before the Iraq-Iran cease fire, to produce and use them. A reported agreement, said to have come into effect early in 1988, to provide Libya's Kadaffi with chemical weapons in return for deliveries of missiles, would indicate that Iran is already producing.[23]

Syria was reported in the spring of 1988 to have received a visit by General Pikalov, Commander of Soviet Chemical Forces, and that subsequently Syrian Frog and Scud missiles were armed with payloads of Vx – the highly toxic nerve agent. If this is confirmed, it will illustrate a new policy direction from Moscow far removed from the spirit of the Paris Meeting and present a risk of major destabilization in the Middle East and Gulf area.[24]

Libya. Colonel Kadaffi is alleged to have used chemical agents in Chad against Hissene Habre's defenders and to have been involved in Uganda in like manner. Libya does have a production capability in Matan-as-Sarra and, more recently constructed, at Rabitah, 55 kilometres southwest of Tripoli, although there is no confirmation of actual manufacture.

All four nations support, supply and harbour international terrorists.

The portent of CBW in the Middle East is not new: Egypt had the potential as early as 1950, perfected by importing East German technicians, and "field tested" in the Yemen Civil War. Since that time, the Arab world has divided into two camps, the pro-Iraq (Egypt, Jordan and the Gulf States) and pro-Iran (Libya and Syria). Both camps have developed their missile arsenals and both have opted for acquisition of CBW. It was to be Iraq's use of chemical weapons, however, that introduced them to inter-Islamic conflict. Initially they converted "smoke" ammunition to chemical munitions; then they were supplied with Soviet-made chemical weapons, including diversified delivery systems. By 1985, Egypt had assisted Iraq in converting a pesticide plant at Samarra into a nerve agent facility – making Iraq the principal producer of toxic chemicals in the region. In the volatility of the Middle East, it is difficult to believe that once such weapons are introduced they will not become the norm. It is a pattern that risks recurring throughout the developing world. How to contain its implications will be a major problem not only for the West but eventually for the Soviet Union as well.

Industrial Disasters

Most thought is given to the military and subversive application of CBW and its effect upon the military and civilian population. The question of commercial (industrial) disasters must also be taken into consideration, however. No better example of the problem can be given than the tragedy in Bhopal. There on December 3, 1984, about forty tons of Methyl Isocyanate (MIC) – an intermediate in the production of insecticide – leaked into the atmosphere.

More than two thousand people died within two days in and around Bhopal and a further twenty thousand were seriously afflicted with lung lesions. There were no textual guidelines for such an occurrence and even the US company concerned, Union Carbide Corporation, was at a loss.

Since that time there have been several industrial accidents, the most recent being in France in 1987, in the Soviet Union in January 1988, when a train carrying hazchem derailed, and in Poole, England, in June 1988. In all cases, hundreds of people were evacuated and although evacuation was conducted in

20

an orderly and controlled fashion, the lack of comprehensive parameters within which to conduct the work or any centralized backup for such specific incidents became painfully obvious. Should evacuation be required under a wartime situation, Civil Defence (volunteers), Fire Brigades and Police would be unable to cope with the situation.

Protecting the Civilian Population

In 1982 the Swedish Government issued the following decree:

The civilian population should in the first case be protected from the effects of conventional weapons. The Defence Committee considers that the continuing armament concerning chemical weapons has increased the risk of these weapons being utilized. Increased attention should therefore be paid to protection against chemical weapons and noted when framing a total defence strategy in conventional war. In order to limit damage, ability to detect, give alarm and to command, as well as knowledge of the effects of these weapons, should be aimed at.[25]

Effective protection of the civilian population is dependent upon plans having been made and implemented based on likely scenarios that may have to be faced. It is perhaps pertinent that we consider such a hypothetical situation here. Let us imagine a toxic cloud. As it moves downwind it mixes with ever increasing amounts of air, becoming larger and more dilute. Diffusion of the vapour vertically and at right angles to direction of motion reduces the exposure to someone standing in its path. Diffusion forward and backwards along the direction of travel in general does not reduce the amount inhaled by someone in the path of the cloud.

The rate of vertical and lateral mixing of the toxic cloud with the surrounding air can vary enormously depending on weather conditions. A bright sunshiny day promoting convection of the atmosphere close to the ground, will cause rapid vertical mixing. A turbulent wind will promote lateral mixing. High windspeeds also reduce the time that a person is im-

21

mersed in a passing cloud and directly reduces the amount he or she will inhale for a given quantity going by. The worst conditions providing the greatest threat to people at the greatest distance downwind occur under conditions of light, steady winds, a clear night with cooling of the ground to cause vertical stability in the atmosphere and the existence of a temperature inversion not too far above the ground to trap the chemical close to it. Conditions very similar to this were responsible for the casualties at the Bhopal incident.

A Warning System. Evaluation of what is happening is a major priority when considering evacuation. Evacuation is a way of increasing the distance between the population and a hazard and is the counter-measure to toxic chemical releases. It is very effective for slowly developing hazards. Slowly developing hazards can include a relatively small leak of a volatile toxic chemical or a large spill of low volatility but highly toxic substance. Or again, a progressive accident such as a fire, which does not at first cause release of toxic chemicals but has the potential of spreading to nearby equipment, tanks and drums containing toxics.

Of course it is evident that there must be an adequate warning system of an attack or hazard. Some chemicals have a strong odour and lower degree of toxicity, such as chlorine and hydrogen sulphide, and would be easily detected. It is the physiologically undetectable agents at low but lethal concentration, such as nerve agents, that would be most worrying. If the agent is released subtly through unobserved corroding of a storage cylinder, or clandestinely – as by a terrorist or saboteur – the only indication that something was amiss would be people collapsing.

Detection apparatus has been developed to very high standards. Particularly is this the case with the British CAM (Chemical Agent Monitor). Hand held, it is specifically developed for the military and, apart from Switzerland and Sweden, no nation outside the Warsaw Pact bloc has any detection and alarm provision for the civilian population.

A Protective System. The bottom line of protection must be the ability to provide shelter, protective clothing (including respiratory aids) medical assistance and alarm systems. These factors are vital whether evacuation is to take place or not.

All are within the realm of possibility. Portable shelters for from five to twenty five people already exist, as do prophylaxis (medical antidotes) and protective clothing. None has been included in any structure within NATO nations' Civil Defence. Nor is there any information on procedure for public distribution or specific training sessions for Civil Defence organizations, Fire Brigades and Police on whose shoulders will fall the awesome responsibility of care and evacuation in time of crisis.

Banning Chemical and Biological Weapons

E fforts to achieve a definitive ban on the production and possession of chemical weapons have been ongoing for ninety years. The Hague Peace Conference of 1899 stipulated that the contracting powers agreed to "abstain from the use of projectiles the sole object of which is the diffusion of asphyxiating or deleterious gases".[26]

The Hague Conference eight years later outlawed the "use of poisons". Use of chemical weapons in the First World War, however, brought clearer definitions in the prohibiting directives incorporated in the texts of Resolutions taken at the 1923 Conference of Central American States and the 1925 Geneva Protocol, supported in 1932 at the League of Nations General Disarmament Conference. Post Second World War saw the issue raised again at the Disarmament Commission of 1953, the Ten Nation Committee on Disarmament of 1960, the Eighteen Nation Committee on Disarmament 1962 and all meetings of the Conference on Disarmament in Geneva since 1969.

Despite such efforts, as analyst Hugh Stringer indicates, agreement to date remains that established in Geneva in 1925 prohibiting "the use in war of asphyxiating, poisonous, or other gases, and all analogous liquids, materials, or devices".[27]

The Geneva Protocol is ratified by 118 nations.

The question of effective control of biological weapons promises to be even more difficult. To a certain extent any negotiations on this problem have been overtaken by events, particularly the emergence of Soviet research and development in "genetic engineering". The Convention on the Prohibition of the Development, Production and Stockpiling of

23

Bacteriological (Biological) and Toxin Weapons and on their Destruction, concluded in 1972 and signed by 111 nations, including the Soviet Union, states that the agreeing parties will

> never develop, produce, stockpile or otherwise acquire or retain microbial or other biological agents or toxins of types and in quantities that have no justification for prophylactic, protective or other peaceful purposes, or weapons, equipment or means of delivery designed to use such agents or toxins for hostile purposes or in armed conflict.

The same regulations oblige signatories

> not to transfer to any recipient, and not to assist, encourage or induce any State, group of States or international organizations, to manufacture or otherwise acquire such agents, toxins, weapons, equipment or means of delivery.

In all those cases the Soviet Union is in violation.

Developments nevertheless took place between 1972 and 1977 when the Committee of the Conference on Disarmament concentrated on banning chemical weapons. A British proposal tabled in 1976 was followed by the Soviet Union and United States agreeing to bilateral negotiations, which were halted in 1980 after verification disagreements between the two parties. It is significant in this context that the Soviet Union only began to show signs of "willingness" for international, then bilateral, talks when it became apparent that Western apprehension about Soviet activities in this field threatened reaction and, in the case of the United States, augured the onset of the US Binary System.

The forty-nation Conference on Disarmament reconvened in 1982 and established the basis for ongoing negotiations comprising:

- A declaration of current chemical weapons stockpiles and production facilities by all States party to the Convention;

- Agreement to destroy over a ten year period all chemical weapons and production facilities;

- Verification of the stockpile declaration and destruction;

24

- Verification that certain industrial chemicals are not being diverted into secret military stockpiles;

- Monitoring of small-scale approved production facilities for protective purposes; and

- Establishment of appropriate international bodies to oversee implementation of the Convention.

The recurrent theme here is one of verification. The West's request that on-site verification should be possible within twenty-four hours notice was immediately dismissed by the Soviet delegate, Viktor Issraelyan, as "provocative".

The visit by specialist teams from within NATO to the Shikhany Proving Grounds in the Soviet Union in 1988 is nonetheless a step forward, even given that the items for examination were old stock and that the Soviets admitted to stockpiling only 50,000 tons – a fraction of what they are known to possess.

There are three major obstacles to obtaining a true and *workable* ban on both chemical and biological agents. First is the question of how to define what constitutes a chemical and biological agent and how to eliminate certain elements within them that are utilized either in commercial practice or as basis for prophylaxis in the civilian field. Second is the problem of verification. Given that both chemical warfare agents and biological toxins can be produced in areas similar to industrial requirement and given that chemical agents can be produced in a small area and easily dissimulated, the possibilities of "hiding" are increased in nations which do not enjoy freedom of the press. Even were some solution found to both problems, the third would remain the most intractable: how to implement sanctions against violators.

All these points were cogently put by a US Arms Control and Disarmament Agency report:

> Given the many technical as well as political difficulties which remain to be resolved, conclusion of a chemical weapons prohibition is not likely to occur in the near term. Verification issues will be difficult to resolve and will require prolonged negotiation. Until the verification and other issues are satisfactorily resolved, an effective and comprehensive

25

chemical weapons prohibition which fully protects
U.S. and Free World interests will not be possible.[28]

It seems unlikely that Mr. Shevardnadze's gesture will fundamentally alter this situation, although it may increase pressure on Western negotiators to accept a less than satisfactory arrangement.

The offer was made during the opening session of the 149-nation Paris Summit Meeting on Chemical Weapons Proliferation, and it was conditional on reciprocation by the United States. It was not a difficult manoeuvre for the USSR, given the enormous publicity generated by the conference, concurrent international tension between the United States and Libya over Rabitah, and in the light of the huge disparity in stock levels between the two superpowers brought about by Soviet production throughout the years covered by the Nixon Moratorium. It is generally perceived that the Soviet Union's proposal would have justified Western optimism had it incorporated a truthful acknowledgment of Soviet stock levels, instead of reiterating the 50,000 tons figure. It is only when both sides trust the figures of the other that negotiations can progress towards abolition.

Conclusions

Political considerations arising from the promise of Glasnost and the relaxing of tension concerning nuclear conflict, have served as a brake to planning for protection against the threat that will take the place of nuclear arms as we go into the 1990's – chemical and biological warfare. In these the Soviet Union has a vast arsenal, well trained forces and decontamination procedures that ensure pursuance of advance in contaminated battlefield conditions, and a program of civilian protection. It has violated commitments under treaties of which it is signatory by providing such weaponry to other nations and has resorted to the use of toxic substances in areas of conflict.

The Western Allies may well find themselves in a "cleft stick" – wishing to protect the civilian population yet not knowing how to introduce the subject to the public during a time of Glasnost and after undeniable success and progress in negotiations with the Soviet Union on nuclear disarmament and other issues. In this respect, there is a danger that the hype produced by the Paris Conference will lead to a false and dangerous assumption of security and optimism. For a long time to come, the West must temper its optimism over East-West relations with the caution that history shows to be essential.

The proliferation of CBW in developing nations could eventually prove a more intransigent problem and risk than that of Soviet possession and intent. Specially dangerous is the portent of usage of CBW in inter-Third World conflict and acquisition of these weapons by terrorist organizations.

Finally, in listing the threats, there is the increased risk of industrial or natural disasters as the world gears itself to more advanced technology and production and manufacturing processes.

For all these reasons, it is vital that Western governments embark on a program to protect their civilian populations against CBW – the threat of the future.

Notes

[1] Recent sources in this field include: M. Dabros, "Canada's Chemical Warfare Policy", *Canadian Defence Quarterly*, Vol. 18, No. 3, Winter 1988; Joseph D. Douglass, Jr and Neil C. Livingstone (i) *America The Vulnerable* (Lexington, Mass: D.C. Heath & Co, 1984); (ii) "CWB: The Poor Man's Atom Bomb", *National Security Paper No. 1* (Cambridge, Mass: Institute for Foreign Policy Analysis, Inc, 1984); Manfred Hamm, *Chemical Warfare: The Growing Threat to Europe* (London: Institute for European Defence and Strategic Studies, 1984); John Hemsley, "The Soviet Bio-Chemical Threat: The Real Issue", *RUSI Journal*, Vol 133, No. 1, Spring 1988; Amoretta M. Hoeber, "The Chemistry of Defeat: Asymmetries in US and Soviet Chemical Warfare Postures", *Special Report* (Cambridge, Mass: Institute for Foreign Policy Analysis, Inc, 1981); Mark C. Storella, "Poisoning Arms Control", *Special Report* (Cambridge, Mass: Institute for Foreign Policy Analysis, Inc, 1984); Hugh Stringer, "Deterring Chemical Warfare: US Policy Options for the 1990s", *Foreign Policy Report* (New York, London: Pergamon-Brassey's, 1986); *Soviet Chemical Weapons Threat* (Washington, DC: Defence Intelligence Agency DST-1620F-051-85, 1986); *Soviet Biological Warfare Threat* (Washington, DC: Defence Intelligence Agency DST-1610F-057-86, 1986).

[2] See, for instance, *Toronto Star*, 7 January 1989, p. A10: the reporter's history begins in 1915 and includes unfounded propaganda accusations of US and UK use.

[3] Colonel G. Alksnis, *Zarubezhnoye Voyennoye Obozreniye* (Moscow), No. 1, January 1980.

[4] Lieutenant-Colonel F. Vladimirov, *Zarubezhnoye Voyennoye Obozreniye*, No.7, July 1983.

[5] Marshal of the Soviet Union V.K. Ogarkov, *Soviet Military Encyclopedia*, (Moscow: Voenizdat, 1976-80), Vol.8, p. 372

[6] Stringer, cited, p. 56.

[7] Colonels Yuri Kudachkin and A. Polyak, *Voyennij Vestnik*, May 1983.

[8] Brigadier Watay quoted Yossef Bodansky, *Soviet Chemical Warfare – Introduction to Use in the Third World* (New York: unpublished paper, 1986).

[9] A.N. Kalitayev, G.A. Zhivet'yev and V.V. Myaskinov, *Defence from Weapons of Mass Destruction: A Handbook* (Moscow: Voenizdat, 1984), p. 111.

[10] E.B. le Chêne, *Chemical Warfare Agents: Protection of the Civilian Population, a Feasibility Study* (London: February 1988, Private paper for restricted circulation), Emphasis added.

[11] Hemsley, cited, p. 59.

[12] Ibid, p. 60.

[13] Ibid. p. 61.

[14] J.P. Perry Robinson, "Chemical Warfare Capabilities of the Warsaw and North Atlantic Treaty Organizations: An Overview from Open Sources", in *Chemical Weapons: Destruction and Conversion* (London: Taylor and Francis, 1980), p. 35.

[15.] General V.K. Pikalov, *Soviet Military Encyclopedia* (Moscow: Voenizdat, 1976-80), Volume 8, p. 372.

[16.] *Soviet Military Power* (Washington, DC: US Department of Defence, 1985), pp. 71-72.

[17.] Martin Elliot Silverstein, "Chemical and Biological Defenses for the Civilian Population", paper to Conference of the Center for Strategic and International Studies, Washington, DC, 1 September 1986, p. 9.

[18.] *Special Reports* Nos. 98 (March 1982) and 104 (November 1982) (Washington, DC: US Department of State).

[19.] UN Security Council Document S 16433, 26 March 1984; Report "The Growing CW Threat" by the Swedish National Defence Research Institute, Spring 1986.

[20.] *NBC Defense and Technology* (New York) May 1986, p.40.

[21.] Report by Aubin Heyndrickx, Head of Toxicology, University of Ghent, submitted to the United Nations Secretary General, March 1988, following investigations in Angola by E.B. le Chêne and Heyndrickx's team, 1986.

[22.] *RUSI Newsbrief*, June 1988, Vol. 8, No. 6, pp. 46-48.

[23.] *Washington Times*, 8 April 1988.

[24.] Ibid.

[25.] Tjorneryd and Svennerstedt, paper, "Swedish Civil Defence Administration", at Second International Symposium on Chemical Warfare Agents, Stockholm, 1986.

[26.] J.B. Scott, *The Hague Conventions and Declarations of 1899 and 1907* (1915) pp. 225-226, cited Stringer, p. 22.

[27.] Stringer, p. 23.

[28.] "US Arms Control", *Annual Report* of the US Arms Control Disarmament Agency, Washington, DC, March 1984, pp. 186-187.

Part III
Radical Palestinian Terrorist Groups

[5]

PALESTINIAN TERRORISM—THE VIOLENT ASPECT OF A POLITICAL STRUGGLE

Anat Kurz

PALESTINIAN ORGANIZATIONS—rejectionist and PLO-mainstream groups alike—have viewed the armed struggle as included in, in fact inseparable from, the comprehensive framework of the struggle itself. Still, for the more pragmatic elements, resorting to terrorism has also involved the persistent dilemma of adjusting the course of the armed fight to immediate and long-term political goals. Related considerations have created diverse preferences regarding modes of operation and geographical scenes.

Palestinian terrorist activity has been traditionally divided into three arenas: activity inside Israel, cross-border infiltrations, and international terrorism.

Terrorist assaults inside Israeli borders have primarily aimed at ending the occupation. They have been perpetrated to inflict direct physical and/or psychological damage to coerce Israel into withdrawing from the West Bank and Gaza Strip. This sphere has been the least influenced by political considerations associated with the legitimacy and image of the struggle, compared with the other two. The only constraints associated with the scope and numbers of attacks have been, especially until the Uprising in the territories started, of a logistical nature.

As in the case of terrorist activity within Israel, choices of targets for cross-border operations and the tactics employed have reflected an effort to use all means available in order to prove devotion to the armed struggle. Cross-border activity has primarily formed the immediate substitute, in terms of geographical scene, for the limited freedom of action inside Israel. It nevertheless has been perceived by Palestinian organizations as being as legitimate as activity in the international arena. Thus, in order to score propaganda gains, infiltrations and infiltration attempts have by and large involved the intention to employ or the actual implementation of spectacular tactics.

> *The attacks . . . have been considered a major factor in gaining the Palestinian cause worldwide public attention and reputation as a principal source of world terror.*

Likewise, operations perpetrated by Palestinian terrorists in the international arena often involved dramatic tactics. The activity in this sphere, though it acquired particular features and objectives throughout the years, basically remained a substitute for the failure to direct a large scale armed struggle against Israel from within. The attacks, mainly those involving innovative and spectacular aspects, have been considered a major factor in gaining the Palestinian cause worldwide public attention (negative in essence) and reputation as a principal source of world terror. In terms of the perceived legitimacy of the armed struggle, terrorist activity in this arena has proved the most dangerous for Palestinian organizations striving to acquire international political recognition.

TERRORIST ACTIVITY INSIDE ISRAEL

When Yasser Arafat, chairman of the Palestine Liberation Organization, denounced terrorism in a public statement made in December 1988 in Geneva following his appearance at the UN General Assembly, he actually referred to terrorism in the international arena, as far as the PLO was involved.

A major cause for the distinction made by Arafat and other PLO spokesmen between international terrorism and activities conducted in other arenas does not exclusively stem from the different measures of attributed legitimacy regarding the perpetration of terrorism in each of them. Rather, it apparently also reflects various degrees of self-imposed commitments.

In this vein, Arafat has maintained that the *intifada* will continue. Indeed, the popular Uprising in the territories has been viewed as the legitimate, the most desired, and hopefully effective mode of war against the occupation. Yet even within the context of the popular Uprising, the PLO strove to confine the tactics of the struggle to non-armed ones.

In leaflets issued by the PLO-backed Unified National Leadership of the Uprising, residents of the territories were called on to refrain from using arms. True, the popular Uprising has principally been characterized by mass, non-armed participation of the territories' population in protests and in generating self reliance. This non-armed aspect, basically associated with the fundamental features of the Uprising, has created an image that the PLO has sought to preserve. In fact, the non-armed demonstrators of the *intifada* became the most effective means for gaining world sympathy for the Palestinian cause.

However, against the backdrop of continuous tension prevailing in the territories, one could expect more frequent use of terrorist tactics than the present rates. The policy advocated by the *intifada's* leadership has presumably proved a significant factor in preserving the Uprising's popular image, through the influence it evidently has over the daily activities of the inhabitants and the political precepts they share.

Yet another factor that undoubtedly plays a dominant role in directing the present course of the struggle relates to the logistical limitations imposed on the deeds of radical elements wihtin the territories. Thus, lack of arms and ammunition, as manifested through the increased use of homemade and improvised weapons, as well as the routine security measures of the Israeli authorities, have apparently made it extremely difficult for radical elements to increase the violent aspect of the *intifada*. Extreme nationalists and religious fundamentalists have called for escalation of the fight, in terms of increasing the use of arms. The Islamic Resistance Movement, Hamas, which has gained prominence in the Gaza Strip since the start of the Uprising, has repeatedly stressed the goal of

liberating the whole of Palestine through Jihad, an.. firmly objected to any political moves by the PLO. Within this context, considerations such as those that direct the *intifada's* leadership to restrict terrorist activities have little weight, if any, among others shared by the Hamas. Ultra nationalists also advocated intensifying frictions between the Israeli authorities and the territories' population, and calls for escalating the armed struggle were broadcasted on the radio station operated by Ahmed Jibril's PFLP-General Command from Lebanon.

Whether directly or indirectly, such calls have inspired extremist elements responsible for the increased activity evident in Israel, especially in the territories, since the start of the Uprising in December 1987.

Compared with previous years' rates, armed assaults which in most cases have been carried out by locally organized elements of no affiliation, have radically increased, as well as bombings. Thus, attacks including the use of firearms, grenades and cold weapons [knives, etc.] increased a hundred percent, and accounted for some hundred incidents from the start of the Uprising through its first year, compared to the previous year's statistics. Bombing attacks actually doubled as well, to about 80 incidents.

These records, however, do not include the hurling of petrol bombs, when not resulting in casualties. This tactic has been widely used by demonstrators during clashes with military forces, as well as in attacks against Israeli civilian objectives in the territories. Including it in the overall figures may therefore bias the illustrated inclination towards terrorism. Interestingly, but not incidentally, the Leadership of the Uprising also does not consider the use of petrol bombs as potentially harmful to the popular image of the Uprising as other terrorist tactics.

The intifada . . . has also proved effective in generating worldwide criticism for Israel's stand concerning the issue, and in eroding Israel's prestige as the threatened side of the Middle East conflict.

The very continuation of the Uprising has been considered essential as a backdrop for any progress toward achieving political gains for the PLO, because it has added the crucial component of emergency to the Palestinian problem. The *intifada*, and especially its popular features, has also proved effective in generating worldwide criticism for Israel's stand concerning the issue, and in eroding Israel's prestige as the threatened side of the Middle East conflict. In December 1988, within days after he made the political concessions that gained the PLO the desired U.S. recognition, Arafat stated, as he had many times before, that the *intifada* will continue. During a visit to Belgrade, he declared: "Our decision was and has been to continue the *intifada* until the occupier is pushed from our territories, and until our people get a chance to employ their sovereignty under PLO leadership on their national soil."

Vowing dedication to the *intifada* demonstrates the PLO policy both in internal and external terms. Besides realizing its value as political leverage, the leadership of the PLO has also recognized its own limited ability to switch off and on the Uprising, which erupted from below. In other words, trying to calm down the *intifada,* including its violent manifestations, is not politically necessary and apparently not practically possible.

The armed struggle, however, could not be totally abandoned. Over the years, it has in effect been a test for Palestinian organizations to prove their dedication to the war against Israel, and provided a means for scoring propaganda gains within the context of the intraorganizational rivalries. Since the start of the *intifada,* self-imposed restrictions on the use of arms in the territories and the increasingly dominant role played by the territories' population in leading the struggle, have enhanced Palestinian groups' desire to score military gains elsewhere.

CROSS BORDER TERRORIST ACTIVITY

Intensified efforts to infiltrate terrorist teams into Israel by Palestinian organizations, PLO-mainstream and radical groups alike, were already evident at the early stages of the *intifada* and this trend has continued. About 35 infiltration attempts were recorded during the period December 1987 and March 1989. In comparison, about ten cross-border attempted attacks were recorded in 1987, during the months preceding the eruption of the *intifada.*

Lebanon has been the preferred, in fact the only available, arena for the escaping infiltration campaign, due to the relative freedom of action enjoyed by Palestinian organizations in that country, and their operational infrastructure existing there. Yet, the principal obstacle facing terrorist teams trying to cross the border from Lebanon to the Galilee has been the routine security activity conducted by the IDF in the

area of South Lebanon. In fact, the only two successful attempts recorded since the start of the *intifada* by early March 1989, were initiated from Egypt. One of them, perpetrated by a Fatah unit, turned into a barricade-hostage episode and resulted in civilian casualties.

Divided into waves, border activity clearly shows the prominent role played by PLO mainstream groups during the first half of 1988. From the summer onwards, both radical and mainstream groups were equally active; yet the number of opposition groups within the PLO also increased, while the Fatah evidently reduced its part in infiltration attempts.

The escalated activity of Palestinian groups operating under Syrian auspices toward the end of 1988 attested to their opposition to diplomatic moves carried out by the PLO in advance of the convening of the Palestine National Council in Algiers in November, and further political gestures made by Arafat afterwards.

A principal motive behind this course of activity, apparently shared by PLO affiliated radical groups and pro-Syrian rejectionist organizations, has probably been the wish to make it difficult for the Fatah to avoid confrontation with Israel in Southern Lebanon. Provoking Israeli military operations or retaliatory raids in the region was probably meant to make it even harder for the Fatah to refrain from action.

Indeed, the Fatah has been treading a fine line in this arena, considering its potential to damage the peaceseeking facade it has attempted to present. Thus a statement allegedly made by Arafat in late November 1988 calling a halt to attacks against Israel from Lebanon was neither officially confirmed nor denied, indicating the probable implications of endorsing either policy at this time of political opportunities.

The border arena, however, has turned into a test for the credibility of Arafat's public promise to avoid terrorist activity. In addition, infiltration attempts also threatened to demonstrate the PLO's limited control over its radical factions. The Damascus-based groups, the DFLP and the PFLP, have not considered themselves committed to political concessions made by Arafat in the aftermath of the PNC meeting. George Habash, leader of the PFLP as well as Naif Hawatmeh, leader of the DFLP, vowed to continue the armed struggle from Lebanon. Renouncing terrorism has been perceived as an effort "to call an end to the military struggle against the Zionist enemy," maintained a PFLP official statement, following the interception of the organization's infiltration attempt in Southern Lebanon in early February 1989. Calling Arafat a traitor, Habash also promised to step up attacks on Israel from across the border. Speaking at a news conference in Damascus on March 7, he said that "there is no resolution (by the PNC) . . . providing for a truce in South Lebanon between us and the Israelis."

Trying to project internal consensus, a PLO official spokesman from Tunis defended recent infiltration attempts carried out by the PFLP and Talaat Yaakub's Palestine Liberation Front. The public statement, issued in early February 1989, said that the intercepted teams were on a military mission that did not violate chairman Arafat's renunciation of terrorism in Geneva in December.

The most apparent ramificaton of ongoing border drives by PLO groups is their possible impact on the PLO-U.S. dialogue. Yet, even the U.S. administration's stand in this regard has apparently been inconsistent. State Department spokesman Charles Redman said, as quoted by the *Jerusalem Post* on March 2, 1989, that "attacks against Israeli civilians and military targets inside or outside of Israel are contrary to the peaceful objectives of the dialogue." However, several days later Secretary of State James Baker maintained that attacks by the PLO against Israel in Southern Lebanon are not acts of terrorism requiring a break-off of U.S. talks with Yasser Arafat's organization.

Although the PLO has repeatedly described related operations as planned to hit military targets, all cells intercepted trying to infiltrate the border were proved to be on killing or barricade-hostage missions against civilians. Disguising the actual objective of such teams' missions has traditionally been meant to serve propaganda purposes and appeal to world opinion. Therefore, since the PLO mainstream apparently cannot bring infiltration attempts from Lebanon to a halt, it paradoxically should share Israel's hope that they will continue to be foiled. In any event, it appears as though the U.S. administration is unlikely to rely on formal definitions of terrorism as a pretext for stopping the dialogue with Arafat, and other considerations, related to the broader context of the conflict, will determine the continuation and direction of the contacts.

Beyond the effects a continuation of cross-border assaults may have on the PLO's international prestige, there is the possibility that they would lead, through international pressures aimed at bringing them to an end, to splits within the organization. Increased pressures by the U.S. on Arafat to commit himself to far-raching concessions, even if of no immediate practical implications, would shake his intra-PLO status, and may therefore leave the administration with no partner for negotiations.

Palestinian International Terrorism.

While Palestinian terrorist activity in and from Southern Lebanon may be tolerated by world public opinion, though not by the Israeli public and government, perceptions and possible ramifications in the case of Palestinian international terrorism seem to be totally different.

Correspondingly, political consideratons led PLO mainstream groups to avoid exacerbating relations with western states by refraining from direct attacks on western objectives, or the perpetration of spectacular assaults on their soil. The principal motive behind this policy has been the PLO's consistent drive to acquire international recognition and develop a political option for its participation in a Middle East settlement.

Thus since 1974 the PLO has denounced international terrorism. Yet at the same time Fatah never totally ceased carrying out attacks, even though they comprised only a minor portion of its activity, and the great part of them targeted Arab objectives. Fatah's self-imposed restrictions on the carrying out of international terrorism produced a fundamental dilemma: international terrorism was the very activity that had generated immediate and much needed publicity. After all, it was Fatah's terrorism that contributed considerably to the widely accepted image of the PLO as the representative of the Palestinian people.

These conflicting elements were clearly illustrated in the most recent spate of Fatah's spectacular activity in the international arena. On September 25, 1985, three Israelis were assassinated aboard their yacht in Larnaca, Cyprus, by a team of Fatah's Force-17. On October 5, 1985, two Israeli seamen were murdered

---

The timing of this wave of international terrorism by Fatah coincided with a rapprochement between Syria and Jordan.

---

in Barcelona, Spain, again by a team of Fatah's Force-17. Fatah was also involved in the October 7, 1985 hijacking of the Italian cruise ship Achille Lauro. That attack was carried out by the Abu al-Abbas faction of the PLF, and was planned as a strictly anti-Israeli operation. By virtue of close links between al-Abbas and Arafat it has been widely assessed that it could not have been carried out without the latter's approval.

The timing of this wave of international terrorism by Fatah coincided with a rapprochement between Syria and Jordan. This development seemed to lower the PLO's prospects of joining the political process, because it undermined the agreement signed by King Hussein and Arafat in February of 1985. This in turn motivated Arafat to demonstrate his determination to continue the struggle through alternative means—i.e., terrorism.

Yet Fatah's spectacular spate of attacks in 1985 was shortlived. Arafat's involvement in the Achille Lauro affair brought intense pressure on him by Egypt and Jordan to change course. In November 1985, in Cairo, Arafat promised to avoid international terrorism. Since then, Fatah has by and large refrained from carrying out attacks that might have provoked further blows to its international diplomatic standing, or broadened the gap between the PLO and moderate Arab States. In fact, the organization never totally abandoned the option of terrorism in the international arena, and has maintained its infrastructure abroad. Allegations linking Fatah to the April 1986 explosion aboard a TWA airliner over Greece were made later, but were not fully confirmed.

Unlike PLO groups, radical Palestinian organizations sponsored by rejectionist Arab states have maintained a persistent international terrorist drive

---

In 1985 and 1986, related terrorist activity reached a peak in terms of volume and the lethal impact of incidents. World public opinion was shocked by blatant incidents . . .

---

throughout the years. The timing and choice of objectives for operations have usually been associated with developments linked with the Middle East political process and the activity escalated whenever there were signs of progress. Attacks were motivated by the wish to disrupt any prospect for a negotiated solution to the Palestinian problem, and to foil Arafat's attempts to be recognized as a partner for a future settlement.

Palestinian terrorist attacks carried out during recent years have resulted in political ramifications involving both the affected states and the sponsoring states of the perpetrating organizations. In 1985 and 1986, related terrorist activity reached a peak in terms of volume and the lethal impact of incidents. World

public opinion was shocked by blatant incidents, including the simultaneous attacks perpetrated by Abu Nidal's FRC [Fatah — the Revolutionary Council] in the Rome and Vienna airports on December 25, 1985, the Syrian-directed bombing attack on a disco frequented by American soldiers in West Berlin on April 5, 1986, and the attempt to blow up an El-Al airliner which was thwarted at Heathrow Airport on April 17, 1986.

Not incidentally, the most spectacular terrorist events in recent years were those that reflected direct or indirect state involvement. Relevant evidence and associated political impact concerning the increased use made by Middle Eastern states of terrorism in the international arena culminated in 1986 in growing international determination to curb state-sponsored terrorism. It should be noted, however, that Iranian sponsorship of Shi'ite international terrorism also was a factor in generating the Western States' sense of emergency regarding the need to actively respond to the threat. In any event, Libya and Syria, the principal sponsors of Palestinian radical elements, were the objects of retaliatory and deterrence measures taken during 1986. Libya's involvement in a series of major terrorist attacks perpetrated by the FRC prompted the U.S. to carry out an air raid on terrorist and strategic targets in Tripoli and Benghazi on April 15. Later that year, economic and diplomatic sanctions were imposed on Syria by the United Kingdom, the U.S., Canada, and other European states, after its direct involvement in the attempt to blow up an El-Al passenger plane was disclosed in a London court. These moves constituted a high point in the increased international determination to curb state-sponsored terrorism. They presumably influenced Syria and Libya to modify their attitude toward the use of terrorism as a strategic tool.

Correspondingly, the drastic reduction evident during 1987 in the activities of radical Palestinian organizations could be attributed, to a great extent, to the changing policies of their sponsoring states.

Another factor that apparently reduced the relative benefit from the use of terrorism for advancing political goals was the very lack of progress in the regional political process. During 1987, neither Syria nor Libya nor the Palestinian radical camp was faced with immediate challenges of the nature of the 1984-85 rapprochement between the PLO and Jordan, which resulted in efforts to assemble an international forum to deal with the Palestinian and the territories' problem. Thus the political stalemate, combined with the previous year's countermeasures, rendered the international terrorist strategy unjustifiably costly and risky.

The state of affairs, together with intra-organizational factors, also facilitated the reintegration of Palestinian groups into the PLO which resulted in the expanded front achieved at the April 1987 PNC meeting in Algiers. Prior to the convening of the PNC, in March 1987, Abu Nidal promised Abu Iyad that "for a determined time, for ten months, he would not carry out terrorist actions." At the same time, Abu Nidal did not attend the PNC, apparently because he had been denied a place on the PLO's Executive Committee.

The concurrent decline in the FRC's international terrorist activity apparently was the result of political-tactical considerations, and did not reflect a profound change of policy. Renewal of international terrorist

> ### The first year of the intifada was marked by a significant increase in rates of Palestinian international terrorism . . .

campaigns has been expected since the eruption of the *intifada* in late 1987, creating challenges for the Palestinian national movement. Some of them stemmed directly from the intensified American efforts to revive the peace process and find a new formula for negotiating a solution to the conflict.

Whenever a political process was underway in the past, it closely affected the diverse Palestinian factions' policies, and forced them and their state sponsors to address both the possibility of their own participation, as well as the converse issue of the form of their opposition to the process. In this sense, the renewal of a political process is likely to alter the cost-benefit considerations of radical Arab states regarding the use of terrorism as a strategic tool. These might combine with mounting pressure from within the organizations to produce fresh spates of international terrorist activity.

The first year of the *intifada* was marked by a significant increase in rates of Palestinian international terrorism, compared with the previous year's records. Yet a more remarkable feature was the recurrence of indiscriminate mass assaults. In terms of tactics and choice of targets, these resembled the attacks that in 1986 resulted in retaliatory measures by the affected states against Syria and Libya. Some of the incidents indicated a spectacular comeback of Palestinian radical elements to the international scene, for example:

A Greek cruiser was attacked by a lone assailant, a member of FRC, in the Aegean Sea on July 11, 1988. Eighty persons on the ship were injured, and nine others were killed. The attack was carried out shortly after a premature explosion in a car in Athens foiled an alleged scheme to hit a U.S. Navy ship in Piraeus;

On April 15, 1988, the second anniversary of the U.S. air raid on Libya, an explosive charge went off near a club frequented by U.S. Navy personnel in Naples, Italy. The incident, in which ten people were killed, was carried out by the Anti-Imperialist-International-Brigades, affiliated with the Japanese Red Army and the PFLP;

A premature explosion in an explosives-laden car, on May 11 in Nicosia, Cyprus, apparently foiled a plan of Abu Nidal's FRC to attack the Israeli Embassy there;

Four days later, on May 15, the FRC carried out simultaneous attacks on a club and a hotel lobby in Khartoum, Sudan. Seven people, all British citizens, were killed in these incidents;

The interception of an FRC team on July 17 in Lima, Peru, allegedly foiled a plot to operate against the Israeli, Belgian and British embassies and the American consulate there.

Another planned operation was probably foiled when a 14-man team of Jibril's PFLP-GC was captured in November in Frankfurt, West Germany. The team was in possession of the Czech-made explosive Semtax and barometric fuses, similar to the device allegedly used in the December 21, 1988 explosion aboard a Pan Am airliner over England that killed 259 passengers and crew, and 11 persons on the ground.

The organizational affiliation of the perpetrators of that incident had not been definitely established by early 1989. And though the possibility of Iranian involvement was not ruled out, Palestinian extremists remained the prime suspects. Among those who appear to have a motive, the PFLP-GC has still been held the most probable perpetrator, due to its past record in carrying out such highly sophisticated attacks.

The recent spate of international terrorism incidents was in effect one aspect of the ongoing intra-Palestinian struggle over strategy for advancing the cause, with the current developments associated with the process generated by the *intifada*. The less cautious conduct of rejectionist Palestinian groups, sponsored by radical Arab states, may be interpreted as a show of intent to resort to extremes, in order to disrupt a process that might lead to a negotiated solution.

This recent terrorist drive has most probably not yet been exhausted. Further attacks can be expected in advance of future political moves, with Israel, other states involved in the process, and pragmatic Palestinians as the most likely targets.

Barring unexpected dramatic developments, PLO affiliated elements are likely to refrain from association with terrorist activity, especially in the international arena. Even before events culminated in the December 1988 reassurance given by Arafat regarding the PLO engagement in terrorism, the organization remained reluctant to provide the parties to a political process with excuses to negotiate a solution without it.

Related considerations apparently prevailed even in the face of what might have been perceived as direct provocations. On February 14, 1988, three prominent Fatah operatives were killed in Limasol, Cyprus, when a bomb went off in their car. They had arrived in Cyprus to conclude leasing arrangements for a ship which the PLO planned to sail toward the Israeli shore carrying Palestinian deportees and refugees. A day later, the ship itself was damaged by a mine explosion. These two coordinated attacks in fact foiled the spectacular Palestinian propaganda operation and apparently generated demands within Fatah to retaliate against Israel, which was held responsible by the organization in both incidents. A Fatah spokesman declared in Tunis that the organization was no longer committed to the pledge not to engage in international terrorism that Arafat had given in Cairo in November 1985. Yet this statement was soon officially denied. A similar dilemma regarding the PLO response to internal pressure for vengeance was generated by the assassination of Fatah's military chief, Khalil al-Wazir (alias Abu Jihad) in Tunis, on April 17, 1988.

Thus PLO groups are unlikely to resort to blatant terrorist campaigns as long as their role in future talks has not been ruled out. However, if the political momentum slows down or promises few prospects for PLO independent participation, then reaction by Fatah's radical elements might involve international terrorism. If this happens, terrorist incidents would probably be perpetrated, even if unauthorized by the higher echelon of the organization, with the aim both of demonstrating the PLO's indispensability for peace talks, and of expressing Palestinian disappointment and frustration. Another cause for impatient elements associated with the PLO mainstream to activate their international terrorist infrastructure might be linked with shifts in the balance of power within the Palestinian national movement. Were a new Palestinian leadership, most probably from within the Israeli-administered territories, to acquire international recognition and influence along the Palestinian people at the expense of the PLO, then the more extreme elements of the Fatah or the PLO as a whole might feel obliged to defend their historical position. Correspondingly, they may conclude that they had little to lose in terms of international political prestige and credibility.

Prospects for such developments seem currently remote, and the political opportunities offered to the PLO as the representative of the Palestinian people appear far from being exhausted.

However, radical Palestinian groups' inclination to respond to political developments regarding the Palestinian issue has formed a source of deep concern for the leadership for the PLO mainstream. Escalating indiscriminate campaigns perpetrated in the international arena may well hamper the organization's efforts to preserve its political prestige and leading status. Incidents will presumably result in growing opposition in Israel as well as in other states to a suggested solution that includes the PLO as partner, and might also result in destabilizing its position within the Palestinian community, if its political orientation fails to bear fruit.

Against this backdrop, doubts will be raised, if not concerning the PLO's genuine peacekeeping intentions, then regarding its ability to control extremists and to guarantee peaceful implementation of an agreement.

[6]

PLO Policy in Lebanon: Legacies and Lessons

Rex Brynen[*]

Introduction[1]

Lebanon has long occupied a particularly important place in the Palestinian struggle. Over 350,000 Palestinians reside there, it borders on Israel/Palestine, and for some twelve years—from 1970 until the Israeli invasion of June 1982—Lebanon served as the political and military center of gravity of the Palestinian movement. It did so, in one sense, in the classic manner of all external guerrilla sanctuaries: it provided shelter, a logistical base, and a departure point for military activities. More importantly, however, Lebanon offered the Palestinian movement—long constrained by the interests and interventions of others—its first period of sustained political freedom. In Lebanon, the Palestinian movement grew uniquely free to construct its own institutions, to promote its own identity, and to choose its own, Palestinian paths to the dream of national liberation.

Equally, the PLO's evacuation from Beirut in August 1982 represented a turning point for the Palestinian resistance movement. In organizational terms, the loss of a semi-autonomous territorial base severely weakened the PLO, increasing its dependence on Arab regimes and exacerbating internal

[*]Rex Brynen is assistant professor of political science at McGill University, Montreal, Canada. This article is based on a forthcoming book, *Sanctuary and Survival: The PLO in Lebanon*, for which support from the Social Sciences and Humanities Research Council is gratefully acknowledged.

divisions to the point of a bitter and open split in its ranks from 1983 until the eighteenth session of the Palestine National Council in April 1987. In Lebanon, Palestinian residents now found themselves largely bereft of protection, surrounded by Israeli forces and hostile militias. The Sabra and Shatila massacres, a campaign of terror in the south, and three rounds of the "camps war" followed.

For these very reasons, issues of Lebanese policy were prominent in the acrimonious debate that accompanied the split. Events in Lebanon—the "Battle of Tripoli" between Arafat and his opponents; competition for the political loyalties of Palestinian camp populations; the defense of the Lebanese camps against Amal (and its Syrian backers)—dominated the next several years of Palestinian politics. The camps war itself played a major role in the eventual reunification of the PLO, and Lebanese issues occupied a prominent position on the PLO policy agenda both at, and after, the eighteenth session of the Palestine National Council.[2]

Since then, the eruption of a sustained popular uprising against the Israeli occupation of the West Bank and Gaza Strip has tended to overshadow issues of Lebanese policy. Yet, despite the changes wrought by the 1982 invasion, the *intifadah*, and the changing nature of Palestinian political strategy, Lebanon remains important to the Palestinian movement. The challenges facing the Palestinian population and movement in Lebanon are severe, and comments made by George Habash of the Popular Front for the Liberation of Palestine are as true now as when they were uttered in November 1987:

> [The Palestinian movement] must answer the following questions: What do we want from Lebanon? Why do we insist on maintaining a Palestinian armed presence in Lebanon? How do we perceive our relations with the LNM [Lebanese National Movement]? If the Palestinian revolution fails to provide a clear answer to these questions, the Palestinian presence in Lebanon will not grow the way we hope. . . . During its presence in Lebanon throughout the seventies and until 1982, the Palestinian revolution made mistakes. A bold reexamination process is in order. These mistakes must be identified, acknowledged, and rectified. . .[3]

To a significant extent, the lessons of the present are to be found in the legacies of the past, in particular, in the crucial period from the June 1967 Arab–Israeli war to the June 1982 Israeli invasion of Lebanon.

The PLO in Lebanon 1967–82: An Assessment

At the outset, it must be noted that Lebanon has been a severe test for the PLO. It was (and is) a country suffering from deep social, economic, and political divisions. The Palestinian armed presence certainly exacerbated the contradictions of the Lebanese system, contradictions which exploded into the Lebanese civil war of 1975–76 and which have continued to rend the country to the present day. But it did not create them. After all, Lebanon had fought an earlier civil war in 1958 over many of the same issues six years before the PLO was founded.[4]

Lebanon has also always been something of a battleground for regional, great, and superpowers. Once again, it is true that the PLO presence aggravated this. Certainly the PLO attracted greater levels of Israeli and Arab intervention in Lebanon, the inevitable consequence of the regional importance and permeability of the Palestine issue. But Lebanon had been a battleground long before this: in the preceding century alone, the Ottomans had ruled over it; European powers had intervened and finally gained control of it; Arab, Syrian, and Lebanese nationalists and the early Zionist movement had laid claim to it; the United States had landed troops to "protect" it; Arab regimes had fought out their differences in it; and years prior to the formation of the PLO, Israeli leaders had discussed the best way to gaining influence or control over it. Outside involvement in Lebanese affairs—often at the request of Lebanese actors—was hardly new.

On top of all this, Lebanon's weakness vis-à-vis Israel allowed the latter to embark on a deliberate and sustained series of massive punitive raids against it, intervention designed to destabilize both the Palestinian presence in Lebanon and Lebanon itself. This in itself placed severe limits on the policy options open to the PLO leadership in its attempts to maintain satisfactory Palestinian–Lebanese relations.

It is undeniable that the PLO was successful in overcoming many of the formidable obstacles it faced in Lebanon. After the June 1967 Arab–Israeli war, the Palestinian *fida'iyyin* exploded onto the regional scene, winning mass support not only from their people but also from the broader Arab population. In the spring and summer of 1969 this support, coupled with external pressures from Egypt and Syria, allowed the Palestinian movement to resist the attempts of the Lebanese army to suppress its activities in Lebanon. The end result was the Cairo Agreement of 3 November 1969, a document of central importance to PLO policy in Lebanon over the next thirteen years. Under its terms the PLO recognized the requirements of Lebanese "sovereignty and security," and undertook to coordinate its activities from Lebanon with the Lebanese army. In exchange, the PLO gained official recognition of the legitimacy of a Palestinian armed presence in Lebanon, freedom of movement in the Arqub district in the south, and the establishment of autonomous institutions in the refugee camps.[5]

From 1969 to 1973, and especially after the loss of its position in Jordan in 1970–71, the importance of Lebanon to the PLO grew. When a second attempt to suppress the PLO was made by the Lebanese army in 1973, the Palestinian resistance, coupled with internal and external support from its Lebanese and Arab allies, was such that the authorities were forced to accept a return to the status quo ante—the Cairo Agreement, as interpreted by the so-called "Milkart protocols."[6]

From May 1973 to April 1975, tensions in Lebanon mounted. When civil war erupted, the PLO's military defense of its positions, together with its internal alliance with the parties of the Lebanese National Movement and assistance from external Arab allies, succeeded in safeguarding the security of the Palestinian refugee camps during the first nine months of fighting. The situation deteriorated in January 1976 with attacks by the Lebanese Front (LF) on Palestinian camps in Beirut. In response, the PLO and the LNM launched a counteroffensive, securing a partially effective cease-fire. That spring, continued political stalemate led the PLO to support the LNM's "mountain offensive" against the LF heartland. But the PLO would not be allowed to restructure Lebanese politics. Syrian military intervention on behalf of the Lebanese Front came in June, setting the stage for the massacre of thousands of Palestinian civilians in the Tall al-Za'tar camp in East Beirut by the LF in August. In September, the Riyadh summit brought the civil war to an "end."[7]

The PLO and the bulk of the Palestinian population in Lebanon managed to emerge from the civil war battered but intact, despite their precarious military position. In 1976–77, through careful diplomacy and the counterbalancing use of external Arab allies, the PLO resisted hegemonic pressures from Syria. It also retained its arms, and its geographic position in south Lebanon. The PLO-LNM "Joint Forces" fought a proxy war in the south against Israeli-backed militias with increasing effectiveness, despite growing levels of Israeli intervention and the countless air raids, shellings, ground incursions, airborne and seaborne commando attacks, bombings, and assassination attempts directed against them. The Joint Forces resisted an Israeli invasion in 1978. And, in the end, the PLO was dislodged (imperfectly at that) only after a massive Israeli invasion of Lebanon and seventy-day siege of Beirut—a period of resistance longer than that offered by the Arab armies of 1956, 1967, and 1973 combined.

These political and military achievements were complemented by social and organizational ones. Through the 1970s and early 1980s the PLO's administrative structure had seen considerable expansion, such that by the spring of 1982 it constituted a virtual Palestinian "para-state" in Lebanon.[8]

The PLO's military forces—over ten thousand well-armed fighters in semi-regular formations, backed by thousands more militia—were but one element of this. On the political front, West Beirut had become the headquarters of the Palestinian leadership and the nerve center of a vast international network of diplomatic and information offices and personnel. Lebanon had also become the center of a vast array of PLO social support institutions constructed to aid Palestinians in Lebanon and throughout the diaspora. With the collapse of the Lebanese government in 1975–76, the PLO undertook (in cooperation with the LNM) the task of maintaining a skeleton of essential services in those areas under the Joint Forces' control. In the camps, the initiatives undertaken by Palestinian popular committees after the 1969 Cairo Agreement grew into a range of programs, from the supply of electricity and water to public sanitation. An extensive system of hospitals and clinics, open to Lebanese and Palestinians alike, was built and maintained by the Palestine Red Crescent Society. Palestinian mass organizations flourished, grouping together Palestinian workers, women, youth, professionals, and other groups within common frameworks under the aegis of the PLO. Most importantly, Palestinians were able to institutionalize their own national consciousness, to solidify the sense of resurgent Palestinianism which had accompanied the rise of the modern Palestinian resistance movement after the 1967 Arab–Israeli war.

All of these were fundamental and impressive accomplishments given the difficulties the Palestinian movement faced. Yet PLO policy was also less coherent, and less effective, than it might have been.

The most important casualty was Lebanese public opinion. In 1969, widespread public support for the Palestinian movement in all Lebanon's confessional communities had effectively hamstrung the Lebanese government's attempts to suppress the *fida'iyyin*. Lebanese progressive parties played a particular role in mobilizing this support, and in turn found their growth catalyzed by the Palestinian presence. But even many conservative leaders, and especially the traditional Sunni urban leadership, had little choice but to echo cries for "freedom of action for the *fida'iyyin*" if they were to not risk their own political bases.

By the eve of the 1982 Israeli invasion, however, a significant degree of alienation between the PLO and its traditional Lebanese supporters had set in. Constant Israeli military pressure on Lebanon, resulting in the deaths of thousands and the displacement of hundreds of thousands from the south, was a major, perhaps the major, reason for this. Anti-Palestinian propaganda disseminated by Israel and the PLO's Lebanese opponents had fed this growing dissatisfaction. But so too had certain types of Palestinian behavior and policy.

As Rashid Khalidi has noted, the weakening of the PLO's popular Lebanese position had "a vital impact on the PLO when the Israeli invasion began."[9] But it was to be in the aftermath of the August 1982 evacuation of PLO personnel from Beirut that the full legacy—and cost—of earlier PLO policy in Lebanon made itself felt. Amal, in an effort to prevent any resurgence of the Palestinian armed presence in Beirut or the south, launched a series of bloody attacks on the weakened Palestinian refugee camps in 1985–87 in which three thousand or more Palestinians died. Even such erstwhile Palestinian allies as the Lebanese Communist party and Progressive Socialist party declared that there would not be, under any circumstances, a return to pre-1982 conditions. The PLO thus faced an up-hill battle to defend Palestinian refugee camps in Lebanon, let alone reestablish even a modicum of its previous influence, capability, and infrastructure.[10]

External factors have contributed to Lebanese opposition to a return of the PLO. Israel, for example, tied its post-1982 withdrawal from the Shuf and south Lebanon to commitments by the Druze and Amal respectively to keep these areas free from any resurgent Palestinian armed presence. Similarly, Syria, engaged in an open struggle with Arafat's Fateh for control of the Palestinian movement after the Fateh rebellion of 1983, encouraged both PLO dissidents and Amal in their attacks as a means of pressuring the Palestinian movement and preventing Fateh's reacquisition of a semi-autonomous Lebanese base. But Lebanese resentment of past Palestinian behavior has played a major part too, such that no significant Lebanese organization could support the large-scale return of the PLO without seriously compromising its popular support.

A great many Lebanese fought, and died, alongside the Palestinians in resisting the 1982 Israeli invasion. Most still support the Palestinian cause. Lebanese and Palestinians alike have participated in the post-1982 guerrilla campaign against the Israeli occupation of Lebanon as part of the Lebanese National Resistance Front.[11] Still, after 1982, few Lebanese have any desire to return to the pre-1982 situation.

Lebanese Alliances: Friends and Enemies

The growth of the Palestinian movement in Lebanon in the late 1960s had been viewed with alarm by the conservative Lebanese elite, Christian and Muslim alike. The Palestinian presence attracted increased Israeli military action against Lebanon, action which inflicted not only a human but also an economic toll on the service-oriented Lebanese economy. The Palestinian presence was disruptive in other ways too, with armed Palestinian guerrillas disturbing public order or flaunting Lebanese law and authority. More fundamentally, however, the Palestinian resistance movement was dangerous to the Lebanese system itself. However much the "revolutionary" nature of the PLO (and more specifically, its Fateh mainstream) may have been questioned by some,[12] the very presence of a militant, generally progressive, and avowedly non-sectarian popular movement in an unequal *laissez-faire* society wherein the privileges of a relatively small number of leading families were sustained by a precarious sectarian political order, was clearly a destabilizing element. The mass popularity of the *fida'iyyin* only heightened this danger, as did the intensification of Lebanon's own domestic economic and political crisis in the early 1970s. It is in this context that attempts by the Lebanese state (and later by the Phalange, Lebanese Forces, and other self-appointed defenders of the status quo) to suppress the PLO should be seen.

In response, the PLO/Fateh mainstream adopted two main sets of policies designed to reduce tensions with the Lebanese government and conservative parties. The first of these—what might be termed a strategy of Palestinian "self-restraint"—involved limitations on potentially provocative Palestinian activities. Beginning in the early 1970s, the PLO announced (but rarely adhered to) a series of temporary freezes on cross-border activity in south Lebanon. It also attempted to regulate the behavior of Palestinian guerrillas through its own military police (the Palestine Armed Struggle Command), judicial system, and internal security forces (Force 17). At the same time, dialogue was initiated with the Phalange party and Christian leaders, in an effort to ease the Christian right's concerns over the Palestinian armed presence.[13]

Ultimately, however, such policies were limited in what they could achieve. Although the overall cost of the Palestinian presence to Lebanese decisionmakers might be mitigated by reducing transitory PLO-related costs—Israeli retaliation, Palestinian misbehavior, and so forth—the structural component of this cost represented by the PLO's role as a revolutionary catalyst was in essence irreducible. The PLO was an indirect danger to the economic, political, and confessional privileges of the Lebanese elite by its very existence. Conflict with the Lebanese government, and with its defenders, was therefore inevitable, even more so as the PLO increasingly (and necessarily) allied itself with the reformist and revolutionary parties of the Lebanese National Movement. At best a strategy of self-restraint might postpone such conflict or reduce its intensity. It could not forestall it completely. Those who argued that the PLO could avoid being drawn into Lebanese issues—a view encapsulated in Fateh's slogan of "non-interference" in the internal affairs of Arab regimes—underestimated the degree to which the Palestinian presence and struggle was, in and of itself, a Lebanese issue. The PLO could refrain from intervening in other inter-Lebanese political conflicts, but it could not prevent itself from becoming the focus of one.

The PFLP and DFLP had always known this, although their enthusiasm for the Lebanese social struggle often led them to aggravate the problem. In the belief that Palestinian liberation required a broader, revolutionary transformation of the surrounding Arab countries, both were active in their support of sister parties in the LNM. The Arab-sponsored resistance organizations—Syria's al-Sa'iqah, Iraq's Arab Liberation Front (ALF)—also became active in Lebanese politics through their local Ba'thist wings in support of the foreign policy objectives of their respective patron regimes. This in turn undercut much of the effectiveness of the PLO's nominal policy of self-restraint, since Palestinian involvement in Lebanese politics was fundamentally provocative to the Lebanese right. After September 1970, however, it was a moot point. For the Palestinian movement, the major lesson of Black September in Jordan was clear: the continued survival of the Palestinian resistance required the mobilization of a broad base of Arab support, one which would both sustain the PLO and constrain the ability of certain regimes to strike at it. The 1973 clashes with the Lebanese army reinforced the point. Fateh became as active as any Palestinian organization in promoting alliances with Lebanese actors; indeed, as the largest Palestinian organization, it became the most heavily involved.

At the same time, the various progressive parties comprised by the LNM were only too anxious to tie their fortunes to that of the Palestinian resistance. The PLO was progressive and popular. It was also seen as a partial guarantee against suppression of the left by a conservative Lebanese state.

Was this inevitable "Lebanization" of the Palestinian issue a carte blanche for the PLO to involve itself in Lebanese politics? Did it invalidate any strategy of Palestinian self-restraint? Lebanese opposition to the Palestinian armed presence was initially weak and divided, a weakness evident in the PLO's ability to wrest from the authorities terms as advantageous as those contained in the Cairo Agreement of 1969. Active (and often gratuitous) Palestinian intervention in Lebanese political affairs, coupled with cross-border firing, the lack of regard for Lebanese sovereignty, the visibility and poor public behavior of some guerrillas—all of this only served to solidify opposition to the *fida'iyyin* while weakening the PLO's own essential Lebanese popular base of support. Pressures exerted first by Kamal Junblatt as Lebanese interior minister in the early 1970s, and later by the LNM, to restrict certain Palestinian activities was a reflection of their genuine concern regarding the damage being done to the PLO (and themselves) by the guerrillas' tendency to showmanship and weak discipline. But this pressure was resisted, and eventually overcome, by the PLO in the name of freedom of action—to the PLO's ultimate detriment.

Did the inevitability of conflict imply that dialogue with the Lebanese right was useless? The Palestinian left sometimes argued that it did. But to accept this is to grant the Lebanese ruling class—a category embracing Maronite leaders, Sunni urban bosses, semi-feudal Shi'i leaders in the south, and many others—a homogeneity and unity of purpose that it simply did not have. Such differences might even have been exploited to the PLO's advantage. The problem with dialogue lay not with the principle, but with the underlying absence of a clear Lebanese policy.

Given the limitations on the use of the strategies of self-restraint and communication, it was the PLO's internal alliances that had to assume overriding importance in Palestinian policy in Lebanon. As the clashes of 1969, 1973, and 1975–76 showed, the PLO's Lebanese opponents were unable to suppress a Palestinian movement which enjoyed broad support from the Lebanese population and the parties of the LNM. Israel and Syria were similarly limited. Throughout this period, the PLO's ties with the LNM and Lebanese masses were strong and productive.

From the mid-1970s onward, however, the PLO's Lebanese support and the strength it derived from its internal alliance with the Lebanese National Movement began to dwindle. Objective factors beyond the PLO's immediate control—the 1977 assassination of LNM leader Kamal Junblatt, political sectarianization, Arab interference, Israeli retaliatory policy—all played a major role in this. But so too did important aspects of PLO behavior. Continued Palestinian cross-border military action in the face of a clear Israeli policy of massive retaliation shifted much of the blame for the destruction of south Lebanon from Israel to the easier and more accessible scapegoat of the Palestinian armed presence. With the PLO-dominated Joint Forces in de facto control of West Beirut and large portions of the south, the impact of negative aspects of Palestinian guerrilla behavior was magnified. Finally, the PLO's ever-increasing influence in the LNM undercut that organization's political status and further damaged the reputation of the Palestinian resistance in the eyes of its erstwhile supporters.

In an attempt to increase its local influence, Fateh increasingly engaged in the creation of marginal but compliant Lebanese organizations, "shops" (*dakakin*), owing primary loyalty to Palestinian paymasters. Many were little more than local street gangs, armed and financed by Fateh and operating under grandiose Islamic or Nasserite titles. These groups, although addressing short-term requirements of local military and political influence, were in the longer term unable to address the social and political problems facing the LNM. Their inability to confront these tasks weakened the LNM from within, burdening the PLO with Lebanese responsibilities that it was neither able nor willing to undertake.

In the south, a related problem marred Palestinian relations with the Lebanese Shi'i movement Amal. The Shi'a of south Beirut and south Lebanon had, in the late 1960s, been among the primary supporters of the Palestinian movement. Fateh had been a major sponsor of Amal when it was first established by Imam Musa Sadr in the 1970s. But as the scale of Israeli destruction in the south grew, many Shi'a began to resist the deployment of Palestinian forces around their farms and villages. Amal increasingly became the umbrella for this resistance. Conflict between elements of the Shi'i community and LNM groups also arose as a result of Libya's perceived involvement in Sadr's 1978 disappearance, the Iran–Iraq war, and political competition for supporters.[14] Amal was heavily penetrated by Syrian intelligence, and many within Fateh, the PFLP, ALF, and LNM saw the growing number of incidents between Amal and the Joint Forces as part of a Syrian attempt to extend its influence at the PLO and LNM's expense. Fateh responded with increasingly heavy military force against Amal and pro-Amal Shi'i villages in the south, a move that further exacerbated tensions. By 1981–82, clashes between the two sides were commonplace.

Thus, instead of building on the mass base that had allowed the Palestinian movement to survive multiple challenges to its position between 1969 and the civil war, the chief focus of the PLO's Lebanon policy after 1976 shifted elsewhere, to one of *force majeure*. Palestinian military preponderance, not the LNM or the sympathies of the Lebanese population, became the primary means upon which Palestinian political power and independence in Lebanon rested—joint PLO-LNM commands, consultation, and stirring declarations of solidarity notwithstanding.

Such emphasis on a strategy of "defense" maintained the security and status of the PLO in Lebanon for some six years, from 1976 to 1982. It came at the cost of further Lebanese resentment of what now appeared to be a Palestinian state-within-a-state. Unlike the PLO's previous reliance on internal allies, the foundation of its post-civil war position was essentially a political house of cards. By removing one material element—the PLO's armed superiority—the PLO's position in Lebanon could be brought tumbling down. And this, of course, is precisely what happened in the summer of 1982.

Armed Struggle: Means Or Ends?

When modern Palestinian guerrilla action was initiated in the 1960s, its objectives were threefold: to revitalize Palestinian identity; to remind Israel and the world of the Palestinians' existence; and to stoke the intensity of Arab–Israeli confrontation as part of a long-term war of liberation embracing both the Arab states and the Palestinian people. [15] These goals had, in the aftermath of the June 1967 defeat, struck a particularly defiant and receptive popular note, catapulting the resistance to the political forefront of the Palestinian issue. The appeal of the *fida'iyyin* intensified.

As the 1970s progressed, objective and subjective circumstances led to a gradual change in Palestinian political strategies. Black September of 1970, the limited objectives set for the October 1973 Arab–Israeli war, clashes with the Lebanese government, and the PLO's reluctant envelopment in civil strife there all served to underscore the ambiguous nature of the Palestinian movement's relations with Arab regimes. At the same time, the Rabat summit declaration of 1974 recognizing the PLO as the sole, legitimate representative of the Palestinian people and the entrance that same year of the PLO into the United Nations reflected the heightened Arab and international profile of the organization and its cause. These two developments, coupled with the continued strength of Israel and the unlikelihood of achieving the PLO's initial maximalist program of liberating all of Palestine, led to a revision of PLO objectives. Specifically, the immediate goal (if not the dream) of a non-sectarian democratic state in all of Palestine was set aside in favor of a more achievable objective. In 1974, the twelfth session of the Palestine National Council endorsed such an approach when it called for the establishment of a "national authority" on any portion of liberated Palestinian land. After 1977 this objective crystalized into the establishment of an independent Palestinian state on the West Bank and Gaza Strip.

All of this had several implications for the Palestinian armed presence in Lebanon. First, it cast Palestinian operations from Lebanon against northern Israel in a new light. Such attacks, even at their height, had never posed a serious threat to Israeli national security, whatever their internal Palestinian value or other political achievements.[16] After 1977 even the political significance of these operations declined: if the West Bank and Gaza Strip were to be the target of immediate Palestinian liberation efforts, it was here, too, that Palestinian armed struggle should be concentrated, in an effort to render Israeli occupation as costly as possible. At best, Lebanese cross-border operations could be used sporadically, as an *acte de presence* intended to derail specific regional developments (such as the Egyptian–Israeli negotiations) inimical to Palestinian interests. At worst, such operations actually undermined the PLO's own objectives: they diverted attention and energy away from the occupied territories.[17] By striking at pre-1967 Israel, they obscured the PLO's new acceptance of an independent Palestinian state. Given the civilian nature of many of the targets attacked, cross-border "terrorism" damaged the PLO's international reputation, and hence devalued the very diplomatic currency it increasingly sought to use in the post-October War period. Most important in Lebanese terms, Palestinian operations from Lebanon invited (or provided a pretext for) Israeli retaliation aimed at destabilizing the Palestinian movement's Lebanese base.

For the PLO, the deterioration of its position in Lebanon caused by cross-border attacks might have been tolerable had they represented a major source of military pressure on Israel. But they did not; on the contrary, Lebanon's real importance lay elsewhere. By the very nature of the Palestinians' own evolving political objectives, Lebanon had become important, not as a military front, but as a headquarters for Palestinian diplomatic activity and a coordinating point for popular, diplomatic, and armed struggle in the occupied territories and elsewhere. All of this required a substantial, secure, and independent Palestinian infrastructure. Indeed, the very essence of the PLO's claim to an independent Palestinian state as it was being put forward necessitated steadfastness in the occupied territories and a demonstrably independent Palestinian polity-in-exile and national identity, and hence, a largely autonomous territorial base free from external interference. This the Palestine Liberation Organization found in Lebanon and only in Lebanon.

This latter point—that the importance of Lebanon to the PLO was political, not military—was fully understood by then-Prime Minister Menahem Begin and Defense Minister Ariel Sharon, who confronted it directly in June 1982. The Israeli invasion of Lebanon sought to weaken the PLO's politico-military power and its territorial and political autonomy.[18]

After this, the *coup de grâce* would be left to others, notably Syria and Jordan, who could be expected to spare little effort in attempting to exert hegemony over the weakened Palestinians and PLO. "Operation Peace for Galilee" was not an effort to halt Palestinian attacks on northern Israel. Rather, it was an attempt to produce a severely weakened, more radical PLO under Syrian dominance that would become preoccupied with a struggle for Palestinian loyalties with the Hashimite regime in Jordan: a PLO which would pose a lesser political threat to Israel, and one with which Israel would feel less international pressure eventually to negotiate. The invasion of 1982 thus illustrated Israeli fears of the dangers posed by an independent Palestinian movement, especially one whose status and security had been enhanced since July 1981 by the conclusion and maintenance of a cease-fire on the Israeli–Lebanese border.

Within the PLO, the Lebanese implications of this were long debated. Some pressed for freezes on military operations in the south, pointing to both military and political imperatives. Others argued that this was a mistake: that a cease-fire with the enemy was unthinkable; that Israel would attack in any case; that a cease-fire would represent a surrender of the rights the PLO had acquired through the Cairo Agreement; and that it would send the wrong message to the Lebanese people, suggesting that the PLO, and not an aggressive, expansionist, Israel, was responsible for their misfortunes. But regardless of the pros and cons of the debate, it was the mystique of armed struggle that dominated Palestinian political discourse in and about Lebanon through much of the 1970s. This was in turn reinforced by the internal political dynamics of the Palestinian movement which, until the end of the decade, made any real suspension of cross-border operations tantamount to political suicide.

Thus, in many respects military action became a veritable end in itself. Accordingly, until 1978, no freeze on PLO cross-border military operations endured longer than a few weeks. And, in fairness, Palestinian field commanders and fighters could be excused much of their confusion regarding the political rationale that lay behind the conduct or non-conduct of military action. Pursuing the politics of ambiguity in an effort to maintain internal unity, the Palestinian leadership never clearly set forth the strategy that underpinned such decisions. If the PLO leadership understood the importance of Lebanon—and it is clear from their intense effort to preserve the PLO's position there that they certainly did—that understanding and the needs stemming from it were never clearly articulated to Palestinian cadres or public.

Such confusion was manifest, among other places, in the organizational and doctrinal development of Palestinian military forces. To protect the Palestinian presence against Lebanese opponents, and to increase political control over military ranks, PLO guerrilla forces were gradually "regularized" in the 1970s and early 1980s. Larger, battalion- and brigade-sized units were established; formal ranks and command structures were established; and heavy weapons, artillery, and (most controversial of all) a number of obsolete, Second World War-era T-34 tanks were acquired. But the more visible nature of such units and weapons made them more vulnerable to Israel and more provocative to many Lebanese than *fida'i* guerrilla bands had ever been. This was particularly true of Palestinian artillery, acquired to circumvent UNIFIL and Israeli border defenses, deter Israeli attacks, and strike back against the Haddad border zone. Palestinian cross-border shelling, rather than cross-border infiltration, hardly seemed heroic to the beleaguered Lebanese who usually bore the brunt of Israeli retaliation. [19]

It was in this context and against the threat of a massive Israeli invasion that the PLO eventually did begin to deemphasize Lebanese operations, a process marked by its acceptance of UNIFIL deployment in 1978 and the cross-border cease-fire agreement of July 1981. In fact, these decisions were taken as much to calm Lebanese public opinion as to abort Israeli military intervention. Pressures on the PLO to deescalate the confrontation with Israel in the south came not only from the Lebanese government and Lebanese opponents of the Palestinian presence, but from the PLO's chief Lebanese allies as well. [20]

Tajawuzat

If Israel's scorched-earth policies in south Lebanon were doing serious and intended damage to the PLO's position in Lebanon, almost equal damage was being done by the behavior of the Palestinian movement itself. Even such a strong supporter of the Palestinian movement as Kamal Junblatt was moved to comment shortly before his death in 1977:

> It has to be said that the Palestinians themselves, by violating Lebanese law, bearing arms as they chose and policing certain important points of access to the capital, actually furthered the plot that had been hatched against them. They carelessly exposed themselves to criticism and even hatred. High officials and administrators were occasionally stopped and asked for their identity papers by Palestinian patrols. From time to time, Lebanese citizens were arrested and imprisoned, on the true or false pretext of having posed a threat to the

> Palestinian revolution. Such actions were, at first, forgiven, but became increasingly difficult to tolerate. Outsiders making the law in Lebanon, armed demonstrations and ceremonies, military funerals for martyrs of the revolution, it all mounted up and began to alienate public opinion, especially conservative opinion, which was particularly concerned about security. . . . I never saw a less discreet, less cautious revolution.[21]

Amidst the chaos of the civil war, the collapse of state authority, heavy fighting in urban areas, and the proliferation of arms and organizations contributed to a veritable explosion of lawlessness. For some Lebanese militias, emerging from the *qabada'i* (strong-arm) tradition of Lebanese politics, looting, extortion, and smuggling represented as much their *raison d'être* as did any political objectives or beliefs. This was not the case for Palestinian organizations, which as organizations formally condemned such behavior. Still, a significant number of cadres and leaders alike did exploit the situation for personal gain. Their conspicuous wealth at a time when ordinary Palestinians and Lebanese were facing bombings, shellings, and social hardship had a severely corrosive affect on the PLO's status, largely overshadowing the popular image of a decade earlier of the self-sacrificing *fida'i* struggling to regain usurped rights.[22]

This problem of lawlessness, damaging enough in its own right, was compounded by other aspects of political chaos. Arab regimes continued to use Palestinian and Lebanese organizations to settle scores on Lebanese territory. Several bouts of fighting between Palestinian organizations themselves resulted in dozens of Lebanese casualties. And last, but by no means least, the situation was constantly fuelled by Israel and the Lebanese Front which, in the early 1980s, embarked on a sustained terrorist campaign of car bombings against Joint Forces-controlled areas.

Tajawuzat (excesses) was the generic title given to such militia lawlessness, corruption, extortion, internecine fighting, violations of the Cairo Agreement, and friction arising from Palestinian military deployments in the south. Palestinian leaders protested that the PLO was not responsible for much of what transpired, that *agents provocateurs* were at work, and that the situation was being exploited by Israel and others opposed to the Palestinian armed presence in Lebanon. And much of this was undoubtedly true. Certainly the PLO could point to an effective campaign against it and its image by the Phalangist Voice of Lebanon, the right-wing press, and Israel.[23] In the Sunni, Shi'i, and Druze communities, many traditional figures used popular irritation with the PLO as a means of recycling their own political influence among their co-religionists. So too did Amal.

But it made little difference. Car bombings were car bombings. Israeli attacks were apparently the product of the PLO presence, Palestinian allegations of long-term Zionist aspirations in south Lebanon notwithstanding. And lawlessness or political violence (whether committed by Palestinians or Lebanese, officially or as "private enterprise") was seen as occurring under the PLO's security "umbrella," a view reinforced by the often hazy lines of demarcation between Palestinian and Lebanese organizations, and between "security" forces and neighborhood street gangs. The hostile propaganda, however exaggerated, retained enough basis in day-to-day experience that it was readily accepted by large segments of Lebanese public opinion, Christian and Muslim alike.

The dangers of all this were recognized. But the problem was never solved, for several reasons. Much of the chaos was externally instigated, beyond the PLO's control, and the PLO was constantly and deliberately distracted by the ongoing confrontation with Israel in the south. Paradoxically, the very security measures necessary to contain *tajawuzat* were themselves provocative to Lebanese opinion, being seen as further evidence of the Palestinian construction of a "state-within-a-state." Most important in terms of policy, the PLO's ability to deal with *tajawuzat* was limited by the nature of the organization, its political dynamics, and the perennial problem of Palestinian unity.

Internal Weaknesses: The Impact of Disunity

All told, the impact of Palestinian disunity on pre-1982 Palestinian policy in Lebanon was severe. Weak internal cohesion, control, and coordination severely undermined the effectiveness of Palestinian policy, creating inconsistencies that undermined the PLO's credibility in the eyes of its allies and opponents alike. They also created the organizational and political gaps that allowed the *tajawuzat* to grow, with serious negative consequences for the PLO's popular image.

To the extent that much of this was a result of the inevitable penetration of the PLO by Arab regimes and their proxies, there was little that could be done to rectify the situation. Nevertheless, the independent nature of the major, mass-based resistance organizations—Fateh, the PFLP, and DFLP—endowed them with a special responsibility to address the weaknesses stemming from Palestinian disunity. To the extent that they failed to do so, they bore significant responsibility for the political atmosphere within which *tajawuzat* and lack of coordination endured.

In the case of Fateh, political maneuverability and ambiguity, adopted so as to preserve the unity of the broad-based Fateh movement and the PLO as a whole, have often come at the cost of a clear political program and course of political action. Because of the very different ideological and political currents that make up its nationalist membership (and that of the PLO as a whole), the Fateh leadership has felt limited in its ability to publicly elucidate policies. One effect of this has been to encourage clique formation among Fateh subgroups, and the use of patronage and private structures of authority to assure policy compliance. In Lebanon, fealty often came to be prized over competence; corruption by local Palestinian (and Lebanese) commanders and ill-disciplined behavior by guerrillas was overlooked in the interests of power. This approach was eventually applied to Lebanese politics too, with damaging consequences to both the LNM and the PLO-LNM alliance.

Such behavior was criticized by the PFLP and the DFLP. In contrast to Fateh, in which *tajawuzat* were usually the product of its loose organization, the DFLP and PFLP were less vulnerable to this by virtue of their Leninist internal structures. But they were not entirely innocent of such practices either. Ideological commitment could be negatively manifest in adventurism, disregard for Lebanese law, and a lack of sensitivity to the religious sensibilities and moral conservatism of the south Lebanese peasantry. Moreover, these organizations were themselves a major reason for Fateh's actions, having acted throughout the early 1970s as (in the words of one senior Fateh member) a "militant irritant" to the PLO's official policy.[24] Freed from the responsibilities that Fateh bore as the leading Palestinian organization, smaller groups sought to extend their political support by outbidding the mainstream PLO leadership, a process for which Fateh, and not they, often bore the political costs. In turn, Fateh adopted policy unilateralism and ambiguity to achieve its goals, a practice that only increased the suspicion of other Palestinian groups. One result of this was to encourage further PFLP and DFLP criticism of Fateh policies, often not so much on the grounds of staunch opposition, but out of concern regarding exactly what they meant.[25]

Thus, multiple centers of authority coexisted and even competed, while organization and discipline suffered. Reflecting both this and the crisis-laden atmosphere of the times, Lebanese decisionmaking was generally ad hoc and fragmented in nature. Those supposedly "unified" decisions that were taken were usually little more than paper exercises.

The most notable example of this was the PLO's efforts to reduce friction by removing Palestinian offices and military deployments from heavily populated Lebanese urban areas. This commitment was made, in various forms, perhaps two dozen times between 1969 and 1982. Yet, whether because of changing conditions, inefficiency, or quite deliberate inertia, it was never really implemented. By the early 1980s, it was understandable if many Lebanese no longer believed what the PLO said, and turned to the simple but effective anti-Palestinian propaganda of its opponents.

Retrospect and Prospects

In April 1987 Syrian troops entered West Beirut, taking up positions around Palestinian camps there and bringing to an end Amal's attacks upon the camps. That same month, negotiations between the Palestinians and Amal took place with the aim of achieving a cease-fire around the refugee camps in Sidon and Tyre.

April 1987 also saw the reunification of the PLO at the eighteenth session of the Palestine National Council in Algiers. The political resolutions adopted by the eighteenth PNC made specific reference to the PLO's position in Lebanon, calling for "reinforcing the unity of action regarding the situation in our camps in Lebanon"; "rejecting the attempts to expel and disarm our people"; "insisting on our people's rights in Lebanon regarding residence, work, movement, and the freedom of political and social action"; and stressing the PLO's right to defend the camps and struggle against Israel in accordance with the (obsolete) Cairo Agreement and its annexes. It also praised the steadfastness of the camps and reiterated its commitment to its alliance with the largely defunct Lebanese National Movement.[26]

Yet 1987 and 1988 have also shown that the difficulties facing the Palestinian movement in Lebanon remain intense. In the context of continued tensions between the PLO and Damascus, the Syrian (and Amal) presence in Beirut meant the continuation of a *de facto* siege of the West Beirut refugee camps. Tens of thousands of displaced Palestinians (most of them from Beirut or from the camps around Tyre) crowded into uncertain refuge in Sidon and elsewhere.[27] Amidst this insecurity, on 21 May 1987 the Lebanese Chamber of Deputies voted (with the blessings of Amal, Syria, and the Phalange) to abrogate the Cairo Agreement. Lebanese president Amin al-Jumayyil confirmed the act in June. The summer of 1987 then saw a renewal of the camps war in the south, ending only with a new agreement between the PLO and the pro-Syrian Lebanese "Unification and Liberation Front" (including Amal) on 11 September.[28] It was not until January 1988 that Amal leader Nabih Berri, having failed to overcome the camps' resistance over the course of more than two and a half years, announced a formal end to the camps war as a "gift" to the Palestinian uprising.

Meanwhile, Israeli intervention in Lebanon has continued unabated. In addition to its continued military actions in and around its self-declared "security zone" in south Lebanon, some two dozen air attacks were launched against Palestinian refugee camps and positions by the Israeli Defense Forces in 1987, and seventeen more in the first ten months of 1988. Ships traveling from Cyprus to Lebanon are regularly stopped and boarded by Israeli naval patrols in search of Palestinian cadres and material. In February 1988 a senior member of the PLO's military command in Lebanon was killed (along with two other Palestinian officers) by a car bomb in Cyprus. Two months later, Fateh's Khalil al-Wazir (Abu Jihad), deputy commander of PLO military forces responsible for both Lebanon and the occupied territories, was assassinated by Israeli forces at his home in Tunis. Given these pressures, and perhaps, in the belief that cross-border actions will only divert attention from the *intifadah* in the occupied territories, only sporadic efforts have been made by Palestinian guerrillas to infiltrate Israel from south Lebanon. Still fewer forays have succeeded in penetrating Israel's Lebanese security zone and border defenses.

Meanwhile, there is ample evidence that the internal weaknesses that have plagued past PLO policy in Lebanon have not disappeared. In Beirut, fighting erupted between Arafat loyalists and Abu Musa's pro-Syrian Fateh dissidents in May 1988, ending two months later with the capture of Shatila (27 June) and Burj al-Barajinah (8 July) camps by the latter. In Sidon, where Syria's writ does not reach and where Palestinian military and political power is strongest, a rash of incidents have signaled local power struggles and the reemergence of *tajawuzat*.[29]

In the reexamination of Palestinian policy that has taken place since 1982, a number of key issues have emerged. For the PFLP, the major mistakes of the 1970s and early 1980s were "that the very nature of the Lebanese-Palestinian national alliance . . . was guided by the Palestinian revolution" and "*tajawuzat* and misuse of arms." In the future, the PLO "ought to make it clear that we do not wish to flaunt our Palestinian armed presence in Lebanon nor do we wish to set up a Palestinian authority in Lebanon or to fly in the face of the Lebanese National Movement program." The DFLP's analysis is similar, although it extends to criticism of pre-1982 Palestinian military pressure on Amal. Fateh leaders, on the other hand, are much more likely to stress the impact of organizational disunity and the role of external (Israeli and Arab) interference, although some extend the critique to tolerance of "incompetence" by Fateh itself.[30]

If past experience is a guide, the rectification of such PLO policy weaknesses in Lebanon will be no simple and painless affair. It is difficult to see how, in the anarchical and multi-polar context of contemporary Lebanese politics, the PLO can reestablish firm internal alliances. A strategy driven by opportunism alone (evident today in Fateh's ties with both Hizballah and the Lebanese Forces) may be useful in the short term. In the longer term, however, it seems likely only to reinforce both suspicion of Palestinian motives and Syrian antipathy.

Similarly, the strengthening of Palestinian "unity of action" will require considerably more than mere PNC resolutions. It will require substantial reform of the structure and process of Palestinian decisionmaking. The obstacles to this—the inherent tensions between democratic debate and revolutionary authority; the competing cross-currents of inter-Palestinian and inter-Arab politics; the firm entrenchment of a leadership style and political dynamic—are severe. If the end of the camps war was a tacit admission by the PLO's Lebanese opponents of the tenacity of Palestinian resistance and the strength of its hard-won military skills, the summer's fratricidal fighting in the Beirut camps has been testimony to serious weaknesses within.

Indeed, such difficulties are so severe that the day-to-day defense of the camps against external threat may, paradoxically, be easier to secure. Yet the military defense of a siege perimeter is "security" in only the narrowest, short-term sense. Promoting an atmosphere within which Palestinians in Lebanon enjoy real security is the more important and more difficult task. Central to this is the need to move cautiously, and to avoid the temptation to deploy the PLO's considerable finances and military potential in pursuit of an assertive role in the internal Lebanese balance of power. It is here that there is much to be learnt from the lessons of the past.

1. The research of which this article is a part has greatly benefited from comments and other assistance from Ibrahim Abu-Lughod, Paul Noble, As'ad Abd al-Rahman, Nabil Sha'th, Yusuf 'Umar, Alex Brynen, Lamis Andoni, and Halla S. It is the author alone, however, who is solely responsible for the views presented herein.

2. The importance of Lebanon in Palestinian policy and political discourse is emphasized

by Rashid Khalidi, "The Palestinians Twenty Years After," *MERIP Middle East Report* 146 (May–June 1987), 11–12. On the emergence of the Palestinian movement in Lebanon, see Rosemary Sayigh, *Palestinians: From Peasants to Revolutionaries* (London: Zed, 1979).

3. George Habash in *al-Khalij* (Abu Dhabi), 4 October 1987 (in FBIS/JPRS, 19 November 1987).

4. Multiple accounts of the Lebanese civil war exist. With regard to the Palestinian role in the conflict, see: Michael Hudson, "The Palestinian Factor in the Lebanese Civil War," *Middle East Journal* 32, no. 3 (Summer 1978), 261–78; Walid Khalidi, *Conflict and Violence in Lebanon.* (Cambridge, Mass.: Harvard University Center for International Affairs, 1979); Tony Khater, "Lebanese Politics and the Palestinian Resistance Movement, 1967–1976." (unpublished Ph.D. thesis, State University of New York—Buffalo, 1982).

5. The text of the Cairo Agreement can be found in Khalidi, *Conflict and Violence in Lebanon*, Appendix 1.

6. Named after the hotel within which the discussions took place, the Milkart Protocols were not a formal agreement but rather the minutes of discussions between the PLO and the Lebanese army regarding a mutually acceptable interpretation of the Cairo Agreement's often vague provisions. They brought to an end two weeks of fighting between the *fida'iyyin* and the army in May 1973, which in turn had been sparked by the Lebanese army's failure to intercept an Israeli raiding party that on 10 April had assassinated PLO spokesman Kamal Nasir, and Fateh Central Committee members Muhammad al-Najjar and Kamal 'Udwan.

7. The Riyadh summit brought together PLO chairman Yasir Arafat, Lebanese president Ilyas Sarkis, Syrian president Hafiz al-Asad, and Egyptian president Anwar al-Sadat under Saudi and Kuwaiti auspices. Agreement by these key regional actors on ending the Lebanese civil war, obtained at Riyadh, was later endorsed by the Arab League as a whole. An Arab Deterrent Force—consisting almost entirely of Syrian troops—was mandated to help implement the agreement reached. For the translated text of the Riyadh summit, see *Journal of Palestine Studies* 6, no. 2 (Winter 1977), 192–94.

8. The term is used by Rashid Khalidi in his *Under Siege: PLO Decisionmaking During the 1982 War* (New York: Columbia University Press, 1986), 28–36. On the PLO's prewar infrastructure in Lebanon, see: Cheryl Rubenberg, *The Palestine Liberation Organization: Its Institutional Infrastructure* (Belmont Mass.: Institute of Arab Studies, 1983). Mona Yunis, "L'invasion du Liban et la situation sanitaire des palestiniens," *Revue d'Études Palestiniennes* 8 (Summer 1983), 39–52 provides an excellent overview of the health-care component of this infrastructure, as does Fathi Arafat, *al-Sihhah w-al-Harb [Health and War]* (Nicosia: Palestine Red Crescent Society, 1984).

9. Khalidi, *Under Siege*, 17.

10. For an overview on the Palestinians' post-1982 situation in Lebanon, see: Marie Christine Aulas, "Lebanon's Palestinians: Life at Ground Level," *MERIP Middle East Report* 119 (November–December 1983), 24–26; Rashid Khalidi, "The Palestinians in Lebanon: Social Repercussions of the Israeli Invasion," *Middle East Journal* 38, no. 2 (Spring 1984), 255–66; "Le siège des camps palestiniens de Beyrouth," *Revue d'Études Palestiniennes* 17 (Autumn 1985), 67–128; Elaine C. Hagopian (ed.), *Amal and the Palestinians: Understanding the Battle of the Camps* (Belmont, Mass.: AAUG Press, 1985); "Documents and Source Material," *Journal of Palestine Studies* 16, no. 3 (Spring 1987), 223–230; Yezid Sayigh, "Shatila: the Irony and the Hypocrisy," *Middle East International*, 7 October 1988.

11. The LNRF was initially founded in September 1982 by several Lebanese leftist organizations, with other groups joining it later. "From its inception, the Front was heavily funded and supported by materials and men from the Popular Front for the Liberation of Palestine and Democratic Front for the Liberation of Palestine. Trying to learn from the tragic pre-1982 experience of the Palestinian resistance in south Lebanon, both groups shunned publicity and accepted

to give all credit for their operations to the Front." Asad AbuKhalil, "Druze, Sunni, and Shi'ite Political Leadership in Present-Day Lebanon," *Arab Studies Quarterly* 7, no. 4 (Fall 1985), 51–53.

12. Samir Franjieh, "How Revolutionary is the Palestinian Resistance? A Marxist interpretation," *Journal of Palestine Studies* 1, no. 2 (Winter 1972), 52–60.

13. On the latter, see Abu Ivad, *My Home, My Land: A Narrative of the Palestinian Struggle* (New York: Times Books, 1981), 161–63.

14. Augustus Richard Norton, *Amal and the Shi'a: Struggle for the Soul of Lebanon* (Austin: University of Texas Press, 1987); AbuKhalil, "Druze, Sunni, and Shi'ite Political Leadership in Present-Day Lebanon," 45–48; Camille Mansour, "Au delà du siège des camps palestiniens de Beyrouth: la montée en puissance du mouvement Amal et ses limites," *Maghreb-Machrek* 109 (July–September 1985), 64–82.

15. Yezid Sayigh, "Palestinian Armed Struggle: Means and Ends," *Journal of Palestine Studies* 16, no. 1 (Autumn 1986), 95–112.

16. At their peak in 1970, Israeli sources reported some 390 Palestinian operations from Lebanon resulting in some 174 Israeli casualties. The effectiveness of Palestinian cross-border attacks declined thereafter. In 1981 (a year which saw two weeks of intense cross-border fighting in July), the IDF reported 141 cross-border incidents with a much lower casualty toll. Although Palestinian shelling did provoke significant panic in Kiryat Shemona and other Israeli "development towns" on the northern frontier, by this time the locus of confrontation had been pushed northward into south Lebanon.

17. Although others would disagree, at least some West Bank PLO figures hold this view. Interview with Mustafa Milhem (PLO Central Council), Amman, 25 December 1986.

18. Avner Yaniv, *Dilemmas of Security: Politics, Strategy, and the Israeli Experience in Lebanon* (Oxford: Oxford University Press, 1987), 100–101.

19. On the development of Palestinian military forces see Sayigh, "Palestinian Armed

Struggle," and "Palestinian Military Performance in the 1982 War," *Journal of Palestine Studies* 12, no. 4 (Summer 1983), 3–24. According to Khalil al-Wazir ("Abu Jihad," deputy commander of PLO forces until his assassination in April 1988) the "regularization" (*tajyish*) of PLO forces was a natural development, unmotivated by any desire to augment political command and control (interview, Baghdad, 30 December 1986). A similar evolutionary view was expressed by the late Sa'd Sayil, chief of the PLO Central Operations room, in an article in *Shu'un Filastiniyyah* 105 (August 1980), 33–48. But two former members of the PLO Executive Committee interviewed by the author suggested otherwise, stating that the ability to exert tighter political control over Palestinian units in the field was a primary consideration at this time, particularly in view of the need to avoid incidents with UNIFIL and maintain the July 1981 cease-fire.

20. Significantly, when Ahmad Jibril's PFLP-General Command attempted to renege on its earlier commitment to the July 1981 cease-fire, Arafat confronted Jibril on the matter in the presence of National Movement figures. According to then-member of the Fateh Central Committee (interview with Samih Abu Kuwayk [Qadri], Damascus, 17 December 1986), Arafat was prepared to "liquidate" the PFLP-GC if they attempted to sabotage the agreement. Similarly, a member of the PFLP Politbureau (interview, Damascus, 18 December 1986) confirmed that his organization too reached the "edge of [military] conflict" with Fateh over the matter. Fateh's efforts to assure compliance with the agreement are detailed in Ze'ev Schiff and Ehud Ya'ari, *Israel's Lebanon War* (New York: Simon and Schuster, 1984), 84–86.

21. Kamal Joumblatt [Junblatt], *I Speak for Lebanon* (London: Zed, 1982), 55.

22. See Khalidi, *Under Siege*, 32–33; Fouad Moughrabi, "The Palestinians after Lebanon," *Arab Studies Quarterly* 5, no. 3 (Summer 1983), 212, 214–15.

23. Nabil Hadi, "al-I'lam al-In'izali al-Lubnani w-al-Muqawamah al-Filastiniyyah" [Leba-

nese Isolationist Propaganda and the Palestinian Resistance], *Shu'un Filastiniyyah* 102 (May 1980), 5–30. The even greater unreliability of many "progressive" radio stations helped *Voice of Lebanon* gain a wider listenership.

24. Interview with Dr. Nabil Sha'th, Cairo, 8 January 1987. Toward the latter part of the 1970s, this problem was supplanted by the "adjunct irritant" of Arab-sponsored organizations.

25. Both the DFLP and PFLP, for example, were publicly critical of attempts by Salah Khalaf of Fateh to resurrect the PLO-Phalange dialogue in 1978. Privately, however, members of the senior leadership of both groups suggest that they did not have a problem with dialogue *per se*, but rather with the way in which it was being conducted (interviews, Damascus, December 1986–February 1987).

26. Text in *Journal of Palestine Studies* 16, no. 4 (Summer 1987), 196–201.

27. According to a report prepared by the DFLP in December 1986, the camps war had destroyed some 3,000 Palestinian homes in Rashidiyyah camp near Tyre, 80 percent of the homes in Shatila camp in Beirut, and 50 percent of the homes in Burj al-Barajinah. By June 1987 UNRWA was reporting some 33,210 homeless Palestinians displaced from Tyre and Beirut, most temporarily located in Sidon or villages to its north. For their condition, see: Rosemary Sayigh, "Jidra: A Microcosm of Palestinian Insecurity," *Middle East International*, 26 September 1987, 13–15.

28. Text of the agreement in *Journal of Palestine Studies* 17, no. 2 (Winter 1988), 211–12.

29. Syrian forces (in Tripoli, the Biqa', and West Beirut) and Amal forces (in West Beirut and Tyre) have severely hampered the freedom of action of the Palestinian movement in most areas. In contrast, the PLO achieved significant military success against Amal around Sidon in 1986–87. Yet with success have come severe organizational difficulties. In August 1987 the commander of "Force 17" in Lebanon, Rasim al-Ghul, was assassinated. In September an attempt was made on the life of Fateh's local political chief, Abu 'Ali Shahin. Shahin and Fateh's military commander in Lebanon were subsequently recalled to Tunis. Later that month fifty Palestinian fighters were poisoned in 'Ayn al-Hilwah camp, an act attributed to revenge for al-Ghul's killing. In November, fighting broke out between Palestinian guerrillas and the local Popular Nasserite Organization. In February 1988 a local dispute led to the kidnapping of two Scandinavian UNRWA workers by Fateh guerrillas for over three weeks despite Arafat's efforts to secure their immediate release. In March, two Oxfam officials were "detained" for five days by Abu Nidal's Fateh-Revolutionary Council. On 26 March another Palestinian military commander, Farid Hawrani, was killed in an ambush. This latter incident sparked further internal clashes, leading to a Fateh clamp-down in 'Ayn al-Hilwah camp.

30. *Al-Khalij*, 4 October 1987; interviews with members of PFLP and DFLP politbureaus, Damascus, December 1986, February 1987. Fateh's view based on interviews with Yasir Arafat and Abu Jihad, Baghdad, 29–30 December 1986; criticism of internal Fateh "incompetence" from interview with Abu Iyad, Fateh Central Committee, Tunis, 24, 27 January 1987. Although many Fateh dissidents offer analyses similar to those above (albeit with greater emphasis on problems of Fateh organization), dissident leader Abu Musa tends to emphasize Yasir Arafat's personal role and his efforts to "hijack" Lebanon. Interview, Damascus, 10 February 1987.

Part IV
Islamic Fundamentalist Groups

Terrorism, Volume 12, pp. 401–416
Printed in the UK. All rights reserved.

Iran's Islamic Fundamentalism and Terrorism:
A View from the Pulpit

Abstract *This paper examines the Friday prayer sermons delivered by Iran's new leadership to answer the question of whether Iran's Islamic fundamentalism has crested with the death of its spiritual leader Ayatollah Khomeini in June 1989. The analysis shows that an attempt is underway to articulate the Islamic identity of post-Khomeini Iran in economic, political, and social relations. The study concludes that although President Rafsanjani is willing to reevaluate Iran's domestic and foreign relations, the totalitarian, Islamic, and revolutionary structure that Khomeini helped build is still intact. As such, the regime's tendencies toward radicalism and export of the Islamic revolution remain unchanged. In this scenario, resort to terrorism by the Islamic Republic in order to maintain its structure and tendencies cannot be ruled out.*

Keywords: Iran, Islam, Shi'a fundamentalism, President Rafsanjani, state-sponsored terrorism.

The consolidation of an Islamic theocracy in Iran occurred immediately after Khomeini's return to Iran in 1979. Since then, the clerics have established their control over civil society by conducting extensive purges of the army, state bureaucracy, and the school and university systems. They have taken over the Iranian parliament (Majlis), and changed its name to the Islamic Consultative Assembly. Additionally, they have created new institutions, like the Corps of the Guardians of the Islamic Revolution—including the creation of a ministry for them—and the Council of Guardians of the Constitution, a special judicial body empowered to veto parliamentary enactments it finds to be inimical to Islamic doctrines. They have integrated the revolutionary courts into the Ministry of Justice in order to ensure that the penal code reflects Islamic norms of testimony, culpability, and punishment. And finally, the clerics have created the Ministry of Islamic Guidance as the chief governmental agency in charge of Islamic propaganda. In short, they have managed to create a system that is structurally totalitarian, Islamic, and revolutionary.[1]

Another core institution is the Friday congregational prayer (*namaz-e-jomeh*). Since 1979, the Friday prayer sermon has been vigorously revived, and fully institutionalized as one of the main pillars of the theocratic state. The importance of this institution was emphasized early on by Khomeini in a speech after his return to Iran:

> I have often recommended that the congregational imams and the distinguished preachers should be looked after. The great nation should realize that if the status of this group, which is the guardian of the Koran and Islam, be undermined the plundering foreigners will achieve their aspirations and the grip on affairs will be lost.[2]

Today the Friday prayers are a major event in the week and the addresses have become an important politico-religious organ seeking to perpetuate clerical rule by advocating particular governmental policies and mobilizing public support for them. The

The author is a consultant and lives in Washington, D.C.

media regularly cover the Friday congregational prayers, which are routinely described as "the unity-creating and enemy-smashing congregational prayer" held in "the meeting-place of lovers of God."[3] In short, since 1979, the spectrum of Islamic political institutions has lengthened to include the Friday prayer sermon, which acts as a motivator, legitimator, and justifier for the domestic and foreign policies of the regime.

What does a reading of the Friday prayer sermons suggest about post-Khomeini Iran? Has Iran settled on a clear course in its domestic and foreign policies? Or has the multiplicity of centers of power impeded the decision-making process? How have the events in the Soviet Union and Eastern Europe affected the attitude of the clerical regime on such issues as freedom, women's rights, and democracy? And finally, to the extent that the structure and tendencies of the system may have changed, has Iran's Islamic fundamentalism crested? This is the key question in determining whether terrorism has been removed from the arsenal of the Islamic Republic as a means to further its revolutionary objectives worldwide.

Historical Context

Until Khomeini's return to Iran and the establishment of an Islamic Republic in that country, the Friday congregational prayer never held the same importance among Shi'ites as it has among Sunnis.[4] According to Shi'ite tradition, the function of leading the Friday congregational prayer was one of the functions of the Twelfth Imam which the early Shi'ite jurists declared in abeyance during Occultation. This situation was reversed with the ascension of Shah Tahmasp, the second Safavid monarch, to the throne in 1524. His long reign (1524–1576) was of crucial importance to the institutionalization of Shi'ism and the definitive penetration of Iran by Shi'ite clerics. One such cleric was Sheikh Ali Abd al-Ali al-Karaki (d. 1534), whom Shah Tahmasp granted the title "deputy of the Imam" giving him broad religious and political authority. Exercising his authority specifically as the deputy of the Imam, al-Karaki instituted the Friday congregational prayer—hitherto considered in abeyance during the Occultation of the Imam by many jurists—and appointed congregational prayer leaders throughout Iran. Safavid monarchs themselves occasionally prayed behind the congregational prayer leaders.[5]

During the Qajar period (1794–1925), the Friday congregational prayer lost much of its sociopolitical significance because the prayer leaders were among the very few religious functionaries appointed by the Shah, and therefore had an ambiguous relationship with the autonomous Shi'ite hierarchy headed by doctors of religious jurisprudence (*mujtahids*).[6]

During the Pahlavi era, an activist cleric by the name of Sheikh Mohammad Khalisi made the resuscitation of the congregational prayer the centerpiece of his Islamic revivalist mission. Khalisi was alarmed by the menace of secularism which he considered the chief weapon of British imperialism in Iran. He argued that the European powers, and Britain especially, have a grand design for the Islamic countries: to connect them to Christianity, and failing that, to turn them away from Islam into materialism and naturalism. As the secularizing intentions of Reza Shah's government became unmistakable in the late 1920s, Khalisi intensified his campaign and attacked the central government in his sermons. Reza Shah, however, reacted firmly, and Khalisi was persecuted and banished. He resumed his activity after the fall of Reza Shah in 1941. He continued to write, preach, and hold Friday congregational prayers. Khalisi regarded the revival of the Friday congregational prayer as the cornerstone of his mission, and attacked the majority of the Shi'ite ulema who questioned its incumbency during the Occultation of the Imam.[7]

His death in 1963 ended efforts to institutionalize the Friday prayer sermons, something the Ayatollah Khomeini would do with the overthrow of the monarchy in 1979.

One of Khomeini's earliest acts after returning to Iran in 1979 was the revival of the Friday prayer congregational prayer and its full utilization as a political platform, despite reservations from some Shi'ite ulema who questioned its incumbency during the Occultation of the Imam. In order to institutionalize the Friday prayer he appointed prayer leaders in all large and small towns to lead the congregational prayer on Fridays and deliver a political sermon. From Autumn of 1983 onward, Friday sermons of the prayer leaders of large and small towns were extensively covered in the media with the intent to perpetuate clerical rule by preaching the ideas of Khomeini. The importance of this institution was elaborated upon in October 1984 by then-President Khamenei when he duly referred to the prayer leaders as "the great pillars of the Revolution, the speaking tongue of the Leader [Ayatollah Khomeini] and the strong arm of general mobilization."[8]

The Friday Prayer Sermons: June–December 1989

Since Khomeini's death on June 7, 1989, through the end of the year, 30 sermons have been delivered by notables of the regime. Ayatollah Ali Khamenei, the new supreme religious leader of Iran, has delivered two key addresses. Hojatolislam Ali Akbar Hashemi Rafsanjani, the newly elected president, has had seven occasions to deliver his message to the Iranian public. Ayatollah Musavi Ardebili, the former revolutionary prosecutor and chief spokesman for the hardliners, has addressed the crowds at Tehran University eight times. Hojatolislam Imami-Kashani, a member of the Council of Guardians, has delivered eight sermons. And finally, Ayatollah Mohammad Yazdi, Iran's chief justice and Rafsanjani's mentor, has delivered five Friday prayer sermons.

Although a wide variety of issues has been on the agenda of the Friday prayer sermons, a few have dominated the debates ove the last seven months. Chief among them has been the issue of leadership in the post-Khomeini era, with particular emphasis on the revolutionary credentials of the new leadership and their qualifications to serve as the vanguard of Khomeini's legacy. The question of how to rebuild Iran's war-torn economy without foregoing the Islamic identity of the country has been a major issue in the Friday prayer sermons. The limits of freedom in Islam, the role of women in the Islamic Republic, and the level of tolerance for opposition to the regime have also been elaborated upon by the leaders of the Friday prayer sermons. And finally, one of the most contentious issues raised in the Friday prayer sermons by the current leadership in Tehran has been the future direction of the Islamic Republic's foreign policy.

Despite the diversity of topics, a common feature of all the sermons has been the need to articulate the Islamic Republic's post-Khomeini identity. The question has been: Who shall have primacy in this process and how shall change be brought about, if indeed it should at all?

The most prominent theme of the first four Friday prayer sermons was the need to unify behind the newly appointed religious leader of the Islamic Republic, Ayatollah Ali Khamenei. Rafsanjani's sermon of June 9 stressed the importance of two points: first, the need for the Islamic Republic to have a supreme religious leader in order to safeguard the "viability of the [Islamic] system." Without a religious leader, he argued, the regime would lose its legitimacy. Second, Rafsanjani emphasized the importance of placing experienced individuals with a proven track record in positions of leadership as opposed to a *marja-e-taqlid* (the highest religious authority in Shi'ite law). In a clear reference to Ardebili's insistence that seminarians be given positions of power within the decision-making process, Rafsanjani asked the following question: "Now that we are talking about ijtihad [as a requirement for assuming a position of leadership], should not those individuals with experience in social, economic, cultural, and foreign policy have priority over seminarians with no expertise? The rational mind says that in this case one go along with the experienced individual."[9] The difference of opinion between Rafsanjani and Ardebili on this particular point, however, was overshadowed by their overwhelming support for Khamenei, recognizing the importance of rallying behind him as the vanguard of Khomeini's legacy. This sentiment was echoed by Imami-Kashani in the congregational prayer held on June 16:

> The appointment of Ayatollah Khamenei as leader of the Islamic Republic met with approval from everyone. All the great sources of emulation, all great seminarians, all the eminent Islamic dignitaries, various states, the university staff, and the students, approved of him. And today, the leadership of our dear leader is potent, stable, and steadfast, and the entire nation who believe in Islam and the revolution, are today his followers.[10]

Kashani's remarks were a clear signal to all contentious parties within the Islamic Republic to put their differences aside in order to demonstrate the regime's capacity to provide for a smooth transition from one religious leader to another. Not surprisingly, therefore, Ardebili commended the decision by the Council of Guardians to appoint Khamenei in his sermon on June 23. He compared the death of Khomeini to that of the prophet Muhammad, arguing that even "after the prophet's death Islam survived and so will the Islamic Republic." Then, in order to demonstrate the significance of this point, he stated that despite the death of Khomeini, the death sentence on Salman Rushdie was still in effect, and urged the new leadership to pledge their allegiance to Khomeini's legacy.[11] Rafsanjani's remarks in his sermon of June 30 offers an international dimension to Khamenei's appointment, suggesting that the Islamic world is in full agreement with the decision to give Khamenei the role once assumed by Khomeini:

> Reports from all over the world and information from outside Iran indicated that mourning for the tragic demise of the great leader of the Islamic revolution and the founder of the Islamic Republic, and obedience to His Eminence, Ayatollah Khamenei the leader of the Islamic revolution was impressive in all countries and regions such as Pakistan, Kashmir, India, Lebanon, Saudi Arabia, the south of the Persian Gulf, and Baku.[12]

A reading of the Friday prayer sermons after Khomeini's death suggests that the potentially divisive factor of succession was kept at bay by absorbing the energies of moderates and hardliners in achieving a smooth transition, thus ensuring that the structure of the Islamic Republic remain intact.

Closely related to the question of succession was the time devoted by the congregational prayer leaders of Tehran in stressing the importance of elections for a new president and the referendum on constitutional amendments scheduled for July 28 throughout the country. The sermons by Imami-Kashani on July 21 and Ardebili on July 28 are of importance in this regard. Realizing the significance of a strong turnout by the Iranian people as an endorsement of the post-Khomeini system, Kashani urged the nation to participate in the elections by invoking the memory of Khomeini:

The Imam [Khomeini] always told us that safeguarding the governing process is more important than the secondary pillars of Islam. Therefore, it is the duty of each and every citizen to contribute to a massive presence and to participate actively in the presidential election and the constitutional referendum in order to demonstrate respect and esteem for Islam, the Koran, independence, and freedom. As such, you must all accept the invitation of the leader of the Islamic Republic of Iran.[13]

Ardebili delivered his Friday prayer sermon on July 28, the day of the election. He discussed the role of elections and referenda in Islam as well as the duties of the people with regard to them. He said, "Nonparticipation in elections is tantamount to failure to discharge one's Islamic duty—it means turning away from and stabbing at the regime."[14] Recognizing the direct relationship between participation in the elections and the legitimacy of the regime, the remarks by leaders of Iran's congregational prayers are similar to a speech Khomeini made to the Iranian people on the eve of the first referendum to decide on the establishment of an Islamic Republic in Iran on March 29, 1979: "Tomorrow is the day of the referendum. It is the day when your destiny will be shaped. It is the day when 'yes' is for Islam and 'no' is against Islam."[15]

With the transfer of power to Ayatollah Khamenei as the new supreme religious leader, the election of a new president, and the ratification of new amendments to the constitution, the key question that remained was: Would the new leadership preserve or modify the basic structure of the Islamic Republic and its tendency toward radicalism that was the trademark of Iran under Khomeini?

Taking Khamenei's Friday prayer sermon of July 14 as a point of reference, it would appear that both the structure of the system, which is essentially totalitarian, Islamic, and revolutionary, as well as its tendencies toward radicalism and export of the Islamic revolution are less likely to change in the post-Khomeini period. In his sermon, Khamenei outlined the ten most significant contributions made by Khomeini in terms of their role as guidelines for the future direction of Iran in the post-Khomeini era. They are as follows: First, the revival of Islam. Second, the renewal of pride for the Muslim world. Third, the revival of the idea of one Muslim nation. Fourth, the removal of 2500 years of monarchical rule from Iran. Fifth, the creation of a government founded on Islam. Sixth, the creation of an Islamic movement as a model for liberation movements around the world. Seventh, a new thinking on Shi'ite theology with an emphasis on the inseparability of politics from religion. Eighth, bringing back piety to the position of leadership. Ninth, creating a sense of pride for the "oppressed masses." And tenth, proving that the principle of "neither East nor West, only the Islamic Republic" is a viable and enforceable foreign policy objective. Khamenei concluded his sermon with a key policy statement: "We shall follow the Imam's [Khomeini's] legacy in our domestic affairs and foreign relations, and will not deviate from revolutionary and Islamic ideals."[16]

As the guardian of Khomeini's legacy, it is clear that Iran's new supreme religious leader is committed to keeping the structure of the Islamic Republic and its tendencies intact. An important part of that legacy, it should be noted, is Khomeini's idiosyncratic interpretation of the Koran, blessing and sanctifying violence in God's name. Therefore, by committing himself to his mentor's legacy, Khamenei's sanction of terrorism to "protect the Imam's legacy" cannot be ruled out. Furthermore, by pledging himself to Khomeini's "contributions," it appears that he hopes to carve the premier spot for himself in the decision-making process. This should allow Khamenei to maintain checks and balances against Rafsanjani and his opponents, thus reinforcing his own position.

Another dominant topic of Tehran's Friday congregational prayers has been the rebuilding of Iran's war-torn economy. Of the 30 sermons delivered since Khomeini's death, ten have been devoted to the question of how to rebuild Iran's economy while safeguarding the legacy of Khomeini's disdain for Western assistance.

Rafsanjani laid out his general plan for the reconstruction of the country's economy at the Friday prayer sermon held on August 4. His new economic initiative, which he referred to as "the decade of reconstruction," is composed of two five-year programs with an emphasis on indigenous industry and infrastructure. Rafsanjani's current five-year economic plan calls for a minimal expenditure of $70 billion to $80 billion. However, Iran's income from the five years will not exceed $50 billion to $55 billion, virtually all of it from oil exports, which guarantee Tehran about $10 billion a year. The actual amount needed to repair the war damage to Iran's economy and significantly improve living conditions is estimated at $400 billion.[17] The success of the current five-year program, therefore, is contingent upon financial assistance from abroad, something hardliners like Ardebili oppose. It appears therefore that Rafsanjani is falling prey to that old and tenacious tendency of Iranian political culture to set unrealizable goals through inappropriate means.

This tendency was reinforced by Imami-Kashani in his sermon the following week, endorsing Rafsanjani's plans to raise the standard of living for Iranians: "We are now in the reconstruction era. I hope, God willing, that our dear brother, Hashemi-Rafsanjani will be successful and carry out reconstruction with the help of the people."[18]

Ardebili made his opposition to Rafsanjani's economic plans known at the Friday prayer sermon held on August 25. By invoking Khomeini's remarks that in the Islamic Republic of Iran the Majlis is the most important decision-making institution with veto power over the executive branch, Ardebili sent a clear signal to Rafsanjani that he must contend with an influential minority of as many as 130 so-called radicals in Iran's 270-member parliament. It should be noted that the Speaker of the Majlis, Ayatollah Karrubi, is a militant cleric and an ardent opponent of Rafsanjani. In his sermon, Ardebili argued that in the process of reconstruction more funding should be allocated to the seminaries in Qom because as key institutions of the Islamic Republic they keep the Islamic structure of the system intact. Ardebili ended his sermon with an implicit warning to his opponents: "Although I may be in Qom, if there ever arises the need to lend my support [to the followers of Khomeini's legacy] I will do so."[19]

In order to appease his opponents, Rafsanjani's sermon of September 1 made reference to accounts in the Western press concerning his plans for restructuring Iran's economy. He stated that "since the new administration is called the 'Rebuilding Administration' by the West, there is an impression that Iran will need to cultivate closer ties to the West." He then went on to say that "the reconstruction of Iran will not be done at the expense of deviating from the Imam's [Khomeini's] path and the ideals of the Islamic revolution."[20] In what appeared to be an endorsement of Rafsanjani's sermon the week before, at the congregational prayer of September 8 Imami-Kashani said: "Safe-guarding the ideals of the revolution is not contradictory to stabilizing the economy."[21]

The debate over the future course of Iran's economy intensified at the Friday prayer sermon delivered by Ardebili on September 22. He told the congregation that "the people of Iran who have witnessed hardships over the last eight years will not feel bad if things do not get better on the economic front. The important thing is not to retreat from the Imam's [Khomeini's] line." He then went on to say that "as a supporter and sympathizer of the Islamic Republic I recommend that we do not give a chance for other viewpoints to develop and to [oppose] those who think other than the Imam's line."[22]

Rafsanjani responded to Ardebili's hardline stance on September 29. In his sermon, Rafsanjani argued that in order for the Iranian people to improve their living standards they would have to rid themselves of the notion that poor is beautiful because poor nations will remain forever subject to humiliation and exploitation by other nations. This view is clearly at odds with the tenet upon which Ayatollah Khomeini built his revolutionary model of the power of the dispossessed, strongly emphasizing the happiness and rewards of afterlife.[23]

Rafsanjani came under attack again, but this time by the guest speaker at Ardebili's November 3 sermon, Hojatolislam Khoeniha, leader of the militant students who took over the United States embassy in 1979. In a direct reference to Rafsanjani's "decade of reconstruction" and his attempts at obtaining financial assistance from the West, Khoeniha argued that "we have to get rid of this notion that the struggle against the United States is here today and gone the next or that one decade is devoted to this struggle and another is not, and is instead devoted to rebuilding."[24]

As the debate over Rafsanjani's rebuilding program intensified in the Majlis and the press, Ayatollah Yazdi delivered a stern warning to the opponents of economic reconstruction in his sermon on November 10. He said, "Those who in their speeches and writings argue that Mr. Rafsanjani's recent moves have hurt the ideal of neither East nor West are misfits who do not wish to see him succeed."[25]

Buoyed by Yazdi's remarks, Rafsanjani's Friday prayer sermon of November 17 was an attempt to explain the limitations of improving Iran's economy: "The basic problem with our society," he said, "is that it is not creative and does not have the foundations for self-sufficiency." He then went on to attack his opponents for blocking his efforts at cultivating ties to the West in order to improve Iran's standard of living: "There are those who think that we can survive by cutting ties with the world. They do not know that with strong relations [to the world community] we can better defend ourselves and [influence events]."[26] Rafsanjani's urgency is highlighted by his growing realization that the gap between the resources Iran commands and what it needs is so wide that it cannot be bridged without foreign help. For example, in December of 1989, the managing director of the National Iron Ore Company stated that Iran needs to import six million tons of iron ore in order to implement the government's plans to rebuild the country's infrastructure.[27]

In a clear reference to Rafsanjani's remarks concerning economic self-sufficiency, Imami-Kashani devoted his sermon of November 24 to the Japanese economy. He argued that in order for Iranians to become productive they would have to emulate the Japanese work ethic as opposed to the "culture of sitting behind a desk."[28] And as Rafsanjani's first five-year program was being debated in the Majlis, in his Friday prayer sermon on December 8 Ayatollah Yazdi urged the nation and its leaders to support his pupil: "I hope the members of Parliament will endorse Mr. Rafsanjani's programs soon in order to solve [our] domestic problems."[29]

By December it was clear to Rafsanjani that without foreign assistance his plans for rebuilding Iran's economy would fail. Therefore, after returning from a visit to the war-torn province of Khuzestan in the south, he held an important congregational prayer service on December 15. With reference to the need to build new dams in Khuzestan in order to enhance that province's self-sufficiency he asked the following quesion: "Is it in our advantage to build these dams with other peoples' support? Yes, we believe that given the strategic importance of Khuzestan it is."[30]

A review of the Friday prayer sermons on the issue of Iran's post-Khomeini efforts at reconstruction seems to suggest that the Islamization of the process of nation-building by hardliners has acted as a constraint on Rafsanjani's tendency toward cultivating closer economic ties to the West. Indeed, the hardliners seem to be echoing Khomeini's position on this subject immediately following his return to Iran in 1979: "Some people have come to me and said that now that the revolution has succeeded we have to think about restructuring the economy, but our people rose for Islam, not for economic revitalization."[31] The question is: Why has Rafsanjani not been more forceful in opposing the hardliners if he genuinely seeks to bring prosperity to Iran? The answer may be that he fails to understand, or perhaps understands all too well, what this would require. He would have to overhaul drastically the entire economic and political structure of the Islamic Republic in ways that would loosen the regime's control over the people—something he is unwilling to do. A look at the Friday prayer sermons since Khomeini's death on the issues of freedom, women's rights, and tolerance for political opposition, seems to suggest that this is indeed the case.

While the topic of political and intellectual conversation in 1989 was the democratization of Eastern Europe, the Friday prayer leaders of the Islamic Republic of Iran lectured on the containment of freedom. In his July 7 sermon, Ardebili talked about the limits to freedom in the context of Khomeini's death sentence against Salman Rushdie. His remarks are instructive and offer an insight into the mindset of the current post-Khomeini leadership:

> The Western version of freedom is unrestrained and devoid of limits. We do not have such freedom in Islam. In Islam we have freedom which is controlled and limited. The best example is that of Salman Rushdie. According to Islamic culture, Salman Rushdie has gone past the limit. He forsook God, insulted the prophet, and mocked the sanctities. It is at this juncture that we do not give an arena of freedom. This is an arena for a clash.[32]

In addition to his intolerance for freedom of expression and support for intellectual terrorism, Ardebili has not hesitated to warn the regime's opponents of the consequences of their opposition. For example, in that same sermon he indicated that "in the next few days we will strike a heavy blow against the enemy." Although it may have been unrelated to Ardebili's warning, a few days later the regime assassinated dissident Kurdish leader Abdul Rahman Qassemlou in Vienna and a former military intelligence colonel under the shah, Ataellah Bayahmadi, in Dubai.

Imami-Kashani in his sermon of November 24 echoed Ardebili's opinions on freedom and democracy in the Islamic Republic by asking the question, "Is it possible, in a country of 50 million, to have 50 million opinions and expectations?" He then answered his own question: "This is impossible and we have instead a unified opinion in Islam. Islam speaks for all."[33]

In addition to setting limits to the freedom of expression, the Islamic Republic has set strict guidelines for Iranian women as well. For example, Ayatollah Yazdi in his Friday prayer sermon of September 15 urged the authorities to get tough on women who do not abide by the Islamic dress code. "It is essential," he said "to combat unveiled women because they threaten the security of the state."[34] He then revisited the issue of the veil in his sermon on December 8, warning the women of Iran to cover themselves according to the guidelines set forth by the regime: "In our Islamic society a women's hair should definitely be fully covered."[35]

Rafsanjani's endorsement of his mentor's position a week later raises an interesting question about the mindset of Iran's prototypical moderate. In the sermon he delivered on

December 15, Rafsanjani cautioned Iranian women against nonconformity to the Islamic dress code. "This sign of opposition to the regime," he said, "will cause them problems such as not getting a job." He ended his sermon with a warning to the opponents of the regime: "Do not try to divide our society or do things that will have negative consequences for yourselves."[36]

What does Rafsanjani's advocacy of suppressing women's rights, and the noticeable absence of any reference to events in Eastern Europe in his sermons since Khomeini's death, reveal about the leading moderate in the Islamic Republic of Iran? Although a number of observers have likened Rafsanjani to Mikhail Gorbachev, a better analogy would be Nikita Khrushchev. Khrushchev was the man who took significant steps towards making the Soviet Union a European country through his policy of "peaceful coexistence." But he was also the man who built the Berlin Wall and brutally suppressed a people's revolt against Communist rule in Hungary in 1956.[37] Like Khrushchev, therefore, Rafsanjani is a pragmatist. He is the embodiment of the Soviet adjective *khitryi*. It means sly, cunning, artful, unscrupulous, smart, clever, and quick-witted. Not surprisingly, he has assumed the regime's highest political and military positions over the last 11 years. He is a manipulator par excellence, who has shown a softer side of the regime both inside and outside of Iran when circumstances have demanded. Therefore, while it is true that Rafsanjani is more moderate than others in the regime—during the post-Khomeini period he has opened up the debate on the future course of Iran's economy and made suggestions that Iran cannot survive in isolation—he has reserved for himself the right to determine what can and cannot be criticized. He plays the role of a pragmatist within a structurally totalitarian system that cannot become democratic in the sense that the term is usually understood, i.e., a political system that is relatively open, that allows for political participation, and which respects basic human rights.

The most widely debated issue of the Friday congregational prayers since Khomeini's death has been the future direction of Iran's foreign policy. The key question has been whether to articulate a new identity for Iran's post-Khomeini foreign affairs, and if so, to determine who shall have primacy in this process.

Ardebili was the first Friday prayer leader to elaborate on Iran's post-Khomeini foreign policy. In his sermon on June 23, Ardebili invoked the legacy of Ayatollah Khomeini's "struggle against imperialism and support for the disinherited of the world." He then asked that the nation continue to follow "the Imam's [Khomeini's] struggles; the most important of which is the struggle against the United States and our blood enemy [Israel]."[38] Based on past experience with Iran under Khomeini, one has to assume from Ardebili's sermon that resort to terrorism, as a means to fulfill the "Islamic duty of opposing the United States," has been included in the arsenal of Iran's post-Khomeini leadership as well.

The Friday prayer sermon of July 7 was devoted to the contentious relations between the Islamic Republic and Saudi Arabia. Responding to Saudia Arabia's claims that there were not enough facilities to accept 150,000 Iranian pilgrims for the annual pilgrimage to Mecca (*hajj*), Ardebili said the Saudis were giving baseless excuses to justify a quota of just 45,000 Iranian pilgrims and pledged that Iran would do whatever it could to remove the "corpse of Taghut" (earthly power opposed to God; a derogatory term used in reference to the Saudi royal family) from the holy shrines in Saudi Arabia.[39] His comments followed an earlier hajj message from Ayatollah Khamenei, who blasted the Saudi hajj policy, which he said was intended to "gratify the United States and Israel."[40] The pilgrimage dispute between Iran and Saudi Arabia is the most persistent, and potentially most challenging, to the Saudi royal family because it involves a difference in the doctrinal view of the nature of the hajj, which Khomeini expressed with unusual forcefulness in 1984:

> Those palace-appointed preachers in the region and elsewhere who say that hajj should be separated from its political content are denouncing the prophet of God, the Islamic Khulafa [Caliphs] and God's saints. Islam's political aspects are several times greater than its aspects relating to the act of worship, for political aspects are related to acts of worship. . . . The fundamental aspect of the hajj philosophy lies in its political dimension. Criminal hands from all corners of the globe are busy attacking this aspect.[41]

In view of the Islamic Republic's insistence that religion and politics not be separated at the annual pilgrimage to Mecca, its attacks against Saudi Arabia, both overt and covert, will in all probability continue unabated as long as the Saudi royal family rules that country. For example, in October Khamenei assured the families of the 16 Kuwaiti Shi'ites executed by Saudi authorities for the bombings in Mecca during hajj ceremonies that "the blood-spilling rulers of Saudi Arabia will without doubt suffer the effects and consequences of their murderous act." Therefore, Saudi Arabia will remain a prime target for the export of Iran's Islamic fundamentalism and state-sponsored terrorism.

The theme of exporting Iran's Islamic revolution abroad was expounded by Ardebili in his Friday prayer sermon of July 28. In his sermon he referred to Khomeini's final wish and said,

> Islam must be translated into action and people must conform to the Koran. The hands of foreigners and aliens must be cut off from the Islamic countries and the fate of Muslims. We pledge our word to employ all our forces and resources to protect the meek and the deprived and never to abandon our objective until the Imam [Khomeini's] wishes and demands are met.[42]

Although Ardebili does not elaborate on how the "hands of the foreigners" will be "cut off from Islamic countries," one cannot rule out the use of terrorism as a means towards this end.

Following the abduction of Sheikh Obeid by Israeli commandos on July 31, 1989, the Iranian leadership stepped up its attacks on Israel and the United States at the Friday congregational prayers. Both Imami-Kashani in his sermon on August 11 and Ayatollah Yazdi in his sermon on August 18 condemned Israel's "intervention" in Lebanon and urged all the pro-Iranian factions in Lebanon to continue their struggle against Israel. A more revealing sermon was delivered by Ardebili on August 25, in which he warned France against intervening in Lebanon. He said, "France, with all its pride and naval flotilla, will back away when confronted by individuals whose priorities are God, Islam, and martyrdom."[43] On September 19, a French UTA airliner was destroyed on a flight over the Tenere desert in Niger, killing 171 people. According to intelligence sources, the government of Iran was responsible for this bombing. It appears, therefore, that the tendency to use state-sponsored terrorism as an instrument to advance Iran's foreign policy objectives has not changed with the death of Khomeini.

Despite Iran's ideologically driven foreign policy, Rafsanjani's Friday prayer sermons seem to indicate a willingness to rethink Iran's position in the international system, particularly in light of the changing nature of U.S.–Soviet relations. This new thinking is reflected in his comments concerning the state of Soviet–Iranian relations. Reporting on

his visit to Moscow and meetings with Mikhail Gorbachev, Rafsanjani laid out the rationale for Tehran's Moscow connection at the Friday prayer sermon on June 30:

> By changing their policy, that is, by withdrawing from Afghanistan, and
> weakening their support for leftist currents in Iran, the changes in the leftist
> view of the world, the exposure of international Marxism as an empty ideolo-
> gy, the Soviet leadership brought about the necessary ground for such a rela-
> tionship. The path [to a renewal of Iranian-Soviet relations] was opened by
> His Eminence, the Imam [Khomeini]. . . . If the two countries maintain re-
> lations as two truly free countries, if they maintain relations with no undue
> demands and with no ill intentions, then the region could witness security in
> whose shade we could obstruct many plundering interests. That is why the
> Westerners have taken so much fright.[44]

Three months later, on September 29, Rafsanjani used his Friday prayer sermon to
deliver a major foreign policy address aimed both at silencing his critics and justifying his
new foreign policy approach. He stated that a new international system is emerging with
an emphasis on cooperation and the peaceful resolution of regional conflicts. He cited the
recent dismantling of nuclear and chemical weapons by the United States and the Soviet
Union, and their "stabilizing roles" in Afghanistan, Lebanon, and the Arab-Israeli conflict as examples of the lessening of international conflict. According to Rafsanjani, these
developments require a reevaluation of Iran's relations with its adversaries. "Iran's enemies," he argued, "realize that they cannot defeat the Islamic Republic and wish to
cultivate closer ties to Tehran. The country no longer lives in a hostile regional and
international environment."[45] This characterization of the international system and Iran's
position within it poignantly illustrates Rafsanjani's realization that in order for clerical
regime to end its isolation and assume a constructive role in the international community,
Khomeini's legacy of "neither East nor West" must be exorcised from Iran's foreign
policy.

Rafsanjani's attempts to chart a new course in Iran's foreign policy were contested in
a major speech by Ayatollah Khamenei. In his sermon on October 20, Iran's supreme
religious leader took exception to Rafsanjani's point concerning the lessening of world
tension by expounding on a number of regional issues, specifically the Islamic Republic's
opposition to both the Taif accords and Yasir Arafat's overtures to Israel. He then went
on to explain the main objective of Iran's post-Khomeini foreign policy:

> If, for a brief moment, you glance at the world, you will see the methods of
> the global arrogance, the policy adopted by the United States against Muslim
> nations, specifically in the Middle East, the current events in Lebanon, and
> the conspiracy which has been hatched [by the Taif Accords] against those
> innocent and Muslim people in that country. You witnessed the Palestinian
> issue and the treachery a number of Arab leaders [like King Hussein of Jor-
> dan and King Fahd of Saudi Arabia] and dignitaries and those powerful men
> of the Arab countries committed in collaboration with some of the appointed
> leaders to Palestine [like Arafat] within the occupied territories.
>
> What I intend to say concerns the fact that you and I shoulder a divine
> commitment: that is, to inspire hope in the people of the world. This is our
> main task: to maintain that point of hope in the hearts of Muslim nations.
> From now on our words and deeds must also be such that the same hope may

remain [in] the hearts of the oppressed. Indeed, fear must also remain in the hearts of the enemies. This is my point.[46]

Although Khamenei refrained from mentioning terrorism, it is clear that what he meant by instilling "fear in the hearts of the enemies [of the regime]" is the systematic use of terror as a means of coercion. It would appear that a prime target of Iranian-sponsored terrorism will be the United States, for in the same sermon, in reference to the recent decision by the U.S. Department of Justice to prosecute those individuals who have committed acts of violence against Americans in U.S. courts, Khamenei said,

When the United States announces that it has the prerogative to prosecute those criminals who have been sentenced in U.S. courts, wherever they may be in the world, or in other words, a universal capitulation for all countries in the world, then the world's general opinion fails to attain the necessary progression. This indicates that those who are powerful and arrogant have created a world which is tainted with tyranny and malevolence. Nations are also prepared to rise up against such bullying, but they need hope, leadership, and guidance. Nations need a role model in order to see that it is possible to stand firm against the global arrogance. This role model today is Islamic Iran.[47]

From Khamenei's perspective the current international system has not changed, and therefore the basic tenets of Iran's post-Khomeini foreign policy remain basically unchanged: the ideological challenge to the United States and its allies in the Middle East; the conflict between the camp of the oppressors, which includes the United States, "Zionists, Fascists, Phalangists, and Communists," and that of the oppressed, with the Islamic Republic of Iran as the vanguard of the powerless; the export of Iran's Islamic revolution around the world; and the Islamization of regional conflicts.

The one country in which all of Tehran's foreign policy objectives converge is Lebanon. Indeed, Lebanon has a special role in the revolutionary regime's commitment to the export of Khomeini's brand of Islamic fundamentalism. For example, according to the former Iranian ambassador to Beirut, Hojatolislam Fakhr Rouhani, Lebanon "is the most important hope for the export of the Islamic revolution."[48] A reading of the Friday prayer sermons suggests that this ideological commitment to Lebanon has not diminished with the passing away of Khomeini. Prior to Khamenei's October 20 sermon, for example, the Friday prayer leaders attacked the Saudi royal family for organizing the Taif summit to discuss the future of Lebanon. In his sermon on October 6, Imami-Kashani pointed out that the Taif conference did not take into consideration the fact that the majority of the Lebanese are Muslims. Therefore, he argued, the "Maronites should be stripped of their leadership [position] and the Lebanese should very soon form an Islamic state."[49] The following Friday, Ayatollah Yazdi told the congregation that ethnicity should be banished from Lebanon, and the Lebanese constitution be revised according to the wishes of the Muslim majority.[50]

Following Khamenei's sermon on October 20 in which he condemned the Taif accords, the question of Lebanon was more forcefully addressed by Tehran's Friday prayer leaders. In his sermon on October 27, Imami-Kashani rejected the decision by delegates at the Taif summit meeting to appoint Renee Mu'awwad, a non-Muslim, as the president of Lebanon. Imami-Kashani's special guest was Sheikh Mohammad Hussein Fadallah, the spiritual leader of Hizbollah in Lebanon, who met with Rafsanjani two days later, issuing a joint statement condemning the Taif accords. And in his Friday prayer sermon of November 3, commemorating the takeover of the American embassy in Tehran, Ardebili attacked the Taif accords in the strongest language, wishing death and banishment to all who "participated in this inhuman gathering."[51] It should be noted that prior to Ardebili's sermon, on October 30, Iran's foreign minister Ali Akbar Velayati met with Hafiz Assad in Damascus to deliver a message from Rafsanjani. He later met with Sheikh Sha'ban, leader of a militant Islamic group, Walid Jumballat, leader of the Druze, Abu Musa, leader of revolutionary Fatah, and Ahmad Jibril, head of the Popular Front for the Liberation of Palestine—General Command (PFLP-GC).[52] Less than 20 days after Ardebili's sermon, Renee Mu'awwad and 24 others were killed in a car bomb in Beirut.

The last Friday prayer sermon of the calender year was delivered on December 29 by Ardebili, in which he reiterated the Islamic Republic's continued struggle against the "conspiracies of East and West to weaken Islam and the oppressed."[53] The common denominator of this sermon, and those delivered by Tehran's other Friday prayer leaders on foreign policy issues, has been the need for a scapegoat. This is reflective, in part, of a major feature of the Shi'ite worldview. The international milieu, to an Iranian Shi'ite, is seen as threatening due to its anarchic nature, a perception in which the directionality involved is from the unruly environment toward the person, so that he is viewed as an effect, and various external factors as cause. A person in such a cultural situation would not likely hold himself accountable when things go wrong and would generally react by turning anger and hostility outward toward others—perceived Sunni oppressors, an arbitrary and unjust government, imperialists, agents of change and modernization, minority groups such as Jews and Baha'is.[54] This worldview has been expounded by the Friday prayer leaders, who, as the spokesmen for the regime, have directed the people as to the identity of the scapegoat. Therefore since 1979, "the Ba'athist government of Iraq, American imperialism, international Zionism, and the Wahhabis of Saudi Arabia" have become the major external scapegoats of the Islamic Republic. A major implication of this interpretation is that, unlike other terrorisms interested in influencing Western opinion and winning support for their cause, the Islamic Republic's fundamentalist terrorism is not concerned with dialogue with the modern world but with expelling or eliminating its external scapegoats—especially the United States.

To sum up, the major objectives of Iran's foreign policy seem to have changed very little since the death of Khomeini. Although Rafsanjani has attempted to chart a new course for Iran's foreign policy, he has been rebuffed by those whose mindset is closer to the traditional Shi'ite perception of the world. The worldview of an anarchic international system in which the United States and the non-Muslim world are conspiring to destroy Islam is an integral part of this thinking. As such, the main guiding principles for the conduct of Iranian foreign policy seem to include absolute independence from East and West, identification of the United States as the principal enemy of the Islamic Republic, exportation of the Islamic revolution, and support for reactionary forces around the world whose aim is to disrupt the status quo. To the extent that it advances these objectives, terrorism will remain an essential element of the clerical regime's foreign policy.

Conclusion

The fluidity, complexity, and confusion of the state of the Islamic Republic since Khomeini's death make it impossible to end this study with any definitive answer to the question of whether Iran's Islamic fundamentalism has crested or not. The initial answer immediately following Khomeini's death may indeed have been affirmative. After all,

Ayatollah Khomeini sat athwart the totalitarian, Islamic, and revolutionary structure he helped build. He was constitutionally empowered to exercise supreme authority in Iran. Moreover, his charisma had been the key to the regime's ability to consolidate its power over the last 11 years. As such, domestic and foreign policy debates between radicals and moderates would not lead to political stalemates because, unlike post-Khomeini Iran where there exists a proliferation of ideologies of both conservative and radical varieties, Khomeini's interpretation of Islam prevailed on both the domestic and international levels.

However, another way of answering the question of whether Iran's Islamic fundamentalism has crested is to ask a more fundamental question: How has the system, both in terms of structure and tendency, changed since the death of Khomeini?

A review of the Friday prayer sermons suggests that the nature of the system has changed very little despite the death of its spiritual leader. In the first place, the perpetuation of an essentially totalitarian structure driven by Islamic ideology has been endorsed by the new establishment. In turn, the institution of leadership—Ayatollah Khamenei as supreme religious leader, Hojatolislam Rafsanjani as president, Ayatollah Karrubi as speaker of the parliament, and Ayatollah Yazdi as chief justice—has been consolidated through general "elections," thus legitimizing its absolute control of the decision-making process. For example, in their sermons, bitter rivals such as Rafsanjani and Arbedili have urged the nation to pledge its allegiance to the rulers of post-Khomeini Iran. Therefore, while some in the new leadership may be factional rivals on some issues like foreign policy or the economy, there is no disagreement on the need for keeping these differences at bay when the survival of the system is at stake.

Second, the 30 congregational prayers since June 7 seem to suggest that most of the themes expounded by Khomeini during his rule, such as "defending the rights of the world's disinherited" or the "struggle against the United States and the Zionist-entity," have not been exorcised from Iranian foreign policy objectives. This ideologically driven agenda aims at the establishment of an Islamic world order to serve as a cordon sanitaire against Western imperialism. Toward that end, the new leadership, with the exception of Rafsanjani, advocate the export of the Islamic revolution to other countries by every means available, including terrorism.

Third, there is hardly any disagreement among the new leadership on the need for maintaining Islamic norms of social and political relations that exclude freedom of expression and suppression of political opposition, whether it be unveiled women or dissident groups abroad. Not surprisingly, there has been a noticeable absence of reference to events in Eastern Europe in the context of transitions to more open societies in sermons by Iran's Friday prayer leaders. This is reflective of an embedded fear of pluralization, and the consequent relinquishing of power to the people. In short, what has happened since Khomeini's death makes it clearer than ever that the Islamic Republic has rested over the last 11 years not only on popularity and persuasion, but on coercion and terror as well.

A major conclusion that may be drawn from a reading of Friday prayer sermons since the death of Khomeini is that to ariculate a new identity for post-Khomeini Iran, whether in the area of foreign policy, the economy, or social norms, would be anathema to the essence of the Islamic Republic. The raison d'être of the system is to be an Islamic revolutionary regime, and, as such, it cannot change. Thus, while the pendulum of domestic and foreign policy may swing from radicalism to pragmatism and vice versa, it will do so within the confines of a rigid, dogmatic, and ideologically driven structure. From this vantage point, Iran's Islamic fundamentalism has not crested, and never will unless the entire system is changed.

Notes

1. For a discussion of the institutions of the Islamic Republic of Iran, see Said Amir Arjomand, *The Turban for the Crown: The Islamic Revolution in Iran* (New York: Oxford University Press, 1988).

2. *FBIS/MEA*, Mar. 1, 1979.

3. Said Amir Arjomand, *The Turban for the Crown*, p. 167.

4. Moojan Momen, *An Introduction to Shi'i Islam* (New Haven: Yale Univeristy Press, 1985), p. 181.

5. See Said Amir Arjomand, "Ideological Revolution in Shi'ism," in *Authority and Political Culture in Shi'ism.* ed. Said Amir Arjomand (Albany: State University of New York Press, 1988), p. 198.

6. Arjomand. *Authority and Political Culture in Shi'ism*, p. 199.

7. Ibid., p. 188.

8. Quoted in Arjomand. *The Turban for the Crown*, p. 168.

9. *Kayhan Hava'i*, June 14, 1989.

10. *FBIS/NES*, June 16, 1989.

11. *Kayhan Hava'i*, June 28, 1989.

12. *FBIS/NES*, June 30, 1989.

13. *FBIS/NES*. Oct. 23, 1989.

14. *FBIS/NES*, July 28, 1989.

15. *FBIS/NES*. Mar. 29, 1979.

16. *Kayhan Hava'i*, July 19, 1989.

17. See *New York Times*, Oct. 10, 1989.

18. *FBIS/NES*. Aug. 11, 1989.

19. *Kayhan Hava'i*, Aug. 30, 1989.

20. *Kayhan Hava'i*, Sept. 6, 1989.

21. *Kayhan Hava'i*, Sept. 13, 1989.

22. *Kayhan Hava'i*, Sept. 27, 1989.

23. For an account of Rafsanjani's remarks see *New York Times*. Oct. 10, 1989.

24. *Kayhan Hava'i*, Nov. 8, 1989.

25. *Kayhan Hava'i*, Nov. 15, 1989.

26. *Kayhan Hava'i*, Nov. 22, 1989.

27. *Kayhan Hava'i*, Nov. 8, 1989.

28. *Kayhan Hava'i*, Nov. 29, 1989.

29. *Kayhan Hava'i*, Dec. 13, 1989.

30. *Kayhan Hava'i*, Dec. 20, 1989.

31. *FBIS/MEA*, Feb. 6, 1979.

32. *FBIS/NES*, July 10, 1989.

33. *Kayhan Hava'i*, Nov. 29, 1989.

34. *Kayhan Hava'i*, Sept. 20, 1989.

35. *Kayhan Hava'i*, Dec. 13, 1989.

36. *Kayhan Hava'i*, Dec. 20, 1989.

37. Richard Nixon, *Leaders* (New York: Warner Books, 1982), pp. 178–179.

38. *Kayhan Hava'i*, June 28, 1989.

39. *FBIS/NES*, July 10, 1989.

40. Ibid.

41. Quoted in R.K. Ramazani, *Revolutionary Iran* (Baltimore: Johns Hopkins University Press, 1986), p. 96.

42. *FBIS/NES*, July 28, 1989.

43. *Kayhan Hava'i*, Aug. 30, 1989.

44. *FBIS/NES*, June 30, 1989.

45. *Kayhan Hava'i*, Oct. 4, 1989.

46. *FBIS/NES*, Oct. 23, 1989.

47. Ibid.

416   *Terrorism*

48. Ramazani, *Revolutionary Iran*, p. 183.

49. *Kayhan Hava'i*, Oct. 11, 1989.

50. *Kayhan Hava'i*, Oct. 18, 1989.

51. *Kayhan Hava'i*, Nov. 8, 1989.

52. The account of Velayati's visit to Damascus is in *Kayhan Hava'i*, Nov. 8, 1989.

53. *Kayhan Hava'i*, Jan. 3, 1990.

54. For a discussion of the Shi'ite worldview see Momen, *An Introduction to Shi'i Islam*, pp. 233–37.

[8]

ISLAMIZATION IN SUDAN: A CRITICAL ASSESSMENT

Carolyn Fluehr-Lobban

SUDAN has offered one of the more provocative cases of state-supported Islamization in recent years because of the government's swiftness and readiness to apply the *hudud* punishments after the *sharia* was decreed to be the national law in September 1983. This Islamization, using the coercive apparatus of the state, must be distinguished from the sociocultural process of conversion to Islam that has been a major part of Sudanese history for the past five centuries.

A number of scholars have described the political context in which Islamization took place,[1] while others have examined the legal effect of this dramatic and far-reaching development.[2] Only a few works have been devoted specifically to southern Sudanese views of Islamization,[3] despite their being a critical dimension to a comprehensive understanding of Sudan. The strongly politicized nature of the north-south divide has made dialogue on the subject infrequent and emotionally charged.

This article seeks to examine the political Islamization trend in its more

1. John L. Esposito, "Sudan's Islamic Experiment," *The Muslim World*, vol. 76, nos. 3–4 (1986); John O. Voll, "Revivalism and Social Transformation in Islamic History," *The Muslim World*, vol. 76, nos. 3–4 (1986); Mahmoud Mohamed Taha, *The Second Message of Islam*, trans. and introduction by Abdullahi Ahmed An-Na'im (Syracuse NY: Syracuse University Press, 1987).

2. Carolyn Fluehr-Lobban, *Islamic Law and Society in the Sudan* (London: Frank Cass, 1987); and idem., "Islamization of Law in the Sudan," *Legal Studies Forum*, vol. 11, no. 2 (1987); Carey N. Gordon, "The Islamic Legal Revolution: The Case of the Sudan," *The International Lawyer*, vol. 19, no. 3 (1985).

3. David D. Chand, "The Imposition of Shari'a Law in 1983 and the Civil War in the Sudan" (Paper presented at the eighth annual conference of the Sudan Studies Association, Providence, RI, April 1989).

Carolyn Fluehr-Lobban is professor of anthropology at Rhode Island College and president of the Sudan Studies Association. A Rockefeller Fellow in the Ethics Institute at Dartmouth College during 1990, she is currently conducting field research in Tunisia.

complex character by discussing the deep historical roots of Islamization in northern regions and the fears of Islamization throughout the southern regions. These roots follow a course that is parallel to the formation of Sudan as an entity in the nineteenth century, and it could be readily suggested that the historical examples of the triumph of Islamist forces have been matched by fear and defensive withdrawal of people in the southern regions. Today, the future integrity of Sudan hinges upon the outcome of the current civil war and political debate regarding Islamization. The retention or the abrogation of the sharia is the central issue that divides north and south and prevents an end to the bloodiest and most devastating episode of Sudan's 24 years of protracted civil war.

While journalistic accounts focus on the centrality of racial and religious differences—Arab versus African, or Muslim versus Christian—historical examination of the divisions between north and south reveals deeper patterns of uneven economic opportunity and development. Similarly, the complex role that the nineteenth-century slave trade played in laying the foundation for the fear of the foreigner and the trader from the north, together with a belief that the trade was Muslim and condoned by Islam, laid the basis and set the agenda for north-south suspicions and divisions that have continued to define relations from the nineteenth century to the present. The dichotomy between Islamization—with all of its genuine nationalist and religious aspirations and historical triumphs—and the fear of Islamization—with all of its bitter history of slavery, economic exploitation, and political isolation—yields a more complex, but comprehensible, picture of the origin and the future of the Sudanese national entity.

NINETEENTH-CENTURY FOUNDATIONS: THE SLAVE TRADE, ARABS, AND ISLAM

Although the British outlawed the Atlantic slave trade in 1833, in that same year Britain's Anti-Slavery Society reported that the Turco-Egyptian troops of Muhammad Ali continued to bring out of Sudan 20,000 slaves annually. Often a companion to, or a secondary effect of the ivory trade, the slave hunt—or *ghazwa* as it came to be called—became a common fact of life for the non-Muslim groups south and west of Sennar prior to 1860 and for the people of Bahr al-Ghazal and Darfur after 1865. Originally attracted to the lucrative ivory trade, European and Ottoman merchants recruited private armies from northern groups, such as the Danagla and Shayqiyya, who built fortified trading stations known as *zaribas*, named after their thorn fences.[4] Slaves were required to service these stations and were used as "currency" to pay the merchants' retainers. Raiding of cattle, needed to trade for ivory, and of humans produced interethnic hostility and general societal breakdown by the mid-nineteenth century.

---

4. P.M. Holt and Martin W. Daly, *The History of the Sudan from the Coming of Islam to the Present Day*, 3rd ed. (Boulder, CO: Westview Press, 1989).

For a period, Europeans dominated the White Nile trade, while the southern Sudan province of Bahr al-Ghazal was penetrated by Egyptian and Syrian traders, using the same zariba system. The role of the *jellaba*, small-scale Muslim traders from the north, expanded with the growth of predatory commerce in the region, and they often acted as agents for wealthier merchants. As the trade "matured," it came to be controlled by a cadre of merchant-princes, one of the most powerful of whom was Al-Zubayr Rahma Mansur, who controlled the trade in Bahr al-Ghazal and the trading routes to Kordofan and Darfur; such was his power that he was appointed by the khedive as provincial governor in 1873. Frequently the ghazwa was the only contact that indigenous people had with foreigners, and it was a terrorizing one. Slavery was conducted for both military and commercial purposes. The Turco-Egyptian armies depended on regular slave raiding, and the demand for domestic slaves in Egypt, the Ottoman Empire, and Arabia was continuous.

With the growing economic interest in Sudan as an extension of Egypt on the part of the British and growing antislavery sentiment at home, a contradiction developed between legitimate commercial interests and activities that might lend support to the condemned slave trade. The contradiction was resolved, in part, by a concerted effort to associate the slave trade with Muslims and with Islam. A literature arose that formulated and articulated this view. In 1840, Sir Thomas Buxton wrote that "Mohamedanism gives the sanction of religion to the slave trade and even enjoins it as a mode of converting the heathen."[5] Others asserted that "slavery is inherent in the religion and social system of Mohamedanism and is congenial to the ideas and customs of Musulman nations."[6] The Anti-Slavery Society readily adopted the view that Islam was a central force behind the slave trade and slavery, a view that fitted nicely with the Christian campaign to suppress the trade and slavery in Sudan.

Today, the reference to "Mohamedanism" is recognized as offensive to Muslims and a fundamental error in the interpretation of Muhammad as divine. The association of slavery with Islam is also erroneous and offensive; while Islam emerged within Arabian society where slavery was already an established institution, the message of Islam stressed manumition as an act of piety and a means of conversion. Neither in the Quran nor the Sunna is there countenance for slavery or the slave trade, although there are numerous references to proper conduct regarding slaves as members of households. The spirit of Islam toward the traffic in human beings is conveyed in a tradition ascribed to the Prophet Muhammad, "Sharr al-nas man ba' al-nas" (the wickedest of people are those who sell people).[7]

---

5. As quoted in Abbas Ibrahim Muhammad Ali, *The British, the Slave Trade and Slavery in the Sudan, 1820–1881* (Khartoum: Khartoum University Press, 1972), p. 67.

6. *Ibid.*, p. 68.

7. Yusuf Fadl Hasan, "Some Aspects of the Arab Slave Trade from the Sudan 7–19th Centuries," *Sudan Notes and Records*. vol. 58 (1977), p. 80.

For their part, the Turco-Egyptians fostered an interpretation of the slave raids—for instance, by calling them ghazwa—that would give the impression that they were military campaigns carried out in the name of Islam against the unbelievers. Although most of the Turco-Egyptian rulers in the Nile valley during the nineteenth century responded to British pressure to condemn the trade and officially to attempt to eradicate it, inevitably some rulers, with economic self-interest, claimed that Islam sanctioned slavery.[8]

In nineteenth-century North and East Africa, slavery was practiced in the Muslim north, in Christian Ethiopia, and in the "pagan" south, and Europe was just emerging—rather self-righteously, it might be argued—from four centuries of involvement with slaving, including the Great Atlantic Slave Trade. Later European writers found in the religion and culture of Islam a convenient scapegoat for the continuation of slavery and the slave trade.

The unquestioned assumption that Islam sanctioned slavery created an ideology that justified expanding British interests in Sudan and helped to engender the mood of a Christian crusade to emancipate the region during the Mahdist uprisings and their aftermath. From Omdurman, Mahdist invasions at the frontiers of the religious state were conducted as *jihad* in the west, in the east, and in the south to bring the last vestige of Turco-Egyptian rule in Equatoria under Mahdist control.

Many southern intellectuals and scholars of the southern Sudan contend that the result of this last encounter in the nineteenth century between southern and northern Sudanese was one of bitterness, hatred, and fear of Arabs and Muslims and that this outlook has persisted to the present day in the minds of southern peoples.[9] Oliver Albino writes of an "inborn feeling of dislike and uneasiness in every Southerner about the *mundukuru* or jallaba—Southern names for Northern Sudanese Arabs."[10] Even the most dispassionate southern accounts of the memory of the Mahdiyya recall the khalifa's 13-year rule as "the time when the world was spoiled."[11]

Islamic Purification and Early Sudanese Nationalism

Islamic messianism made a strong appearance in nineteenth-century sudanic Africa, a phenomenon that was reinforced by the pilgrimage tradition.[12] Apart

8. Muhammad Ali, *British and Slavery*, p. 69.

9. Robert O. Collins, *The Southern Sudan, 1883–1898* (New Haven, CT: Yale University Press, 1962); Dunstan M. Wai, *The African-Arab Conflict in the Sudan* (New York: Africana Publishing Co., 1981).

10. Oliver Albino, *The Sudan: A Southern Viewpoint* (London: Oxford University Press for the Institute of Race Relations, 1970), p. 77.

11. Francis M. Deng, *The Man Called Deng Majok* (New Haven, CT: Yale University Press, 1986), p. 41.

12. Umar al-Naqar, *The Pilgrimage Tradition in West Africa* (Khartoum: Khartoum University Press, 1972); M. Hiskett, "The Nineteenth-Century Jihads in West Africa," in *The Cambridge History*

from the breeding ground that the economic and political upheavals of the last century made of Sudan, revivalism has been a persistent and logical feature of Islamic history.[13] In Sudan, Islamic revival and nationalist pride derive from the period of Muhammad Ahmad al-Mahdi. He is referred to by present-day northern Sudanese as "Abu al-Istiqlal," the Father of Independence, for uniting various Sudanese peoples in the northern regions and driving out the alien rulers.[14]

The mahdist state was the first modern Sudanese national entity, governing vast and diverse regions from a central capital at Omdurman, with a centralized legal and political apparatus and its own currency. It was also an Islamic state fashioned to revive the concept and practice of the early Islamic community of Muhammad and his companions. Although the roots of the Islamic revolution, which swept Sudan in the late nineteenth century, are usually traced to the harshness of Turco-Egyptian rule and a nascent Sudanese nationalist response, contemporary scholarship takes a more complex view, one that incorporates internal tensions within the Muslim community at the time, as well as external variables of foreign interests and rule. Peter Holt and Martin Daly argue that the timing of the Sudanese revolt, 60 years after the imposition of Turco-Egyptian rule, was related to the weakening of the empire's hold in Sudan caused by the removal from office of the khedive, Ismail, in 1879 and the British occupation of Egypt in 1882.[15] Gabriel Warburg describes some of the tensions within nineteenth-century Islam in Sudan that played a central role in the dual nature of the Mahdiyya: Islamic purification and revival and nationalist political mobilization.[16]

By the nineteenth century, the sociocultural process of Islamization was in its fourth century in Sudan, with populist Sufi orders the main agents in the spread of Islam. The Sufi brotherhoods, *tariqa*s, generally decentralized and egalitarian, were challenged by the imposition of Turco-Egyptian rule, as formal sharia courts, headed by Egyptian *qadi*s, were established, and local education became a central government concern. Anticipating antagonism between state-supported and popular Islam, three Egyptian *ulama* were sent with the Turco-Egyptian expeditionary force of 1821 to explain to Sudanese Muslims that their conquest was a legitimate act supported by principles of Islamic government and law.[17] After 1822, increasing numbers of Sudanese ulama were trained formally at al-Azhar University, thereby further undermining local Sufi leaders. The mahdist uprisings of the 1880s, undertaken to rid Sudan of foreign influence, included assaults against Turco-Egyptian state religious personnel and institutions, as well as against its military forces. That conflict between Sudan's indigenous popular

---

of Africa, vol. 5, from c. 1790 to c. 1870, ed. John E. Flint (London: Cambridge University Press, 1976).

    13. John O. Voll, "Revivalism and Social Transformation."
    14. Holt and Daly, *History of the Sudan*, p. 87.
    15. *Ibid.*, p. 86.
    16. Gabriel Warburg, *Islam, Nationalism and Communism in a Traditional Society: The Case of the Sudan* (London: Frank Cass, 1978). See the introduction.
    17. *Ibid.*, p. 8.

Islam and state-supported Islam was resolved by the triumph of the mahdi—the epitome of populist, purifying, revivalist sentiment.

The mahdist state was the only truly anti-imperialist, Islamic republic of its time in Africa, and more than one observer has noted its vanguard role in this respect, while others have drawn parallels to Iran's Islamic revolution. The death of Britain's General Charles Gordon at the hands of the mahdist forces as they overran Khartoum in January 1885 unleashed a furor in England that would not subside until the reconquest of Sudan in 1898. Nearly a century of scholarship, increasingly by Sudanese, has documented the achievements as well as the shortcomings of the independent Sudanese state, which lasted from 1885 until 1898 when an Anglo-Egyptian army retook Khartoum. The mahdist effort to conquer and Islamize the south is still recalled in southern political discourse as a bitter moment in their history. In the context of Sudanese nationalist history, it is important to note that southern Sudanese fought against the Turco-Egyptian presence in the south and joined forces with the mahdists to expel it from Sudan. In the north, however, the recollection of the mahdi's triumph over the foreign intruder is still capable of mobilizing masses of northern Sudanese; since independence, the great-grandson of the mahdi, Sadiq al-Mahdi, has twice been prime minister, 1967–69 and 1986–89.

Islamization, with its overtly political dimension, has historical roots in Sudan and the rest of Africa beyond today's headlines. In the nineteenth century, the framework of Islamic solidarity produced a bulwark against the penetration of non-Muslim elements—a message that has renewed meaning and importance in contemporary times.

POLARIZATION OF MUSLIM AND NON-MUSLIM IN THE TWENTIETH CENTURY

There is little disagreement that during the period of the Anglo-Egyptian Condominium, 1898–1956, relations between north and south did not improve; in fact there was a consciously different and unequal treatment of the regions. From the beginning of British rule, the northern regions were administered separately, with a political policy of indirect rule that incorporated local shaykhs and a separate Sharia Division of the Judiciary that was parallel to the British-derived Civil Division.[18] Although the mahdi's family was initially confined and closely observed for possible insurrectionary activity, by the time of World War I the son of the mahdi, Abd al-Rahman al-Mahdi, rejected the call for jihad by Britain's Ottoman enemies and swore allegiance to the crown. The British developed the rich Gezira land between the Niles for cotton and other commercial crops, while an administrative and transport infrastructure was built to support this key economic activity. Thus, central riverain Sudan developed, while little effort was

---

18. Fluehr-Lobban, *Islamic Law in the Sudan*, p. 36.

expended on Darfur or southern Kordofan, the east (excepting the port of Suakin and later Port Sudan), or the southern provinces of Bahr al-Ghazal, Upper Nile, and Equatoria.

As early as 1922, with the Passports and Permits Ordinance, and more clearly from 1933 on, the official policy of the British resulted in the separation of the south from the north through the "Closed Districts Ordinance," which forbade the use of Arabic and Arab-influenced education, dress, or settlement in the south. An important exception permitted the continued presence of the jellaba merchants—the symbols of the nineteenth-century slave trade. This complex dynamic, as Francis Deng writes, was such that the British tried to give the impression that there was a great difference between the south and the north. "You Northerners," they would say, "are slave traders and you treat the Southerners like *Abeed* [slaves]. Don't call them Abeed! They are slaves no longer. And then they would turn around and say that the Southerners are lazy people and are impervious to progress."[19]

The problem of the south for the British was one of effective political administration, not economic development. Their limited resources required assistance from other sources. Education and health services were largely provided through Christian missionary stations that were established by concession in the south with freedom to proselytize. English, not Arabic, was the language of administration and education. The protection of the region from Islam, and, by extension, the prevention of its penetration into central Africa, made the southern Sudan a kind of bastion of Christian missions.

Islam and Modern Nationalism

Significant nationalist activism began in the 1920s with the rise of the White Flag Society to challenge British occupation; the first demonstrations in Sudanese history were those motivated by political speeches from the mosques.[20] A revolt in Egypt in 1924 inspired mutinies within Egyptian garrisons all over Sudan, but most significantly in Khartoum, where a demonstration was led by a southerner, Ali Abd al-Latif. Others erupted in Wau in Bahr al-Ghazal and Talodi in southern Kordofan. The defeat of the White Flag movement ended its militant confrontation with the British and the possibility of a unified north-south, anti-imperialist front. Thereafter, nationalist sentiments were expressed in Arabic literature and poetry, with references to Arab and Islamic history as well as popular songs.

The Graduates Congress, organized by a group of northern intellectuals—prominent among them, Muhammad Ahmad Mahgoub—gave a framework, a set of terms, and an ideology to continued nationalist aspirations in the 1940s. The

19. Francis M. Deng and Robert O. Collins, *The British in the Sudan, 1898–1956* (Stanford, CA: Hoover Institution Press, 1984), p. 231.
20. Muddathir Abd al-Rahim, *Imperialism and Nationalism in the Sudan* (Oxford: Clarendon Press, 1969), p. 106.

national identity of Sudan was conceived of as based upon Islam and Arab culture and founded in African soil and traditions.[21] Yet in their first memorandum to the government, they called for an end to north-south divisions and to Britain's southern policy in Sudan.

The traditionally powerful tariqas became mobilized in the growing nationalist movement. In 1945 the Umma Party—whose name carries a strong reference to the Muslim community—was organized by the mahdist Ansar to give voice to an independent and Islamic future for Sudan. The pro-unionist Khatmiyya sect also depended upon the common ideology of Arabism and Islam, but its political program supported unity with Egypt. The secular nationalist Communist Party was established in 1946, while the Muslim Brotherhood was founded in 1953 with a clear program for an Islamic state.

The discussions prior to independence in 1956 were dominated by the issue of union or separation of Sudan and Egypt. Concerning the issue of the constitutional make-up of an independent Sudan, virtually all of the key political parties, except for the Communist Party, called for a more central role for Islam than had existed under British rule. Northern politicians dominated the transition to independence, and, again, only the Sudanese Communist Party recognized the seriousness of the southern question and the role that religion should play in the future secular state. A feeling of isolation on the part of southerners from the nationalist political process resulted in resentment and isolation. The post-independence constitution committee, for example, rejected southern requests for federation and called, instead, for a united Islamic Sudan.

Islam and Sudanese Constitutional Development, 1956–1983

After more than five decades of British rule—1898–1956—the political agenda was set to expand the role of Islam in government. The Muslim Brotherhood, through its lobbying group, the Islamic Front for the Constitution, advocated that Sudan should become an Islamic state, basing both constitution and law solely on the Quran and Sunna. In 1957, a year after independence, the Umma Party and Khatmiyya sect issued a joint statement in which they called for Sudan to develop an Islamic parliamentary republic, with the sharia serving as the sole source of legislation. The first prime minister, Ismail al-Azhari, who ruled from 1956 to 1958, declared that Sudan would be made an Islamic republic from within parliament.[22] The call for an Islamic state did not move beyond the stage of political rhetoric, because in November 1958 the first of Sudan's three military governments—that of General Ibrahim Abbud—took control and held power for the next six years until it was overthrown by a populist revolution in October 1964.

---

21. Muddathir Abd al-Rahim, "Arabism, Africanism and Self-Identification in the Sudan," in *The Southern Sudan and the Problem of National Integration*, ed. Dunstan M. Wai (London: Frank Cass, 1973), p. 41.
22. "An Islamic Constitution," *Sudanow*, November 1979, p. 12.

The deep-seated fear among southerners of Islamization and Arabization was accelerated under Abbud's rule whereby official government policy was national integration through the enforced spread of Islamic education and conversion and the promotion of Arabic as the national language. Missionary schools were nationalized, foreign missionaries expelled, and the day of rest changed from Sunday to Friday, provoking resistance and region-wide student strikes in 1960.[23] By 1963, the Anya-Nya guerrilla army was founded, and the first period of civil war began in earnest.

After the 1964 revolution, various unresolved political questions raised at the time of independence were subjected to fresh examination in the light of the new Sudanese democracy. The National Committee to Establish a Constitution—the country was still without a permanent constitution—recommended that the constitution be derived from the principles and spirit of Islam and that the sharia be the basis of all legislation. Meanwhile, the Round Table Conference convened in 1965 to discuss the southern question, and although it advanced the critical dialogue between northern and southern politicians—agreeing to a nonseparatist future for the south—it nevertheless failed to reach agreement on the constitutional issue of the status of the south vis-à-vis federation, regional autonomy, or any other configuration in a unified Sudan.[24]

It was left to the second military ruler, Jaafar al-Numayri—who seized power in 1969—to implement a policy of regional autonomy for the south, and, ultimately, to negotiate the Addis Ababa accords that formally ended the civil war and brought about the integration of southern institutions and leaders into the government and society of the entire Sudan. Freedom of religion was ensured and Arabic became the national language, with English the principal language of the southern region.

The first Permanent Constitution of Sudan was adopted in 1973 during the early years of Numayri's rule. It states that "Islamic law and custom shall be the main sources of legislation; personal matters of non-Muslims shall be governed by their personal laws" (article 9). Under article 16, Islam, Christianity, and "heavenly" religions are equally protected. This latter reference to the protection of the "heavenly" religions of the south, formerly viewed as pagan and therefore potential converts to either of the competing world religions, was considered a victory for southerners—many are neither Christian nor Muslim.

FROM PEACE TO WAR, STATE-SUPPORTED ISLAMIZATION: 1983 TO THE PRESENT

Events in 1983 represent a turning point in Sudanese history and epitomize the assertion that Islamization and the fear of Islamic domination are deeply and

23. Dunstan M. Wai, *The African-Arab Conflict*, pp. 88–89.
24. Mohamed Omer Beshir, *The Southern Sudan: From Conflict to Peace* (London: C. Hurst and Co., 1975), p. 100.

profoundly related in Sudan. Further, it is also clear that a distinctly anti-Islamist political agenda is the result of the advocacy of an Islamist agenda in Sudan. Two events serve to illustrate this powerful relationship: in May 1983, some southern troops mutinied, and the second period of civil war ensued; in September 1983, Numayri decreed that the sharia henceforth would be state law. A contributing factor to the renewal of civil war was southerners' disappointment with the regime's failure to fulfill the Addis Ababa accords, especially regarding economic development and the issue of the discovery of oil in the south that would be refined in and exported from the north. The increased reliance of an ever more isolated Numayri on the political agenda of the Islamic right resulted in the convergence of these two powerful opposing forces in the transforming events of 1983 with which Sudan is now coping and, ultimately, must reconcile.

The specific events leading to Numayri's Islamization through the now infamous "September Laws" have been adequately summarized elsewhere.[25] Upon further reflection, however, what had been viewed as a dramatic new move by Numayri had actually been anticipated by events dating at least to the post-1976 coup attempt that Numayri survived and that resulted in a personal revival of Islam explained in his book, *Why the Islamic Path?* By 1977 a committee to bring Sudanese law into conformity with the sharia had been formed and had drafted various pieces of legislation, including a ban on alcohol and the institution of *zakat*, and the Muslim Brotherhood had taken control of most university student political groups.[26] Legislative attempts to Islamize Sudanese law through the use of democratic means—that is, via the single party, the Sudan Socialist Union's People's Assembly—were less than completely successful because of the strength of the opposition mounted in the assembly, chiefly from its southern constituents. The political estrangement of southern politicians from Numayri over the Islamization issue was already well established by the time southern forces mutinied at Pibor and Bor on May 19, 1983.

Having engaged the Sudanese army loyal to Numayri on a number of occasions and having seized foreign hostages, especially those associated with the government-approved development projects—Jonglei Canal and Chevron Oil— the new southern movement's military potential was manifest. Its political agenda was announced with the founding of the Sudan People's Liberation Movement (SPLM) and the Sudan People's Liberation Army (SPLA) on March 3, 1984, whereby the nonseparatist, nationalist, pan-Sudan character of the movement was declared. From the outset, a clear and consistent demand of the SPLM has been the removal of the sharia as state law.

25. Gordon, "Islamic Legal Revolution"; Esposito, "Sudan's Islamic Experiment"; Fluehr-Lobban, "Islamization of Law"; Abdullahi Ahmed An-Na'im, "Constitutionalism and Islamization in the Sudan," *Africa Today*, vol. 36, nos. 3–4 (1989).

26. Carolyn Fluehr-Lobban, "Shari'a Law in the Sudan: History and Trends since Independence," *Africa Today*, vol. 28, no. 2 (1981).

Southern rebels and politicians were not the only groups opposed to the Numayri-imposed Islamization. Northern secular and religious voices—long subdued by the repression under Numayri, beginning largely in 1983—began to criticize the imposition because of the government's undemocratic method of introducing the sharia and for the failure to employ the Islamic method of *shura* (consultation) in its implementation. Sadiq al-Mahdi was arrested shortly after the announcement of the September Laws for his opposition to this move. The judiciary, with its tradition of independence and respect for the rule of law, was reluctant to accept the sweeping changes Islamization meant, and many judges refused to implement mandated changes. Numayri's response—to sack the judges and appoint new ones, often recruits from the ranks of the Muslim Brotherhood— exposed the bias of the "new order." In response, Numayri created his own "Courts of Prompt Justice," whose excesses in applying the harsh hudud penalties, with amputations for relatively simple theft and whippings for alcohol offenses, became notorious. These measures amounted to a reign of terror engineered in the name of Islam, which some Muslim intellectuals, such as Sadiq al-Mahdi and the Republican Brotherhood leader, Mahmud Muhammad Taha, could not countenance. Ultimately, Taha was hanged for his opposition to the Islamization, and within 18 months of Sudan's "Islamic Experiment,"[27] popular opposition to it and to Numayri reached the point of massive demonstrations, leading to the overthrow of the regime.

During the one-year transitional government headed by Jazuli Dafa'allah, the September Laws and their apparatus for application were frozen. The job of removal or reform of the sharia was left to a coalition government elected in 1986 and led by Umma Party head, Sadiq al-Mahdi. Although Sadiq had been jailed by Numayri for his opposition to the September Laws, as prime minister he was less decisive. His public position was for moderation and compromise. He considered that Islamization under Numayri was improperly imposed and, in practice, un-Islamic, but abrogation of the sharia was not a political option that he entertained. On this point the pressure exerted on Sadiq al-Mahdi by the National Islamic Front (NIF), headed by his brother-in-law, Hasan al-Turabi, was keenly felt. In some respects his middle of the road position was a replay of party politics at the time of independence when the Umma Party called for a greater role for Islam within the context of a parliamentary republic; at that time, however, the Islamic Right was less powerful and more isolated. Until his last days in office, Sadiq was promising to introduce new Islamic laws or revise or reform them in such a way as to protect Sudan's non-Muslim minority. Impatient with these seemingly empty promises and with his failure to initiate talks with the SPLM/SPLA, Sadiq's coalition partner and the constituent assembly called for the resignation of the government. A move to circumvent Sadiq's position and abrogate the September Laws in June 1989 may have been what precipitated the

27. Esposito, "Sudan's Islamic Experiment."

30 June coup, which is now widely recognized to have had the support of the NIF. This view has been confirmed by one insider, the former speaker of the constituent assembly, Mohamed Ibrahim Khalil.[28]

The NIF, a direct outgrowth of the Muslim Brotherhood whose image was somewhat tarnished by its close association with the Numayri regime in its last years, was organized in 1985 just after the demonstrations and the coup. Its charter, drafted in 1987, recognizes that Muslims are the majority in Sudan and, therefore, that Islamic jurisprudence should be the general source of law for the nation because it represents the will of the democratic majority (II.B). Further, the Sudanese nation is a diverse yet unified whole, and regional self-rule is best accomplished through a federal system of power sharing (III.A).[29] Although the NIF accepts the central principles of national unity and regional government, in practice it did not enter into any consensus agreement with the other major parties regarding peace talks with the SPLM before the June 1989 coup, nor has it succeeded since in fulfilling its promise to begin the peace process. Indeed, editorials in the few legal government publications hint that the current regime is prepared to leave the south to the "secessionists." Even scholars sympathetic to the NIF are writing that "the desirability of maintaining this unitary state is doubtful"[30] if a unified Islamic republic does not succeed in bringing an end to the conflict.

From a southerner's viewpoint, accustomed to disappointment and disillusionment from northern politicians, this represents a new dimension of the "jellaba mentality" that has seen the south as a source for the extraction of wealth but never as a real political partner in the future of Sudan. The southerner's deep distrust and long-held fear of Arab Muslims has intensified during the past seven years of civil war with its massive dislocation of people, a war-induced famine that affects hundreds of thousands of Sudanese, and with mutual recriminations among each of the four governments in Khartoum since 1983 and the SPLM/SPLA.

Added to the breakdown of official contacts between Khartoum and the SPLM/SPLA are reports of marauding Arab militias, especially among two sections of the Baqqara armed by Sadiq's government, and who have allegedly engaged in slavery. These activities were first reported in 1987 by a University of Khartoum professor, Ushari Mahmud,[31] who was arrested by both Sadiq and Umar al-Bashir governments for his exposé. A more recent report by the human

28. Mohamed Ibrahim Khalil, "Crisis of Democracy and National Reconciliation" (Banquet lecture at the ninth annual conference of the Sudan Studies Association, Lexington, KY, April 1990).

29. National Islamic Front, *Sudan Charter, National Unity and Diversity*, January 1987, reprinted in *Management of the Crisis in the Sudan*, Proceedings of the Bergen Forum, February 1989, eds. Abdel Ghaffar M. Ahmed and Gunnar Sorbø, University of Bergen, 1989, pp. 133–144.

30. Abdelwahab Osman El-Affendi, "Islam and Legitimacy in the Sudanese State" (Paper presented at the ninth annual conference of the Sudan Studies Association, University of Kentucky, Lexington, KY, April 1990.

31. Ushari Ahmed Mahmud and Suleyman Ali Baldo, *Al Diein Massacre: Slavery in the Sudan* (Khartoum 1987).

rights group, Africa Watch, concludes that there is sufficient evidence from reports of kidnapping, hostage-taking, pawn brokering, and other monetary transactions involving human beings "on a sufficiently serious scale as to represent a resurgence of slavery."[32] The Khartoum government's failure to enforce the Sudanese law against slavery has been cited as negligence or complicity, while the central government responds that these practices are part of the customary law of the Baqqara with which it has no right to interfere. Even if these allegations prove to be false, the exacerbation of fear and hatred of the "Arab" northerner by the southerner that they represent has only served to sharpen the polarization of this deeply divided nation.

CONCLUSIONS

This new level of polarization that Sudan has been experiencing is not without its ironies. In the immediate post-independence period the southern resistance, Anya-Nya, fought to separate from the north, while the current movement, SPLM/SPLA, is struggling for a unified, democratic, and secular Sudan. The Islamists, who had visions of a unified "Islamic Republic of the Sudan," are apparently concluding, with considerable frustration, that this may be impossible and that a separated south might be the only solution. For the NIF-backed current regime, there can be no compromise on the question of sharia and Islamization. Before meeting with the SPLM they are demanding a cease-fire, which the SPLM/SPLA refuses unless the sharia is withdrawn. This stalemate amounts to a showdown over the future of Sudan as a national entity. Long-term observers of Sudan are reluctantly reaching the unpleasant conclusion that the issue is no longer who will rule Sudan but whether or not Sudan will be able to survive in any meaningful fashion.[33]

The distrust between those who have come from the north to exploit or to rule and the peoples of the south has a historical time frame of at least 150 years, spanning Ottoman and British colonial control of Sudan and 34 years of independence. While the jellaba may have exploited the southern Sudanese in an internal colonial-like relationship, the northerner was formally defeated and colonized by powers such as the British, who were seen as anti-Muslim, or the Turko-Egyptians, who, in the mahdist view, betrayed Islam. In both views Islam was a powerful mobilizing force against the enemy outsider. Today the "enemies" of Islamization are Sudanese nationals—southerners and northern secularists—who present a far more complicated case. The mobilizing effect of calls to Islamic solidarity confront and confound the integrity and unity of the nation-state. Pursuit of the Islamist agenda in Sudan has been and will continue to be met with

---

32. Africa Watch. *Denying "the Honor of Living." Sudan: A Human Rights Disaster* (New York: Africa Watch. 1990.
33. John O. Voll, "Political Crisis in Sudan." *Current History,* vol. 89 (1990), p. 179.

forceful resistance and, ultimately, will be found to be inconsistent with the maintenance of national unity. Excepting the NIF, in effect currently in power, this fact has been substantially recognized by all of the major political parties, including the SPLM, in joint declarations signed at Koka Dam in Ethiopia on March 24, 1986, in the National Democratic Alliance Charter of 1989, and in a recent joint statement signed in Cairo in March 1990.[34]

The Islamist agenda has been pursued farther in Sudan than in many of the better-known examples of contemporary Islamic republics with respect to Islamization of law and application of the hudud penalties. Sudan may have some unique features with respect to its large non-Muslim minority population and years of civil war, but it nonetheless shares in the regional and global phenomenon of Islamic revival. The issues that Sudanese Islamization raises—among them the protection of the rights of non-Muslim minorities and the serious problem that issue presents for the future of the nation-state—would benefit from more research and evaluation by scholars of Islam and the Middle East.

34. The Koka Dam declaration (A Proposed Programme for National Action) was signed by all of the major political parties in the Sudan, including the SPLM and, at a later date, the Democratic Unionist Party, but not the National Islamic Front. The text of the declaration is reprinted in Ahmed and Sorbø, *Management of the Crisis in the Sudan,* pp. 130–32.

[9]

MODERN ISLAMIC REFORM MOVEMENTS: THE MUSLIM BROTHERHOOD IN CONTEMPORARY EGYPT

Abd al-Monein Said Aly and Manfred W. Wenner

The coming to power of Ayatollah Ruhollah Khomeini in Iran in February of 1979, the seizure of the Grand Mosque in November of 1979, the Soviet invasion of Afghanistan in December of the same year, as well as the recent assassination of Anwar al-Sadat in Egypt have all contributed to an obsession with Islam on the part of the Western world. In these reports, misunderstandings of Islam and its theories and practices are rife, fundamental errors concerning the history of Islam are continually repeated, and a very confusing picture of the historical and political perspectives which influence the views of Muslims is presented.

Even more important, however, is the fact that much of what has been written—in both the popular and the serious press—treats these developments as representative of *all* Islamic "political" movements, and whatever changes in the theory and practice of Islam may be taking place in other arenas not currently afflicted with political violence are either ignored or misunderstood. In this essay, we wish to provide a brief historical introduction to the growth and development of modern Islamic reform movements, and then outline, using the example of the Muslim Brotherhood in Egypt, some important developments which have taken place recently. Last, but not least, we will suggest what the non-Muslim world may expect in the near future if our analyses are correct.

Abd al-Monein Said Aly is currently a Ph.D. candidate at Northern Illinois University in DeKalb, and a Research Associate of the Al-Ahram Centre in Cairo.
Manfred W. Wenner is Associate Professor of Political Science at Northern Illinois University in DeKalb. His previous studies have focused on Yemen and the Arabian Peninsula.

HISTORICAL BACKGROUND

Others have competently and extensively documented and explained the intellectual heritage of modern (20th century) Islam. What is important here is that the reader understand,

(1) that the role of Islam in any reform of current conditions—most of which are the result of the increasingly dominant role of the West in all aspects of life—is subject to many and quite varied interpretations;

(2) that Islamic reformist thought coexisted with other ideologies seeking change, including European liberalism and local nationalisms (as was the case, for example, in Egypt); and,

(3) that with only isolated examples (of which the early career of Taha Husayn is perhaps the best), there was very little doubt expressed concerning the importance of Islam, if only as a culture and civilization. In general, adherents of the various interpretations of history and Islam's role in it did not seek a confrontation; indeed, the intellectual climate (especially in Egypt) is marked by a peaceful coexistence between these (in the Western mind) seemingly irreconcilable ideologies.

HASAN AL-BANNA AND THE BIRTH OF THE MUSLIM BROTHERHOOD

It was in an atmosphere of intellectual ferment about the role and the future of Islam in contemporary society that Hasan al-Banna—the founder of the Muslim Brotherhood—was born. Exposed, due to the intellectual/religious orientation of his family, to the most "traditional" of Islamic legal doctrines (the Hanbali), he nevertheless became acquainted with several alternative orientations toward Islam, including the Sufi and the more modern views of several contemporaries. After completing his education, al-Banna gravitated toward Cairo, where he first came into direct contact with the cosmopolitan influences which were prevalent in all the urban centers of the Middle East at the time. Here he encountered the intellectual, political, and social problems and conflicts which the process of "Westernization" seems to engender: an emphasis upon materialism, the often ostentatious display of wealth, the new standards of prestige and status (which emulated Western criteria), the laxity of adherence to Muslim principles, the moral decay, and the like, to which so many other Muslims leaders have alluded.

After further studies, and association with others in (largely intellectual) Islamic associations, Banna began a program of teaching and writing in which he stressed the need for general reform along Islamic lines—of the social system, of the economic system, as well as the political system. In 1928, he founded the *Jam'iyyat al-Ikhwān al-Muslimīn* in Isma'iliyya (sometimes given as *Ikhwān al-Muslimūn* and today variously translated as Muslim Brotherhood, Muslim Brothers, or Muslim Brethren), to accomplish these goals.

As the organization grew. Banna moved its headquarters to Cairo, and began to organize on a full-time basis and undertake more extensive and diverse activities. Included among these were: (1) the building of neighborhood mosques; (2) creating small educational institutions, which offered courses in religion and literacy; (3) small hospitals and dispensaries for the public; (4) small industrial and commercial enterprises, designed to provide employment as well as income for the organization; and, (5) social clubs and organizations—a brilliant stroke, since Banna apparently recognized that people join organizations with public goals for reasons other than the achievement of these public goals, i.e., to satisfy private needs as well. Perhaps of no less importance, the Brotherhood undertook a large-scale publishing program—books, magazines, pamphlets, etc., and finally, after World War II, a mass-circulation newspaper.

Later, the Brotherhood began to take up other causes; among these in the 1930s was that of the Palestinians, which resulted in a spread of its influence into Syria, Transjordan, and to a lesser degree, Lebanon. While the Brotherhood continued its educational, social, economic and religious activities, it became increasingly concerned with, and an influential factor in, the *political* life of Egypt. One result was that Banna was imprisoned by the British authorities for his activities in the early 1940s.[1]

THE RELIGIO-POLITICAL THOUGHT OF BANNA

In the 1920s, when Banna started his movement, Islamic political thought was divided among three schools: (1) the traditionalists, or the conservative elements of al-Azhar, who theoretically refused any compromise with modernization and secularization, but who, pragmatically, dealt and compromised with the Egyptian crown and the British authorities; (2) the modernizers, or the students of Muhammad Abduh, who tried to modify the tenets of Islam to the requirements of Western "modernizing" norms, and their logical end, the secularization of Islamic society; and, (3) the conservative reformers (the students of Rashid Rida), who agreed with the second "school" on the necessity of purifying Islam from innovations (*bid'a*) which made Muslims depart from the "true" Islam, on opposition to *taqlīd* (accepting previous scholarly opinion as binding), and on following the path of *ijtihād* (personal interpretation of the basic elements of the faith). However, they disagreed completely on the value of Western political ideas, and argued the necessity of returning to the ideas and practices of the first generation of Islamic rulers for inspiration. For them, the Islamic Caliphate was

1. The literature on the Brotherhood, its origins and its founder, is extensive; we have drawn here from the three major studies in English: C. P. Harris. *Nationalism and Revolution in Egypt.* (The Hague, 1964); I. M. Husaini. *The Moslem Brethren.* (Beirut, 1956); and, R. P. Mitchell. *The Society of the Muslim Brothers.* (London, 1969).

the ideal government, and the great age of early Islam served as a model of what the world should be.[2]

Hasan al-Banna was attracted to this latter school: his vision was a response to the failure of the liberal institutions (which emerged from the Egyptian Constitution of 1923) to free the country from the British. Probably it was no coincidence that Banna's call started in Isma'iliyya, where all the signs of Western civilization, oppression and colonization were most clearly visible. Banna himself recognized the importance of Isma'iliyya to his organization, because the Suez Canal Zone and the extensive British facilities and influence there had created a sense of alienation in the Egyptian in his own country; for him and others the Zone had become a (perhaps *the*) symbol of the sickness of the country.[3] In general terms, Egypt lost confidence in the Western ideas of modernization and liberalism; it was a time for rising militancy among many elements of the population, as indicated by such organizations as *Shubbān al-Muslimūn* (Muslim Youth), *Misr al-Fatat* (Young Egypt), and, eventually, the *Ikhwān al-Muslimūn*—all seeking major changes in Egypt.

It was a time in which even the most liberal of Egyptians—Taha Husayn, Abbas al-Aqqad, Muhammad Husayn Haykal, and Tawfiq al-Hakim—expressed their disappointment in liberal institutions and their inspiration and possible answers.

Although Banna was intellectually a combination of Muhammad Abduh reformism, Rashid Rida conservatism, and al-Afghani's political activism, he conceived his mission as a more comprehensive vision of Islam. One of his followers summarized his view of al-Afghani as "merely a cry of warning against problems," of Abduh as "merely a teacher and philosopher," and of Rashid Rida as "merely a historian and a recorder."[4] The Muslim Brotherhood, on the contrary, "means *jihād*, struggle and work—it is not merely a philosophical message."[5]

For Banna, the Islamic ideal was represented by the first generation of Muslims, when Qur'anic principles were adhered to and Islam was the principal "nationality." For him, the distance between current Islamic societies and the true Islamic path is the cause of the decadence in the Muslim *umma* (community). His basic questions were: do Muslims carry out the Qur'anic commandments? Do they have faith and belief in the divine doctrines contained in the Qur'an? Does any sphere of their life accord with the social laws prescribed in it? Having answered all these questions in the negative, the mission of the Brotherhood,

2. R. al-Sa'id, *Hasan al-Banna*. (Cairo, 1977), p. 29 (in Arabic); see also Albert Hourani, *Arabic Thought in the Liberal Age: 1798–1939*. (London, 1962), pp. 7–8.
3. Hasan al-Banna, *Risalāt al-Mu'tamar al-Khamis*. (Beirut, n.d.), p. 30 (in Arabic); see also M. S. Agwani, "Religion and Politics in Egypt," *International Studies*, 14 (July 1974): 379.
4. Sa'id, *op. cit.*, p. 30.
5. *Ibid.*, p. 31.

therefore, is to "lead Mankind towards truth, call humanity to the path of goodness and illuminate the entire world with the light of Islam."[6]

The revival of Islam, then, is not only a defensive mission to rescue Muslim societies from the West; it is also an offer to bring humanity, "which has gone astray, to the right course."[7] "It is the culture and civilization of Islam which deserve to be adopted and not the materialistic philosophy of Europe."[8]

In his book on the Brotherhood, Ishak Musa Husaini argued that the Brotherhood has six principles. The first is scientific: to provide a precise explanation of the Qur'an, and defend it against misinterpretation. The second is pragmatic: to unify Egypt and the Islamic nations around these Qur'anic principles, and to renew their noble and profound influence. The third is economic: the growth and protection of the national wealth, raising the standard of living, the realization of social justice for individuals and classes, social security for all citizens, and a guarantee of equal opportunity for all. The fourth is socio-philanthropic: the struggle against ignorance, disease and poverty. The fifth is patriotic and nationalistic: the liberation of the Nile Valley, all Arab countries, and all parts of the Islamic fatherland from foreigners. The sixth is humanitarian and universal: the promotion of universal peace and a humanitarian civilization on a new basis, both materially and spiritually, through the medium of the principles of Islam.[9]

To achieve these principles, Banna emphasized the *political* nature of Islam. He stated, in his message to the Fifth Conference of the Brotherhood:

> We believe the rules and teachings of Islam to be comprehensive, to include the people's affairs in the world and the hereafter. Those who believe that these teachings deal only with the spiritual side of life are mistaken. Islam is an ideology and a worship, a home and a nationality, a religion and a state, a spirit and work, and a book and sword.[10]

Governing, in other words, is in the very nature and origins of Islam. The role of the Muslim reformer is to act as legislator, educator, judge, and executive: he cannot be only a missionary, but must seek power and authority in order to apply the tenets and laws of Islam. If he does *not* seek power to that end, he commits an "Islamic crime."[11]

The method to achieve these goals is to spread the call of *jihād*. As one of the fundamental duties of the true Muslim, *jihād* has two aspects: power and argument. Banna stated explicitly:

6. H. al-Banna. *What is our Message* (Karachi, 1968), p. 10.
7. *Ibid.*, p. 3.
8. *Ibid.*
9. Husaini, *op. cit.*
10. Banna. *Risalät.* p. 10.
11. *Ibid.*, pp. 37–38.

Allāh Almighty commanded the Muslims to do *jihād* for his sake . . . Only if the people refuse to listen to this call and resort to defiance, oppression and revolt, then, as a last resort, recourse should be had to the word to disseminate the call.[12]

In general, Banna's strategy can be summarized as follows: (1) avoid the battleground of theological disputes; (2) avoid domination by notables and important men; (3) avoid divisive political organizations such as parties; (4) emphasize gradualness because every movement must pass through several stages before arriving at its goal; (5) seek power in order to realize goals, including if necessary armed force; (6) set up a religious government, because government is one of Islam's cornerstones, and includes education, legislation, adjudication, and implementation and action—all of which are inseparable from one another; (7) belief in Arab *and* Islamic unity; (8) revival of the caliphate, because the caliph is *the* symbol of Islamic unity; and (9) consider and treat every country which aggresses against the Islamic homeland as a tyrannical state which must be resisted in every way.

As this summary makes clear, Banna placed great emphasis upon *action* in his call to the faithful, because he firmly believed that political action was absolutely necessary if the weakness of the Islamic community were to be overcome.[13]

THE BROTHERHOOD AND POLITICAL ACTION

As a result of his imprisonment by the British authorities, Banna founded a more secret "sub-group" within the Brotherhood known as the "Secret Apparatus." While the Brotherhood made its influence felt on the national political scene, especially after World War II, because of its size, its organization, its array of activities and the discipline of its members, this more violent wing of the movement undertook its own campaign to bring about the policy results it sought. As a result of its utter contempt for the ruling authorities after the Palestinian debacle, this wing assassinated the Prime Minister in 1949. In return, the government's political police assassinated Banna a few weeks later.

Though forced into placing more emphasis upon its underground operations as a result, the Brotherhood had ties to a variety of other secret associations and groups bent upon bringing about change in Egypt; one of these was the Free Officers group, with whom ties were maintained through an unknown junior officer by the name of Anwar al-Sadat. Despite the necessity of maintaining a low profile, members of the Brotherhood were prominent participants in the watershed event known as Black Saturday (January 26, 1952, when central Cairo was

12. Banna, *Message*, p. 14.
13. Husaini, *op. cit.*, pp. 42–43.

burned in an orgy of anti-Western violence). Because of its links to the Free Officers, it was the only organized group which was permitted to operate publicly after the Revolution of July 1952.[14]

THE MUSLIM BROTHERHOOD IN THE NASSER ERA (1952–1970)

After July 23, 1952, the relationship between the Muslim Brotherhood and the Egyptian government developed through several stages: (1) The period between July 1952 and March 1954 was a stage of conciliation between the Brotherhood and the Free Officers. Conciliatory gestures were adopted by the regime, such as releasing all the Brothers who had been imprisoned under the old regime, and opening an official inquiry to search for the murderers of Hassan al-Banna. Additionally, after the promulgation of the law banning political activities on January 16, 1953, the officers authorized the Brotherhood to continue its activities under the pretext that it was an association with religious aims.[15] (2) The period between 1954 and 1970 was a period of tension in the relationship between the movement and Nasser. In 1954, six members of the Brotherhood were executed, the Supreme Guide (then as now Hasan al-Hudaybi) was condemned to labor for life and more than 800 Brothers were given long prison sentences while many thousands were imprisoned without trial. Nonetheless, in 1964 Nasser decided to order a general amnesty, freeing all the Brothers, to counterbalance the influence of the communists, who had been freed as well. Again, in 1965, the Brothers were accused of planning to overthrow Nasser; many were arrested throughout the remainder of 1965 and the first half of 1966, and in late August 1966 three of the major leaders were hanged.[16] (3) The period from 1970 to 1981, when the Muslim Brothers were allowed to play an increasing role in Egyptian political life.

Many (though not all) scholars agree that Nasser's regime (1952–1970) was the most significant attempt at the modernization and secularization of Egypt since Muhammad Ali. Nasser was not satisfied with merely creating new institutions parallel with the traditional ones; his aim was to modernize the bases of legitimacy using Western and nationalist concepts, in addition to modernizing the panoply of other traditional institutions.

Nasser ideologically rejected the theocratic notion of the State without rejecting Islam altogether. He propagated an eclectic formula based on Egyptian nationalism, Islamic principles, Arabism and Marxism. His major theme was to raise the level of mass Egyptian consciousness through the propagation of Arab

14. On the major events in this sequence, see the works cited in footnote 1.
15. *Al-Nahar Arab Report*, "The Muslim Brotherhood in Egypt II," May 1975, p. 26.
16. *Ibid.* See also, Maxim Rodinson, "The Political System," in P. J. Vatikiotis, ed., *Egypt Since the Revolution*, (New York, 1968), p. 108.

unity nationalism (Pan-Arabism).[17] His social and economic policies were designed to place Islam at the service of the state. He frequently attacked "reactionary Muslims," and at the same time tried to subordinate Islam to socialism by alternatively emphasizing "Arab socialism" and "Islamic socialism." The keynote of this campaign was sounded by Nasser on March 12, 1965, when he stated: "The Muslim religion is a religion that is 100 percent socialist."[18]

Practically speaking, under Nasser all significant religious institutions were made subject to the control of the state. The *awqāf* (personal, public and mixed) were either abolished or brought under the control of the Ministry of *Awqāf*.[19] The *sharī'a* courts were next: in 1955 the government announced the abolition of all communal judicial systems and the transfer of their jurisdiction to the national courts. This development was seen as symbolic of a "national spirit" which found expression in the consolidation of the state.[20]

The next, and probably most important step, was the reform of al-Azhar, the last stronghold of the conservative *'ulamā'*. According to a 1964 law, al-Azhar was attached to the Presidency of the Republic, and a Minister of al-Azhar was appointed by the President. Its various departments were placed under the leadership of men who would follow the government line, its curriculum was reformed, and four modern secular faculties (Medicine, Engineering, Agriculture, Commerce) were added. The new curriculum was designed to produce a new set of values, simultaneously in accord with the faith and the demands of modern life.

In addition, the Ministry of *Awqāf* was directed to take charge of all mosques ". . . and guid[e] the leaders in such a way that they [the mosques] would fulfill their religious mission in the proper way."[21] Nasser was, in effect, nationalizing religion in the same way as he had land, industrial, and commercial enterprises.

The "nationalization" of the religious institution was accompanied by a withering attack against the *'ulamā'*; they were charged with being "oldfashioned," "obstructionist," "obscurantist" and forming a "priestly" caste. They were also charged with being unable to cope with modern times, and this, the government said, was turning people away from Islam.

Although Nasser was not as drastic as Atatürk in attempting to distinguish between politics and Islam, he had his own formula for legitimacy which he sought to base on a unique mixture of the Egyptian national movement and Islam. This did not, however, accord with what the Muslim Brothers would accept as the

17. H. R. Dekmejian, "The Anatomy of Islamic Revival: Legitimacy Crisis, Ethnic Conflict and the Search for Islamic Alternatives," *The Middle East Journal*, 34 (Winter 1980): 5.

18. D. N. Wilber, *United Arab Republic* (New Haven, 1969), p. 74.

19. B. Borthwick, "Religion and Politics in Israel and Egypt," *The Middle East Journal*, 33 (Spring 1979): 156.

20. D. Crecelius, "Al-Azhar in the Revolution," *The Middle East Journal*, 20 (Winter 1966): 40–42.

21. Borthwick, *op. cit.*, pp. 157ff.

bases for legitimacy in the society. They denounced Nasser as a "traitor" after the signing of the Egyptian-British Treaty of 1954, and tried to assassinate him. Their propaganda establishment, through different means, orchestrated an attack upon Nasser's Arabism and Arab socialism as "foreign doctrines" and devoted much of their energy to a denunciation of what they described as the infiltration of the Egyptian spirit by "atheist" ideas.[22] However, the Brothers had to pay the price for their principles in 1954 and 1966. It was only under the new regime of Anwar al-Sadat that their political fortunes revived.

THE MUSLIM BROTHERHOOD IN THE SADAT ERA (1970–1981)

A number of factors may be adduced to explain the revival of the Brotherhood under Sadat; some are external in origin, some are domestic. We would suggest the following breakdown:

External factors: (1) the aftermath of the Egyptian participation in the Yemen War (1962–1967); (2) the aftermath of the Egyptian defeat in the 1967 Arab-Israeli War; and, (3) the role of Saudi Arabia, and its relationship with the Brotherhood. In the list of internal factors: (1) the continuing economic crisis which has plagued the Egyptian economy for more than a decade; and, (2) the role of the Egyptian Left in domestic politics since the death of Nasser.

The Yemen War

In order to demonstrate Egypt's support for progressive development in the Arab states, and the positive results which could be achieved for Arab nationalism if and when the rule of "reactionary forces" could be eliminated, Nasser committed himself to the defense of the new Yemeni Republic (proclaimed in September 1962). Over the next five years, this decision (taken for a variety of political reasons) cost Egypt dearly.[23] Instead of demonstrating that Egypt was capable of effectively supporting and assisting other Arab states bent upon modernization, this adventure eventually made Egypt increasingly dependent upon Saudi Arabia after the 1967 defeat by Israel.

The June 1967 Arab-Israeli War

The June defeat raised serious questions about the legitimacy and competence of the regime. Just as the 1948 debacle had thrown a merciless light on the

---

22. *Al-Nahar Arab Report, op. cit.*
23. On the Egyptians in the Yemen war, see: M. W. Wenner. *Modern Yemen 1918–1966.* (Baltimore, 1967); and, E. O'Ballance, *The War in the Yemen.* (Hamden, Conn., 1971). It should be noted that a substantial portion of the war costs were, in the long run, borne by the Soviet Union through its liberal extension of credits to Egypt.

incapacity of the country's leaders of that period, so the June defeat raised doubts about the capacity of the Nasser regime to deal with the country's major political and security problems. A serious debate as to the relevance of the country's major values took place; usually Islam was seen as the only alternative to such other ideologies as socialism and Arab nationalism, even by high-ranking members of the government who had been involved in the campaign. For example, Vice President Husayn al-Shaf'i wrote:

> Islam will remain the greatest and most powerful social concept ever known in the history of man. When the Muslims are attacked, *jihād* becomes the sixth pillar of Islam. As the Muslims were ordered to fast, so also they are ordered to fight, because a belief needs power to protect it, and power needs a belief to push it.[24]

The Brotherhood's analysis was quite simple: Egypt lost because she strayed from the Qur'an, which had been replaced by the National Charter. Even more important, the Brotherhood saw the defeat as: (1) an effective condemnation of the secular social, economic, political, and intellectual characteristics of the regime—all of which ignored or violated the principles of *shari'a;* (2) a sign of God's revenge for the oppression which they had endured under Nasser; and, (3) God's punishment for the alliance which the government had made with an atheist state (the USSR) in order to advance its secular interests.

The Brotherhood's complementary analysis of the nature of Israeli society was used to argue for the necessity of creating an Islamic state: Israel is a religious state, based upon the tenets of Judaism. The Egyptians, who had depended upon a secular ideology, could not hope (and had not been able) to withstand the power of religious faith. This particular analysis had great appeal for many Egyptians, who were quite divided as a result of the defeat.

Saudi Arabia and the Brotherhood

The relationship between the Brotherhood and Saudi Arabia, especially since World War II, has been complex and varied. In the contemporary era, this relationship shows clearly during the 1954 conflict between Colonel Nasser and General Muhammad Najib (Naguib) over leadership of the Revolutionary Command Council. The Brotherhood took the side of General Najib, primarily because of the Council's limitations on Brotherhood activities. King Saud, then the Saudi monarch, intervened on their behalf, extracting a promise from the RCC to permit the Brotherhood to operate openly once again.[25]

---

24. S. A. Hanna, "Islam, Socialism and National Trials," *The Muslim World.* 68 (October 1968): 293–294.

25. Husaini, *op. cit.,* p. 135.

Saudi influence on the Brotherhood's activities surfaced again in 1965; at that time, the fact that President Nasser and King Faysal were on opposite sides of the Yemeni War contributed to the perception that a major split had developed in the Arab world—between Nasser and the "progressive" states, and Faysal and the "conservative" states, including Iran and Morocco. The Brotherhood supported Faysal and, as noted above, is alleged to have planned to overthrow Nasser. According to their accusers in the later trials, they were to have received both funds and arms from Saudi Arabia for this purpose (although the evidence presented must be seen in the light of the conflict).[26]

In fact, there has often been a clear relationship between the intensity and closeness of Saudi-Egyptian relations, and the level of Brotherhood activity. As Saudi influence grew during Nasser's later years (the result of increasing economic power), and then undertook a quantum leap under Sadat, the Brotherhood's activities also expanded and grew, as evidenced by their vastly increased publishing program.

In order to understand the changes in the Brotherhood after the death of Nasser, as well as the role of Saudi Arabia, one must keep in mind the special status of the Saudis. First, the Saudi social and political system has been cited by the Brotherhood as the example of a more truly Islamic state. Second, the fact that Saudi Arabia accepts only the *shari'a* as a source of legislation as well as a guide to punishment for criminal activity is ritually cited by the Brotherhood; this is particularly true when the Brotherhood cites Saudi crime statistics and suggests that the low level of "serious crime" is the result of the canonical punishments which the Saudi authorities mete out.[27] Supporters of the Brotherhood consequently suggest that it is not necessary to depend upon outside sources for legislation or inspiration for dealing with contemporary issues and problems. Last but not least, the Brotherhood has been able to find refuge in Saudi Arabia when things do not go well in Egypt.

From the Saudi point of view, their support for the Brotherhood is quite deliberate and calculated. First, the Saudis ideologically approve of the "Islamization" of Egypt, which they view as having been for too long under the influence of left-wing ideologies. Second, therefore, increased support of the Brotherhood provides an effective check against too great an influence on the part of the Egyptian Left on domestic or foreign policy—something usually inimical to Saudi interests and objectives.[28]

It is at this point that some of the foreign and the domestic factors which have contributed to the Brotherhood's revival overlap.

26. *Al-Nahar Arab Report, op. cit.*
27. J. R. O'Kane. "Islam in the New Egyptian Constitution." *The Middle East Journal.* 26 (Spring 1972): 147; See also *al-Da'wa.* August 1976. p. 36.
28. Ali Rustum, *Saudi Arabia and Oil Diplomacy.* (New York, 1976), pp. 75-76.

The Egyptian Economy

The continuing population and land pressures which afflict Egypt require massive infusions of capital in order to develop the kind of infrastructure and economy which can begin to cope effectively with these problems: or such, at least, is the view of the Egyptian government. Under Sadat, the government's relations with Saudi Arabia improved markedly, and the latter became a major contributor to Egypt's finances, especially for development programs, until the Camp David Accords and the subsequent Arab League "boycott" of Egypt. While this was damaging to Egypt, Sadat believed that only the financial and technical resources of the Western nations could undertake the massive program of infrastructural and industrial development which he saw as necessary. He therefore substantially modified the economic policies of his predecessor, adopting what has become known as the "open door" policy in an effort to attract extensive foreign investment as well as to promote expanded domestic industrial investment. Unfortunately for Sadat, the net result was not what he had hoped for. Furthermore, one of the side-effects was the rise of a new class of importers, real estate agents, etc., who enjoy a lifestyle which has aroused widespread resentment among the urban poor *and* the urban middle class, an unusual combination. Both groups have been severely affected by high inflation and widespread unemployment and underemployment and have become increasingly disenchanted with the government.

One analyst has noted that although the Brothers had a large rural and urban class membership, middle class, white-collar professionals dominate the activist membership. The growth of urbanization without any parallel growth in the economy has created a very large segment of the population which no longer believes it is sharing equitably in the wealth of the country. Among these, no matter what their original socio-economic class, the Brotherhood can spread its message; many of them accept a revolutionary ideology eagerly, especially one which permits them to support radical change without losing any of their traditional beliefs.[29]

There is another dimension to this: the escalation of corruption in Egyptian society in recent years. As has been recently and eloquently noted, corruption in developing countries comes in multiple forms: the most important are (a) endemic, (b) developmental, and (c) planned. It seems reasonably clear that Egypt has all three types, and in the popular mind, the life-style of President Sadat and his family suggested that it affected every level of the ruling establishment.[30]

29. E. Davis, "Islam and Political Change in Egypt," Paper Presented to the 1980 American Political Science Association Convention, Washington, D.C.
30. J. Waterbury, "Corruption, Political Stability and Development: Egypt and Morocco," *Government and Opposition*, 11 (Autumn 1976).

However, it is another form of corruption which is probably far more serious, and even more evident to the public eye. This is what we may call, for lack of a more precise term, moral corruption. It is most evident in the large number of night clubs, the soaring incidence of prostitution, the emerging gambling clubs, and ostentatious and expensive restaurants and cabarets of every variety. These characteristics of contemporary Cairo have deeply offended the more religious among the population, and the Brotherhood has skillfully exploited this sentiment.

The Role of the Egyptian Left

Last but not least, one must consider the nature of the confrontation which developed between Sadat and the Left. As noted above, the latter's role in domestic affairs has been of concern to Saudi Arabia. At the same time, under Nasser, the ascendancy of the Left and its emphasis upon Arab nationalism (in foreign policy) and on egalitarian reforms (in domestic policy) in large measure neutralized the appeal of the Brotherhood to many of the socio-economic elements at the bottom of the social pyramid.

Upon achieving power, Sadat was forced to develop and promote some ideological emphasis to fill the void left by Nasser's death; Sadat opted to use Islam. In part, the decision to do so was motivated by a fear that the Egyptian Left would be able to pre-empt his new position: in order to neutralize any alternative group trying to grasp the reins of power (and the Left was the only political faction which had a visible organization considered able and likely to do so), Sadat had to take the only alternative course. He announced that Egypt was a state of "Science and Faith," an obvious attempt to combine the two strains of Islamic thought outlined above, and bitterly attacked the Left generally as inappropriate and irrelevant to Egyptian and Islamic conditions.[31]

The result was that Sadat found a tactical ally in the Brotherhood (especially with respect to his confrontation with the Left during the period between the "Corrective Revolution" of May 1971 and 1977); he released the Brothers from prison, including the Supreme Guide, Hasan al-Hudaybi. And, in the preparatory work for his own, new Constitution for Egypt, he invited their participation in the drafting of relevant articles and sections.[32]

THE BROTHERHOOD'S POLITICAL ACTIVISM

In his analysis of the most effective way for the Brotherhood to achieve its goals, Banna had outlined the three-stage process through which the movement

31. O'Kane. *op. cit.*, p. 137.
32. *The Economist* (London), "Cairo's Caliph," July 16, 1977; see also M. C. Aulas. "Sadat's Egypt," *New Left Review*, 98 (July 1976).

must pass: (1) the propaganda stage, which concentrated upon the education of the people; (2) the stage of attracting and selecting supporters, the drilling of recruits, and the mobilization of those who answer "the call"; and, finally, (3) the stage of action. But, throughout this process, the basic aims of the Brotherhood should never change: obtain explicit recognition of its political existence, and then, as the most crucial step toward other social goals, the implementation of the *sharī'a* as a matter of public policy.[33]

In the discussions preceding the promulgation of the Sadat Constitution, the Brotherhood became an active participant, and enunciated a series of demands (in exchange for its support): (1) that Islam be declared the official state religion; (2) that the *sharī'a* be recognized as the primary source of legislation, especially with respect to the constitutionality of other laws; and, (3) that the *sharī'a* be made the sole source of personal status laws, and that any laws which contradicted the *sharī'a* be declared void; in this connection, the Brotherhood suggested that the liberation of women be accomplished within the framework of religion.[34]

The result, that is, the text of the Constitution as accepted and promulgated, was unsatisfactory to the Brotherhood (and other traditionalists). Although Article One said that "Islam is the religion of the state; Arabic is its official language, and the principles of the Islamic *sharī'a* are (a) principal source of legislation,"[35] this was not acceptable because of the Brotherhood's insistence that the *sharī'a* be the *only* source of legislation.

Furthermore, the text of Article Two, which read:

> The state shall be responsible for maintaining the balance between women's duties toward the family and her activity in society, as well as for her equality with man in the fields of political, social, cultural and economic life, without detriment to the Islamic *sharī'a*.

was also deemed unacceptable, since it overemphasized equality in socio-cultural matters.

Unsuccessful in their attempt to have the new Constitution written to their specifications, the Brotherhood moved their campaign for changes to their liking into two new avenues: (1) the People's Assembly, and, (2) the mass media.

In the Assembly, the Brotherhood offered a series of legislative proposals; among them were, (1) imposition of the *sharī'a* punishment for theft (cutting off a convicted thief's hand); (2) requiring memorization of the Qur'an in all governmental bodies; (3) the imposition of a dress code for women; (4) forbidding the employment of men in hair dressing salons for women; (5) the prohibition of

---

33. Husaini, *op. cit.*, p. 39.
34. O'Kane, *op. cit.*, pp. 138–140.
35. Text of the Egyptian Constitution of 1971; *The Middle East Journal*, 26 (Winter 1972); 55–68. This article was amended in the Constitution of May 1980 to be the *only* source of legislation.

alcohol. The Assembly responded by consigning (1) through (4) to committee, and passing (5) in a form so riddled with exceptions and loopholes as to make it totally ineffective. The result was predictable: the Brotherhood and its supporters concluded that the Assembly was useless for their purposes; what was needed was a complete and total rewriting of the Constitution with the *shari'a* as the only source of legislation. The Brotherhood decided to turn to the media as a way of exercising greater influence over public policy in Sadat's Egypt.[36]

Although one mass circulation publication by the Brotherhood had been available for some time. *al-'Itisām*. it was decided that another major effort at reaching greater audiences and obtaining additional public support should be made. As a result, after obtaining the required permission in 1976. the Brotherhood launched *al-Da'wa* (The Call, the traditional Islamic term for proselytizing activities by Islam) as a monthly journal of commentary, news. and opinion. The principal spokesmen represented were 'Umar al-Tilmasani and Salih 'Ashmawi: the latter was a former aide to Banna. and became the editor-in-chief of *al-Da'wa*. No independent or objectively verifiable circulation figures are available: the only figure ever given was published in the second issue of *al-Da'wa* itself: 100,000.[37]

In any event, a study of *al-Da'wa*'s content indicates that there has been an appreciable change in the views of the Brotherhood. from Banna to the present. Though the articles which appeared in the journal continued to stress the superiority of Islam, the evils of communism and liberalism. the necessity of applying the *shari'a* to cure society's ills, the requirement of participation in the *jihād* as a condition of being a real Muslim. etc., a review of recent articles shows that the current level of religious zealotry among the Brothers is considerably higher than earlier: "The Revival of Islam."[38] "The Intellectual Invasion from the West,"[39] "Secularism is the Conspiracy from the West against the Islamic East,"[40] are just some of the titles from recent issues.

CHANGES IN THE BROTHERHOOD'S IDEOLOGY

In fact, we are led to the conclusion that some important changes took place in the Brotherhood during Anwar al-Sadat's tenure. What are these changes? What contributed to their appearance? Our analysis would seem to show that the Brotherhood modified its views on three major items: (1) the appropriate economic system: (2) the role of Arab unity: and. (3) the political party system.

---

36. *Al-Da'wa*. August 1976. pp. 12–13.
37. *Ibid*. Effective circulation was probably much higher.
38. *Ibid*., pp. 2–3.
39. *Ibid*.. November 1976. pp. 26–27.
40. *Ibid*.. January 1977. pp. 4–6.

The Economic System

An earlier writer on the Brotherhood observed that the "old" Brotherhood saw economic reform in terms of two factors: (a) economic independence as the foundation of genuine political independence; and, (b) economic improvement: some form of economic and social security for the poverty-stricken masses of Egypt was necessary in order to close the gaps in the class structure to avoid further national disunity.[41] In his program, Banna advocated a kind of socialism as necessary for Muslim society. The abolition of usury; the nationalization of natural resources; industrialization; the nationalization of the National Bank of Egypt; the abolition of the stock market; land reform; the progressive application of the *zakāt* (tithe) on capital as well as profits, and a host of similar steps were the main components of Banna's program for socio-economic reform.[42] Many of these proposals were implemented in the Nasser era but were labeled as "socialist." Further, it is necessary to add, the "old" Brothers believed in the necessity of public, as well as private ownership of manufacturing industries and businesses.[43]

The "new" Brotherhood, on the other hand, appears to have adopted the diametrically opposite point of view on what constitutes the "proper Islamic" economic system. In practical terms, they appear to have moved completely into the "capitalist" camp: recent publications argue that private ownership (with only a few exceptions) is one of the bases of Islam, and that any doubt about this is a doubt concerning the validity of the *sharī'a*, because private ownership is the origin of the *zakāt*, *kaffāra* and inheritance; it is the ideal system of economic activity.[44]

Apparently, the justification for this change stems from the social functions which private ownership performs in Islam.[45] One of the conclusions which the Brotherhood has drawn for the contemporary situation is that such private ownership of the means of production (industries of all types) as well as of land means that both producers and workers should become stock-holders.[46]

Arab Nationalism and Arab Unity

The "old" Brotherhood believed in the importance of Arab nationalism *(qawmiyya)*, even though their understanding of the term Arabism was quite

41. Mitchell, *op. cit.*, p. 272.

42. *Ibid.*, p. 274.

43. Husaini, *op. cit.*, p. 146. Husaini adds that in Banna's view, communism has a fundamental and irreconcilable clash with Islam even though both believe in the evils of capitalism as an economic system.

44. E. Abduh, "Ownership in Islam," *al-Da'wa*, August 1976, pp. 14–15.

45. M. Kamal Wasfi, "Liberty in Islam," *al-Da'wa*, November 1976, pp. 16–17.

46. "Islam or no Islam: An Overview of the Algerian Charter," *al-Da'wa*, November 1976, pp. 41–43.

different from the secular thought associated with Pan-Arabism. They considered Arab unification as an essential prerequisite for the revival of Islam, since the Prophet had said, "Arabs are the first Muslims; if the Arabs are humiliated, so is Islam." The Brotherhood found it easy to accept the unity of faith and language represented by the term "The Arab World," and believed that a liberation of all Muslim lands, especially Arab lands, had to precede a truly Islamic renaissance. In serving the cause of Arabism, then, the Muslim Brotherhood was "serving Islam and the welfare of the entire world."[47]

This "Arab" dimension is absent in the recent writing of the Brotherhood. In addition to the traditional attack on the secularism of Pan-Arabism, represented by the Ba'th Party (which the Brotherhood considers a tool of the Christian, colonial West),[48] the new Brotherhood views the Palestine issue as a conflict between Islam and Judaism, which needs to be resolved as part of a Pan-Islamic solution. Palestine was, in the current view, not lost in 1948, but rather in 1909, when Sultan Abd al-Hamid II was forced to abdicate the caliphate by a combined force of "Crusaders" (the Brotherhood catchword for Christians), Zionists, and Free Masons. In their view, Zionism had failed to make any progress in Palestine (in the Ottoman period) because of the Sultan's Pan-Islamic views, and his reluctance to alienate Islamic lands.[49]

The Role of Political Parties

The "old" Brotherhood specifically condemned the factionalism of political parties; it considered the existence of multiple parties as essentially a "tool" of the West for dividing the "Brotherhood of Islam." The mission of Islam is to gather together, not to tear apart the fabric of society, and it is not possible to further the Brotherhood's mission unless one is devoid of factionalism and has become utterly devoted to God.[50]

The "new" Brotherhood has altered its political tactics, and has adopted a stand first enunciated in 1954, when the Supreme Guide supported General Najib's call for a "clean" party system. At the present time, as their journal *al-Da'wa* insisted, the Brotherhood demands a complete, free and competitive party system in which it is permitted to have its own Islamic party. Furthermore, the new Brotherhood explicitly calls for, and promises to install, democracy as a political system: democracy is the system "which opens the door for all thoughts and minds, as opposed to dictatorship, in which no ideas are permitted except those of the ruler." Democracy is "able to uncover every mistake, and no one is

47. Mitchell, *op. cit.*, p. 267.
48. "The Ba'th Party and its Role," *al-Da'wa*, November 1976, pp. 58–59.
49. G. Rizk, "Why did Sultan Abd al-Hamid Refuse to sell Palestine to the Jews?," *al-Da'wa*, November 1978, pp. 10–12.
50. Husaini, *op. cit.*, p. 43.

above criticism, while in a dictatorship the decisions are all orders from the ruler, and everyone must obey without discussion or criticism."[51]

What has brought about these changes in the stand of the Brotherhood? A number of explanations may be offered, most of which are quite easily related to contemporary developments in Egypt. In the first instance, it would appear that the Brotherhood wishes to distance itself as much as possible from the principles and programs associated with the Nasser Era, during which time it suffered its greatest setbacks—pragmatically as well as ideologically. Indeed, this hypothesis serves well to explain the Brotherhood's change regarding both the nationalization programs of Nasser, as well as the Supreme Guide's stand on certain international issues.[52]

The last change in their principles is clearly tactical: the Brothers have realized, particularly since 1954, that individually and as an organization they are not safe if the whole political system is not "safe", i.e., democratic. The Brotherhood realized that it utterly failed to influence the Free Officers regime, and the time has come to use democracy as a tool for keeping its mission alive.

Another reason for the very real change in the Brotherhood's economic orientation may be traced to a perceived change in its primary constituency within the Egyptian population. Its early appeal (in the Canal Zone) appears to have been to those most affected by Britain's overwhelming economic superiority within the Egyptian economy. As the economy developed and Britain's role diminished, there is evidence that the population to which the Brotherhood appealed underwent a shift. Whereas in the past it appealed to those whose livelihood seemed overwhelmingly dependent upon the actions of the British, and therefore the ideology emphasized nationalization, today the majority of its membership seems to be among the petit bourgeois of the towns and cities, that is, that portion of the population which resents the concentration of immense wealth in a small elite, but which just as firmly believes in private property and capitalist ideology as the only ideology/program which recognizes their interests. The very limited records we have of the Brotherhood's membership would appear to indicate that the activist portion of its support is primarily found among engineers, doctors, and other professionals, i.e., other elements of the social structure who tend to benefit from a "capitalist" rather than a "socialist" economic system.[53] This provides an interesting confirmation of some of the evidence which has come to light concerning who supports the Islamic Republic in Iran.

---

51. M. Abd al-Kudus. "Warning: The Jews are Coming: The Impossible Peace between Egypt and Israel," *al-Da'wa,* September 1979, p. 57.

52. Those who see politics in the Middle East in personal terms will, however, likely attribute these changes to Hudaybi's relationship with certain members of the royal family and some of the wealthier families. See: Husaini, *op. cit.,* pp. 113–116.

53. Davis, *op. cit.*

This also suggests that the Brotherhood. while continuing to emphasize certain basic principles concerning the role of Islam in society, has become a *pragmatic* political organization in contemporary Egypt. We believe that this has important consequences for its ability to play a more important role in Egyptian politics in the future.

THE BROTHERHOOD AND THE SADAT GOVERNMENT

As we have implied. the relationship between the Brotherhood and Sadat underwent additional changes during the latter's tenure as President. We would distinguish between the period 1970–1978. which can be characterized as a time of "peaceful coexistence" between them. and 1978 to 1981. which was marked by confrontation due to two factors: (1) the Egyptian-Israeli Peace Treaty: and. (2) the Iranian revolution and the Khomeini phenomenon.

During the first period. Sadat was involved in two sensitive political situations. First. he was interested in bringing Egypt into the Western camp in general. and into an alliance with the United States in particular. This was occasioned in large part by his belief that only the United States had the resources and ability to aid the faltering Egyptian economy, and that only the United States had the power to solve the Arab-Israeli conflict by applying sufficient pressure on Israel. whether economic. political. or military. In order to accomplish this. Sadat opted for what was known as the "open door" (*infitāh*) policy, which simply meant that Egypt was open for investments and ideas from the West (without the kinds of restrictions which previously existed).

Secondly. and at the same time. Sadat was also crucially dependent upon Saudi Arabia and its financial assistance to cover many current operating costs of the Egyptian government. Moreover. Sadat seems to have been aware from the very outset of the potentially high social costs involved in the open door policy. The increasing gap between the classes in Egypt. and the slow erosion of the position of the middle class has always been fertile ground for the political left. As we have tried to show. this situation led to Sadat's decision to use religion. and specifically the Brotherhood. as a curb upon the ambitions of the left. and its attempts to exploit the situation.

At the same time. the Brotherhood was in a critical situation. It wanted to maximize its political benefits on the one hand without. on the other hand. provoking Sadat. Since the Brothers did not consider Sadat sufficiently Islamic. due to their experience with the Constitution. they adopted a strategy of peaceful coexistence. in the hope that more propitious days lay ahead.[54]

---

54. *Al-Da'wa* never referred to Sadat as "the believer." the term used in the rest of the Egyptian media. Furthermore. they rarely used his name. preferring to refer to him as "the president

The turning point in this carefully balanced association came in 1978. The signing of the Egyptian-Israeli Peace Treaty alienated Saudi Arabia on one hand, which in turn sharply curtailed its support to Egypt; on the other hand, the rift with Saudi Arabia relieved Sadat of one of the major constraints with respect to his policies toward the Brotherhood. At almost exactly the same time, the Iranian revolution gave the Brotherhood increased confidence, and a new hope in the possibility of establishing an Islamic society in Egypt. To Sadat, these developments represented the dangers of Islamic fundamentalism, especially to his own government. The result was that the relationship between the Brotherhood and Sadat changed, and took on entirely new characteristics.

The arenas of conflict were four in number:

First, Sadat announced that he would not permit the establishment of an Islamic party along the lines and principles advocated by the Muslim Brotherhood. He gave as his reasons that such a party would (a) possibly frighten away Western investments; and, (b) provoke the Coptic Christian minority, whose status in contemporary Egypt appears somewhat ambiguous in any event (as a result of a spate of attacks on Coptic institutions and individuals in recent years). The Brotherhood, on the other hand, in line with its new position on political parties, believed it was the only party capable of bringing into being an Islamic state in Egypt (which it feels is widely desired), and that such a prohibition directly contradicted the alleged move toward greater socio-political freedoms enunciated as a policy objective by Sadat.

Second, Sadat found himself in a complex conflict growing out of his open door policy. A major concern of the Brotherhood is, as we have said, the enormous growth of night clubs, prostitution, gambling, alcoholic beverage consumption, and like activities; it is precisely such establishments which were eventually attacked in the January 1977 violence.*[55] Sadat could not offer any concessions in this regard, however, since the motive behind the open door policy was to increase tourism and foreign investment, and these licentious activities were among the ways for tourists to contribute to the local economy; in other words, Sadat's economic goals simply could not be achieved in what the Brotherhood saw as a righteous and moral Islamic society.

Third, no longer as restrained by the Brotherhood as before, Sadat embarked on a liberation program for women which almost completely alienated the Ikhwān. One might suggest that Sadat sought a new constituency; in the summer

---

of the republic." This would seem to imply strongly no more than minimal respect for the office, and very little for the individual actually in that office.

    * These events began with riots over the price of bread. The casino burnings followed, and were directed against Saudi and Gulf Arabs as well as against drink. [Ed.]

    55. S. Shadi. "Is it a Conspiracy against the Islamic Sharī'a?." *al-Da'wa*. January 1977. pp. 6–7.

of 1979 he announced a new set of laws concerning the status of women: (1) at least 30 representatives in the National Assembly had to be women. and (2) new restrictions limited divorce and made polygamy nearly impossible.[56]

Fourth, and perhaps most important, was the conflict which arose over Sadat's handling of the Arab-Israeli conflict. The Brotherhood attacked every attempt by Sadat to solve the problem peacefully, since in their terms it is a religious confrontation between Islam and Judaism. The only possible solution is a *jihād* which will rescue lost Islamic territory. The arguments presented in *al-Da'wa* were unremitting in their logic and their bitterness with regard to Sadat. who, because "Palestine is an Islamic question," had no right to give or offer concessions. since he cannot legitimately speak for Islam.[57] After the signing of the peace treaty, the Brotherhood intensified its attacks. especially with regard to the "normalization" of relations between Egypt and Israel; it called for a campaign to boycott Israeli banks. goods. and any other kind of dealing which might grow out of the relationship. since it believes that acquiescing therein would simply promote (Israel/Jewish) economic and cultural imperialism.[58]

It was these four conflicts which set the stage for the confrontation between Sadat and the Brotherhood. The latter, as early as 1977, chose to participate heavily in the strikes. demonstrations, and riots which took place in January of that year; the Brothers were prominent among the "puritans" who systematically but *selectively* smashed and burned the casinos. night clubs, and other pleasure spots of the rich and foreign along the Pyramids Road in that year.[59] In spite of the fact that Sadat attributed the riots to the Left. specifically to communists and Soviet agents who were attempting to overthrow his government. Sadat was informed by the Brotherhood that it would not limit its "call" to speeches and publications; in fact. they had just begun their campaign for further political influence.

The Brotherhood began its expanded "call" on the campuses of the Egyptian universities through the medium of a variety of Islamic groups, perhaps the best known of which is the Islamic Society *(al-Jāmi'a al-Islamiyya)*, which played a prominent role in recent student demonstrations. In late 1977, the society won nearly all the seats in the Student Union elections in every university in the country.[60] as well as in the National Student Union.[61] Demonstrations against the government were widespread. but particularly severe at Minya and Asyut. The

56. *Al-'Itisām*, August 1979. pp. 5–10.
57. See the issues of *al-Da'wa* for August 1976; January, April. September. and December 1977; and January 1978.
58. Abd al-Kudus. *op. cit..* p. 57; and Umar al-Tilmisani. "The Normalization of Relations and the Exchange of Ambassadors." *Al-Da'wa.* January 1980. p. 5.
59. *The Economist* (London). "Voices from Egypt's Bottomless Pit." January 29, 1977.
60. *Christian Science Monitor,* April 10, 1980. p. 7.
61. *Al-Da'wa.* January 1978.

result was that the old and much-disliked "University Guard," designed to check up and report on dissident activities, was re-introduced to the Egyptian campus scene.

OTHER ISLAMIC GROUPS

One of the government's problems has been the fact that more than half-a-dozen small but militant Islamic groups (collectively known as *al-Jāmi'āt al-Islamiyya*) are operating in Egypt in addition to the Brethren. And, it is not at all clear which actions should be attributed to which group, nor how strong these other groups are, either in terms of numbers or resources.

What was clear by the end of the decade, however, was that one of the strongest and perhaps the best organized of these other groupings was the one known as *al-Takfīr wal-Hijra*, probably best translated as "Penance and Retreat," both words with strong Islamic connotations. The group appears to have been organized in the early 1970s, and first became known when some of its members participated in the attack on the Army's Military Technical College in Cairo in 1974. At that time, it seems to have supported an effort by another radical Islamic group, the Islamic Liberation Party, to mount a serious threat to the government. The attackers made a number of demands which have continued as a *leitmotif* since then for groups even more radical than the Brotherhood: (1) specific protests against Sadat's pro-American policies; (2) demands that a "pure" Islamic state be set up in Egypt, with the *sharī'a* as state law; (3) demands that "sin" and "crime" be made synonymous. (It should perhaps be added that the political system of the first century AH would be the model for the Egyptian political system, as well as for the entire Muslim world.)

Although considered a minor splinter group at that time, by August 1976 it was clear that *al-Takfīr wal-Hijra* was far larger than originally thought. It was then estimated to have around 500 members, and to be concentrating its activities on propagandizing and recruiting in the high schools and universities. The fact that it had far more serious and extensive goals in mind was made clear in July of 1977, when it kidnapped and later killed the former Minister of *Awqāf* and instructor at al-Azhar, Shaykh Muḥammad Ḥusayn al-Dhahabī. By assassinating a prominent figure associated with the government's religious policies, *al-Takfīr wal-Hijra* made clear to the public and the government that it was not a tame organization, and that it believed that the government's policies could only be changed through the use of political violence.

It would appear that *al-Takfīr wal-Hijra* has borrowed heavily from the Brotherhood: organized on hierarchical lines in cells, each headed by an "amir," its head is known as the Amir al-Mu'minīn (Commander of the Faithful, the traditional title of the head of the Islamic community). Until his arrest and execution by the government, this was Shukri Ahmad Mustafa, an engineer who had written a number of religious tracts, and advocated a kind of "hijra" analagous to that of Muhammad, especially to Arabia, to the disaffected and uncertain. Although the Brotherhood (in early 1979) specifically condemned the terrorism of *al-Takfīr wal-Hijra*, the real relationship between the two in view of their organizational history and goals remains unclear and unknown. *Al-Da'wa*, however, defended the members of the group, who were termed "victims" of the religious vacuum which existed in the country; it specifically refused to call them criminals. Furthermore. *al-Da'wa* rejected the trials of the participants in the violence as unconstitutional, since they were conducted under military and not civilian law, and called for a dialogue with them, since they were clearly good, though misled, Muslims.[62]

By 1979, the increasing militancy of Islam in Iran was also having its effect upon developments in Egypt. In that year, knowing the important role which students played in the Iranian revolution, Sadat dissolved the National Student Union and severely curtailed the scope of student unions in the individual universities. Further, government funding which had formerly made it possible for Islamic organizations to conduct summer camps, publish magazines and other materials, as well as carry out additional activities. was abruptly cut off.[63] It is highly likely that Sadat's insistence upon providing aid and asylum for the deposed and discredited Shah of Iran further alienated whatever low level of Islamic support may still have existed among the politically aware and active portion of the population.

THE ASSASSINATION OF SADAT AND ITS AFTERMATH

By early 1980, the signs of an increasing sympathy and even active support for the multitude of Islamic groups was quite widespread; only the very brave were not openly making some sort of peace with the growing wave of Islamic militancy now evident in all strata of society. All the signs pointed toward an eventual clash between Sadat and the Islamic associations.

One of Sadat's problems at this time was almost totally overlooked in the Western press and by Western analysts: the significant upsurge in the political consciousness and activity of the Coptic community—its determined effort to resurrect the Coptic language (at the expense of Arabic), its efforts to proselytize and to develop new churches, schools, and socio-political organizations. Ironically, the United States encouraged this: the visit by the Coptic Patriarch Pope Senuda III to President Jimmy Carter in 1977 increased his visibility and prestige. In other words, although the activities of the Islamic groups helped to arouse the Copts, the latters' increased militancy in turn further stimulated the Muslim

62. *Ibid.*, September 1977.
63. *Christian Science Monitor, op. cit.*

resurgence. and created the fear of a vastly increased social and political role for the Copts and the Church.

By 1981. Sadat had reneged on many of his earlier promises regarding political dissent and opposition—in the press. in the National Assembly. as well as other forms of political organization. In fact. the wide spectrum of viewpoints represented in the arrests in the summer of 1981 showed how seriously Sadat had eroded his bases of support: politicians of the right and the left. members of the various Islamic associations. as well as leaders of the Coptic Church. elements of the business elite as well as journalists. professors. media personalities, and so forth.

It has. of course. become a cliché to point out that as the Shah ruthlessly suppressed opportunities for dissent. for participation in decision-making on the part of the "middle classes" (broadly defined), and for those disadvantaged by rising inflation and the various programs for development which did not produce the promised results. it was to be expected that the one channel which the regime could not afford to totally control. much less alienate, the mosque. became the major avenue of opposition to the government. It was. and is, our opinion that by the summer of 1981, Sadat had created a situation which inevitably produced the outcome which so shocked the world: his assassination by militant Muslims belonging to one (or more) of the Islamic groups. The question has now become. what will the role of these organizations be under President Husni Mubarak?

At this point, we can only suggest that it depends heavily on Mubarak's responses to the demands of the same constellation of groups and interests which played such an important role in Sadat's downfall. The basic problems remain: the basic groups with specific interests and goals remain. In a very real sense, President Mubarak controls his own destiny: he may be able to alter the power relationships which exist, or he may face the same kind of confrontations which preceded the Iranian revolution. Does that mean that we may expect another "Iran" in Egypt?

COMMENTS AND CONCLUSIONS

We can answer that question by answering another: how does Egypt differ from Iran?

First, in Egypt. unlike Iran. an Islamic political organization has been in existence for more than 50 years, and in that time developed a far more sophisticated and extensive network of affiliated organizations and economic activities than we have been able to discern in Iran.

Second. in Egypt. unlike Iran. the Islamic political organization is better prepared to govern after its seizure of power. Whereas in Iran the various religious associations and groupings (with greater or lesser degrees of commitment to Islam) have had slowly to learn the intricacies of governing (especially in a multiethnic and highly diverse society spread over a large territory), we would suggest that the Brotherhood at least has exercised substantial political influence over a sizeable portion of the educated and professional population.

Third, in Egypt, unlike Iran, the Islamic political organization has demonstrated a far more pragmatic approach to the acceptance of technology and related phenomena which stems from the West and which can contribute to its success. Although it is clear that the Ayatollah and his supporters, for all their intemperate attacks upon the attributes of Western civilization, could not have come to power without the cassette recorder, the jet aircraft, and a host of other Western technological developments, Egyptian Islam is heir to a long tradition of "accepting" and using such technology when it can effectively contribute to efforts to resist the West, and especially the latter's culture, ideologies, economic and political policies, and goals in the area.

Fourth, in Egypt unlike Iran, there is no overwhelmingly dominant individual to play the role of an Ayatollah Khomeini. In part, this may be due to the fact that Egypt is a Sunni society, and Iran is a Shi'a society; in part, however, it is also due to the long experience of the Brotherhood without a charismatic leader: it has been forced to rely far more heavily upon organization, upon control over and access to various modes of power. Note that the Muslim movement in Egypt has survived the death of Hasan al-Banna, the major ideologue of the Brotherhood (Sayyid Qutb), many additional "martyrs" such as Shukri Ahmad Mustafa, Mustafa Abd al-Maqsud Ghazi, Ahmad Tariq Abd al-Alim, as well as the imprisonment (incommunicado) of such figures as Shaykh Abd al-Hamid Kishk, Hilmi al-Jazzar, and more recently, Umar al-Tilmasani. It would seem possible to suggest, therefore, that if the Brotherhood were to come to power in Egypt, it would be able to retain the reins of power longer than we believe the Ayatollah and his allies will be able to do in Iran. (A note of caution: as of this writing, the Islamic Republic is about three years old, and seems capable of maintaining itself for some time to come, despite the evident fissures in the government and the campaigns against it domestically and externally; it is at least holding its own against Iraq, and appears to have adjusted to the severe dislocations caused by the cutbacks in petroleum exports. All these should be perceived by the West as a warning against hasty judgments on the resolution and staying power of Islamic political movements in the contemporary world.)

On the other hand, we would note those factors which would seem to argue against the long-term success of any Islamic revolution in Egypt and can be major assets for Mubarak.

First, Egypt has a lengthy liberal political tradition which, whatever its origins, was often inhibited by the British presence and yet led a healthy existence for many decades. In fact, it may be suggested that the necessity of keeping this tradition alive in the face of British opposition may have succeeded in nurturing a far more healthy political tradition than might otherwise have been the case.

Second, a considerable part of the Egyptian middle class and intellectual elite have a far longer tradition of associating themselves with indigenous nationalist and progressive movements than was the case in Iran, where the "Four Hundred Families" were so clearly tied to a regressive monarchy and political tradition. In fact, some of the leading intellectual figures in the Egyptian liberal and Islamic traditions have come out of this socio-economic class.

Third, the Egyptian economic system in its current form is not the result of a very few years of rapid and dislocating development, as was clearly the case in Iran in the last few years of the Shah. Indeed, with the exception of the years of the Middle East Supply Center, it would be fair to say that the Egyptian masses and even its formerly much smaller land-owning elite managed to develop the economy fairly organically since the days of Muhammad Ali. This is not to argue that its system of allocations is just, nor sufficient to meet basic needs; it is only to make the point that it is far more clearly the result of a long-term process with which many elements of the population have been socialized into coping.

Nevertheless, we are led to conclude that should Islam in the form of the Brotherhood or other organization make a concerted effort to take over the Egyptian system, we could expect substantial political changes throughout the Islamic world that would be far more significant in their impact than those which resulted from the creation of the Islamic Republic in Iran. The Western world would probably over-react again; there would be the usual massive effort at analysis of the "new Islam" and what it means for the West. We fully expect these analyses to be no more sophisticated and analytical than most of those we have seen to date. Furthermore, in its effort to understand the new "vitalism" of Islam there would be little effort to see that a similar phenomenon was occurring elsewhere, including the United States. While we would caution against over-simplistic comparisons between the Islamic and Christian worldviews, it remains a truism that we are by and large incapable of religious self-analysis. When some aberration of Islamic doctrines and principles occurs, as it will among the adherents of any ideology, we are quick to blame Islam—as a religion, as a culture, and as a threat of substantial proportions to the values of Western civilization. On the other hand, when what can only be considered as an aberration of Christian doctrines and principles occurs (*vide* Jonestown), we are quick to blame this on the work of the individuals involved, and not the culture from and in which they arose. Unless and until we are willing to see that what Clifford Geertz called the "primordial sentiments" continue to have clear and immediate value to people, we will not understand Islam, we will not understand the Moral Majority, we will not understand the Gush Emunim—in a word, we will fail to understand the politico-religious motivations of millions of people in the contemporary world.[64]

64. Clifford Geertz, "The Integrative Revolution: Primordial Sentiments and Civil Politics in the New States," in C. Geertz, ed., *Old Societies and New States* (New York, 1963).

[10]

THE THEOLOGICAL ROOTS OF PEACE AND WAR ACCORDING TO ISLAM

William C. Chittick

Few topics seem so pressing as the threat of war. Eager to establish peace and prevent a world-wide conflagration, people want to "do something" as soon as possible. Many of them look to religion with the idea that its help should be enlisted in accomplishing this most urgent of tasks. But religion - if one may speak in generalities - does not acknowledge any principles higher than its own, not even the survival of the human race. Asked to help establish peace, it will do so in its own way or not at all.

In the general Western view., which has certainly not been altered by certain recent events, Islam is one of the most warlike of all religions. Stereotyped opinions and the fact that few people have the patience to delve into the principles and "myths" underlying the surface appearance make the task of bringing out Islam's actual views on peace and war especially difficult. But only by probing deeply into Islamic ways of looking at things can we hope to understand how Muslims view the current situation. Once we have taken a step towards understanding Islam, perhaps we will find the appropriate language with which to "enlist" its help in establishing true peace in the world.

The aim of the present paper is to clarify the basic Islamic view of peace and war on the assumption that real and effective cooperation with Muslims can only be undertaken after we have reached a genuine understanding of how they perceive the current human situation. We cannot ask followers of Islam to propose "practical" and "concrete" cures for the present crisis unless we first listen with a sympathetic ear to their diagnosis of the disease.

It is important for the reader to realize at the outset that what is being discussed here is the religion of Islam as set down in its fundamental texts, not necessarily the opinions of contemporary Muslims. No Muslim today would claim that the community as a whole lives up to the ideals established by the Qur'ān and the Prophet`s-Sunnah. All agree that a distinction must be made between what Islam teaches and what Muslims think and do. At the same time, differences of opinion among present-day Muslims as to what in fact Islam does teach - especially when it is a question of applying these teachings to the contemporary situation - run deep. Any attempt to sort out these different opinions, even in the limited domain of peace and war, would require a book-length study.[1] Hence the present paper deals only with the normative and underlying Islamic principles that are more or less agreed upon by all Muslims, whether or not everyone would express them in the terms employed here. The question of how to deal with the present situation on a practical level will have to be answered by those Muslims who wish to live in accordance with their own tradition.

* * *

To discuss the political reality of peace and war within the Islamic context, we need to understand how Islam views these two concepts in a general sense. Peace can be defined as "freedom from war", while war can be called "a state of hostility, conflict, opposition, or antagonism between mental, physical, social, or other forces" (cf. *Webster`s Third New International Dictionary*). These definitions prove a starting point from which to approach the specifically Islamic way of looking at peace and war as set down in the fundamental source for all Islamic thought and activity, i.e., the Qur'ān which is the Word of God as revealed to the Prophet Muhammad by means of the angel Gabriel. Once the general Islamic sense of the two terms is clear, we can turn to the specific issue of how traditional and normative Islam would strive to establish peace in the world.

All Islamic thought begins with God, or more specifically, with the "attestation of faith" (*Shahāda*), the statement that "There is no god but God," which is considered a unique certainty upon which all other truths depend. Hence our initial task is to answer the question, "In the Islamic view, how do peace and war relate to God and to the attestation of faith?"

"Peace" (*al-salām*) is a name of God. The Qur'ān calls God "Peace" in the passage,

> He is God; there is no god but He. He is King, Holy, Peace,

> Faithful, Preserver, Mighty, Compeller, Sublime. Glory be to
> God above everything they associate with Him. He is God, the
> Creator, the Maker, the Form-giver. To Him belong the Names
> Most Beautiful. All that is in the heavens and the earth glorifies
> Him. He is Mighty, Wise. (59:23)

These few sentences epitomize Islamic theology. More specifically, they
express two ideas about God found throughout the holy book: the
transcendence of the Divine Reality, and His immanence in created things.
"Peace," for example, fits into the category of the "negative" (*salbī*) names
of God (also called the names of "incomparability" [*tanzīh*]). It signifies that
God is free from and infinitely exalted above all defects and imperfection,
since these are attributes of the creatures, not the Creator. In Himself God
knows no "hostility, conflict, opposition, or antagonism." As for God's
immanence, this is expressed by the mention of His creativity, the fact that
He is close enough to the creatures - in spite of His transcendence - to shape
and form all things. All attributes and qualities found in the world derive
from Him; so true is this that "Whithersoever you turn, there is the Face of
God" (2:115). If "all that is in the heaven and the earth glorifies Him," this
is not only because all things alert us to the fact that he is exalted beyond
their imperfections, but also because they tell us that every positive attribute
comes from Him. As the Qur'ān constantly reminds us, everything in the
universe displays God's "signs" (*āyāt*).

> Surely in the creation of the heavens and the earth, and the
> alternation of night and day, and the ship that runs in the sea, ...
> and the clouds compelled between heaven and earth - surely
> there are signs for a people who understand. (2:164)

In short, the name "Peace" signifies that no imperfection or conflict is to be
found in God. By implication, "There is no god but God" means that "There
is no peace but God" and "There is no perfection but God." Moreover,
"everything other than God" (*mā siwā Allāh*), which is how Muslim thinkers
define the "world" (*al-ʿālam*), is different from God and therefore opposed to
Peace in some sense. In other words, everything other than God is imperfect
by definition - "All things perish except His Face" (Qur'ān 28:88). True
peace belongs to God alone, while any peace possessed by His creatures can
only be imperfect and perishing.

God's Peace follows upon His Unity: He is one in every respect, so there is
nothing in Himself other than Himself that could oppose or contradict Him.
His Self is totally unlike the human self, which is constantly flooded with
conflicting thoughts and feelings. Human beings are never wholly at peace
with themselves because they are made up of opposing faculties and
energies. And this is as it must be, since peace as such belongs only to God,
while its opposite - war, that is "hostility, conflict, opposition, and

antagonism" - is to some extent intrinsic to everything other than God, to all created things.

If God is absolute Peace, is the world "absolute war" ? Certainly not, since that would demand strife and conflict so deep and so far reaching that no two things in the universe could exist together in harmony. It would be total chaos if not pure nothingness. Hence the world is only "relative war," but as such it is also "relative peace". The world's peace - the harmony and equilibrium that exist among its opposing forces - is, in Qur'ānic terms, a "sign" or reflection of God's Absolute Peace. The world is a mixture of opposing forces that may conflict or harmonize depending on the situation. If its relative peace is to be increased, this can only be done by bringing it closer to the Absolute Peace of God.

But is "war" understood as a "state of hostility, conflict, opposition, and antagonism" necessarily bad? No, says Islam, since war in this general sense is inherent to the world, and the world is God's good creation. Hence all conflicts must be working towards God's ends, even if they appears evil in our eyes. In other words, conflicts and opposition may in fact make up the different dimensions of an equilibrium that escapes our view.

It was stated above that God is Peace but not war, since this would demand conflict and opposition within His One Self. But many Muslim theologians provide a much more sophisticated explanation of the divine nature. In fact, they say, conflict and opposition must ultimately derive from God since He created the world and accomplishes His aims through all the opposing forces found within it. To understand the theological roots of conflict, we need to turn again to the doctrine of the divine names.

Though God in Himself is One, He takes on a variety of relationships with His creatures. He is the Life-Giver and Slayer, the Exalter and the Abaser, the Benefiter and the Harmer, the Forgiver and the Avenger. At any given moment every creature is related to these and other pairs of opposing divine names. Life has been given to us in this world and before long it will be taken away. We are exalted above some of our fellow creatures in wealth, power, and intelligence, but abased before others. We have received many benefits and suffered many ills. The ontological roots of every situation we experience derives from the divine nature. The fact that we undergo constant change shows that God continuously bestows upon us new relationships with these and other names. Perfect equilibrium (*i'tidāl*) among the divine names is found only in God Himself, who is the Coincidence of Opposites (*jam' al-addad*). "He is the First and the Last, the Outwardly Manifest and the Inwardly Hidden" (Qur'ān 57:3). But the creation of the universe demands that the names display their opposite properties in unequal proportions, or else the properties would cancel each other out.

The Theological Roots of Peace and War   149

Though a certain "disequilibrium" of the divine Names allows the individual things of the world to exist in their infinite variety and constant change, it remains true that the world as a whole - "everything other than God" - represents and equilibrium among all the divine names. Each name conveys to us a mode in which the Divine Reality establishes relationships between Himself and the creatures. The modes may conflict at any given moment and in any given existent, but the totality of existence represents a harmony of all the different modes, since existence gushes forth from Reality, Sheer Being, just as light comes forth from the sun. If one ray is perceived as green and another as red, this does not contradict the underlying unity of light.

In short, the archetype of peace *in divinis* is the Unity of the Divine Self, while the archetype of war considered as a positive reality is the multiplicity of the divine names. In God Himself the names coexist in perfect harmony and equilibrium, since the names are not different from His Being. The "Forgiver" is God, and the "Vengeful" is also God; the Life-Giver is God, and so also is the Slayer. But the properties of the names reflected in the world display opposition and conflict, since, for example, God as the Forgiver displays Himself differently to His creatures than God the Vengeful. Nevertheless, all opposition works within the context of the Divine Unity that gives birth to it. Vision of things as they are in themselves is to see all things as God's creatures within the context of His one Being. It is to see all the colours of the spectrum as manifestations of the One Light.

It was pointed out that God is the Absolute Peace, while creation is relative peace and relative war. The world displays a certain conflict and strife as a result of the opposition among divine names such as the Abaser and the Exalter, even though the activities of these two names go back to the One God. This sort of opposition among the names might be called "horizontal", since in the long run neither of the opposing names dominates over the other, while each name manifests the Divine Peace through its harmonious relationship with its opposite on the same level.

But there is a second kind of opposition among the names that might be called "vertical". In the present context, this means that certain names display the Divine Peace, while their opposites bring about opposition and conflict. For example, God is both "Merciful" and "Wrathful". Though at first sight it might appear that these two names stand on the same level, in fact, as the Prophet reported, "God`s Mercy precedes [i.e., has priority over] His Wrath". Mercy is prior to Wrath because Mercy represents the divine nature itself, while Wrath is an attribute that God assumes only in relationship to certain creatures. In other words, God is Merciful toward all creatures and Wrathful only toward some. In the last analysis His Wrath must be considered an extension of His Mercy, just as a father's anger toward his child displays his love. The constantly repeated Qur'ānic formula, "In the Name of God, the Merciful (*al-raḥman*), the "Compassionate (*al-raḥim*)," expresses the priority of Mercy (*raḥma*) in the divine nature. (Note that Merciful and Compassionate both derive from the word *raḥma*).

Names and attributes of God connected to Mercy represent God as He is in Himself, while names and attributes connected to Wrath represent specific attitudes that God assumes in relation to certain creatures for special reasons. Mercy is closely allied to such divine attributes as unity, beneficence, bounty, guidance, forgiveness, and equilibrium, while Wrath is allied to multiplicity, harm, error, vengeance, and deviation. The eschatological fruit of Mercy is paradise (i.e., nearness to God), while that of Wrath is hell (i.e., distance from Him). In the cosmos, Mercy is made manifest by the prophets, who express the divine name the Guide (*al-hādī*), while Wrath do not work on the same level. That which manifests Mercy is made manifest by Satan and his attendant demons, who express the divine name the Misguider (*al-muḍill*). Note that in Islam Satan is the ape of the prophets, not of God; all things in existence, even the negative and dispersive tendencies, come under the sway of the Divine Unity. [2]

The vertical opposition between Mercy and Wrath is fundamentally different from the horizontal opposition between, for example, the Life-Giver and the Slayer. In the case of horizontal opposition, all creatures and activities that manifest it remain at the same "distance" from God; the two opposing names bring into existence a kind of "yin-yang" relationship between forces in the world, an opposition which is in fact a complementarity, since both forces work toward the same end. But Mercy and Wrath do not work on the same level. That which manifests Mercy is "closer" to God than that which manifests Wrath. If a being moves from Mercy to Wrath, it leaves unity and harmony and enters into multiplicity and disequilibrium. If it moves in the other direction, it travels away from conflict into harmony. In other words, "Peace" or freedom from conflict lies at the centre of a circle: the centre is God Himself, while the circumference is as near to chaos as can be imagined. All creatures are situated on the radii. If they move centripetally, they travel closer to Peace, Unity, Bounty, Forgiveness, and Mercy; if they move centrifugally, they journey toward war, dispersion, harm, vengeance, and wrath.

*   *   *

The horizontal conflict among the names is taken into account in the verse repeated several times in the Qur'ān, "Everything in the heavens and the

The Theological Roots of Peace and War   151

earth glorifies God" (24:1, 57:1, 61:1, etc.). This means that all creatures work in harmony toward the end for which they were created, even though a certain strife and opposition can be perceived on every level of created existence. But a second kind of conflict, peculiar to human beings, derives from the vertical opposition between Mercy and Wrath. It is alluded to in the Qur'ānic verse,

> Have you not seen how to God bow down all who are in the heavens and all who are in the earth, the sun and the moon, the stars and the mountains, the trees and the beasts, and many of mankind? (Qur'ān 22:18).

Not all of human beings bow to God. Those who do not bow have turned away from Mercy and Guidance and embraced wrath and error. In other words, they have rejected the purpose for which they were brought into the world, a purpose explained in the verse,

> I have not created jinn and mankind except to worship Me [or "to serve Me"] (Qur'ān 51:56).

The first kind of war and conflict is inherent to the universe; it is willed by God because it displays the opposing qualities of His Names. It results from the divine command that brings all creatures into existence: "His only command to a thing, when He desires it, is to say to it 'Be!', and it is" (Qur'ān 36:82). All conflicts and wars that derive from this "engendering command" (*al-amr al-takwīnī*), simply manifest the diverse possibilities of existence latent within the Divine Creativity.

But God has created human beings in His own image, giving them freedom to choose between good and evil. Since He has given freedom only to mankind (and the jinn[3]). He directs at them alone a different kind of command: "He has commanded that you worship none but Him. That is the right religion, but most men know not" (Qur'ān 12:40). This "prescriptive command" (*al-amr al-taklīfī*) differs totally from the engendering command in that it can be disobeyed by those toward whom it is directed. The creatures cannot disobey God when He says "Be!", since this engendering command determines their existence and their nature. If horizontal conflict arises as a result of the engendering command - if lions devour lambs and waves smash against the shore - this only shows that hostility, opposition, antagonism, and "war" are inherent to the created world. But human beings can choose to ignore the prescriptive command, and as a result a new kind of conflict arises in existence, a vertical conflict between the creatures and the guidance desired for them by their Creator.

Given the fall of the human race and mankind's subsequent "forgetfulness" (*ghaflah*) of God, this kind of war may be inherent to the human situation, but it works counter to the divine purpose for mankind, which is "worship" or "service" of God. It removes human beings ever farther from their own Centre, which is Mercy and Peace, and hence it calls down upon them God's Wrath; in other words, it takes them ever closer to the circumference, which is dispersion, multiplicity, deviation, and disequilibrium.[4]

When God created human beings, He made them His vicegerents or representatives (*khalīfah*) on earth (Qur'ān 2:30). The human vicegerency, called by the Qur'ān the "Trust" that no other creature was able to carry (33:72), means that human disobedience results in evil consequences not only for those individuals who turn away from God but also for the whole of creation, over which mankind was given power (cf. the repeated Qur'ānic declaration that all things were "subjected" [*taskhīr*] to human beings, e.g., 14:32-33; 31:20; 45:12-13). Conflict and war between mankind and God results in the corruption and ruin of the earth itself. The closer human beings stand to Divine Mercy, the more they are put into harmony with the Divine Peace. When they are at peace with God, they fulfill their functions as vicegerents and therefore govern and control the earth in a manner that brings all creatures under the sway of God's Peace. But if people move toward the periphery of existence - toward the circumference which is war and conflict - they fail to control the earth in the manner set down themselves, they call it down upon their own wards as well, that is, the creatures of the natural world.[5]

These ideas are expressed clearly in the Qur'ānic doctrine of the "corruption" (*fasād*) of the earth. According to the Qur'ān, God told the angels, "I am setting in the earth a vicegerent." They replied, "What, wilt Thou set therein one who will work corruption and shed blood?" (2:30). "Working corruption in the earth" is a possibility reserved for human beings, since only they can turn against the Divine Mercy and their own natures by disobeying the prescriptive command, that is, by refusing to serve and worship God. The Qur'ān employs various forms of the word "corruption" fifty times, and in every case where actual corruption is envisaged it results from human activity. In short, "Corruption has became manifest an the land and in the sea through what men's hands have earned, so that He may let them taste some part of what they have done. Haply they may return [to Him]" (Qur'ān 30:41).

God allows corruption to appear because human beings have been given the free will to chose their own destinies: at the same time it can serve to remind them of their responsibility toward Him as His vicegerents. "Repentance" or "turning toward God" is seen as corruption's only remedy; to repair the ill results of disobedience, people must once again follow the religion that God has sent down for them.

Obedience, through which human beings can carry the Trust, depends upon

The Theological Roots of Peace and War   153

right faith and practice, which in the Islamic view can be defined as the
"profession of God's Unity" (*tawḥīd*) on all levels - in the heart, mind, soul,
and body. God's One Reality is the source of peace and harmony, while
obedience to Him roots out corruption from the earth. The connection
between the Divine Unity and the disappearance of corruption is clearly
expressed in the verse, "Why, were there gods in earth and heaven other
than God, earth and heaven would surely be corrupted" (Qur'ān 21:22).

Human disobedience and the resulting corruption in the earth grow up out of
the failure to affirm God's Unity, also called the "association of other
divinities with God" (*shirk*), the only sin that cannot be forgiven (Qur'ān
4:48, 116). This erroneous introduction of multiplicity into the Single
Source and Centre leads to disequilibrium and dispersion - or an encounter
with the full force of the Divine Wrath - since the "associator" or
"idol-worshipper" (*mushrik*) in effect negates any possibility of linking
himself with the Centre; he cannot possibly achieve peace, which depends
upon contact and harmony with Unity, so he remains in conflict and war.
More often than not the false divinity that a person "associates" with God is
self-will, ego-centric desires, or "caprice" (*hawā*). In the words of the
Qur'ān.

> Have you seen him who has taken his caprice to be his god?
> (Qur'ān 25:43, 45:23).

> Who is further astray than he who follows his caprice without
> guidance from God? (Qur'ān 28:5).

Once people begin to obey their own whims and desires instead of following
God's revealed guidance, they are acting "as if there were gods in earth and
heaven other than God". The result can only be the earth's corruption, the
dissolution of the kingdom over which they were made vicegerents. Hence
the Qur'ān says,

> Had the Real (*al-ḥaqq*) followed their caprices the heavens and
> the earth and whosoever is in them would have been corrupted
> (Qur'ān 23:71).

Only God's Mercy keeps the universe intact despite people's rejection of the
Divine Command and their eager attempts to embrace His Wrath.

The opposite of *fasād* "corruption" is *ṣalāh* "soundness, rightness, goodness,
wholeness, wholesomeness, holiness". The Arabic term most commonly
used for peace among nations is *ṣulḥ* , a word derived from the same root
and closely connected in meaning. The literal sense of *ṣulḥ* is to set things
right or to make things good, sound, and whole. To establish *ṣulḥ* in a
conflict is to bring about a reconciliation between the opposing parties. The

Qur'ān employs the word in a single instance, in the sense of reconciliation between husband and wife (4:128). More importantly, the Qur'ān employs the term *ṣalāh* and the adjectival form *salih* in more than 120 instances to refer to an ideal activity or situation which human beings must strive to achieve. "Wholesome works" (*'amal salih or salihat*) is the Qur'ānic term for that activity which brings human beings into harmony with the divine command. In other word, it is the activity which erases corruption and establishes peace.

> Obey not the commandment of the prodigal, who work corruption in the earth and fail to make things wholesome (Qur'ān 26:152).

Or again, the Qur'ān quotes Moses' words to his brother Aaron:

> Be my successor among my people, and make things wholesome; do not follow the way of the workers of corruption! (Qur'ān 7:142).

The expression, "Those who have faith and perform wholesome works", employed in the Qur'ān fifty-three times, has become a set phrase referring to good Muslims.

Through wholesome works the faithful are able to overcome corruption and dispersion and move toward peace, harmony, and wholeness. This "vertical" movement toward God is referred to in the Qur'ānic verse, "To Him good words go up, and the wholesome work - He uplifts it" (35:10). In short, those who move toward God's Mercy and avoid His Wrath, who strive to achieve His Peace and avoid conflict with Him, will reach nearness to Him and Paradise.

> Surely those who have faith, and those of the Jewry, the Sabaeans, and the Christians, whosoever has faith in God and the Last Day and performs wholesome works - no fear shall be upon them, neither shall they sorrow. (Qur'ān 5:69).

> Whosoever, male or female, does a wholesome deed, having faith, We shall assuredly give them to live a goodly life. (Qur'ān 16:97).

> I [God] am All-forgiving to him who repents, has faith, does wholesome deeds, and follows guidance (Qur'ān 20:82).

Though a certain opposition and strife is inherent to existence, the world remains in relative equilibrium so long as human beings attempt to carry out their duties as God's vicegerents upon the earth by performing wholesome

The Theological Roots of Peace and War   155

works. These duties are summarized by the term *islām*, which means literaly "submission", that is, to the Will of God, or to His command. Since there are two commands, there are two kinds of submission: On the one hand all things submit to the engendering command. In other words, all things in the universe are "submitters" or "Muslims" through their created natures. That is why everything in the heavens and the earth sings God's praises. On the other hand only those human beings who submit themselves to the prescriptive command can be called "Muslims" in the more specific sense of having submitted their own wills to God's Will. (The Qur'ān does not limit this term to the followers of Islam, since for example, it applies it to Abraham and the apostles of Jesus [3:67, 5:111].)

The word *islām* derives from the same root as *salām*, "peace". The literal sense of the term is to become free or safe from something, or to gain peace in respect to it. The implication is that through submitting one's will to God's Will, one gains safety from error, deviation, and corruption. One is integrated into the Divine Unity and hence put into harmony with the opposing yet complementary properties of the Divine Names. One has faith and performs wholesome works, which provide a remedy for the corruption that has taken place in the land and the sea at the hands of those human beings who have not carried the Trust. Hence submission to God brings about peace in the sense of *salām* and *ṣulḥ* : In the first sense, one gains the Peace of God, and in the second one gains a wholesome and peaceful relationship with all His creatures, a relationship through which the created world is put into correct equilibrium with its Divine Source.

* * *

In order to understand the Islamic idea of peace (*ṣulḥ*) in the world, we need a clear conception of the preliminary peace (*salām*) which must be established between human beings and God. In the Qur'ānic view, peace with God necessitates "war" against all tendencies that tend to dispersion and disequilibrium. It demands a movement towards the Center - Mercy and Peace - and an active opposition against all forces that draw away the Center. In other words, to be at peace with God is to be at war with error and caprice, which are the tendencies within ourselves which try to draw us away from Him.

But "peace" is not necessarily good, since itself the word merely define a relationship among various forces. We have to ask about the nature of those forces. Peace cannot be good if it means harmony and equilibrium with dispersion, whether of the inward kind, which the Qur'ān calls "caprice," or the outward kind, which it calls "this world" (*al-dunyā*). "Satan" personifies both the inward and the outward dispersive movements, since he works in the world as well as in ourselves.

Nor is "war" necessarily good, since in fact most people fight not against dispersive tendencies but along with them. In other words, most people follow the natural movement of "thisworld", the "path of least resistance" that draws them away from the Centre. The Qur'ān refers to them as "those who have gone astray" (*al-ḍāllūn*) if not "those toward whom God is Wrathful" (*al-maghḍūbūn ʿalayhim*), whom it also calls God's "enemies" (aʿdaʾ).

It is important to note that "peace with this world" is not the same as "peace with creation". In fact, the two are diametrically opposed. To live in peace with this world (*al-dunyā*) is to be in harmony with those tendencies in the created world which take human beings away from God, while to live in peace with creation (*al-khaq*) is to act as God's vicegerent on the basis of having been integrated into the Divine Unity and Peace; it is to contribute towards bringing all creatures under the sway of equilibrium and harmony.

In order to give a bare introduction to some of the basic Qur'ānic ideas concerning peace and war, we will outline here two kinds of peace and two kind of war:

1. Peace with God.
2. Peace with caprice and this world.
3. War for God's sake.
4. War against God.

1. Peace with God. Strictly speaking, peace belongs to God alone. But nearness to God, however envisaged, results in harmony with Him and therefore relative peace. Hence the Qur'ān refers to Paradise as the Abode of Peace (6:127, 10:25). The Muslim greeting, "Peace be upon you", is the formula of welcome by which the angles accept the blessed into Paradise, and there the blessed exchange it among themeselves (Qur'ān: 7:46, 10:10, 13:24, 14:23, etc.). This may be interpreted to mean, "May you and your religion be free from defects and imperfections"; or, more simply, "May Peace, God, be with you." To achieve peace in this world and the next, people must follow God's guidance, which will take them back to the luminous Centre, far from the shadows of dispersion and error.

> There has come to you from God a Light and a Book Manifest, whereby God guides whosoever follows His good pleasure in the

ways of Peace; He brings them forth from the shadows into the Light by His leave; and He guides them to a Straight Path,. (Qur'a–n 5:16).

The Straight Path is the path of Islam, that is, submission to God's Will and obedience to His prescriptive command.

Obey God, and obey the Messenger; ... if you obey the Messenger, you will be guided. (Qur'ān 24:54)

Whoso obeys God and His Messenger, He will admit him into gardens underneath which rivers flow, therein dwelling forever; that is the mighty triumph. (Qur'ān 4:13)

The faithful ... obey God and His Messenger. Those, upon them God will have Mercy. (Qur'ān 9:71)

God ever guides those who have faith to a Straight Path (Qur'ān 22:54)

Those who have been guided to God and who have reached peace with Him are called His "friends". "Surely God's friends, no fear shall be upon them, neither shall they sorrow" (Qur'ān 10:62). Their hearts are "at rest" with God, or more specifically, with His "remembrance" (*dhikr*).

God wrought this not, save as good tidings, and that your hearts might be at rest; victory comes only from God. (Qur'ān 8:10)

In God's remembrance are at rest the hearts of those who have faith and do wholesome deeds. (Qur'ān 13:28)

O soul at rest with God, return to thy Lord, well-pleased, well pleasing! (Qur'ān 89:28)

When God is pleased with His servants, they also are pleased with Him; this is a "mighty triumph" (Qur'ān 5:119, 9:100, 58:22).

2. Peace with caprice and this world. If a person is at peace with this lower world, he or she is one of the unbelievers, who have made their own caprice into a god. Paradise is the Abode of Peace, while life in this world is "naught but a sport and a diversion; surely the Last Abode is better for those who are [4]godfearing" (6:32). One cannot take the rectification of this world's situation as one's goal, since this world in itself, considered independently of the God who gives it subsistence, has no stability or permanence.

> The likeness of this life is as water that We send down out of
> heaven; the plants of the earth, whereof men and cattle eat,
> mingle with it, till, when the earth has taken on its glitter and has
> decked itself fair, and its inhabitants think they have power over
> it, our command comes upon it by night or day, and We make it
> stubble, as though yesterday it flourished not. (Qur'ān 10:24)

The unbelievers see nothing but this world and their own egocentric desires;
they are heedless of God (*ghafala*), never remembering Him. The faithful
are at rest with Him and pleased with Him, while the unbelievers are pleased
with this world:

> Surely those who look not to encounter Us and are well-pleased
> with the present life and are at rest in it, and those who are
> heedless of Our signs, those, their refuge is the Fire. (Qur'ān
> 10:7)

The "submission" of such people is to their own lower selves: "The
evildoers follow their own caprices, without knowledge ... They have no
helpers" (Qur'ān 30:29).

3. War for God's sake. "peace with God" is a goal that the faithful must
strive to reach, not their actual situation. It cannot be actualized if they take
a passive stance toward existence, that is, if they accept their own situation
as good and desirable. Peace can only come from obedience toward God
and submission to His command. Hence it demands great activity. Human
beings must apply God's commands and prohibitions to every dimension of
life. The basic practice that Islam requires of all its followers are known as
the Five Pillars: the attestation of Divine Unity (*shahāda*), the daily prayers,
paying the alms tax, fasting during the month of Ramadan, and making the
pilgrimage to Makka. But these and the other rules and regulations set
down in the Shari'ah or Divine Law are only the outward shell of Islam; the
full enactment of Islam's requirements demands also the perfection of virtue
(*iḥsan*) through the actualization of the human theomorphic nature (*ta'alluh*).
In other words, to be "Muslims" in the true and full sense, people must
dedicate themselves to God on every level of their existence; this is the only
way that *tawhid* or the "profession of God's Unity" can be realized. God's
Oneness demands that human beings conform to His nature not only in their
deeds and activities but also in their hearts, minds, and souls. People must
strive to gain nearness to God not only through wholesome works, which
eliminate corruption and establish peace in the outside world, but also
through the perfection of the inside world of their own souls.

One Qur'ānic term that describes human efforts to realize *tawhid* on all
levels is *jihad*, which means literally "to struggle, to strive". This term

commonly refers to the most outward and obvious kind of struggle, the war against the unbelievers on the field of battle. In this sense it has often been translated as "holy war", an expression that is unsatisfactory for a number of reasons, not least being the fact that it conjures up a stereotyped picture in the minds of most Westerners.[6] The term *jihad* has been used in Islamic history for practically any war fought by a Muslim king, whatever the motives for engaging in the war might have been. To suggest that these motives have always been considred "holy" is to ignore the fact that in many cases religious authorities did not consider these wars valid, since Islamic law lays down stringent rules that must be followed before *jihad* can be undertaken; moreover kings rarely consulted with those religious authorities who might put the objective standards of the Law before the subjective interests of the kingdom. "Holy war" can be a satisfactory translation of *jihad* only in the deepest and most inward sense of the term, that is, the struggle against God's enemies within the soul in the effort to attain human perfection and sanctity. In the present context we will translate the term in its literal sense as "struggle" in order to bring out its broad implications.

The Qur'ān employs the word *jihad* and its derivatives thirty-five times, often with obvious reference to specific historical situations and the outward fight (*qital*) against the unbelievers who were opposed to the early Muslim community. But several verses have a clear significance transcending specific events, e.g., "Struggle for God as is His due" (22:78). In explaining the meaning of this verse the commentators distinguish between the outward and inward struggles and cite the saying of the Prophet when he came back from the Battle of Tabuk in 631, one year before his death: "I have returned from the Lesser Struggle to the Greater Struggle", that is, from the struggle against the unbelievers to the struggle against caprice and the lower soul. The same sources cite a saying 'Ali, the Prophet's son-in-law, according to which struggle is of three kinds: with the hand (i.e., the sword), the tongue (by "commanding good and forbidding evil"; cf. Qur'ān 3:110, 9:71, etc.) and the heart (by remembering God).[7] Most authorities agree that the inward and greater struggle takes precedence over the outward and lesser struggle, since the inward struggle is incument upon the faithful at all times and in all places, while the outward struggle depends upon circumstances; generations or centuries may pass before the authorities of the Law are able to agree on an instance in which the outward struggle may be fought.

The Law or Shari'ah deals only with the domain of action, not with intentions and spirituality, which are the domain of the inward struggle. Those authorities who specialized in the inward and spiritual domain usually described the greater struggle in terms of the transformation of the soul to be achieved through spiritual practice, referring to it by the term mujahada, which is a different form of the term jihad.[8] Hence the distinction between the outward and inward kinds of struggle came to be reflected in these two forms of a single word: the authorities who speak about one or the other refer to the same Qur'ānic verses and prophetic sayings to prove their points. Thus, for example, the great al-Ghazali (d. 1111) hardly mentions *jihad* in his four volume masterpiece *Ihya' 'ulum al-din* except to show that the inward struggle is more fundamental to the religious life than the outward struggle; but he refers to *mujahada* in detail. [9]

In short, the way to God is to struggle against oneself and against those who are opposed to Him.

> Obey not the unbelievers, but struggle against them mightily (Qur'ān 25:52).

> Whosoever struggles, struggles only for his own soul; surely God is independent of all the worlds (Qur'ān 29:6).

Like "struggle", the word "fight" is used frequently in the Qur'ān and is interpreted in both an outward and inward sense.

"So let them who sell the present life for the next world fight in the way of God ... Those who have faith fight in the way of God, and the unbelievers fight in the idols' way. Fight you therefore against the friends of Satan" (4:74-76).

The aim of the inward warfare is to attain peace with God, while the aim of the outward warfare is to rectify the corruption worked in the earth by those who have failed to live up to their responsibilities as God's vicegerents. Only then can relative peace and harmony be established among the contending forces of this world. The Qur'ān makes this point in retelling the story of David and Goliath:

"And they routed them, by the leave of God. David slew Goliath and God gave him the kingship and Wisdom, and He taught him such as He willed. Had God not driven back the people, some by means of others, the earth had surely been corrupted; but God is bounteous unto all the worlds" (2:251; cf. 5:33).

The faithful are at peace with God, and with the friends of God, but at war with His enemies:

> Muhammad is the Messenger of God, and those who are with him are hard against the unbelievers, merciful to one another (Qur'ān 48:29).

> Oh you who have faith, whosoever of you turns from his religion, God will assuredly bring a people whom He loves and who love Him, humble towards the faithful, disdainful toward

the unbelievers, men who struggle in the way of God, not fearing the reproach of any reproacher (Qur'ān 5:54).

4. War against God. War against God, like struggling in God's path, may be outward or inward. The outward war takes place with the sword, the inward with the heart. In both cases those who fight this war have been overcome by unbelief (*kufr* - literally, "Ingratitude") and disobedience toward God's prescriptive command. The unbelievers consider God their enemy (2:98, 8:60, 9:114), and their recompense is the Fire (41:28). The faithful struggle in the path of God, while the unbelievers strive to prevent others from entering this path. "Surely those who disbelieve and bar from the way of God have gone astray into far error" (4:167; cf. 9:34, 11:19, 16:88, etc. They have taken up the work of Satan, who "desires to precipitate enmity and hatred among you ... and to bar you from the remembrance of God and from prayer" (5:91).

* * *

This first survey of Qur'ānic imagery could be extended indefinitely by further quotations from the Qur'ān, the Hadith, and Islamic literature in general. But our conclusion would be the same: Islam considers peace in God as the goal of human life, while war against His enemies - in particular against the caprice of the human soul - is the only way to achieve this peace. But people cannot have peace at the present moment as long as they remain distant from God. To be with Him - and thus to become fully human - they have to struggle against everything hat turns them away from their duties as His vicegerents. Only the greatest human beings - the prophets and those men and women who have sttained to God's good pleasure and proximity already in this life - have attained peace with God, their hearts being "at rest" with Him. But this inward peace does not contradict outward effort and strife, as the life of the Prophet Muhammad proves. Long after he had won the inward and greater struggle, he had to continue with the lesser struggle. Moreover, he never for a moment gave up the outward forms of the greater struggle. e.g., prayer, fasting, and other duties incumbent upon all Muslims. That is why the Muslim authorities point out that *jihad/mujahada* remains the lot of human beings as long as they continue to exist within the domain where God has prescribed (*taklif*) religious duties for them, that is, as long as they live in this world. Full and total peace will not be achieved until they reach the Abode of Peace, which cannot be found on this plane of existence.

War and strife accompany human beings in the present world because they and all created things are evanescent and perishing. The changing nature of all creatures brings about opposition and conflict. To make the most of this conflict people must put themselves in harmony with Peace, the Divine Reality. In function of Peace they can struggle to bring relative harmony into the world by performing wholesome works and thereby eliminating "corruption". As long as people want to remain human, they are forced to engage in the greater and inward struggle. If they do not carry the Trust, they will enter into the ranks of the ungrateful and irresponsible infidels, and "their refuge will be the Fire".

That the world is full of war and strife is a sign of God's Mercy, which always precedes His Wrath. War and conflict remind human beings that God alone is Peace. If people want peace, they must struggle in the way of God, not in the way of their own desires, no matter how grand may be their vision of a "better society" or a "happier world". They cannot escape turmoil by seeking to overcome it on its own level; the more they try to do so, the more it will engulf them. The history of the world during the past 200 years is all the proof this statement needs.

Islam offers no simple method of establishing peace on earth; the causes of the enormous social disequilibriums that face us throughout the world are built into the presuppositions upon which modern culture and contemporary life-styles are based. To solve the "problem of Islam" that faces us in the Middle East today, we have to solve the "problem of the human race" that faces us wherever we look, especially inside our own hearts. We cannot achieve real peace in the Middle East or anywhere else until we find it in oureselves.

Notes :

1. For a recent attempt to sort out opinion relating to the political domain. cf. R. Peters. *Islam and Colonialism: The Doctrine of Jihad in Modern History.* The Hague: Mouton, 1979.

2. This fact is no way negates human responsibility for evil, as most Muslim theologians have taken pains to demonstrate Cf.. for example, the doctrine of *kasb* according to the Ash'aries (H.A. Wolfson, *The Philosophy of the Kalam*, Cambridge and London: Harvard University Press, 1976, pp. 663-716).

3. Jinn are beings made of fire, while angels are made of light and human beings are made of clay. Jinn are semi-spiritual and semi-corporeal, just as fire neither pure light nor pure clay. They were given free will by God and therefore can disobey His commands like mankind. Iblis or Satan was one of the jinn, which explains why he was able to disobey God. But the angels cannot disobey Him,

The Theological Roots of Peace and War 163

since they always "act as He commands" (Qur'an 21:27).

In the final analysis Satan's rebellion and human disobedience also play a positive role in the divine plan, but most Muslim authorities have not considered it opportune to emphasize this fact, since the unbelievers cannot avoid the negative consequences of God's Wrath.

In the Islamic view, this is the root of the "ecological crisis." See Chittick, " 'God Surrounds All Things': An Islamic Perspective on the Environment," The World and I, I/6, June 1986, pp. 671-678.

On *jihad* cf. M. Khaddury, *The Islamic Conception of Justice*, Baltimore and London: The Johns Hopkins University Press, 1984, chapter 7; and Peters, *Islam and Colonialism*. Peters' summary of Western stereotype (pp. 4-5) is worth quoting: "The Islamic doctrine of jihad has always appealed to Western imagination. The image of the dreadful Turk, clad in a long robe and brandishing his scimitar, ready to slaughter any infidel that might come his way and would refuse to be converted to the religion of Mahomet, has been a stereotype in Western literture for a long time. Nowadays this image has been replaced by that of the Arab 'terrorist' in battledress, armed with a Kalashnikov gun and prepared to murder in cold blood innocent Jewish and Christian women and children. The assumption underlying these stereotypes is that Moslems, often loosely called Arabs, are innately bloodthirsty and inimical towards persons of a different persuasion, and that owing to their religion, which allegedly preaches intolerance, fanaticism and continuous warfare against unbelievers. This view of Islam and Moslems, which developed in the Middle Ages, acquired new life and vigour in the era of European imperialism. Moslems were depicted as backward, fanatic and bellicose, in order to justify colonial expansion with the argument that it served the spread of civilization, which the French called *mission civilisatrice*. At the same time, this offered a convenient pretext for use of force against the indigenous population, for behind the outward appearance of submissiveness of the colonized Moslems, the colonizers saw the continuous danger of rebelliousness lurking, nourished by the idea of jihad and waiting for an opportunity to manifest itself."

Cf. Maybudi, *Kashf al-asrār*, ed. A. A. Ḥikmat. Tehran, VI. p. 405; III, p. 213; also Baydāwi, *Tafsir*, on Qur'an 22:78.

Both *jihād* and *mujāhada* are *maṣdars* or verbal nouns representing the third form of the Arabic verb. Either may be used to refer to the "struggle" that the Qur'an usually mentions in verbal form.

E.g. *Ihya' 'ulūm al-dīn*. Cairo, 1309/1939, III, pp. 42, 57.

[11]

THE POLITICS OF MILITANT ISLAMIC MOVEMENTS IN THE MIDDLE EAST
Nazih N. M. Ayubi

Islam means different things to different people, and this applies to politics as it applies to other areas of social life.[1] To some, Islam may serve as a means for legitimizing and preserving the status quo, while for others it may provide a vehicle for protest or even a spearhead for revolution.

The Political Roles of Islam

Both trends are inherent in the Muslim political tradition. On the one hand, much of Islamic political philosophy has been related to a doctrine of civil obedience. The caliph performed some religious duties but was basically no more than a political figurehead, and thus a de facto separation between religion and state developed. The ulama (religious scholars) often taught that anyone in effective possession of political power had to be obeyed, that "an unjust ruler is better than civil strife". This was particularly true of the mainstream Sunni tradition.

Among the most obvious contemporary examples of religion as a vehicle for legitimization are Saudi Arabia and Egypt. In Saudi Arabia, Islam masks and counterbalances the regime's excessive military and cultural dependence on the West, as well as the hedonistic and indulgent pursuits of some sectors of the elite. Islam was also used as a "mask" by the late President Anwar Sadat of Egypt to disguise the rather offensive manifestations of the "open door" economic policy and the growing corruption that surrounded it. Sadat also managed to get a fatwa (religio-legal counsel) from the ulama to justify the Egypt-Israel peace treaty.

Rulers may sometimes be successful in trying to use religion for their own political purposes, but they may also be forced to swallow their own poison. The Saudis, for example, have always used religion to justify their own policies and to resist the spread of radical influences, especially from Egypt. They have not only financed Islamic organizations in Egypt but have also provided refuge for Islamic militants fleeing from this country. During the time of Nasser, this was particularly true, but such trends continued. In 1977 certain members of the Egyptian neo-fundamentalist group al-Takfir w'al-Hijra (to be analyzed below) escaped to Saudi Arabia after killing a former minister. The Saudis, in accordance with their previous norm, refused to return them to Egypt. Two years later, some members of Takfir were reported to have been among those who participated, in the name of Islam, in the violent takeover of the Most Sacred Mosque at Mecca.[2]

In Egypt, the story is more intricate. After Sadat came to power, he perceived Nasserists and leftists as being his real political enemies, and to counterbalance them, he released all members of al-Ikhwan al-Muslimun (the Muslim Brothers, a fundamentalist organization first formed in 1929) who were still in detention, permitted their publications to circulate, and discreetly gave all

1. See the valuable article by Michael C. Hudson, "Islam and Political Development", in John L. Esposito (ed.), Islam and Development: Religion and Sociopolitical Change (Syracuse: Syracuse University Press, 1980), esp. pp. 13-24.
2. Cf. Al-Siyasa, 27 November 1979; Al-Nahar, 28 November 1979; Al-Safir, 28 November 1979.

0022-197x/82/1314-0001$01.50/0

Journal of International Affairs

manner of encouragement to what was then called "the Islamic trend". Partly as a result of this, Islamic groups were eventually to become enormously powerful and to get completely out of hand, turning against Sadat himself. It was members of one of these groups (*al-Jihad* organization) who eventually assassinated him.

Just as religion can be utilized as a tool for preserving the status quo, it can also work as a catalyst for change. Islam has always maintained within it a certain tradition of revolt. The socio-political unrest of the first century of Islam (especially following the death of the Prophet Mohammed in A.D. 632, led, among other things, to the emergence of the *Shi'a* sect. This might have been partly motivated by the need among non-Arabic speaking groups, especially the Persians, for a measure of equality and self-realization vis-à-vis the dominant Arabs. In any event, Shiism was soon to attract the sympathy of the underprivileged classes. The Shiites eventually developed a rather elaborate clerical hierarchy and their *ulama* collaborated with those in political power, especially as Shiism became the state religion of Persia in the 16th century. Nevertheless, Shiism continued to host a rich literature on the justification of revolt against unfair and corrupt rulers, a heritage that Ayatollah Khomeini and his colleagues could invoke and draw upon for the purposes of the 1978-79 Iranian revolution; this revolution started as a social revolution of the professional middle class, the Bazaari merchants, and the urban lumpen proletariat, but is increasingly being turned into a clergy-led religio-nationalistic revolution.[3]

Quite a few militant Islamic groups, or neo-fundamentalist protest movements have made their presence felt in many Middle Eastern countries recently. Although such movements are not strong enough to seize political power in any of these countries at the present time, they are certainly capable of challenging and destabilizing existing governments. In both Saudi Arabia and Egypt they have come into violent confrontation with the ruling authorities. Furthermore, a "surprise" can never be ruled out; for who, after all, expected five years ago that Iran could become an Islamic republic? The purpose of the rest of this essay will be to analyze some of the main characteristics of both the "ideology" and the membership of such militant Islamic groups, and to try to understand from within the theological controversies, the political significance of such movements.

Islamic Protest Groups.

To a large extent the flourishing of militant Islamic groups is an indication of the existence of a disillusioned youth revolt in many countries of the Middle East. In the fifties and sixties, the hopes of people in the Arab world hinged upon socialism and pan-Arabism. When these failed there was a strong "return to Islam", but this time with a right-wing orientation. Outside the Arab world, neither Kemalism in Turkey, nor the "White Revolution" in Iran appear to have succeeded as a developmental model. Islamic revival is therefore at least partly a function of the eclipse of the Arab-nationalist movement, and of other developmental experiments in the Middle East. In the uncertainty created by the demise of such experiments, it was

---

3. On Shiism and politics in Iran see in particular: Shahrough Akhavi, *Religion and Politics in Contemporary Iran* (Albany: SUNY Press, 1980); Nikki R. Keddie, *Roots of Revolution: An Interpretive History of Modern Iran* (New Haven: Yale University Press, 1981).

natural to seek refuge in older and more familiar concepts: for the Egyptians, for instance, it is an identity based on Egyptian patriotism and religion (with revival among both Muslims and Christians); to Saudi Arabians, an identity based on Arab ethnicism and Islamic guardianship.

In theological terms, the main intellectual inspiration for most neo-fundamentalist movements, both in Saudi Arabia and Egypt, comes from the Islamic thinker, Ibn Taimiya (1263-1338) who lived in Syria during the eclipse of the Abbasid dynasty. In his book *Al-Siyasa al-Shar'iyya* [Politics According to Religious Law], and in other books, he gives strong justifications for disobeying corrupt rulers. Ibn Taimiya's teachings have always had an impact on puritanical, militant movements that expressed a kind of Islam more oriented towards the past. Among his disciples, in one way or another, were Mohammed ibn Abd al-Wahhab in Arabia in the 19th century, and to some extent Rashid Rida, the Syrian Islamic thinker of conservative inclination, who lived in Egypt during the earlier part of this century.[4]

Many of the Egyptian militant Islamic groups were also influenced by two contemporary Islamic thinkers: the Pakistani Abu al-Ala al-Mawdudi, and the Egyptian Sayyid Qutb. The main thrust of the ideas of these thinkers is an adherence to the principle of "God's absolute rulership" *(al-hakimiyya l'illah)* and a belief in the total pagan ignorance *(jahiliyya)* of all contemporary governments because of their failure to apply this principle and to enforce the application of *shari'a* (religious law). The solution, say the neo-fundamentalists, is to go back to the primary sources of *shari'a*: the Koran, and the *Sunna* (sayings and traditions of the Prophet), discarding *fiqh* (jurisprudence) which has

been "polluted" with human and political vested interests over time.

As in Protestantism, the importance of discarding the church's teachings and "going back to the sources" is the egalitarian and participatory ethos that makes everybody capable of understanding and interpreting the word of God without barriers based on clerical ranks or theological education. The idea is to exclude the *ulama* who have, for all intents and purposes become part of the ruling establishment and therefore, from the neo-fundamentalists' point of view, unable to see things properly. Traditionally, the *ulama* were in charge of an important source of the *shari'a*: *ijma'* (consensus of the learned). This permitted a fair amount of improvisation and innovation in interpreting religion. Neo-fundamentalists reject such philosophical and logical "tricks", and with them the main source of the *ulama's* influence. As they confront the scholars of the thousand-year-old Al-Azhar mosque-university, for example, they claim that nobody has a monopoly over interpretation, that all Muslims are *mujtahid's* (those who apply *ijtihad* — independent interpretation), and that indeed they have overwhelming arguments that are unknown to the *ulama* and to which these would have no reply.[5]

In order to understand further the characteristics and activities of such neo-fundamentalist groups, it is useful at this point to look more closely at the cases of two countries where these groups have been involved in

---

4. Cf. Malcolm H. Kerr, *Islamic Reform* (Berkeley and Los Angeles: University of California Press, 1966), Chapters 5 and 6.
5. Discussions between religious scholars and Islamic neo-fundamentalists, reported in *Al-Liwa' al-Islami*, no. 19, 3 June 1982, and no. 20, 10 June 1982.

Journal of International Affairs

certain violent political acts against the authorities in recent years: namely, Saudi Arabia and Egypt.

Saudi Arabia's Neo-Fundamentalists and the Mecca Takeover, 1979

The armed takeover in November 1979 of the Most Sacred Mosque at Meccca by a militant Islamic group took many by surprise, and proved beyond doubt that even "very Islamic" Saudi Arabia cannot be considered immune to an "Islamic resurgence".

In Saudi Arabia religion is a major instrument for social control and political legitimacy. This is achieved through institutions such as the *shar'i* (religious) courts, the Organization for the Enforcement of Good and the Prevention of Evil (established in 1929), and the moral police (*mutawwi'*) system.[6] Furthermore, the Saudi royal family has historically allied itself with the *Wahhabi* movement which is a puritanical Sunni movement that follows to a large extent the strict *Hanbali* school of Sunni jurisprudence. It has also relied significantly on the support of the prestigious *ulama* body inside the country.

But in the same way in which the rulers use Islam to legitimize their rule, several opposition movements in Saudi Arabia also tend to express themselves in religious terms. The "Islamic Revolution Organization" emerged after the riots in the eastern region in 1979. Its adherents believe in creating an Islamic republic in Arabia based on popular participation and full independence in foreign policy. There is also, apparently, a radical branch of the Muslim Brothers *(al-Ikhwan al-Muslimun)*, formed initially in Egypt in the twenties, whose Saudi members believe that *salafi* Islam is being utilized in Arabia today to mask corruption and oppression.

The existence of such Islamic groupings indicates

that Saudi Arabia also seems to be witnessing certain aspects of the general phenomenon of political revival of religion that now involves most parts of the Middle East. Many observers wondered why there should be an "Islamic revival" in a country that is supposed to be so strictly Islamic. But such movements are more often movements of socio-political protest, in spite of their religious appearance, and they are often related to socio-economic contradictions, cultural alienation, and to generation differences. The people who launched the takeover were members of puritanical movement who, in invoking strict "fundamentalist" teachings, were actually expressing social criticism of, and political protest against, what they regarded as the false and opportunistic utilization of Islam to hide corruption, decadence, and oppression, as well as subservience to the "foreigner".

There is little doubt that the *Ikwhan* movement (which should not be confused with the Muslim Brothers of Egypt) was behind the dramatic Mecca events. This movement emerged in the second decade of this century among the deprived tribes of the Najd region of Arabia, partly in an attempt to revive the simplicity and austerity of the *Wahhabi* call. The House of Saud allied itself with the movement but conflicts, especially in their tribal dimension, were never completely resolved until the *Ikhwan* were defeated by Ibn Saud in 1929-30.

The group of three to five hundred rebels that took over the Mecca mosque for a number of days in November 1979 was an offshoot of the *Ikhwan* movement. Ideologically they may be seen as representing "a position of rejection" of the cultural challenges of the twentieth century, under the pretext that "Islamic

6. Compare James P. Piscatori, "The roles of Islam in Saudi Arabia's Political Development" in James Esposito, (ed.), op. cit., pp. 123-138.

society is in no need of change". It is a position that "almost takes one back to the *Wahhabi* movement, and which reflects a prevalent perception within Saudi Arabia: renewal is a misleading word that expresses a trick of the Devil—and why shouldn't the twentieth century acclimatize itself to Islam?"[7] In theological details, however, the Mecca takeover group shares a great deal with the *Takfir* group of Egypt, especially in the concept of direct reliance on the Koran and the *Sunna*. They also cast aside public employment and normal education, criticize the existing religious establishment, and call for retreat from public life in order to prepare for the great struggle.[8] As far as political issues are concerned, those who took over the Most Sacred Mosque are reported to have condemned financial and social corruption, political oppression, and subservience to the United States of America. They also asked for the election of a "commander of the faithful" and for strict moral codes.[9]

Although the leader of the movement was definitely Juhaiman Saif al-Utaiba, other reports maintain that the mosque-takers also announced the arrival of the long-awaited *mahdi* (the rightly-guided one) in the person of Mohammed Abdallah al-Qahtani; but even if he existed, he must have been secondary to Juhaiman. Juhaiman was a forty-three year-old Najdi who had studied for four years at the Mecca Islamic University and who had worked with the National Guard for some eighteen years before resigning to dedicate the last six years of his life to religious activism. Most of his followers were students or graduates in their twenties or thirties, and the majority came from the Islamic University of Madina (established in 1960), and from other universities. They used to meet with him in mosques and houses in Mecca, Madina, and other cities, to study and discuss, among other things, the *rasa'il* (mono-

graphs) of his own writings or of his interpretations of Ibn Taimiya that he used to publish. The role of the Islamic university at Madina also highlights the rather "pan-Islamic" nature of the movement, not only in terms of the similarity of a number of its ideas to those of neo-fundamentalist groups in other countries—like Egypt—as we have seen, but also in terms of the multinational membership of the Mecca group. Among the sixty-three who were eventually executed for their part in the takeover plot were one Iraqi, one Sudanese, three Kuwaitis, seven Yemenis, and most remarkably, ten Egyptians.

In short, therefore, participants in the Mecca takeover can be described as being young, urban, and educated. In addition, there is also evidence that the rewards of the oil boom have not been spread evenly among the various tribes and regions.[10] Of the forty-one Saudi citizens who were executed in January 1980, seventy percent were from the relatively underprivileged Najd region, and twenty-five percent were from the less-than-friendly Utaiba tribe alone.[11]

As was to be expected, the Mecca takeover was put down in the name of Islam. The rebels were classified as *kharijite* deviants, and a *fatwa* was obtained from the *ulama* justifying the storming of the Mecca sanctuary in their pursuit.

7.   Hamid Rabi' *Al-Islam w'al-quwa al-dawiyya* [Islam and International Forces], (Cairo: Al-Mawqif al-Arabi, 1981). pp. 19-24.
8.   The main detailed source on the Mecca events is the clandestine book: Abu-Dhurr (pseud.), *Thawra fi rihab makka* [Revolution in the Precinct of Mecca], (Dar Sawt al-Tali'a, 1980). A summary of Juhaiman's monograph is given on pp. 265-273.
9.   *Le Monde*, 1, 2, and 3 December 1979.
10.   Because of the sensitivity of the tribal issue the Saudi authorities denied that the dissident organization had had any tribal or even familial dimension. Cf. *Al-Riyad*, 9 December 1979.
11.   Abu-Dhurr, op. cit., p. 248ff. et passim.

Journal of International Affairs

The Mecca events are also significant in a wider sense. They revived the controversy as to the Islamic legitimacy of the monarchical form of government (since many fundamentalists believe that Islam does not sanction the rule of kings). These events highlighted the problems of "corruption on earth", magnified in the Saudi case by the impact of the oil bonanza.

This phenomenon combined with the nature of the existing socio-political system has led to widening disparities among the various social classes, among the religiously educated, the secularly educated, and the illiterates, and also between the urban centers on the one hand and the Bedouin and the rural centers on the other.[12] Residents of the latter areas have had an increasingly uncomfortable time in recent years as drought has crept into most of the desert and as the government's policies have become more biased towards the urban centers to the detriment of the desert and country dwellers. If religion is to be used again as a vehicle for protest and a catalyst for revolt in Saudi Arabia, it is most likely to be such "relatively deprived" groups who will resort to its use.

Having thus considered the case of Saudi Arabia, let us now turn to an examination of the Egyptian case.

Egypt's Neo-Fundamentalists and the Assassination of Sadat, 1981

The assassination in October 1981 of President Anwar Sadat by members of a militant Islamic group illustrated the importance of these groups in present-day Egypt. Indeed, many believe that had these groups not "pre-empted themselves" by the assassination of Sadat, a more serious Islamic revolution, not unlike the Iranian one in many respects, might well have taken place in Egypt sooner or later. These secretive "Islamic groups" had, in fact, become so influential that, in addi-

tion to their strongholds in university campuses, they had managed to penetrate some of the legal "Muslim societies",[13] and to secure the support of some older religious preachers.

The problem was that Sadat had gone too far in his attempts to use the "religious weapon" for his own political purposes, failing to realize that the Islamic movement had acquired an independent life and logic of its own. Religious associations were originally encouraged by the government in the early seventies in an attempt to counterbalance the Nasserist and socialist trends, and were supported organizationally and financially by the authorities.[14] By 1977, the militant Islamic groups felt strong enough to go their own way, first by persecuting Christian students, then by harassing secularist faculty, and finally by challenging the government authorities directly. The social outcome of the economic policies of Sadat's regime, especially the so-called "open door" policy, *infitah*, helped only to fuel the frustration and anger of the religious youth.[15]

In the meantime, Sadat continued to put on his religious face, in which the dedicated did not believe. As

12. For further details see: Nazih Ayubi, "Vulnerability of the Rich: The Political Economy of Defense and Development in Saudi Arabia and the Gulf", *The Gulf Project*, Center for Strategic and International Studies, Georgetown University, Washington D.C., June 1982, and references cited.

13. In Arabic the first type is known as *jama'at islamiyya* while the second is known as *jam'iyyat islamiyya*.

14. See for example the detailed testimonies by important academic officials reported in *Sabah al-Khair*, no. 1350, 19 November 1981.

15. See on this policy: Nazih Ayubi, "Implementation Capability and Political Feasibility of the Open Door Policy in Egypt" in Malcolm H. Kerr and El Sayed Yassin (eds.), *Rich and Poor States in the Middle East* (Boulder: Westview Press, 1982). For an Islamic critique of this policy see: A. 'Abd al-Latif, "Al-Infitah al-istihlaki w'al-akhlaq" [Ethics and the Consumerist 'Open Door'], *Al-Da'wa* no. 26. July 1978, pp. 30-31.

the Islamic thinker of Egypt, Hasan Hanafi, wrote sarcastically:

> President Sadat has been given the title 'the Believer-President'. He is always called by his first name, Muhammad. He is shown in the mass media in his white *jallabiya*, going to the mosque or coming out of it, with a rosary in one hand, Moses' stick in the other, and with a prayer mark on his forehead . . . He murmurs in prayer, closes his eyes and shows signs of humility and devotion. He begins his speeches with 'In the Name of God', and ends them with Qur'anic verses signifying modesty and asking for forgiveness.[16]

Apparently believing that a cultivated image of piety and religiosity would impress people, Sadat gradually lost touch with his own folk, not realizing that to the Islamic youth such affectations could not camouflage the economic crisis and the lack of jobs, the indulgent consumerism and unabashed corruption, and the uncritical subservience to the Israelis and the Americans. He seems to have realized the potential danger of the militant Islamic groups only in mid-1981. This led him in a pre-emptive move, to arrest over fifteen hundred people in September 1981 (most of whom were neo-fundamentalists, although many secularist opponents of all political shades were included), and to threaten that he would arrest five thousand more if the fundamentalists did not behave themselves. Trying in turn to pre-empt any further action by Sadat, some members of the militant Islamic groups, led by one whose brother was being detained, assassinated the president barely a month later. For a few days after the assassination of Sadat there were sporadic, and in some instances, vicious armed encounters with members of other militant Islamic groups as the government set out to arrest thousands of suspected members and sympathizers. This has calmed down to an extent since then, but nobody can be absolutely sure about future prospects.

It may be useful at this point to consider in some detail certain features of these secretive, underground Islamic movements. To start with, there are several such groups (around twenty, according to an announcement in June 1982 by the Minister of the Interior). Most of them have philosophical or organizational roots that branched off at some point or other from the older fundamentalist societies of the thirties and onwards, namely the Muslim Brothers and the more extreme Mohammed's Youth. The most widely publicized of the neo-fundamentalist groups, and the one originally suspected of Sadat's murder, is the group known by the authorities as *al-Takfir w'al-Hijra*. This title has normally been translated as "Repentance and Flight", although a more faithful translation would be something like "Excommunication and Emigration". Another important group is *al-Jihad* (struggle or crusade), some of whose members were actually convicted of, and executed for, the assassination of Sadat.

It is believed by some that such offshoots from the older fundamentalist groups date back to around 1965, when young members of the Muslim Brothers were arrested in a conspiracy against the Nasser government and were cruelly tortured. This resulted in a detention camp mutiny in May 1967 that led to the isolation of the younger and more rebellious elements. This circumstance gave them the opportunity for intensive discussion of religious and political matters, and they started from the proposition that rulers who tortured people simply because they were sincere believers in their own religion could not be real Muslims even if they were nominally so. Hence there emerged the basic

---

16. Hasan Hanafi, "The Relevance of the Islamic Alternative in Egypt", *Arab Studies Quarterly*, vol. 4, nos. 1 and 2, Spring 1982, p. 63.

concept of *"takfir"*—that is, to judge somebody as being infidel (or as I have termed it for brevity, "excommunication")—which was very much influenced by the writings of Sayyid Qutb.

The Arab states were badly defeated in the Six Day War of 1967 at the hands of the Israelis. The Muslim youth in detention saw this as an indication of the total corruption of regimes that "deserted God and so were let down by God". The solution was to work for a real Islamic society and to fight anybody who might stand in the way. Deliberations as to how this goal was to be achieved led, however, to the emergence of at least two trends; one group believed that the situation was not yet ripe for radical change. They thought in terms of stages, and called their movement "action through understanding" *(al-haraka bil mafhum)*, in the sense that they would not yet declare their total rejection of the society.[17]

The other group calling itself the "believers' community" *(jam'at al-mu'minin)*, opted for immediate action and open confrontation, using a strategy of retreat in order to reconquer (emulating the practice of the Prophet Mohammed in emigrating to Madina in A.D. 622). They therefore had to flee into the deserts or the mountains of Egypt or Arabia in preparation for a victorious comeback, under absolute and unquestioning allegiance to their *imam* (leader and guide), and following a very strict code of conduct covering all the details of life and behavior.

This group advocated the total rejection of the present order, but it also stressed the role of an almost messianic leader who would come to save his people. The movement was tightly organized in small cell-like units *(majmu'at)* with a certain degree of specialization: missionary units *(da'wa)*, survival units *(i'asha)*, as well as units for arms training, intelligence, and so on.

The organization was based mainly on personal allegiance *(bay'a)*, strong internal discipline, and severe punishment of deserters. It was also the only neofundamentalist organization to have included a relatively large number of girls (with rumors about semi-communal social relations within the group).

Although discovered by the government in 1973, *Takfir* came into open confrontation with the authorities only when its members took a former minister of religious affairs hostage, and after demanding the release of some of their jailed comrades, they eventually killed him. Following their trial, their *imam*, Shukri Mustafa, and three other leaders were hanged, and 36 of the 204 who had been tried were imprisoned. The others, as well as possibly hundreds of supporters and sympathizers, were left at large—many of them to be arrested at the time of Sadat's assassination.

The organization to which Sadat's assassins belonged was reported by the government to be *al-Jihad*, an organization that was first uncovered in 1978 when some of its members were involved in anti-Christian sabotage. Five people directly responsible for the assassination were sentenced to death and seventeen others to imprisonment in March 1982. Some three hundred other members of *al-Jihad* are still awaiting trial.

As an organization, *al-Jihad* seems to lay less emphasis on a leadership cult than *Takfir*, being more oriented towards organized action, and rather than withdrawing, it seems to be interested in infiltrating governmental and military institutions. Internally it is based on a kind

17. This information is based on the account given by a counselor-at-law who had access to the files of the *Takfir* case. CF. Mamduh Tawfiq, Al-Ijram al-siyasi [Political Criminality], (Cairo: Dar al-Jil, 1977), pp. 163-187.

of "democratic centralism". and a system of commis-sars (*mas'uli tanzim*). On the central level the organiza-tion is said to have had a governing "scholars' council", a "consultation council", and three commissions: one for armament, one for finance, and one for preaching. At a lower level there are believed to have been revolutionary committees and mosque units, as well as militias formed of student and skilled worker ele-ments and provided with significant amounts of arms and ammunition.[18]

Although not as unorthodox as *al-Takfir*, members of this organization seem also to believe that those who do not abide by the details of the *shari'a* should be considered infidels. One distinction is that, whereas *Takfir* believes in stages of struggle. *Jihad* believes in levels of struggle which decide the worth of everybody in the eyes of God. They consider that the crusading spirit is a more important factor for Islam than learning and education. for "what did the Ulama of Al-Azhar do when the troops of Napoleon were desecrating the Muslim soil of Egypt?" Such ideas were incorporated in *Al-Farida al-gha'iba* [The Absent Commandment], a monograph written by one of their leaders, 'Abd al-Salam Faraj, and heavily influenced by the teaching of Ibn Taimiya.[19]

Although there seems not to have been a dominant personalized leadership in the *Jihad* organization. Abbud al-Zumur, a young army officer, appears to have played an important organizational role. He in fact believed that the group should delay political action for two or three years until an Islamic revolution could count on the popular support that would give it the same kind of success that had been enjoyed by the Iranian revolution. Another important figure—and one of the few middle-aged leaders of the neo-fundamen-talists was a blind professor at the Theological College

in Asyut, 'Umar 'Abd al-Rahman, who is said by the authorities to have issued the group with religious *fatwas* justifying things like stealing money and per-secuting Christians.

Ideologically, such groups share two notions: belief in the non-separation of religion from politics, and in the necessity of applying *shari'a* by force. Concerning foreign affairs they tend to agree with the older funda-mentalists that Muslims are confronted by a conspiracy whose partners are the "atheists" (i.e., Communists). "Crusaders" (i.e., Christians), and "Zionists" (i.e., Jews).[20]

An interesting aspect of militant Islamic groups is that many of their members seem to have a fairly sketchy knowledge of the finer points of their religion. According to 'Umar 'Abd al-Rahman, one of the few religiously educated people associated with the militant groups. "most members of *al-Takfir w'al-Hijra* do not remember the Qur'an, do not know the rules of gram-mar, and are often mistaken even in the names of the books on which they base their arguments."[21].

An equally significant aspect of the militant Islamic groups is the composition of their personnel.[22] They

18. According to government sources as reported in *Mayu*, 2 November 1981.
19. A brief summary of this monograph was published in *Al-Ahram*, 8 December 1981.
20. Cf. e.g. Jabir Rizq. "Al-Wad' al-'arabi al-mumazzaq" [The Sundered Arab Situation], *Al-Da'wa*, no. 57, January 1981. pp. 16-17. This magazine is the official publication of the Muslim Brothers, but its publication—together with other religious magazines—was pro-hibited in September 1981.
21. Interviewed in *Al-Musawwar*, no. 3013, 9 July 1982.
22. For further details see: Nazih Ayubi. "The Political Revival of Islam: The Case of Egypt"; and Saad Eddin Ibrahim, "Anatomy of Egypt's Militant Islamic Groups: Methodological Note and Pre-liminary Findings", both in *International Journal of Middle East Studies*, vol. 12. no. 4, December 1980.

Journal of International Affairs

reflect the following characteristics: (1)their leaders tend to be in their twenties or early thirties and their members in their late teens or early twenties; (2)they are mostly university graduates or students, especially in scientific subjects; (3)they tend to come from a lower-middle class background; and (4)they tend to be urban but of rural or small town backgrounds, with a proportionately higher percentage coming from Upper rather than Lower Egypt (i.e., the Delta).

A closer look at the leadership indicates that the fourteen *amirs* (or commanders) of militant Islamic groups who were arrested in September 1981 display the following features:.

—the median age was twenty-eight years; only one of them was fifty;

—most of them were born in the countryside—especially in upper Egypt—but were active in the cities;

—they were employed as physicians, civil servants, teachers, among other principally white-collar occupations.

The age factor reveals that this is to an extent a typical youth revolt, reflecting a real generation gap and a profound mood of disillusionment and frustration. The rural-urban factor points to a development crisis and to the tensions and pressures of recent immigration into decaying cities that have serious and escalating problems. Activities of the neo-fundamentalists are indeed most obvious in the three major cities of Egypt—Cairo, Alexandria, and Asyut—where the mere size, as well as the concentration of business, leads to many practices that would be easily defined as morally corrupt by such people, and where the existence of

sizeable Christian minorities would increase the chances for sectarian competition, friction, and agitation.[23] The occupational breakdown of the leadership clearly indicates that these are not just peasant-type traditionalist movements, but basically militant movements of the petit-bourgeoisie. Among the members, the percentage of university students, particularly in the sciences, is especially high: their belonging to such groups may, therefore, reflect anxiety over career prospects, especially as unemployment of the educated has become a very serious problem under the impact of the economic liberalization policies followed in the seventies.

One can therefore suggest that although the jargon is theological and the symbolism is religious, the real worries and concerns of many members of the militant Islamic groups may indeed be social and economic, and that the real interests and pursuits may indeed be political.

Major Concerns of the "Islamic Movement"

Behind the theological controversies and religious terminology, there are basic political issues and socio-economic grievances. The neo-fundamentalist groups

23. The town of Asyut in Upper Egypt is particularly significant since the leader of *Takfir* and several of the leaders of *Jihad* came from there and since it also witnessed some of the bloodiest armed confrontations between the militant Islamic groups and the government security forces shortly after the assassination of Sadat. In this town, situated in a harsh desert environment, Christians are numerically important and economically have been in the ascendant since the mid-nineteenth century, a situation that is apt to stimulate Fascist-type reactions in times of socio-economic strain. The town also has several strong institutions of Islamic education, and furthermore, the governorate of which Asyut is the capital was entrusted by Sadat for many years to an official known for his pro-Muslim Brothers sympathies and his anti-Christian views; he is said to have given serious support to the activities of the militant Islamic groups.

represent both a quest for authenticity and a quest for participation.[24] The search for justice and equity (*'adl*) is still present but has been relegated to the background. Let us now examine the first two of these major concerns.

a. *The Quest for Authenticity.*

It is not really surprising that the Islamic revolution in Iran has turned into a movement for native self-assertion. Islam had played a similar role in the Algerian war of independence against the French. In resisting foreign dominance (political and/or cultural), Islam can provide a sense of cultural nationalism that is both defiant and self-assuring. This explains why Khomeini was joined by many secular (but nationalistically-oriented) people such as Abul-Hasan Bani-Sadr and Sadiq Qutbzadah. It also explains why Islam was so revered by many non-Muslim nationalists in the Arab world, such as Michel 'Aflaq, a leader of the Baath party in Syria, and William Makram 'Ubaid, a leader of the Wafd party in Egypt. Indeed, it explains why several Christian Arabs, such as the Egyptian Anwar Abdel-Malek and the Palestinian Edward Said, have been foremost among those who are affronted by the frequent distortion of the image of "Islam" in the West.[25]

"Political Islam", as Abdel-Malek calls it, can therefore serve as an effective weapon against the "cultural dependency" that often results from the Westernization policies which various Middle Eastern rulers pass off as developmental policies.[26] The anti-Western flavor of the Islamic revolution in Iran should thus come as no surprise. Nor should one find it strange that after decades of Kemalist cultural disfiguration in Turkey, the main *Islamic* organization in that country should be called the *National* Salvation party. The rather anti-

Western coloring of many of the slogans of the neo-fundamentalists both in Saudi Arabia and in Egypt should also be understood, in the same way, as being a reaction to various alienating policies that were enforced by the ruling elite in the name of modernization but from which the majority of the people never really benefited.

b. *The Quest for Participation*

In different ways and to varying degrees the Iranian regime under the Pahlavis, the Saudi Arabian regime under the House of Saud, and the Egyptian regime under Nasser and Sadat, were "closed" systems that did not allow genuine political participation, especially from the youth. A generation gap has often developed and young people have found it possible to be listened to only if they oblige the listener by claiming more knowledge of and dedication to, the word of the Almighty. In Egypt, for example, where Sadat managed to silence most people by his resort to the prohibitionary concept of *'aib* (taboo, extremely shameful and "not done"), it was only the young members of the militant Islamic groups who could dare to challenge him in public by doing so in the name of religious righteousness. These youths also challenged religious

---

24. Compare the interesting discussion in Fouad Ajami, *The Arab Predicament* (Cambridge: Cambridge University Press, 1982), esp. pp. 50-75 and Chapter 3.
25. "Curiously", maintains Bernard Lewis, "most of those involved are members of the Christian minorities in Arab countries and are themselves resident in Western Europe or the United States". He then takes to task both A. Abdel-Malek and E. Said, but does not explain why he considers their position curious. See his, "The Question of Orientalism", *The New York Review,* 24 July 1982, p. 50ff.
26. For further details see: Nazih Ayubi, "Secularism and Modernization in Islam", *Free Inquiry,* Vol. 2, no. 2, Winter 1981.

Journal of International Affairs

scholars of the establishment, confidently asserting that they knew their religion better than the scholars. There was, as well, a rather perverse sense of joy in being able to stop a respectable university professor in mid-lecture as a member of an Islamic group would stand up in the classroom to announce loudly "the call to prayers".

The invention of and adherence to a so-called Islamic costume by many neo-fundamentalist groups also emphasizes the sense of participation and sharing, and colors it by a shade of simple equality with the insiders on the one hand and an element of defiant distinction from the outsider on the other. In fact, this participatory aspect distinguishes the neo-fundamentalists even from slightly older fundamentalists (such as the Muslim Brothers) who had more respect for learning and age, and is reminiscent of the participatory brotherhood of some of the protestant movements in Christianity.

The Christians of Egypt (the Copts) also resorted to religion to counteract the lack of political participation but they did this, ironically, in a completely different way. While militant Muslims to a large extent revolted against their own religious establishment and formed their own neo-fundamentalist groups, militant Copts turned to their clergy, not only for religious but also for political leadership.[27] This development partly explains the deterioration in relations between President Sadat and the Coptic patriarch which led to Sadat's official suspension of the patriarch in September 1981. It is interesting to note that among the religious agitators whom he subsequently arrested, most Muslims were young, anti-establishment militants, while most Christians were middle-aged and rather sedate church clerics.

A month after these extensive arrests, Sadat was assassinated. "I killed the Pharoah," shouted one of the assassins, indicating how the lack of participation

must have been among the major grievances of these people.

In summary, one can say that behind the religious language of the Islamic groups, two major political concerns are to be observed: a quest for authenticity and a quest for participation. It is possible at this juncture to raise the point that neither of these two concerns is exclusively confined to the Muslim world. In Western Europe and North America too, the quest for participation was central to the youth movements of the sixties, while in the Third World at large, the quest for authenticity does indeed represent one of the major concerns now prevalent among many intellectuals and politicians of these predominantly non-Western countries. While we agree that the militant Islamic groups share with the youth of the sixties a yearning for participation and also share with other popular movements of the Third World a search for authenticity, we maintain that the Islamic movement still keeps a distinctive character and a particular vigor of its own. This, we believe, is due to the specific historical experience of the Muslim world.

Firstly, Islamic institutional and intellectual development has promoted a holistic, all-encompassing view of life that does not easily separate the religious from the political. Islam is therefore well-equipped with a quasi-political vocabulary and literature.

Secondly, there is the history of rivalry and conflict between Christendom and *Dar al-Islam* (the Household of Islam). Of all the world's existing civilizations, only the Islamic civilization was a direct source of learning for the West, and of all the Eastern civilizations, only the Islamic Empire ruled parts of Europe. The recent

---

27. Milad Hanna. *Na'am aqbat lakin misriyyun* [Yes Copts, But Egyptians], (Cairo: Madbuli, 1980), pp. 94-98.

domination by the West of Muslim societies, which had themselves been superior to Europe and dominant over parts of it not so long ago, has been particularly painful and hurtful to Muslims. This gives particular depth and vigor to the call for authenticity in the Muslim world.

A third element central to the Muslim experience is the creation of Israel. On the one hand, it was painful to watch the determined implantation of this "foreign" body in the heart of the Arab world, and to the detriment of the majority of the people who inhabited that land, i.e., Muslim and Christian Palestinians. A further affront was the occupation of Jerusalem in 1967.[28] On the other hand, it was felt that if the Israelis could succeed because of their ardent adherence to their religion, Muslims would be all the more victorious if they were to adhere to their own religion. As one Islamic writer in Egypt put it:

The Pioneers of Zionism say that 'Jewish religious life is more than anything else the secret behind the eternity of Israel' . . . So if only we would wake up and realize that the sole path for salvation, victory and supremacy starts by making Islam a full lifestyle for all Muslims.[29]

The contemporary Muslim world is indeed starting to experiment with its own blend of "religion-cum-politics". In its own way, the Iranian revolution is increasingly emphasizing religion as the primary basis for political identity and allegiance. To a large extent the future of all aspiring Islamic movements in the Middle East will depend on what may come of the Iranian experiment. In the meantime, however, this new "religionization" of politics is certain to create difficulties for non-Shiites within Iran, and to cause trouble for Middle Eastern countries with significant Shiite communities (such as Iraq, Bahrain, Lebanon and Saudi Arabia).

With two varieties of religious nationalism now in place in both Israel and Iran, the temptations and/or pressures to go in similar directions are escalating throughout the Arab world. Even within the ardently secularist Palestinian movement, the "religious trend" seems to be gaining ground, while in most Arab countries, Islamic movements have increasingly become a reality of political life. If religion is indeed to become the paramount political force in the Arab world, more tormenting conflicts can be expected, both within individual countries, and throughout the region as a whole.

28. Significantly, it was only after the defeat of 1967 and the arson in Al-Aqsa Mosque of Jerusalem in 1969 that the first Islamic summit was held (in September of that year), leading to the creation of the Organization of Islamic Conference with forty-two member states and with headquarters in Jeddah, Saudi Arabia. Cf. Hamid H. Kizilbash, "The Islamic Conference: Retrospect and Prospect". *Arab Studies Quarterly*, vol. 4, nos. 1 and 2, Spring 1982.
29. Muhammad al-Khatib, "Ghazwat badr" [The Conquest of Badr], *Al-Da'wa*, no. 27, December 1978, p. 19.

[12]

Muslim Fundamentalism

Anthony Hyman

'A spectre is haunting the world – the spectre of Muslim Fundamentalism' – thus we could paraphrase Marx and Engels. Like communism in the 1840s, Muslim fundamentalism has inspired both fear and awe, being treated often in the Western media with an unusual degree of prejudice, ignorance and sensationalism. There are aspects of the political impact of Muslim fundamentalism which recall the lurid imaginings in the European press from the late nineteenth century about the Pan–Islamic threat to Europe's colonial empires. One of the most prevalent misconceptions has been that Muslim fundamentalism (like Pan–Islam before it) represents a monolithic force, threatening Western civilisation and ultimately seeking world domination, and many distinct Islamic tendencies have been wrongly viewed as one political movement.

The phenomenon of Muslim fundamentalism has been variously described as the 'renewal', 'resurgence', 'revival' or 'repoliticisation' of Islam, and as 'militant Islam', but often the exact position of Islam itself as a factor in socio-political change remains hazy. It is clear, though, that religion has re-emerged from the shadows as a major component in our understanding of contemporary political development in Muslim countries and societies in the Middle East, Asia and Africa.

It would be quite wrong, however, to imagine the spread of fundamentalist ideas as being uniquely Muslim. Fundamentalist religious views are in fact flourishing openly in many different societies, with religion and politics intertwined for, (among others), Zionists in Israel, Sikhs in India and 'born-again' Christians in the USA. In the USA a vigorous Christian fundamentalist revival is going on, ranging from the New Right Christian Churches to Creationism, the rejection of Darwinism in favour of a literal interpretation of the Genesis account of creation. A revivalist crusade for the 1980s, against the 'permissive society' and current liberal or humanist ideas, has been launched – not by Muslims but by Christian preachers in the USA.

It is plain that the return to religious roots, and the mobilisation of religious faith to reform a corrupt or decadent society, are far from being limited to Third World countries, let alone to Muslims. Its manifestation and symbolism vary from religion to religion and culture to culture, but despite the differences, there are some intriguing parallels in the organisation of fundamentalist groups, and in the methods used by activists to rouse popular response.

REVIVAL OF ISLAM

Muslim fundamentalism has grown under the pressures and challenge of foreign – and specifically Western – influences in Muslim lands. It is distinct from the influential rival modernist trend among Muslims, by which,

3

4   *The Institute for the Study of Conflict*

fundamentalism has, however, been greatly influenced. It is no less distinct from traditional conservatism, typified by the *ulama*, the Muslim religious establishment. In the last two centuries, the *ulama* have fulfilled their role as conservative guardians of Islamic doctrine, but have proved incapable of integrating modern ideas with traditional Islamic culture. In modern times many brave attempts have been made to reconcile the two cultures, all led by lay Muslims, rather than the *ulama*. Laymen, often professionals of liberal background educated in Western colleges or secular institutions, tried to fill the vacuum in the leading Muslim countries, but their ideas percolated through only to a small class.

The Muslim modernist movement lost much of its impetus, and most of its self-confidence, with the first world war. It soon split into two mutually contradictory trends: whole-hearted secularism and Islamic revivalism. Disenchanted secularists among Muslims, as well as conservative traditionalists, have become increasingly attracted to fundamentalism in recent decades. Central to the fundamentalist outlook is the conviction that Islam is a total philosophy affecting all areas of human activity. They believe that Islam is a complete social and economic system in its own right, distinct from capitalism and socialism alike – one, moreover, containing the answers to current problems facing humanity.

The Muslim world has spawned many mass movements of religious revival and many sects of Islam in its time. Modern fundamentalism is essentially different from its earlier manifestations, seen in the puritanical Wahhabite movement in Arabia and other linked revivalist Islamic movements from the eighteenth century. The Muslim Brotherhood in Egypt and other countries of the Middle East, the *Jamaat-i-Islami* (Islamic party) in Pakistan and many other fundamentalist groups are all concerned with capturing political power in their respective countries, and establishing a model Islamic state. But few of these parties forming the so-called 'Islamic movement' have access to state power, most being in opposition to established governments, while in some important cases (as in Egypt) their legal existence as parties is banned by law.

Fundamentalists accept only rarely the term *fundamentalist*, preferring that of *Islamist*. As the Afghan resistance leader, Professor B Rabbani, has stated: "It is a word we do not use. We are Islamists, that is to say, that for us Islam is a driving force which concerns every aspect of our life. It is an ideal – of social justice, for struggle against poverty, for peace. But also, on the personal level, it is an ideal of piety, and of purity. Ours is a spiritual revolution, and we are, above all else, believers".[1]

It is the ability of fundamentalists to articulate – on moral grounds and in religious terms – popular grievances on political, economic and social issues which gives them political clout. In the past decade, and especially since Iran's Islamic revolution in 1979, secular-minded modernist governments in most Muslim countries have been put on the defensive by a rising Islamic tide. Even though Muslim fundamentalists only rarely have power, some at least of their 'Islamic' demands have been accepted by governments throughout the Middle East in recent years who were anxious to appease the protesters. As a result, popular 'non-Islamic' practices such as horse-racing, betting, sale and consumption of alcohol and the establishment of city night clubs have been banned or restricted in some states. Even the centuries-old custom of raising pigs for their own use by Christian Arabs has been the object of demonstrations and harrassment by Islamists, showing their abhorrence of this meat which is *haram* (forbidden to Muslims).

In numerous petty ways daily life in Muslim cities has been affected by the shrill, insistent demands of activists demanding reforms. Changes in dress are probably the most dramatic and surprising development as far as women are concerned. Even if the remarkable switch in Egypt to *shari* dress (*al-ziyy al-shari*: lawful dress), together with the *chadar*, the veiling or covering of the female body and face in contemporary Iran and Pakistan, are not simply inspired by a fundamentalist revival,[2] this development since the late 1970s is evidently linked to it. The paradox is that it was precisely in these countries that women from the same middle class, urban backgrounds had until the 1970s led Muslim women of more conservative lands in the struggle for social emancipation, in which Western-style dress in itself was often seen as a badge of progress.

PROGRESS OR REGRESSION?

An important part of the attraction of fundamentalist ideas lies in the current retreat from secularism or liberalism in the Muslim world. For many people of the younger generation, the search for cultural and religious roots has led to an intensification of Islamic identity. Both in changes in personal behaviour of individual Muslims, and the response of governments, it can be argued that there is a positive side to this process. Moral standards, at least in theory, improve towards a sober Islamic ideal, while the state may undertake a programme of mosque building, accompanied by law reforms of an Islamic type – typically, so far, in taxation and criminal law.

For many progressive-minded Muslims with deep roots in their culture, however, modern fundamentalism often looks totally negative. Many trace the reactionary nature of fundamentalism to the colonial experience of Muslim societies, shaking the self-confidence of many Muslim thinkers and resulting in an inferiority complex. Unlike modernists of an earlier generation, they usually lack roots in their own traditions. Defining as 'neo-fundamentalist' the organised groups emerging from the 1930s, the Pakistani professor, Fazlur Rahman, writes that they reveal an intellectual poverty, "a pathological preoccupation with exhibiting the great masterpiece that Islam once was – in the fields of science, philosophy, literature and art." What it does have in abundance, he goes on, is intensity: "It is vibrant, it pulsates with anger and enthusiasm, and it is exuberant and full of righteous hatred. Its ethical dynamism is genuine, its integrity remarkable. Some of its expressions may be disconcerting or even grotesque, but should it find enough content, it could prove to be a great, even decisive force in a world torn by individual, national, racist and communal selfishness and narrowmindedness".[3]

There are many Muslims who would agree with Fazlur Rahman's bitter view that fundamentalists appear to have a "divine mission to shut down Islamic intellectual life". Such impact as they have had so far has, indeed, been largely destructive or negative. In the field of education, for example, they have closed departments in colleges, banned certain subjects, dismissed teachers or demanded segregated classes for female students hitherto attending joint classes in colleges. In many Muslim countries mobs led by bearded fundamentalist activists have burned down newspaper offices after the publication of articles deemed offensive to Islam, while many books and films have fallen foul of self-appointed Islamic censors. This willingness to use violence together with righteous fury over 'insults to religion' have together proved highly effective in mobilising urban mobs to intimidate holders of differing views.

THE APPEAL OF FUNDAMENTALISM

Numerous explanations have been advanced for the popular response to the various radical Islamic revival movements which can be classified as fundamentalist, and detailed studies have been made of the impact of Muslim fundamentalism in specific societies. Sociological and psychological explanations have rightly emphasised the element of order, authority and discipline offered by fundamentalism to members of those societies facing rapid and confusing change.

The resurgence of Islam in national life in many Muslim countries has shown the attraction fundamentalist ideas have for a wide span of classes. The urban poor – some of them recent migrant families from the villages – provide many activists, but its strength among the educated youth in colleges reflects also the disillusionment of educated people in general with those secular ideologies – Arab nationalism, state socialism and liberal democracy – all seen to have failed to produce the anticipated fruits. Social upheaval, growing economic problems such as inflation, serious unemployment and shortage of housing in the rapidly expanding capital cities, have combined to produce an environment highly favourable to the propaganda of fundamentalists. The traditionalism, piety and social conservatism of recent rural Muslim migrants to the cities, in particular, often seems to be outraged by the naked exploitation and moral degradation of urban life. Fundamentalist groups have tried to mobilise the popular attachment to Islam by exploiting religious sentiments as a political ideology, often in opposition to the state's drive towards secularisation.

Muslim radicals emphasise the goals of Islam in terms of social justice, and the abolition of economic exploitation within the Muslim *umma* (community), in accordance with the Quran and Sunna, (the model pattern of behaviour of the Prophet Muhammad). Though most Muslims have legitimate doubts about the viability in a complex modern world of an ancient, traditional code of conduct, for millions of other Muslims there is a confidence and firm faith that these early laws are valid for all time. In analysing the currents of Islamic politics, we cannot ignore the element of faith and hope, the attraction for millions of Muslims of a recreated 'Golden Age' of virtuous Caliphs and pious Muslims, located in the few decades around 632 AD, the year of death of the Prophet Muhammad. The nature of faith in Muslim fundamentalist circles is sometimes akin to that of millenarian sects among Christians: "Its followers are not makers of revolution. They expect it to make itself, by divine revelation, by announcement from on high, by a miracle – they expect it to happen somehow. The part of the people is to gather together, to prepare itself, to watch for the signs of the coming doom . . . ."[4]

Passivity is, however, far from being typical political behaviour in the inner circle of committed activists in Muslim fundamentalist parties. In many Muslim countries fundamentalist ideology inspires political movements or parties, with a mass following and organised cadres. In Egypt, Syria, Iraq and other Arab countries, there are fundamentalist terrorist organisations driven underground by rival ruling regimes.

Modernisation and Islamic revivalism

The current atmosphere of radical puritanism or revivalism evident in many Muslim societies is intimately linked to the process of modernisation, the rapid, sweeping social and economic changes in recent decades. The phenomenal growth of cities, with the uprooting of millions of villagers, seen in Egypt, Iran and elsewhere, is a major factor, together with the related expansion of education and industrial sectors of the economy. In many of the interpretations of contemporary Islamic revivalism, the key points have been urbanisation and the hectic pace of change during the 1970s in the oil-rich states. What remains more obscure, or at least more debatable, is whether Islam is the convenient vehicle – rather than the actual inspiration – of the political demands of new urban groups.

Six years ago, the organised power of the new city dwellers in Tehran and other huge new Iranian cities, who were mainly rural migrants, played a decisive part in the Iranian revolution, toppling a ruler who seemed to many observers entrenched in power, besides being backed by the USA. This essentially new class in Iran still counts as a force in the Islamic revolution. "Who are the Muslims?", enquired a sociologist in Iran, soon after the overthrow of the Shah. "The Muslims are the poor", was the revealing answer, showing the explosive blend of populism with religion. Rapid urban growth in Iran, as in Egypt and Turkey, has created a huge underclass of aspiring townsmen, often living in slum conditions and deeply resentful of the privileged, Westernised elite, whose lifestyle of conspicuous consumption, secular tastes or Western dress is a permanent affront to religious puritans. The popular identification of Islam itself with the poor and the exploited classes of Muslims, which seems to have occurred in Iran at least, has helped rouse Muslim masses into political activity.

Among the sociological explanations advanced by specialists for the rise of Islamic fundamentalism or puritanism is that of Professor Ernest Gellner, of the London School of Economics, who views it in terms of world civilisation, as the transformation of the central 'great tradition' of Islam into the majoritarian folk tradition: "It allows it to assume a triple role in affirming a continuous old identity, in repudiating a humiliating past and poverty and in rejecting the foreigner, and yet it also provides a charter for purification and self-discipline".

Gellner sees this past tension between the two traditions as having prevented Islamic society from fully entering the modern world, and views its contemporary transformation, by the emergence of a majoritarian folk tradition, as meeting the requirement of continuity as well as of revolution.

Other observers think this is an unduly philosophical approach, which ignores the negative, anti-rational tendency to be found since the first appearance of Muslim fundamentalist groups.

THE RISE OF FUNDAMENTALIST GROUPS

It is no accident that the earliest and most influential Muslim fundamentalist groups emerged in British-ruled India and Egypt. These were two key centres of Muslim population and intellectual life, and both had been profoundly shaken up by social and economic changes under direct British imperial rule (Indian subcontinent), or under *de facto* British control (Egypt). Already strong nationalist movements were claiming independence under the banner of democracy in both countries, led by secular-minded politicians of the Wafd in Egypt, and of the Indian National Congress in India.

This background of overwhelming British power, and the far-reaching effects of imported Western models in virtually all spheres of modern life in the towns, is essential in understanding the rise of fundamentalism. Egypt's Muslim Brotherhood, which was to penetrate every Muslim land of the Middle East, began in the Suez Canal Zone, a part of Egypt administered by the British Army until as late as 1954, when British military HQ for the Middle East was transferred to Cyprus. Fundamentalist ideas grew in the shadow of British military power, which was at its peak throughout the Middle East region during the second world war, with most Muslim lands under British occupation. Even when from the late 1940s the staged withdrawal from the region of British military bases and power began, British and French influence remained while the USA rapidly became involved in the region. Three factors which were to dominate relations were Western help for the newly-founded state of Israel from 1948, their search for reliable allies against the spread of Soviet communist influence, and the oil and gas interests of international companies.

The movement of the Muslim Brothers

Founded at Ismailiya in Egypt in 1928, *Al-Ikhwan al-Muslimun* (Muslim Brothers or Brethren) developed from a youth club into an influential political organisation during the second world war. Its founder was a young Arabic school teacher, Hasan al-Banna (1906–1949), who rejected alike the values and institutions of Egypt's politicians and Western-dominated cities. In their place the Muslim Brothers preached a fundamentalist view of society and politics. "You are a new soul in the heart of this nation to give it life by means of the Quran", activists of the Brethren were told by their charismatic leader Hasan al-Banna in 1943.

The movement's startling success in attracting membership – estimated at some 500,000 members and at least as many sympathisers by 1949 – is due, in part at least, to its millenarian streak: the consciousness of being part of an elect, pure group of true Muslims set apart from the corrupt, decadent society of 'nominal Muslims' has been characteristic of the Muslim Brothers. The principal theoretician of the Brothers, Sayyid Qutb, (executed in 1966), stated this concept firmly in an inspiring book, *Signposts on the Road*, rejecting, along with other Arab systems, the modern Egyptian social system as *al-nizam al-jahili*, the brutish, ignorant order of the kind known in pre-Islamic Arabia – the touchstone of all that is base for pious Muslims. This decadence was contrasted with the ideal Islamic rule, *al-nizam al-islami*, the type of society which the Muslim Brothers hope (and still pray) to introduce.

In the past 30 years, the Muslim Brothers have had to work in opposition, often outlawed and forced to organise clandestinely in small cells.[5] In Egypt they were driven underground in 1954, after an unsuccessful assassination attempt on President Nasser. The Brothers continued to grow quietly, expanding membership fast in Syria, Iraq and many Middle Eastern states.

Throughout the Muslim world, but especially in Arab lands, the Egyptian *Ikhwan* won fame in the war over Palestine from 1947–1949. Volunteer cadres of Muslim Brothers had fought there side by side with units of the Egyptian Army against the Zionists, earning respect and approval on all sides of the Arab political spectrum. The Palestinian issue has remained a central concern of all fundamentalists, providing also a rallying-point, and common ground on a symbolic issue about whose justice there was rare agreement among Arabs. It was, of course, President Sadat's compromise over Israel's occupation of Palestinian land by the Camp David agreement – seen as a betrayal of the Palestinians and the Arab 'nation' – which was the catalyst for the plot to assassinate Sadat in 1981, carried out by a tiny fanatical offshoot of the *Ikhwan*.

In Egypt itself, the *Ikhwan* was extremely active in organising political demonstrations against British occupation of the Canal Zone. It became generally recognised as a major anti-imperialist force, its brand of Islamic activism serving as the vehicle for popular anti-colonialism. But from 1954 the Muslim Brotherhood lost out in Egypt, in the power contest with Gamal Abdul Nasser. Under Nasser, Egypt experimented with socialism and non-alignment, and Islam as a political ideology was missing, just as the Islamic identity was the least important in Nasser's once-famous theory of Egypt's three circles of national identity converging on Cairo, coming after both the Arab and African circles.

Political rivals of the *Ikhwan* in Egypt and elsewhere have often claimed that the Brotherhood was the creation of British colonialism, and has been used by imperialists as a counterpoise to communist influence in Muslim lands. Though the early record of political activism by the *Ikhwan* would seem to disprove this theory, in practice fundamentalist parties have been given funds or encouragement by various Muslim governments from time to time, to check the progress of left-wing parties. Sadat himself tried this approach in Egypt in the late 1970s. In Egypt at the present time, the *Ikhwan* is split, and numerous radical offshoots of it flourish underground. In spite of an official ban, fundamentalist activists of the 'Islamic Trend' contested the 1984 elections, under the cover of membership of the New Wafd Party, winning ten seats in the

Egyptian Parliament. Since 1981, several hundred more fundamentalists have been imprisoned, charged with murder or plotting to overthrow the government and replace it by an Islamic order. There can be little doubt that the *Ikhwan* and other fundamentalist groups would become stronger in Egypt, if permitted to organise freely.

Muslim Brothers in Syria and Sudan

It is Syria which provides the most striking example of fundamentalist political activism of all the Arab countries. Various factions of the original Brotherhood in Syria (loosely grouped as the 'Islamic Front of Syria') have waged a bitter and bloody struggle since 1976 against President Assad's regime. Fundamentalists have mass-support from Syria's Sunni Muslim community, but their cadres suffered terrible losses in the aftermath of the wholesale insurrection in the northern cities of Hama and Aleppo in 1980. Although a brutal repression and massacres by Syrian troops in 1980, and, since then, executions of *Ikhwan* members caught by the security forces, may well have convinced many earlier backers of the fundamentalists from among the prosperous traders of Aleppo that it was futile to take on an army, the Islamic underground in Syria has not given up its opposition to a hated military regime. The large costly stocks of weapons used by activists in the northern cities could only have been smuggled in by help from outside Syria – probably from Iraq. Since the Assad regime is surrounded on all sides by enemies, its internal opponents are unlikely to remain cowed for long, or be short of weapons and money.

In the Sudan the Muslim Brothers have become partners in the military government of President Numeiri since 1977, in what was claimed to be a policy of 'national reconciliation' – an ironic term for policies which have caused immense controversy among Sudanese Muslims, and dangerously alienated Christians in south Sudan. Strains can be seen in a revival of insurgency in the south, while in the Muslim north, modernists and Sufi leaders have opposed what the Muslim Brothers call the 'constitutionalisation of Islam'. The hanging in Khartoum in January 1985 of a vociferous critic, Mahmoud Muhammad Taha, (veteran Muslim politician and leader of the reformist Republican Brothers, and a strong defender of Christian rights), looked like a desperate measure of the government. Sudan's 'Islamisation' measures have altered the tax structure, greatly reducing state revenues without, however, attracting the large bounty anticipated from Saudi Arabia. There are some parallels between Sudanese and Pakistani attempts to impose 'Islamisation' from above.

Jamaat-i Islami of Pakistan

The influential position in Pakistan of the *Jamaat-i Islami* (community of Islam) is due largely to the lifework of Abu'l A'la Maududi (1903–1979), the major theoretician of fundamentalism in the Indian subcontinent, and also well known in the Arab countries. Maududi's concept of Islam, as well as the organisation and strategy of the *Jamaat*, was heavily influenced by Marxism, besides his independent study of Islam. Maududi's stress upon the ideal of

Islamic revolution as the goal of the pious Muslim arose out of the challenge of new systems of thought from Europe, and in particular communism. Activism and vigorous propaganda by party workers were enjoined on its membership by the *Jamaat* – founded in 1941 in India, but gaining political influence only after 1947, when Maududi migrated to Pakistan – whose creation he had opposed.

Maududi's call for activism and agitation reminds some observers of Marxist Agitprop, but he claimed the Quran as his authority, writing: "Quran does not contain mere opinions and abstract thoughts so that you can peruse it sitting in your padded armchair and understand all that it wants. It is not a book discussing theology . . . it is a book of agitation and movement, and by its very revelation it shook a meek and complacent man", that is, the Prophet Muhammad.

Maududi's understanding of Islam was as a worldwide revolutionary movement led by the true Muslims. He scorned the narrow concept of nationalism – this was the basis for his rejection of the partition scheme of India in 1947 – believing instead that the Muslim community (*ummah*) as a whole was the sole valid identity for true Muslims: "Islam demands the earth, and will not settle for a part or a section of it".

The considerable success of the *Jamaat-i Islami* in Pakistan, compared with many of its fundamentalist counterparts elsewhere, had much to do with Maududi's flair for journalism (his early profession in India), plus his ability to communicate a coherent theory of the Islamic state, and to inspire party activists. But the *Jamaat* had many advantages in Pakistan, was permitted to operate openly and never banned even when its activists committed violent acts against the law, or harshly criticised each of Pakistan's governments in turn of being 'un-Islamic'. Pakistan, created in the name of Islam, could hardly afford to be seen to suppress the *Jamaat-i-Islami*, even when its rulers had a secular approach to society.

The *Jamaat* has been acknowledged even by its enemies in Pakistan to be the best organised political party, with a cadre structure owing something to the example of communist parties. The *Jamaat*'s student wing, *Islami Jamiat-i-Talaba*, has regularly won power in most of Pakistan's college elections in the past decade, giving the *Jamaat* thousands of activists in the cities for demonstrations, and boosting its national showing. In truth, though, the *Jamaat* has never achieved national electoral success in Pakistan, despite its tight organisation and mass-base. Its candidates have been humiliated regularly at elections, even in the cities of Lahore and Karachi, where the *Jamaat* has a large following.

A large part of the explanation for the *Jamaat*'s impact in Pakistan is due to funding from outside the country, and to its activists' willingness to use violence in coercing opponents. Those who visit the *Jamaat*'s magnificent centre ouside Lahore, or who observe the various activities and the stream of booklets for free distribution besides the many newspapers it publishes, may well wonder about its source of finance. Saudi Arabia has long been the generous patron of the *Jamaat*'s work – describing it as the "Islamic movement in Pakistan",[6] in the Saudi press. Saudi funds have greatly helped the *Jamaat*, as they have other fundamentalist-inclined parties and groups around the world.

Violence has been a characteristic of the *Jamaat* since its first steps in Pakistani politics. It was far from being the only offender, but the *Jamaat* and its student wing often proved more successful in street violence than groups with left-wing or secular tendencies. Claiming to fight for Islamic causes, the *Jamaat* attracted support from other conservative Muslim parties.

Islamisation by decree

The *Jamaat-i Islami* under the leadership of Mian Tufail Muhammad has taken a gamble in backing the military dictatorship of General Ziaul-Haq since 1977. In its hopes of seeing an Islamic system in Pakistan, the *Jamaat* wholeheartedly backed the military government's reforms, and now runs the distinct risk of being blamed for continued military rule and postponement of national elections, as well as the hanging of ex-Prime Minister Z A Bhutto in 1979, without, however, getting anything approaching its ideal Islamic state. Probably the party's isolation from the mainstream of Pakistani politics was the main reason why the *Jamaat*'s leader finally made a public breach with the government in 1984, without, however, joining or giving even token support for the Movement for Restoration of Democracy, a platform of eleven parties demanding elections.

"Islamisation from above" is how many Pakistanis describe the current programme introduced by General Zia since 1977. In its heavy-handed attempts to create an Islamic society, the government has so far clearly failed to unite Pakistan's parties behind it as well as the majority of the public. Critics may be right in complaining that religion by decree is dividing the nation, and actually endangering its fragile unity. State intervention into what has been a private sphere, (observance of religion), has produced sharp tensions, contributing to destructive rioting between Sunni and Shia Muslims in Karachi in 1983.

The position of Pakistan's biggest religious minority, the allegedly heretical Ahmedia or Qadiani sect, has worsened recently, after the government gave in to a shrill campaign led by conservative mullahs and fundamentalists. In May 1984 Ahmedias were prohibited from calling themselves Muslims, or using many Muslim terms to describe their religious practices. A further object of the persecution, as yet unrealised, is to remove all Ahmedias from their posts in state service. In this atmosphere of growing religious bigotry and fanaticism, Christians and other minority groups fear for the future in Pakistan. Though the impact of the 'Islamisation' laws is by no means all attributable to the *Jamaat* and fundamentalist ideology – the process, in fact, began under the secular-minded Bhutto – fundamentalism has much to answer for.

Pakistan's hesitant progress towards 'Islamisation' is far from being the Islamic revolution desired by fundamentalists. Some of the reforms in taxation, banking and criminal law are meaningful, but others are merely symbolic and still remain on paper years after being decreed. It is the very fact that a military regime is introducing the reforms which vitiates them for some Muslims. Besides the primary need to keep the armed forces behind the regime, there is a sizeable political constituency formed from the the religious classes (*mullahs* and *maulvis*) and the lower middle class Muslims of the towns, which in virtually all Muslim lands has shown itself susceptible to the ideology of fundamentalism. In Pakistan, religious sentiments and passions are being shrewdly exploited to help keep in power a narrowly-based military regime.

THE SHI'ITE CHALLENGE

The Islamic revolution in Iran has produced dramatic effects throughout the Muslim world. As a rare example of a genuine 'people's revolution' – instead of the customary army coup dressed up as revolution – the struggle against the Shah was indeed remarkable enough. Its combination of Shi'ite religious zeal for martyrdom, ferocious Iranian nationalism and strong xenophobia, fascinated the world. Understanding how Iran's fundamentalist tendency emerged as the dominant force of an ephemeral coalition against the Shah is vital to an assessment of its potential influence or lasting strength inside Iran.

For many shrewd observers, Iran's revolution conforms to the pattern of the French revolution, having already reached the final of four phases in six years: moderate opposition; ascendancy of the extremists; the reign of terror and virtue; and Thermidor, or 'convalescence from revolutionary fever'. And like revolutionary France, Iran has a foreign war to fight.

History is written by the victors too. Leading members of Iran's clergy have been too flushed with their outright victory, by the dictatorship of the Islamic Republican Party (IRP) from 1981, coolly to analyse the stages by which power was obtained. The clergy have naturally appropriated all the credit for the people's revolution, conveniently forgetting the role of Iran's secular parties and pressure groups. For Ayatollah Murtaza Mutahari, (assassinated shortly after the triumphal return of Ayatollah Khomeini to Iran in 1979), it was a unique event, comparable only with earlier movements led by prophets inspired by God. He wrote in an influential book, *The Islamic Movement in the Twentieth Century*:

"The nature of the Islamic movement is in no way similar to the French revolution, or to the great October revolution of Russia. This movement is one of those glaring historical events that prove false the concept of the materialistic interpretation of history and that of the dialectics of materialism, according to which the economy is recognised as the corner-stone of social structure, and a social movement considered a reflection of class struggle".

One does not have to agree with such a bold claim as this to assess the Iranian revolution as indeed unique in modern history. In 1981 it brought to power – after the shake-out with Bazergan, Bani Sadr and other politicians – a class which had never previously controlled the country, "traditional clergy armed with mosque pulpits and claiming the divine right to supervise all temporal authority, even the country's highest elected representatives".[7]

Whether the fundamentalist dominance lasts long in Iran, however, is another matter. Much of the present government's confidence comes from the towering authority of one old man, Ayatollah Ruhollah Khomeini, who as *Vilayat-i-Faqih* (religious guide) exercises ultimate control under the 1979 constitution. There are grounds for believing there is an inherent instability in the regime. There is no consensus within the leadership of the IRP about policies, with a fundamentalist faction opposed by more moderate clergy. The very unity of the IRP could fall apart on the death of Khomeini, over the question of peace overtures or military setbacks and correct strategy over the hugely costly war with Iraq. There is a continuing controversy over the type of Islamic economy to be created in Iran, which has vital implications for the prosperity of the large *bazaari* or merchant class.

It is not altogether cynical to assert that the ending of the Iran–Iraq war would be against the interests of Iran's ruling party. The war economy has soaked up some two million unemployed, and the war crisis provided the excuse for establishing a dictatorship and crushing all internal centres of opposition. Without the patriotic war and the cause of endangered national unity, Iran's government would face greater public discontent, and probably a much higher level of terrorist activity, besides open rebellion in the Kurdish region.

'True Shi'ism' as the religion of protest

Iran's revolution has some key elements in common with other Third World societies, where protest movements against economic and cultural imperialism of the West have developed. The neologism 'Che Khomeinism' conveys the international, transcultural flavour still to be found in Iran's atmosphere, overlaying the specific Shia Muslim component. The most influential single source of these ideas has been a French-educated Iranian sociologist, Dr Ali Shariat (1933–1937), who became the ideological mentor of Iranian youth from the 1960s. Shariati's hugely popular lectures, tapes, books and pamphlets circulated widely, commanding mass appeal among the urban educated classes. The views of Third Worldists like Che Guevara, Franz Fanon and the existentialist philosopher Jean-Paul Sartre, and indirectly Marxism, all contributed to form Shariati's outlook, along with Islamic writings.

Though claimed by the present clergy-dominated government as one of their own, Shariati was very hostile towards the traditional *ulama*. Far from sharing the wish to impose on Iran the rule of the clergy and of Khomeini, Shariati had an opposed vision: Shi'ism was intrinsically radical, he claimed, and this religious culture if led by Iran's intelligentsia could carry out two essential revolutions, national and social, leading to a modern, enlightened and just society. The impact of Shariati's ideas on Iran's youth has been described well as re-activating the millenarian tradition. Certainly he helped revive intense interest and respect for Shia Islam in the younger generation. Compared with those of Shariati, Khomeini's ideas were less known and of less appeal in Iran until his return there in 1979.

The clergy backing the IRP government have since then presented a highly selective picture of the popular Shariati, which really amounts to a travesty of his ideas. Because of his popularity in Iran, Shariati is also claimed by various rival left-wing political groups as their spiritual mentor: among them the Muslim guerrillas, *Mujahidin-i-Khalq*, and the small terrorist group *Furqan* (Salvation). His admirers are to be found in opposite camps, each quoting Shariati's texts to support their own actions.

Among those who have popularised further some key concepts of Shariati is Ayatollah Khomeini himself, who, however, has remained an extreme traditionalist – more so, incidentally, than the leading fundamentalists of Pakistan and Egypt. Khomeini is far from being a typical, orthodox member of the senior Shia clergy of Iran. He first came to national prominence in 1963, as one of the rare public critics from the *ulama* of the Shah's regime, which he branded as US controlled. An international issue, the crucial American support for Israel, was also made a ground for protest in Qum, and disturbances spread to the capital on Khomeini's arrest. Khomeini's view of the relation between religion and politics is distinct from other traditional Shia *ulama*, and close to that held by Sunni Muslim theologians.

For the great majority of Iranians, though, nice points of theology have been of less importance than a few simple, plain ideas associated with Khomeini and the revolution. Political activism in the right cause is urged as the duty of every pious Muslim. Significantly, Imam Husain was characterised by Khomeini as an heroic rebel against tyrannical kingship, not as a martyr, as is common with Twelver (or *Imami*) Shias. Khomeini capitalised on the fact that Shia Islam is a religion of authority, in which belief in the Imam and submission to him is the third article of faith, after belief in God and the Prophet. Though not claiming to be the Imam (in the Shi'ite sense), Khomeini has never repudiated the title awarded him by popular acclaim, and it undoubtedly adds to his stature and moral authority over Shia Muslims. Until 1979 Khomeini was one among other Ayatollahs, ('sign of God', an honorific title of respect given to leading Shia theologians), but since then has been elevated far above his peers, receiving respect verging on adulation.

In most areas of society, the fundamentalist ideals of the traditionalist *ulama* led by Khomeini are being practised with zeal. Mosques have become Iran's centres of power as well as of piety. The future in Iran looks bleak for those Iranians suffering from the 'disease' of *Gharbzadegi*, ('Westitis', or intoxication with Western ways or values). The tolerance of dissent and public debate in Iran during the early period of the revolution was replaced by a narrow dictatorship of the IRP. Its censors strangled expression of divergent views in the media within two years of the Shah's fall from power. The closing down of the country's universities was ordered as part of a bid to purify Iran of Western influences, to be replaced by an Islamic system. The repressive agencies of the state have been fully employed in Iran to enforce this traditionalist pattern of society on recalcitrant citizens as well as to repress the political opposition, but it must be admitted that the great majority of Iranians appear to support the government's policies. Enjoying a vast base of support and confident of the rightness of its policies, Iran's government cares nothing for international criticism of its grim human rights record.

All Iran's religious minorities have been greatly concerned over the militantly Shia pattern of the Islamic republic, though their status is recognised under the Iranian constitution. The Baha'i religion, however, has faced persecution – not for the first time in Iran, where the 300,000 members of the Baha'i community are generally regarded as apostates from Islam and agents of imperialism. Their property has been confiscated, institutions banned, their marriages are not recognised as legal and Baha'is have been dismissed from state employment. Community leaders have been imprisoned and some executed. There are aspects of this persecution which recall the Nuremberg Laws directed against German Jews under the Third Reich.

Exporting the Islamic revolution

Iran's revolution has had an undeniable impact in the Muslim world of some 700 million people, spread right across Asia and Africa, from China to Morocco. It has had special appeal for Shia Muslims, estimates of whose total numbers go as high as 140 million, mostly living as sectarian minorities in Sunni-dominated states. In Iran itself – the sole state ruled by Twelver (*Imami*) Shias – there are 35 million. In all the states close to Iran there are considerable Shia minorities: in the Gulf, Pakistan, India, Afghanistan, Soviet Azerbaijan and the Caucasus, Turkey and Lebanon. In Iraq, Persian-speaking Shias actually form a majority. What these Shias have in common are political grievances against their various governments, which often treat Shias as second-class citizens, failing to share power, or the fruits of power in economic benefits. What they have all also had since 1978–1979 is the inspiration from Iran of Imam Khomeini's Islamic revolution.

Iran expected to rouse its co-religionists among the Shia majority in Iraq into open rebellion against 'a godless tyrant', the Ba'ath Socialist Party. Tehran mounted a provocative propaganda campaign by radio in 1979, but even under the strain of a lengthy and terribly destructive war (from September 1980), Iraqi Shias have failed to respond en masse to Tehran's calls for *jihad* (holy war). A small scale Shia agitation in Iraq was easily suppressed by the Ba'ath regime, and activists of Iraq's Al-Dawa group of fundamentalists have been forced to flee to Tehran, from where they publish rhetorical statements revealing their complete dependence on Iranian patronage, and their inability to grasp the real situation in Iraq and the Middle East in general. Meanwhile, Shia conscripts fight and die like other Iraqis, against the mainly Shia armed forces of Iran.

Iran's media maintains that Saddam Hussein's regime in Iraq in fighting the war is acting as part of an imperialist plot devised by the 'Great Satan', the USA, to destroy the revolution. This version of events is widely credited by Iranians, as well as by sympathisers of Iran and fundamentalists generally. Shia militants hope to replace the Saddam Hussein Ba'athist regime by an Islamic one in Baghdad. According to some reports, Al-Dawa militants and other Shias dream of creating a new Shia-dominated state, based on the Shia holy cities of Najaf and Karbela in southern Iraq.

Such a state could come about – if at all – only after a crushing victory by Iran over Iraqi forces, which looks unlikely in the present stalemate. It would mean the first significant change, (apart, of course, from Palestine), in territorial frontiers of the new states established after the first world war out of the Ottoman empire. Such outcome would greatly increase Iran's influence in the region, and at the same time boost the prestige of the Shia communities. It would also bring into question Iran's relations with the Gulf states – independent, rich but militarily puny.

LEBANON AND THE GULF STATES

Revolutionary Shi'ism, inspired and aided from Iran, has had more success in Lebanon and the Gulf. Lebanon's civil war problems were compounded in 1982 by the Israeli invasion and temporary occupation of south Lebanon. Iranian money, arms and even a token contingent of revolutionary guards (*pasdaran*) reached Lebanon with the co-operation of Iran's ally Syria. Since 1979, pro-Iranian groups of Lebanon's one million-odd Shias have hived off from the independent nationalist Shia movement *Amal*, led by Nabih Berri. Of these, *Islamic Amal* and *Hizbullah* (Party of God) are well known. The most sinister development has been the recent organisation (even basic details of which are uncertain) of the terrorist group *Islamic Jihad*, whose suicide attacks against US. French and Israeli targets in Lebanon since April 1983 were devastating blows to the foreign policies and prestige of these states in the Middle East. *Islamic Jihad* has thrived on the spirit of sacrifice, the 'death wish' or eager willingness to embrace martyrdom in the 'just cause' of Islam, which is now to be found in young Shias of the Lebanon – until the mid-1970s a poor, politically submissive community.

Some shrewd observers question any direct Iranian link with *Islamic Jihad*, noting the strange immunity from attack of Soviet or other communist targets in the Middle East. Though it is true that Soviet policy in the region is not seen as pro-Israel, and does not rouse such passions as the USA's policies, Ayatollah Khomeini and all fundamentalists agree on the dangers posed by godless communism. After all, one of the principal attractions of fundamentalist ideology for the youth of the Middle East is the promise it presents of confronting, and beating, their three *bêtes noires* – Zionism, imperialism and communism.

In the Gulf states and in the Eastern province of Saudi Arabia too, Shia militancy and fundamentalist ideas have grown hand in hand. Iran's revolution was not only next door, but something of a parallel situation with Lebanon existed. Large Shia minorities, many of them of Persian extraction, live under Sunni or Wahhabite domination. However, there can be no real comparison between the two, as far as political effects are concerned. There is, indeed, a 'special relationship', an affinity and sympathy for Iran, the Shi'ite motherland, felt in varying degree by Shias in general, but popular Shia response of a political kind in the Gulf states seems muted. The shadowy Shia terrorist international Islamic *Jihad* carried out a suicide bombing of the US embassy in Kuwait in 1983, with agents apparently from the Iraqi Al-Dawa organisation. Their imprisonment provoked a further terrorist strike, the hijacking of a Kuwaiti airliner to Tehran, which cost many lives.

Kuwait is the richest and the most populated of the Gulf sheikdoms with 1·3 million, of whom less than half are Kuwaiti nationals. It allows a degree of press and political freedom unusual in the region, which has meant that fundamentalists there have not needed to operate underground. The pressure of the fundamentalists in Kuwait comes mainly from young men and women, some of whom have studied in Western colleges, and activists present a united front, of Shias and Sunnis. Some observers believe that fundamentalist pressure was responsible for the refusal of the Emir of Kuwait to veto a law banning sale or consumption of alcohol, passed by the national assembly.

In Bahrain – where Iran has a longstanding territorial claim – a group of Shias were put on trial and imprisoned in 1982, after an attempt to overthrow the government. The plot allegedly had Iranian backing. A recent study of the Gulf region maintains that stability of the conservative, pro-Western mini-states is likely to continue, in the short term, at least, and that the oil-rich but weak governments are capable of handling the problem of subversion from Iran – or Iraq, for that matter.[8] As long as the war between these two major regional powers continues, their energies are fully engaged, giving more time for Saudi Arabia and the Gulf Co-operation Council to develop further collective defence capabilities.

Contradiction within the kingdom

Saudi Arabia's government won a psychological victory in mid-1984, and also its first test of combat in modern warfare, when its air force shot down an Iranian fighter plane in Saudi air space. Observers had not expected the Saudis to act decisively, as the Iran–Iraq war spilt over their borders. But fears for the future were evident in increases in the already huge military budget for 1984–1985, at a time of financial cutbacks. The fabulously rich oil-exporting kingdom has reduced oil production to some 4·4 million barrels a day, resulting in a drop of some 20 per cent of its budgeted income of 60,000 million dollars.

Great oil wealth, combined with a small population, has given Saudi Arabia (like Libya and Kuwait) potential political influence throughout the Muslim world. The changes brought by massive oil revenues to Saudi Arabia's archaic society have caused tensions. Even more, the tight monopoly of power and state riches by members of the 5000-strong royal family, together with the blatant corruption and immorality of some of the princes, has bred dissatisfaction – at least among the rich business classes and technocrats. However, it is difficult for outsiders to be sure what is happening beneath the surface of this rigidly-controlled society. The puritanical tradition of the Wahhabi sect makes sure that the interpretation of the Shari'a law is stricter than any other Muslim countries. Nevertheless, Saudi Arabia is no theocracy, and the *ulama*, powerful though they are as a class, are really junior partners to the Islamic monarchy of the Saudi leading princes.

The seizure by an armed band of Muslim fanatics of the Great Mosque in Mecca focussed attention on some of the contradictions abounding in Saudi Arabian society. This act of sacrilege at the holiest place of Islam (towards which Muslims the world over turn five times daily at prayer) took place on a highly significant day – 20 November 1979 – the first day of the new century in the Muslim calendar, 1400 of the *Hegira*. The Mecca insurgents, composed of Saudis, Egyptians and other Muslims, were led by a young fundamentalist, Juhaiman al-Oteibi, educated at Medina University, an ultra-conservative theological seminary created by Egyptian activists of the Ikhwan who had been forced into exile. The small group apparently believed that one of their companions was the long-awaited Mahdi, who would deliver the Muslims from their wicked, immoral and corrupt rulers. They regarded the Saudi *ulama*, as having sold out to the monarchy, betraying its duty.

The shock of this bloody siege greatly harmed the prestige of the Saudi monarchy, which prided itself on being the guardians of Islam's holiest shrines. It was soon followed by rioting in the oil-rich eastern province by members of the 120,000-strong Shia minority, a despised and oppressed group. Instigation from Iran was alleged, and in fact at this very time a new radio station was set up in Iran, calling itself 'The Voice of the Islamic Revolution in Saudi Arabia'. The voice of Ayatollah Khomeini urged workers in the vital oilfields of Saudi Arabia to revolt, directed essentially at the Shia one-third of Aramco's workforce.

The challenge to the conservative Saudi monarchy comes from radical Islamic puritanism, all the more grave because the House of Saud claims to represent Islam. The contradictions of Saudi policies, both domestic and foreign, have been exposed in particular by its fundamentalist critics. In spite of a reasonably successful drive for economic diversification and education, Saudi Arabia remains almost entirely dependent on foreign expertise, labour and investment income, the *rentier* state par excellence. Since the shocks of 1979, a new Saudi assertiveness has been in evidence in foreign policy, as Riyadh distanced itself from Washington's overtly pro-Israeli stance, trying to prove that it could make a foreign policy of its own after all.

The radical fundamentalist challenge comes home every year, during the *Hadj* (pilgrimage season) to Mecca and Medina, as hundreds of thousands of Muslim pilgrims converge on the holy cities. Ever since 1979, this has been made the occasion for rowdy and dramatic demonstrations by huge contingents of Iranian pilgrims, carrying posters, and distributing pro-Khomeini leaflets which bitterly criticise the Saudi rulers. The very institution of monarchy is reviled as unIslamic. In 1984 the Iranians numbered 150,000 led by Ayatollah Taheri of Isfahan. The moral pretensions of the House of Saud do not permit it to exclude any country's Muslims from making *Hadj* – their religious right and duty – reserving only the right to confiscate any weapons found.

Conservative counter-attack

Oil wealth has given the House of Saud many means of spreading its conservative version of fundamentalism. From the 1960s this hitherto peripheral and petty kingdom began to counter Nasser's various moves in the Middle East, and after 1973 its quadrupled oil revenues gave it the means to be more ambitious. Saudi Arabia dominates the Organisation of the Islamic Conference (OIC), which was founded in 1969, and is based in Jeddah – though Jerusalem is claimed as its future base, after its 'return' to Arab control. The OIC has 13 subsidiary organisations, seven affiliated institutions and six specialised committees. It has tried to provide a framework for positive action in ending disputes and wars between Muslim states – with conspicuous failure. It has played a big part in promoting an Islamic (ic, non-interest) banking system, Islamic universities in various countries of Africa and Asia as well as economic co-operation between rich and poor Muslim states. At the third

Islamic Summit Conference in 1981, held in Taif in Saudi Arabia, the Saudis offered one billion dollars towards a three billion dollar programme.

A proliferation of Islamic conferences funded by Saudi organisations take place each year in the various cities of Muslim countries. Lavish patronage of 'Islamic' enquiries into the social sciences have begun to produce a new breed of researcher and teacher at universities. Posts with high salaries in new universities in the kingdom and in the Gulf attract many Egyptian and other Arab graduates, some of them adopting neo-fundamentalist views for the first time in their lives.

Opposition to communism, to Soviet influence and other radical or revolutionary ideologies, as well as to Zionism, is one negative plank of Saudi strategy. The positive side is seen in persuading other Muslim states to move towards what the Saudis claim are authentic Islamic policies, by abandoning Western models and codes and adopting instead Shari'a laws. Here Saudi Arabia can point to some successes, as some of the Gulf states move closer to the Shari'a code, and Pakistan, Mauritania and Sudan renounce, at least in part, the legal systems of the colonial era. These changes, however, have been so far more of style and rhetoric than of substance, critics maintain. What is certain is that many near-bankrupt military regimes in Muslim countries have gone along some way with applying Shari'a laws, promising gradual 'Islamification' of their societies – and receiving often large loans and grants from Saudi-based institutions. A symbolic change common to many ex-colonial states has been the substitution of Friday, the Muslim Sabbath, for the Sunday holiday imposed by Christian colonial administrations.

Saudi funds from state and private sources promote a wide range of contacts at different levels, from the teaching of Arabic in non-Arab countries to the building of mosques and cultural centres as well as provision for scholarships for foreign students to study Islamic subjects in the kingdom. The Muslim World League (*Rabitat al-Alam al-Islami*) is very active in these fields.

'Propaganda pro fide' is carried on from Riyadh on a scale which bears comparison with Moscow's effort for communism. Islamic radio programmes are funded for many languages. At the end of 1984 a printing press was opened in Medina, designed to produce seven million copies of the Quran each year. As well as copies of the Quran in fine calligraphy, it will print translations for the great majority of the world's Muslims who cannot read Arabic. The centre will also produce 30,000 sets of audio and video cassettes annually, at a total cost of 140 million dollars.

CLASHING IDEOLOGIES IN THE MAGHREB

North Africa contains in miniature the complexities of the international political scene. The four countries of the Maghreb represent the different tendencies to be found elsewhere in the Muslim world, and some of the contradictions too. Fundamentalist groups have grown in popular appeal in the 1980s, but nowhere do they really threaten a government. Algeria's state socialism has tried to control and supervise religion by appointing salaried official mullahs for mosques, but the faithful prefer to attend unofficial mosques. Algeria's fundamentalist *Ahl al-Da'wa* movement has created disturbances, notably in 1981 at Algiers university, but the root causes seem to have been economic and social, rather than religious. The same could be said of the serious rioting in cities of Tunisia and Morocco in January 1984, after news of sharp price rises in bread, because of the removal of state subsidies. Both governments found it essential to keep bread priced artificially low, giving poor Moroccans and Tunisians at least their staple food, like citizens of the Roman empire.

The treaty of unity between the Maghreb's most unlikely partners, Morocco and Libya, surprised all observers, alarming some. Morocco's conservative monarchy, with close ties to the USA and France, pledged in August 1984 to work towards unity with the radical Islamic Socialist republic of Libya. It was the latest in a series of ephemeral 'unities' promoted by Colonel (or 'Brother') Qadhafi – one which has some mutual political benefits, and little substance.

Qadhafi's unique brand of radical ideology has attracted attention not for its intrinsic interest, but because Libya's booming oil revenues combined with its small population give ample scope for foreign adventures. Qadhafi has been quite wrongly cast as a fundamentalist by some writers, yet Islam is only one ingredient in Qadhafi's philosophy, along with Arab nationalism, anarchism, populism and Marxism, as expressed in Libya's actions. *The Green Book* of Qadhafi advocates a system of direct democracy on the anarchist model, with spontaneous 'people's committees' and syndicates uniting to rule Libya without the need for either party politics or a state bureaucracy. The reality is very different, with a repressive, brutal dictatorship. Libya's instability is especially evident in its adventurist foreign policy. Its 'foreign legion' of mainly African mercenaries has suffered one reverse after another in erratic interventions around Africa. Aid and training for terrorists has gone to many groups claiming to fight imperialism, again without much effect.

For many young fundamentalists, however, Qadhafi's Libya seems a beacon of radical, anti-imperialist activity. Libya is remote, and Qadhafi a revolutionary genius. They would not agree that the Libyan leader has failed to heed the advice of his idol Nasser: "Don't try to invent electricity, it has been done already". The image of Qadhafi outside Libya is often that of a clown, a *naif* simpleton like Voltaire's Candide. He has, however, succeeded in communicating his vision of the future to Muslims around the world: "a vision of the need to develop his country, transform the society, rediscover the true Islam, regenerate the Arab world, and unite it, and fire his generation with the same compulsions".[9] Though Qadhafi has never favoured the Muslim Brotherhood's activities, often attacking it as a tool of imperialism, his name is linked to the spread of fundamentalism.

INDEPENDENCE STRUGGLES AND THE HOLY WAR

In various countries Muslims are engaged in struggles for independence or separatism, in which fundamentalism plays a significant role, along with nationalism, Sufism and traditional, tribal Islam. In Afghanistan, where a struggle popularly regarded as a *jihad* has been going on against the Soviet invasion at the end of 1979, fundamentalists have provided a positive ideology, organisation to fight, and also channelled Arab and Western money and arms to the internal Afghan guerrilla resistance. Afghan fundamentalists reflect the indirect influence of Pakistan's *Jamaat-i Islami* and the Muslim Brotherhood, and the Shia minority contains elements inspired by Iran's Revolution, subsidised from Iran.

In three states of Asia, Muslim minorities are at war with their governments, seeking autonomy or independence. In the Philippines Libyan-backed rebels of the Moro National Liberation Front have been fighting in Mindanao since 1972. Their struggle is claimed to be on behalf of the country's 2·5 million Muslims, and received aid from Libya and other Arab states.

In Thailand and Burma there are also Muslim insurgencies, aided by Arab states. Fundamentalists play a part as individuals in all these struggles, but they started because of specific, local grievances, often to do with land or alleged discrimination. In Burma it was anti-Muslim riots in towns in the summer of 1983, and discriminatory citizenship laws passed that same year which roused Muslim leaders to struggle for a protected place in Burma, not for a separate Islamic state.

In Yugoslavia, Europe's largest Muslim community of four millions centred in Bosnia, there has been a growing Islamic revival since 1970. Money for a mosque building programme and Islamic cultural centres has been provided by Saudi Arabia, Kuwait, Libya and other oil-rich Muslim states, keen to help Islam in a communist state. Eleven Muslims were recently jailed in Sarajevo, convicted of being members of a counter-revolutionary group, "attacking the brotherhood of the nation of Yugoslavia", and spreading propaganda about an alternative "Islamic order". Allegations of Iranian aid for these Bosnian Muslims were, however, less than convincing, as brutal police methods were used to obtain 'evidence'.

In Western Europe and North America there are some striking recent initiatives of a fundamentalist or Pan–Islamic inspiration, nearly always relying on funds from one or more Muslim state. The Muslim Institute of London is a centre of Islamic research, aiming at making a positive presentation of Islam in the West, but concerned basically with Muslims living in the West and the young generation born there, which is seen as in danger of assimilation. The Muslim Institute is linked to *The Crescent International* based in Toronto, which started in 1980 as, 'news magazine of the Islamic movement". Both have a shrill, strongly anti-Western bias, and are enthusiastic supporters of the Iranian revolution. The director of the Muslim Institute, a journalist called Kalim Siddiqui, claims, in one of many booklets, that: "Western civilisation is in fact a plague and a pestilence. It is no civilisation at all. It is a disease . . ."

A more ambitious, sophisticated and independent venture is the lively monthly *Arabia: The Islamic World Review*, which started from London in 1981. Founded by a group of rich Saudi businessmen, (as part of the Islamic Press Agency), it is intended to provoke a dialogue, and a meeting of minds in a badly split world. The new English-language monthly declared its aims to be to provide, "more accurate information and more informed and perceptive comment from predominantly Muslim perspectives and to provide a forum for dialogue between Muslims and others on the whole range of issues affecting the contemporary world".

The time seemed auspicious to launch *Arabia*. Two years later. however. an editor complained. "in every Muslim country there is a heightened tendency to believe in conspiracy theories and to ascribe ulterior motives to those questioning state policies and social practices". *Arabia*'s editor criticised a trend in the Muslim world which he described as. "political and intellectual introversion". And by 1985. the fundamentalist tendency seemed to dominate this international Islamic monthly.

Modern technological change, and in particular the transistor radio. has helped spread ideas as never before. across national frontiers and into remote rural communities where few people can read. One effect has been to make the Muslim *umma* (community of believers) more of a reality. Village Islam. Sufism and other expressions of religion or politics co-exist with various models of fundamentalist Islam. in a battle for minds. In this, the female half of the population has hardly counted. as yet.

WOMEN'S PLACE IN THE ISLAMIC SOCIETY

There are few areas of life where Muslims are more sensitive to Western or liberal criticism than the place of women in society. Fundamentalists tend to have an obsessive concern over women's role. making regulations for all kinds of situations. While traditionalist Muslims have understood education to be reserved for men. fundamentalists do not believe education should be closed to women – but that women should attend segregated institutions.

The principle of female segregation lies at the root of the Islamic social order. Iran is one of the rare contemporary Muslim countries. along with Saudi Arabia, where the state takes it upon itself to define and regulate this code of female behaviour. The legal status and basic freedoms of women have been severely reduced in Iran, by the revocation of the Family Protection Law of 1967 (a piece of legislation on Western lines. giving protection to wives against arbitrary divorce and other rights given husbands under Shari'a law). A puritanical attitude to the display of feminine charms in public has led to organised patrols of men and women monitoring the streets of Tehran. Women caught using cosmetics. failing to cover all their hair with a scarf or those whom the Islamic prudes judge to be indecently dressed. can be beaten or put in prison. A prominent member of Iran's Supreme Judicial Council. Moussavi Bojnurdi. in 1984 described women who did not cover themselves fully as "public prostitutes". warning that the law of *Ta'azir* (religious punishment) allotted 74 lashes to women for failing to wear the *hejab*. and dressing decently. In Iran women still keep their jobs in state offices. though senior appointments are the monopoly of men.

Outside Iran. it is the full purdah system of female segregation which is propagated by most fundamentalists. Maududi's book on *Purdah*. (first published in India in 1939 in Urdu. and since in numerous editions and translations), is one of very few books written by a Muslim about this institution. being also unusually systematic and detailed. Maududi eloquently defends all traditional social restrictions on Muslim women, arguing that nature itself has made women unfit to take an active role in society, outside the home where she belongs. Nature decreed that woman is passive, and man active, claimed Maududi. Woman has such a degree of biological disabilities, and such huge family responsibilities as to preclude her leaving purdah in a well-ordered society.

"Is it justice that, besides performing their natural functions in which the male cannot share, women should also be burdened with those civic and cultural responsibilities, for the performance of which nature has freed man from all other (ie biological) functions? . . . This is not justice, but injustice, not equality but inequality". Thus purdah accords with a 'natural' dichotomy of sexual capabilities, according to Maududi. Like most Muslim writers of apologetics, Maududi attacks the Western ideals of equality of the sexes and female emancipation by quoting lurid and sensational extracts from European writers on immorality, sexual anarchy and lewd behaviour in the West – as if to warn that this way of life does not work in the West, it is unnatural and not for us.[10]

These unashamedly male chauvinist views on women can be found, even if less systematically argued, in many other fundamentalist Muslim circles. In Turkey, one of the most secularised Muslim lands where women have been to a large extent emancipated since the reforms of Kemal Ataturk in the 1920s, such views are held among members of the National Salvation Party and linked right-wing 'Islamic' parties. For these Turkish men, the mixing of the sexes is shameful and dangerous too. Women are like roses, they explain – beautiful but fragile, they need men's protection.

The example of Turkey is intriguing, for many reasons. In this stridently secular state, where wearing the Muslim *hejab* (headscarf) is banned in colleges and law courts – as violating "the spirit of the Constitution" a few bold Turkish professional women of fundamentalist views led the way from the later 1960s, offering up themselves as martyrs to Muslim modesty. Unable to teach or practise law, except in Western dress, they prefer to obey their religion, as they understand it.

Signs of an Islamic revival in Turkey have been common since the late 1960s, with religious seminaries, a state-promoted revival of Islamic clergy and also (illegal) Quran classes, as well as a thriving fundamentalist press, ultra-conservative rather than radical. It is Turkey's many small towns in the provinces which are the seedbeds of religious conservatism, as indeed seems to be the case in Egypt. At the same time there is an increasing secularism in the cities, and Islamic militants are an unrepresentative minority. Underground cells of fundamentalists flourish, but in Turkish politics, neo-Islamic parties have made little impact.

Probably the most surprising aspect of the Islamic revival is how the fundamentalist ranks have been swelled from the 1970s by many well educated young women – often coming from modernist, middle class families. The eager adoption of the traditional *chador* or other forms of Muslim dress by young women in Egypt, Tunisia, Iran, Malaysia and elsewhere has been explained by some of these women as stemming from a desire for full identification with their society, a cultural rather than a religious reaction against the 'international style' of blue jeans, Western dress and pop music. But equally for many women, the rejection of tight-fitting Western dress for the anonymity of the *chador* is a rejection of the modernisation linked with the West, and a corresponding identification with the brand of Islam presented by fundamentalist groups.

In Indonesia and Bangladesh, the two largest Muslim nations, women do not appear to have a prominent place in fundamentalist groups, which are anyway poorly developed. There are many educated Muslim women in all the societies where religion is an issue who are ranged passionately against fundamentalism, some of whom are extremely active in organising feminist modernist and secular-minded Muslims to come out openly against what they fear could be the curtailment of women's progress as equal citizens. As could be expected, it is notably in Pakistan and Egypt that womens' groups have started to defend their rights against the fundamentalists. If modernists often claim too that their cause is based on Islam, it should cause no surprise. The name of Islam is invoked, on the one hand to justify and legitimate an existing order, and on the other to condemn it and replace it. Why, after all, in the 20th century AD – or 15th century AH – should we expect Islam to be any more one-dimensional than its ideological rivals, such as Christianity and Marxism?

REVIVAL – OR FALSE DAWN FOR ISLAM?

"Religion is as effectually destroyed by bigotry as by indifference", wrote Ralph Waldo Emerson. There are many severe Muslim critics of the trend to fundamentalism, who name the Islamic activists fanatics and derisively call them, *Ikhwan al-Shaitan* or 'Brothers of the Devil' (Satan). Some call them fascists. How accurate is such a judgment?

At first sight, there are indeed close parallels between the phenomenon of fascism and the rise of Muslim fundamentalism. The class appeal, as in fascism, has been largely to the lower middle classes – poorly paid civil servants, small traders, skilled workers and young army officers. The frustrations, discontent and economic insecurity of these classes have been ably exploited by fundamentalist politicians, producing in some Muslim societies solid support. Another common element is charismatic leadership – that rare quality which Max Weber defined as being founded upon: "A certain quality of an individual personality by which he is set apart from ordinary men and treated as endowed with supernatural, superhuman or at least specifically exceptional powers or qualities". The mystical cult of the leader is most evident in contemporary Iran, where Ayatollah Khomeini attracts blind obedience and adoration by the masses.

At the time when Muslim fundamentalism spread its roots by parties or small groups in Egypt, Lebanon and India, fascism was fashionable and even glamorous; Mussolini's Blackshirts and Hitler's invincible armies seemed to many people to represent a brave new future, which would sweep away the corrupt old order. Key themes for both ideologies are discipline, order, authority and tradition. Where not actually opposed to the principle of parliamentary democracy, or contemptuous of it as 'unIslamic', fundamentalist ideologies have in mind 'guided democracy' of an authoritarian type. They praise the merits of firm leadership and obedience to the appointed leader.

In some fundamentalist parties there is a strong emphasis on hierarchy, with defined grades of authority within their structure, as fascist parties are organised. Their activities often display a narrow intolerance of opposition, and a willingness to use violence in pursuit of 'Islamic' causes. For both ideologies, there is little scope for women outside the home, where the domestic duties of raising children, cooking and running the home are believed to best suit women's nature.

This may seem a formidable catalogue of parallel characteristics, but it is insufficient to identify fundamentalism with fascism, because of the absence of certain crucial fascist elements. Many specialists agree that fascism is a phenomenon seen in developed industrial states, with close links forged between capitalism and fascism. As for agricultural or Third World societies, warns Martin Kitchen: "to analyse such regimes in terms of fascism does nothing to provide a true understanding of the nature and dynamics of such systems of domination".[11]

Among the key elements in fascism have been the rejection of religious authority, and the substitution of the party and leader for religious belief. Fascist parties have also tended to be ultra-nationalist, rather than internationalist, as the fundamentalist orientation certainly is. The distinguished German historian of fascism, Ernst Nolte, defined it as: "anti-Marxism which seeks to destroy the enemy by the evolvement of a radically opposed and yet related ideology and by the use of almost identical and yet typically modified methods, always, however, within the unyielding framework of national self-assertion and autonomy".[12]

Even if it is true that outside the mainstream of European fascism, there have been examples of fascist parties closely allied to churches, (as was the Falange in Spain), by no stretch of the imagination could fundamentalists be accurately described as ultra-nationalist, claiming as they do membership of and loyalties to the Muslim world community (or 'Arab nation') rather than the nation state. Nor has racialism as such been an essential ingredient of fundamentalist movements. Instead they share a sense of the uniqueness, a special God-given quality of the Muslim community. Fundamentalists also have in common, as we have seen, a strong belief in the conspiracy theory of history, which is one of the characteristic elements of populism.

The fundamentalist phenomenon, now endemic in Muslim societies, is probably closer to populism than to fascism. It may not fit easily with definitions of the concept of populism as developed in non-Muslim societies, but Muslim fundamentalism can take its place alongside a whole range of populist movements, differing greatly in content, ideology (or the absence of it) or class appeal. As we have seen, there is in fascism a substantial populist content, varying in importance in the various manifestations of fascism in Europe. The many different Muslim fundamentalist movements naturally vary somewhat in their populist and totalitarian aspects, yet they do agree – in their propaganda at least – to the populist premise that virtue resides in the simple people, who are the overwhelming majority, and in their collective religious traditions.[13]

Muslim Fundamentalism 27

As far as the prospect for Muslim fundamentalism is concerned, it will surely depend largely on the political and economic fortunes of the major, prestigious Muslim states, either indirectly encouraging or directly patronising the spread of the various rival versions of fundamentalism. These ideas are in fashion at present, but they represent one extreme only. In the long term, moderation is more typical of Islamic culture. If fundamentalist ideas for solving the manifold problems of society are seen to fail, others will come into fashion in their place. It is too early yet to write off Islamic modernism as a force for progress in the Muslim world.

NOTES

[1] *Le Monde*, 18 April 1984, and see further Malcolm Yapp, *Contemporary Islamic Revivalism*, in *Asian Affairs*, London, June 1980.
[2] J W Williams, veiling in Egypt, in Esposito (Ed) *Islam and Development*, Syracuse, USA, 1980.
[3] Fazlur Rahman, Islamic neo-fundamentalism, in D. Stoddard (Ed) *Change and the Muslim World*, USA, 1981 and D Khalid, *Reislamisierung und Entwicklungspolitik*, Koln, West Germany, 1982.
[4] E J Hobsbawm, *Primitive Rebels*, London, p 58.
[5] Richard Mitchell, *The Society of the Muslim Brothers*, London, 1969.
[6] Duran Khalid, the final replacement of parliamentary democracy by the 'Islamic System' in Pakistan, in W-P Zingel, *Pakistan in its fourth decade*, Hamburg, West Germany, 1983.
[7] Ervand Abrahamian, *Iran between two Revolutions*, Princeton, USA, 1982, p 530.
[8] A H Cordesman, *The Gulf and the Search for Strategic Stability*, Boulder, Col., USA, 1984.
[9] Ruth First, *Libya the elusive revolution*, London, 1974, p 21.
[10] A Maududi, *Purdah and the status of women in Islam*, Lahore, Pakistan, 1972, and for a modernist Muslim critique, see Mazhar ul Haq Khan, *Purdah and polygamy*, Peshawar, 1972.
[11] Martin Kitchen, *Fascism*, London, 1976.
[12] Ernst Nolte, *Three Faces of Fascism*, New York, USA, 1969, p 40.
[13] See further G Ionescu and E Gellner, (Ed) *Populism, its meanings and national characteristics*, section 7 by Peter Wiles, section 10 by Peter Worsley, also Worsley's *The Third World*, London, 1967.

SELECTED READING LIST OF GENERAL INTEREST

Hamid Enayat, *Modern Islamic Political Thought*, London, 1982.
J L Esposito (Ed), *Islam and Development: Religion and Sociopolitical change*, Syracuse, USA, 1980.
Albert Hourani, *Arabic Thought in the Liberal Age*, London, 1970.
G H Jansen, *Militant Islam*, London, 1979.
Edward Mortimer, *Faith and Power: The Politics of Islam*, London, 1982.
James Piscatori (Ed), *Islam in the Political Process*, Cambridge, 1983.
Maxime Rodinson, *Marxism and the Muslim world*, London, 1980.

Part V
Christian Terrorist Groups

[13]

Messianic Sanctions for Terror

David C. Rapoport

A most striking development in recent years has been the use of theological concepts to justify terrorist activity, a phenomenon which I have called "holy terror."[1] The most notorious instance has occurred among the Shia, where the attempt to revive *jihad* (holy war) doctrines has produced some remarkable incidents in Lebanon and elsewhere. A major feature of the Shia episodes has been a striking willingness, even eagerness, to die, a disposition sustained by the belief that one who is killed while fighting in a *jihad* is guaranteed a place in paradise. This promise of an extraordinary personal benefit for assailants who die (a perversion, incidentally, of the traditional doctrine) gives Shia terror an awesome dimension in the eyes of potential victims.[2]

In the United States abortion clinic bombers regularly cite scripture to justify their deeds, and several scripture-based, messianic, right-wing terrorist groups have emerged in the last few years, the most prominent being "The Covenant, the Sword and the Arm of the Lord" and "The Order."[3]

Another and most interesting case came to light in Israel in 1984 when the government convicted Jewish terrorists who had organized the "Temple Mount Plot," a conspiracy to destroy Muslim sacred shrines built on Judaism's holiest site, that of the second temple. If the shrines were obliterated, the construction of a third temple would be possible at last, a circumstance which some visualize to be a precondition of the coming of the Messiah.[4] It has been alleged, too, that American Christian messianic groups (who may be interested in creating conditions for Armageddon) have furnished funds for third temple enterprises, a project which has certainly been very dear to some Christian elements for more than a century.[5] I do not know whether the Messiah will come if the third temple is built, but I do know that if the Muslim holy sites are blown up catastrophic results could ensue which may indeed put us one step closer to an Armageddon. But will it be the one scripture describes?

Holy terror seems new to us, but prior to the French Revolution it was the dominant, perhaps only form of terror. And holy terror, whenever it appears, is usually linked to messianism. Two well-known historical examples are the Assassins (*Nizaris*) or *Fidayeen* of Islam[6] and the Jewish Zealots and *Sicarii*. The Assassins emerged in the eleventh century, persisted for two hundred years, and are the first known example of an international conspiracy organized by a state, a conspiracy which threatened the governments of several Islamic realms.[7] The Zealots, who lived earlier in the first century, survived for a shorter period, some sixty years, but they had enormous significance. They successfully provoked a massive rebellion against Rome, one which ended in catastrophe, for the second temple, the ritual center of Judaism, was destroyed. The final act in the rebellion was a gruesome mass suicide at Masada. Subsequently, the revolt inspired two more massive uprisings in successive generations. As a result Judea was depopulated, large Jewish centers in Roman-controlled Cyprus and Egypt were decimated, and the final tragedy of the second

Comparative Politics   January 1988

exile or Diaspora occurred, whose traumatic impact on Jewish consciousness became the central Jewish experience for the next two thousand years and altered virtually every institution of Jewish life.

No single messianic terror group has occupied such a prominent place in Christianity. Christian messianic movements have been numerous and episodic and have had comparatively less effect. Still, the Christian examples are much better documented than those in Islam and Judaism, and they are important and instructive, too, because Christian terror is not so intimately connected to underground organizations. The Crusades, for example, had an essential messianic component which produced some grotesque forms of violence, especially among the poor who launched what some historians have called Peoples' Crusades.[8] And for brief moments in the late medieval period the Taborites and the Anabaptists created public arrangements which could be called systems of state terror.

It is, of course, a commonplace among the historians and sociologists of messianic movements that they often produce terror. But two key issues have been ignored which I want to address. Most messianic groups have not engaged in terror, and indeed they are often committed to pacifism, especially those in the Christian tradition. One wants to know therefore why a group behaves in one way rather than the other and what the relationship is between such seemingly different matters as pacifism and terrorism.

Bryan Wilson's admirable *Magic and the Millennium* comes closest to discussing these issues, but he is concerned mainly with external circumstances—the impact of colonialism upon indigenous peoples—and rarely focuses on those elements of beliefs which predispose some messianists to terror.[9] Furthermore, he makes no distinction between violence and terror, a difficulty he shares with many students of messianism.[10]

The principal question I want to discuss, then, is why messianism produces terror sometimes, or, better still, what the logical and psychological links are between specific messianic motifs and terror. The problem of external circumstances will *not* be treated; my concern is with the internal dynamics. Although I will use a few examples from Islam and from primitive societies, I will focus on traditional Jewish and Christian experiences which have always provided the basic paradigms for the rest of the world.

Let us begin by making clear how I shall be using the two key terms, terror and messianism. Most academics see the terrorist as one who uses violence unlawfully for political purposes, and there is a strong tendency to describe terrorists as members of small underground rebel groups that employ hit and disappear (that is, guerrilla-like) tactics.[11] I prefer the more traditional conception, which, as we shall see, is especially appropriate for messianic experiences. In this view, terror is understood as extranormal or extramoral violence, a type which goes beyond the conventions or boundaries particular societies establish to regulate coercion. These conventions identify justifications and establish limits and immunities which enable one to distinguish between the appropriate and inappropriate social responses to criminal as opposed to belligerent activities.

Rebels sometimes accept the same restraints that governments do. It would be very difficult, for example, to distinguish the methods of the major protagonists in our own revolutionary and civil wars. But other times they do not. The distinguishing characteristic of the terrorist, therefore, is a deliberate decision to abandon these restraints or to refuse to accept as binding the prevailing moral distinctions between belligerents and neutrals, combatants and noncombatants, appropriate and inappropriate targets, legitimate and

David C. Rapoport

illegitimate methods. The terrorist *knows* that others will regard his actions as shocking or as atrocities, and this is one reason why he acts as he does, for his object in using terror for messianic ends is to create a "new consciousness" by methods which provoke extreme emotional reactions—panic, horror, revulsion, outrage, and sympathy. In this respect, any person or group may commit terrorist acts; certainly rebels may do so, but so can large armies and established authorities, as the cases of the Crusades and the Zealot-*Sicarii* revolt illustrate. The nature of the act, not the status of the persons who commit it, is the critical feature.

What will be meant by messianism? One who believes in messianism is one who has faith that there will be a day in which history or life on *this* earth will be transformed totally and irreversibly from the condition of perpetual strife which we have all experienced to one of perfect harmony that many dream about. In some messianic visions it is imagined that there will be no sickness and no tears, that we will all be wholly *liberated* from government, a condition of perfect freedom. History ends in all messianic visions *because* God has promised us that it would. At His appointed time He will intervene in our affairs, saving a "righteous remnant," all those who deserve to be saved.[12]

If I may be permitted a brief digression, one should note that, while messianic movements are worth studying in their own right, understanding them also has value for the light they may throw on related phenomena. Certain terrorist groups, like those which came out of the student movements in the 1960s, are often called messianic for good reason, though they have no religious underpinning. Stripped of its theological dimension, the messianic aspiration, moreover, bears an extraordinary similarity to those of the "great" revolutions of France, Russia, and China, and a kinship between messianism and revolution has been recognized by persons as different as Burke and Engels, Talmon and Hobsbawm. It was the French Revolution, too, which gave terror its first secular justification, and terror was an essential part of the Russian and Chinese experiences.

Hobsbawm makes the *minimum* case for linking messianism to revolution and to revolutionary terror. Messianism is a necessary social illusion for generating the "superhuman efforts" revolutions require. "Would the Bolsheviks have [made the revolution] to exchange the Russia of Tchekov for that of Khrushchev?" For a moment within the small group of revolutionaries, messianism produces an ideal society, and, "when normal modes of behavior creep in again," the disappointed revolutionaries use terror, for they want to believe the ideal is betrayed, not that it is flawed.[13]

I will provide some more material concerning these parallels as we go along, mostly in the footnotes, but I must return to our basic concern, the subject of religious messianism. Each messianic vision or paradigm contains its own particular details, which pertain to matters like timing, agents, process, and signs. Some of these details, and hence, some of the visions, seem peculiarly conducive to terror. But no matter what the particular content of a belief may be, its significance depends initially on two conditions. Believers must think that the day of deliverance is near or imminent, and they must also think that their actions can or must consummate the process. When these conditions are fulfilled, then and only then will six substantive details of a messianic vision influence the recourse to terror. They are (1) the nature of the desired action, (2) the cause or character of the messianic aspiration, (3) the proof that believers think may be necessary to demonstrate sufficient faith, (4) the moral qualities ascribed to participants in the messianic struggle, (5) the "signs" or "portents" of

Comparative Politics   January 1988

a messianic intervention, and (6) the character of the deity's involvement. Messianic beliefs, it should be stressed, rarely form a coherent whole and are usually sufficiently ambiguous to allow participants to choose between alternatives or abandon one course for another when this appears more productive. Finally, a particular religious culture often has a variety of paradigms to choose from.

Imminence and Human Agency: The Necessary Conditions

Clearly, one can believe both that a messianic era is predestined and that the day of deliverance is neither near nor predictable. But it does seem unreasonable to think that in all times in all circumstances those who believe that a day of reckoning must occur will also remain content with a doctrine that says that this day is always very far off and/or unknowable. The histories of religions with messianic components seem to confirm both propositions. While a sense of imminence is not present usually, it does appear intermittently and sometimes after very long periods of absence. Eight centuries after the messianic vision became firmly rooted in Jewish consciousness through the prophet Isaiah, a sense of imminence finally was aroused in the generation before the Zealot-*Sicarii* revolt and shortly before the development of Christianity. The first five centuries of Christianity exhibited numerous Christian and Jewish messianic episodes, which then ceased until the Crusades in the eleventh century when they began again. A third period occurred in the sixteenth and seventeenth centuries, a fourth during the French Revolution, and another one is apparently developing today.

The hope which a messianic vision supplies is obviously important for the orthodox revealed religions, because without it the rest of the religious tradition may seem onerous or meaningless, and it is quite conceivable that a messianic vision is necessary for the survival of some revealed religions. Judaism had good reason, therefore, to retain its faith that a messiah would come,[14] and the conception was passed on to Christianity and to a lesser extent Islam, where it is known as Mahdism and is especially significant among the Shia. For the Sunni the line between the *Mahdi* and a *mujaddid* is often blurred, the latter being a "renewer of the faith" who revitalizes the community Mohammed established and in effect becomes a state-builder.

While the value of a messianic belief may be self-evident, when a sense of imminence takes over, when some believe that the world will end tomorrow or within a foreseeable future, a variety of dangerous reactions may occur just because so much anxiety will be generated concerning who will be saved and how. Hugh Schonfield's description of the Jews in the first century is not farfetched. "The whole condition of the Jewish people was psychologically abnormal. The strangest tales and imaginings could find ready credence. . . . Almost every event was seized upon to discover how and in what ways it represented a Sign of the Times and threw light on the approach of the End of the Days."[15]

Such anxieties can uproot the orthodox religion itself. Certainly the first targets, and most of the time the *only* targets, of messianists are coreligionists whom they believe are corrupted or contaminated. Since the traditional religion, moreover, is the initial source of the messianic belief, disappointment may induce an exodus from the parent religion altogether. In a messianic episode in Crete (476), many, believing that the sea would part for

David C. Rapoport

them as it did for Moses, threw themselves in and drowned. "Many of the Jews of Crete," an eyewitness observed, "subsequently embraced Christianity."[16]

Orthodox religious leaders attempt to forestall messianic anxieties and explosions in a variety of ways. The most direct way is to deny some of the central tenets of messianism. The Council of Ephesus (431) went right to the root of the matter: it denounced the doctrine of collective salvation on earth as heretical error and fantasy, asserting that the messianic promise pertains only to individuals and to their life after death, an event in the spiritual world. Normally, most Christians have accepted this view, but the relevant Biblical passages can be interpreted differently, and no council could prevent Christians from occasionally believing different interpretations.

Never being able to deny that messianism was a collective phenomena pertaining to the "righteous remnant" who were to continue inhabiting this world, the Jewish tradition was in a weaker position. The rabbis did try to defuse potential tensions by making the Jew's primary responsibility to attend to ordinary living even in the face of clear evidence of a messianic presence. "If you have a sapling in your hand," Rabbi Yochanan Ben Zakkai taught, "and they tell you that the Messiah has come, first plant the sapling and then welcome the Messiah." Sound advice, but not advice always followed.

Spokesmen for the orthodox religions always find it necessary to deny that one could ever know the time for a messianic epoch, and they sometimes even make strenuous efforts to prevent individuals from publicizing contrary views. In England during the Restoration it was a criminal offense to speculate on the date of the Second Coming.[17] Shia authorities in the ninth century denounced the "time determiners" as "liars" who spread "disillusionment and despair."[18] And an early medieval rabbi wrote, "May the curse of heaven fall upon those who calculate the advent of the Messiah and thus create political and social unrest among the people."[19] Each of these cases provides evidence that, as soon as the speculation about the date of the great event becomes a popular activity, there is an inevitable tendency (based I suppose on wishful thinking) to believe that it will happen sooner and sooner or become more and more imminent.[20]

In England speculation was an integral part of seventeenth-century upheavals, just as it was an essential element in the three disastrous rebellions which Jews waged against the Romans much earlier. When a date has been fixed by an existing messianic tradition, one can expect anxieties to intensify as centuries pass and the imminence of the date becomes more apparent.

> Many misfortunes would have been prevented. Many blood stained pages of our history would have been left unwritten, if the rabbinic injunction against calculating the date of the Messiah's appearance had been heeded. As it was, the arrival of *every* date suggested by one or the other of the rabbis caused general excitement among the people. At such times there was never wanting an imposter or a self-deluded dreamer to come forward and take advantage of the opportunity, and thereby bring misery and horror upon thousands.[21]

In Islam the *hadith*, or traditions of Mohammed and his companions, is "a framework for defining what the community is, a framework which is the basis of education and learning as much as practical life."[22] One of these traditions is that the *Mahdi* will emerge at the beginning of a new century according to the Islamic calendar. The startling attack in 1979 on

Comparative Politics   January 1988

the Grand Mosque of Mecca, Islam's holiest shrine, which staggered the Saudi dynasty, occurred in the first hour of the first day of the Islamic year 1400. The assailants, who came from twelve countries including the U.S., named one of their number the *Mahdi*, and nearly every detail in the assault seemed contrived to follow a well-known Islamic tradition.[23] This same tradition has produced other examples. A century ago Chinese Gordon's army was massacred in Khartoum by the Sudanese *Mahdi* who had staked his claim to be the *Mahdi* on the first day of the Islamic year 1300. In the same period several *Mahdi* movements emerged elsewhere, the most conspicuous being the Sanusi movement in Libya, utilizing the same general expectation that that century was *the* century. In Egypt today three messianic groups (one of which assassinated Sadat) have appealed to this dating tradition.[24] It is conceivable that the Iranian revolution may be linked to it too.

Dating traditions in the past created a sense of imminence, and they will continue to do so in the future. I suspect, for instance, that as we approach the year 2000, which is an important date for Christian speculators, messianic expectations will spread rapidly. Does one need to be reminded that messianic expectations at the end of the millenium following Christ were an essential part of the passions which created the Crusades?

There are, in addition to dating traditions, other elements of beliefs relevant to the question of imminence which can be illustrated by looking at the contemporary situation. A most conspicuous characteristic of our world since the 1950s is a general revival of religious enthusiasms,[25] and this revival, like earlier ones, necessarily draws attention to the messianic component in the revealed religions, a component which is usually ignored. Clearly, religious enthusiasm is not messianism, but each religious revival probably stimulates dormant sentiments that a messianic delivery could be imminent.[26]

Messianism is always associated with the presence of "signs," and in our day it is easy for the believer to see two of the most prominent signs in messianic eschatology. In most Jewish, Christian, and Islamic messianic visions, the "Last Days" emerge in the context of world catastrophe, and the spectre of such a possibility has haunted everybody's imagination ever since World War II, most of all in the form of nuclear holocaust but also as ecological, technological, and demographic disasters. Indeed, "end of the world" thinking has become so striking in secular circles that the apocalyptic theme in religious thought has gained some intellectual respectability, as Carl Jung's fascinating *Answer to Job* demonstrates. Never before has the end of the world seemed so feasible, and, since messianism often functions as a device to explain catastrophe, one would expect it to emerge naturally whenever catastrophe is either experienced or anticipated.[27]

A second sign is the restoration of the state of Israel, a common theme in apocalyptic prophecies. The reestablishment of Israel, especially after the Six Days War when the holy places were regained, has had an enormous impact on various American Christian messianic groups loosely lumped together as "fundamentalists." Their interest goes back to the early nineteenth century, when the extraordinary and humiliating failures of millenarians in using Biblical dating schemes to predict the Second Coming compelled them instead to emphasize more the significance of signs or portents, the most important being the restoration of Israel to its ancient homeland.[28] Indeed, in America Zionist activity may have developed among Christians before it did among Jews.[29]

The return to the Land has excited Jewish messianic expectations, as one should have anticipated, and the Six Days War produced the first important genuine Jewish messianic

David C. Rapoport

movement since the seventeenth century, the Gush Emunim (Bloc of the Faithful). Indeed, anticipated possession of the Land is a *sine qua non* of Jewish messianic movements, and in the past its actual repossession after an exile has had enormous consequences. In the First and Second Commonwealths messianic sentiments were stirred too, as they have been today, and it is conceivable that every restoration of Israel will tend in time to generate messianic movements.[30]

Parenthetically, one should note that Islamic messianic expectations are linked to Christian and Judaic ones too. At least in some traditions the *Mahdi* is supposed to appear soon after Christ returns, though it is a moot point just what effects Second Coming anticipations among Christians have had on messianic activity in Islam.

A messianic belief becomes imminent, one might conclude, either because one of its components (such as dating traditions) leads a believer directly to that position regardless of events in the real world or when one of its components can be used as a sign to interpret events of the world as indicators of imminence. But even if the obstacles to making imminence credible are overcome, no action will ensue until the believer also thinks that he can influence messianic events, which means he must deny directly the teachings of the religious establishments on this issue. Among the Jews, for example, a rabbinic tradition persists that the Messiah's advent was fixed in the creation of the world, and even God therefore cannot hasten or retard the process.[31] The problem, however, is that messianism makes sense or is attractive largely *because* we believe that the righteous and the wicked must have different fates. Consequently some believers will conclude, despite what the authorities want us to think, that what we do must count after all. When a sense of imminence takes root, some believers must find it psychologically impossible to regard their actions as irrelevant, because the consequences of being mistaken are so immediate and momentous. *At the very least*, they will act to secure their own salvation. And once the initial barrier to action has been overcome, it will only be a matter of time before different kinds of action make sense too. Soon they may think they can shape the speed or timing of the process.

Range of Conceivable Actions

Clearly, there is no one prescribed way to accomplish these purposes. Messianic speculators have suggested various possibilities, not all consistent with each other, and in the past different movements have tried different courses. One can speak of a range of plausible actions. Believers may make choices, swinging radically sometimes from one alternative to another.

Some activities are patently nonviolent. Proselytizing is common. One may give property away to discharge debts, finance missionary work, and show one's love for humanity as did the Millerites, an American messianic movement (predecessor of the Seventh Day Adventists) in upstate New York in the 1840s. Messianic groups sometimes travel great distances to a sacred site where redemption is supposed to begin. After the Jews were dispersed in the wake of the second temple's destruction, messianic episodes for the next nineteen centuries normally induced a collective exodus to the Holy Land. Groups of Indians in Brazil periodically would peacefully migrate to find "The Land of No Evil." Numerous

Comparative Politics   January 1988

Melanesian cargo cults in the twentieth century awaited deliverance in designated spots. In Jamaica not long ago the Ras Tafari, a black group, organized several times to go to Ethiopia, which they believed the Bible had identified as the site for the Messiah to appear.[32] The Doukhobors, a Russian pacifist sect that was established in the eighteenth century and moved to Canada a century later, began a trek in late autumn 1902 to find a "land of ever-lasting sunshine."[33] Those who have seen the film *Close Encounters of the Third Kind* may recall that the migration to the site of messianic deliverance was a central theme there too.

Action to signify a change of identity or the purification of community often accompanies migration: crops, livestock, and all means of gaining livelihood may be destroyed in a holocaust. Because these objects are mechanisms we use to discharge normal or daily obligations, their destruction symbolizes or represents the emergence of the "new" form of humanity and a faith that one has taken an irreversible step into the new world. In nineteenth-century Russia, the Skoptsi (who numbered tens of thousands, including nobles, officials, rich merchants, and peasants) believed that the messianic period would be populated by sexless beings; therefore, to prove that one really believed, the condition for joining the movement was castration for the men and the cutting of the breasts for the women.

The purification and migration process are more familiar as part of the western experiences in another form. When believers think that an advent is not immediate, they often create a sacred community which tries to separate itself completely from the profane world. These groups initially are characterized by hypernomian behavior, that is, asceticism, excessive self-discipline, and a stringent observation of rules which comprehend every aspect of the individual's life. Sometimes they distinguish themselves from the existing society further by violating conventions sanctified by intense emotional sentiments. The Adamites and Doukhobors were nudists, and many groups attacked sexual and marital conventions by becoming celibate or instituting plural marriages. The ethos of this hypernomian community—and the persecution which may ensue—gives messianists cause to identify themselves as the "righteous remnant."

In Islam the term *Mahdi* (the "right-guided one") connotes "rising from concealment" and/or "rebellion against constituted authority."[34] A group which withdraws has as another purpose the intention to find a better and more secure base in order to organize a violent return. For this reason, perhaps, it might be better to call an Islamic group a hypernomian "counter-society," for the term counter-society seems to have, in the academic literature, the connotation that a violent confrontation is intended.[35] The pattern is reflected in Mohammed's own career which probably provides the archetype or model. When he failed to convert his own people in Mecca, he fled to Medina (*Yathrib*), from which he returned later in triumph.

The significance of that event is indicated by the fact that Islam's calendar begins with it and that Muslims are obliged to set themselves apart or migrate (*hajara*) if they cannot practice their religion suitably. This tradition of creating counter-societies is a way of recapitulating the circumstances of Islam's birth—a pattern which is observable in very different kinds of communities as well.[36] The Assassins (1090–1275) organized Islam's most notorious counter-society, but they were not the first to do so, and the formula is

David C. Rapoport

repeated over and over again through to our own century, as indicated by the examples of the major Egyptian terrorist organizations in the 1970s, one of which assassinated Sadat.

So expected is the messianic recourse to violence in the Islamic world that even Jewish messianism there is often violent too. It is interesting to note, by way of contrast, that in the diaspora circumstances of the Christian world, Jewish messianism rarely has been violent.

The fate of hypernomian groups which withdraw seems more complicated in the Christian world than in Islam. Christian groups usually withdraw not so much to fight as to wait. If society does not leave them alone or compels them to participate, they may resist initially by pacifist methods, even accepting martyrdom, perhaps to remind God of the price being paid for His tardiness! Sometimes, after a difficult period, the groups change their course and actively engage the larger society, moving in the process directly from pacifism to terror. The Anabaptists and Taborites of medieval Europe come to mind as examples,[37] and they were apparently preceded by the Jewish Essenes in the first century. A more recent instance is the case of the Doukhobors' "Sons of Freedom" element which broke the pacifist traditions of the main body in Canada to engage in terror intermittently for several decades after World War II.[38]

The striking change appears puzzling, so much so that one eminent authority has described the process as a "mutation," a term which seems inappropriate for it means a "new species" not able, or at least not likely, to resume its earlier character.[39] But earlier ways are resumed, and therefore there is a "doctrinal logic" to these changes. Whether one chooses pacifism or terror, one still is rejecting the existing conventions governing coercion, and thus there is some consistency in the dynamic. Also because messianism is doomed to failure in its own terms, its life has to be episodic, and it would be quite surprising for the hope to persist and reappear again and again unless there were alternative ways to strive for it. In the messianic visions of the revealed religions, there are several possible courses of action suggested. Believers, thus, can choose to do different things or different things at different phases of the process. The two dominant images in these paradigms are that of the "suffering servant" and that of the "avenging angel," the latter most often representing the final days or the days of destruction.

Pacifism, then, can be understood as activity appropriate only while waiting for messianic activity to begin, behavior which in the case of Christian offshoots also seems to embody the spirit of original religion. To usher in the new age another kind of behavior is necessary. It should be remembered that Christianity, which originally was probably a messianic offshoot of Judaism, developed its own pacifist tradition in the wake of the terror in the Zealot-*Sicarii* revolt, and many of these early pacifists believed that in His Second Coming Christ would have a sword. It is not surprising, therefore, to find that, when messianists who abandon pacifism become convinced that they were mistaken about the timing of the process, they often revert to pacifist traditions. Anabaptist history reflects this rationale: the group returned to pacifism after a gruesome experience with terror during the Reformation.

The pattern occurs infrequently in Islam, though the sword is supposed to be used as a last resort and for defensive purposes only. Nonetheless, Islam has a few striking examples to parallel the Christian practice. Some observers have interpreted the dynamics of Shia life in a similar way. Although pacifism and terror may not be appropriate terms, "Shi'ism can . . . accord legitimacy both to passive submissiveness and explosive activism . . . at times [it] has been understood . . . to justify submission to oppression and injustice, since the

Comparative Politics   January 1988

prevalence of injustice might be interpreted as a sign of the imminent return of the Twelfth Imam (and the messianic era). On the other hand, certain clerics have argued that active opposition to corrupt sovereign power and a positive emphasis on restoring justice will hasten the return of the Twelfth Imam."[40] In nineteenth-century Iran the Babi messianic movement began in a terror campaign but upon defeat transformed itself into the Bahai, a pacifist group. And there seem to be examples of primitive peoples in North America and Africa doing the same thing in the wake of the decisive failure of their insurrections to extricate themselves from western domination.[41]

Bryan Wilson's study of the Christadelphians, a contemporary British messianic movement, emphasizes something else which is relevant as well, namely, that pacifism sometimes can be nourished by a profound hatred and not simply by love.

> Christadelphianism is basically a revolutionary organization, vigorously opposed to the social order. . . . . But this attitude is not translated into social action, although at the appointed time there would be disposition to do so. . . . The Christadelphian is in conflict with the prevailing social order but powerless to organize its overthrow. . . . Reform [is] useless . . . he [does] not want the world to get better; he [is] opposed to peace, and he want[s] war. Misery was the world's lot and his pronouncement of the fact [falls] little short of active rejoicing. He was emotionally involved in his predictions for disaster out of which he alone would emerge triumphant.[42]

A study of the sequence of events in the Zealot-*Sicarii* uprisings, which were preceded by an extensive passive resistance campaign, reveals another reason, based on what I would call psychological circumstances and not belief. Angry unarmed demonstrations will tax superbly disciplined troops, the Romans learned. When this discipline breaks down, the atrocities which result, especially when women and children participate, may so disturb a community that virtually any countermeasure seems justified. There are comparable instances in the modern world (such as Northern Ireland and Cyprus) which suggest that there is a connection between passive resistance and terror which is independent of the messianic ethos.

The Cause

If a messianic believer thinks that he must participate in a struggle to "force the end," the nature of the messianic aspiration itself or the cause will become a factor conducive to terror. This is our second element of belief. It would seem rather obvious that, when the stakes of any struggle are perceived as being great, the conventional restraints on violence diminish accordingly. For example, wars which threaten the very existence of the belligerent parties are normally more savage than those for territory or trade, and it is common knowledge that the appearance of revolutionary states in an existing international order introduces a new level of ruthlessness in world politics. If nothing else were involved, the extraordinary image messianists often sketch of the future—the transformation of human existence itself—can induce one to waive limits. While the details of the messianic existence

David C. Rapoport

may differ, since the outcome is always a perfected society, the effect on the scope of violence would seem to be uniform in all cases.

One reason why restraints on conflict are sometimes accepted by belligerents is that they anticipate that there will be more wars in the future and that therefore it would be advantageous for all parties to accept limits. The messianic struggle, on the other hand, will end all wars. To accept restraints for humane or prudential reasons might only delay the outcome.

Unreal expectations necessarily create bitter disappointments and savage responses. Perhaps the most common one is the hunt for the "traitors" responsible. The Zealots-*Sicarii* and the Anabaptists had their reigns of terror which resemble those which came later in the great revolutions of France, Russia, and China. Another natural response may be a group decision that the messianic date is not imminent as the group had thought initially. Accordingly, it adopts a less aggressive attitude toward the world, and this attitude sometimes incites a dissenting element to engage in desperate actions against the larger society hoping that the latter's response might compel the messianic group to resume its initial stance. This *may* have been the motive behind the frenzied mutilation murders of whites in San Francisco (1973–1974) by the Fruit of Islam, an element which broke away from the Black Muslim movement when this movement began moderating its extraordinary militancy. There are secular parallels too. The origin of the Italian Red Brigades has usually been understood as an attempt to make the Communist Party believe in revolution again.

The belief that a purge will be beneficial can take other forms. In Israel when the Camp David Accords were struck, it seemed to a few members of the Gush Emunim that a process of relinquishing the Land had begun, that God was allowing the messianic opportunity to slip from Israel's grasp because the people had sinned in allowing Muslims to retain sacred shrines on Israel's holy sites.

> It [Camp David] was a direct signal from Heaven that a major national offense was committed, a sin that was responsible for the political disaster and its spiritual consequences. Only one prominent act of desecration could match the magnitude of the setback: the presence of the Muslims and their shrine on Temple Mount, the holiest Jewish site, the sacred place of the first, second and third (future) Temples.[43]

Proof

A third element, which contains a range of variable details, would be the "evidence" needed to demonstrate faith. If hypernomian behavior or traditional tests seem ineffective, new tests to prove moral worthiness might be contrived. In the first century some believed the condition of God's intervention to be His conviction that the believer's faith was unshakeable, and perhaps the most striking single action in this regard occurred when the Zealots decided to burn their own food supplies after Jerusalem was taken, signifying that they had indeed placed all their trust in Him. In being bound by His promise to rescue the righteous remnant, He had to act. While the Zealots thought that there was no better way to demonstrate commitment, most rabbis subsequently interpreted this as an effort to blackmail God which could not possibly succeed.

Comparative Politics   January 1988

A similar process has been observed in some nineteenth-century rebellions in Algeria. "The apocalyptic could interpret concern for practical organizational considerations as a sign of doubt about the ultimate arrival of divine assistance. Strategic planning, military training and the building up of supplies appeared as distractions from the true task of the apocalyptic, namely the preaching of hope, deliverance, ... the realm of justice, [and] the superiority of faith over common sense."[44]

The most striking quality of the religious terrorist in Islam, especially among the ancient Assassins, whose ritual and method effectively prevented escape, seems to be an eagerness to seek martyrdom.[45] The reward in paradise is the most common explanation, but to be a martyr, as the term itself indicates, is "to bear *witness* for the truth," and martyrdom, hence, is a mechanism to demonstrate fidelity, an act which also dispels the doubts of believers and aids proselytizing efforts. Among the Jews in the period preceding the Zealot uprisings a similar kind of martyrdom developed for the first time.

The line between martyrdom and suicide obviously is not always clear, as the gruesome spectacle at Masada indicates. In Christian messianic sects suicides of this sort occurred especially in Russia during the seventeenth century. The most recent example occurred at Jonestown, which has been called a case of revolutionary "suicide," a testament to the belief that the act would have consequences in both the natural and supernatural worlds.[46]

Josephus, who is our only source, suggests that, as the course of the Zealot revolt developed, a rather extraordinary process unfolded. The rebels began to act in ways directly antithetical to the spirit of hypernomianism, as though they thought that true fidelity was not measured by unswerving commitment to religious norms as much as it was by willingness to violate religious taboos, by one's ability to deny limits. When the *Sicarii*, for example, mounted their assassination campaign against Jewish priests who they charged had succumbed to Hellenistic influences, the attacks normally occurred on the most holy days. The message was clear; even the most sacred occasion or circumstance could not provide immunity.[47] Josephus' description of the deplorable fate of a Roman garrison illustrates this point again. After receiving a safe passage agreement secured by a covenant, the most inviolable pledge Jews could make, the troops surrendered.

> When they had laid down their arms, the rebels massacred them; the Romans neither resisting nor suing for mercy but merely appealing to the Covenant!. . .The whole city was a scene of dejection, and among the moderates everyone was racked with the thought that he should personally have to suffer for the rebels' crime. For to add to its heinousness, the massacre took place on the sabbath, a day on which from religious scruples Jews abstain from the most innocent acts.[48]

As the assailants in such situations obviously understand, the aggrieved will perceive violence of this sort as atrocities and are likely to respond in kind, providing the original assailant with a fresh justification for new atrocities. Thus, when the news of the massacre reached the Greeks of Caesarea, the Roman capital of Judea and a major source of military recruitment, they massacred the entire Jewish population there. The Jews elsewhere took revenge by indiscriminate attacks on Greeks wherever they could find them, and the Greeks responded in kind. By such means the conflict involved more and more participants who

David C. Rapoport

were pulled into an ever-escalating struggle by atrocities which manipulated their fear, outrage, sympathy, and guilt.

The antinomian ethos implied by these acts is a strikingly common feature of messianic movements.[49] Gershom Sholem's analysis of the Sabbatian movement which inflamed seventeenth-century Jewry demonstrates that its participants believed that the condition of liberation was the systematic violation of every sacred precept.

> When fulfilling each commandment the pious Jews says a blessing. But according to the new messianic formulation introduced by Sabbatai Zevi himself, he says: "Praised be He who permits the forbidden," a formula which the defenders of the Jewish tradition rightly regarded as the epitome of this revolutionary heresy.[50]

> Through a revolution of values what was formerly sacred became profane and what was formerly profane [became] sacred. . . . More than anything else . . . the "radicals" insisted on the potential holiness of sin. . . . The Gordian knot of the exilic Jew had been cut and a vertigo that ultimately was to be his undoing seized the newly liberated individual: genuine desires for a reconsecration of life mingled indiscriminately with all kinds of destructive and libidinal forces tossed up from the depths by an inexpressible ground swell that undulated wildly between the earthly and the divine.[51]

An Islamic parallel may be the attack described above on the Grand Mosque in Mecca in 1979. The shrine is the holiest in Islam. The assault occurred during a uniquely holy period, the beginning of the year when Mohammed's *hijra* occurred, and also during a holy moment, a time of prayer. Fighting in that place or during those times has always been prohibited.[52]

The process at work in these examples reminds one of the term coined by the French theologian Jacques Ellul to describe the more bizarre activities of student radicals in the 1960s, "desacralization," the pressing need for those who see themselves involved in the creation of a new world to profane all the sacred symbols and norms of the old.[53] Nineteenth-century Russian anarchists were engaged in an identical effort, and those familiar with Isaac Bashevis Singer's *Satan in Goray* will remember that the desacralization process among the Sabbatians is its major theme.

The Sabbatians did not employ or teach terror: their antinomianism was a secret affair. But a doctrine of this sort must in time create an interest in terror, and the Frankists, a Sabbatian offshoot, though they did not practice it, did preach that terror was holy, and their language strikingly resembles that of the Russian anarchist Nechaev, usually considered the creator of modern revolutionary terror.[54]

Medieval Christian antinomianism was practiced more publicly. The Brethren of the Free Spirits and the Adamites, who moved from a phase of hypernomianism during which they were known as Flagellants, believed that they had entered into a state of grace or had literally become gods incapable of sin. "A man who has a conscience is himself Devil and hell and purgatory." The Adamites declared that "blood must flood the world to the height of a horse's head. . . . From their island stronghold" they "waged what they called a Holy War. . . . They set villages on fire and cut down or burnt alive every man, woman, and child they could find," justifying their acts "with a quotation from Scripture: 'And at midnight there was a cry made. Behold, the bridegroom cometh.' "[55] In the first crusade the

Comparative Politics   January 1988

Tafurs who "represented" the poor, and as such "exalted as a Holy People worth far more than the knights," normally massacred all the inhabitants of places captured. One incident bears a striking resemblance to Josephus' description of the fate of the Roman garrison which surrendered to the *Sicarii*, and perhaps it was no accident that it took place on the same spot in Jerusalem. Among the Tafur atrocities reported by Christian sources were instances of cannibalism to signify superior commitment or to prove themselves free of sin.[56]

Signs or Portents

The fourth element consists of the various "signs" or visible proof that a deliverance is in process. Most messianic visions associate the destruction of the old order and the birth pangs of the new with a series of cataclysms so profound and so unique that they appear to dissolve both the laws of nature and of mortality. The world appears to be in the grip of uncontrollable forces: earthquakes, floods, volcanic eruptions, falling stars, widespread famines, raging epidemics, revolutionary wars, gruesome massacres, the dissolution of the most elementary social units, and, above all, the unprecedented persecution of the righteous. The terror and horror described is meant to distinguish this struggle from those which have always engaged men. When we believe that a sign of deliverance is a period of inconceivable woe and that the period has not yet occurred, there will be some eager to do their part, and both the commission and provocation of atrocities seem to be means admirably designed for that end. If the road to Paradise runs through Hell, if the fulfillment of the Promise depends upon life becoming as unbearable as possible, violence can have no limits because it cannot be associated with a principle that tells us when to stop because we have either succeeded or we have failed. When disasters do not bring redemption, the obvious remedy is to make the suffering even more profound, but in principle there is no way to demonstrate that our situation is as horrible as it can be.

The Participants

The fifth element is the description provided of the participants' moral nature, for our picture of the enemy always shapes our view of the kind of struggle we must wage. In the language of Dead Sea scrolls, the struggle is seen as a war against the Sons of Darkness, or in other messianic contexts against Amalek,[57] Satan, and the Anti-Christ. The enemy is wholly evil, always dangerous, in short, something other than human. Binding agreements are impossible to make because the restraints which the enemy accepts or proposes are designed for the sole purpose of lulling us into complacency. Against such an antagonist the temptation becomes overwhelming to argue that everything is permissible, that he must be mercilessly destroyed.

In Islam the Holy War or *jihad* which normally is waged against people who are not Moslems has always been governed by rules protecting the rights of noncombatants and prisoners. But in the eyes of Islamic terrorists, those who profess Islam but are essentially

David C. Rapoport

hypocrites or apostates have always been the epitome of evil and as such have forfeited all rights, as an influential contemporary terrorist theorist has made clear.

> Governments in the Islamic world today are in a state of apostacy. . . . Of Islam they preserve nothing but its sheer name, although they pray, fast and pretend to be Muslims. Our *sunna* has determined that the apostate be punished more severely than he who has always been an infidel. *The apostate must be killed even if he is in no position to fight while an infidel does not merit death in such a case.*[58]

Justifications for unlimited violence are strengthened when we see *ourselves*, and not simply our cause, as wholly righteous, an essential feature of antinomianism, indeed part of its very definition. The medieval Christian Free Spirits and Adamites literally believed themselves to be gods and hence able to commit acts which were grotesque by conventional moral standards. Similar phenomena are central issues of Dostoevski's novels *Crime and Punishment* and *The Possessed* which treat the nineteenth-century anarchists who are the architects of modern secular terror. The picture of the participants in the cases of both the Christians and Dostoevski reminds one of claims often made by contemporary secular terrorists that the enemy is a symbol or beast, not a person, and that the freedom fighter cannot be a terrorist regardless of the methods employed.

God's Role

The sixth and final element is the character of divine intervention. Will God participate in the struggle? In ancient Israel the wars in which God participates are always different from those between human forces only. Whether we are talking about messianic activities or of the earlier wars to gain the Promised Land, which seem to be a model for the messianic conflict, these differences are sustained.

The simple fact of divine participation produces a paralyzing terror or dread which dissolves the enemy's resolution and negates his advantage of superior numbers and equipment. God fights by means of famine, pestilence, and other natural disasters which spread devastation indiscriminately. At its worst, a violent conflict between humans gives the victor a choice concerning the lives and fortunes of the defeated, and normally conquerors preserve in order to possess. At their best, such wars may be subject to conventions concerning the disposition of populations and properties never engaged or no longer involved in the conflict. But in sharp contrast to this practice, the enemy and its properties had to be exterminated completely in Israel's early holy wars, lest its continued existence corrupt Israel. In the later messianic wars terror seems to be violence without restraint or violence that transcends those limits which ordinary concerns for utility and morality dictate.

Jung's description of John's vision of the apocalyptic wars in *Revelation*, a book which is essential to a variety of Christian messianic movements, is worth citing.

> [It] is a terrifying picture that blatantly contradicts all ideas of Christian humility, tolerance, love of your neighbor and your enemies, and makes nonsense of a loving father in heaven and rescuer

209

Comparative Politics   January 1988

of mankind. A veritable orgy of hatred, wrath, vindictiveness and blind destructive fury that revels in fantastic images of terror and fire overwhelms a world which Christ had just endeavoured to restore to the original state of innocence and loving communion with God. . . . In all my experience I have never observed anything like it, except in cases of severe psychoses and criminal insanity.[59]

Let me conclude quickly. Once a messianic advent appears imminent, preexisting paradigms guide the expectations and, therefore, the actions of believers, paradigms which, for the most part, are the creation of the dominant or orthodox religious cultures, such as Judaism, Christianity, and Islam. When the paradigms are vague and conflicting, believers must make choices and may abandon some for others more promising and equally legitimate. This also means that there will be differences between single movements and distinct phases which seem contradictory within a single movement. Yet in every case powerful impulses towards terror are inherent in the beliefs of a world about to be destroyed, the gains imagined, the character of the participants, and God's methods. Beyond all this, and I cannot emphasize the point enough, terror is attractive in itself to messianists just *because* it is outside the normal range of violence and for this reason represents a break with the past, epitomizing the antinomianism or complete liberation which is the essence of the messianic expectation.

NOTES

1. David C. Rapoport, "Fear and Trembling: Terrorism in Three Religious Traditions," *American Political Science Review*, 78 (September 1984), 658–77.

2. The somewhat panicky concern to protect government buildings in Washington after Shia suicide attacks in Lebanon is indicative. In December 1983 the *Los Angeles Times* reported that a four minute bomb warning in Coast Guard headquarters provoked a mass exodus of officers leaving the enlisted men behind. In several television interviews after the U.S. embassy in Kuwait was destroyed in 1984, all my interviewers seemed convinced that there was no defense against suicide attacks and that the supply of martyrs must be inexhaustible. For an interesting study of suicidal terrorism which explodes some myths associated with it, see Ariel Merrari, "The Readiness to Kill and Die: Suicidal Terrorism and Indiscriminate Violence in the Middle East," unpublished paper, Psychology of Terrorism Conference, Woodrow Wilson International Center for Scholars, Washington, D.C., March 16–18, 1987. I describe the Shia tactic in Lebanon as a perversion because it entails suicide, which the Islamic tradition prohibits. For an interesting parallel perversion, see Rapoport, "Fear and Trembling."

3. Bruce Hoffman, "Right Wing Terror in the U.S.," *Violence, Aggression and Terror*, 1 (January 1987), 1–25.

4. A very thorough account of the plot is contained in Ehud Sprinzak, "Fundamentalism, Terrorism and Democracy," colloquium paper, Woodrow Wilson International Center for Scholars, September 15, 1986. A later version of this paper entitled "From Messianic Pioneering to Vigilante Terrorism: The Case of the Gush Emunim Underground" will be published in *The Journal of Strategic Studies*, 10 (September 1987).

5. The allegations are made by Barbara and Michael Ledeen, "The Temple Mount Plot," *The New Republic* (June 18, 1984), 20–23, but the parties identified have denied all these allegations. Cf. Eti Ronel, "The Battle over the Temple Mount," *New Outlook*, 27 (February 1984), 11–14, and Janet Aviad, "Israel: New Fanatics and Old," *Dissent*, 31 (Summer 1984), 11–14. Neither Aviad nor Ronel discusses this issue, but they do refer to the moral support by some diaspora Jews.

6. The Assassins called themselves Nizari and were an offshoot of the Ismaili who came out of the Shia. Nizari assailants were known as *fidayeen*, dedicated or consecrated ones. See Rapoport, "Fear and Trembling," pp. 664ff.

7. Assassin communities were located in remote mountain fortresses, which M. G. S. Hodgson describes as a "league of city states." *The Order of Assassins* (The Hague: Mouton, 1955), p. 99.

8. See Norman Cohn, *The Pursuit of the Millennium*, rev. ed. (New York: Oxford University Press, 1970), pp. 61–71, 98–108. Particularly interesting is the discussion of the Tafurs (vagabonds?) in the first crusade who sometimes seem to have roasted and eaten the corpses of their enemies.

9. Bryan Wilson, *Magic and the Millennium* (London: Heinemann, 1973), chap. 8.

David C. Rapoport

10. Kenelm Burridge and Michael Barkun do distinguish violence and terror, and their suggestions are interesting though confined to terror as an element in the antinomian ethos. See Kenelm Burridge, *New Heaven, New Earth: A Study of Millenarian Activities* (Oxford: Blackwell, 1969); Michael Barkun, *Disaster and the Millennium* (New Haven: Yale University Press, 1984).

11. The earliest contemporary discussion of terrorism emphasized the extranormal character of the violence as its distinguishing feature. See Thomas P. Thornton, "Terror as a Weapon of Political Agitation," in Harry Eckstein, ed., *Internal War* (New York: Free Press, 1964); E. V. Walter, *Terror and Resistance: A Study of Political Violence* (New York: Oxford University Press, 1969); David C. Rapoport, "The Politics of Atrocity," in Yonah Alexander and Seymore Finger, eds., *Terrorism: Interdisciplinary Perspectives* (New York: John Jay, 1977); and H. Price, Jr., "The Strategy and Tactics of Revolutionary Terrorism," *Comparative Studies in Society and History*, 19 (1977), 52–65. The more common recent definitions do not distinguish between violence and terror. See, for example, Charles A. Russell, L. J. Banker, and Bowman Miller, "Out Inventing the Terrorist," in Yonah Alexander, David Carlton, and Paul Wilkinson, eds., *Terrorism, Theory and Practice* (Boulder: Westview, 1979).

12. We have excluded two other messianic forms, one which posits salvation as an event in the spiritual or unseen world, the orthodox Christian doctrine, and another which is wholly secular, such as Marxism. My characterization corresponds roughly to Yonina Talmon's description of millenarism. But she speaks of movements, not beliefs, and therefore specifies imminence as a necessary feature. See "Millenarism," *Encyclopedia of the Social Sciences* (New York: Macmillan, 1968). While the notion of a personal savior was once essential to the definition, the term presently is virtually interchangeable with millenarism and chiliasm. The apocalyptic group is a particular kind of messianic group. In this paper I have not distinguished between "premillenarian" and "postmillenarian" doctrines. The first visualizes a single, sudden, dramatic destructive advent, while the second sees an initial advent which is spiritual and/or gradual, which is displayed in the unfolding of history and may or may not be followed by a violent occurrence. The postmillenarian view, which is the source of the secular doctrine of progress, was characteristic of nineteenth-century messianic groups like the Mormons. See Stow Persons, *American Minds* (New York: Henry Holt, 1958), pp. 176–77. The Gush Emunim, an Israeli messianic group which has a fundamental concern to settle the West Bank, has a postmillenarian view which reserves an essential role for violence.

13. Eric J. Hobsbawm, *Primitive Rebels* (Manchester: University Press, 1959), pp. 60ff. Hobsbawm uses the term millenarianism instead. Wilhelm Muhlman calls such situations "charismatic," a context of collective excitement, belief in miracles and wonders, and extreme sensitivity to signs. Wilhelm Muhlman, *Messianismes révolutionnaires du tiers monde* (Paris: Gallimard, 1968), pp. 186–87. Hobsbawm notes a similar phenomenon among nineteenth and twentieth century Andalusian anarchists. An uprising broke out every ten years for some eighty years "when something in the local situation made action imperative or when some impetus from outside fanned the glow of latent revolutionism into a flame. Some piece of news, some portent or comet, proving that the time had come would penetrate into the village. It might be the original arrival of the Bakunist apostles in the early 1870s, the garbled news of the Russian Revolution, the news that a Republic has been proclaimed or that an Agrarian Reform Law was under discussion." Hobsbawm, *Primitive Rebels*, pp. 86–8. It seems that in the general analysis of revolution, too, the notion of imminence is a necessary but rarely appreciated concept.

14. The place of the messianic hope in Jewish liturgy is discussed in Julius Greenstone, *The Messiah Idea in Jewish History* (Philadelphia: Jewish Publication Society, 1906), appendix.

15. Hugh J. Schonfield, *The Passover Plot* (New York: Geis, 1965), p. 19.

16. Greenstone, *The Messiah Idea*, p. 111.

17. Christopher Hill, "Till the Conversion of the Jews," UCLA Clark Library Lecture, October 30, 1981, in Richard Popkin, *Millenarianism* (Los Angeles: University of California Press, forthcoming).

18. Wilson D. Wallis, *Messiahs: Their Role in Civilization* (Washington, D.C.: American Council on Public Affairs, 1943), pp. 85–86.

19. *Babylonian Talmud, Sanhedrin* 97a.

20. A leader's description of how the Millerites, an American messianic movement in the 1840s, were impelled by the demands of their followers to fix a date for the Second Coming is interesting in this regard. "At first a definite time was generally opposed; but there seemed to be an irresistible power attending its proclamation, which prostrated all before it. It swept over the land with the velocity of a tornado, and it reached hearts in different and distinct places almost simultaneously, and in a manner which can be accounted for only on the supposition that God was [in] it. The lecturers among the Adventists were the last to embrace the views of the time . . . [but ultimately they] could but exclaim, 'What were we, that we should resist God. It seemed to us to have been so independent of human agency that we could but regard it as a fulfillment of the midnight cry.' " Quoted in Leon Festinger et al., *When Prophecy Fails* (Minneapolis: University of Minnesota Press, 1958) p. 20. Note how Raphael Patai explains the hostility towards the time speculator: "The results of all these efforts in widely different periods to discover a method of calculating the date of the advent had a common conclusion—that the Messiah would come soon, not in a distant and indefinite future but in their own (the calculators') lifetime." *The Messiah Texts* (New York: Avon, 1979). p. XXXVIII.

21. Greenstone, *The Messiah Idea*, p. 108.

22. Ayman Al-Yassini, *Religion and State in Saudi Arabia* (Boulder: Westview, 1985), pp. 124–9. The tradition is

Comparative Politics   January 1988

discussed in detail in Abdulaziz Abdulhussein Sachedina, *Islamic Messianism: The Idea of the Mahdi in Twelve Shiism* (Albany: S.U.N.Y. Press, 1981), pp. 150–180.

23. Michael Gilsenan, *Recognizing Islam* (London: Croom Helm, 1982), p. 17.

24. Edward Mortimer, *Faith and Power: The Politics of Islam* (New York: Vintage, 1982), pp. 75–9, 181–2.

25. Gottfried Osterwal writes, "Contemporaneous history is to a large extent the history and growth of new religions and cults. There is hardly a region in the world that in the last two or three [decades] has not given birth to a new religious movement or that has not seen the sudden revival of some old messianic belief. And hardly a week passes . . . somewhere where another prophet arises whose message of a soon coming 'messiah' and the imminent destruction of the 'present world' becomes the basis of a new messianic movement or religious awakening. Over 6000 of such new religious movements have been reported from Africa. Since the Second World War hundreds of new religions arose in Japan and a similar number has been reported from the Philippines. The thousands of cargo cults and prophetic movements in New Guinea and Oceania are well-known, Southeast Asia . . . Latin America . . . North America and Europe [show] that the expectation of the soon coming Messiah . . . is a universal phenomenon." *Modern Messianic Movements as a Theological and Missionary Challenge* (Elkhart: Institute of Mennonite Studies, 1973), p. 7.

26. "Millenarian enthusiasm [has] always flourished when men thought and cared deeply about religion and when political convulsions tempted them to deduce that the Time of the End was approaching." P. G. Roger, *The Fifth Monarchy Men* (London: Oxford University Press, 1966), p. 132. One also could argue the reverse position, that catastrophe breeds messianism which then produces an interest in religion.

27. Michael Barkun, "Divided Apocalypse: Thinking about the End in Contemporary America," *Soundings: An Interdisciplinary Journal*, 66 (Fall 1983), 257–280. Barkun's perceptive essay is the source for the themes in this paragraph. In the eyes of those who experienced it, the fall of Rome probably provided an early parallel to our sense that the world can be destroyed.

28. Timothy P. Weber, *Living in the Shadow of the Second Coming: American Premillenialism 1875–1982*, enl. ed. (Grand Rapids: Zonderwan, 1983), ch. 6. The restoration of Israel has, of course, been interpreted in different ways at various times. In the Crusades it was understood to be the conquest of the holy places. In the late medieval period, groups like the Taborites and Anabaptists imagined themselves to be the new Israel, and seventeenth-century English Protestants agitated to send the Jews back to Zion. See note 32 for an African version.

29. W. E. Blackstone in 1891 got 413 of the most prominent Americans, headed by the Chief Justice, J. P. Morgan, and John D. Rockefeller, to sign a "memorial" on behalf of the Russian Jews urging President Harrison to pressure the Turks to give Palestine back to the Jews. This was five years before Herzl's *Der Judenstaat* and six before the first international Zionist conference! See Weber, pp. 138ff.

30. Sprinzak, "Fundamentalism."

31. *Babylonian Talmud, Sanhedrin* 97b.

32. "Ethiopia shall soon stretch her hands unto God." *Psalms*, 68:31. Some African messianic sects have called themselves Ethiopian. See George Shepperson, "Ethiopianism and African Nationalism" *Phylon*, 14 (1953), 9–18.

33. George Woodcock and Ivan Avakumovic, *The Doukhobors* (London: Faber and Faber, 1968), pp. 173–82.

34. D. S. Margoliouth, "On Mahdis and Mahdism." *Proceedings of the British Academy* (London: Oxford University Press, n.d.), p. 213.

35. Emmanuel Sivan suggests using the term counter-society, which was originally employed by Kriegel to describe the French Communist Party and then by students of Islam. " 'A counter-society is a mirosociety which constitutes a closed society while maintaining some ties with society as a whole. The counter-society must be capable of being self-enclosed in order to avoid fragmentation or abdication. It must prevent alien influences from penetrating it yet must remain sufficiently open and aggressive to draw from the outside whatever it cannot itself produce. It must pursue the dream of ultimately becoming a majority. It struggles to demolish the old society while at the same time hoping to become heir to that society: radical destruction on the one hand, preservation for the sake of the new order on the other.' Joined to these two major functions is a third one, the counter-society as a model for the future." Emmanuel Sivan, *Radical Islam* (New Haven: Yale University Press, 1985), p. 85. Sivan notes further that Dannawi describes Muhammed's original group of followers as an exemplary " 'countersociety,' . . . operating in the heart of the *jahili* (corrupt?) society . . . and engaged in battle against the latter, 'for the barbaric society tends to react harshly using all the means at its disposal: murder and banishment, torture and pressures, ridicule and seduction.' "

36. Examples of archetype imitations in different periods are discussed by Hodgson, *The Order of Assassins*, pp. 77–80; Rapoport, "Fear and Trembling;" T. Hodgkin, "Mahdism, Messianism and Marxism in the African Setting," in P. Gutkind and P. Waterman, eds., *African Social Studies: A Radical Reader* (New York: 1977); Sivan, *Radical Islam*, chap. 4; Gilsenan, *Recognizing Islam*, chap. 7; Peter Von Sivers, "The Realm of Justice: Apocalyptic Revolts in Algeria (1849–1879)," *Humaniora Islamica*, 1 (1973), 47–60; and Marilyn Robinson Waldman, "The Popular Appeal of the Prophetic Paradigm in West Africa," *Contributions to Asian Studies*, 17 (1983), 110–14.

37. Cohn, *The Pursuit of the Millenium*, pp. 198–281.

38. See Simma Holt, *Terror in the Name of God: The Story of the Sons of Freedom Doukhobors* (Toronto: McClelland and Stewart, 1964), and Woodcock and Avakumovic, *The Doukhobors*, chap. 13.

39. Wilson, pp. 36–37.

David C. Rapoport

40. Marvin Zonis and Daniel Brumberg. "Shiism as Interpreted by T. Khomeini: An Ideology of Revolutionary Violence," in Martin Kramer, ed., *Shiism, Resistance and Revolution* (Boulder: Westview, 1987), p. 49.

41. Ibid., chaps. 8 and 9. Wilson suggests that the normal course of revolutionary messianism is *from* "military" to "pacific" values, but I cannot tell whether his evidence would support the terms terrorism and pacifism as substitutes. Von Sivers, "The Realm of Justice," p. 50, speaks of the "oscillation" between "revolutionary activity" and a retreat into "quietist brotherhoods" which he has informed me is widespread in Islam. He also told me that the "brotherhoods" have pacifist elements but did not believe there was evidence that the different activities referred to different phases visualized for the messianic process; the brotherhoods are models for life in the transformed society. This picture does not seem fundamentally different from my own.

42. Bryan Wilson, *Sects and Society* (Berkeley: University of California Press, 1961), p. 351.

43. Sprinzak, "Fundamentalism," p. 8.

44. Von Sivers, "The Realm of Justice," p. 56.

45. See Rapoport, "Fear and Trembling."

46. John R. Hall, "The Apocalypse at Jonestown," in Ken Levi, *Violence and Religious Commitment* (University Park: Pennsylvania State University Press, 1982), pp. 36–54.

47. Josephus, *Antiquities of the Jews*, H. St. Thackeray, transl., *Loeb Classical Library*. (London: Heinemann, 1962), XVII, p. 23.

48. Josephus, *The Jewish War*, ibid., II, p. 457.

49. The Oxford English Dictionary defines an antinomian as "one who maintains that the moral law is not binding upon Christians under the law of grace," and the word generally refers to persons who do not believe themselves bound by social rules or standards.

50. Gersom Scholem, *The Messianic Idea in Judaism* (New York: Schocken, 1971), p. 75.

51. Ibid., p. 112.

52. I am grateful to Ibrahim Karawan who suggested the parallel.

53. Jacques Ellul, *The New Demons* (London: Mowbray, 1975), pp. 48–87. Nineteenth-century anarchists often "desanctified" themselves by committing acts that they regarded as personally obscene, the object being to break the hold of society's moral conventions over their feelings. For a similar process among the Weathermen and the Japanese Red Army, see Rapoport, "Politics of Atrocity."

54. Scholem, *The Messianic Idea*, pp. 126–34. "The annihilation of every religion and positive system of belief—this was the 'true way' the 'believers' were expected to follow. Concerning the redemptive powers of havoc, Frank's imagination knew no limits: 'Wherever Adam trod a city was built but wherever I set foot all will be destroyed for I came into the world only to destroy and annihilate.' " Ibid., p. 130. Compare this with Nechaev: "The revolutionary . . . knows only one science: the science of destruction. . . . He enters the world . . . only because he has faith in its speedy and total destruction. . . . He must not hesitate to destroy any position, any place, or any man in this world—all must be equally detested. . . . If he has parents, friends, and loved ones, he is no longer a revolutionary if they can stay his hand." "Revolutionary Catechism" in David C. Rapoport, *Assassination and Terrorism* (Toronto: CBC, 1971), pp. 79–81.

55. Cohn, pp. 148–63.

56. Ibid., pp. 65–7.

57. The Amalekites who attacked a weak and exhausted Israel in a particularly cruel fashion personify a boundless evil which God has obliged Israel to exterminate. For the use of Amalek by the Gush Emunin, see Uriel Tal, "Foundations of a Political Messianic Trend in Israel," *Jerusalem Quarterly*, 35 (Spring 1985), 43ff.

58. My emphasis. The quotation is from Faraj's *The Absent Precept*, quoted by Sivan, who says that Sadat's assassins "meditated" on the work. Sivan, *Radical Islam*, pp. 128, 103. See my discussion of a similar theme among early Muslim terrorists in Rapoport, "Fear and Trembling."

59. Carl Jung, *Answer to Job* (Princeton: Princeton University Press, 1973), pp. 76, 95.

[14]

LEBANON: A CONFLICT OF MINORITIES

JANET HANCOCK

Lecture given to the Society on 22 October 1986. Ms. Hancock is a Principal Research Officer in the Foreign and Commonwealth Office Research Department. She has worked in the Lebanon several times, most recently from May to July 1986. The opinions expressed are the author's own.

THE HISTORY of the region now known as Lebanon has been marked by a series of political transformations aimed at securing some form of stable and peaceful administration over a variety of peoples whose sense of identity based on religion or nation has often been much stronger than any identification with a nation state. The Ottoman Turks, who incorporated Lebanon into the Empire in the early 16th Century, recognised that the central areas of Lebanon, populated by the hardy mountain Druze and Maronites, was something of a special case and required different treatment from the other provinces. Druze feudal lords were given authority over the Mountain within the structure of the Empire and subsequently Druze and Maronite feudal lords shared power, vying with each other for the upper hand until the 19th century.

In Lebanon history has a habit of repeating itself; bloody massacres in the 19th century have contributed towards Christian suspicions of other communities and to the intransigence of some factions which in turn contributed to massacres in the 1980s; the potential power of a united Lebanon has alarmed her neighbours in the past. Charles Churchill, writing in 1862 of Lebanon's relationship with the Turks, remarked: "The Lebanon is in fact a *point d'appui*, a nucleus around which the various mountain tribes naturally congest. Should, therefore, its population ever be bound together by feelings of mutual trust and confidence, the danger to the supremacy of the Porte would be imminent". (*The Druzes and the Maronites*, London 1862.) The recent history of Lebanon has shown that her neighbours have felt constrained to act whenever one faction has appeared to be gaining the upper hand too strongly. Similarly Lebanon has been seen as offering opportunities to neighbours who might wish to extend their area of influence or neutralise that of a rival. Strong independent communities have long been seen as a dangerous channel through which a rival could establish a foothold. To quote Churchill again: " In the Christians of the Lebanon they [the Turks] saw a ready nucleus for the intrusion and permanent preponderance of a foreign power, gradually enabling them to advance new pretensions, to acquire new rights, and finally, perhaps, to establish a quasi-independence, formidable and menacing to their own political existence ". It is hard not to see in this a mirror of the Syrian attitude towards the Maronites and their Israeli patrons in the

LEBANON: A CONFLICT OF MINORITIES   31

1980s. It is Lebanon's misfortune that no one of her largest communities is strong enough to assert control unaided, but all are too strong to be allowed to coalesce.

Lebanon's conflicts have been those of communities carving out their patches, intermingled with struggles for regional domination and overlaid by the conflicts of remote nations. Lebanon has seen many armies come and go, as the inscriptions at the Nahr al-Kalb testify. Some, such as the ill-fated US marines, stay for only a short time. Others, perhaps more directly concerned, outstay their welcome. The relative weakness of the communities dictates that each requires an outside backer if it is to prevail or even maintain its position. In the past the Maronites have sought out the French, and later the Israelis; the Sunni relied on the ruling authorities until the First World War and the awarding of the Mandate for Lebanon to France in 1920 altered their world picture; the Druze, it is widely believed, relied on the British for support (and the memory of this lingers on). The Shi'a, cast adrift in a world of Sunni Islam, lacked a natural protector until very recently. The coming to power of Ayatollah Khomeini and the new assertiveness of Shi'a Islam has profoundly changed the outlook of many Lebanese Shi'a, who, fuelled by new confidence, have thrust themselves into the Lebanese power play from which they had previously been excluded. It can be said that in many ways the emergence of the militant Shi'a on to the political scene is part of the natural order of things Lebanese: it is simply their turn now.

The small area of Lebanon is shared by 22 religious sects, including Nestorian Christians, Presbyterians, Jews and Baha'is. Of these, four in particular stand out in the socio-political geography: the Maronites, the Druze, the Sunni and the Shi'a. In addition, a number of separately identifiable peoples have sought refuge in Lebanon over the years, principally Armenians fleeing Turkish persecution, Kurds and Palestinians. It is not possible to give an authoritative figure for the numbers of each sect or minority in Lebanon since no official national census has been held since 1932; it is indeed in the interests of many concerned to maintain the uncertainty. Current estimates are that the Shi'a Moslems have now emerged as the largest single group, with the Sunnis probably as the second largest, and the Maronites, if emigrés are excluded from the figures, the third. The Druze have always constituted a small percentage of the population.

In the nineteen-fifties and sixties Lebanon was held up to the world as a model for multi-ethnic and multi-confessional societies, a nation where a heterogeneous mix of sects and nations, many of them having originally arrived seeking refuge from wars or persecution, had succeeded in working together to establish a prosperous, forward-looking nation state. The picture today is very different. Lebanon presents a sorry spectacle of warring factions, large areas of its territory occupied by foreign forces, its capital divided and its commercial centre destroyed. The reasons why all this has come to pass are many and complex, and it is of course a gross over-simplification to see Lebanon's present circumstances as the result of

32   LEBANON: A CONFLICT OF MINORITIES

trying to cram too many different groups together into one small area and
to expect conflicts and diversities of, in some cases, hundreds of years
standing to resolve themselves into harmonious unity after forty-odd
years. It is, however, part of the story. It is not new: sectarian conflict,
whether for religious, economic or social reasons, has helped shape the
part of the world which is now known as Lebanon, and what is happening
today could be seen as a mere continuation of processes which have been
determining political and social patterns over the years. The struggle to
hold ground against the competing claims of others is a constant feature
of co-existence, a form of normality within which periods of absence of
conflict have allowed tensions to build up as a prelude to another explosion.

Over the years one group or another has briefly emerged dominant:
each in turn has been pushed back, most often with the assistance of a
strong outside protector whose support is needed if the balance is to be
tipped. Lebanon has in the past decade been witnessing just such another
upheaval, but one which has produced an unexpected turn: what began as
a socio-economic revolution driven by progressive and nationalistic
notions elaborated on university campuses and within Palestinian circles
has spawned a new revolution spearheaded by Shi'ite clerics and fighters
whose ultimate vision is of the restoration of all Arab lands to Shi'a
Islamic rule. This is admittedly an extremist view and one not necessarily
held by any but a minority of Shi'a in Lebanon, but it is nonetheless true
that of all the parties engaged in the struggle for political power which
followed the 1975–76 conflicts it is the Shi'a, who originally played little or
no part in the wars, who have taken up the running.

A vitally important rôle in all this has been played by the Druze. For
the 400 years of Ottoman domination the Druze vied with the Maronites
for control of Lebanon, that is the central mountainous heartland of the
present day state of Lebanon. The Druze themselves are something of an
anomaly. The smallest Moslem sect in Lebanon (they constitute about 7
per cent of the population) they are also extremely small in terms of
numbers among Moselems as a whole and have no large community
outside the region to which they could turn for backing, their numbers
being concentrated in Lebanon, Syria and the Israeli-occupied Golan.

In the late 18th century Maronites living amongst the Druze did so in
peace and prosperity: as Charles Churchill points out, the relationship
between the two communities in the early years of the 19th century was
relatively harmonious. "The situation and general condition of the Christians amongst the Druzes and indeed amongst all the mountain tribes,
was, up to this period, as satisfactory as could be expected in a Moham-
medan state". He goes on to note that the Christians were prized as
tenants by their Druze landowners and had themselves become property
owners, living in far better conditions than their co-religionists in the
cities. Peaceful co-existence was in many ways a product of the common
hostility felt by Druze and Christians towards the Ottomans: both were
tolerated, but both were seen by their Sunni rulers as heterodox. The

Christians suffered various impositions, while the Druze frequently proved themselves to be rebellious and subversive and were treated accordingly.

The Ottoman rulers originally recognised the established tradition of Druze independence under Druze emirs and accordingly awarded Government of Druze regions to Druze princely families, but it was not long before Druze governors clashed with the Ottoman authorities, the first such conflict occuring as early as 1523. From then on there was a constant struggle on the part of the Druze to maintain as much autonomy as possible within the Ottoman system, a struggle which from time to time spilled over into open insurrection. As Ottoman power began to decline, so the Druze became stronger in their own regions; in the 17th and 18th centuries the Druze social organisation was the norm, their political structure was the law of the land and their feudal chiefs ruled under the title of Emir. As Najla Abu Izzedin points out in her book *The Druzes*, the Druze imprint was so strong on the mountain region that the name Druze came to be applied to all the Mountain's inhabitants irrespective of religious affiliation. Much of this was due to the legacy of one man: Emir Fakhreddin Ma'n II, who ruled from 1586–1633, whose autonomous principality included Beirut and the Beqa'a and whose reign was marked by peace and prosperity, toleration and outward-looking policy (his principal foreign relationship being with the Italian states, in particular Tuscany). Inevitably Fakhreddin's evident power and renown attracted the attention of the Ottomans: he was eventually brought down by military force and murdered in 1635.

After Fakhreddin no other Druze ruler attained similar powers, partly because the Ottomans ensured that they did not and partly because no other ruler of the same calibre emerged until the late 18th century when the Shehabist Amir Bashir II (who reigned for 52 years) came to power. The Shehab family won support of both Maronite and Druze mainly through having disguised their religious convictions, and it is still not entirely clear whether the Emir was Christian or Moslem. His most powerful ally among the Druze princes was Sheikh Bashir Junblatt, whose family had played a leading role in the region's history since the days of Fakhreddin and, of course continues to do so today. Under Bashir the Mountain enjoyed self rule, but his relationship with the Druze feudal leaders fell victim to other forces at play within the Ottoman Empire, namely the powerful Egyptian pasha Muhammad Ali, whose leadership in Egypt was threatening the integrity of the increasingly weak Empire and who extended his control to Lebanon for a period of nine years (1831–1840). Bashir II sided with Muhammad Ali. Bashir Junblatt, unusually for the Druze, supported the Ottoman authorities. Following the Egyptian victory the Junblatts and their supporters lost their land holdings and were forced to leave the Shuf, only returning after the fall of Bashir in 1840.

The suppression of the Druze feudal princes allowed the Maronites to assert themselves and become landowners, while Egyptian rule allowed

34   LEBANON: A CONFLICT OF MINORITIES

greater flexibility and openings to the West. Christian missionary activity was tolerated, and for the first time in many years the Maronites found themselves in contact with their European co-religionists. Despite these advantages the Christians made common cause with the Druze against their Egyptian overlords, whose demands for high taxes and military conscription proved onerous, and gained the support of the European Powers who put pressure on Muhammad Ali to leave. Trouble soon flared between the Maronites, who wished to hold on to the privileges attained under Egyptian rule, and the Druze whose princes were allowed to return and who wished to regain their earlier rights. This culminated in 1840 in the first series of massacres of Christians which still exercise such sway over Christian perceptions. The massacres of 1840 were halted following the intervention of the European powers, whose influence in the region by that time was great enough to enable them to impose yet another system of Government on the Mountain, still within the ever weakening structure of the Empire. This was known as the Double Qaimaqamate, established in 1842, under which the Northern sector was ruled by a Maronite and the Southern sector by a Druze, both owing allegiance to the Ottoman pasha of Sidon. Tensions persisted, however, since many Maronites continued to live and work under Druze overlords.

Long standing resentments were fanned by the activities of the Maronite peasantry in the north who, in 1859, rebelled against their feudal overlords; dissidence spread to Maronite peasants living in the southern sector and in 1860 widespread massacres took place (in which the Turks had a hand) which led to the deaths of some 11,000 Christians in four weeks. The uprising destroyed the Qaimaqamate and ensured that the Western powers, principally Britain and France, would have a say in the political complexion of Lebanon from then on. Yet another system of Government was tried, this time known as the Mutessarifate, under which power was vested in a Christian but non-Lebanese ruler advised by an Administrative Assembly composed of representatives of the different sects according to number. This arrangement foreshadowed the system which was to come into being when Lebanon eventually achieved independence.

Two overwhelming ideas came together to form the basis for the Lebanese state as constituted in the nineteen-forties: the Maronite concept of a country set apart from the rest of the Arab world by religion and by its relationship with Europe and "Christendom" and the Sunni Moslem vision of Lebanon as an integral part of the Arab world, bound to the Arab hinterland by common language, culture and religion. Within this apparently irreconcilable dual vision of Lebanon were the politicians and businessmen who believed that matters of common interest, such as national prosperity and the limited aspirations of the majority to live in peace, could override the divisions and lead to national integration and the establishment of a unified state where diversity would be a positive factor leading to the common good. Nonetheless these wholly admirable aspirations were often subject to certain caveats which led to the ultimate

LEBANON: A CONFLICT OF MINORITIES   35

collapse of the system. The Maronites were determined that the sovereignty of Lebanon and the integrity of the Christian communities should
not be threatened, while the Sunnis were concerned that the dominant
position that they had assumed under the Ottomans should not be put at
risk by encroachment of the other Moslem sects. The Constitution written
for the most part by a Maronite businessman Michel Chiha, provided for
a Presidential system with a Chamber of Deputies having seats allocated
to the Communities according to size. The Constitution was later underpinned by the oral agreement between the most prominent Maronite
leader, Bishara Khoury, and his Sunni counterpart, Rashid al-Solh, which
came to be known as the National Pact. The underlying principle of the
National Pact was a basic compromise: that the Lebanese Christians
would accept Lebanon's Arab nature and refrain from allegiances with
European powers, and the Moslems would respect Lebanon's uniqueness
and not press for it to be merged with any other part of the Arab world. In
the mid nineteen-forties such a compromise no doubt appeared workable;
cataclysmic events such as the establishment of the State of Israel and the
expulsion of thousands of Palestinians had yet to take place, nor was there
any indication that the Shi'a, who had not previously been parties to the
struggle for dominance, would do other than accept their lot.

The Shi'a had long been regarded as constituting the most impover-
ished and powerless section of Lebanese society. As Fuad Ajami points
out in his article *Lebanon and its Inheritors* (*Foreign Affairs,* Spring 1985)
the area where many Shi'a live – South Lebanon – was a marginal corner
of the Syrian region, ignored and underdeveloped by Ottoman rulers and
remote from the centres of power of the Empire. It was not always so; at
the end of the sixteenth century the Shi'ites occupied much of the area of
Mount Lebanon which is today the heart of the state of Lebanon. The
Maronites lived to the north and the Druze to the south, many of them in
the Shuf mountains which remain their stronghold today. During the 17th
and 18th centuries the Maronites moved south and the Druze moved
north, and thus squeezed, the Shi'ites were forced out of the centre and
into the periphery, where they remained until new circumstances relating
to the conflict between Israel and the Palestinians forced new migrations
upon them. The Shi'a are now back in the centre and are gradually
attempting to impose a Shi'a character on the Western half of Beirut itself.
In attempts to formulate some form of workable political system for the
whole of Lebanon it is Shi'a demands and aspirations which have to be
accommodated. In order to achieve this some fairly radical revisions
would have to be made to the pattern of power-sharing formulated under
the National Pact. The Shi'a were of course accorded a place within the
system which could be said to have corresponded to their place in the
socio-political geography of Lebanon at the time. Other minorities were
then dominant: the Maronites particularly, who had benefited from the
special relationship which they enjoyed (and to a certain extent still do)
with the French, and the Sunni partly because they constituted the largest
Moslem community in Lebanon and partly because they belonged to the

36   LEBANON: A CONFLICT OF MINORITIES

mainstream Moslem sect which dominated the surrounding region. Their historical role ensures that the Druze too would be influential, even though the small size of their community precluded their inclusion in the formal power-sharing framework. The Shi'a themselves were isolated from the main centre of Shi'a Islam which lay further to the East; the only state which had Shi'ism as the State religion was Iran. The Shi'a in Lebanon felt themselves to be completely marginalised and saw themselves (as they still do) as a minority community in regional terms. Memories of Ottoman domination and of the inability of Shi'a community leaders to assert themselves encouraged the Shi'a to believe that political action was futile.

Two major events conspired to alter this perception: successive Israeli invasions of Shi'a regions which followed the establishment there of large numbers of Palestinian fighters, and the success of the Iranian revolution. The first provided the Shi'a with a genuine grievance which touched directly on their self interest; the second provided the inspiration and confidence that Shi'a protest and self-assertion could succeed. Another major factor was the emergence of an attractive and charismatic leader, the Imam Musa Sadr, whose energy and intellectual dynamism helped to change drastically Shi'a perceptions of themselves. His disappearance in 1978 gave to the Shi'a community a powerful myth and martyr figure, whose legend was to feed the popular imagination. As a result of the disruption caused by Palestinian and Israeli military activities in the South, many Shi'ites migrated north to Beirut; some joined the Shi'a community in the Beqa'a. A large and ever increasing Shi'a presence was established in Beirut, the political heartland of Lebanon, and thus ensured that the Shi'a could no longer be ignored. The outcome of all this remains to be determined; what is clear is that the political map of Lebanon is in the throes of experiencing yet another transformation which could be the most drastic of all.

BIBLIOGRAPHY

Abu Izzedin. Najla: The Druzes (E. J. Brill. 1984)
Ajami. Fouad: Lebanon and its Inheritors (Foreign Affairs. Spring 1985)
Churchill. Charles: The Druzes and the Maronites (Bernard Quaritch. 1862)
Gordon. David C.: The Republic of Lebanon (Croom Helm. 1983)
Hitti. Philip K.: History of Syria (Macmillan. 1951)
Salibi. Kamal: The History of Modern Lebanon (Caravan Books. 1977)
Sofer. Arnon: Lebanon. Where Demography is the Core of Politics (Middle Eastern Studies. April 1986).

[15]

Articles

SECTARIAN CONFLICT IN EGYPT AND THE POLITICAL EXPEDIENCY OF RELIGION

Hamied Ansari

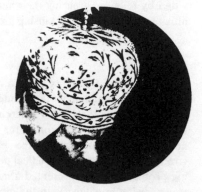

The ideal of a secular-democratic state in the Middle East is now more remote than ever because of the Lebanese civil war and the Iranian revolution. In fact, most states in the region today face political instability and violent disturbances as a consequence of the intensification of ethnic and religious consciousness. Even Egypt has experienced sectarian conflict in recent years, despite the strong secular impulse which has traditionally kept the Muslim majority and the Coptic Christians united behind national goals.

In Egypt, any discussion of the communal conflicts between Muslims and Copts is generally regarded as a taboo.[1] Most Egyptian writers insist that clashes between members of the two communities are aberrations in a society characterized by a long lasting harmony among its national components. But the conflicts are real, and in the last decade religious fervor has invaded all groups and associations in Egypt, inflaming communal feelings while weakening national bonds. Extreme piety among the militant Islamic fraternities has given rise to uncompromising attitudes which have been matched by Coptic student militancy. Against this background, the authorities, from the President down to minor of-

---

1. Jamal Badawi, *al-Fitna al-Ta'ifiyya fi Misr* (Cairo: Arabic Press Center, 1980), p. 21.

Hamied Ansari is Assistant Professor and Acting Director of the Middle East Studies Program at the John Hopkins University School for Advanced International Studies. This article is based on a paper delivered at the Middle East Studies Association Annual Meeting in Chicago in November 1983.

ficials in local government, rival each other in showing their religious devotion. Behind this upsurge is the use of religion as a means to consolidate power and mobilize society. Its adverse consequences were reflected in the polarization of the society which came to a climax with the assassination of President Anwar Sadat.

I hope that this essay will contribute in a modest way toward understanding the cleavages behind the turmoil in many areas of the Middle East, that it will show how appeal to religion by the authorities was carried out at the cost of national consensus, and how this exacerbated tension between communities divided by religion, arousing their mutual fears and compelling the militant fraternities to forge links with kinship groups to confront a common peril.

II

The Coptic Orthodox Church has experienced in the past decade a revolutionary transformation in its attitude toward the state authorities. The election of Shenouda III as the 117th Patriarch in 1971 marked the beginning of an activist Church determined to protect the rights of the community as a whole. Shenouda, even before assuming the spiritual mantle of this ancient community, was strongly inclined to take a radical position with the authorities on some outstanding problems.[2] He represented a movement within the Church hierarchy which was growing impatient with the moderate lay members, who traditionally acted as unofficial representatives on matters directly affecting the interests of the Church. His activities, however, alarmed the traditionalists within both the Christian and Muslim communities.

Behind the growing militancy of the Church were the government restrictions and the various bureaucratic bottlenecks which severely limited the building of new churches. The restrictions imposed by the government are derived from old Ottoman laws which permit Christians free worship but deny them the right to expand their activities, especially missionary activities. A frequent complaint voiced by the Church leaders was that the existing churches were not sufficient to meet the growing needs of the community. Drawing on information provided by the Census Bureau, a committee set up by the People's Assembly in 1972 to investigate the Coptic grievances noted that the number of churches in the country, including all denominations, was 1442. On the other hand, sources at the Ministry of the Interior provided a much lower estimate of 500 churches, of which 286 were Coptic. According to one source, the difference in the figures quoted by the Census Bureau and the Ministry of the Interior reflected how many churches had been built without official permission—a recurrent problem of il-

---

2. See Mohamed Heikal, *The Autumn of Fury: The Assassination of Sadat* (New York: Random House, 1983), pp. 156–65.

legality which became a bone of contention between the State and Church leadership.[3]

Most claims advanced by the militant Copts were based on their own estimate of their proportion of the population, but like all minorities they tend to inflate their numbers. The official census is more likely to provide an estimate that is too low. The various estimates range between the 1976 official census of 2.3 million in a population of 36.6 million (6.2%), to the unofficial Church figure of 8 million.[4] The Copts are not evenly distributed and their concentration in some of the provinces of Upper Egypt is strongly correlated with the rise of the Islamic militant phenomenon and the recurrence of sectarian clashes. What lends special significance to this observation is that Upper Egypt has been slow in catching up with the modernizing trends of Lower Egypt. Of the Upper Egyptian provinces, Minya and Asyut have the highest concentration of Copts (18.6% and 20%, respectively) and, as will be observed later, the sectarian conflict has been most intense in those areas.

The building of new churches has been the subject of prolonged negotiations between the state authorities and the Patriarchal heads of the Coptic Church. The need for more churches was first brought to the attention of President Nasser by Shenouda's predecessor, Pope Kirollos VI. The compromise formula worked out between them in the early 1960s granted the Copts official permission to build 25 churches every year. In the event, however, only 68 Coptic churches (out of a total of 127 belonging to all sects) received official building permits in the 1960s.[5] Sadat tried to compromise by expanding the number of churches to be built every year to 50, but this decision alienated the Muslim fundamentalists and militants, while it left Shenouda unsatisfied.[6]

In recent years the Coptic leaders have resorted to the establishment of philanthropic societies to compensate for the small number of churches, but these were regarded by the authorities and the Islamic militants as subterfuges to disguise church services. Muslim fundamentalists and militants who became alarmed by the increasing number of Christian philanthropic societies started to form their own. In 1972, sources at the Ministry of Social Affairs indicated that the number of philanthropic societies belonging to the Coptic Christians was 438, and that they received financial aid from the government amounting to roughly

3. See Badawi, *al-Fitna al-Ta'ifiyya fi Misr*, p. 74. According to Badawi, the Ministry of the Interior refused to acknowledge the legality of churches built without official licenses.

4. *al-Da'wa*, June 1980, wrote that "although the Copts constituted less than two and a half million, they insist that they have as high a proportion of the population as eight million. They are using this claim to advance other claims such as eight ministerial positions, one-fourth of all top posts in the army and the police as well as the civil service. They even want a university of their own." Sadat also quoted the figure of eight million in condemnation of the exaggerated claims made by Pope Shenouda. See his speech of May 14, 1980.

5. Badawi, *al-Fitna al-Ta'ifiyya fi Misr*, p. 74.

6. Heikal, *The Autumn of Fury*, p. 164.

LE25,000. By comparison, the number of Islamic philanthropic societies was slightly higher (679) and their share of government aid was LE50,000.[7]

In contrast, Robert Bianchi has provided higher figures on the number of associations belonging to members of both communities. According to him, in 1980 the number of Muslim groups (1600) was more than double the number of Christian groups (600) of all denominations. In population terms, Bianchi's figures would mean that per 100,000 adherents to each faith there were 26 associations for Christians versus 4.3 associations for Muslims (using the 1976 official census figures). In addition to the religious-philanthropic groups, Bianchi's figures include the less privately and voluntarily operated public welfare and multi-functional groups. Nevertheless, in terms of regional configuration in the formation of associations, he makes the interesting observation that the high concentration of associations among Muslims in the traditional areas of Upper Egypt is strongly associated with the size of the Christian population. This finding suggests "a chain reaction of organization and counter-organization among Christian and Muslim communities engaged in highly competitive and mutually reinforcing processes of association formation."[8]

The first sectarian conflict during the Sadat regime took place at Khanqa, a town of 22,000 inhabitants 20 kilometers north of Cairo. The main cause of the conflict was the attempt of local Muslim inhabitants to forestall the conversion of the quarters of one of the philanthropic societies, the Holy Book Society at Khanqa, into a Coptic church. On November 6, 1972, some unknown persons set the premises of the Society on fire. On the following Sunday, a large number of Coptic clergy and laity arrived from Cairo to hold protest meetings and, in defiance of a ban imposed by the local authorities, held prayers on the burned out site. That same evening, Muslim militants went on a rampage, burning and destroying Coptic property in Khanqa. The government intervened to restore order and a committee composed of members of the People's Assembly was set up to investigate. Subsequently, the Assembly adopted legislation for the "protection of national unity" which empowered the President to take any steps necessary to prevent sectarian conflict. But the core issue of the official restrictions on the building of churches remained unresolved.

The election of Shenouda and the Khanqa affair took place amid rumors of a grand Christian conspiracy designed to offset the population imbalance. The alleged conspiracy was supposedly hatched at a conference called by Shenouda in March 1972. After Shenouda was deposed by a presidential decree in September 1981, *al-Ahrar*, the Liberal Socialist Party organ, for some reason published a full length report of the conference without attribution. The report said that Pope Shenouda

---

7. See Badawi, *al-Fitna al-Ta'ifiyya fi Misr*, p. 71.
8. Robert Bianchi, "Changing Patterns of Interest Representation in Modern Egypt." Paper delivered at the 1983 Annual Conference of the American Political Science Association in Chicago.

held a meeting of the leading members of the Coptic minority at St. Mark's Cathedral in Alexandria, to discuss ways and means to increase the Coptic population with the view of establishing equality with the Muslim population. The plan for increasing the Coptic population included a strict enforcement of the Church's prohibition of birth control, while encouraging it among Muslims. It also included the provision of material incentives to increase family size through improvement of health standards, encouragement of early marriages, reduction in the cost of church weddings, and conversion of Muslims.[9] According to one writer, the discussions at the conference were officially reported at the time by the secret police and when the contents were leaked they aroused the indignation of the Muslim fundamentalists and Islamic fraternities.[10]

The sensitive issue of conversion was the subject of another official report drawn by a deputy at the Ministry of Awqaf on the circumstances leading to the conversion of two young men to Christianity in Alexandria. This report also somehow reached the independent imams in Alexandria mosques, who denounced in a provocative manner "the dangers to which Muslim youths were exposed due to missionary activities."[11] No attempt was made to make an official refutation of the circulating reports or to challenge their contents. In reaction to these reports, however, the Islamic militants were mobilized, and this in turn aroused the sensitivities of the Copts. The situation became so unbearable to the latter that some of their leaders convened a conference in Alexandria on July 17, 1972, at which they appealed to the authorities to take urgent steps to safeguard their rights.

Relations between the authorities and the militant Church leaders began to worsen when the People's Assembly enacted legislation in conformity with the *Sharia*. The so-called permanent constitution promulgated by Sadat in 1971 included a clause which declared that the Shari'a constituted *one of the sources* of legislation.[12] Behind the official religious mask the government wanted to placate the Muslim fundamentalists, while seeking to undermine the influence of the left among Marxists and Nasserists. Ironically, many leftists thought that Islamically-inspired legislation, such as the apostasy law punishing conversions from Islam, was aimed at them. The Copts were affected too, and Pope Shenouda convened a conference in January 1977 to discuss the consequences of application

9. *Al-Ahrar*, September 14, 1981.
10. See the statement of the Islamic jama'at in the response to the alleged report in *al-Da'wa*, June 1980, pp. 22–23.
11. Badawi, *al-Fitna al-Ta'ifiyya*, p. 11. *Al-Ahrar* of September 14, 1981, quoted Shenouda as saying that while conversion efforts must be doubled, attempts must also be made to spread doubts about Islamic beliefs. He was quoted as saying that "people with shaken beliefs may not be good for us, but they will not be against us either."
12. This clause was amended in 1979 to make it *the principal source* of legislation. See *al-Da'wa*, May 1980. The amendment in the constitution adopted by the People's Assembly on July 19, 1979, said that "Islam is the religion of the state. Arabic is its official language and principles of Islamic laws are the main sources of legislation."

of Islamic laws to non-Muslims.[13] The conference condemned the government action because it violated human rights guaranteed by the United Nations Charter and the liberal ideals of Islam, which rejected coercion. A resolution adopted by the conference maintained that Islamic laws had harmful effects on marital ties within the Coptic community. For example, it was observed that some Christian men converted to Islam to avoid stringent Coptic divorce laws, then apostatized once proceedings were over.

The conference also condemned the unfair treatment of Copts in the government bureaucracy and the public sector. The main accusation was that Copts were frequently denied promotions. Another sensitive issue raised by the conference was the near absence of Coptic representation in the People's Assembly. It must be observed that this phenomenon is of recent origin. During the Monarchy, many of the leading members of the Chamber of Deputies were Copts. Minority representation has declined very sharply since 1952, however, due to a drop in Coptic rural population as a consequence of migration to urban areas and overseas. It should be noted that distribution of parliamentary seats is heavily in favor of rural areas. The situation has deteriorated to such an extent that no Copt was returned to the People's Assembly in the 1976 elections. The poor level of representation is also noticeable at the local government levels.

III

What aroused the hostility of the militant Copts and compelled them to adopt defensive measures was the rise of Islamic militancy. The most visible sign of the latter was the proliferation, with some government encouragement, of autonomous Islamic fraternities or jama'at *(jamā'āt)* which became prominent after Sadat came to power. Their elan and purpose were derived from a fundamental Quranic tenet calling on all Muslims to observe the principle of "enjoining the good and prohibiting the evil." This is "an unconditional duty incumbent on every individual Muslim—which means that no Muslim, even one who lacks proper knowledge of religious principles, is exonerated from the obligation to do all he can to secure the adherence of his fellow Muslims to those principles."[14] The jama'at further derived their legitimacy from the Prophetic model enshrined in the example of the small circle of faithful followers out of whose nucleus Islam spread to the far reaches of the earth. The belief in the jama'at as a legitimate group dedicated to carrying out God's injunctions and prohibitions is thus grounded in the solid Islamic tradition of the Quran and the Prophetic Sunna. But

13. The proceedings of the conference and its adopted resolutions are in Badawi's *al-Fitna al-Ta'ifiyya.* pp. 79–90.
14. Hamid Enayat, "Iran: Khumayni's Concept of the Guardianship of the Jurisconsult," in James P. Piscatori, ed., *Islam in the Political Process* (London: Cambridge University Press, 1983), p. 161.

it should be noted that interpretations of this tradition and the extent to which adherents were willing to go in fulfilling their obligations varied from group to group.[15]

The jama'at further justified their presence on political and ethical grounds. The various leaders of the different jama'at mobilized their followers in response to what they perceived as the moral laxity of the times and the defeatist spirit which came as a consequence of the June war defeat in 1967. Thus the jama'at were circles and coteries of varied internal cohesion and rituals, whose attitudes were a reaction to the circumstances in which they found themselves at the time. These attitudes were visible in the strong reaction against the secularist tendencies of Nasserist rule rooted in the ideas of nationalism and socialism. Their leaders expressed severe disappointment with the traditional *ulama* for their failure to combat atheism and corruption and to stem moral degeneration. In this moral vacuum, marked by the absence of the traditional leadership of Islam vested in the ulama, some of the leaders of the fraternities came to believe their mission to be as sacrosanct as religion itself.[16] Thus, a distinguishing feature of the jama'at was their willingness to take an activist role and to adapt doctrinal matters to political objectives.

Of the activitists, the extremists were those militant jama'at which invoked jihad (struggle) as a fundamental obligation. These jama'at came to be known by their adopted or externally imposed names, such as al-Takfir wa al-Hijra and the Jihad group, to which we will refer shortly. Their militant doctrine harked back to that of the old Kharijites, which drew "perilous conclusion about a man's inner faith on the basis of external acts."[17] On the basis of this doctrine, the Islamic militants justified rebellion against a Muslim ruler whose actions do not conform with Islamic laws. These militants must be distinguished from other jama'at which expressed moderate views on relations between faith and behavior, and those with a sufi outlook which preached withdrawal and cultivation of inner spirituality.

It will be a mistake to assume that the fraternities were confined to Muslims. It has been pointed out that Coptic students on university campuses began after 1967 to establish their own fraternities in reaction to the Islamic jama'at, and also in response to the atmosphere of religiosity which characterized the post-1967 war era.[18] Tension between the two communities was thus exacerbated by the rivalry between Muslim and Coptic students in setting up their own

15. For a fuller discussion of the jama'at, see the author's article "The Islamic Militants in Egyptian Politics" in the March 1984 (Vol. 16, No. 1) issue of the *International Journal of Middle East Studies*, pp. 123–144.
16. See Mohammad Abd al-Qudus's interview with Essam al-'Aryan in *al-Da'wa*, November 1980, p. 46.
17. Fazlur Rahman, *Islam* (Chicago: The University of Chicago Press, 1979), p. 131.
18. Milad Hanna, *Na'am Aqbat, Lakina Masriun* (Cairo: Madbuli Press, 1980), pp. 114–15.

'Usar (fraternities). This tension reached a climax in March 1980, when, as a consequence of a series of bomb explosions and attacks on Christian property in several cities in Upper Egypt and Cairo, Pope Shenouda decided to cancel all Easter celebrations. The repercussions of the sectarian conflict were even felt in the United States, where thousands of Copts living there staged demonstrations during Sadat's visit to Washington in May 1980. The international press further began to reveal in embarrassing detail the "physical threats to which the Copts were exposed."[19]

IV

The first open and direct attack on Shenouda was made by Sadat after his return from the United States in May 1980 on the anniversary of the "Corrective Revolution." The protest of the expatriate Copts had damaged Sadat's stage-managed plans to present to the West an image of a president whose regional and international commitments enjoyed the unflinching support of his people. He thought that Shenouda was behind the protest in the United States, which had been designed to exploit the deep Christian beliefs of President Carter. Sadat had been further exposed as a weak president who invoked Islam and encouraged the jama'at in order to bolster his regime.

In the course of his speech Sadat attacked Shenouda in terms which were later repeated by the jama'at in their own condemnation of the militant Copts. He, for example, confirmed the allegations that some Copts wanted to create a state of their own parallel to the Maronite attempts in Lebanon. He went further to claim that some Copts were discovered fighting alongside the Phalangists against the Palestinian resistance. Another accusation which inflamed the Muslim fundamentalists was Sadat's remark that through their world-wide connections Copts were bringing pressure to bear on the Egyptian government to abandon the Islamic character of the state.

Sadat unwittingly set the militants in both communities against each other by his accusation that outspoken Copts were impeding government plans to enforce Islamic laws. In his final statement of his May speech, Sadat reminded the Copts that he was a Muslim ruler of an Islamic country and that he would oppose any attempt to dilute the Islamic identity of Egypt. This statement was met with thundering applause. Sadat may have succeeded in winning the approval of his audience, but he alienated the Copts.

19. See, for example, *The International Herald Tribune*, September 9, 1981.

V

It was not only the Coptic minority which felt threatened by the jama'at. Political movements on the left and right of the political spectrum shared the same feelings. However, they held the state to be the cause of their common complaint. A critic of the Sadat regime once remarked that "the Islamic jama'at enjoyed privileges reminiscent of the privileges granted to foreigners under the capitulation treaties."[20] Many liberal Egyptians likewise believed that the role of the jama'at at an early stage of Sadat's rule was in harmony with the political goals of the regime, which included the neutralization of extremists across the political spectrum.

The extreme right, represented by the Ikhwan or Muslim Brotherhood, viewed the officially-sponsored fraternities with suspicion. Its leader, Omar Tilmisani, thought that they were created to counter-balance his movement.[21] The negative reaction to the jama'at was also apparent among the conservative and traditional leaders of the Muslim community. A representative view was Shaykh Mutwali Shaarawi's remark that "the jama'at were created not to defend Islam *per se*, but to preserve the political system."[22]

The Egyptian left represented by the *Tajamu'*, a loose association of Marxists, Communists and Nasserists, expressed the view that political expediency was behind the official creation of the jama'at. It stated further that the official policy behind the encouragement of the jama'at set in motion adverse reactions throughout the Coptic community, although the primary objective was the elimination of the influence of the left on university campuses.[23]

Rather than undermining the influence of the left or the right, the militant activities of the jama'at spread to provincial cities and to peripheral areas of the major urban center, where they encountered some resistance from militant Copts. But, contrary to the impressions of the threatened political movements, the jama'at were diverse, divided entities, lacking common political objectives, and their relations with the state and the Ikhwan were varied and conflicting. While some jama'at forged some links with the state, others fell under the influence of the Ikhwan. Nevertheless, many groups either turned their attention to other worldly interests or took to extremism in order to establish by means of force the kingdom of God on earth.[24]

20. Salah Hafiz in *Rose al-Yusif*, October 26, 1982, pp. 7–9.
21. Interview of Omar Tilmisani in *Al-Ahrar*, February 15, 1982.
22. Shaykh Mutwali Shaarawi in *al-Ahram*, November 8, 1981.
23. From the internal journal *al-Taqaddum*, June 25, 1981 and August 19, 1981.
24. It is difficult to know the exact number of the Islamic fraternities or how many individuals joined them. According to *al-Ahrar*, January 2, 1982, there were altogether 30 different types of Islamic fraternities. However, the paper does not mention its source of information. A report in *al-Musawwar*, January 29, 1982, said that inside al-Liman—Egypt's most notorious prison camp—there were 99 different Islamic groups. President Sadat, presumably relying on figures provided by the Ministry of the

Despite their diversity, the majority of the jama'at had a common ancestry. They were rooted in the Ikhwan movement, and many jama'at members were either former members of the Ikhwan or came from the same social origins.[25] Furthermore, the notion of *takfir* (the appellation of unbelief) which served as the basis of the militant doctrine of rebellion against the established authority was inspired by the writings of the Ikhwan leader, Sayyid Qutb.[26] Because of these common bonds, many observers arrived at the erroneous conclusion that the jama'at and the Ikhwan were one and the same. Thus, when relations between the state and the Ikhwan turned sour, Sadat himself denounced the militant jama'at, declaring them to be the secret army of the Ikhwan.

I have argued elsewhere that fundamental differences emerged between the Ikhwan leadership and the militant jama'at after 1971.[27] The cultivation of religious values by Sadat and the affirmation of the Islamic character of the state came in response to the challenge posed by leftists and Nasserists. In a bid to placate the right, Sadat ordered the release of Ikhwan leaders and followers who were serving long prison sentences during the Nasserist regime. He even went further by permitting the Ikhwan to reorganize and to publish its journal, *al-Da'wa*. The new leadership under Tilmisani also seemed reconciled to acting in the role of an advisor to the authorities and to confining the activities of the movement to propagation of Islamic values.

The growing disenchantment of the militants with the Ikhwan had at its basis the conviction that the Ikhwan leaders, the majority of whom belonged to the older generation, had grown tired of the repression that they had continued to suffer for at least three decades and were ready to compromise true beliefs in order to win some favors from the political authority. Although the Ikhwan was able to win to its side the Islamic jama'at which dominated the student unions in the Egyptian universities, many jama'at which adopted the concept of takfir rejected the Ikhwan leadership.[28]

In contrast to the Ikhwan and the moderate jama'at, the militants believed that Sadat's attempts to establish Islamic rule were a sham. Most of them

---

Interior, said that the militants among the Islamic fraternities were in the range of 7000 to 8000. Undoubtedly Sadat's figures included members of both the militant and moderate fraternities.

25. It should be noted that the moderate and the extremist jama'at were of the same social origins and paradoxically were inspired by the same doctrinal sources. For example, Essam al-'Aryan and Colonel Abbud al-Zomor in the militant Jihad group came from the same district in Giza. The former, however, expressed moderate views on authority and rebellion in Islam. The Muslim Brotherhood movement was the legitimate father of many groups which turned toward extremism. For instance, Shukri Mustafa, the leader of the militant Takfir wa al-Higra, was imprisoned in the 1960s because he was a member of the Ikhwan. It may also be noted that the militant doctrine of establishing Islamic rule by force was inspired by the writings of the Ikhwan leader, Sayyid Qutb.

26. See Sayyid Qutb, *Ma'alim fi al-Tariq* (Cairo: Dar al-Shuruq, 1981).

27. Hamied Ansari, op cit.

28. See the critique of the militant doctrine by the leader of the Islamic fraternities at Cairo University in *al-Da'wa*, November 1980.

adopted the extreme position that Sadat was not a Muslim ruler nor did his rule represent a step toward the establishment of Islamic rule. They defended the purity of their beliefs and attacked the Muslim Brotherhood for its willingness to reach a *modus vivendi* with the authorities. It was even rumored within militant circles that Tilmisani was cooperating with the security department, something he came close to admitting in an interview with *al-Musawwar*.[29] Also, the groups which were originally encouraged by the state in the universities could not escape the stigma of their former association.

VI

After 1973, the government came to the recognition that the Islamic jama'at were a bad idea after all. This happened long after Sadat had got rid of his rivals identified with the left during the Corrective Revolution of May 1971. The brief successes in the October War consolidated the regime further and even brought to it a measure of popularity. All these obviated the need for a strategy that was heavily dependent on appealing to the right in order to suppress the left. But in the meantime the Islamic jama'at had gained autonomy and a momentum which lay beyond state control, and some of them were able to forge links with rural migrants of similar origins in the outskirts of Cairo and the provincial cities in Upper Egypt.

Beginning with the Military Technical College in 1974, the Islamic militants launched a series of attacks on what they considered symbols of authority. The scope of their hostilities was expanded further to include those conservative ulama who were critical of the militant doctrine. For example, a former Minister of al-Awqaf was kidnapped and killed in 1977 by al-Takfir wa al-Hijra.[30] The discovery of each group led to its immediate suppression. But this did not prevent the emergence of similarly inclined groups. However, it must be remembered that these groups were not connected with each other in any formal sense. The last group to emerge was Tanzim al-Jihad, which figured prominently in the period between the sectarian disturbances at Zawiya al-Hamra in June 1981 and Sadat's assassination in October of the same year.

The turning point in the anti-Copt activities of members of the Tanzim al-Jihad was the affair at Zawiya al-Hamra. Some of its members formed the impression there that the militant Copts were fully armed and thus a serious threat

29. Interview with Omar Tilmisani in *al-Musawwar*, January 22, 1982. See also denials of complicity with the Ministry of the Interior in *al-Da'wa*, March 1981. Hilmi al-Jazzar, the leader of the Islamic jama'at, who was most closely associated with the Ikhwan, said that he was personally requested by the Minister of the Interior to go to Minya to calm Muslim feelings after the occurrence of sectarian clashes there. See *al-Da'wa*, June 1980, p. 61.

30. See Saad al-Din Ibrahim, "Anatomy of Egypt's Militant Islamic Groups: Methodological Note and Preliminary Findings." *International Journal of Middle East Studies* 12(1980), pp. 423–499.

to Islam.[31] This drove them to devise ways to acquire arms and undergo military training. The regime was also blamed for not providing protection to defenseless Muslims and for letting the Copts become aggressive through its appeasement policy. Thus, the sectarian disturbances at Zawiya al-Hamra propelled members of Tanzim al-Jihad to carry out their violent activities behind the scenes to eliminate those they regarded as the enemies of Islam. It may be observed that the disturbances set off a chain reaction which ended in Sadat's assassination. The militant response of Tanzim al-Jihad to the events at Zawiya al-Hamra in the form of attacks on churches and Coptic property exposed some of its members to the security apparatus. Because of the threat of imprisonment or fear of exposure, the remaining members felt compelled to act against the President, for they considered him to be ultimately responsible for their persecution by the police. On the other hand, the reaction of the Muslim Brotherhood and the moderate Islamic fraternities to the events at Zawiya al-Hamra was comparatively mild. They were prepared to take measures against the Copts, but not physical violence and threats of annihilation.

VII

Zawiya al-Hamra, in the northeastern part of Cairo, comes under the administration of the Local Council of North Cairo. Politically, the area is under the control of the Local Committee of the National Democratic Party (NDP) in al-Sharabiyya district. The area (about 40 feddans) was originally a Waqf property which became state land when Waqf properties were abolished. Encroachments on state land increased as more settlers came to live in the area. The first settlers came from Upper Egypt in 1945, but since then rural migrants have come from different parts of the country. Some of the new migrants forged common links with the old settlers, but the community, given its heterogenous character, began to feel growing tensions arising from increased population density. A local Coptic priest remarked that most of the trouble began after the arrival of rural migrants from Minya.[32] The significance of this remark will become apparent when the social origins of members of Tanzim al-Jihad are examined. Suffice it now to say that Minya province had a long history of sectarian conflict. Thus it seems that the rural migrants brought to the city their ancient prejudices and petty feuds.

The immediate cause of the sectarian conflict lay in the government's decision to use the little space left in Zawiya al-Hamra to relocate the inhabitants of slums in other parts of the city. In 1979 a decision was taken by the Governor

---

31. Based on transcripts of interrogations held by the Office of the Public Prosecutor. These transcripts are accessible to the public and can be obtained from the Ministry of Justice in Cairo.
32. See *al-Musawwar*, July 10, 1981.

of Cairo to pull down the slums of Eshash al-Torgoman ('Ishāsh al-Turjumān) and Arab al-Mohammadi and to relocate their inhabitants in Zawiya al-Hamra and in a new settlement on the outskirts of Heliopolis. Eshash al-Torgoman was a slum area in the center of the business district in Cairo, while the Arab al-Mohammadi slum was in the eastern part of the city, close to 'Ain Shams University. The area was vacated to make room for the construction of business offices and upper class residences. Two sociologists who observed the attitudes of the slum dwellers before their evacuation said that they were very resentful for many reasons, including loss of livelihood which they had earned by providing menial services in the area.[33] They were also embittered by the prospects of a breakdown in their social relations, since they were relocated in two faraway places. Furthermore, it was observed that coercion was used to evacuate the inhabitants. It is no surprise, as a sociologist concluded, that after the settlers arrived in Zawiya al-Hamra they nursed bitter feelings because of the conditions of their alienation.[34]

The evacuation began in 1979 and was carried out in two stages which ended in 1981. The plan aimed at resettling 5,000 families or 30,000 individuals.[35] A sociologist who visited Zawiya al-Hamra before the occurrence of the sectarian clashes observed that families who came from Eshash al-Torgoman were living under appalling conditions due to lack of space. Her estimate was that on the average there were seven individuals per room and in the majority of cases there were two or three related families in the same apartment.[36]

Sadat, however, gave a different version. He said to *Mayo*, the official publication of the National Democratic Party, that two years before, when he was in Alexandria, he summoned the Minister of Construction, Engineer Hasaballah al-Kafrawi, and gave him the following instructions:

> Listen, for thirty years, from before the 23 July revolution to this day, we have been facing a big problem called the problem of Eshash al-Torgoman and Arab al-Mohammadi in the center of Cairo. It is a major problem and it gives a very bad picture of the people's standard of living. I have summoned you to tell you that the time has come to solve this problem immediately. I will no longer allow the continuation of this problem . . . Al-Kafrawi acted immediately. He chose al-Zawiya al-Hamra and decided to move the inhabitants of Eshash al-Torgoman and Arab al-Mohammadi there. Last year I went to al-Zawiya al-Hamra, toured the area, entered some houses and talked to their owners . I was really pleased to see happiness in the faces

33. Aly Fahmi and Madiha el-Safty. "Anxiety and Deviance in the Arab City." Unpublished paper presented at the Tenth International Congress on Social Defense, Salonika, September 28 to October 2, 1981.

34. Madiha El Safty. "Sociological Perspectives on Urban Housing." *Cairo Papers* (The American University in Cairo: 1983.

35. See a report in *Akher Sa'a*. May 23, 1979. Also, *Akhbar al-Youm*, May 19, 1979.

36. Madiha El-Safty. "Sociological Studies in Urban Housing." See also the criticism raised by the Labor M.P. Hamdi Ahmad in *al-Sha'ab*, July 21, 1981.

of the new residents. They had left their shacks and now lived in healthy houses in an area that was rebuilt in accordance with the modern system.[37]

Contrary to the impressions formed by the President, the inhabitants of Zawiya al-Hamra were deeply affected by other policies adopted by the government. In particular, it was observed that *al-Infitah*, the economic liberalization policy, had led to a spiraling increase in the cost of living, while widening the gap between the few individuals who were able to profit from selling imported goods on the one hand and the deprived majority on the other. The Islamic fraternities sharpened religious differences by disseminating information on the high level of prosperity achieved by Coptic businesses under the umbrella of al-Infitah. (It should be noted that during the riots at Zawiya al-Hamra some of the shops owned by Copts were looted or destroyed.)

There are different versions of the reasons behind the outbreak of sectarian clashes. Sadat said in one of his speeches that the clashes began as a result of a petty feud between two neighbors which was exploited by religious extremists and politicians to advance political goals.[38] In a typical fashion, he blamed communists and misguided members of the opposition for fomenting the sectarian disturbances. Actually, it was the ruling party (NDP) which was engaged in the deadly game of promoting political objectives at the cost of national consensus. At that time, the NDP's local committee, composed of parliamentary deputies and party officials, was still excited by the victory it had won against the opposition during the elections of the People's Assembly a month earlier. The ruling party's local committees normally become active at election times, after which their activities begin to subside until they come to a complete standstill. In the case of Zawiya al-Hamra, however, the pre-electoral tension was still having some lingering effects. This was evident in the local committee's ill-advised intervention to settle a dispute between a Muslim and a Copt over a piece of land of about 1800 square meters.[39] The reasons which it gave for intervening were explained in a leaflet which was distributed in the area two days before the outbreak of violence.

The leaflet was addressed to the people of al-Sharabiyya district and al-Zawiya al-Hamra. It began with a quotation from the *Hadith*: "Let sedition lie asleep for God curses whoever awakens it." The NDP then went on to say that on "12 and 13 June a citizen claimed a piece of land on the basis that he had a

37. See *Mayo*, June 22, 1981.
38. See text of Sadat's speech in *al-Ahram*, September 15, 1981. See also *Mayo*, September 7, 1981 and *al-Sha'ab*, June 30, 1981.
39. According to Milad Hanna, a prominent member of the left-wing Nationalist Progressive Unionist Party (Tajamu'), the local committee of the NDP had no business to meddle in matters that were best left in the hands of the courts of law, but the shortsightedness of the NDP was due to its political opportunism. See *al-Taqaddum*, June 26, 1981. See also the statement of Minister of the Interior Nabawi Ismail in *Akher Sa'a*, June 24, 1981. He also confirmed that the Copt had a legal claim to the land under dispute.

court ruling (in his favor). The security forces intervened in cooperation with the NDP to examine the claim and found that it was invalid. The local Popular Council of North Cairo had already decided to let a poultry firm use part of the land for the purposes of the firm and the rest was to be utilized for building a mosque.'' The leaflet ended by saying that the ''NDP is vigilant and attentive in the interests of the masses, [works to] instill spiritual values and maintain law and order.'' The names of the secretary general of the NDP, two members of the People's Assembly and local committee members were appended at the bottom of the leaflet.

The decision of the Local Council undoubtedly infuriated the Coptic family whose right to the disputed land was upheld by a court of law. Thus blinded by fury and outrage, the Coptic family members opened fire on Muslims gathered on the disputed land for the evening prayers. As a consequence, moderate and extremist jama'at were quickly mobilized. In the ensuing clashes, 17 people died and 112 were injured. Also, a total of 171 shops and public places were ransacked or destroyed. Sources at the Ministry of the Interior said that 266 persons were arrested; some of them were carrying stolen property. The Minister of the Interior personally appealed to Omar Tilmisani and other fundamentalist leaders closely connected with the jama'at to step in to calm the situation and to soothe the feelings of the embittered Muslims. A High Council of the Permanent Islamic Propagation Conference was established to monitor the situation closely and to recommend action to the Minister of the Interior. The Council included two of the prominent Ikhwan leaders, Omar Tilmisani and Mohammad al-Ghazali, and Abdul Latif Mushtahri and Attiyeh Khamis, among other Muslim leaders.

Those jama'at which rejected the militant doctrine and were closely connected with the Ikhwan held a conference at Zawiya al-Hamra on June 20. But, as one can tell from the recorded speeches, there was little in their denunciation of Copts which distinguished them from the militants.[40] They too seemed to have succumbed to the evils of uncompromise. Hilmi al-Jazzar, speaking on behalf of the jama'at in the Egyptian universities, attributed the ''Christian militancy to the absence of Islamic rule which alone could put an end to aggressions committed against Muslims.'' He called on Muslims to boycott Christian businesses as one of the means to prevent them from accumulating money in order to arm themselves.

The speakers at the conference repeated the allegations made by Sadat in his speech on the anniversary of the Corrective Movement. Most inflammatory,

40. To my knowledge these speeches have never been published anywhere. Nevertheless, apart from the secret police who recorded the speeches of the leading members of the fraternities on various occasions, the militant members of what came to be known as Tanzim al-Jihad recorded the speeches. As revealed by the transcripts of the interrogations held for members of Tanzim al-Jihad, a machine to mass produce cassettes was bought in an effort to emulate the Iranian revolution.

however, was the speech of Shaykh Hafiz Salama, the independent Imam from Suez and a leading critic of Sadat. He said that Sadat's own words revealed the existence of a conspiracy hatched in the Vatican and in New York against Islam. Another leading member of the jama'at in the Egyptian universities, Essam al-'Aryan, said that Shenouda was playing the same role as Major Sa'd Haddad in Lebanon so that sufficient havoc would be caused in the country to invite foreign intervention under the pretext of protecting the minority.[41] He added that Copts never gave up the old ambition of establishing a state with Asyut as its capital. Some Christians were fully armed and some of them were trained in Lebanon as declared by the president. As an evidence of the state of preparedness of the militant Copts, al-'Aryan pointed out that the Christians used firearms in their attack in Zawiya al-Hamra, while Muslims fought back with sticks and any sharp instrument they could get hold of.

Essam al-'Aryan, however, admonished those who were responsible for the destruction of homes and shops, because in his opinion such activities exposed the weaknesses of the perpetrators. He added that at any rate the government would compensate the owners as it did in the past when owners of casinos and night clubs were compensated. (He presumably was referring to the destruction of places of entertainment during the food riots in January 1977.)

The resolutions of the conference called on the authorities to dismiss Shenouda, disarm the Christians, stop the building of churches, bring to trial the attackers at Zawiya al-Hamra and put an end to the missionary activities. The conference also called on Muslims to stay away from Christian shops and places of business. It can hardly be said that these resolutions were hammered out by a moderate group prepared to defuse the conflict. On the contrary, there is a good reason to suspect that the moderate jama'at were rivaling the extremists in showing their hostility to the Copts. Somehow in the fracas caused by the Zawiya al-Hamra affair, the Islamic teachings which extol the virtue of tolerance and call on Muslims to respect the integrity of Christians were forgotten.

But the speakers at the conference tended to distinguish themselves from the more radical groups present in the audience. It was revealed that the militant elements were exerting pressure behind the scene for strong measures against Christians. Shaykh Attiyeh Khamis, for example, said that some extremists tried to put pressure on the leaders of the community to take a more militant stand. But he thought they were presumptuous to think that they were more zealous

---

41. Essam al-'Aryan, a medical doctor age 27, was born in Nahia village, Imbaba district, in Giza. To this village also belonged Colonel Abbud al-Zomor, the top-ranking member of Tanzim al-Jihad who stood trial for his part in the plot to assassinate President Sadat. Al-'Aryan was married to the sister of one of the accused in the attack on the Military Technical College in 1974. He was the former Amir al-'Am of the Islamic fraternities of the Egyptian universities. Although he held regular sermons in which he preached the enforcement of Islamic laws, he rejected the militant doctrine of *takfir*. For an explanation of this doctrine which distinguishes the moderates from the extremists see my "The Islamic Militants in Egyptian Politics."

about Islam than the traditional leaders of the community. He further condemned them as a superficial bunch of youth devoid of sound understanding of the principles of faith. Similarly, the Chairman of the Local Council of North Cairo, speaking at the conference, also warned against subversive elements who were splitting the Muslim movement. (It was not clear then who these speakers meant until the identities of members of Tanzim al-Jihad became known publicly as the autonomous group responsible for President Sadat's assassination. Through signed confessions, each member revealed his role, beginning with attacks on Copts in Upper Egypt and Cairo and ending with the assassination.)

VIII

The response of members of the Jihad to the sectarian disturbances was revealed by Tariq al-Zomor in his confession. He said that two days after the events at Zawiya al-Hamra, a resident of the area approached the Tanzim with the request to provide protection for the Muslim inhabitants in the area against further provocations by the militant Copts. A group of five armed men, including Tariq al-Zomor, were dispatched to guard the area but no incidents of violence took place.[42]

Nevertheless, the various confessions indicate that the anti-Christian activities of Tanzim al-Jihad began in Upper Egypt and slowly spread through its members in the capital. Throughout the period between 1977–1980, Minya and Asyut became the hotbed of sectarian clashes. The Islamic jama'at there accused the Copts of hoarding weapons in their churches. They also objected to mixing between the sexes and the sale of alcohol. The confrontation between the Copts and the jama'at reached a climax during Easter in 1980, when the jama'at warned against Muslim observance of the Coptic celebration of the Spring festival of Sham al-Nasim, which is also traditionally observed by Muslims.

Many Amirs (princes of the fraternities), inflamed by Sadat's allegations against Shenouda in his May 1980 speech, devoted their Friday sermons to attacks on Copts. One such Amir who fanned anti-Christian hostilities was Karam Zuhdi. In his confession statement, Zuhdi revealed his responsibility for spreading hostilities against Copts from Upper Egypt to Cairo. According to police records, Zuhdi was the main instigator of the clashes with Copts in Minya before his escape to Cairo in 1980.[43] In Cairo he sought the shelter of the jama'at at Cairo University. There he began to spread anti-Christian views and to advocate

---

42. Based on transcripts of interrogations held by the Public Prosecutor.
43. Police records in Minya show that Karam Zuhdi with others attacked the Orthodox Church in an area locally referred to as "Sultan" land in 1978. He assaulted Coptic couples on several occasions because he believed that Islamic norms prohibited men and women from walking together. He attacked Coptic employees of a cultural center in Minya for showing a film on the life of Dr. Taha Hussein.

the establishment of Islamic rule through violent means. It was also during his stay in Cairo, which lasted two summer months, that he met like-minded men such as Mohammad Abd al-Salam Farag, the chief ideologue of Tanzim al-Jihad. Both agreed on the principles of jihad as the means to establish Islamic rule. Zuhdi then went back to Upper Egypt to spread the new doctrine of violence among members of the Islamic fraternities. How he escaped detection by the security apparatus despite the order for his arrest remains an enigma. At any rate, this was the background behind the formation of the loosely structured Tanzim al-Jihad, with a majlis al-shura or a consultative council, composed of the leaders of some of the militant groups in Cairo and Upper Egypt. It included Omar Abd al-Rahman, a blind Shaykh educated at al-Azhar who acted as the chief *mujtahid* or Sharia law interpreter of the Tanzim, Mohammad Abd al-Salam Farag, an engineer employed at Cairo University and the author of the Tanzim's doctrinal statement, *al-Farida al-Gha'iba* (the absent obligation), Colonel 'Abbud al-Zomor of Military Intelligence and the top ranking officer in the Tanzim, whose responsibility was military planning and training, and Karam Zuhdi, a graduate of the Agricultural Institute in Asyut living in Minya. These were the most prominent members, but there were others who were set on a collision course with the authorities.[44]

The militants in the Jihad group presented a clear divergence from the methods advocated by the other Islamic groups for the establishment of Islamic rule. In his confession, Zuhdi said that the Muslim Brotherhood opted to create a Muslim society by means of inculcating Islamic values at the grass roots. The Islamicization of the society must come before the establishment of Islamic rule. Zuhdi said that the Jihad group believed in the exact opposite: "We proceed from the top to the bottom because we believe that a good ruler can create everything in the society." As for the other Islamic fraternities, Zuhdi said that his group believed in jihad as the means to overthrow the repressive regime. By contrast, the Islamic fraternities which eschewed the principle of armed struggle through jihad showed opposition to the regime by merely holding demonstrations, protest meetings, and delivering speeches at mosques and public gatherings.

As noted earlier, after the disturbance at Zawiya al-Hamra, the militants became convinced that the activist Copts were fully armed and that they were not a match for them unless they obtained arms. They knew, however, that acquir-

---

44. The activities of Tanzim al-Jihad became particularly ominous when it was joined by Nabil al-Maghrabi, an employee of the Ministry of Culture in al-Shurabiyya district. He was a former army officer and worked part-time as an editor of the Muslim Brotherhood organ *al-I'tisam*. In his interrogations, al-Maghrabi revealed that in February or March 1980, he visited St. Mark's Cathedral in Cairo to draw a plan of the quarters of Pope Shenouda in preparation for an attack. He admitted that he was working under the order of Colonel Abbud al-Zomor. He further participated in the attack on a jewelry store owned by a Copt in Shoubra al-Khaima on the outskirts of Cairo. He was arrested on September 25, 1981 as he was carrying a suitcase full of explosives. His arrest propelled his brother-in-law, Hussein Abbas, to join Khalid al-Islambuli in the attack on Sadat on October 6.

ing arms from the blackmarket would cost them money beyond their meager resources. The solution was found in attacking Christian jewelry stores. They sought the opinion of Shaykh Omar Abd al-Rahman in order to be certain that they were not violating Islamic tenets. His *fatwa* (edict) was as follows: "Christians belong to three categories: Those who kill Muslims, those who support the Church with money and arms in order to harm Muslims, and those who do not cause any harm to Muslims. An eye for an eye must be exacted from Christians in the first category, while Christians in the second category must be deprived of their wealth. But no harm should come to Christians in the third category."

The fatwa of Omar Abd al-Rahman was interpreted by the militants to mean that Islam legitimized taking booty from Christians so long as it could be proved that they aided the Church to harm Muslims. As a consequence, members of the Tanzim al-Jihad robbed two Christian jewelry stores in Naga' Hammadi in the deep south and in Shubra al-Khaima north of Cairo. The latter was also the scene of a bomb explosion at a Coptic wedding in July, where police discovered a sophisticated explosive device originated within the army. This led the authorities to speculate that Islamic fundamentalists had penetrated the officer corps of the armed forces.

When he was finally convinced to act, Sadat made the fatal mistake of treating all the opposition as one monolithic entity bent upon destroying the regime. Sadat himself announced in the wake of the crackdown in September that there was no difference between the Muslim Brotherhood and the militant jama'at. Indeed, as noted above, he said that the militant fraternities were the military arm of the Muslim Brotherhood. Sadat also made the serious mistake of treating the secular and religious opposition to his regime on equal footing. There are two possible explanations for the indiscriminate treatment of the opposition. One was Sadat's ignorance of the real differences dividing the various opposition movements. The other explanation was that Sadat exploited the escalating sectarian conflict to put behind bars his critics among secularists and moderate religious elements alike. I am inclined to accept the latter explanation, given Sadat's impatience with the growing criticism of his policies. Nevertheless, Sadat's political opportunism proved to be disastrous. While it united the secular and religious opposition, it also forced the militant members of Tanzim al-Jihad to act rapidly before the security forces closed in on them. Some of their leaders from Upper Egypt were already in hiding when orders were issued for their arrest.

In the first two weeks of September, Sadat issued his famous decrees which included the detention of prominent religious leaders in both the Muslim and Coptic communities. Bishops, priests, shaykhs and imams were put behind bars. The detention list included such important men as Tilmisani, Abdul Salam Zayyat, Milad Hanna, Ismail Sabri Abdullah, Hilmi Murad, Shaykh Mahalawi and Shaykh Kishk. These men represented diverse ideologies and political movements. The only common thing among them was their opposition to Sadat's controversial domestic and foreign policies. At any rate, they were not united to overthrow the regime as it was claimed. Of dubious legality was Sadat's sacking of Pope Shenouda and his exile to a monastery in the desert. He was replaced by a five-man committee of bishops. The outspoken Coptic and Muslim philanthropic groups and societies were closed and their journals and bulletins banned. Journalists and university professors were either imprisoned or transferred because of their criticism of Sadat. Indeed, Sadat's repressive policy was unprecedented since it affected a wide cross section of the society. It also unleashed some forces which lay beyond the control of the government. On October 6 members of the Tanzim al-Jihad assassinated President Sadat while he was reviewing the military parade held on the anniversary of the October War.

IX

The sectarian disturbances had a destabilizing effect on the political system, aroused hostility and bitterness among members of the Muslim and Coptic communities and gave rise to problems which pose a difficult dilemma for President Mubarak. What do we learn from the past events which may be helpful for understanding religious consciousness, how it is aroused and transformed into an obstacle on the path of national integration and political development?

Sadat abandoned the Nasserist formula of political mobilization based on secular ideals and adopted instead a formula which was designed to win the support of the traditional and conservative elements in his struggle with the left. Sadat's formula had two disastrous consequences to the stability of the political system: first, it alienated the Coptic minority and forced the traditionally acquiescent Coptic Church to take a militant stand.

Secondly, the politically expedient appeal to religion had the unintended consequence of arousing Islamic militancy. It has repeatedly been observed, even by some of the conservative ulama closely connected with the government, that Sadat's religious appeals were window-dressings. His primary concern had been to consolidate his rule and to silence the secular opposition by means of Islamic symbolism. The traditional constituency to which Sadat had appealed also came under the influence of the Islamic militant groups, who, like the secularists and the moderate religious groups, fully understood Sadat's political motives. Let us not forget that some of the militants were originally Sadat's own creation. It is also no surprise that the Governor of Asyut, who was ousted from his post by President Mubarak when he came to power, boasted at one time that he knew personally the leaders of the militant jama'at in his province. Nevertheless, a reasonable explanation of Sadat's policies cannot be realized without fully analyzing the context within which these policies were carried out. Egypt in the past decade has experienced a tremendous social transformation reflected in a high level of urbanization due to rural migration. But to say that rural migration

416

and the expansion of Cairo and Alexandria beyond imaginable limits have affected the stability of the political system is not a novel thesis. Egypt in this regard fits a general Middle Eastern pattern, where rural migrants forged links with the old settlers of the same social origins against the established classes, transplanted traditional values and transformed the periphery of the city into rural settlements.

We must, however, go beyond this level of generalities to focus on the links between political mobilization and the use of religion as a political tool. In his bid to mobilize rural migrants and conservative elements, Sadat committed the fatal error of appealing to traditional sensibilities and narrow prejudices rather than adopting an enlightened policy designed to win a broad social base. Nowhere was this more apparent than in the attempt of the ruling party to "outbid" the Islamic militants in Zawiya al-Hamra, which led to the ugliest sectarian clashes in recent memory. When social harmony was threatened as a consequence of this policy, Sadat resorted to the opposite extreme of launching a widespread repression. Sadat, in trying to restore social balance, treated the Islamic opposition as one entity. Here he made the fatal mistake of not drawing the necessary distinctions among Islamic groups and secular opposition as grounds for political action.

We need to watch carefully the consequences of recent developments under Mubarak. His first act as President was the release of all the leading members of the secular and moderate religious opposition. Also, in a gesture of good will, Mubarak invited the opposition for consultation at the Presidential Palace in November 1981. The main concern expressed by the President was how to establish constructive relations with the opposition and how to avoid recourse to measures which have perpetuated in the past the cycle of violence and repression. Almost everyone present at the meeting expressed the view that the panacea for Egypt's ills was the adoption of genuine democracy. In response, Mubarak seems to have embarked on a new course that will lend strength to the liberal-secular impulse.

Mubarak called for new elections to the People's Assembly in May 1984 on the basis of proportional representation and voting by party slates instead of the traditional two-member district constituencies and absolute majority. The ruling party won 391 of the 448 contested seats; it received 87.3 per cent of the popular votes. By contrast, the only opposition party which survived the elections was the newly reconstituted New Wafd. The party won 57 seats in the Assembly and received 12.7 per cent of the popular votes. The other opposition parties—the Labor Party, the Liberal Party and the left-wing Tagamu'—were eliminated due to a clause in the electoral procedure which barred any party from holding seats if it received less than 8 per cent of the votes cast. Thus, the ruling party has maintained its hegemony and the opposition remains comparatively weak.

417

Nevertheless, the May elections may be regarded as revolutionary in comparison with previous elections. They created a viable opposition represented by one of the oldest parties in the Middle East which takes pride in its secular-liberal past. It can be surmised from the above that liberalism is once again on the march in Egypt. But obstacles continue to exist which pose a barrier toward the realization of a real democracy. No attempt has been made to repeal the laws which impose heavy constraints on freedom of speech and assembly and Pope Shenouda has not been reinstated as head of the Coptic Church. There can be no genuine democracy without the right of association for the pursuance of political objectives.

The New Wafd continues to function under a leadership that has not divorced itself from the past or learned anything since the time it had lost power to the army officers. The leaders of the New Wafd evoke memories of a bygone age long buried under the historical heap. The New Wafd won a substantial number of seats largely because of its nationalist-secularist past. It was a strange spectacle indeed when in a recent gathering of the Wafdists men in the audience shouted "long live the Wafd the Enemy of the British" and "Down with the [British] occupation," and its future orientation is unclear, particularly in the light of its electoral alliance with the Ikhwan.

The return of the Wafd is likely to lead to polarization between the Nasserists—the beneficiaries of the agrarian reforms and the socialist decrees and the employees of the public sector—on the one hand, and the old class of bourgeoisie and the new class which has prospered thanks to Sadat's economic liberalization on the other. Wafd leaders have privately expressed the apprehension that polarization is likely to open the door to direct military intervention, given the existence of social affinities between the supporters of the Mubarak regime and the military apparatus.

Threats which imperil liberalism are also present in the large number of lower middle class people of rural origins on the periphery of urban society whose political extremism has been fully revealed in the assassination of President Sadat. The parties competing for their support may find the temptation to appeal to this traditionally-minded segment by resorting to Islamic symbolism too strong to resist. The repercussions of such an appeal have already been witnessed in the eruption of sectarian conflicts between the Coptic minority and the Islamic groups in Zawiya al-Hamra.

Part VI
Jewish Terrorist Groups

[16]

Avraham ('Yair') Stern (1907–1942): Myth and Reality

Joseph Heller

As a rule it is in the nature of a political leadership to develop before the eyes of the world, and even if the nuances of its nature are made clear only with the passage of time, its most salient and significant features become readily apparent soon after its inception. This rule does not apply, however, to the political leadership of underground movements; here, the protagonists aim to conceal their activities, until such time as they attain the breakthrough for which they struggle and yearn. Our central character never succeeded either in reaching this stage, or in surpassing the level of a conspirator. Herein lies the difficulty in producing a comprehensive biographical study of the man, insofar as the researcher must separate between the two distinct spheres in which any given leadership exists – the realm of myth and legend, and historical reality. It is the function of historical research to provide a balanced view of images from the past, and assemble, to the best of one's ability, a 'true' picture, one that fits into the broad context of historical and long-term developments.

In Israel, engagé historical literature is a device which is most often characteristic of the political right, although the left is by no means entirely innocent in this regard. At any rate, it has proved a hindrance to serious research and to any satisfactory treatment of the subject of the Zionist leadership. With respect to the systema-

* Joseph Heller teaches International Relations and Modern History of the Jewish People, at the Hebrew University of Jerusalem. A major book by him on Lehi ('The Stern "Gang": 1940–1949. From Radical Right to National Bolshevism'), is due to be published (in Hebrew) soon by the Z. Shazar Center (The Historical Society of Israel), Jerusalem.

[*The Jerusalem Quarterly*, Number Forty-Nine, Winter 1989]

tic construction of myths, Avraham Stern is perhaps the most typical case in point. Interestingly, the adherents of this mythology include those of Stern's disciples who turned leftward and, in particular, to the radical right. All viewed him as a charismatic leader who provided ample evidence of his magnetic powers.

The point of the following essay will be to demonstrate that, contrary to the beliefs of his disciples, Avraham Stern, the prime revolutionary, was not in fact the leader of an unprecedented revolution, but rather a link in a chain of revolutionary leaders of the maximalist Revisionist school, that is, the radical Zionist right. His efforts followed those of Abba Aḥimeir, Uri-Zvi Greenberg, Yehoshua Heschel Yeivin, and Uriel Heilperin (Yonatan Ratosh). But unlike these men, who published the principles of their beliefs under their own names and signatures, Avraham Stern, insofar as he published the basic principles of his ideology, did this under a pseudonym, Elazar Ben-Yair (after the Masada hero) rather than his own signature. In general, he tended to conceal his long-range aims, as befitting a true underground fighter, a man who originated in the underground and aimed to use it as a device in the pursuit of influence and power. In other words, for him, the underground did not represent an end in itself, but rather, the means to an end. His inability to achieve complete success with respect to his means and his total inability to achieve his goal, meant, in essence, that his personality as a leader never grew beyond the initial stages of development. Hence there was a special need to invent the myths, a need that was inseparably linked to the fact of his personal sacrifice. Although his foremost mentor, Ze'ev Jabotinsky, was also wrapped by his disciples in layer upon layer of myth and legend despite the fact that he, too, died without seeing his goal fulfilled, Jabotinsky, unlike Stern, succeeded in building a political movement, and imparting an ideology to this movement. Stern only succeeded in laying the foundations for a future movement and its ideology. Having said this, however, there is nothing to prevent us from elucidating the roots of his ideological and political emergence, examining his attempt to establish a new leadership for the radical right, and addressing the question of whether or not he can, in fact, be viewed as a truly charismatic leader, as defined by criteria that are generally accepted by political researches.

The following statements were printed in *HeḤazit* (The Front), the journalistic mouthpiece of Stern's organization, the Lehi acronym for Lohamei Herut Israel, commonly known in English as the Stern Group, [or Gang]), in the first issue published after the re-establishment of the organization in the summer of 1943:

> ...He [Avraham Stern] was the world's first truly free Jew. His Zionism was not just excess baggage to the aims of Churchill or Stalin...

...Stern was not prepared to serve either of the combatant sides. To him this was simply a war of Gog and Magog inasmuch as neither side had declared support for the national aspirations of the Jews, and both had done harm to our people in one way or another. Nevertheless, the willing slaves of all the Zionist camps hastened to prove their loyalty to the Ruler...

...and they did not care to consider the fearsome danger that awaited the masses of the House of Israel in the event of a declaration of war on the part of the Jews against Nazi Germany. Who can tell whether all these declarations and recruitment drives of the Jewish Agency and the New Zionist Organization, and that terrifying propaganda that was already being orchestrated in the earliest days of the war – who knows whether these reasons were not the very ones that caused the intensified persecution of the Jews in Europe?[1]

Less than a year later, on the second anniversary of Stern's death and just a few days after the start of the 'Revolt' of the IZL (acronym for Irgun Zva'i Leumi, commonly referred to in English as the 'Irgun') under the command of Menachem Begin, the following was written by Lehi in a booklet dedicated to the memory of the founding father:

...He was a lion, and the cravings of the foxes were foreign to him. He was an eagle who did not know how to fly low... He was not of those who live and die, like all human beings. He was a Prometheus, one who appears but once over many generations...[2]

...How great was the hatred aimed at Copernicus and how fierce the battle against him, when we publicized his simple discovery! Yair [Stern's *nom de guèrre*] was the dialectician of the Hebrew freedom movement; the Euclid of the national geometry...

...a man of vision and a believer. These were the virtues that made Yair the first Hebrew statesman of the Land of Israel since David HaReuveni.[3]

In response to this unique apotheosis, the following statement appeared in the IZL journal *BaḤerev* (By the Sword):

...You are hereby attempting to turn a great patriotic figure into a sacred idol. A new Jesus. One can state with certainty

[1] [E. Katz], 'The Person in the Attic', *HeḤazit*, 1, Tammuz 5703 (1943); republished in: Lehi, *Lehi Writings*, 1, Tel Aviv, 1959, p. 125.

[2] [Eldad?], 'The Way of his Life and Death', In: *Yair*, 25 Shevat 5704 (1944); republished in *Lehi Writings*, op. cit., p. 376.

[3] 'His Portrait', *ibid.*, pp. 379, 382. In the Lehi, the image of David HaReuveni came to be favorably regarded, against the judgment of Aḥimeir. See 'Letter to the Zionist Youth', *Doar HaYom*, October 21, 1930

that such a campaign would have disgusted Yair himself had he still been alive... But you were driven to create yourselves a 'leader'... since, the Great Leader, who was a leader to multitudes among the people... you destroyed, you disqualified, you tarnished his reputation. You made Jabotinsky into Yair's student!...

...You thus have an example you can emulate: this is what they did in Russia, by turning Stalin into a living idol. In order to destroy the memory of Trotsky... But even the brazenness of these [Russians] had its limits... Even *they* did not dare to taint the name of Lenin, the true leader, recognized by the masses...[4]

A senior member of the IZL, most probably Menachem Begin himself, went even further, taking issue with Stern's disciples in reference to the Lehi's maxim at the beginning of 1944: 'Kill or be killed – never get arrested', and asked:

In light of the maxim of *HeḤazit*, the difficult and troubling question arises: why did Yair not keep a pistol in his room, and why didn't he prepare himself for a battle with the police? The authors of *HeḤazit* write that he was a man of *absolute* logic: he knew it all and understood it all. We may therefore assume that he understood that the danger of *elimination* awaited him...

The IZL member was of the opinion that

Yair did not wish to die this way, Yair did not want to be involved in a shoot-out with a policeman – a drunken assassin. Yair was prepared to be arrested, and to die as well. But he was hoping – hoping against hope – that he would be made to *stand trial*, that he would be granted the opportunity to tell the world about his demands, and then go to his death like [the IZL's martyr Shlomo] Ben-Yosef, with heroism and with joy, thus serving as an example to the fighting youth. But fate denied him even this favor, as he himself wrote in his magnificent poem just before his tragic death. He was felled by the bullet of a criminal in a policeman's uniform.[5]

---

[4] 'Letter to the Editors of *HeḤazit*', in: *BaḤerev*, Nisan 5704 (1944), pp. 27–28.
[5] 'Revolutionary Hysteria', *ibid.*, p. 35. Ben-Yosef was executed by the authorities in June 1938 after a failed anti-Arab retaliatory operation conducted by members of the Betar Company in Rosh Pinah. The poem was quoted by Y. Shamir, on the eighth anniversary of Stern's death, in: *LaHaver* (internal, February 1950), p. 6:

Perhaps even this favor will not be granted by fate:
Not against the wall will I be made to stand – upon a gallows
Beheaded at the neck like a wretched criminal
I will let my soul blow away between Earth and Heaven.

So much for the legend of Avraham Stern as a revolutionary of the radical right. But perhaps as a result of the fact that the Lehi had adopted a new policy of National Bolshevism' in 1944–49, its leftist 'wing' began to construct a new myth – the myth of a leftist Stern.

In late February 1949, Natan Friedman-Yellin, chief of Lehi's Center (in 1949 he changed his name to Yellin-Mor), spoke at the conference of the 'Loḥamim' (Fighters) Party (Lehi), that in the spring of 1939 it was suggested to Stern that Abba Aḥimeir (Yair's main mentor) be invited to participate in the publication of the IZL newspaper in Poland, *Di Tat* (Yiddish: The Act):

> Yair expressed his reservations... *Di Tat* must not publish anything that represents a war against socialism. His clarification on this point aroused the anger of Abba Aḥimeir. Yair did not yield even an inch. The conversation ended with Aḥimeir slamming the door as he left the meeting place enraged and dejected. This was not simply a case of arbitrary antagonism on a personal level. It was in fact a clash between two schools of thought ... one made anti-socialism into its religion. And the other school may be defined as 'anti-anti-socialism' ...opposition to the view of socialism as an intrinsically anti-nationalist outlook. And implicitly one may reveal [in this opposition] an additional component – namely, that there is no reason to insist that nationalism and socialism cannot coexist ... Yair recommended that members of the movement join the Histadrut [the General Federation of Labor]. One may, of course, regard this recommendation as a tactic, aimed at penetrating the Histadrut in order to seek converts under camouflage. [6]

Aḥimeir did not deny that there were differences of opinion between himself and Stern. Whereas the former believed that there should be two fronts, namely internal and external, the latter was of the opinion that there was but one – external – front, until the foreign power was expelled:

> On the main points, Yair agreed with Aḥimeir's position: (1) absolute neutrality with respect to internal 'gentile' affairs; (2) a boycott of products of the Reich; and (3) a war against the general leftist slant dominating the Jewish journalistic establishment. However, Yair was opposed to the title 'anti-Ma'[rxism], Yair's reasons being, by his own account, not ideological, but strictly tactical: 'Our newspaper must capture the Bundist youth, and let us not repel them from the

---

[*] Natan Friedman-Yellin (Gera), 'On Problems of Government and Society (February 25, 1949), in: Archives of Beit 'Yair', Lohamim (Fighters) Party Files, File No. 4. See also, *BaMaḥteret*, 6 (republished in: Lehi, *Lehi Writings*, op. cit., 1, p. 71.)

start with titles that are unfamiliar to them.[7]

Nevertheless, it was not just Dr. Israel Eldad (Scheib), now expelled from the Fighters Party, and Yellin-Mor who went to the trouble of constructing the Stern legend. In 1949, they were joined by Yitzhak Shamir, their partner in the leadership of the Lehi, who relied on his comrades to build the legend. He himself, as a pragmatic leader who had little patience for ideologies but had a thirst for power, was inclined to put an end to the ideological rivalry at the conference at which the Lehi was split. He also tried to repudiate some of the dissenting views of Yellin-Mor, whom he supported not only ideologically but also as he needed an organizational framework for continuing his political career. He did not 'spare the rod' from Stern himself, albeit implicitly, when he pointed out that

> No combative activity will be possible even outside Israel without the existence of strong bases inside the country. Whoever thinks differently is detached from reality. This is a manner of thought especially characteristic of a type of people who are known in political movements as 'the intelligent ones'... These 'intelligent' individuals play an important and necessary role in any political movement, but they have a tendency to show detachment and disregard for realistic factors when implementing their ideas. Without their ideas we are nothing, but without an understanding of reality, their ideas will forever remain strictly in the realm of theory.

Shamir did not reserve these statements strictly for his opponents at the Fighters' conference of 1949, but intended them for Stern as well, who had also considered, on the basis of unrealistic judgment, the possibility of attacking the British minister of state in the Middle East (1941–1942), Oliver Lyttelton; the 'proper' action which was not detached from reality, was carried out by the Lehi in November 1944, with the assassination of Lord Moyne.[8]

II

What is then the true image of 'Yair' Stern? Regarding the distinction between legend and historical reality with respect to the Ba'al-Shem-Tov and Herzl, the late Professor Ben-Zion Dinur

[7] Abba Sikra [Aḥimeir], "'Tvarda" and "Gilboa" (Two meetings with Yair, May the Lord Avenge his Blood)', *Ḥerut*, May 27, 1949; see also the response of Yellin-Mor: N. Friedman-Yellin, 'Not a deliberate distortion – Just a Weakness of Memory... (response to Abba Sikra from *Ḥerut*)', HaMa'as, 4(86), 5 Sivan 5709 (June 2, 1949).

[8] P. Ginosar, 'Lehi Revealed. Minutes of the Conference of the Fighters for the Freedom of Israel (March, 1949)', Ramat Gan (Bar-Ilan University) 1985, pp. 97–98.

stated in 1962 that 'the legend surrounding the former is the historical reality known to us, and the historical reality concerning the latter has become legend'.[9] Can the same be truthfully said of Stern? In other words, was 'Yair' a 'born' revolutionary? Was he a revolutionary of the right or the left? Did he really rebel against Jabotinsky's outlook in its entirety, or only against parts of it? Were the 'Principles of Renaissance' truly a revolutionary innovation, as maintained by the official historiography of the Lehi? Was his orientation indeed geared solely to the independent Hebrew nation, or did he perhaps also tie his fate to other powers? Was his attempt to establish connections with the Axis Powers a tactical misjudgment or a strategic error? Did he wish to die the way he did, achieving an end result that was calculated from the start, or is it possible that his former comrades from the IZL were correct in asserting that he would have preferred to stand trial as a political defendant? Was the myth built around his personality after his death intended to serve the interests of the revived Lehi, struggling for its ideological and political uniqueness, or was it perhaps faithful, at least in part, to the historical reality?

To begin with, a distinction must be made between Stern's intellectual wellsprings, and his development as a political leader. Secondly, although there is evidence of mutual influence between the two, there are also dichotomies between his intellectual growth and his growth as a leader. Thirdly, unlike some political leaders, Stern could not always calculate the course of his future development. The special political dynamism and multifarious intrigues of the years 1936–39 were required in order for his historical personality to become fully crystallized. In contrast, apart from the heavy load of romantic baggage of Polish and Russian revolutionary literature that he brought with him when he arrived in Palestine in 1925, the principal period of his intellectual development was in the years 1932–38. Two major schools of thought influenced him: the revolutionary Russian, Polish, Italian, and Irish; and the Jewish nationalistic-messianic.

The first school, namely the Russian, comprised three distinct elements: first, the *Narodnaya Volya* (People's Will), from which he inherited the compulsion towards personal sacrifice (a sentiment powerful enough to find lyrical expression in his poetry) that was inextricably linked to individual terrorism as strategy for attaining redemption. People like Timofei Mikhailov, Andrei Zelyabov, Sofya Petrovskaya, and Sergey Kibalchich were undoubtedly on his mind when he wrote his poems of the early thirties; second, the 'Fighting Brigade' of the Social-Revolutionaries under the leadership of Boris Savinkov, and its deeds; third, Lenin's tactics in seizing power, as well as his foreign-policy

---

[9] *The Great Man and His Age. Lectures Delivered at the Eighth Convention of the Historical Society of Israel, December 1962*, Jerusalem (The Historical Society of Israel) 1963, p. 11.

strategy as exemplified during the Brest Litovsk negotiations at the close of the First World War.

The Polish school also comprised a number of elements: first, Poland's romantic rebellions of the nineteenth century; Second, the patriotic legacy of Adam Mickiewicz *Konrad Wallenrod*, Juliusz Slowacki, and Adam Skwarczinski; and third, the edicts of the leader for whom Stern's reverence was perhaps the greatest, Pilsudski: 'How do we educate towards a battle of national liberation?' For instance,

> The blood that was spilt today, the lives that were extinguished today, shall produce their bountiful yield only in the future. But let us heed this fact: no political ideal, no system in this world ever came into being without gaining notoriety at the outset; and we always find that those trends that were most abhorred were the ones that triumphed. Such was the destiny of the banner of armed rebellion... the sooner we arrive at the realization that there is no way out of the present situation other than armed warfare – the better off we will be...[10]

Stern was enchanted by the Italian revolutionary movement, as expressed through the images of Garibaldi, Mazzini, and in a different sense, Mussolini,[11] as well as by the Irish Struggle for independence, especially with respect to the martyrology of the Easter Rising of 1916.[12]

No less than the above, Stern was influenced by the Jewish national struggle, particulary those that possessed messianic tendencies. These heroes of his began with the Hasmoneans and the Zealots, most notably such figures as Elazar Ben-Yair, hero of Masada, and Bar-Kokhba, who was, in his eyes, the most prominent representative of the kind of 'realistic-activistic messianism' that inspires the people and strives for their freedom. Along with this, Stern was captivated by the legends surrounding the Messiah Son-of-Joseph, who 'must fall, and then a dreadful world war will break out... and with the termination of this war the Messiah, the

---

[10] *Omer La'Am* (Evening paper) July 29, 1939. W.T. Drymmer's Memoirs, *Historical Notebooks*, XIII (in Polish), Paris, 1968, pp. 70–71, 76–77.

[11] Garibaldi and Mazzini were adopted as role models for the Revisionist movement, largely thanks to Jabotinsky. See his article: 'Rebel of Light' of 1912 (*Uma VeHevra* [Nation and Society], Jerusalem, 5719 [1959], pp. 99–110). On Garibaldi, see also *Liberated Jerusalem* (in Polish: *Jerozolima Wyzwolona*), No. 20(28), June 1939, pp. 11–12. With reference to the influence of Mussolini, cf. A. Stern to H.S. Halevi from February 15, 1934, in: *HaUma*, 82 (1986), pp. 86–89.

[12] P.S. O'Hegarty, 'The Victory of Sinn Fein (The Rising of 1916)', *BaMaḥteret*, 5, Shevat 5701 (1941, also in: *Lehi Writings*, op. cit., 1, pp. 53–56. With reference to IZL's esteem for Sir Roger Casement, cf. 'From the Lives of Great Revolutionaries: Sir Roger Casement', in *BaḤerev*, Adar 5702 (1942), pp. 4–6. The anonymous writer seems to have had Stern in mind. See also F.X. Martin, 'The Evolution of a Myth: The Easter Rising, Dublin 1916' in: E. Kamenka (ed.), *The Nature and Evolution of an Idea*, N.Y., 1976, pp. 57–80.

Messiah Son-of-David, will appear at the head of his troops, and he will make the Hebrew nation sovereign over the entire world'. Finally, Stern referred to the writings of Maimonides, who gave three clear signals marking the success of the Messianic King: victory over the surrounding nations, the building of the Holy Temple, and the ingathering of the exiles of Israel.[13]

Stern rebelled against the approach of evolutionary Zionism. In this respect he followed in the footsteps of Jabotinsky, whom he adored with an admiration which also included the master's qualities as a politician, as expressed in his reliance on England, and as evidenced by his support for the 'Petition' (1934). He certainly shared Jabotinsky's determination to build an image of a new kind of Jew: 'people with a healthy imagination and a strong will, aspiring to express themselves in the battle of life', and as such, coined slogans such as 'Die or capture the mountain'.[14] But much as he revered Jabotinsky, a man like Stern could not stand behind a political leader who, even in the turbulent period of 1936–39, put his trust in diplomacy and conscience, and pinned his faith on the democratic world, without preparing a political alternative. The declining leader was, gradually but consistently, clearing the way for people who symbolized personal sacrifice, figures such as Sarah and Aaron Aaronsohn. Furthermore, he was now presenting Nili (acronym for the secret organization, of which the Aaronsohns were members, of Jews in Palestine who, during World War I, worked for the Allied intelligence in the hope of ensuring future Jewish settlement) as a model for the future rebellion, no less than the Irish Easter Rising of 1916.[15] These latter figures were preceded not only by Jabotinsky, but also by two additional teachers whose influence on Stern was decisive: Uri-Zvi Greenberg and Abba Aḥimeir. Greenberg provided Stern with the messianic, masterly dimension of the new Sicarii (Jewish terrorists of the late Second Temple period, who assassinated collaborators with the Roman authorities) which he regarded as necessary for the contemporary political situation: 'The Jewish community that eagerly anticipated the coming of the Messiah... and the Jewish community under siege are surrounded by the hostile forces of Christianity and Islam...'[16] But Stern had not yet been influenced by Greenberg in the direction of the idea of England's 'treachery' ('Thou hast betrayed me, O King'). Nevertheless, he was influ-

[13] S[tern], 'The Messianic Movements in Israel', *BaMaḥteret*, 4, Tevet 5701 (1940); 5, Shevat 5701 (1941); and 6, Adar 5701 (1941). (republished in *Lehi Writings*, op. cit., 1, pp. 47–48, 55–56 and 63–66 respectively.)

[14] Z. Jabotinsky, 'Sienkiewicz', *Hadashot HaHretz*, October 8, 1919 (also published in *On Literature and Art* (Hebrew), Jerusalem, 5708 (1948), p. 164. Cf. also Jabotinsky's play *Samson* (1927). The 'Song of Betar' was published for the first time in *Ḥazit HaAm*, March 22, 1932.

[15] *BaMaḥteret*, 4, Tevet 5701 (1940), dedicated to Avshalom Feinberg, in *Lehi Writings*, op. cit., 1, pp. 43–44.

[16] U.Z. Greenberg, *The Book of Indictment and Faith*, Jerusalem 5697 (1937), pp. 53–58.

enced by him in another respect: a view of the Arabs as an enemy that must be battled till the bitter end:

> 'Thou shalt not triumph over My Jerusalem, O Daughter of Arabia!'...
> 'A Jewish soldier prays for your peace with a rifle
> May it please you to be charmed more by a rifle than by the playing of a pipe organ.'[17]

The missing link that connected Jabotinsky, whose outlook was revolutionary in part while still expressing faith in England, and Greenberg, who held that Zionism would be fulfilled strictly through messianic mysticism, was Abba Aḥimeir, who preached in favor of a war of national liberation along the lines of integral nationalism and European fascism, beginning in 1928. But it was the riots of 1929 that gave him a particular impetus to disseminate his ideas in a vigorous effort to transform the Revisionist movement from a champion of parliamentary democracy into a revolutionary liberation movement, and a fighting force that relies on bloodshed. Jabotinsky himself was, according to this scheme, to be made into a *Duce*. Aḥimeir's influence on Stern was actually long-term rather than short-term, as Stern himself would admit in a private letter dated June 1936.[18] However, Aḥimeir influenced this particular student of his not only by recommending the recourse to a war of national liberation, but also by proposing the method of individual terrorism.[19] He, along with Professor Joseph Klausner, taught Stern that the fact of national defeat does not necessarily represent the final word, and heroism is destined to triumph.[20]

The last of Stern's intellectual mentors was Uriel Heilperin (Ratosh), with whom he maintained intimate contact from 1936 onward. Heilperin bequeathed to him his booklet *We Lift Up Our Eyes to Sovereignty* as a revolutionary program *par excellence*, largely abandoning Jabotinsky's policies by insisting that sovereignty must have priority over the will of the majority, and further suggesting that the rule of the revolutionary [elitist] minority be implemented: the theory of 'the Sons of the Caste', the revolutionary avant-garde, the 'circle within a circle' that will

[17] U.Z. Greenberg, *Ezor Magen uNe'um Ben-HaDam* (The Zone of Defense and Address of the Son of Blood), Jerusalem 5690 (1930), pp. 5–6, 15, 30. Cf. articles by Stern in *HaMetzudah*, Nos 3–6 (1932–1933), 'We and Our Neighbors', which provide evidence for a concept of eternal confrontation.

[18] Cf. his letter to Ronnie Burstein, June 11, 1936 (in the possession of Ronnie Zamir). With reference to Aḥimeir's political doctrine and his dispute with Jabotinsky, cf. my 'Ends and Means – The Ideological and Political Debate between Jabotinsky and Achimeir, 1928–1933', in *Zion*, 5747 (1987), issue 3, pp. 315–369.

[19] Cf. his 'The Sicarii Scroll', in A. Aḥimeir, *The League of the Sicarii* (Hebrew), Tel Aviv, 1972, pp. 217–223.

[20] On Klausner, cf. his *When a Nation Fights for its freedom* (in Hebrew), 1st printing 5696 (1936); 2nd printing, Jerusalem, 5699 (1939).

arouse the masses and send them off to battle. When he finally despaired of imparting his program to the Revisionist movement from which he originated, Heilperin proposed an alternative scheme that subsequently became known as 'Canaanite',[21] but the latter would be rejected by Stern, on account of its rejection of the Jewish heritage. But he enthusiastically adopted Heilperin's revolutionary theory, which acquired a new practical and dialectic significance in light of the report of the Peel Commission (July 1937) extolling the vigor of the Jews of Palestine. The revolutionary approach seemingly became even more relevant after the hanging of Shlomo Ben-Yosef.

The summer of 1938 was to witness Stern's final intellectual crystallization. It began with the recognition of the need for a new war for freedom under the title given by Heilperin, 'The Sovereign Will', which came as a consequence of Ben-Yosef's execution, and continued with a personal clash with Jabotinsky, who refused to support Stern's request for a war of the IZL against the Hagana and the Arabs. It ended that same summer with a dispute over strategy between Jabotinsky and Begin at the Third World Convention of Betar (the Revisionist youth organization) in Warsaw; on this occasion, Begin, then leader of Betar, demanded that Jabotinsky adopt the conception of 'Military Zionism', because, in his words, indeed 'Cavour would not have attained the liberation of Italy without Garibaldi'.[22] 'Yair' was dissatisfied by the ambivalence that characterized Jabotinsky's position: on one hand, explicit support for regarding Ben-Yosef's failed mission as a model worthy of emulation ('the dew that renders the soil fruitful'), and on the other hand, the insulting rejection of Begin's proposal to revise the Oath of Betar from 'defense' to 'defense and conquest'. Such a revision, had it been adopted in practice and not simply on paper, could have represented a revolutionary change in the political position and fundamental approach of the leader of the New Zionist Organization.[23]

From this point onward – that is, from the summer of 1938 – with the conclusion of the period in which his ideological position was consolidated, Stern went off on his own independent path. He

[21] Platform for the World Convention. *HaMedinah*, Warsaw. 13, Tammuz 5698 (July 12, 1938), and a more complete text in Jabotinsky Institute 3/1/2/2; A final echo of the 'honeymoon' between Heilperin and Stern is to be found in the article 'The Hebrew as Colonialists and Fighters', *BaMaḥteret*, 6, Adar 5701 (1941), republished in *Lehi Writings*, op. cit., 1, pp. 31–34.

[22] Protocol of the Third World Conference of Betar (Bucharest, 1940), p. 60. For the conversation between Jabotinsky and Stern, cf. 'Conversation with Pitt [Jabotinsky]', ['Yair' to Raziel'], August 19, 1938, *'HaKad'* Archives ('Yair's' personal manuscripts found hidden in a milk pitcher [*kad* in Hebrew], now in the possession of his brother, David Stern. (Henceforth: Yair's 'Milk Pitcher

[23] Cf. Dr. I. Eldad (Scheib), *The First Tithe: Chapters from Memoirs and Moral*, 2nd ed., Tel Aviv, 5723 (1963), pp. 19–26; and my 'Jabotinsky and the Question of "Self-Restraint" (1939–1986)', in: *Transition and Change in Modern Jewish History* (essays presented in honor of Shmuel Ettinger), Jerusalem, 5747 (1987), pp. 283–320.

was now free to reinforce his position as a political leader, thus
assuming the role which he had been called upon to fill, according
to his own conception, built on the assumption that Jabotinsky's
course had 'failed'. Until now he had lacked the outlet for his
political aspirations, although it was clear to him that the principal instrument for this purpose was the IZL, reorganized after the
split that occurred in 1937. His functions as adjutant to Avraham
Tehomi [the founder of IZL and its Head of Command (1931–
1937), before it became a Revisionist organization], as Command
secretary, and as a member of the Command, ostensibly provided
him with the wellsprings of power, but only in the event that he
could successfully manipulate the Head of Command. Theoretically, conditions for such developments existed from the time the
IZL became an arm of the Revisionist movement. But Jabotinsky
was serving as president of the New Zionist Organization and as
supreme commander of the IZL, as well as the Head of Betar.
Consequently he had to manoever between the maximalists and
the more moderate elements. Thus it was clear that the IZL was
having problems getting its own house in order with respect to its
independent policy, especially in view of the fact that Jabotinsky
himself persisted in maintaining support first and foremost for a
policy of 'self-restraint', and would not relinquish his orientation
towards Britain. The constraints that forced the 'Supreme commander' to accept the change of direction on the question of the
'self-restraint' enabled the continued cooperation between the
Command and the 'Supreme Commander'. However, it soon
became evident that the differences were considerable, extending to the issue of the leader's authority.

Jabotinsky attempted to overcome this nagging difficulty by
means of the 'Paris Agreement' in early 1939, intensifying his
control over the IZL. It was no coincidence that Stern abstained
from this agreement. Nor was David Raziel (1910–1941), Head of
the Command, satisfied by the state of affairs, but he did not dare
to voice his dissent regarding the 'grand strategy' of the 'Supreme
Commander'. Stern, in contrast, by the spring of 1939, had begun
to regard Jabotinsky as an 'ex-activist'.

However, at a press conference which he convened in Warsaw,
he spoke mainly of the need to break the Arab resistance, to
enlarge the Yishuv [the Jewish population of Palestine] by means
of illegal immigration, to nurture the 'reservoir' of the Jewish
people through mass education, and to attract sympathizers and
gather support from 'states whose interests are directly or indirectly compatible with the realization of the goals of the *IZL*'. But
even before the time had arrived to declare Britain an incorrig-
ible, implacable enemy, hints could be discerned: 'If England, out
of inertia and as a consequence of the contradictions in her policy,
surrenders to the Arab rebellion, which is, after all, directed
against the vital interests of the Empire, then to our good fortune,

132

we have states that are objectively potential allies of the Jewish liberation movement'. This was one wish. Another goal was expressed as follows: 'On the other hand, the states of Eastern Europe objectively also represent potential allies, inasmuch as a Jewish problem objectively exists in these countries, and there is no desire to solve this problem by barbaric means in the form of annihilations and pogroms, but rather through constructive cooperation in order to eliminate the Diaspora and establish Jewish independence in the Land of Israel'.[24]

At the same time, Stern came into contact with the Polish authorities (at the bureaucratic, not the ministerial level, as his disciple would have us believe), indeed as a result of a recommendation from Jabotinsky, who did not at first suspect that Stern was undermining his authority. Nor did Jabotinsky know that the IZL was organizing a commanders' training course in Andrychow, Poland, to prepare the cadre for the program which would enlist forty thousand young people who would be ready to capture the Land of Israel at the opportune moment.[25] Thus, Stern's leadership was now headed in a new direction. Would this be a dead-end course, or would it be the starting point for the longed-for redemption?

It was the White Paper of May 1939 that confirmed Stern's prediction regarding Britain's 'treachery' once and for all. Nevertheless, his operative conclusions were not yet clear, and we have no evidence to suggest that he sought the cooperation of the Axis powers at this early stage. But he did rephrase his warning to Britain in harsher terms, while taking pains to explain that the 'enemy' was the Arabs and not Britain. The British were, in any case, 'pro-British', and concerned with one thing only, namely the protection of their own interests. Ostensibly, he still spoke of the same basic, desired solution espoused by the Jabotinsky school, namely 'a covenant between the Empire and the Hebrew state'. It is inconceivable that he was still deluding himself and his friends with respect to the nature of the true enemy. It is possible that he adopted this tactics in order to deceive the political leadership of the New Zionist Organization, while at the same time attempting to inform the British that ...'the moment it becomes clear that it is not the intention of Great Britain to fulfil this condition [a Hebrew state], the Jews shall cease to be loyal to Britain – ally of the Arabs – and in any case, they will have no choice: they will find themselves other allies'.[26] The die was cast, but an ally was yet to be found.

[24] Y. Slutzki, *The History of the Haganah*, 3(1), Tel Aviv, 5732 (1972), pp. 62–63. Cf. also: *Di Tat* (in Yiddish), March 10, 1939, where France and Turkey are mentioned as potential allies.

[25] J.B. Shechtman, *Ze'ev Jabotinsky – The Story of his Life*, 3 (Tel Aviv, 1959), pp. 233–236.

[26] E[lazar] B[en-]Y[air] (i.e., Stern), *The Enemy*, K12/4-4, Jabotinsky Institute; and manuscripts amended by Stern, P3A/223, Jabotinsky Institute.

Stern's leadership was put to the test on the final day before the
outbreak of World War II, when Jabotinsky proposed a plan for
the staging of a 'symbolic' rebellion, a proposal which Stern
rejected outright, suspecting that its real aim was the elimination
of the IZL.[27] Just one month earlier Stern had publicly clarified
his own intentions, and defined the basic principles that would
guide his actions. By the end of May, it became possible for him to
express his views freely, in the wake of Raziel's arrest and the
appointment of his close friend, Hanoch Kalay [who had been
commander of the Kfar Sava cell of Betar and the IZL commander
for the Haifa district and the Moshavot (settlements) as Head of
Command. He was now presenting himself and his organization
as the 'true leadership' of the Yishuv, owing to the capitulation of
the Yishuv in the face of the White Paper. Thus, he felt justified in
referring to his following as the 'New Israelite Liberation Movement'. At the end of July 1939, he again denounced Jabotinsky,
by insisting that there was no difference between the New Zionist
Organization and the Jewish Agency. With regard to the fundamental principles, which pointed in the direction of Social Darwinism, as befitting the radical right, he stated that

> force is always the decisive factor in the lives of the con-
> querors of lands and of those who fight for freedom. Force
> has always shaped the fate of nations... Fiume, Vilna (Vil-
> nius), Ethiopia, Austria, the Sudetenland, China, Spain and
> Czechoslovakia. Such force would be forged in the under-
> ground by dreamers and fighters, by those who would
> betray oaths of allegiance and relieve themselves of the
> burden of agreements, by opponents of law and order, and
> by national revolutionaries.

The IZL is the Hebrew army, the 'army of freedom and royalty'. It
shall be the one to establish the 'Kingdom of Israel'. Stern now
proceeded to formulate the model upon which this kingdom
would be established. As was the fortune of T.E. Lawrence and the
Bedouin tribes in the course of the First World War, so will be the
destiny of the People of Israel: 'When the imminent war breaks
out, foreign diplomats and officers will come to us...and strive to
draw us to their side...'[28]

Here, for the first time, Stern was undoubtedly trying to publicly
hint at his ultimate intentions, namely, to assume the political
leadership of both the Revisionist movement and the Yishuv in
general, operating under the inspiration of his ideological men-

[27] *The History of the Haganah*, 3(3), op. cit., p. 1615 (in a note to line 9)
[28] E[lazar] B[en-]Y[air], 'Principles and Conclusions'. *Omer La'am*, July 29,
1939; cf. also, 'A Most Respectable Gentleman', P3A/223, Jabotinsky Institute. Y. Zelnik, Stern's close confidant at the time, claims that Stern was
influenced by T.E. Lawrence's *Seven Pillars of Wisdom*. On the influence of
Social Darwinism on the radical right, cf. S.G. Payne, *Fascism, Comparison
and Definition*, Madison, 1980.

tors Greenberg and Yeivin. But although he was sure of his basic aims, the ally that would assist him, when the need arose, in adopting the role of the Messiah Son-of-Joseph had yet to appear on the horizon. He had not yet developed any feeling of sympathy towards Germany. On the contrary, his own sympathies, as well as those of the IZL in general in Poland and in Palestine, were directed towards Poland, who in those days was struggling against Nazi Germany by peaceful means over the issue of Danzig and the Polish Corridor.[29]

His arrest on the day before the outbreak of the Second World War prevented him from realizing his ambitions of national revolutionary leadership, but, during the period of his internment, and especially during his confinement in Mazra Prison from February to June 1940, he found his ally. His admiration for Germany's victories on land and at sea influenced him to examine the possibility of forging a treaty with one or two of the Axis powers. At the same time, he sought to take command of the IZL, with the support of the maximalist 'Indictment and Faith' faction of the New Zionist Organization. The poems he wrote while in prison (*To Our Motherhood* and *The Messiah*) resound with his spirit of self-sacrifice, as exemplified by Shlomo Ben-Yosef, Ya'acov Raz, and Arieh Yitzhaki.[30]

By this stage, this principle had assumed political significance and could be viewed as something that was likely to be actualized; judging from the IZL organ *BaḤerev*, published just prior to Stern's release from prison, opposition to England was steadily growing within the organization, as evidenced by the attitude to the draft.[31] Neither Jabotinsky nor Dr. Arieh Altman, chairman of the Revisionist movement in Palestine, had any idea of Stern's real intentions. In any case, they had already made up their minds to support England, as David Raziel had already done under their inspiration when he signed an agreement with Police Inspector-General Allan Saunders.

Nevertheless, Order No. 112 (June 26, 1940) should not be viewed as the beginning of the split and the establishment of the IZL in Israel, despite the fact that in this document, Stern called for evasion of the draft, and announced that the 'IZL forges alliances within Israel and with the nations, but does not sacrifice

---

[29] Cf. U.Z. Greenberg, 'The Legend of Ya'acov Raz', in: *Omer La'am*, op. cit. 'In My Blood Shall You Live Forever' in: A. Stern – 'Yair', *Poems* (no date), pp. 105–114, 130–131.

[30] Ya'acov Raz attempted to plant a bomb in the Arab market in the course of an IZL mission in the summer of 1938, but was captured and beaten to death. Arieh Yitzhaki was killed in the summer of 1939 in the process of preparing a mine while on a retaliatory mission on behalf of the IZL.

[31] 'The War Aims of the Jewish People', *BaḤerev* (May 1940). With reference to Stern's admiration for Hitler's victories, cf. accounts given by his comrades in the IZL Command: B. Zeroni, A. Heichman, H. Lubinski, and H. Kalay; the Haganah Archives.

its freedom'.[32] The split had not yet begun here, because Stern still had hopes at this point of taking over the IZL in its entirety. Among other things, these hopes were based on his own efforts to convince Jabotinsky that Raziel was no longer fit to command the IZL. Stern pointed to no fewer than ten faults and errors of which Raziel was guilty, in his opinion, each of which should have served as sufficient evidence, both internally and externally, of Raziel's failure as Head of IZL Command. The Command had lost confidence in him, he insisted, even before the issue of opposition to England and support for Italy had arisen.[33] Jabotinsky, who at that time was living in the United States, was depressed over the setbacks that the Allied forces had suffered in the war, and over the failure of the New Zionist Organization and the IZL to establish a new center of power in the United States. With this in mind, Stern probably assumed that Jabotinsky would be unable to control the affairs of the IZL from afar.[34] Eventually, at any rate, Jabotinsky's death seemed to provide him with an opportunity to put himself forward as replacement, not Raziel.

The IZL in Israel was established on September 3, 1940, when the command published its first communiqué. This communiqué was, in itself, an admission of hopelessness with respect to the chances of gaining control of the IZL; in view of the meager number of recruits, there was no alternative other than the establishment of an 'Underground of Revolutionaries'. Although it was promised that the new organization would have to take control of the entire country by force of arms at the earliest opportunity, and that it would eventually become clear to all the world that it was the single legitimate spokesman for the fighting Jewish nation,[35] it was also clear that its star would rise only in response to a revolutionary political act. Inasmuch as Stern, since the summer of 1939, had been strictly anti-British (as he himself indicated already at the time of the IZL's proclamation of a ceasefire, dated September 10, 1939), it was obvious that the only way to break through the thick wall of British opposition to the aspirations of the Hebrew nation for freedom, was by means of a treaty with a power hostile to Britain.

Thus, Stern was now taking his life in his hands, and placing his future as a political leader in the balance. At this point, the battle against England was being transformed from a stratagem to a fundamental principle; England as the occupier of the homeland was now a very real 'enemy', in contrast to Hitler, who was

[31] 'Announcement of the Command No. 112', *Lehi Writings*, op. cit., 1, pp. 17–18.
[33] Stern's letter to Jabotinsky, unsigned and undate (July 5, 1940), from Weinshal's book (2nd ed., 1976), between p. 165 and p. 168.
[34] Merlin to Raziel [?], July 11, 1940, Yair's 'Milk Pitcher', File No. 40; Stern to Merlin, July 22, 1940, *ibid*.
[35] The Command of the IZL in Israel, No. 1, eve of Rosh HaShanah 5701 (September 3, 1940), *Lehi Writings*, op. cit., 1, pp. 19–20.

simply an 'troublemaker'.[36] It was a decision which would set
Stern on an irreversible course, apparently one which could not
be abandoned even in the face of an initial failure. The Italians –
the first candidates for an alliance – obviously also belonged in the
category of 'troublemakers', but Stern was unable to make any
significiant contacts with them. However, the document that was
drafted for the 'double agent' provided further evidence of Stern's
readiness to be content with a limited version of the 'Kingdom of
Israel', one which would be dependent on an ally. But in any
event, Italy's downfall in North Africa and Greece put an end to
her candidacy.[37]

It was the proposal delivered to the Germans (in early January
1941) that rendered Stern hopelessly entrapped. His willingness
to forge an ideological-political treaty with Hitler can be partly
explained by the fact that the extent of the Holocaust was as yet
unknown. Nevertheless, it was Stern's insistence that the ideological and practical aspects of Nazi anti-Semitism could be separated from Hitler's international politics in general and his policy
with respect to England in particular,[38] that confirm his ignorance of the earliest signs of the impending calamity. He believed
that the issue at hand was simply an additional link in the chain of
events whose roots were to be found in the likes of Plehve, Petlyura, and the Transfer Agreement. The treaty proposal was
proof of the limitations of radical politics, not only on the tactical
level, but also on the strategic level. The negative reply sent by
Stern's emissary, Naftali Lubenchik, was an indication that
among the decision-makers in Germany, *Idealpolitik* (that is, the
trend of extermination of the Jews) had prevailed over *Realpoli-
tik* (that is, the trend of expelling them). These events brought
about the first split within the 'Underground of Revolutionaries',
with the desertion of two members of the command, at least one of
whom decided to leave in protest over the attempted treaty with
Germany, and over the domination of radical elements over
Stern. Stern had become nothing more than a political 'supreme
leader'[39] over a small band of people, fanatical elitists – at least in

---

[36] With reference to the terms 'troublemaker' and 'enemy', cf. account given by
Moshe Svorai in: Y. Banai, *Unknown Soldiers*, Tel Aviv, undated [1958], p.
72.

[37] The Italian document appears in: D. Niv, *Battle for Freedom: The Irgun Zvai
Leumi*, 3, Tel Aviv, 1967, p. 177. Cf. also M. Roten (Rothstein), 'Italian Espio-
nage in the Land [of Israel]', secret evidence, Haganah Archives, File of Secret
Evidences.

[38] The German document appears in: D. Ysraeli, *The Palestine Problem in German Politics, 1889-1945*, Ramat Gan, 1974, pp. 315–317. Ada Amichal-Yei-
vin did in fact cite most of the German document in her book, but she missed
the point by underestimating the document's dire significance, owing to her
blind devotion to Stern: *In the Purple: The Life of Yair – Avraham Stern*, Tel
Aviv, 1986, p. 226 and Appendix 12. (The following statement was deleted:
'In its philosophical outlook and its structure, the IZL feels itself closest to the
totalitarian movements of Europe.')

[39] Ya'acov (Yashka) Eliav, *Wanted*, Tel Aviv, 1983, pp. 190–93.

terms of their own self-perception – who still believed in the
course he was taking. Henceforth, he would be obliged to prove
the validity of his basic assumptions; not only did he resume his
efforts to establish ties with the Germans, but he also began to
resort to individual terror, adopting the concept of 'expropria-
tion' (i.e., mainly bank robberies) as befitting a revolutionary
underground. Within just a little over a month's time, his underground movement reached its bitter end, for even if its members
truly believed that 'the ends justify the means', the means at their
disposal were too meager to ensure a meaningful success in any
shape or form.

The tragic end that befell Avraham Stern and his friends was
seemingly inevitable. It was not just Order No. 1 and the conceptions of 'trouble-makes' and 'enemy' that brought it about, but
also the 'Principles of Renaissance'. The reference here is not to
those principles that simply represented a return to the basic doctrines of Revisionist maximalism (particulary those inspired by
Uri-Zvi Greenberg and Yehoshua H. Yeivin), but rather to operative clauses such as 'the forging of treaties with all parties that
have an interest in the organization's battle, and are prepared to
lend it direct assistance' (Paragraph No. 7), and 'a never-ending
battle against all who intend to stand in the way of the fulfillment
of the destiny' (Paragraph No. 9). It was no coincidence that Stern
separated the Principles of Renaissance into two categories, specifically those that apply to 'the Era of War and Conquest' and
those that pertain to 'the Era of Rule and Redemption'.[40] The
operational failures were not enough to undermine Stern's
mystical and 'realistic' fundamental assumptions, as had happened to his deputy, Hanoch Kalay.

It should also be pointed out that Stern did not harbor the sligh-
test trace of socialist sentiment, as demonstrated by the paragraph (No. 12) relating to 'the Regime of Justice': 'The establishment of a social regime, in the spirit of the morality of Israel and
prophetic justice; under this regime, no one shall be hungry nor
unemployed. Here, all sons of the Nation, by virtue of being her
sons, shall live a life of freedom, honor, and friendship. It shall
be a symbol and a model to the nations.' This was written under
the inspiration of Professor Joseph Klausner. There was no ideological or political significance to Stern's recommendation to his
comrades to join the Histadrut, beyond his hope of subverting
the foundations established by the left, which he despised; for he
was in total agreement with the rejection of the concept of *mif'al
a-binyan* [literally: 'industrial enterprise and construction'; a
contemptuous anti-socialist slogan used by the Revisionists)
with all its social, economic, and political connotations, as evidenced by his proclamations against the Jewish Agency and the

[40] In: *BaMaḥteret*, 5, Shevat 5701 (1941); in Yair's 'Milk Pitcher', File No. 89.

Haganah in the years 1938–39.[41] His support for the 'National Worker's Front' was intended as a means of taking advantage of every force that was opposed to the Revisionist movement which, in his opinion, had failed. As one who had truly and wholeheartedly believed that 'the ends justify the means', and 'let the judgment breach the mountain', he was unable to sit and wait for any form of pause in the action, or for a more opportune moment, in order to translate his ideology into politics, despite the sparse means at his disposal.

Nevertheless, throughout the various stages of Stern's development as a leader, the theme of personal sacrifice did not always appear as the central motif, so dominant in his poetry ('Only Death can rescue one from the ranks'; 'It is our dream to die for our nation' [1932]; 'Let us greet him [the redeemer of Zion]: let our blood be a red carpet in the streets, and on this carpet, our minds shall be like white lilies' [1934]). This theme did not always bear an unequivocal political significance, since he was, at the same time, campaigning on behalf of Jabotinsky's Petition (the 'Bridge of Paper', in the words of Abba Aḥimeir). It was indeed his intellectual mentors Yeiven and Aḥimeir who warned him against the German connection, albeit in vain. Yeivin, to whom he had stated that he would re-establish Nili, asked him the following:

> Is he fully aware of the odds, and of the immensity of the danger? With awe and compassion, we pay tribute to the memory and the mighty heroism of the people of Nili. But they were battling against the Turks, who were despised by Jews throughout the world, whereas the enemies of the Turks were the *English*. But you want to fight the English, whom the Jewish people regard as allies in the war against Hitler. They will speak of you as one who is lending assistance to Hitler... They will cover your memory with spit and with contempt. You will be hated and despised by the people whom you are attempting to liberate. He [Stern] responded simply: 'I know this. And I will do it nonetheless'. He took the path of destruction and the torment of Hell which he created for himself.[42]

His other mentor, Aḥimeir, also warned him:

> It would have yet been understandable had the Lehi succeeded in aligning themselves with the *Sam*[mael, the

[41] [A.Stern], 'The Crimes of the Jewish Agency', Jabotinsky Institute Archives, P233. See also, E[lazar] B[en-]Y[air], *BaḤerev*, Nisan 5699 (1939). For Stern's hostility towards communism, cf. his article: 'Israel in the Lands of Dispersion (A Historical Review)', *HaMetzudah*, 1 (1932, ed. H.S. HaLevy), (Tel Aviv, 1978), pp. 19–20.

[42] Dr. Y.H. Yeivin, 'The Inception of the Movement for the Kingdom of Israel: Yair – the "Bar-Mitzvah" of his Death', *Sullam*, 11 (71), Year 6, Adar 5715 (1955), p. 23. (The meeting took place in the winter of 1940, according to Yeivin.)

Satan] in the hope of preventing the slaughter of the European Diaspora... War against Britain under the present circumstances is nothing less than the creation of a fifth column for the benefit of the *Sam*.

Yair: We shall somehow manage to get along with the Germans once they capture the Land. Even the Soviets managed to reach a settlement with them when the need arose.

Aḥimeir: You remind me of the marksman who shoots and then draws a circle around the spot where the bullet hit...'[43]

Stern's self-indoctrination with respect to 'troublemaker' and 'enemy' was the factor that prevented him from comprehending the events unfolding in Europe; thus he believed that Hitler was simply an ordinary pogrom monger in the style of Haman or Petlyura, as evidenced by his response to the Madagascar Plan, as well as his response to the events that were taking place in the Warsaw Ghetto in March of 1941:

> ...It is incumbent upon us to seek the least of all evils... The Jews of the Middle Ages lived in the ghetto for hundreds of years... From this same ghetto came the Jewry that later... succeeded, with one hand, in establishing a great part of modern industry and international trade, while at the same time, with the second hand, nurtured Marx and Lassalle. Tens of internationally renowned scholars, great thinkers, writers, and artists were produced by her [i.e., Medieval Jewry] within this space of time... If the day comes when he [the Jew] leaves the ghetto a second time after being fired in the crucible of affliction, refined and purified of assimilated impurities, he will again capture a place in the sun, to live a life of creativity and sovereignty in his Hebrew homeland. Because if the nation wishes to leave the ghetto once and for all, it must leave the Diaspora. For in times of war or on the eve of peacetime, neither within the walls of the actual ghetto, nor within the walls of hatred that preceded the ghetto, can there be redemption in the Diaspora.[44]

[43] Abba Sikra, "'Tvarda" and "Gilboa" – Two Meetings With Yair, May the Lord Avenge his Blood', *Ḥerut* May 27, 1949. (The meetings took place at the end of the summer of 1941 according to Aḥimeir.) Also, in a meeting with Ya'acov Orenstein (*In Chains*, Tel Aviv, 5733 [1973], p. 148), Stern mentioned the example of Lenin and Brest Litovsk. In a conversation with Dr. H. Rosenblum (*Barkai*, Johannesburg, February-March 1950, p. 5–9) he spoke of Pilsudski's journey to Japan during the First World War. N. Friedman-Yellin's response to Aḥimeir, 'Not a Deliberate Distortion – Just a Weakness of Memory... (response tò Abba Sikra from *Ḥerut*)', *HaMa'as*, 4 (86), 5 Sivan 5709 (June 2, 1949).

[44] 'Diaspora and Redemption (On the Question of the Ghetto)', *BaMaḥteret* 6, pp. 20–23, in: Yair's 'Milk Pitcher', File 89 (deleted from the *Lehi Writings*).

Paradoxically, it was Jabotinsky, of all people, Stern had rebelled against, who managed to convince Stern of the relevance of 'the anti-Semitism of things' and 'the anti-Semitism of human beings' to the situation of 1940. In other words, although Polish anti-Semitism was more severe than the German variety, there was a remedy for both. Like Stern, Jabotinsky had in no way predicted the Holocaust, and believed that his 'evacuation plan', along with the rehabilitation of the European Diaspora, would still be relevant in the aftermath of the war. But unlike Stern, he never had any doubts regarding the orientation that the Jewish people must adopt.[45]

III

What, then, is Stern's proper place in history in relation to his political opponents in the Zionist leadership? Was his failure actually 'a victory in defeat' as his followers insist till this day? In a sense it was, inasmuch as there are grounds to the assertion that the Lehi in its later revival would not have arisen had it not been for his ideological and political legacy. But despite the legends that they themselves spun around his personality, under the harsh constraints of the underground they, too, understood and admitted among themselves that they must shake themselves free of his failures. Nevertheless, they felt justified in regarding these failures strictly as tactical errors, especially in view of the fact that the 'war' that Stern declared on England 'proved' itself to be warranted, even in the opinion of the IZL and the Jewish Agency (in the period of the 'United Hebrew Resistance Movement'). But they conveniently ignored a number of details, namely, that Stern's declaration of war was premature, and his plans were based on an intention to capitalize on an anticipated victory of the Axis powers. The official Zionist leadership and the Revisionist opposition, whom he vigorously denounced as quislings, managed to survive as leaders because they did not regard the White Paper of 1939 as spelling the end of Zionism, and they considered the outbreak of the war as actually offering an opportune moment for the strengthening of Zionism. Ben-Gurion, Weizmann, and Jabotinsky, unlike Stern, did not make the assumption that the White Paper and the war, as critical as these events may have been, were the final word in the history of the Jewish people. Unlike Stern, they believed that the only criterion for the use of violence, if indeed there is one, must be a symmetry between will and ability.

In his article on Franklin D. Roosevelt, Isaiah Berlin distinguished between two types of statesmen, without making the essential distinction between right and left. One type is that of a

---

[45] Z. Jabotinsky, *The Jewish War Front*, London, 1940, Chapters 4–5.

man of single principle and fanatical vision. Possessed by
his own bright, coherent dream, he usually understands
neither people nor events. He has no doubts or hesitations
and by concentration of will-power, directness and
strength he is able to ignore a great deal of what goes on
outside him... The second type of politician possesses ante-
nae of the greatest possible delicacy, which convey to him,
in way difficult or impossible to analyse, the perpetually
changing contours of events and feelings and human activities round them – they are gifted with a peculiar, political
sense fed on a capacity to take in minute impressions, to
integrate a vast multitude of small evanescent unseizable
details, such as artists possess in relation to their material...[46]

It seems that a third category can be added here, of those who are
devoured by the fire of their own revolutions, people of the left
and the right, each in his own way, figures such as Zelyabov,
Patrick Pearse, and Drieu La Rochelle, and not least among them,
Avraham Stern. When he had already realized that his end was
near, in the summer of 1941, he wrote:

At times when nations struggle and collapse, in times of war
and on the eve of revolutions, many search for the single
one, and the masses [search] for a leader. The yearning
hearts, the hopeful eyes, all turn towards the great anonymous one, he who bears the idea of freedom. When faith is
lost in the rule of law, when the sense of security in the
power of the public collapses, the primordial instinct, fixed
deeply within the hearts of human beings, comes to the fore:
total surrender to the mighty, blind following on the heels
of the leader. The decay of democracy in Athens preceded
the arrival of Alexander the Great, the destruction of the
French Revolution led to the rise of Napoleon, and in our
own time we are witnessing the helplessness of the majorities and of the rulers of many lands, beginning with Soviet
Russia and Nazi Germany and ending with Fascist Italy and
democratic England. In the annals of the Hebrew nation,
the rule of the mighty hand – of the fighter, the judge, and
the king – has become a tradition. Interwoven throughout
many generations as glorious links in the chain of rule are
the names of [Moses] Son-of-Amram and Joshua Son-of-
Nun, of King David and Mattathias the Hasmonean, of Bar
Kokhba and David HaReuveni, all the way to Herzl and his
successors... Now, as well, the nation is calling for an anonymous leader who will guide them along the path of redemption. The Hebrew freedom movement which dwells in the

---

[46] Isaiah Berlin, *Personal Impressions*, London (The Hogarth Press), 1980,
p. 27.

underground awaits the arrival of the commander. It does not make the fulfillment of the destiny dependent on the name of that man, for [the movement] knows in advance that agony and the gallows await its commander, and... [that] another shall take his place, to confine his life to austerity in the name of an idea. The *idea* is the pillar of the fire that goes before the camp of the freedom fighters...[47]

By the time he recorded these words, he had already despaired of using T.E. Lawrence, Lenin, and Pilsudski as leadership models. Their places were taken by the sacrificial models of Masada, Nili, and the Irish Easter Rebellion of 1916. His ten-year dialogue with death in the name of national liberation had now come to an end.

IV

Beyond his belief in the ability of personality to impose its will upon reality, Stern embraced the idea of the influence of one single, impersonal, historical process, that of Social Darwinism. In practice, this meant that although the Hebrew nation had abundant military strength and vigor at its disposal, this was still insufficient; thus, a pact with a victorious power was necessary in order to fill the needs. Stern was politically and psychologically prepared to leap from revolutionary thoughts to revolutionary deeds. But his essential nature was that of a romantic leader. As such, in his own way, he interpreted the ideology of the conservative right of Jabotinsky, the first of his mentors, as he did with the ideology of the radical authoritarian right, as imparted to him by his teachers Ahimeir, Yeivin and Ratosh. His disciples – Natan Friedman-Yellin (Mor), Yitzhak Yezernicki (Shamir), and Dr. Yisrael Eldad (Scheib) – would learn the appropriate lessons, and would seek to emphasize the need for a suitable balance between ideology and politics. But because of new circumstances and changing times, they were constrained to foster a new ideology, one of National Bolshevism. Stern never dreamed of any such ideology; he sought to be the one who ignites the Hebrew revolution (the same revolution sought by Jabotinsky since 1912),[48] but of his own will, he was consumed by its fire because of the failure of his ideological concepts.[49] The nimbus of charisma that was later spun around his personality by his successors was simply the product of the ideological, political, and practical necessities of the times, in the face of a hostile environment. But there was no

---

[47] 'The Leader', in: 'Yair, 25 Shevat 5702 – 25 Shevat 5704 (early 1942 – early 1944)', in: *Lehi Writings*, op, cit., 1, pp. 395–96.

[48] Z Jabotinsky, 'The Igniter' (1912), in: Z. Jabotinsky, *Reshimot* (Notes), Tel Aviv (no date), pp. 13–17.

[49] 'Let us Greet the Redeemer of Zion.../ let our blood be a red carpet in the streets,/ and on this carpet, our brains shall be like white lilies.' A. Stern – Yair, 'In Thy Blood Shalt Thou Live Forever', *Poems* (no date), p. 33.

basis for it in the reality of Stern's life and times. In essence he had been a revolutionary typical of the radical right and a victim of its Zionist version.

Part VII
State Sponsors of Terrorism

[17]

ANNALS, *AAPSS*, 463, September 1982

Aspects of Terrorism in Iran

By SEPEHR ZABIH

ABSTRACT: Even prior to the Constitutional Revolution of 1905-11, acts of terrorism were a commonly accepted form of political and religious struggle in Iran. Since the 1978-79 turmoil, terrorism has been used frequently by governments in power and has attained a transnational dimension. Beginning in the early 1900s, the composition and ideological orientation of violent groups have changed dramatically from religious fundamentalist in the forties and fifties to Marxist and Marxist-Islamic since the mid-sixties. After the 1979 revolution began, there was a significant realignment of all political terrorist forces. In order to overthrow the Shah, these groups joined Khomeini and staged a successful insurrection. Two years later, the more secular groups deserted the Islamic Republic in order to wage an armed struggle for its overthrow. The transnational dimension of terrorism in Iran has also changed. Such states or entities as Libya, Lebanon, the Palestine Liberation Organization (PLO), and Shia Lebanese Amal are no longer on the side of either Khomeini or his arch opponents. For the foreseeable future, political terrorism will continue to be a common feature of the Iranian scene.

Sepher Zabih holds a degree from the London School of Journalism and a Ph.D. in political science from the University of California at Berkeley. He has written five books and numerous articles on Iranian politics. Since the revolution he has been a regular commentator for the McNeil-Lehrer program of the Public Broadcasting Service. He is currently a professor of government at Saint Mary's College of California and a research associate in the Institute of International Studies, University of California at Berkeley.

TERRORISM as a means of political struggle has had a long history in modern Iran. Prior to the Iranian constitutional movement in the early 1900s, individual acts of assassination were perpetrated against Qajar kings and several ministers. Additionally, assassination was often used with government collusion as a means of repressing such religious minorities as the followers of Bab, the precursor to Bahaullah, ever since their faith was declared in the mid-nineteenth century.

Evidence of organized acts of political terrorism came sometime later, between the 1905 revolution and the advent of Reza Shah to power in 1925. Several political groups were formed in this period to eliminate politicians, newsmen, and even some religious leaders accused of working for foreign powers, notably Great Britain and Tsarist Russia.

The best known of these was called Komitehe Mojazat (Punishment Committee), which pursued a nationalistic Islamic ideology and was responsible for scores of attempted or successful assassinations of politicians between 1910 and 1919. Another political movement known as Jamiyate Islami (Islamic Society) was begun by Mirza Kuchek Khan in the same period and had similar goals but later changed into a separatist political movement in the Caspian province of Gilan. It was this movement that welcomed the intervention of the newly formed Soviet Red Army in 1920 and declared the First Communist Republic in Enzeli. In the process of that transformation, the movement acquired every characteristic of a guerrilla organization fighting against the weak central government of the last Qajar Shah.[1]

With the successful coup d'état of Reza Khan in February 1920, and the subsequent abolition of that dynasty five years later, acts of political terrorism did not completely cease. In his struggle to consolidate power and prepare the way for his new Pahlavi dynasty, Reza Khan authorized political assassination of some of his outspoken enemies, such as Mirzadeh Eshghi, the well-known liberal journalist and poet. His first chief of national police, Brigadier Mohammad Dargahi, was nicknamed "Mohammad the Knife" because of his control of clandestine political assassinations of the new Shah's enemies.[2]

Such acts became unnecessary with the progressive consolidation of the Pahlavi's first dictatorship. Laws for repression of political opposition in the name of fighting subversion were enacted. His secret police, known as "Taaminat" or security, enforced them ruthlessly, and except for desperate acts of defiance and resistance by some tribal and leftist opposition groups, political terrorism did not plague Iran in the last years of his reign.

TERRORISM DURING WORLD WAR II

The Anglo-Soviet military occupation of Iran in late August 1941 brought the Reza Shah dictatorship and relative stability of the country to an abrupt and violent end. Not only was the machinery of government totally shattered, but a state of

---

1. As yet the best available study of this period in West European languages is Edward G. Brown, *The Persian Revolution of 1905-1909* (Cambridge: Cambridge University Press, 1911). On the Babi and Bahai religions, consult Moojan Momen, ed., *The Babi and Bahai Religions: Some Contemporary Western Accounts* (Oxford: George Ronald, 1981).

2. See Ibrahim Khajenouri, *Bazigaran Asre Talai* (Performers of the Golden Era), 1(12) (Tehran, 1943).

near-anarchy so conducive to individual or organized acts of political terrorism was ushered in. While the occupation lasted, the presence of foreign troops both aided and impeded large-scale acts of terrorism, particularly in militarily sensitive regions of the country. It encouraged terrorism because both occupying powers, particularly the Soviet Union, gave free rein to political groups supporting their cause. When the Soviets refused to evacuate Iran's northern provinces under the 1942 tripartite treaty at the end of World War II, leftist terrorism became rampant throughout the country.[3]

Indeed, the process of setting up Communist regimes in Azarbayjan and Kurdistan involved a systematic and well-organized campaign of political assassination of Iranian politicians opposed to Soviet policies. Perhaps this was the first clear manifestation of transnational terrorism on a large and organized scale in this period. Not only did hundreds of Iranian Communists return home in the shadow of the Red Army, but literally thousands of Armenian and Azarbayjani and Tajiki citizens of the Soviet Union rushed into Iran to help promote Soviet policies. Ethnic, linguistic, and facial similarities made this cross-national infiltration extremely easy.

Along with the pro-Soviet groups, terrorism was also exercised by a new group of fundamentalists known as Fedayeen Islam, with well-established ties to Ikhvanel-Muslemin in Egypt and other Arab/Moslem countries. In this sense, transnational terrorism became a multilateral operation involving not

3. See Sepehr Zabih, *The Communist Movement in Iran* (Berkeley and Los Angeles: University of California Press, 1966).

only the Soviet Union and political groups supporting it in Iran but also Moslem fundamentalist groups throughout the region from Egypt to Pakistan.

The Fedayeen pursued an ideology that was at once nationalistic and pan-Islamic. It was nationalistic in the sense that they opposed the great powers controlling Iran, in particular Great Britain. Consequently, the targets of their political terrorism included government officials, journalists, and statesmen who were known for their pro-British sympathies. In the period between 1942 and 1953 they were responsible for the assassination of at least ten prominent Iranian politicians. The most important of these was General Ali Razmara, who was killed in March 1951, thus paving the way for the assumption of power by Mossadegh two months later. In recognition of this "heroic" act of terrorism, the assassin Khalil Tahmasebi was freed by the Iranian parliament in 1952, only to be subsequently tried and executed some three years later.[4]

The group was also pan-Islamic in the sense that it advocated close cooperation with all Islamic countries, whether Arab or non-Arab, that accepted the two minimum goals of emancipation from alien British rule and dedication to some form of Islamic government. Evidence that became available after the 1979 revolution indicates that the group established financial, political, and other ties with branches of Ikhvan throughout the Arab world, in particular Egypt, Lebanon, Iraq, and to a lesser extent in the Persian Gulf regions. Bearing in mind that most of these countries were in the throes of a national liber-

4. *Times* (London), 12 Mar. 1951.

ation struggle, the group had little difficulty in finding new recruits and locating facilities for ideological and military training.

THE FEDAYEEN DURING THE MOSSADEGH ERA

The advent of the nationalist government to power in April 1951 created both opportunity and problems for this Islamic fundamentalist terrorist group. On the one hand, the group was denied its common enemy, namely, as always in the past, the pro-British government. On the other hand, the government, fearing the disruption of law and order, not only refused to recognize it as a legitimate political force but decided to restrict its activities radically. In a dramatic move typical of his political career, Mossadegh took refuge in the parliament building barely a month after he was in office for fear of his life and the threat of retaliation by the Fedayeen. The impact of this move was so drastic that even the religious supporters of the group, among them Ayatollah Abolghassem Kashani, decided to underplay their ties with the Fedayeen and rally to the support of the prime minister.[5]

Toward the end of Mossadegh's first term in office in the early summer of 1952, the group reorganized and reestablished its close ties with the more politicized Shia leaders. The events at the end of July that suspended Mossadegh's government and brought into power Ahmad Ghavam, a notoriously anti-cleric prime minister, necessitated a complete alignment of all anti-Shah

political forces. The Fedayeen joined nationalists, Communists, and religious groups in a broad coalition to reinstate Mossadegh to power. The result was the uprising of July 17 which did precisely that. With the inauguration of Mossadegh's second term, the Fedayeen resumed its political activity, but this time aimed at the elimination of several non-Shia "heretic" groups. The followers of the notable historian and scholar, Ahmad Kasravi, who was murdered in the chamber of the trial judge in 1948, were targeted. A number of Bahai leaders were also victims of the politicoreligious terrorism.

However, the coalition that reinstated Mossadegh to power began to disintegrate by early 1953. Precisely because Kashani and his followers had deserted Mossadegh and progressively moved to the side of the Shah, the Fedayeen also reappraised its position and policies.

After some soul-searching, the Fedayeen became agents for the new rightist, royalist coalition dedicated to the overthrow of the Mossadegh regime. In doing so, the Fedayeen in reality became de facto agents for U.S. and British policies, as revealed in numerous documents about this period detailing the Central Intelligence Agency-Secret Intelligence Service (CIA-SIS) cooperation with anti-Mossadegh forces.

Ironically, not only were their services inadequately rewarded, but when they attempted to assassinate prime minister Hossein Ala in early 1955 as he was about to leave for Iraq to sign the Baghdad Pact, the security forces turned against them. The assailant of the prime minister, the killer of General Razmara, and the recognized leader of the group, Navrab Safavi, were rounded up,

5. For an inside account of this period, consult Sepehr Zabih, *The Mossadegh Era: Roots of the Iranian Revolution* (Chicago: Lake View Press, 1982).

88   THE ANNALS OF THE AMERICAN ACADEMY

tried before a military tribunal, and executed.[6]

DECLINE OF THE FEDAYEEN

Thus began the era of underground and clandestine activities that lasted until the early 1960s. A critical phenomenon during this period was the establishment of Iran's state security and information organization, "Savak." The organization, trained and advised by the CIA and U.S. military intelligence, began a systematic campaign to eradicate all political clandestine groups. By the summer of 1963 it appeared that the Savak had successfully attained its objectives.

However, in June of that year there was a major religious upheaval in which the present leader of Iran, Ayatollah Rouhollah Khomeini, the Fedayeen and other similar groups, as well as considerable segments of the population were involved. The government had little difficulty in using maximum military force to crush the religious uprising. Khomeini was sent into exile and notorious centers of political agitation in the holy cities of Qom and Mashad and the baazars in several cities were placed under tight military control.

For all practical purposes, acts of terrorism by this and similar groups seemed to have come to an end. In early 1965, a member of the Fedayeen Islam assassinated Prime Minister Hassanali Mansur as he was about to pronounce new oil and other commercial agreements with the Western powers. This last act of terrorism led to a systematic effort to eradicate the leadership of the group and cut off its ties with neighboring or distant Arab-Islamic countries. One reason that a consid-

6. *Ettelaat* (Tehran), 3 Feb. 1955, p. 4.

erable measure of success accompanied these efforts was the relative stability of the regime and the fairly close ties with these countries, which made cooperation with the Iranian security authorities mutually beneficial.

Thus, in the period between 1965 and early 1978, this group became virtually marginal to the Iranian political scene. Looking back at its records, one can say that in isolation the group could use political terrorism on a limited and nonsystematic scale. Working together with other political groups and committing individual acts of terrorism when the sociopolitical conditions were conducive, the Fedayeen achieved significant success.[7]

NON-ISLAMIC GROUPS

Beginning in the mid-sixties, the fundamentalist Islamic group lost its monopoly as a relatively successful and long-standing underground political organization. Instead, new groups espousing different pseudo-Marxist ideologies began to challenge the regime by systematic and frequently quite successful acts of political terrorism. Indeed, these new organizations succeeded in monopolizing the allegiance and frequently the active support of a significant cross-section of politically articulate Iranians. Needless to say, the government's attitude toward this new source of threat was severe repression combined with acts of counterterrorism when necessary,

7. No definitive study of the Fedayeen is available in European languages. After the 1979 revolution, some of the early participants and returnees to Iran have written extensively on the organization, but always from a subjective perspective. See *"Salhaye Khun dar rahe Islam"* (Years of Blood in the Path of Islam), in *Fedayeen Islam* (Qom and Tehran, 21 Apr. 1979), p. 35.

but at no time during this period was the security organization able to eradicate these groups completely.

During the revolutionary upheaval, remnants of the leadership cadres of these groups dominated urban guerrilla warfare against the government in a surprisingly quick and efficient manner. A contributing factor to their success was the government's liberalization policy, initiated and supported by the United States, which led to premature release of some of their cadres. Thus, in November-December 1978 it was not uncommon for prisoners to leave the notorious Evin prison in the morning and lead street riots and other acts of violence next morning in full view of foreign and occasionally domestic media.

Ideologically speaking, these underground organizations can be divided into two groups: the Fedayeen Khalgh (People's Devotees) and the Mojahedine Khalgh (People's Crusaders). Since its inception in the mid-sixties, the Fedayeen Khalgh has pursued a Marxist but not necessarily pro-Soviet ideological orientation. It is only recently that the pressure from the Islamic regime caused several splits in its ranks and file, causing one faction to embrace a pro-Soviet posture. This organization differed from the better-known Soviet-led Tudeh Party by its acceptance of armed struggle as a legitimate means of fighting the Shah. In this sense it was obviously to the left of the Tudeh party and as such was renounced and even occasionally betrayed by that traditionally pro-Soviet group.

As to the attitude of the Soviet Union concerning this group, it should be noted that the determining factor was, as always, formal relations between the Soviet Union and Iran. When these relations were correct and amicable, as indeed they were in the last decade of the Shah's reign, Moscow had no difficulty in condemning the group as a "bunch of naive terrorists."

On the other hand, Moscow would—at least since the 1979 revolution, when it wished to pressure the Islamic Republic—support and encourage this group in favor of a particular objective. Interestingly enough, even when a major split resulted in the formation of a pro-Tudeh faction, the group did not integrate itself with the latter. For all practical purposes, in the last year and a half the two groups, the Tudeh and the majority faction of the Fedayeen, have pursued identical goals and policies.[8]

The second group that emerged about the same time were the Mojahedine Khalgh, with a pronounced Islamic-Marxist ideology. Even though Communism is known as an atheistic ideology, the group found sufficient common grounds between the original teaching of Marx and a more liberal interpretation of some of the Islamic principles and concepts.

The Mojahedin has been responsible for numerous acts of terrorism since 1965.[9] It joined the first group

8. For a perceptive, albeit slightly sympathetic, analysis of opposition forces in the early phase of revolution, see Ervand Abrahimian, "Iran in Revolution: The Opposition Forces," MERIP Reports, No. 75/76, 9 (Mar./Apr.), pp. 3-8. For an up-to-date study of the same, see Sepehr Zabih, *Iran Since the Revolution*, (London: Croom-Helm, 1982) especially Chapter 8, "The Left and the Islamic Republic."

9. Data on their operations and casualties may be found in Sepehr Zabih, *Iran's Revolution* (London: Croom-Helm, 1982), *Essay* (San Francisco: Alchemy Books, 1979), p. 42. Also Shahram Chubin, "Leftist Forces in Iran," *Problems of Communism*, 29:1-25 (Jul.-Aug. 1980).

in a systematic struggle to transform the final phase of the 1979 revolution into a bloody insurrection. The fact that it could appeal to Islam as the common denominator of the masses of Iranians supporting Khomeini proved of tremendous value. As a matter of fact, the Mojahedin came very close to dominating totally the politics of the left with the advent of the Khomeini regime. That they failed to do so and instead, in a matter of less than a year, split with the Islamic Republic is something deserving closer scrutiny. Suffice it to state that in its prerevolution existence, the organization had no difficulty recruiting from a very representative cross-section of basically urban Iranians.

Available data indicate that the Mojahedin were also in close contact with non-Iranian underground organizations in the Middle East and elsewhere. Thus, for example, a segment of its leadership after receiving undergraduate education in Iran would be sent abroad, often on government scholarship, and either after completion of graduate education or before doing so would end up in Cuban, Palestinian, Libyan, or Leftist Lebanese training camps.

One group that not only provided camp and training facilities for the Mojahedin but also established a network of operatives for smuggling men and weapons in and out of the country was Amal, the well-known Lebanese Shia organization. A number of prominent Mojahedin thus trained in urban guerrilla warfare returned to Iran in the latter part of the year-long turmoil, 1978 to 1979. Those who could be trusted by the provisional government and by a close circuit of Khomeini associates achieved important leadership positions. Those who preferred

anonymity and/or did not fully agree with the regime never gave up their arms and their ambitions to fully dominate the new Iran. The best representative of the first group is Mostafa Chamran, the Berkeley-educated engineer who left the United States in the mid-sixties, received initial training in Cuba, and joined the Palestine Liberation Organization (PLO) and the Amal camps as a skillful guerrilla organizer. After serving as defense minister of the Islamic Republic, he was put in charge of underground operations behind Iraq-Iran war fronts in September 1980. He was mysteriously killed in action the summer of 1981.[10]

Smaller groups who have joined the anti-Khomeini armed struggle since June 1981 include the Ranjbaran (Toilers), with a Maoist ideology; the Peykar (Combat), a Trotskyite organization; and of course various Kurdish and other ethnic dissident groups. The Ranjbaran, which claims to be the sole genuinely Communist group, is led by a number of U.S.-educated individuals, such as Berkeley-trained physicist Iraj Farhumand, who was executed in February 1982 after six months of imprisonment.[11]

GOVERNMENT-SPONSORED TERRORISM

Throughout this era the government also exercised political terror-

10. His killing has been attributed to the Pasdaran by at least one knowledgeable Iran specialist, Fred Halliday, when suspicion of cooperation with the deposed president Abolhassan Banisadr was aroused. Interview, Berkeley, California, 8 Feb. 1982.

11. "Voice and Image of Islamic Republic" (official title of Iran's State Radio and Television System), monitored by Sepehr Zabih, 23 Feb. 1982.

ism, some of which had trans-national ramifications. A notable example is the entrapment-assassination of General Teymour Bakhtiyar, Savak's first director in Iraqi territory in 1964. The general, who was related to ex-queen Soraya, was lured to the mountainous region of Kurdistan near the Iranian border and assassinated by a group of Iranian military intelligence agents who had been planted in Iraq months earlier in a faked hijacking episode. This event is also significant because Iraqi territory was also used as a haven for Communist and other opponents of the Shah, including agents of Khomeini who had just been sent into exile in Iraq.[12] This situation changed with rapprochement between the two countries in 1975.

Transnational terrorism, in which security agencies in various countries of the region not only performed the routine intelligence-gathering and identification and location of enemies of their respective states but actually used terrorism as a means of eliminating them, became an accepted form of coexistence.

While the exact nature of the multilateral relations of Iranian, Iraqi, Israeli, Turkish, and American security organizations is beyond the scope of this article, it is important to note that acts of transnational terrorism both began and occurred before the 1978-79 upheaval.

TERRORISM AND THE REVOLUTION

With the advent of revolution, however, government-sponsored

12. Best account of this James Bondish episode is given by Gerard de Villiers's *L'Irresistable Ascension de Mohammad Reza Shah d'Iran* (Paris: Plon, 1975).

terrorism acquired wider application and in some sense even a sort of legitimacy. This is due to three factors.

First, foreign-trained guerrilla movements, as noted earlier, were among the chief claimants to succeed the Shah after 1979. When these claims could not be satisfied, some guerrilla groups turned against the Islamic Republic and justified the use of terrorism as a legitimate means of satisfying their grievances. Indeed, their official position of armed resistance to the present regime, pronounced from the safety of their foreign exile in France and elsewhere, eschewed terrorism and claimed the struggle to be a legitimate resistance to an oppressive regime.

Second, the government justifies its repressive retaliatory measures in the name of the inherent right of self-defense. Thus terror and counterterror, which have greatly intensified since June 1981, are explained away by a logic either revolutionary or counterrevolutionary, depending on one's perspective.

A third factor legitimating government-sponsored terrorism is the pan-Islamic ideology of the regime. The espousal of this ideology enables the regime to support and initiate political terrorism anywhere in Islamic countries in pursuance of its goal. Lebanon, in particular, has become the main arena where pro-Khomeini Shia groups, in affiliation with a much better armed Amal, have been engaged in many acts of violence.

The Iran-Iraq war has given government-sponsored terrorism a new dimension. For one, it has injected into the traditional Shia-Sunni feud the element of territorial nationalism. For another, it has created objective conditions for expression of transnational loyalties. The combination of these has made the distinction between acts of war and defense on the one hand and acts of political terrorism on the other extremely difficult.

Thus, for example, pro-Khomeini Shia Lebanese will destroy the Iraqi embassy in Beirut as an act of solidarity with the present Iranian regime. In doing so, they also serve Israeli interests, which leads to the speculation that Israeli intelligence is in an unholy alliance with Shia fundamentalists not only in Lebanon but also in Iran, where the Jews have not fared any better than other minorities.[13]

Similarly, the PLO connection to Iran-based transnational terrorism was seriously affected by this war. On the one hand, to support a fundamentalist Shia but nonetheless non-Arab Iran would be anathema to Arab nationalists. On the other, to side with the Iraqis against Iran, in whose regime many of the Palestinian-trained guerrillas still serve, would be incomprehensible. This dilemma compounded Palestinian-Iranian relations further when the more radical groups within the PLO began to side with the Mojahedin and other political groups that have been engaged in armed struggle against Khomeini since June 1981.

The hostage crisis introduced a new element in Iran's long history of political terrorism. Irrespective of the ultimate outcome of the crisis, there is little doubt that from the outset it was deeply entangled with internal political developments in the infant Islamic Republic. The government sponsorship of that

blatant act of international terrorism simply made the Islamic Republic an international outlaw. It also contributed heavily to the utility, if not the legitimacy, of acts of terrorism by all groups, whether in opposition or in support of the government. Thus, the loser in this ill-conceived act of outlawry was Iran itself, not only because of significant financial losses but also for giving credibility and legitimacy to a form of terrorism of which the country itself has become the prime victim.[14]

GOVERNMENT BY EXECUTION

By June 1981 the struggle with anti-government organizations greatly expanded political terrorism as an acceptable form of deciding who would rule the country. In less than a month, close to 1000 government and ruling clergy officials, ranging from revolutionary guards to an incumbent president, prime minister, chief justice, and prosecutor general of revolutionary tribunals, were killed, often in well-organized, inside jobs of bombing by infiltrating the highest sanctum of government. In the same period, close to 6000 of the activists of the various armed groups were either caught and summarily tried and executed or fell in numerous street fighting with security forces. As a rule, the largest and best organized of these, namely, the Mojahedin, bore the brunt of ferocious government reprisals. The terror and counterterror continue to date.[15] Whether it will lead to a conven-

13. Some aspects of the Israeli connection with Iran before and after the revolution are covered in Zabih, *Iran Since the Revolution.*

14. The internal dimension of this crisis has been emphasized in my book, among others.

15. While data given by either side are generally over- or understated, the *Amnesty International Report,* issued 24 Feb. in London, generally supports these figures.

tional civil war or a decisive victory of one side over the other is unknown. What is evident is that Iran is in for a long period of the illegitimate use of violence in its efforts to resolve political disputes. The most long-lasting and perhaps devastating consequence of Khomeini's rise to power and dogged determination to retain power is the degree of acceptability that political terrorism has gained over the last four years.

A further development since June 1981 relates to the transnational dimension of terrorism. By seeking and receiving asylum in France, the leadership of the Mojahedin and the looser organization, the National Resistance Council, have reinforced this dimension of terrorism in Iran. If the granting of asylum could be justified, the continuous exercise of command and control of acts of violence, particularly by the Mojahedin, from a foreign soil can only be construed as at least acquiescence to the terrorism against the government of Iran, with which France still retains diplomatic ties. But by the same token, acts of transnational terrorism, airplane hijacking, and assassination of government opponents in exile have continued unabated, indicating the Iranian government's dedication to a policy of state-sponsored terrorism beyond its borders.

As this brief review indicates, terrorism defined as the illegitimate use of violence for political or religiously inspired objectives has deep roots in Iran's recent history. It has often been characterized by a transnational dimension, which since the mid-sixties has become a significant factor. The year-long revolutionary upheaval of 1978 to 1979 and the political development in Iran at least since that November 1979 taking of the American hostages simply intensified and compounded this important dimension. In a real sense, contemporary Iran has placed itself outside the bounds of international law and order, for not only armed opposition groups but also the state commit acts of terrorism in their relentless struggle to destroy one another.

* * *

QUESTIONS AND ANSWERS

COMMENT (Wolfgang): Before turning to questions, I would like to make a comment. I understand that Miss Gomer from the Phelps Institute made a commentary in the last session and the first session about land purchases by Arab nationals in Kansas and other parts of the Western United States. I think that comment needs to be recognized, and I should like to say, Miss Gomer, that I do not have significant information to provide an intelligent response to that. However, I think the issue you are raising about the capability or the potential of some terroristic activities occurring by reason of any kind of massive kind of purchasing of land in the United States by groups that may or may not have had some association with terrorism in the past is one to which we need to give attention.

COMMENT (Zabih): I would like really to direct my comments to my fellow panelists who spoke on El Salvador. It seems to me the basic question that comes to mind is that in a war of that nature, atrocities are committed on both sides. My general impression from your presentation was that you were rather one-sided. One could document atrocities on either side. In this type of war, giving sanctuary to those who are escaping or running away from pursuing forces has always been a major question. Do you go and ask the family that owns the house or a village if it will consent to have these people seek refuge there? There are all kinds of complicated problems in guerrilla warfare. To overemphasize the atrocities on one side and say nothing really about the other side, I think, is an injustice to a very difficult problem.

[18]

WHY ASAD'S TERROR WORKS AND QADHDHAFI'S DOES NOT

by Daniel Pipes

The Middle East has special importance for terrorism. It is the region that hosts the greatest number of agents engaged in terrorism, and these terrorists promote the widest variety of ideologies. The Middle East has also witnessed by far the most incidents of an international character, and most new trends develop first in the Middle East, then spread to other areas.

In recent years, the most important new development in Middle East terrorism has been the adoption of terrorist methods by state authorities. Politically motivated violence against noncombatants has evolved from a tool used exclusively against the state into an instrument of the state. Thus, in addition to helping clandestine groups fight against central authority, terror now serves weak states against more powerful ones, and in this sense constitutes a novel form of military conflict. This development makes terrorism far more important politically than it would be if confined to small organizations hiding from the law.

The following survey offers a political-military analysis of the major Middle East sponsors of terrorism. It includes three states — Libya, Iran, and Syria — and one movement, the Palestine Liberation Organization (PLO). It excludes less important, though still significant, sponsors of terrorism such as South Yemen and Iraq.

The PLO — though not a state (and indeed not a single movement, but a coalition of several autonomous groups) — clearly deserves inclusion here. In the matter of employing terrorism, it resembles a government more than it does the usual irredentist movement. Its financial means resemble those of a state and its wide diplomatic recognition (greater than Israel's) gives it a unique international presence. Further, the PLO has controlled large areas of territory over extended periods, in both Jordan and Lebanon.

To look at state-sponsored terrorism, we begin with an assessment of the four sponsors' effectiveness and then consider the reasons for their very different records.

Daniel Pipes is the editor of ORBIS. His most recent book is *The Long Shadow: Culture and Politics in the Middle East* (Transaction, 1989).

PIPES

Libya

Mu'ammar al-Qadhdhafi's goal from the time he came to power in September 1969 was to make himself the most powerful leader of the Middle East. A man with unusual views and a turbulent temperament, he pursued radical solutions on a host of issues, including Israel, Islam, and the good society. (His views on this last were incorporated in the "Third Theory," which he expounded widely and tried to apply in Libya.) But three limitations frustrated his ambitions: the small and unskilled population of Libya, the difficulty of turning cash from oil sales into power, and widespread resistance to his views, especially outside Libya.

Terrorism offered a way to solve these problems. Because it required only a few operatives, it solved the problem of demographic limitations. Because foreigners were hired for operations, it allowed money to be used to good effect. And because it permitted direct action far away, it allowed Qadhdhafi to exert pressure around the globe.

Qadhdhafi proved himself better at creating mischief than achieving political goals. His agents killed people and gained attention, but they changed almost nothing.

Accordingly, the Libyan government began sponsoring terrorism shortly after Qadhdhafi came to power. Besides Israelis, dissident Libyans abroad felt Qadhdhafi's wrath most often, but so did Arabs who disagreed with him, as well as Muslims and Westerners. By 1975-76 Qadhdhafi's hand was nearly everywhere — in the Middle East and Western Europe especially, but also in Africa, the Americas, and the South Pacific.

Nevertheless, Qadhdhafi proved himself better at creating mischief than achieving political goals. His agents killed people and gained attention, but they changed almost nothing. Dissident Libyans continued to work against Tripoli; Israelis endured Libyan-sponsored attacks; Qadhdhafi's neighbors survived his persistent efforts at subversion; Muslim rulers outlasted his efforts at subversion; and Western democratic governments maintained their principles. In short, terrorism's considerable potential eluded Qadhdhafi. Accordingly, his reliance on this tool decreased, beginning in the mid-1970s, and it has not been satisfactorily replaced by anything else. This failure goes far to explain Qadhdhafi's obvious frustration in recent years.

The PLO

The Palestine Liberation Organization seeks to destroy the State of Israel and replace it with an independent Palestinian polity under its own control. Founded in 1964, the PLO began as a tool of the Egyptian government.

TERRORISM

The overwhelming defeat of three conventional armies in the Six Day War of June 1967, however, prompted Arabs to seek an alternate weapon against Israel; and this is what the PLO, with its romantic notions of individual combat, offered. With the support of Arab and communist governments, the organization was quickly transformed from a minor movement into one of the most prominent actors in Middle East politics.

But it was militarily weak. So, rather than tangle with the formidable Israeli Defense Forces, the Palestinians developed an alternate way to destroy Israel, based on terrorism. Inspired by the Front de Libération Nationale in Algeria (and to a lesser degree by the Viet Cong), the PLO hoped to make life so miserable for Israeli civilians that they would eventually give up and abandon the country. This strategy allowed, even encouraged, attacks on the innocent and the undefended — thus the PLO's long record of massacring children and other civilians. In essence, the PLO viewed Israelis as foreign settlers who, like the *pieds noirs*, would opt to leave when the price got too high. (The same analogy was put this way, decades later, by Mu'ammar al-Qadhdhafi: "We consider Palestine today like Algeria yesterday .... There used to be as many French settlers as there are Israelis now in Palestine. And yet those French settlers were expelled, Algeria became Arab, and the Algerian people won full independence.")[1]

But herein lay a basic misconception, for unlike the French in Algeria, very few Israelis have another home to return to. Moreover, Jews live in Palestine not just for reasons of convenience and gain, as did the French in Algeria, but for powerful religious and nationalist motives. Based on this understanding, flawed as it was, the PLO's violence failed to have its intended effect. The acts were spectacular, the attention enormous, but the results were insignificant. Israelis were killed, but the intended political impact of the deaths was not achieved. Concessions or changes in policy by Israel were not forthcoming. Indeed, Arab states have probably been challenged more by PLO terrorism than has Israel.

To be sure, the PLO has much to boast of — its many diplomatic representations, widely accepted legitimacy, a great reserve of funds — but these resulted from its wide support among Arab states and its own political skills, not from the killing of innocents. The Palestinians had a strategic purpose for terrorism but it was flawed, and this deficiency very much reduced the impact of PLO efforts.

Iran

The Islamic Republic of Iran strives to export its eccentric and fundamentalist reading of Islam throughout the Middle East and the Muslim world. Seeking nothing less than a basic re-orientation of public life along strictly Islamic lines, it has used all methods available to achieve this goal.

---

[1] Tripoli Television Service, June 8, 1988.

PIPES

On coming to power in February 1979, Ayatollah Ruhollah Khomeini
and his followers hoped that moral exhortation would be sufficient to rouse
Muslim masses abroad, thereby bringing down what they considered to be
hypocritical Muslim regimes. The ayatollah's stirring rhetoric did have an
impact, especially in the aftermath of the Mecca takeover in November 1979,
when Khomeini's angry response led to assaults on U.S. embassies in half a
dozen countries. Words alone, though, overthrew no government. So, by the
end of 1979, the Iranians began aiding foreign groups to augment their efforts
internationally. These groups engaged in anti-government sabotage and attempted coups d'état, notably in Bahrain, Iraq, and Saudi Arabia. But in September 1980 Iraq attacked Iran, and Iran's main goal for the next eight years
was the defeat of Iraq. Strapped for money and manpower, the luxury of
sponsoring conventional efforts to change foreign regimes lapsed.

Instead, Tehran resorted to terrorism. This tool had the advantages of
requiring little money and few operatives; at the same time, it made good use
of what Iran had in abundance — devoted followers. Tehran also developed
an institution that changed the face of state-sponsored terrorism, the suicide
attack. Yet even Khomeini lacked enough devotees for this form of terror, so
his government had to search for a mechanism to keep up a steady supply of
recruits. Tehran eventually created a virtually unlimited pool of recruits by
relying on the state's intelligence sources to coerce individuals into undertaking suicide operations.

Iranian leaders deployed the terror weapon with intelligence and
strategic purpose. Consequently, Tehran achieved some of its policy goals
through terror. It caused some other states — including Pakistan and Turkey
— to run scared. Most of the small Persian Gulf states bent over backwards
to accommodate Iranian wishes, and many Muslim governments appeased
the ayatollah in hopes of keeping his agents away. Concomitantly, Western
influence was reduced in much of the Middle East.

Iranian efforts have been concentrated on Lebanon, and rightly so, for
a civil war has been raging there since 1975, making the country unusually
open to Iranian influence. Anarchy in Lebanon offers virtually unlimited freedom of action and avoidance of responsibility. Accordingly, most of Tehran's
terror operations have emanated from Lebanon, the site of its training camps.
Further, years of war bred irrationalist impulses, so most of the terror has
been executed by Lebanese Shi'is. Too, the country's political fluidity offers
the possibility of creating a second Islamic republic.

Iranian actions threaten Westerners with special menace. In illustration,
I offer a personal experience that took place in March 1988, when I served
as a U.S. delegate to the United Nations Commission on Human Rights in
Geneva. As one of my duties, I handled the Iran portfolio — attending meetings on this issue and negotiating on behalf of the United States. This commission annually passes a resolution introduced by a West European state
that condemns the abuse of human rights in Iran. But that year, because of
widespread Iranian terrorism against Britons, Frenchmen, Germans, and

TERRORISM

others, no West European state stepped forward to introduce the Iranian resolution. Oh yes, they would all vote for it; but, in United Nations terms, voting is not everything. Introducing a resolution is a stronger action, and customarily every resolution is formally introduced by a member state. (The United States would gladly have introduced the Iran resolution, but in the eyes of many this would have politicized the effort and weakened support for it.)

Europeans worried much more about crossing the ayatollah than the Kremlin. *This* is an effective use of terrorism.

Thus, a slight sense of panic spread each time the subject of Iran came up at a meeting of the Western states. Two-thirds of the representatives would flee the room when the dread name was spoken, not wanting to be associated in any way with the resolution's introduction. The Japanese ambassador muttered, "I want to escape." The French delegate scurried from the room, smiling tightly as he claimed an "urgent" meeting. West German and Italian delegates slunk off without a word. Why did they take off like this? Because their governments feared more terror out of Tehran. When it came time to vote against the Soviet record of human rights abuses in Afghanistan, one could hardly restrain the Europeans, who eagerly looked forward to introducing the resolution. In short, they worried much more about crossing the ayatollah than the Kremlin.

This is an effective use of terrorism. More recently, widespread apprehension in the West in the wake of Khomeini's edict against Salman Rushdie has again proved the power of Iranian threats on a virtually global scale.

Syria

Finally, consider the Syrian government. Hafiz al-Asad aims to control, or gain preponderant influence over, all the territories that make up the region known as Greater Syria — Lebanon, Palestine, and Jordan, in addition to Syria proper.

Asad began to deploy state-sponsored terror in a significant way a few years after coming to power in November 1970, and his judicious use of this instrument is key to his statecraft. Asad never boasts or indulges in media spectaculars, and he always attends carefully to timing. He acts with great secrecy, leaving open the possibility of making public deals that improve his reputation. Asad's hallmark is the closely calculated, low-key, and far-sighted use of terror.

Absent is the usually clear association between sponsor and operatives. Damascus controls a great number of groups, and these, rather than the

PIPES

Syrian government itself, undertake the terrorist operations. In addition to the many Palestinian groups he has brought under the banner of the Palestine National Salvation Front, organizations acting on Syria's behalf include the Syrian Social Nationalist party, the Armenian Secret Army for the Liberation of Armenia, the Kurdish Worker's party (PKK), the (Druze) Progressive Socialist party, the Democratic Front for the Liberation of Somalia, and the Eritrean Liberation Front. Others too (such as the pope's assailant, Mehmet Ali Agca) have received training in Syria. Many of these organizations are based in the Biqa' Valley of Lebanon, nominally in a separate country, but in fact under Syrian control.

Indirect sponsorship offers Asad several advantages. It allows him to call on a greater number of individuals and organizations; he can more plausibly deny culpability when agents are caught; and it permits him to play an intermediary role between the groups and foreign governments. He is able to maintain decent relations with many other states — even those whose citizens suffer his predations.

Asad's efforts have had considerable success, for his use of terror often affects the policies of other states.

Asad's efforts have had considerable success, for his use of terror often affects the policies of other states. In the Arab-Israeli conflict, terror is instrumental in preventing Arab states and 'Arafat from adopting more accommodating policies toward Israel. In Lebanon, it helps Damascus control a majority of the country. In the Persian Gulf, it keeps the money flowing. With Libya and Iran, it boosts an otherwise frail alliance. Terrorism enhances Syrian power, and so increases Asad's value to the Soviet Union; in particular, operations against Turkey help destabilize a key member of the North Atlantic Treaty Organization.

Nowhere, however, is the impact so great as it is vis-à-vis the Jordanian government. It can be argued that the entire Syrian-Jordanian relationship is dominated by the threat of terrorism from Syria. One round of attacks began in late 1983: in India, the Jordanian ambassador was shot on October 25; in Italy, the next day, the ambassador was wounded; in Greece, during November, a security agent was killed; and in Spain, on December 29, submachine-gun fire on two persons killed one and wounded the other. Abu Nidal's group — based in Damascus — was implicated in all of these cases.

The attacks then abated, only to begin again when King al-Husayn and Yasir 'Arafat agreed on February 11, 1985, to work together, a pact that both the Syrian and Soviet governments strongly opposed. A four-month sequence of terrorist activities followed. It included a bomb at the American Research Center in Amman; an explosion in an airliner of the Jordanian carrier, Alia; a

TERRORISM

hand-grenade attack on Alia offices in Athens; a rocket attack on the Jordanian embassy in Rome; a rocket attack on an Alia plane in Athens; an Alia plane hijacked in Beirut and blown up; a bomb attack on Alia offices in Madrid; and the assassination in Turkey of a Jordanian diplomat who also happened to be the brother-in-law of the Jordanian commander in chief.

This campaign had Amman under siege, and it played a major role in the abrogation of the Jordan-PLO accord in February 1986.

The Success of Terror

Two observations follow from the patterns adduced here.

First, when judged by their aims, the four main sponsors of terror have fared very differently. Qadhdhafi remains impossibly far from becoming the most powerful politician of the Middle East; 'Arafat has little prospect of destroying Israel and founding a Palestinian state; the Iranians have some chance of expanding the Islamic Revolution; and Asad has proceeded quite far in the direction of Greater Syria. Significantly, this lineup from frustration to achievement exactly reflects their gains from terrorism.

Second, failure or success has varied according to the coordination of means and ends. Qadhdhafi gained least, for he had no strategy. The least rational leader in this sample, he had only the vaguest of objectives. He reveled in violence for its own sake and was always active, even when there was no apparent goal. The PLO also accomplished little from terrorism (although quite a bit from its other activities), for it too pursued a mistaken strategy. Caught up in the rhetoric and drama of terrorism, it fabricated incidents out of whole cloth and persisted in the use of terror long after this weapon proved counterproductive.

In contrast, the Iranian government deployed terrorism as a means to shake up the region and even to challenge the United States. The Iranians had clear goals and wielded terror to promote these. But the Syrian use of terror has been most crafty. Hafiz al-Asad knew what he wanted and deployed violence with skill. He became a major force in regional affairs — acting and forcing others to react — in large part due to the intelligent use of terror.

The critical factor here concerns the ability to connect means and ends. The failed leaders engage in murder for its own sake; the successful ones make terrorism part of a larger strategy. It is in this sense that Asad is the most competent, Qadhdhafi the least. Asad invariably has a clear sense of what he is trying to achieve; he uses terrorism just as he would any other instrument of state. Qadhdhafi, a radical who cannot long keep his attention on any single matter, has confused ideas or too many ideas, and so hardly makes plans. He wallows in carnage and mayhem and seems to enjoy them in their own right. Asad directs his fire on a few vulnerable targets; Qadhdhafi scatters his around the globe. One has specific goals in mind; the other seeks to spark revolutions.

Put differently, efficacy is inversely proportionate to the irrationality of

PIPES

the leader. A passionate temperament and emotional indulgence make it hard
to control the terrorism tool. The utility of a terrorist undertaking is largely
determined by a leader's cunning, vision, and his ability to relate policy to
strategy.

These observations suggest one major policy implication for the West:
when it comes to terrorism, pay more attention to Syria and Iran, less to Libya
and the PLO. The PLO and Libya garnered early attention, for they had this
field largely to themselves until the late 1970s. By now, however, they are
has-beens; Damascus and Tehran are the sponsors that count most.

Part VIII
Middle East Terrorism Spill-over into Other Regions

[19]

Middle Eastern Terrorist Activity in Western Europe: A Diagnosis and Prognosis

by
Dennis Pluchinsky*

INTRODUCTION

From January 1980 to July 1, 1986, Middle Eastern terrorist groups have carried out over 259 attacks in sixteen West European countries which have resulted in 165 deaths and over 1,569 injuries.[1] Thirty-nine percent of these attacks, 45% of these fatalities, and 62% of these injuries have occurred during 1985-86. Middle Eastern terrorist activity has been and continues to be a major security and political problem for most countries in Western Europe. Many of these countries (West Germany, Spain, Great Britain, France, Italy, Greece, and Portugal) are also confronted with an indigenous terrorist threat from various separatist and Marxist revolutionary groups. The more active and dangerous of these groups are: the Red Army Faction (RAF) and the Revolutionary Cells (RC) in West Germany; the Red Brigades (RB) in Italy; Direct Action (DA) and the Corsican National Liberation Front (FLNC) in France; the Popular Forces of April 25th (FP-25) in Portugal; the Popular Revolutionary Struggle (ELA) and the November 17th Group in Greece; the Basque Fatherland and Liberty movement (ETA-M) in Spain; and the Irish Republican Army (IRA) in Great Britain.

The level of threat posed by any of these groups in their respective countries at a particular time varies, depending primarily upon the number and impact of police arrests and the ideological and operational unity within the groups. While the short-term threat posed by these groups varies, the long-term threat remains high. All of these groups have, at one time or another, been dealt crippling operational blows by police and security forces. The fatal blow, however, has been missing. Many of these groups are already into their third or fourth "generation" — both in terms of membership and leadership. The security threat posed by these indigenous groups will not dissipate any time in the immediate future.

Compounding the indigenous terrorist problem for the European police and security forces is the activity of foreign, primarily Middle Eastern, terrorist groups. It is a unique security problem for Western Europe. No other region in the world is faced with a significant terrorist threat from foreign groups. For Western Europe, it is a problem of "spillover" terrorism. Unfortunately, Western Europe has proven to be a preferred operational area for those Middle Eastern groups. More attacks by Middle Eastern terrorist groups take place in Western Europe than in any other region, excluding, of course, the Middle East. Moreover, there are certain Middle Eastern terrorist elements that prefer operating in Western Europe rather than in the Middle East. The Abu

Nidal group and those entities responsible for assassinating Libyan and Iranian dissident elements are more active in Western Europe. For example, 68% of the attacks attributed to the Abu Nidal group since 1973 have taken place in Western Europe,[2] while over 95% of the terrorist attacks directed at dissident Libyan exiles since 1980 have taken place in Western Europe.[3]

Why this preference for Western Europe? What does this region offer that these groups cannot find in other regions such as Latin America, Africa, the Far East, North America, and, in some cases, even in the Middle East? There are five factors which make Western Europe an attractive operational area for Middle Eastern terrorist groups.

1. **Western Europe provides these groups with a potential manpower pool which facilitates the building and maintenance of a logistical infrastructure.** There are large communities of Palestinians and Arabs in most West European countries. This also includes the large student populations. Moreover, Middle Eastern businessmen and tourists frequently travel to Western Europe. This makes it easy for Middle Eastern terrorist groups to send in operational elements which can not only blend into the environment but can also receive logistical aid from sympathizers and in-country support elements.

2. **Western Europe offers these groups geographic proximity and compactness, excellent transportation facilities, and relatively easy cross-border movement.** In other words, it is easy to get to Western Europe and, once there, to move around between countries.

3. **Western Europe offers these groups abundant, easy, and attractive targets.** Middle East terrorists carry out attacks against three targeting sections: Israeli or Jewish, Western, and Arab or Palestinian. There is a large number of these targets in Western Europe.

4. **Western Europe offers these groups immediate worldwide publicity when they carry out an attack in the region.** The publicity spotlight is broader and brighter in Western Europe than in most other regions. With regard to the Middle East, attacks carried out by Middle Eastern groups in Iran, Syria, Iraq, and Libya receive little publicity because of the state-controlled press in these countries. In Lebanon, the level of political violence literally buries, from a publicity standpoint, all but the most spectacular and lethal incidents.

5. **Western Europe provides these groups with a "substitute battleground" in which to carry out their intra-Palestinian and inter-Arab feuds.** The majority of the attacks carried out by Middle Eastern terrorist groups are aimed at other Arab and Palestinian targets. The authoritarian nature of such states as Libya, Iran, Iraq, and Syria makes it difficult for these groups to operate effectively within these states. Israeli security

6

measures also make it difficult for these groups to operate within Israel. It is less risky and operationally easier to attack Libyan, Syrian, Iranian, Iraqi, and Israeli targets in Western Europe.

DIAGNOSIS

Middle Eastern terrorist activity in Western Europe is a product of the numerous antagonistic relationships which exist in the Middle East between states, ethnic and religious groups, and Palestinian and Arab personalities. More and more of these conflicts, feuds, and disagreements are evolving into "mini-terrorist wars" which are being fought not in the Middle East but in Western Europe — a substitute battlefield. Who are the adversaries in these mini-terrorist wars? What are their motives? What effect do these terrorist attacks have on the security environment in Western Europe? These questions are addressed below.

Last year, Middle Eastern terrorist groups carried out 75 attacks in Western Europe which caused 65 deaths and over 529 injuries.[4] In 1984, the figures were 47 attacks, 18 deaths, and 63 injuries. The 75 Middle Eastern attacks in 1985 were carried out in 14 West European countries, with only Portugal, Luxembourg, Finland, Ireland, Belgium, and Norway being spared. The countries selected most frequently for these attacks were Greece (14), Italy (13), and Cyprus (9). (See chart #1.)

Of these attacks in 1985, 42 were directed at Arab and Palestinian targets, 13 against Israeli and Jewish targets, and 20 against "Western" targets, including 5 aimed at the United States. These are the three major targeting sectors for Middle Eastern terrorist groups. The most significant development was the increase in attacks directed at Western targets. This particular development will be discussed later.

Attacks against other Arab and Palestinian targets

A breakdown of the 42 attacks aimed at Arab and Palestinian targets indicates that:

8 were directed at Libyan exiles
7 against Jordan
6 against PLO moderates and Arafat supporters
6 against Libya
5 against Iran
4 against Syria
2 against Iraq
1 against Tunisia
1 against an Iranian exile
1 against an Iraqi exile
1 against a Palestinian student

The suspected or stated motives for the above attacks are as varied as the targets. The 10 attacks directed at Libyan, Iranian, and Iraqi political exiles were carried out in order to silence or intimidate exiled opponents of these regimes. Libya and Iran are particularly active in these

7

types of state-directed intimidation campaigns. These opposition elements, however, occasionally retaliate against Libya, Iran, or Iraq — sometimes with the support or encouragement of other Arab states which also oppose these regimes. For example, Iranian dissidents and former supporters of the Shah of Iran are believed to have been responsible for five attacks against Iranian targets in Western Europe in 1985. Iraqi dissidents, operating under the name of the "Organization of the Iraqi Islamic Vengeance," and with the suspected support of either Syria or Iran, carried out two attacks against Iraqi interests in Nicosia. Moreover, Libyan opposition elements — occasionally with the suspected support of Iraq, which obviously opposes Libya's support for Iran — carried out six attacks last year against Libyan targets in Western Europe.

The catalyst for the seven attacks against Jordanian targets and the four against Syrian targets appears to have been the Jordanian — PLO agreement signed on February 11, 1985 in Amman. This agreement, which sought a negotiated Middle East peace settlement, was opposed by Syria. Syria was also displeased with Jordan for re-establishing diplomatic ties with Egypt in September 1984 and for agreeing to host the Palestine National Council (PNC) meeting in Amman on November 22, 1984. President Assad had warned Arafat not to convene a meeting of the PNC. The February 1985 agreement and the November 1984 PNC meeting most likely provoked Syria into contracting with the Abu Nidal group to attack Jordanian targets, as a show of "displeasure." The Abu Nidal group has apparently been based in Damascus since November 1983 when the Iraqi government banished it from Baghdad. This symbiotic relationship between the Abu Nidal organization and Syria consisted of Syria providing the group with resources and safehaven and the Abu Nidal group in turn providing Syria with a "terrorist option" when developing and implementing its foreign policy. Ironically, this is the same type of relationship the Abu Nidal group had with Iraq when Baghdad used the group to attack Syrian targets in the mid-1970s.[5]

The Abu Nidal organization has a history of creating commando names for specific terrorist campaigns. The name "Black June" was used in the late 1970s when the group attacked Syrian targets; the "Arab Revolutionary Brigades" was used when the group hit moderate Arab states like Kuwait, the United Arab Emirates, and Jordan; the "Revolutionary Organization of Socialist Moslems" has been used primarily against British targets; and the more formal name for the Abu Nidal organization, "Fatah-Revolutionary Council," is used primarily in attacks against Israeli targets. For the Syrian-backed terrorist campaign against Jordan, and to a lesser extent against moderates within the PLO, the Abu Nidal group used the name "Black September Organization" or BSO — a parody on the name used by the PLO when it sanctioned terrorist attacks in the early 1970s.[6] Abu Nidal's use of this commando name first appeared on December 4, 1984 — two weeks after the start of the Palestine National Council meeting in Amman — when the BSO killed a Jordanian political counselor in Bucharest. The BSO attack communiqué denounced Jordan for plotting with PLO leader Yassir Arafat.

After the signing of the February 1985 PLO/Jordanian agreement in Amman, BSO attacks against Jordanian targets increased. In March, the BSO attacked Jordanian airline offices in Rome, Athens, and Nicosia. In April, anti-tank rockets were fired at the Jordanian embassy in Rome and at a Jordanian airliner in Athens. In July, the BSO carried out a machine gun and grenade attack on the Jordanian airlines office in Madrid, and assassinated a Jordanian diplomat in Ankara. In September, the BSO killed a supporter of Yassir Arafat in Athens. This has been the last attack carried out by the BSO. The PLO-Jordanian agreement was eroding. King Hussein went to Damascus on December 30-31 for discussions with President Assad. On February 19, 1986, Jordan ended political coordination with the PLO in working towards a Middle East peace settlement. The PLO/Jordanian accord no longer threatened Syria's premier position in Lebanon, and the BSO attacks against Jordan stopped — for now.

It was previously stated that there were four terrorist attacks registered against Syrian targets in 1985. In April, the Syrian airline office in Rome was bombed and in Geneva, a bomb exploded in a vehicle driven by the Syrian Chargé and another bomb was found in front of a Syrian diplomat's residence. In June, a bomb was found outside the Syrian embassy in London. These attacks appear to be directed against Syria by PLO elements in retaliation for the Syrian-backed Abu Nidal attacks against Jordan and PLO moderates. As a result, the Syrian/Jordanian/PLO conflict in late 1984 and 1985 was the catalyst for 12 terrorist attacks involving Jordanian, Syrian, and PLO targets in Western Europe. This is a classic example of a Middle Eastern political feud, escalating to the terrorist mode, and spilling over into Western Europe.

It should also be pointed out that there were six terrorist attacks in Western Europe in 1985 against moderate PLO members and supporters of Arafat. One of these attacks was claimed by Abu Nidal's "Black September Organization." Another was claimed by the "Eagles of the Palestinian Revolution" — a Syrian-backed Palestinian group. Consequently, these two attacks were most likely linked to the above-mentioned Syrian/Jordanian/PLO conflict. The remaining four attacks were probably carried out by dissidents from Arafat's "Fatah" organization and other anti-Arafat elements from the "Palestine National Salvation Front," a Syrian supported counterweight to the PLO.

Attacks on Israeli and Jewish Targets

Attacks against Israeli and Jewish targets are a standard part of Middle Eastern terrorist activities in Western Europe. Stringent security measures in Israel make it difficult for these groups to carry out attacks in Israel so Western Europe is an attractive alternative. The number of attacks per year varies, depending primarily on the number of "trigger events" which take place in the Middle East. Any increase in the number of attacks can usually be attributed to specific events such as the Israeli military incursion into Lebanon, the massacres at the Sabra and Shatila refugee camps in 1982 or Israeli retaliatory bombing attacks against PLO

Summer 1986

targets. The unusually high number of attacks against Israeli and Jewish
targets in 1985 can be traced to several events which took place in the
Middle East. Of the 13 attacks which took place in 1985, the author
believes that six of these attacks were terrorist retaliations for three
specific events: (1) the Israeli bombing on July 21, 1985 of a small
Lebanese village called Kabrihka; (2) the Israeli interception in late
August 1985 of two yachts off the northern coast of Israel which contained 13 Fatah and "Force 17" terrorists; and (3) the Israeli bombing of the
PLO's headquarters in Tunis on October 1, 1985. The six attacks and
these three events combined to produce a dialectical spiral of violence
between Israel and Middle Eastern terrorist groups. The October 7, 1985
hijacking of the Italian cruise ship "Achille Lauro" by the Palestine
Liberation Front (PLF) and the subsequent death of Leon Klinghoffer,
an American citizen, were other, unfortunate by-products of this spiral
of violence.

Attacks Against Western Targets

The third and last targeting sector for Middle Eastern terrorist
groups is "Western targets," that is, attacks against U.S. and West
European facilities and personnel. Of the 75 terrorist incidents carried
out by Middle Eastern groups in Europe in 1985, 20 were directed at
Western targets. It was these attacks that attracted the most publicity for
the groups, caused the most casualties, and had the greatest impact on
the political and security environment in Western Europe. The primary
reason that these attacks had more of an impact on the security environment in Western Europe than those directed at Arab, Palestinian, Israeli,
and Jewish targets, is that the attacks aimed at Western targets were
more indiscriminate in nature and clearly designed to cause mass
casualties. These attacks caused 45 deaths, or 66% of all fatalities caused
by Middle Eastern attacks in 1985, and 439 injuries or 83% of the injury
total. The objective of these attacks was to cause shock and then to induce fear. This in turn was to translate into pressure on the European
countries to release imprisoned Middle Eastern terrorists. This was the
primary motive for 13 of the 20 attacks directed at Western targets.

These 13 attacks involved the following terrorist campaigns designed to release imprisoned comrades:

1.   Three incidents directed at Swiss targets by suspected PLO
terrorist elements to pressure the Swiss to release two Palestinian terrorists arrested on April 26, shortly after bombing two
Syrian diplomatic targets in Geneva.

2.   Two attacks against French targets in Paris by suspected
Iranian-backed Shi'ite groups to force the French to release the
terrorists involved in the attempted assassination of former Iranian Prime Minister Bakhtiar in Paris in 1980.

3.   The hijacking of TWA Flight 847 out of Athens by
Lebanese Shi'ite terrorists to force the U.S. to put pressure on
Israelis to release some 700 Lebanese Shi'ite Moslem prisoners.

4.   The December 27 attack on the airport in Vienna by Abu

Nidal to pressure the Austrian government into releasing three Abu Nidal members arrested in Vienna for a 1981 attack on a Vienna synagogue.

5. Four attacks by the Abu Nidal group, operating under the name of the "Revolutionary Organization of Socialist Moslems," against British targets in Greece, Spain, and Italy in order to force the British to release the three Abu Nidal terrorists being held for the attempted assassination of the Israeli ambassador in London in 1982.

6. Two attacks by the Abu Nidal group against Italian targets in Italy in order to pressure the Italian government into releasing an Abu Nidal member arrested in Rome in April 1985 for firing an anti-tank rocket at the Jordanian embassy and because of Italy's request to the Greek government to extradite an Abu Nidal member for the October 1982 attack on a Rome synagogue. Both attacks, the Café de Paris bombing in September and the attack on Fiumicino airport in December, had secondary objectives. The Café de Paris attack was also aimed at the British and the U.S., and the Fiumicino attack was also directed at Israel and the U.S.

The remaining seven attacks directed at Western targets in Western Europe in 1985 were either carried out for other motives, such as support for Iran in the Iran-Iraq war or in retaliation for the Israeli bombing of a small village in southern Lebanon, or were simply not claimed. In fact, there were four attacks in 1985 which have not been attributed to any specific Middle Eastern group or state. However, it is generally agreed that Middle Eastern groups were involved. The first took place on April 12 when a bomb exploded in the El Descanso restaurant near the Torrejon air base outside the Madrid. This particular restaurant is frequented by U.S. military personnel and their dependents. Eighteen Spaniards were killed and 82 persons were injured, including 15 Americans. Several groups, including the "Islamic Jihad" organization, claimed credit for the bombing. However, no viable claim has been received. The second unclaimed incident took place on June 19 when a bomb detonated in the check-in area of the Frankfurt international airport. Three people, including two children, were killed and 42 others injured. Although some 20 groups have claimed credit for the attack, no viable claim has been received.

Another attack occurred on July 1 when a bomb exploded in the transit luggage section of Fiumicino airport in Rome. Twelve people were injured in this bombing. No terrorist group claimed credit for this attack. The possibility exists that in both the Frankfurt and Rome incidents, the bombs detonated prematurely. The targets may not have been the airports but aircraft departing these airports. A fourth unclaimed attack took place on November 24 when a car bomb exploded in a U.S. military commissary area in Frankfurt. Some 36 people, including 32 Americans were injured during this attack. Once again, no group claimed credit, but Middle Eastern terrorists are the primary suspects.

11

Summer 1986

Of all the terrorist developments which took place in 1985, the intensified activities of Middle Eastern terrorists against "Western" targets in
Western Europe was the most significant. This assessment is based on
several factors:

1.   1985 marked a dramatic increase in the number of attacks
against "Western" targets and in the casualties caused by these
attacks.[7] In 1984, only 6 attacks took place against "Western"
targets which resulted in 2 deaths and 26 injuries. In 1985, there
were 20 attacks, 45 deaths and 439 injuries. The attacks last
year clearly indicated a trend towards more indiscriminate attacks designed to cause mass casualties.

2.   There was a significant increase in the number of attacks
directed at U.S. targets. In 1984, there was only one attack carried out against a U.S. target. This was the attempted assassination of the U.S. Consul General in Strasbourg on March 26 by
the Lebanese Armed Revolutionary Faction. In 1985, 5 attacks
were recorded, causing eight U.S. deaths and 74 injuries. The
five attacks were: the June 14 hijacking of TWA Flight 847 out
of Athens; the bombing of a TWA office in Madrid on July 1;
the July 22 bombing of the Northwest Orient airline office in
Copenhagen; the car bombing at a U.S. military shopping area
in Frankfurt on November 24; and the attack at the El Al and
TWA ticket counters at Rome airport on December 27. These
attacks signal a trend of increasing Middle East terrorist attacks
against U.S. targets in Western Europe.

3.   The attacks by Middle Eastern groups against "Western"
targets in 1985 signaled the beginning of a terrorist campaign by
certain groups to focus on a perceived "Achilles heel" of West
European governments — tourism.[8] One of the groups, the
Abu Nidal organization, implied as much in its communiqués.
After the September 16 grenade attack on the Café de Paris on
the Via Veneto in Rome, an Abu Nidal group warned tourists,
especially Arabs, to stay away from Britain, Spain and Italy to
avoid "operations by our heroic strugglers." All three countries are holding Abu Nidal terrorists. This warning was
repeated after the group bombed the British Airways office in
Rome on September 25, as a communiqué advised "tourists to
avoid British, Spanish, and Italian institutions because they will
be targets of our operations." These warnings were possible indicators that attacks, similar to the airport incidents in Rome
and Vienna, were being planned.

Middle Eastern terrorist activity has been a security and political
problem for Western Europe governments since the early 1970s when
Palestinian airplane hijackings dominated the terrorist scene and the
massacre at the 1972 Olympics in Munich testified to the bloody and
desperate nature of Middle Eastern terrorism. Over the years, the threat
of Middle Eastern terrorism in Western Europe has generally oscillated
between the low and moderate levels with an occasional peak into the

high level. Such peaks are most often triggered by a particularly lethal or well-publicized Middle Eastern terrorist attack, such as the Carlos-led raid on the OPEC Ministerial meeting in Vienna in 1975, the seizure of the Iranian embassy in London in October 1980, the attack on the Rue Copernic synagogue in Paris in October 1980, the Carlos threat to the French government in February 1982, and the massacre at the "Jo Goldenberg" restaurant in Paris in August 1982.

In general, Middle Eastern attacks in Western Europe have been directed at other Arab or Palestinian targets or against Israeli or Jewish targets. (See chart #2.) Historically, there have been few attacks against Western targets in Western Europe. In fact, only 28 attacks were recorded during 1980-84. However, the 20 attacks which took place in 1985 indicate that these groups are beginning to concentrate their efforts more on Western targets. Moreover, it appears that these groups may be intentionally designing their attacks to scare tourists away from certain countries in Western Europe. This is most likely not a targeting aberration, but a signal of a dangerous and growing trend.

ACTIVITY IN 1986

The trend toward more indiscriminate attacks by Middle Eastern terrorist groups in Western Europe which began in 1985 has continued into the first six months of 1986. In February and March, a group calling itself the "Committee of Solidarity with Arab and Middle Eastern Political Prisoners in Western Europe" carried out seven indiscriminate bombing attacks in the Paris area which caused two deaths and over 67 injuries.[9] These attacks were directed at stores on the Champs-Elysées and a Paris to Lyon train. Bombs were also found and defused on the Eiffel Tower and in a crowded Paris metro station. The purpose of these attacks was to pressure the French government into releasing three terrorists, one of whom is the suspected leader of the group responsible for the February and March incidents. It would appear that certain Middle Eastern groups have come to realize that they can put more pressure on a West European country by carrying out indiscriminate bombings in the capital of that country than by kidnapping its citizens in Lebanon.

On April 2, a bomb exploded aboard a TWA flight over Athens. Four Americans were killed, including an infant, and six were injured. A group calling itself the "Arab Revolutionary Cells — Al Kassam's Revolutionary Cells" claimed responsibility for the attack. This group claimed that the attack was in retaliation for the March 24 Gulf of Sidra incident in which U.S. Navy planes, on maneuvers in international waters, responded to Libyan missile attacks by attacking Libyan radar installations and sinking several Libyan vessels. Middle Eastern terrorists retaliated against on April 5 when a large bomb exploded in the "La Belle" disco in West Berlin, a place frequented by U.S. servicemen. Three people were killed, including two American servicemen, and 230 were injured. Seventy-two Americans were among the injured. This attack was linked directly to Libya.[10] On the same day, two Libyan diplomats were ordered to leave France because, according to a Ministry

13

of Interior spokesman, "they were in contact with individuals likely to commit attacks on American interests in France." Press reports indicated that one of the targets of these planned attacks was the visa section at the U.S. Embassy in Paris.[11] The U.S. responded in self-defense to these continued actions by Libya to plan and carry out terrorist operations against U.S. and West European targets, and on April 14-15 carried out punitive air strikes against terrorist-related targets in Libya.

Although Libya was clearly implicated in an attempted terrorist attack against a U.S. Air Force officers' club in Ankara on April 18, three days after the U.S. air strikes, this attack was probably planned before the air strikes, during the period when the attacks on the La Belle disco and the U.S. visa section in Paris were being planned.[12] Since April 15, there has been very little Libyan-directed or supported terrorist activity recorded in Western Europe. Other Middle Eastern terrorist activity, however, has continued in the region. There have been 11 Middle Eastern terrorist attacks in Western Europe from April 15 to July 1. The most significant incidents involved attempts to smuggle explosives aboard Israeli El Al planes in London on April 17 and in Madrid on June 26. Both operations were designed to blow up the El Al planes in mid-air. Both operations were thwarted by El Al security officials during luggage check-in inspections. If these bombs had not been detected, over 350 people would have died. Syria has been linked to both of these incidents.[13] In the attempt at Heathrow airport, an Arab was subsequently arrested who claimed that he had the support of the Syrian embassy in London. In the Madrid attempt, the Arab who was later arrested claimed to be a member of the Abu Musa group — an anti-Arafat dissident group supported by Syria. Moreover, on July 5, the Abu Musa group claimed responsibility for the Madrid attempt and also demanded that the Spanish government release the captured terrorist, calling him one of their "freedom fighters."[14]

The other nine Middle Eastern attacks after April 15 consisted of: (1) the previously mentioned Libyan-supported attempt on the U.S. Air Force officers' club on April 18; (2) the April 24 bombing of a British airways office in London (a suspected retaliatory attack for British support during the April 15 air strikes); (3) the April 25 grenade attack on a Saudi Arabian airline office in Vienna; (4) the April 25 attempted grenade attack on a Kuwaiti airline office in Vienna; (5) the May 2 attempt by a suspected Libyan-funded group to bomb a Bank of America office in Madrid; (6) the June 9 assassination of a top-ranking member of the Democratic Front for the Liberation of Palestine (DFLP) in Athens; (7) the June 19 bombing of the Italian Chamber of Commerce Office in Athens; (8) the June 19 attempted bombing of the Italian consulate in Athens (these June 19 attacks were most likely triggered by the start of the "Achille Lauro" hijacking trial in Genoa on June 18); and (9) the June 21 attempt to launch two anti-armor rockets at the Iraqi embassy in Vienna.

From January 1 to July 1, 1986, there have been 25 Middle Eastern terrorist incidents in Western Europe.[15] Fourteen took place before the April 15 air strikes on Libya and 11 occurred afterwards. A brief survey of the most significant of these attacks indicates that the trend toward more indiscriminate attacks by Middle Eastern terrorist groups has continued into 1986. The breakdown of the targets of these attacks also indicates that the trend toward more Middle Eastern attacks on Western targets has continued into the first half of 1986. Sixteen of these attacks were directed at U.S. and West European targets. Two were aimed at Israeli targets, and seven directed at other Arab or Palestinian targets. This would appear to confirm a trend which was started in 1985. For example, of the 158 Middle East terrorist incidents recorded in Western Europe from 1980-1984 (a five-year period), 102 or 65% were directed at other Arab or Palestinian targets, 28 or 17% were directed at Israeli or Jewish targets, 22 or 13% were directed at West European targets, and 6 or 5% were directed at U.S. targets. In comparison, of the 101 attacks recorded from January 1985 to July 1, 1986 (an 18-month period), 50 or 49% of the total were directed at Arab or Palestinian targets, 15 or 15% at Israeli or Jewish targets, 26 or 26% at West European targets, and 10 or 10% at U.S. targets.[16] While the attacks by Middle Eastern groups continue to be aimed primarily at other Arab targets, there is a discernible shift toward more attacks on West European and U.S. targets.[17]

CONCLUSIONS AND PROJECTIONS

Middle Eastern terrorist activity in Western Europe will continue to be a major security concern for Western Europe and the United States in the immediate future. The Middle Eastern groups and states involved in the terrorist activity which took place during 1985 and the first six months of 1986 have given no indications that they are prepared to stop their activities in Western Europe. The region still has operational advantages over the Middle East or other regions. As long as there are inter-Arab conflicts, intra-Palestinian rivalries, Arab disagreement over a Middle East peace settlement, radical Middle Eastern states and groups which oppose the existence of Israel, Middle Eastern terrorists imprisoned in West European jails, and U.S. political and military involvement in the Middle East — especially U.S. support for Israel — there will be Middle Eastern terrorist activity in Western Europe. The political alliances may change and terrorist groups like the Abu Nidal organization may shift clients or patron states, but the use of political terrorism to settle Middle Eastern feuds and conflicts and to influence the Middle East policies of West European states will continue. The level of this activity will alternate between temporary lulls and periods of intensified activity. The lulls should not disarm us and the intensified activity should not surprise us.

After the April 15 U.S. air strikes on Libya it was generally agreed that there would be a period of increased terrorist activity directed either at the United States or some West European countries, especially Great Britain for its direct support of the U.S. raid. These retaliatory attacks did not take place, at least not at the level which was expected. There are reasons for this muted Middle Eastern terrorist response in the West European arena. First, the U.S. raid most likely caused some political confusion within the Qadaffi regime. This confusion prevented any type of well-planned terrorist response to the U.S. air strikes. Second, the post-raid crackdown on Libyan "diplomatic" activities by West European countries no doubt disrupted the Libyan terrorist logistical infrastructure in the region.[18] Third, the linking of Syria by the press to the bombing of the Arab-German club in West Berlin on March 30 and the April 17 attempt to blow up an El Al plane out of London's Heathrow airport has probably caused Syria to pull back temporarily from supporting terrorist activity in Western Europe. Fourth, the increased indigenous terrorist activity in June and July by groups like Action Directe, the Red Army Faction, and the Basque separatist group ETA-M most likely caused some Middle Eastern groups to postpone any operations in specific countries.[19] There appears to be a correlation between periods of increased indigenous terrorist activity in Western Europe and the operational inactivity of Middle Eastern groups and *vice versa*. This is probably linked to the fact that security measures, police searches, and identity checks at border crossings and airports are intensified after bursts of terrorist activity, by either indigenous or Middle Eastern groups, thus making it difficult for other groups to operate.

These four negative factors which have combined to restrain Middle Eastern terrorist activity in Western Europe since the April 15 raid are temporary restraints. In time, the Libyans may develop an appropriate terrorist response to the April 15 raid. Middle Eastern groups may "plug in" to new logistical infrastructures in Western Europe. Moreover, it is possible that some of these groups may foster new ties with indigenous European groups in order to take advantage of the logistical aid these groups could provide. It is doubtful that Syria will permanently sheath its terrorist sword. It will continue to support terrorist attacks against Israeli and Jewish targets and, when the advancement of Syrian political objectives dictates it, against other Arab, European or U.S. targets.

The April 15 U.S. air strikes on Libya did not alleviate the Middle Eastern terrorist threat in Western Europe, for there are many components to this threat. Libya, although a major factor in this threat, is only one of many. The U.S. raid, combined with the subsequent security crackdown on Libyan People's Bureaus in Western Europe, has shown the Libyan regime that further support of terrorist activity against U.S. and West European targets will no longer be cost-free. A price will have to be paid. It is still too early to say if Libya will be willing to pay that price in the future. What can be said is that the U.S. raid has temporarily restrained Libyan support for terrorist activity and most likely caused it to re-evaluate any further support. As a limited form of negative reinforcement, the U.S. raid on April 15 has so far been successful. It is important to remember, however, that there are still other components of the Middle Eastern terrorist threat which must be dealt with. Some of these components are Middle Eastern states. Some are radical Palestinian terrorist groups. Some are deep-rooted, complex, Middle East political issues, emanating from conflicts whose resolutions must be achieved in the Middle East, not in Western Europe or the United States. These other components of the Middle East terrorist threat may be more difficult to contend with than the Libyan factor.

CHART 1

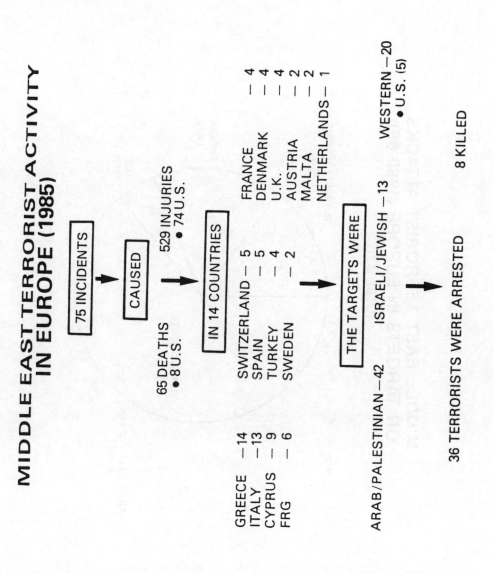

MIDDLE EAST TERRORIST ACTIVITY IN EUROPE (1985)

75 INCIDENTS → CAUSED → 65 DEATHS ● 8 U.S. 529 INJURIES ● 74 U.S.

IN 14 COUNTRIES

GREECE —14
ITALY —13
CYPRUS — 9
FRG — 6

SWITZERLAND — 5
SPAIN — 5
TURKEY — 4
SWEDEN — 2

FRANCE — 4
DENMARK — 4
U.K. — 4
AUSTRIA — 2
MALTA — 2
NETHERLANDS — 1

THE TARGETS WERE

ARAB/PALESTINIAN —42   ISRAELI/JEWISH —13   WESTERN —20 ● U.S. (5)

36 TERRORISTS WERE ARRESTED   8 KILLED

CHART 2

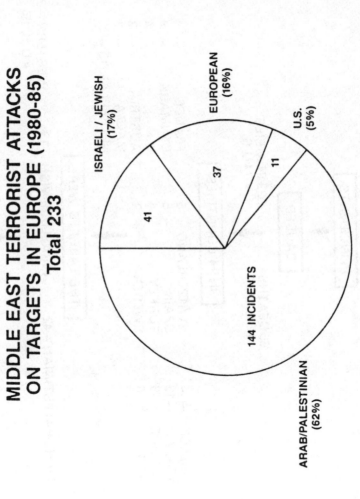

MIDDLE EAST TERRORIST ATTACKS
ON TARGETS IN EUROPE (1980-85)
Total 233

ISRAELI / JEWISH
(17%)

EUROPEAN
(16%)

U.S.
(5%)

41

37

11

144 INCIDENTS

ARAB/PALESTINIAN
(62%)

APPENDIX I

Selected List of Terrorist Incidents in Western Europe
from 1985 to July 1, 1986 Attributed to
Middle Eastern Groups

1985

January 13	**Rome:** A Libyan diplomat was shot and killed.
January 31	**Nicosia:** A Palestinian businessman was shot and wounded in his office.
February 6	**Frankfurt:** A bomb exploded in an Iranian bank.
February 12	**Limassol, Cyprus:** A bomb is defused outside an Israeli shipping company.
February 23	**Paris:** A bomb exploded outside the Marks and Spencer department store. One person was killed and 15 were injured.
February 27	**Madrid:** A bomb exploded in a Jewish-owned travel agency. Five people were injured.
February 28	**Vienna:** A former Libyan ambassador was shot and wounded.
March 1	**Rome:** A Libyan emigre businessman was shot and killed in his office.
March 17	**Groedinge, Sweden:** An Iraqi defector, reportedly a former Iraqi intelligence officer, was murdered.
March 21	**Rome:** A hand grenade was thrown into a Jordanian airline office.
March 21	**Athens:** A hand grenade was thrown into a Jordanian airline office. Three people were injured.
March 21	**Nicosia:** A hand grenade was thrown into a Jordanian airline office.
March 29	**Paris:** A bomb exploded in a movie theatre sponsoring a Jewish film festival.
April 1	**Rome:** A Syrian airline office was bombed. Three people were injured.
April 2	**Nicosia:** A Libyan emigre businessman was shot and killed.
April 3	**Rome:** An anti-tank rocket was fired at the Jordanian embassy.
April 4	**Athens:** An anti-tank rocket was fired at a Jordanian airliner taking off from Athens rocket.
April 6	**Bonn:** A gunman shot and killed a Libyan dissident. Two Germans were also wounded.
April 12	**Madrid:** A bomb exploded at the El Descanso restaurant, just outside Madrid. Eighteen Spaniards were killed and 82 people were injured, including 15 Americans.

19

Summer 1986

April 13	**Aachen, West Germany**: A Moroccan citizen was shot and killed.
April 26	**Geneva**: A bomb exploded in a vehicle driven by a Syrian diplomat. A second bomb was found near another Syrian diplomat's residence.
April 26	**Geneva**: A bomb exploded in front of a Libyan airlines office.
June 2	**Geneva**: A bomb exploded at the Geneva railway station. A second bomb was defused at the Geneva airport.
June 3	**London**: A bomb was found outside the Syrian embassy.
June 5	**Athens**: There was an attempted assassination of a member of the Palestine Liberation Organization (PLO).
June 6	**London**: A bomb exploded at a Jewish-owned travel agency.
June 14	**Athens**: A TWA plane was hijacked to Beirut. One American was killed.
June 15	**London**: A bomb exploded near the "Swiss center."
June 19	**Genoa, Italy**: A bomb exploded next to an Israeli shipping firm.
June 19	**Frankfurt**: A bomb exploded at Frankfurt airport. Three people were killed and 42 injured.
July 1	**Rome**: A bomb exploded in the transit luggage section at Fiumicino airport. Twelve people were injured.
July 1	**Madrid**: A bomb exploded at British airways and TWA offices. One person was killed and 24 injured.
July 1	**Madrid**: The Jordanian airlines office was attacked by terrorists with machine guns and hand grenades. Two people were injured.
July 17	**Nicosia**: A bomb exploded in the home of a PLO representative.
July 22	**Copenhagen**: Bombs exploded at the Northwest Orient airline office and a synagogue. One person was killed and 27 injured.
July 24	**Ankara, Turkey**: A Jordanian diplomat was shot and killed.
August 8	**Glyfada, Greece**: A bomb exploded in the bar of the London hotel. Thirteen people, mostly British tourists, were injured.
August 9	**Bonn**: A letter bomb exploded at the Iranian embassy. One person was injured.
August 18	**Istanbul**: A former Colonel in the Iranian police was shot and killed.
August 27	**Istanbul**: A bomb exploded outside the El Al airlines office.

September 3	**Glyfada, Greece**: Hand grenades were thrown into the Glyfada hotel. Nineteen British tourists were injured.
September 15	**Copenhagen**: Bombs exploded in front of a Jewish food store and a travel agency specializing in trips in Israel. Twelve people were injured.
September 16	**Rome**: Hand grenades were thrown at tourists sitting at the Café de Paris, an outdoor cafe on the Via Veneto. Forty people were injured, including 8 Americans.
September 18	**Athens**: An Arab publisher and personal friend of Yassir Arafat was shot and killed near his office.
September 24	**Stockholm**: A bomb exploded in front of the Iranian ambassador's residence.
September 25	**Rome**: A bomb exploded in a British airways office. One Italian was killed and 14 injured.
September 25	**Larnaca, Cyprus**: Palestinian terrorists killed three Israelis during an attack on a small boat in the harbor.
September 30	**Amsterdam**: A bomb exploded next to the El Al ticket office.
October 6	**Athens**: A Libyan emigre businessman was shot and wounded.
October 7	**Athens**: Three bombs exploded at Libyan-related targets: a Libyan airline office, the Libyan consulate, and a car owned by a Libyan diplomat.
October 7	**Genoa**: The Achille Lauro cruise ship, out of Genoa, was hijacked in the Mediterranean sea by Palestinian terrorists. One American was killed.
October 9	**Barcelona, Spain**: The bodies of two Israeli seamen were found. The PLO terrorist group, "Force 17," claimed credit for the murders.
October 21	**Athens**: A Libyan emigre was shot and killed.
November 5	**Rome**: A bomb was found hidden in a calculator sent as a gift to the Iranian ambassador to the Vatican.
November 8	**Nicosia**: A bomb exploded outside the Iraqi airlines office. A second bomb exploded under the car of the airline office Manager. He was killed.
November 8	**Thessaloniki, Greece**: A hand grenade exploded outside the room of two Palestinian students.
November 18	**Athens**: An Egyptian clerk was shot and killed.
November 23	**Athens/Valleta, Malta**: An Egypt Air plane was hijacked during its flight from Athens to Cairo. The plane was diverted to Malta. The hijackers killed two people, including an American woman, and wounded five others, including two Americans.
November 24	**Frankfurt**: A car packed with explosives explodes in the U.S. military post exchange. Thirty-six people were injured, including 33 Americans.

November 25   **London:** A letter bomb exploded inside the Iranian consulate. One person was injured.

December 7   **Paris:** Firebombs exploded in two French department stores. Thirty-five people were injured.

December 12   **Valletta, Malta:** A bomb exploded at the Libyan cultural center.

December 27   **Vienna:** Terrorists attacked the El Al counter at the airport. Three people were killed, and 31 injured, including 2 Americans.

December 27   **Rome:** Terrorists attack the El Al and TWA check-in counters at the airport. Sixteen people were killed, including 5 Americans. Seventy-four were injured (10 Americans).

December 28   **Nicosia:** There was an attempt to booby-trap the car of the PLO representative.

1986

February 3   **Paris:** A firebomb exploded in a shopping mall on the Champs-Elysées. Eight people were injured.

February 3   **Paris:** A bomb was found and defused on the third level of the Eiffel Tower.

February 4   **Paris:** A firebomb exploded in a crowded bookstore. Four people were injured.

February 5   **Paris:** A firebomb exploded in a shopping mall. Twenty-six people were injured.

February 16   **Rome:** The owner of an anti-Qadaffi radio station was shot and wounded.

March 17   **Paris:** A Paris to Lyon express train was bombed. Nine people were injured.

March 20   **Paris:** A bomb exploded in a shopping gallery on the Champs-Elysées. Two people were killed and 32 injured.

March 20   **Paris:** A bomb, wrapped with nails, was found and defused in a crowded metro station.

March 30   **West Berlin:** A bomb exploded in a German-Arab club. Seven people were injured.

April 2   **Athens:** A bomb exploded aboard a TWA flight over Athens. Four Americans were killed and six injured.

April 3   **Paris:** A bomb exploded outside the home of an Iranian opposition leader.

April 5   **West Berlin:** A bomb exploded in the La Belle disco. Three people were killed, including two U.S. servicemen. Over 230 people were injured, including 72 Americans.

April 7   **Stockholm:** A bomb exploded at a Northwest Orient airline office.

April 10   **Lisbon:** A bomb exploded in front of the Air France ticket office.

April 17   **London**: Security agents at El Al airlines intercepted a hidden bomb in the carry on luggage of an Irish girl at Heathrow airport.

April 18   **Ankara**: Four Libyans were arrested near a U.S. Air Force officers' club. One was carrying a travel bag filled with six hand grenades.

April 24   **London**: A bomb exploded at an office which housed the British airways and American airlines ticket offices.

April 25   **Vienna**: A hand grenade was thrown at the Saudi Arabian airlines office. Another grenade was found outside the Kuwaiti airlines office.

May 2   **Madrid**: Two terrorists were arrested attempting to place a bomb in a Bank of America office. The terrorists were linked to a Middle East group.

June 9   **Athens**: A top level member of the Democratic Front for the Liberation of Palestine was shot and killed.

June 19   **Athens**: A bomb exploded outside the Italian chamber of commerce office. A second bomb was found outside the Italian consulate.

June 21   **Vienna**: Two anti-tank rockets were found aimed at the Iraqi embassy.

June 26   **Madrid**: A bomb, intended to be smuggled aboard an El Al plane, exploded at the luggage check-in area for El Al airlines. Thirteen people were injured.

Endnotes

* The opinions expressed in this paper are solely the author's and should not be interpreted in any way as representing the views or policies of the U.S. Department of State.

1. This figure includes explosive devices discovered by police before they could detonate and devices which failed to detonate due to mechanical failure. The majority of these attacks were either claimed by a Middle Eastern group or subsequent investigation linked a Middle Eastern group to an attack. Some incidents, however, were attributed to a Middle Eastern group through "analysis," that is, the suspected link was made based on the target of the attack, method of operation, area of operation, and the timing of the attack (i.e., did it occur just after a "trigger event" in the Middle East?).

   The annual figures for the number of Middle Eastern terrorist attacks in Western Europe and the fatalities and injuries caused are:

	Incidents	Fatalities	Injuries
1980	33	28	65
1981	20	11	214
1982	34	23	248
1983	24	10	113
1984	47	18	63
1985	75	65	529

   The above figures (based on the author's files) are subject to minor changes as further investigation and subsequent arrests lead to responsibility for past attacks which, at the time, were not attributed to Middle Eastern terrorist groups.

2. Xavier Raufer, "Terrorisme: Les Reseaux Transnationaux Venus Du Moyen-Orient" (Terrorism: The Transnational Networks out of the Middle East), *Le Debat*, 39 (March-May 1986), p. 180.

3. Based on a report issued by the U.S. Department of State in Washington, D.C. on January 9, 1986 entitled "Libya Under Qadaffi: A Pattern of Aggression," pp. 7-11, and the author's article "Political Terrorism in Western Europe: Some Themes and Variations" in Yonah Alexander and Kenneth Myers, *Terrorism in Europe* (Croom Helm: London: 1982), p. 61.

4. This figure *does not* include the 58 passengers killed during the Egyptian counter-terrorist attack on the hijacked Egyptian Air plane in Valletta, Malta on November 24, 1985. For comparative purposes, indigenous terrorist groups in Western Europe (including the IRA and the ETA) were responsible for 133 deaths in 1985. If the IRA and the ETA were excluded, the figure would be 42.

5. The Abu Nidal organization used the commando name of "Black June" (after June 1976 when Syria fought the Palestinians in Lebanon) to attack several Syrian targets during the latter half of 1976. For example, on September 26, Black June terrorists attacked a hotel in Damascus causing 4 deaths and 34 injuries. Three of the terrorists were captured and publicly hanged in Damascus the next day. On October 11 the Syrian embassies in Rome and Islamabad were attacked by Black June. On December 1, Black June terrorists attempted to assassinate the Syrian Foreign Minister in Damascus. The Abu Nidal organization was based in Baghdad at the time of these attacks. For an excellent article on the Abu Nidal group and its relationships with radical Middle East states, see Aaron D. Miller "A Portrait of Abu Nidal: The Man Who Loves to Kill Americans" in the *Washington Post*, March 30, 1986, p. D1.

6. It is possible that the Abu Nidal's use of the commando name "Black September Organization" is a commemoration of the September 17, 1982 massacre in the Sabra and Shatila refugee camps in Lebanon.

7. The number of Middle Eastern terrorist attacks against Western targets in Western Europe from 1980 to July 1, 1986 is as follows:

1980	1
1981	4
1982	8
1983	10
1984	5
1985	20
1986 (as of 7/1)	16

8. With the concurrent fall of the dollar it is difficult to assess accurately the effect of recent Middle Eastern terrorist attacks in Western Europe on tourism. However, it would appear that these attacks have had a major, negative impact on tourist travel to Western Europe, especially the Mediterranean countries — at least during the June 1985 to June 1986 period. Since the hijacking of TWA Flight 847 in June 1985, there has been a dramatic increase in press and magazine articles and television programs dealing with the effect of terrorism on tourism. Various polls indicate that Americans are afraid of traveling to Western Europe. A recent *Newsweek* poll taken between March 26 and 27, 1986 (before the bombing of TWA Flight 840 and the bombing of the disco in West Berlin) indicated that 61% of the Americans interviewed, if they had the opportunity to travel overseas this summer, would refuse to go because of the threat of terrorism. [*Newsweek*, April 7, 1986, p. 23]. See also the article "As U.S. Travel Abroad Declines, Europe Grieves" in the *New York Times*, July 13, 1986, p. 1. However, since the last major Middle Eastern terrorist attack on April 5 — the bombing of the La Belle disco — there has been a three month period of relative calm on the Middle East terrorist front in the Western Europe. There have been recent indications (airline bookings, passport applications) that American tourism may be starting to return to Europe.

9. The "Committee for Solidarity with Arab and Middle East Political Prisoners in Western Europe" is an apparent alias for the Lebanese Armed Revolutionary Faction (LARF). This is a Lebanese Christian group, tinged with Marxism-Leninism, formed in northern Lebanon in 1980. The LARF has claimed credit for six attacks against U.S. and Israeli diplomats in France from 1981-84. The LARF attempted to assassinate three U.S. diplomats in Paris and Strasbourg, and assassinated a U.S. Army attaché in January 1982 in Paris. There are currently three LARF members imprisoned in France and Italy. The group is ostensibly seeking the release of three terrorists being held in France: George Abdallah, the suspected leader of the LARF; an Armenian terrorist; and a pro-Iranian terrorist who attempted to kill former Iranian Prime Minister Bakhtiar in Paris in 1980. In communiqués issued on March 20 and April 7, the group also demanded that Italy release the two LARF members it is holding or else the group would "make the streets of Rome and its people subject to what is being witnessed in Paris."

10. Speech by President Reagan to the American people on April 14, 1986 from the White House.

11. *Washington Post*, April 19, 1986.

12. Reuter, April 18, 1986; Agence France Presse, April 20, 1986; and an interview with the Turkish Minister of Interior in *Cumhuriyet* (Ankara) on April 25, 1986.

13. *Washington Post*, June 1, 1986, p. 1, and the *New York Times*, July 16, 1986, p. A3.

14. Reuter, July 5, 1986.

15. See Appendix I.

16. See the article by Ennio Caretto in *La Stampa* (Rome), July 11, 1986. Caretto's article is based on comments made by the author to a U.S. Information Agency (USIA) seminar on terrorism, held at the U.S. Department of State on July 9, 1986 for members of the foreign press.

17. This shift is fueled somewhat by the fact that 12 West European countries are currently holding Middle Eastern terrorists in jail. Consider also that terrorists from the Abu Nidal group, one of the most active and dangerous Middle Eastern terrorist groups, are being held in Great Britain, Austria, Greece, Spain, Malta, and Italy. On March 2, 1986, the Abu Nidal organization issued a press release in Damascus on the occasion of welcoming back three members of the group who recently received early releases from prisons in France and Portugal. This press release noted that "the official spokesman renewed greetings to our freed comrades and the promise to the other comrades who continue to suffer exceptional circumstances to make every effort for their imminent return to our ranks and for their freedom."

18. A background paper by the U.S. Department of State (dated July 1, 1986) entitled "European Actions Against Libya's Terrorist Network" notes that West European countries have expelled more than 100 so-called Libyan diplomats and businessmen. The European actions reduced the staff of several key Libyan People's Bureaus (LPB) and imposed travel restrictions of those who remained. The LPB's and Libyan student organizations in Europe form the core of the Libyan terrorist network in the region.

[20]

"Death to America" In Lebanon

by Daniel Pipes

THE UNITED STATES FACES A NEW adversary, the radical fundamentalist Shi'i Muslim. He first appeared with the rise to power of Ayatollah Ruhollah Khomeini in 1978 and has grown more dangerous in subsequent years. The ideology, tactics, and goals make this enemy dissimilar to any encountered in the past. The scope of the radical fundamentalist's ambition poses novel problems; and the intensity of his onslaught against the United States makes solutions urgent.

Initially, problems caused by the radical fundamentalists were confined to Iran. These began during the revolt against the Shah of Iran in 1978, when they took occasional actions against Americans to encourage them to leave. (Best known of the American victims were two employees of Ross Perot's E.D.S., who were thrown in a Tehran jail without charges and eventually rescued by a private team hired by Perot.)

Although most Americans had left Iran by the time Khomeini became its ruler, the few who remained faced increasingly unpleasant circumstances. In particular, the U.S. Embassy in Tehran became the symbol of fundamentalist hostility; seized briefly by Khomeini's followers in February 1979, it was then taken for a se-

Daniel Pipes, *Associate Prof. of Strategy at the U.S. Naval War College, is the author of* Slave Soldiers and Islam *and* In the Path of God: Islam and Political Power. *Editor of the* Harvard Middle East Papers. *Dr. Pipes taught at the Univ. of Chicago and Harvard, and served as Special Advisor to the Counselor of the Dept. of State.*

cond time in November and held for 444 days.

The hostage problem received enormous attention in the United States, but Iran was quickly and gratefully forgotten the instant that specific issue was resolved. Bad memories, limited access, and a barrage of hostile propaganda caused Iran to disappear from the national consciousness. The reverse, however, did not take place; Iranians retained their obsession with the United States. The radical fundamentalists ruling Iran, it soon became apparent, saw the eviction of Americans from Iran as only a first step in a more extensive campaign.

Soon after it came to power, Khomeini's regime began fostering and aiding radical fundamentalist groups in other countries; these have since emerged as a force to be reckoned with in several parts of the Middle East. Foremost are Ad-Da'wa in Iraq, the Islamic Front for the Liberation of Bahrain, and several organizations in Lebanon, including Hizbullah (also known as "The Party of God"), Islamic Amal, and Islamic Jihad. In addition to their efforts to win power for Shi'i fundamentalists, several of these groups have taken up arms against the United States.

Although attempted in many places, this effort succeeded just in Lebanon, for obvious reasons. Lebanon offered the radical fundamentalists, as it had the Palestine Liberation Organization (P.L.O.) a decade earlier, the unique advantage of freedom from state control. Anarchic conditions in Lebanon made it an ideal base for Iranian terror against the United States. With determination, forceful groups could establish themselves in portions of Lebanon and operate as quasi-sovereign bodies.

This fringe of Shi'i groups exploited Lebanon's anarchy to engage in a remarkable sequence of attacks against Americans after April 1983. Principal events include: two bombings of the U.S. embassy in Beirut, on 18 April 1983 and 20 September 1984; one bombing of the embassy in Kuwait, on 12 December 1983; and a plot against the embassy in Rome just barely foiled in November 1984. Fundamentalists destroyed the U.S. Marine barracks in Beirut on 23 October 1983, killing 241 soldiers; they kidnapped one president of the American University of Beirut and held him for a year (17 July 1982-21 July 1983), then assassinated another on 18 January 1984; they abducted at least five Americans off the streets of Beirut between March 1984 and January 1985; and they tortured and murdered two Americans on a hijacked plane in Tehran in early December 1984. They also struck targets of other states, especially those of France and Israel. In the aftermath of almost every incident, a fundamentalist group claimed responsibility for the violence.

These assaults raise three principal questions. What do fundamentalists expect to achieve by attacking Americans? What is Iran's role in the violence? And what steps can the United States government take to protect its citizens?

The Goal: Eradication of Western Civilization

ATTACKS ON THE UNITED STATES ARE intended to achieve nothing less than the complete extirpation of American culture from the Middle East. This is so audacious, it may sound implausible; indeed, the alien nature and ambitious scope of fundamentalist aspirations does make it difficult for many Westerners to take them as seriously as they deserve. But few took the Ayatollah Khomeini seriously when he declared his plans to build an Islamic society in Iran, and he did carry through. If nothing else, the radicals' savage record argues for very close attention to their plans.

Fundamentalists approach public life with two characteristic concerns. First, they draw strict dichotomies in every sphere of life, dividing everything into the Islamic and the non-Islamic, the Muslim and the non-Muslim. This applies, for example, to food, culture, individuals, and governments. Second, thy feel painfully the weight of Muslim decline. Glories of the medieval period, real and imagined, are often conjured up to be compared with the backwardness, poverty, and weakness of today. Confronted with this predicament, fundamentalists are obsessed with the challenge to make God's faithful once again great.

They ascribe the Muslims' tribulations in modern times to misguided efforts at emulating the West. Fundamentalists note that from about the year 1800, many Muslims began to adopt Western practices, hoping to attain what the Europeans had by doing as they did. In the process, of course, these Muslims distanced themselves from Islam, a critical mistake from the fundamentalist point of view, which advocates that Muslims seek solutions in Islam. Muslim supremacy will be regained only with strict adherence to Islamic doctrine and regulations.

But enshrining Islam as a guide to modern life entails complications. Although fundamentalists insist that they are only returning to old ways, the solutions they demand from Islam go far beyond the religion's traditional scope, thus transforming its nature. In particular, they seek Islamic guidance concerning the distribution of economic and political power. Accordingly, fundamentalists turn Islam into an ideology, a full-blown alternative to liberalism, communism, fascism, democracy, and the other ideologies from the West. As one of their leaders succinctly put it, "We are not socialist, we are not capitalist, we are Islamic."

America and West Europe, whose influences have had so wide and deep an impact in Muslim countries, are viewed by fundamentalists as the principal obstacle to the application of the Islamic ideology. Their music, movies, video games, comics, education, literature, and art reach throughout the Muslim world, as do their machines, clothing, foods, and furnishings. Western customs regarding the sexes — such as dancing, dating, mixed bathing, and female employment — break down the divisions required by Islamic precepts. Western banks, oil companies, and other corporations beckon ambitious Muslims.

Fundamentalists regard the ways of the West as seductive and evil, luring believers from the true religion, deceiving and debilitating them. To save Muslims, they strive to remove the temptation of Western civilization. Elimination of the Western, and especially the American, presence from Muslim lands is a fundamentalist priority.

America stands out due to its size, dynamism, and moral foreign policy; due to its

A radical fundamentalist Shi'i

unparalleled economic, military, and political power; and due to its cultural pre-eminence. The last has special importance: America exports the largest number of fashions and the greatest technical advances, the most original customs and the critically influential ideas. America stands so often at the leading edge of civilization, the fundamentalists almost inevitably choose it as their premier target.

Although the powerful appeal of American culture disturbs all fundamentalists, few of them are in a position to combat it. Most devote the bulk of their attention to preaching in mosques and staying out of the authorities' way. Only in Iran, where radical fundamentalists have gained power, can the issue of America's cultural threat receive the requisite attention. And Iran's leaders do take this struggle very much to heart. Ashgar Musavi Khoeiny, leader of the 1979 attack on the U.S. embassy in Tehran, for example, recently defined the main objective of the Iranian revolution as the "rooting out" of American culture in Muslim countries.

Terror Against the United States

BUT HOW TO DO SO? DIPLOMATIC, economic, moral, and other methods—of peaceful suasion cannot work, for Americans obviously will not readily pack up and leave the Middle East. Khomeini's followers therefore resort to coercion; and the coercive means most suitable for them is terrorism. Terror reduces differences in power between Iran and the United States, and enables Tehran to take steps not available to Washington. In the words of a Saudi prince: "These small countries know that the only people who have stopped the American superpower have been terrorists. They stopped you in Vietnam. They stopped you in Iran. They are stopping you in Lebanon. That is why they attack you. It is the only way." The many deadly attacks on Americans since 1979 make it clear that Iranian leaders intend to make full use of this advantage.

A pattern emerges as anti-American incidents recur. Fundamentalist Muslims direct terror primarily against those Americans associated with major institutions. Note the affiliations of the five Americans plucked off the streets of Beirut and taken hostage after March 1984: William Buckley, a political officer at the United States embassy; Jeremy Levin, a correspondent for the Cable News Network; Peter Kilburn, a librarian at the American University of Beirut; the Rev. Benjamin Weir, a Presbyterian minister; and the Rev. Lawrence M. Jenco, a Roman Catholic priest. Each of these men represents an institution deemed threatening by the Iranian rulers and their agents: the American government, media, schools, and churches.

Not surprisingly, the government looms as the largest enemy of the fundamentalists. Official American installations have therefore been the target of preference for fundamentalist attacks. The media are intensely resented for what is perceived as anti-Islamic bias; better that they leave the Muslim world and not have information to distort. Universities present special dangers by virtue of the profound influence they exert over young Muslims. As Ayatollah Khomeini explained, "We are not afraid of economic sanctions or military intervention. What we are afraid of is Western universities." Missionaries are seen as spearheading centuries-old Christian efforts to steal Muslims away from their faith.

Assuming that their hatred for the West is reciprocated, radical fundamentalists suspect that all Americans living in the Muslim world engage in espionage. Thus, Islamic Jihad accused the five American hostages in Lebanon of "subversive activities." "These people are using journalism, education and religion as a cover, and they are in fact agents of the CIA." The radicals believe that their efforts threaten the West as much as the West threatens them. They have as much difficulty imagining American indifference to them as Americans have imagining fundamentalist obsession toward themselves.

The fundamentalists do not hide their intentions to continue and even accelerate their aggression against Americans. In November 1984, a member of Islamic Jihad threatened to "blow up all American interests in Lebanon." The spokesman made clear who would be targeted: "We address this warning to every American individual residing in Lebanon." Two months later, this threat was renewed: "After the pledge we have made to the world that no Americans would remain on the soil of Lebanon and after the ultimatum we have served on American citizens to leave Beirut, our answer to the indifferent response was the kidnapping of Mr. Jenco. . . . All Americans should leave Lebanon." In reply, a spokesman for the Department of State declared that "the U.S. is not going to be forced out of Lebanon." Islamic Jihad then answered, the five American hostages "are now in our

custody preliminary to trying them as spies. . . . [They] will get the punishment they deserve." Such trials may well be held.

Future attacks on Americans will probably be directed against all those institutions already hit as well as a significant addition — multinational corporations. The widespread presence in the Middle East of American banks, oil producers, airlines, gasoline retailers, and the like, their exposed position, and their controversial activities make them an inevitable mark.

Such attacks will be severely felt. Commercial organizations will not absorb many blows before giving up on the Middle East; they will leave as soon as the expense and effort of coping with terrorism exceeds the benefits to be gained by staying. Embassies, news bureaus, schools, and churches have no such clear measure; they will presumably remain longer in the Middle East. But they will stay only by becoming more discreet and by adding multiple layers of protection. Such steps work, to be sure, but unlisted numbers and barricades diminish the effectiveness of these institutions — exactly what the fundamentalists want.

Unless steps are soon taken, they will be in a position to force Americans to retreat from many parts of the Middle East. This would not only strengthen the forces of radical fundamentalism, but it would also create extraordinary opportunities for the Soviet Union. What could be more to Soviet advantage than for America's influence to dissipate in this critical region and its institutions go into hiding?

Iranian Responsibility

WHILE EVERY TERRORIST ACT AGAINST Americans cannot be directly or unequivocally connected to the Iranian government, circumstantial evidence compellingly suggests that strong ties exist between Tehran and the radical fundamentalists.

Radical fundamentalist Muslims first arrived from Iran in the Baalbek region of Lebanon in December 1979. Although dispatched to fight Israel, their small numbers and poor training rendered them ineffective. A second contingent of Iranians then went to Lebanon in June 1982; rather than try to take on Israel, these took advantage of the turmoil following the Israeli invasion to organize and galvanize the Shi'is of Southern Lebanon. They formed alliances with Lebanese organizations such as Islamic Amal and eventually established an

Islamic government in Baalbek along Iranian lines. More Iranians were sent to Baalbek; by the end of 1982 they numbered about 1500. Money and arms provided by Iran brought in Lebanese; according to the Lebanese newspaper *An-Nahar*, one fundamentalist organization alone, Hizbullah, disposed of about 3,000 fighters in September 1983; recent estimates put its numbers at about 5,000.

The Lebanese movement publicly proclaims that it is inspired by Khomeini. In the words of a young member of Hizbullah, "We are an Islamic revolution . . . Iran was a big influence on us." When Hizbullah's troops left Friday prayers in Baalbek during September 1983. Tehran television noted that "their procession was led by Muslim religious authorities who were carrying banners proclaiming the necessity to spread the Islamic revolution [of Iran] and fight against the enemies of Islam." More succinct is the graffito found on many walls of Beirut: "We are all Khomeini."

The Lebanese Shi'is frequently adopt the rhetoric and goals of the Iranian government. A member of Hizbullah was recently quoted as saying, "Our slogan is 'death to America in the Islamic world.' " Another was even more ambitious: "The future is for the Muslims. The Soviet Union and the U.S. want to take over the earth. With Imam Khomeini, we can succeed to take these forces out, to destroy these forces."

The two sides agree on the value of terror against the United States. Husayn Musawi, the leader of Islamic Amal, called the 1983 attack on the Marine barracks "a good deed." For its part, the media in Tehran portrayed this attack as an act of "popular resistance." An Iranian editorialist wrote that "the American soldiers had died like Pharaohs under the rubble of their temple," and the Iranian government conspicuously avoided condemning this and other suicide attacks. In the Kuwaiti Airlines hijacking, collusion between the Iranian government and the terrorists appeared almost certain. With regard to this incident, the President of Iran, Seyyid 'Ali Khamene'i acknowledged that "the Islamic movement and the anti-Zionist and anti-U.S. stance of the Lebanese nation is supported by the Islamic Republic of Iran."

Control from Iran, though hard to trace, is

unmistakable. Much of the movements' funding, arms, and organizational expertise comes from Iran. In the words of a Hizbullah leader in Lebanon: "Khomeini is our big chief. He gives the orders to our chiefs, who give them to us. We don't have a precise chief, but a committee."

Diplomatic Solutions

FUNDAMENTALIST TERRORISM REPRESENTS a new challenge for Americans. In other cases, enemies of the United States employ terror to change specific government policies; but the fundamentalists seek nothing less than the expulsion of Americans—private individuals and and organizations as well as government officials—from the Middle East and the Muslim world.

Precisely because fundamentalist Muslim goals are so extravagant, strategies against the Iranian campaign of terror are difficult to formulate. Appeasement, usually the wrong response anyway, is competely

> I nquiry into Syrian desires could produce areas for cooperation.

out of the question here. The United States government cannot abandon the Middle East, much less can it force American citizens to do so. Further, a great majority of Middle Eastern Muslims would not want Americans to depart.

Other than purely defensive measures or appeasement, what steps can the United States take to prevent further incidents? Two approaches offer possible answers: diplomacy and retaliation.

Diplomatic efforts directed toward Tehran or the fundamentalist groups in Lebanon are almost certainly futile. Both are determined to oust Americans and will not accept less. Instead, diplomacy has to concentrate on finding allies in the battle against the radical fundamentalists among those others who fear their power. Many Frenchmen have been killed by them and their violence has spread to Kuwait and Italy; the Israelis, to their shock, find Shi'i groups in South Lebanon more ferocious than the P.L.O.; other factions in Lebanon dread the prospect of increased Shi'i power; and Lebanese Shi'is who are not radical fundamentalists reject the aggressions of their coreligionists.

This list is formidably long, but one must doubt that any of the states would be willing to expend much treasure or blood in Lebanon;

and the other Lebanese have shown that they can no longer contain the fundamentalists.

Only one country could and would intervene: Syria. Were the Syrian authorities inclined to do so, they could crack down on Lebanese fundamentalist power in a number of ways. The conduits that bring money, arms, and other forms of aid from Tehran could be cut. Other Lebanese factions could be assisted against the Shi'is. Or Syrian forces could be used to the same end.

But why should Hafiz al-Asad choose to interfere? For two reasons. Since the Lebanese civil war broke out in 1975, Syria's guiding concern has been to prevent any faction from controlling the country. When Maronites ruled in 1975, Damascus supported the rebel forces; as the rebels, including the P.L.O., threatened in 1976 to take over, it made an abrupt volte-face and supported the Maronites. As the Maronites emerged with new strength in 1976, the Syrians again backed the rebels. One of the rebel factions, the Shi'is, now threaten to control most of Lebanon, and the Syrian leaders must surely be preparing to prevent them.

Shi'i control threatens in another way too. Led by the Muslim Brethren organization, fundamentalists in Syria constitute the most dangerous oppostion to the Syrian government. So feared were the Brethren that the authorities made membership in the group a capital crime in July 1980. In December 1980, Syrian military forces attacked a Muslim Brethren camp at Ajloun in Jordan, bringing the two countries near war. Given this apprehension, Damascus must be extremely concerned that fundamentalists in Lebanon might funnel aid to their Sunni colleagues in Syria. The January 1985 declaration of an amnesty for members of the Muslim Brethren may indicate that the government, fearing a coalition of fundamentalists, seeks to appease its opposition. Should this be the case, Damascus would have clear reason to turn against the Shi'i fundamentalists in Lebanon.

An American deal with President Hafiz al-Asad would not be easy to arrange, if for no

other reason than that their policies have for years run in opposite directions. Nonetheless, these two governments—as well as other states and most Lebanese citizens—may find they have a common interest in suppressing the radical Shi'is of Lebanon.

The United States might encourage the Syrians in this direction, perhaps by indicating a willingness to deal with Damascus on issues outstanding. Inquiry into Syrian desires could produce areas for cooperation. Or the United States could show flexibility about revising the Reagan Initiative to include Syria or more actively mediating between Syria and Israel.

Retaliation

DIPLOMATIC EFFORTS SHOULD BE TRIED but not counted on. These cannot substitute for a willingness to oppose force with force. In

President Hafiz al-Asad with U.S. Secretary of State George Shultz.

contemplating the use of violence, the American objective must be to find steps that discourage further terrorist incidents. As ever, many constraints tie American hands.

To begin with, three considerations rule out a direct strike against Iran. First, the United States cannot take actions that risk bringing the Soviet Union into Iran, for this would facilitate Soviet control of the Persian Gulf and render that region's oil flow even more vulnerable than it already is. Restrictions on the free flow of oil could have the gravest implications for the United States and its allies, possibly leading to the neutralization of Japan and the breakup of NATO. Keeping the Soviet Union out of Iran and the Persian Gulf must have highest priority in United States policy.

This being the case, Washington cannot take chances with measures that might lead to

Iran's territorial disintegration. However obnoxious the ayatollah's policies, American interests require that the government in Tehran retain firm control over the entire country. All actors—the Iraqi military provincial rebels, exiled opposition groups—who reduce Tehran's authority contradict those essential interests. Frustrating as it is, the United States must not harm the Khomeini government's grasp of power.

Second, Iranian military targets are off-bounds. Attacking them would mean in effect joining Iraq's war effort against Iran, entailing many undesirable consequences. This would align Wasington with the aggressor in the Iraq-Iran war and tie it closely to one of the most repressive regimes in the Middle East; it would impel Iran further into the Soviet camp; and, far from reducing acts of terror against American citizens, cooperation with Saddam Husayn would increase them. For these reasons, all Iranian targets with military value, regardless how insignificant or remote, and all important economic facilities, such as the oil-exporting port of Kharg Island, must be inviolate.

Third, the United States is restricted by its own standards of morality; it cannot imitate the Iranians and strike out blindly against civilians. The United States must uphold certain standards of behavior, even when its enemies do not.

These three restrictions effectively exclude American actions against Iran. Striking some targets could endanger the stability of the government; others would make the United States the ally of Iraq; and still others would contravene American ethical standards.

If Iran itself escapes retaliation, its agents abroad—and especially those in Lebanon—need not. Striking the radical fundamentalists in Baalbek avoids the risks associated with striking Iran itself. It would not destabilize the government in Tehran, and the Iranians in Lebanon are not involved in the war with Iraq. But they are actively engaged in terror. For these reasons, they are a suitable target for American retaliation.

The United States government has often threatened retaliation against the radical fundamentalists, but not yet carried through. Philip Taubman explained in *The New York Times* why nothing happened after the September 1984 bombing in Beirut:

> Officials said today [4 October] that President Reagan and his senior aides had not authorized a retaliatory strike against the Party

of God [Hizbullah] both for practical and policy reasons.

Military and intelligence aides, according to the officials, have advised the White House that because the group's leaders and followers do not ever assemble in one place, an air raid would be ineffective and would risk killing innocent civilians.

The White House was told it would also be difficult to introduce American forces covertly into the Bekaa to carry out a commando raid.

Equally important, the officials said, is a widespread belief among Mr. Reagan's aides that a retaliatory strike against the Party of God or Iran would only produce an escalation in terrorist attacks against the United States.

These reasons for inactivity no longer suffice. If the United States lacks the capabilities for air strikes or commando raids, these must be developed immediately. The enemy's practice of surrounding himself with innocents cannot be allowed to inhibit all American use of force. And the fear of provoking more terrorist attacks carries no weight in the aftermath of the Tehran hijacking outrage. As Secretary of State George P. Shultz has noted, "a great power . . . must bear responsibility for the consequences of its inaction as well as for the consequences of its action."

The only serious hesitation with regard to attacking fundamentalist installations in Lebanon has to do with efficacy. Would exacting a heavy price for atrocities against Americans provide a disincentive for the enemy? Or are the means and the will there to rebuild the facilities?

This question is difficult to answer in the abstract, for the adversary is elusive and his means uncertain. Instead, the reverse point should be strongly emphasized: the absence of punishment encourages fundamentalists to challenge the United States. How can they but despise a power that can be hit time after time without fear of retribution, that does not protect its citizens, that does not go beyond verbal indignation?

Time has come for the United States to retaliate. Punishment of the terrorists who are most implicated and most vulnerable—those in the Baalbek region—presents the best opportunity to protect Americans and their interests in the Middle East. If the Syrian government can be induced to cooperate, so much the better; but if this fails, the United States must gird to undertake a costly and unpleasant conflict. □

Part IX
Regional Responses to
Middle East Terrorism

[21]

RESPONDING TO TERRORISM's CHALLENGE: THE CASE OF ISRAELI REPRISALS

by Reuben Miller*

INTRODUCTION

It has often been argued that governments with a declared and practiced harsh policy of "No Ransom, No Concessions," and which also retaliate against terrorists, will be most successful in deterring international terrorism. The argument follows that if you raise the costs and risks for terrorists, you reduce their gains and benefits. Vice President, George Bush summed up this approach by stating, "I think we should reiterate the willingness of our administration to retaliate swiftly when we feel we can punish those who were directly responsible."[1] The thinking of politicians who have delved into the area of combating terrorism has been dominated by this common wisdom.

Supporters of retaliatory strikes argue that such acts will inflict retribution and attrition upon terrorist organizations; will deter their future activity; and will provide credibility to the administration. They claim that retaliations would prove that the administration "means business" and will confirm a long standing policy drawn by the Nixon Administration in September 1972, following the massacre of Israeli athletes in the Olympic Games in Munich.

The purpose of this article is to examine retaliations and reprisals as a facet of harsh policy. The Israeli experience with Palestinian terrorism will serve as a case study to demonstrate the effectiveness of such policy practices.

CONCEPTUAL FRAMEWORK

Because of the existing resemblance, in operational terms, between retaliation and preemptive strike, the demarcation lines have to be drawn.

Unlike preemptive strikes or military rescue missions, retaliations are overt and direct responses to specific acts of terrorism. Though most types of operations are carried out by a qualified military force, a preemptive strike is conducted before an act of hostility can be carried out and is expected to disrupt predetermined plans of an adversary. On the other hand, it could be argued that a preemptive strike, though it precedes the future activities, may also follow previous hostilities and in that sense it becomes a retaliation. Hence, the distinction is somewhat confusing and left as a matter of interpretation.

A retaliatory act responds to one or more acts of terrorism that have been identified by the responding government. When a government retaliates it specifies the goals, the scope and the intentions of its act. However, one important factor pertaining to retaliations is the timing of the public announcement about the operation. If a government releases a statement to the press too early, then the potential target group can take some countermeasures. For example, it can evacuate some sites, retreat to a better location, or fortify its position in preparation for the attack. Thus, the public declarations defeat the initial purpose of the retaliation and provide sufficient warning time to the terrorists. Ultimately, such warnings will reduce the intended effect of such an operation. Obviously, secrecy is imperative and serves as a key to success in this type of activity. But, it is extremely difficult to preserve secrecy simultaneously with overt operations characteristics. Hence, the common practice is to release a public statement shortly after the operation has commenced but before actual contact with the terrorists has been established.

The method, extent and targets in a retaliatory operation may vary. There could be air strikes or artillery barrages as well as naval bombardments. Other methods may involve military commando raids against specific marked targets. Regardless of the method and extent, it should be kept in mind that those acts are always overt operations -- widely reported and covered by the media -- with accepted responsibility by the government. The publicity campaign usually specifies that the operation was carried out as a retaliation to particular acts of terrorism.

On the other hand, covert operations could be used as a method to thwart terrorism. Every state has its various intelligence agencies and other military organizations that carry out clandestine operations. Clearly, not much is known about these kinds of covert activities and probably some of them were designed to penetrate different terrorist groups. Clandestine intelligence operations have various goals. Some are directed at political assassinations. Others gather information which over time becomes useful against the target group. Some can argue correctly that such practices by governments tactically resemble terrorist attack, drawing on anonymity and disguise. Hence, from this perspective, it could be argued that legitimate governments often exercise state terrorism. Naturally, covert and intelligence operations are highly classified and are beyond the focus of this study.

While a distinction has been made between retaliation and a preemptive strike, it is also important to note that there is a difference between retaliation and rescue operations. Probably the most important difference is that there are no hostages at the site of the retaliation, at least none are expected to be there. However, in a rescue operation it is definitely known that there are innocent hostages. At times in rescue operations even the number of hostages is known, as well as their identity and nationality, as in skyjacking incidents. On the other hand, the number of hostages held on a train, or at airport terminals and other public places is often not known; neither is their identity or nationality. Other distinctions between retaliatory operations and rescue missions are tactical and logistical. All retaliation activities are conducted on the enemy's territory where the terrorists enjoy the safety of their location and feel confident and out of reach of their pursuers. The attacking force, though it studies the target site beforehand, is unfamiliar with all the features of the target and must be guided by intelligence reports, as in Entebe, 1976 and Nicosia, 1978 where the rescuers met with hostile fire from the terrorists as well as from other forces of the host country. Thus the strike force is in a disadvantageous position. On the other hand, most of the rescue missions have been conducted in places unfamiliar to the terrorists with the exception of the immediate site, while the rescue teams operated in a "friendly" environment. Examples are the raid on the Sabena plane in Tel-Aviv in 1972 and the raid on the Egyptian plane in Luxur in 1976. A retaliation intends to inflict maximum damage and destruction upon the target site and its terrorist occupants. If intelligence reports indicate the existence of hostages in the midst of a retaliation target area, such operations are usually cancelled because of fear of harm to the hostages. In a rescue operation the only targets are individual terrorists who hold the hostages.

This particular distinction also constitutes a different course of action. Though in rescue missions, as well as retaliations, the element of surprise is the most important, the form of using the force is substantially different. In a rescue mission, emphasis is on a very short confrontation -- as short as possible -- with focus on identifying the individual terrorists. At times such confrontation culminates in a shootout with the terrorists with the intent to kill or capture them. In retaliations, the scope of the operation is broad, with intent to destroy, damage, eliminate, injure and at times even capture terrorists for future interrogation and information. Over all, the concept of retaliation encompasses the notion of inflicting extensive injuries and damage to the target group, thus raising its 'costs,' while a rescue mission has a different goal -- to release hostages. At times, in the process of rescue operations the attacking force also inflicts injuries and damage to the terrorists as well as to the hostages, as in Munich, 1972. But the intention then is not to cause extensive damage to the site of operation. Hence, it could be argued that retaliations have long-range goals while rescue operations have immediate and short-term goals. Both types of operations share tactical similarities. We find such common denominators in a number of incidents: the raid on Entebe, 1976; Mogadishu, 1977; Sabena (Tel-Aviv), 1972; Nicosia, 1978; Luxur (Egypt), 1976; and Malta, 1985. Both types of operations dwell on a surprise attack, forcing the disoriented terrorists to improvise while the initiative is in the hands of the attacking force. The time involved in both is short though the preparations are extensive.

The most important question concerning a retaliation is: What are the goals of such an action? If the objectives are clear, then the rationale behind such a retaliation could be analyzed and argued. There are at least five interwoven objectives: [1] retribution, [2] credibility to a stated policy, [3] attrition, [4] high cost for terrorists, and [5] deterrence.

Retribution. Retribution includes a sense of revenge and the philosophy of an "eye for an eye and a tooth for tooth" as a form of punishment. With this trend of thought it is expected that the loss of human life as well as kidnappings will be punishable through the conduct of retaliatory strike. Recently Congressman Ken Kramer, R-Colorado, introduced legislation that makes capital punishment possible for terrorists who attack and kill Americans abroad.[2] This legislation has been introduced several times in the past through various international agreements.

This simple form of justice fulfills an inner desire to avenge those who are killed in the process of a low-level conflict where there are no rules and the law has not been followed. But, it ought to be remembered that terrorism defies existing laws and regulations by which legitimate governments behave. Simultaneously, there are governments that do not abide by the rules of international law and that use various methods of coercion including terrorism. Retribution may fulfill the desire of the victim's survivors for some form of punitive action in response to terrorist atrocities. Retaliatory legal measures or more coercive types of reaction also may provide a sense of satisfaction to a government (and its constituents), by indicating its ability and resolve to respond rather than being a passive target.

Credibility. Retired Admiral James Holloway, executive director of the Task Force on Combating Terrorism, has said that Americans believe terrorism affects the credibility of the United States as a powerful country and world leader.[3] This statement indicates a shared concern among decision makers pertaining to the self-image of a government. This concern is enhanced especially after a government has taken a tough stand on a particular issue. Any government that has proclaimed its policy in public and reiterated its position has to demonstrate its serious intent to carry out and practice what it stated. If and when terrorist activity directed against such a government continues over time, which is a reflection of terrorists' determination to challenge and defy it, then pressure for action mounts upon that government. When a government fails to follow through with its promises, then its credibility and resolve deteriorate in the eyes of its own public, as well as among the terrorists and other international observers. Failure to adhere to policy guidelines will indicate a lack of determination to carry out a certain policy and that the authorities' prior proclamations were hollow.

However, it should be noted that legitimate governments have operational limitations in waging retaliatory operations. After all, governments are bound by rules and laws of conduct which infringe upon their freedom of action. On the other hand, a terrorist group does not abide by the same rules of law. Such groups have their own "laws." Thus, terrorists are testing the willingness of governments not to break those laws which initially they agreed to follow. Therefore, the credibility of a legitimate government is being tested on two different levels -- on legal and ethical grounds and on the resolve and decisiveness grounds of its leadership to follow through with retaliatory strikes.

Attrition. Acts of retaliations also have tactical and practical objectives to eliminate terrorists and destroy their infrastructure. During such operations, the retaliation forces may seek to capture terrorists alive. Captured terrorists may provide significant information to the attacking force.

The damage in terms of material, property, training facilities, equipment and financial losses inflicted on a terrorist organization by a military strike, may halt its activities for quite some time. It is expected that a retaliation has the same effect on terrorists as acts of terrorism have on innocent soft targets. Retaliatory strikes are intended to be surprise attacks and to utilize terrorist-type tactics against terrorists. Since it strikes at the midst of terrorist "safe ground" at times when they are unprepared and disorganized, retaliation becomes frightening and a form of counter-terror to terrorists. By applying this method of the "stick" it is expected that terrorists, wherever they are, will feel insecure and constantly be on the run. When that occurs, it is thought that such a way of life -- being on the run -- will disrupt terrorists' activity, organization, structure, training and ultimately their operations. Putting the terrorists on the run may deter further action on their part, at least for some time, which would translate into a reduction in the frequency of their activity.

As the cost for terrorists to rebuild their infrastructure may be high, it is expected that the time lost through the destruction will delay terrorist operations. Time must be allocated to rebuild organization and facilities, regroup forces, reestablish training grounds and replace all that was lost during the retaliation. It also may be argued that reprisals against terrorist organizations might reduce the number of new recruits and incoming volunteers. It is thought that a retaliation will cause potential volunteers, especially the undecided ones and those unsure of themselves, to think twice before joining a terrorist group.

It should be noted that many of the most spectacular skyjackings were low-budgeted operations facilitated by a small group of highly charged and committed people. Also, it is argued that terrorists are actually highly motivated and committed people and their organizations draw their recruits from pools of people who have nothing to lose but only to gain. If those potential volunteers actually are considering joining a terrorist group, a retaliation act may be exactly the turning point that will drive them directly into the hands of terrorist organizations, and dedicate their talents, efforts and lives to the goal that the group claims to have.

High Cost. Governments exercising retaliations have a military edge over terrorists, pushing them to fight a conventional battle. Such retaliatory practices eliminate the terrorists' advantage of anonymity and disguise which are their best defense mechanisms. When acts of retaliation occur, terrorists, who usually are not trained to fight a conventional battle, are caught by surprise. Exposure to fight it out with a highly trained military unit, which is familiar with such techniques, does not offer much chance to terrorists. Then the price to a terrorist organization becomes high in terms of the number of terrorists who might be killed, wounded and/or captured. Their human resources might deplete in a short time, while it takes a very long time to build or rebuild an organization with its infrastructure of command, training, economic base, tightness of group, and commitment to a political goal.

Deterrence. It is thought that an act of retaliation may teach terrorists a lesson. And the lesson is that they will constantly be pursued by military task forces if they do not cease their terroristic activity. Ultimately it is expected that retaliation will cause terrorists to rethink their strategy and force them to give up terrorism. Deterrence is achieved by presenting a putative adversary with a credible threat to exact a high price should aggression be attempted.[4]

The last three objectives of attrition, high cost and deterrence are highly interwoven and are tactical goals. On the one hand they attempt to inflict high costs to terrorist groups and thus to reduce the expected benefits that such groups seek from their acts of terrorism. By using its offensive forces and transferring the "war" to terrorists' "territory" a government indicates resolve and determination. Its retaliations intend to demonstrate a government's willingness to take an active role in pursuing terrorists and that there are few limits to what it may do, short of total war.

CHOOSING A RESPONSE -- RETALIATIONS

The act of resorting to counter low-level violence by a government could be interpreted as its frustration or inability to resolve a problem by peaceful means. This assumes that peaceful means have been exhausted before the final stage of resorting to retaliation. Frustration builds up over time when expected results are not being provided. If the expectations are being met, then there will be no frustration. But, when these expectations are not met, a government knows that the public statements and promises it has made

may be viewed as empty. In other words, a government has locked itself in a
no-win situation where it has to take a drastic decision to release the
built-up pressure on itself from unmet expectations.

It could be argued that retaliations are extremely dangerous to a
government since the choice of retaliation is the last one and provides no
other options. In those cases, often hesitancy and fear are reflected in the
decision to retaliate. If the retaliation does not succeed, more frustration
and lack of confidence characterize the political echelons. Military failure
to accomplish the retaliation objectives often has adverse effects since all
hopes had been put on that option.

On the other hand, governments often choose retaliations and reprisals as
a first option. In these cases their choice of response is often perceived
as determination and resolve without frustration initially. If retaliation
becomes a regularly practiced policy of a target government, then pressure
on it is released with each and every operation. The act itself is not
committed to fulfill high expectations as a last resort. Actually, it is
viewed as an ongoing government stand. Thus, the expected utility is also
spread over time across several retaliations rather than representing high
stakes put on one case.

ISRAELI REPRISALS

Israel is the only country in the world that applies its declared harsh
policy and retaliates openly against terrorists. This policy was established
in 1953 by Ben-Gurion and has been practiced ever since by the Israeli
Defense Forces (IDF). This policy has been reiterated numerous times over the
years by all Israeli governments and Prime Minsters as well as Defense
Ministers. Israel stands alone in this form of conflict. Initially, Israel
responded against targets ". . . in the bordering states, ostensibly in
response to acts or omissions on the part of the target governments which
Israel perceived to be provocative."[5] This policy of reprisals was established
as a reaction to Palestinian infiltration across the international borders.
The reprisals ranged from minor operations by small military units of a dozen
men, to brigade-size assaults, artillery shellings, air strikes, and commando
raids. Overall, these retaliations are viewed as an extension of the Arab-
Israeli conflict by other means. Israelis have not distinguished between
independent Palestinian terrorism and/or that of the Arab countries that
harbored their bases. The Israeli perception is one of increasing threat to
its existence. It is assumed that most or all Arab states are part of a
coalition aimed at destroying the state of Israel.[6] Since various Arab
governments have been supporting, harboring, financing and training different
Palestinian groups in their struggle with Israel, Palestinian terrorism has
been incorporated into Israel's general threat perception.

Palestinian terrorism against Israeli targets has assumed over the years
a large array of activity such as bombings, shellings, armed attacks,
sabotage, skyjackings, hijackings, hostage takings, suicidal raids, and
suicidal car bombings. Palestinian terrorism has targeted the Israeli
civilian population within the pre-1967 borders and the territories, Israeli
nationals overseas, Israeli officials in the Middle East Region and abroad,
military personnel in Israel proper and especially in Lebanon, and Jewish
targets around the world. The Palestinian terrorist attacks have been
conducted in four distinct geographical locations: Israel proper -- the pre-

1967 borders; Occupied Territories -- West Bank and Gaza Strip; Middle East Region -- Cyprus, Egypt and Lebanon; and finally attacks in the international arena. However, Alon argues that Palestinian terrorism abroad represents only 2.6% of all terrorist attacks.[7] He says,

> From the Palestinian point of view, international terrorism strikes were the most effective strikes in the sense that they brought the Palestinian issue to the international agenda. The effect was achieved by a few murderous strikes and prolonged hijackings that shocked and fascinated the world through broad and intensive media coverage.[8]

With this broad spectrum of terrorist assaults, Israelis view acts of international Palestinian terrorism and of indigenous terrorism within the context of the Israeli-Palestinian confrontation. Thus, it is extremely difficult to discern between retaliations for particular acts of terrorism abroad or similar attacks within Israeli boundaries. Some of these retaliations were extended in response to Palestinian infiltration, sabotage, and shelling, especially during the War of Attrition (1968-1970) along the Jordan River. At other times it was in direct response to a Palestinian attack abroad. During the War of Attrition, Palestinian infiltration also caused military clashes between Israeli and Jordanian artillery and forces. Often, Jordanian guns and tanks provided cover for Palestinian terrorists. Since the interaction of Israeli forces, Palestinian groups, and the armed forces of the Arab neighboring states are so interwoven, it is difficult to draw demarcation lines between reprisals and border clashes. Table 1 includes all forms of Palestinian terrorism against Israeli targets in all geographical locations. On the other hand, Israeli reprisals mainly have been contained in the Occupied Territories and the Middle East Region, initially in Jordan and later in Lebanon.

When Palestinian terrorism against Israel has spread to the international scene, Israel has been consistent in its harsh approach. Thus, the first Israeli retaliation since the Six Days War took place on December 28, 1968, when Israeli commandos landed at Beirut airport and blew up 13 Arab planes.[9] This action was a direct response to Palestinian terrorism which interfered with civilian air travel to Israel. An Israeli government announcement on the raid of December 28 said that the Arab terrorists had "come from Beirut airport and belonged to the branch of the sabotage organization in Lebanon."[10] The statement warned, "Arab governments that allow the activities of sabotage organizations from their territories must know they bear responsibility for the acts."[11]

TABLE 1
PALESTINIAN TERRORISM AND ISRAELI REPRISALS

Year	Attacks on Israeli Targets	Israeli Reprisals
1968	31	16
1969	40	38
1970	20	12
1971	9	5
1972	49	24
1973	36	11
1974	14	53
1975	28	32
1976	13	2
1977	9	2
1978	22	11
1979	38	48
1980	21	14
1981	22	11
1982	44	6
1983	36	13
1984	52	36
1985	31	24
TOTAL	528	358

Sources: Facts on File, and The Middle East
Journal (Chronologies)

Israel has carried out 358 retaliations between 1968 and 1985 while the terrorist organizations conducted 528 attacks. All retaliations were against terrorist bases and targets in the neighboring Arab states. However, it should be mentioned that often targets were located in the vicinity or in the midst of civilian population centers. Thus, during a retaliation, especially such as air attacks, civilians have been injured in the process. It is interesting to observe that once counter-measures have been employed, usually as an immediate response to a new threat, they are maintained. The high frequency of these acts indicates that Israel has responded constantly.

The figures in Table 1 indicate the high level of military activity between Israeli and Palestinian forces. The War of Attrition was marked with high intensity and is attributed to Palestinian activity on the West Bank and Israel proper in 1968. The high frequency of retaliations in 1969 is attributed to the defeat of the Fatah in the occupied territories and its inevitable outcome of transferring the bases to the confrontation states -- namely Jordan. The sharp drop in attacks on Israeli targets, 50% between 1969 and 1970, indicates the probable effect of Israeli retaliations against Jordan. However, terrorism generated from Jordanian territory practically ceased to exist as of September 1970 with the outbreak of the Jordanian Civil War. Since then King Hussein has curbed Palestinian terrorist activity from

Jordanian soil. It is also argued that the increasing numbers of Palestinian guerrillas and their military capability endangered the King and his throne thus forcing him to take tough measures to curtail Palestinian activity in his kingdom.

The effects of the Jordanian Civil War are reflected in the low number of attacks against Israel in 1971. Most of those were generated from Syrian territory. However, from 1972 until 1975 Palestinian terrorism was transferred to Lebanon, which provided a solid base in the area named "Fatahland" on the southwestern slopes of Mount Hermon. On the other hand, following the Yom Kippur War, Israel engaged in a high activity of reprisals which resulted in 53 counterattacks in 1974. Rabin, the newly elected prime minister, ordered the intensification of the war against terrorism. It is also argued that those retaliations were meant for domestic purposes as well as for the terrorists. The 'Blunder' of Yom Kippur overshadowed the mood in the country and thus provided the stimulus to foster an image of a government determined to quell terrorism with a tough policy. By way of such an approach the new government was to gain credibility amongst the Israeli public. With the outbreak of the Lebanese Civil War in 1975, Palestinian terrorism against Israel decreased, especially in terms of attacks across the borders. In 1976 and 1977, Palestinian attacks dropped to low levels of 13 and 9 incidents respectively. The highlight of the events was the skyjacking of Air France Flight 139 to Entebe. Most of the incidents in these years occurred within the Israeli boundaries. Hence, the level of retaliation also dropped and was incorporated into daily routine and regular security measures practiced by Israel in those areas. Also, it ought to be remembered that political negotiations were underway in Geneva in 1976, and Sadat visited Jerusalem in 1977. Both events overshadowed the activity of Palestinian terrorism and contributed to the sharp drop in the level of terrorist activity against Israel.

In 1978 Palestinian terrorism increased to 22 incidents. Evidently it was an attempt to undermine the Camp David Accord agreement, to isolate Egypt, and to draw Israel into reprisals against the Palestinians in Lebanon. The newly elected Begin government in Israel had understood the underlying intentions of the P.L.O. and carefully maneuvered into position and struck back with 11 counter attacks. Hence, it could be argued that Begin's government found itself in a similar position to the Rabin government of 1974. The peace agreement became a mutual test for Israel, Egypt, and the P.L.O. On the other hand, Begin's government was domestically pressed to indicate that it had not softened its position concerning the P.L.O. This trend and practices were exercised in the next two years with an increase to 48 reprisals in 1979. From 1980 on Israeli reprisals leveled off, though in June 1982 a full scale Israeli invasion of Lebanon took place. It is noted that the number of Israeli reprisals in 1982 dropped to 6 counterattacks. Because of the invasion which was designed to eradicate the terrorist strongholds in Lebanon, the IDF engaged in military clashes on a daily basis with the P.L.O. and other groups operating in Lebanon. The demarcation lines between terrorism and daily military routine activity became blurred. During the next three years of Israeli presences on Lebanese soil the clashes between Israeli troops and either Palestinian or Lebanese forces were considered as military confrontations rather than acts of terrorism. Therefore, they have not been included in the analysis and are not reflected in the table above.

117

During the whole period under study, Israeli retaliations exceeded terrorist attacks only twice. In 1974 and in 1979 Israel responded with 53 and 48 reprisals respectively. In both instances it was a newly elected government which used reprisals to send messages to the P.L.O. and its splinter groups. Furthermore, Rabin and Begin used those retaliations also for domestic political purposes. In both instances attention was drawn from the home political arena which was marred by doubts and speculation about the future of the country and the peace process. Hence, reprisals served as a tool to consolidate their domestic political powers and to gain credibility for their commitment to Israel's national security and its future. By committing the IDF to retaliations they reconfirmed a long-standing policy of deterrence but also helped to fuel the public's perception of threat.

In the early stages of the Palestinian-Israeli War, Israeli reprisals were aimed at Palestinian cells on the West Bank and Gaza Strip and at those who harbored them. The method was one of raids and hot pursuit using infantry and other ground forces. However, when Fatah moved its bases across the river to Jordan, the method and scope of Israeli reprisals changed too. Artillery duels assumed the brunt of the reprisals. Occasionally, the air force was employed when the targets were clearly identified. The method of response changed again after the P.L.O. was forced by King Hussein to move its bases and chose Lebanon as a host country. Then, the Israeli air force became one of the most active tools in the battle against Palestinian terrorism, especially those attacks which originated across the Lebanese border.

Throughout this period, Israel used its military might, usually its air force, as the most effective means to destroy training camps, headquarters, bases and other targets facilitating terrorist activity. Often the targets were located in the midst of civilian centers. Thus, the Israeli air raids at times inflicted damages and injuries on civilians. However, it was found that the air force became a powerful means to retaliate, the quickest one and probably the least costly from an Israeli military perspective. In other instances the Israeli high command decided to use the navy commando units, as well as mechanized forces, in intensive countermeasures across its borders, and along the shoreline with immediate response to terrorist strikes. The tactics of ambushes and patrols were also used frequently along the Jordanian and Lebanese fronts.

In addition to the overt operations of retaliations and reprisals against Palestinian terrorist bases, training camps, commando and control centers, etc. the Israeli Mossad also had launched a campaign in an attempt to abolish Palestinian terrorist activity abroad. A major effort was made to seek out the people who masterminded Black September's attack on Israeli athletes during the Munich Olympic Games in September 1972. This particular operation pursued those individuals throughout all of Europe and the Middle East. However, the Israeli government rejected any responsibility for these assassinations.

Jonas,[12] Tinnin,[13] and Bar-Zohar and Haber,[14] reported that Israeli intelligence -- Mossad -- actively pursued Palestinian terrorists, mainly in Europe and in Lebanon. One of the known cases is the killing of Ahmed Boushiki in Lillehammer, Norway on July 21, 1973. Boushiki was killed after being mistakenly identified as a Black September leader by an Israeli counter-terrorist group.[15] The main effort of Israeli security in the international arena though was placed on preventive and defensive measures

118

such as (a) air marshals on El-Al planes, and (b) security guards in all Israeli official offices and institutions overseas.

Blechman,[16] in a study of Israel's retaliations across the border, indicated that their effectiveness lasted up to 30 days from the Israeli reaction. Blechman's rigorous study concluded:

> The reprisals have not fulfilled their stated
> purpose of compelling Arab states to reduce Arab
> initiated violence directed at Israel, except from
> a relatively short time perspective and with some
> other exceptions, particularly notable before 1956.[17]

However, it should be noted that Blechman's study focuses only on the Israeli reprisals conducted between 1953 and 1956.

Alon[18] points out that in terms of cost and benefit, retaliations did not achieve Israel's ultimate goal of ending terrorism and that those actions actually incurred high costs to Israel. Hoffman[19] reached the same conclusion in his examination of the trend of Palestinian terrorism. He stated, "Israel's invasion of Lebanon in June 1982 actually had little effect on the level of Palestinian terrorist activity."

Ben-Horin argues that "Israelis should not be surprised when deterrence fails (and usually are not)."[20] And Israeli retaliations have multiple goals of which deterrence, high cost, and retaliation are only the most significant ones. But, these retaliations are limited in their overall accomplishments.

EVALUATION OF ISRAEL'S REPRISAL POLICY

The initial purpose of Israeli reprisals was to abolish acts of terrorism against Israeli targets. However, the lessons of this violent experience point to a different direction. Though in the short term those reprisals proved to be effective, in the long run they have not accomplished the set goal. For more than 30 years Israel has been fighting terrorism, often unsuccessfully. The methods of terrorism have changed; so have the targets and the locations. By the early 1970s Israel was confronting terrorism in four distinct areas -- Israel proper, occupied territories, Middle East region and the international arena. And still today Israel is being frequently targeted in these four regions. More recently, since December 1987, the Palestinian-Israeli confrontation has flared up again in a new form and dimension. The Intefada (uprising) emerged in Gaza and spread through the Palestinian community to the West Bank. The Intefada generally involves Palestinian civilian population and does not constitute a military threat to Israel's sovereignty. Thus, unlike in past experiences, the IDF has been facing a major dilemma in terms of effective response. While the tactical options of response are unlimited, the strategy is confined to (a) capital punishment inflicted upon the general population, or (b) singling out individual activists for exemplary punishment. Both approaches appear to be futile and the old practices of reprisals and retribution are counterproductive under the new circumstances which developed in the occupied territories. Hence, one may conclude that the only proper path to resolve the current situation is to resort to political channels and avoid quick military fixes.

119

Though Israel has carried out spectacular and daring retaliations as well as rescue missions like the raid on Entebe in 1976, the data do not indicate a reduction in the frequency of acts of terrorism against Israel. On the contrary, those incidents increased over the years, expanded in scope and method, and became spectacular and daring media events. With the increase of Palestinian terrorism from the occupied territories and the confrontation states Israeli troops attempted to achieve each and every one of the five goals mentioned above. However, the Israeli experience does not bear out the deterrent capability attributed to retaliations and 'Harsh Policies.' The repeated terrorist attacks over the years testify to the failure of this concept.

On the other hand, the reprisals have established the credibility of Israeli governments in the eyes of their constituents, at least for a while. Over the years the harsh policy of reprisals has become institutionalized in Israeli political life. This policy is not questioned anymore in political circles and has become a taboo for any newly elected government. While the policy was in place, the scope, location, and targets were examined before a new reprisal attack was ordered. The 1982 invasion of Lebanon and its aftermath has changed this approach somewhat. The rise of the Intefada on the West Bank and Gaza has refocused the applicability of harsh policy to all types of low level violence. Hence, it could be argued that the cycle of terrorist attacks and reprisals has been perpetuated and the levels of violence has been repeatedly refueled.

The discussion above points out that the Palestinian terrorist groups do not operate in a political vacuum and respond to a large variety of variables surrounding their environment. Thus, the changing political arena in the Middle East, peace talks, domestic politics of the different countries which harbor them, and other circumstances such as international events and conferences on the Middle East have an impact upon these groups and determine their activities. Furthermore, they have dynamics of their own, unrelated to the regional politics. Hence, they react to an inherent internal struggle for power, group competition, and sponsors. Therefore, Israeli retaliations only serve as one variable with which Palestinian groups have to cope.

Since only Israel exercised retaliations, the findings may be fortuitous or a result of some special characteristics of Israeli experience. From the discussion above it is clear that the Israeli experience does not point to the common wisdom about reprisals' effectiveness. However, the perception of Israel's success against terrorism has been reflected in McFarlane's testimony before the Congressional hearings on the Iran-Contra affair.[21] Overall, it could be argued that the Israeli experience is unique in nature and therefore may not be indicative of success or failure in other instances where governments will practice similar policies against international terrorism.

CONCLUSIONS

Thus far, no other country has chosen to follow the counter-terrorist practices of Israel as an established and consistent policy. However, several countries have developed anti-terrorist units that generally operate, within a framework of a policy designed to combat acts of terrorism, while an incident lasts, such as hostage-taking situations. Examples include the British attack on the Iranian embassy in London in April 1980, or the German rescue mission in October 1977 in Somalia, or the Italian rescue mission of General Dozier in January of 1982. But, those acts are considered rescue missions rather than retaliations. No other government has ever actively pursued terrorists and retaliated as post facto action to hijackings, kidnappings, bombings and other forms of non-confrontational attacks such as bombings. However, some could argue that the U.S. bombing attack against Libya on April 15, 1986 is a retaliation attack. This American mission, however, was an isolated incident of flexing muscles against a target state sponsoring terrorism. Hence, the Israeli case provides the sole example for a general retaliatory policy. So far Israel has experienced over 30 years of a harsh policy but those practices have not thwarted or deterred acts of terrorism.

It ought to be borne in mind that retaliations have inherent limitations. The most important one is the high level of expectations vested in these operations, which are supposed to produce immediate results. Retaliations may be observed as long standing policies or as sporadic government reaction. If the government's response has been established as a long-practiced policy, it is viewed then in tactical terms, which often fulfills limited expectations. However, a single retaliation may lift the mood of the decision makers of the responding country and lead them to believe in the long term effects of such an operation. But, if a government dwells on the long term effects that a retaliation produces, then the responding government engages in self-deception since it attempts to satisfy constituents' pressure, expectations, and credibility and achieve deterrence.

The discussion above has examined only overt operations against terrorist groups. Ofri[22] has argued that covert operations would achieve better the desired effect of retaliations. However, many obstacles lie in the path of covert operations. Beside the operational difficulties facing such activities, there are fundamental research problems in the study and analysis of covert operations. By their very definition and nature they are secretive and unavailable for scrutiny and inquiry similar to overt operations. The lack of research data would prevent us from collecting the information necessary for systematic study and analysis of such activities. Ultimately, obstacles will hinder any type of effective measurement of a wide range of variables which are important to complete such studies. Furthermore, the basic question pertaining to the successful effect of retaliations, covert or overt, still remains -- how do we know if and when a terrorist group has been uprooted and its infrastructure destroyed?

The recent reemergence of the Red Brigades in Italy testifies to the inaccurate perception that this particular group had been destroyed. Hence, the issue of verification arises every time that a terrorist act takes place. In light of this background we ought to remember that the inherent nature of terrorism, as a strategy of protracted war, is to be elusive, to operate in disguise, and to exercise endurance. The operational key of terrorist groups with cellular infrastructure is to keep low and operate sporadically for an extended period of time. With those kinds of operations, a terrorist group, or its remnants, can resurface at any given time after its officially reputed destruction. Then, its members can emerge under a new name or under the old name with new members. With such built-in characteristics it is no wonder that terrorism has become analogous with a hydra.

This article professes that retaliations are doomed to fail in the long run, especially against acts of international terrorism. At least in one country's experience, reprisals failed to accomplish the goal of abolishing international or other types of terrorism. However, in the short term, such overt operations often do succeed in achieving their immediate goals. Such accomplishments tend to create a perception of success and increase the level of expectations. Therefore, it is concluded, retaliations often become the only weapon on which politicians can rely. These types of counter-terrorist measures serve political goals, enhance the credibility and rhetoric of those who proclaim harsh policy, and fulfill the sense of retribution.

* Assistant Professor of Political Science, University of Northern Colorado, Greeley, Colorado

ENDNOTES

1. New York Times, March 6, 1986: 3.

2. Rocky Mountain News, March 7, 1986: 62.

3. Ibid.

4. Ben-Horin, Yoav, and Posen, Barry, Israel's Strategic Doctrine (Santa Monica, CA.: Rand Corporation, 1981), p. vii.

5. Blechman, Barry M, "The Impact of Israel's Reprisals on Behavior of the Bordering Arab Nations Directed at Israel," The Journal of Conflict Resolution, Vol. XVI, #2, June 1972, p. 155.

6. Ben-Horin and Posen, Israel's Strategic Doctrine, p. 4.

7. Alon, Hanan, Countering Palestinian Terrorism by Israel (Santa Monica, CA.: Rand Corporation, 1980), p. 151.

8. Ibid., p. 52.

9. New York Times, December 29, 1968, p. 1.

10. Facts on File, 1968, p. 582.

11. New York Times, December 29, 1968, p. 1.

12. Jonas, George, Vengeance (New York: Bantam Books, 1985).

13. Tinnin, David, Hit Man (London: Futura Publications Limited, 1977).

14. Bar-Zohar, Michael and Haber, Eitan, The Quest for the Red Prince (New York: William Monnon & Company, Inc., 1983).

15. Washington Post, August 2, 1973, p. 8.

16. Blechman, "The Impact of Israel's Reprisals," pp. 155-182.

17. Ibid., p. 288.

18. Alon, 1980.

19. Hoffman, Bruce, <u>Recent Trends in Palestinian Terrorism</u> (Santa Monica, CA.: The Rand Corporation, 1984), p. 14.

20. Ben-Horin and Posen, <u>Israel's Strategic Doctrine</u>, p. 13.

21. <u>Washington Post</u>, May 14, 1987, p. 17.

22. Ofri, Arie, "Intelligence and Counterterrorism," <u>Orbis</u>, vol. 28, #1, Spring 1984, pp. 41-52.

[22]

Israel's Counterterror Strategies, 1967-1987

William V. O'Brien

The 1967 June War was initiated as a result of escalating hostilities between Israel, Fatah terrorists, and Syria. Indeed, all of Israel's wars with the exception of the 1973 Yom Kippur War have developed out of terrorist/counterterror hostilities. I propose to review briefly Israel's counterterror strategies in the twenty years since the 1967 June War. I will summarize basic Israeli counterterror strategy and then analyze the challenges posed for Israel by the emergence of the Palestine Liberation Organization (PLO) as a quasi-independent political-military actor. Finally, I will attempt a provisional evaluation of Israel's counterterror strategies over the last twenty years.

Basic Israeli Counterterror Strategy

By 1967, basic Israeli counterterror strategy had been firmly established. It was loosely referred to as a strategy of "retaliation" or "reprisals" for terrorist attacks. The need to reassure the Israeli public that terrorism would not go unpunished frequently resulted in a pattern of terrorist incidents followed by retaliatory counterterror strikes. However, the Israeli strategy against terrorists and their supporters was basically one of deterrence and of preventive/attrition. Though passive defense measures were also taken, Israeli leaders never considered them sufficient. What they considered indispensable, however, was deterrence through preventive/attrition strikes.[1]

These strikes were aimed at three related types of targets. First, they were primarily counterforce attacks on terrorist forces,

Dr. William V. O'Brien is Professor of Government, Georgetown University; and author of *The Conduct of Just and Limited War* (New York: Praeger, 1981).

bases and facilities. Second, they usually inflicted collateral damage since terrorist bases were generally collocated with civilian targets. Israel sought to minimize collateral damage but contended that persons living close to terrorist bases and supporting or tolerating terrorist operations must expect to suffer from Israeli counterterror strikes. Third, Israeli counterterror attacks were generally conducted in the sovereign territory of a neighboring Arab state and were intended to influence that state's behavior.[2]

As with nuclear deterrence, Israeli counterterror deterrence threatened to inflict "unacceptable damage." Unlike nuclear deterrence, this unacceptable damage had to be inflicted from time to time. It was realized that, although prevention/attrition attacks on the terrorists could reduce their capabilities, no deterrent could stop them altogether. Accordingly, the Israelis made a conscious effort to influence the behavior of the people from whose neighborhoods the terrorists operated, as well as their government, in order to deter them from continued cooperation with the terrorists.

This strategy, of course, risked war (for example, the 1967 June War) with states from which the terrorists operated as well as with their allies, but, notwithstanding the risks of escalation, Israel saw no alternative to its counterterror strategy.

The remarkable success of Israel's 1967 June War led, of course, to the occupation of the West Bank and Gaza, as well as the Sinai. Although Nasser was to resume conventional hostilities in the War of Attrition, 1969-70, the prospects of victory for the armies of the Arab states were such that the hopes for the Palestinian cause were dashed. Hence, the PLO emerged as a quasi-independent political-military actor, determined to wage a war of national liberation.

The Challenge of the PLO

The PLO waged its war of national liberation in a number of forms and phases. Initially, the PLO sought to conduct a guerrilla/terrorist campaign within the occupied territories, hoping to emulate the exploits of the Viet Cong and the Algerian FLN. Successful Israeli counterinsurgency and civil affairs operations quickly eliminated any hope of success in this venture. The PLO was obliged to fall back into neighboring Arab countries and resume the kind of terrorist operations previously carried out by the *fedayeen*, who had been largely under the control of Arab governments.[3]

Now, however, the PLO aspired to independent status, with the host state expected to support or at least condone its terrorist operations. Israel's response was to continue preventive/attrition strikes against PLO targets, hoping that these strikes would have the collateral effect of discouraging continued support or toleration of the PLO's terrorist operations by local populations and the host governments.

Naturally, the coercive process of altering public attitudes and government policies in Arab countries took considerable time. In the case of Jordan, the main source for PLO terrorism, 1967-70, the process took three years. Meanwhile, another dimension of PLO terror was added in the form of aerial hijacking. Some of the radical elements within the PLO, notably the Popular Front for the Liberation of Palestine (PFLP), were dissatisfied with the guerrilla/terrorist operations launched against Israeli-occupied territory. They believed that international terrorist attacks against Israel and her friends would have a far greater political/ psychological effect. Although the PFLP and other elements specializing in aerial hijacking often operated independently of the mainstream PLO, Israel was obliged to treat all international terrorism as emanating from the PLO.

The validity of the claim that international terrorism pays greater political and psychological dividends is supported by the surprisingly modest number of PLO hijackings, even at the time of their greatest notoriety. Hanan Alon's useful study of Israel's counterterror measures records only one PLO aerial hijacking in 1968, 3 in 1969, 4 in 1970 and comparably low figures in the early 1970s.[4]

Preventive security measures taken by Israel and other states reduced the vulnerability of international air traffic to terrorist attacks. However, the basic Israeli strategy was put to the test. It was often difficult to determine the "address" of international terrorists. Israel attempted to respond by attacks on PLO targets in countries known to be sanctuaries and bases for anti-Israeli terrorist operations. The most spectacular of these Israeli strikes was that of December 12, 1968, against the Beirut airport where 13 Arab-registered aircraft were destroyed. This raid followed a December 10, 1968 PFLP attack on an El Al plane in Athens in which one passenger was killed. The UN Security Council unanimously condemned the Beirut raid but offered no relief to victims of international terrorism.[5] The Lebanese Government attempted unsuccessfully to curb the PLO's terror operations.[6]

International terrorism of another kind was demonstrated in its full horror by the PLO "Black September" massacre of eleven members of the Israeli Olympic team in Munich, September 5, 1972. Two days later, on September 7, 1972 the IDF made two incursions into Lebanon to attack PLO bases. The following day, September 8, the IDF carried out simultaneous strikes against terrorist bases and naval installations in Lebanon and Syria. On September 9 the IAF downed three Syrian aircraft over the Golan Heights, and the artillery of both sides engaged in duels.[7] The United States vetoed a Security Council resolution which, though it called for an immediate halt to military operations in the Middle East, did not mention the terrorist acts that had led to the Israeli actions.[8]

Following the high drama of September 1970, the international aerial hijacking campaign abated, and terrorist attacks comparable to the Munich massacre became rare. International security measures were partly responsible, but to a great extent the abatement reflected Yasir Arafat's 'peace offensive' to gain international status and respectability. This campaign culminated in the reception of Arafat at the United Nations, the granting of observer status to the PLO at the UN and other international fora, and a large number of "recognitions" of the PLO as the sole representative of the Palestinian people, as proclaimed by the Arab Summit at Rabat, October 29, 1974. The success of Arafat's campaign demonstrated that the road to respectability led away from international terrorism.

Nevertheless, the PFLP terrorist hijacking of an Air France plane leaving Athens June 27, 1976, forced Israel to undertake a different kind of counterterror operation, a mission to rescue civilian passengers held hostage by the terrorists. The Entebbe rescue mission succeeded brilliantly with few losses of life among the hostages and, among the Israeli force, only the tragic death of its commander, Lt. Col. Yonatan Netanyahu.[9]

Early in the 1970s the threat of PLO international terrorism seemed formidable. In retrospect, that threat has been well contained. Though it continues to exist, it is not the main problem in Israel's war with the PLO. The principal threat has been that of terrorist attacks within Israel and the occupied territories.

Terrorist Attacks Within Israel and the Occupied Territories: The Israeli Response

Israel dealt with PLO terrorist attacks from Jordan during 1967-70; from Syria during 1967-74; and from Lebanon throughout the entire twenty-year period since the June War. Israel has continued its deterrence and preventive/attrition strategies, always cognizant that they risk escalation to full-scale war with Arab states.

Terrorism from Jordan, 1967-70. After its short-lived effort to conduct an insurgency war within the West Bank and Gaza, the PLO used Jordan as its main base. Israel responded vigorously with the traditional three-fold objective of deterring and punishing the PLO, the local populations in the areas where the PLO terrorists were based, and the Jordanian government. Had Hussein endorsed the PLO's strategy and trusted their attitude toward his government, he might have committed regular Jordanian forces to support the PLO as he had supported the *fedayeen* prior to the 1967 June War. However, the PLO's arrogant and sometimes bloody challenges to his government did not encourage cobelligerency. Moreover, Israel was inflicting unacceptable damage on people in areas from which the PLO operated against Israel.[10] The "Black September" international hijacking which culminated in the open insurrection of the PLO in Jordan led to Hussein's military defeat of the PLO, with the threat of Syrian intervention being held in check by the prospect of Israeli intervention backed by the United States. Over a period which lasted until the middle of 1971, the PLO was gradually expelled from Jordan. While these events are in part explained by Hussein's need to suppress insurrection, they are also a consequence of the Israeli counterterror strategy.

Terrorism from Syria, 1967-74. In the early 1970s Syria remained Israel's most implacable enemy. PLO terrorist operations continued to originate in Syria, but they were few. Although Syria armed the PLO, permitted it to maintain training bases, and even controlled several of the PLO elements, Assad was clearly reluctant to risk Israeli counterterror attacks within his country for the sake of the PLO. In June 1973 Assad proclaimed his support for the PLO's operations despite Israeli threats of retaliation. But, in fact, by the end of 1973 PLO infiltration into Israel from Syria had virtually stopped.

After the 1973 Yom Kippur War in which Syria was badly beaten, the Syrians kept up low-level conventional hostilities along the

Golan DMZ. These continued right up to the day the Syrian-Israeli disengagement agreement was concluded on May 31, 1974. Just one week before, May 23, there had been a rare case of PLO infiltration into Israel from Syria. The terrorists were prevented from executing a Maalot type of operation in which one or more kibbutzim in the Golan area would be attacked, hostages taken, and the release of PLO prisoners demanded. Israel responded with IAF attacks on Syrian military targets on May 24.[11]

Just before the Syrian-Israeli disengagement agreement was signed in Geneva, Golda Meir stated that the United States had given Israel private assurances of American support for Israeli counterterror measures, notably by vetoing UN Security Council resolutions condemning Israeli counterterror measures. This was said to be required because Syria refused to guarantee that its territory would not be used for the initiation of terrorist attacks on Israel.[12] However, it was then reported that Assad had given Kissinger oral assurances, to be conveyed to Israel, that the PLO would not be permitted to launch attacks on Israel from Syria.[13]

While Syria continues to host PLO bases and operations, attacks on Israel have not originated in Syria since 1974. Given Syria's adamant anti-Israeli policies, the Syrian case seems to constitute another success for Israeli counterterror strategy.

Terrorism from Lebanon, 1967-87. Virtually all the terrorist attacks against Israel since the 1970 expulsion of the PLO from Jordan were launched from Lebanon. The very success of Israeli counterterror strategies against PLO operations from Jordan and Syria forced the PLO to concentrate its forces in Lebanon. Here the Israeli counterterror strategy proved less successful, for the Lebanese government did not have the strength either to evict or to control the PLO as Jordan and Syria had.

From September 1970 until April 1975, Israeli counterterror strategy consisted of maintaining the preventive/attrition pressures on the PLO bases in Lebanon while giving explicit and implicit warning to the local Lebanese population as well as the Lebanese government that there was a high price to be paid for acquiescing in PLO terror operations. The Lebanese government responded with four approaches, all of which failed. First, it tried twice to control the PLO through formal agreements, one concluded on January 16, 1969; the second, the Cairo Accord of October 25, 1969, which the Lebanese government annulled in May 1987.[14] These agreements sought to trade off recognized status for the PLO in exchange for a modicum of control over the areas from which it launched its terrorist attacks on Israel and conducted its relations with the Lebanese government and armed forces. The PLO violated the restrictions in both agreements. Meanwhile the Christians, apprehensive over the PLO's growing strength, developed their own militia forces, and Lebanon's factions prepared for the bloody competition that deteriorated from civil war into perpetual anarchy.[15]

The Lebanese government then resorted to the use of its own armed forces in an attempt to curb the PLO, notably in June and September 1972 and May and June 1973.[16] However, by this time the regime was already too weak to act as forcefully as had Hussein and Assad.

The Lebanese government then sought assistance from the United Nations Security Council. This body passed some resolutions condemning Israel but, of course, they were not sanctioned except by a "world opinion" to whose manifest unfairness Israel had long since become indifferent. Typical of Security Council practice was its handling of the Kiryat Shmona case. On April 11, 1974, PLO raiders seized an apartment building at Kiryat Shmona, killing eighteen residents, among whom were children whom the terrorists had thrown out of windows in the upper floors. The IDF stormed the building and killed the terrorists. Then, on the night of April 12-13, IDF units, striking at the Lebanese villages from which the Kiryat Shmona attack had originated, blew up a number of houses. Defense Minister Dayan declared on April 13 that if the Lebanese government did not prevent terrorist raids from its territory, Israel would continue its punitive raids until South Lebanon was a desert.[17] The Security Council condemned the Israeli raid, refusing to accept a U.S. amendment to the resolution which would have inserted the words "as at Kiryat Shmona" after the words "all acts of violence."[18]

Finally, Lebanon sought assistance from other Arab states. Sadat threatened to send Egyptian Air Force units to Lebanon in June 1974 but did not. On September 4, 1974, the Arab League Council called for international action to end Israel's raids against the PLO in Lebanon, but again nothing was done. By the end of 1974, all approaches by the Government of Lebanon in dealing with the PLO/Israeli conflict had failed.

The 1975-6 Lebanese Civil War led to Syrian intervention in which the PLO and its radical Lebanese allies were defeated. A tacit Syrian-Israeli "Red Line" agreement mediated by the United States limited the conditions and locations of the Syrian occupation of Lebanon. It assured Israel's overflight prerogatives in Lebanon while denying Syria the options of introducing ground-to-air missiles and of using its air power in fighting with Lebanese factions.[19]

However, the barring of Syria from Southern Lebanon, where Lebanese political authority and military power had ceased to exist, created a vacuum which enabled the PLO to strengthen its state-within-a-state. Israel created a buffer zone controlled by the forces of the maverick Lebanese Major Saad Haddad. However, the basic Israeli counterterror strategy remained one of deterrence and preventive attrition. With the advent of the Begin administration in 1977, Israel shifted its strategy from one-for-one retaliation to sustained counterterror operations. Prime Minister Rabin had already indicated his preference for sustained counterterror in June and July 1974, as Dayan, now the Defense Minister, had done in 1970.[20] Nevertheless, increased Israeli counterterror pressures often followed major terrorist attacks.

Such an attack occurred in the "Country Club" raid of March 11, 1978, which resulted in a bloody running fight even to the outskirts of Tel Aviv.[21] A comprehensive Israeli response was attempted during the period March 15-June 13, 1978, by the Litani Operation which, though it inflicted serious damage on the PLO, made no lasting contribution to the problem of removing the terrorists from their South Lebanese bases.[22]

On April 24, 1979, Begin reiterated the Israeli policy of sustained counterterror operations. Meanwhile, the PLO, convinced that there would be more Litani Operations, began a conventional arms build-up of long-range artillery, rockets, tanks, anti-aircraft guns, and other weapons and materiel obtained from Soviet, Libyan and Syrian sources.[23] The PLO's motivation in obtaining these conventional arms may have been a desire to compete with other Lebanese factions and Haddad's forces. Or, it may have been simply an exercise in building the appearance of a serious military force for prestige reasons. Most importantly, however, it was clearly an attempt to develop a new terror weapon against Israel.

Although it was possible to infiltrate through the UNIFIL area established by the UN after the Litani Operation, the PLO lacked assured direct access to the Israeli border.[24] With long-range artillery and rockets, the PLO could launch countervalue attacks on Israeli population centers, thus introducing a new, grim dimension to the terror-counterterror war. Israel reacted to this new threat with prevention/attrition raids by land, sea and air against PLO forces and bases. In the period 1979-81, this sustained counterterror campaign appeared to produce good results, and the PLO threat was contained.[25]

However, the Syrian missile crisis of Spring 1981 threatened to undermine the Israeli counterterror strategy. The introduction of Syrian missiles into Lebanon, in violation of the 1976 Red Line agreement, threatened Israeli overflights. This could have imperilled the entire preventive/attrition strategy which was largely based on IAF air strikes, and the deterrent threat would have lost credibility. In the context of the Syrian missile challenge, the hostilities of July 10-24, 1981, confirmed the dangers implicit in the PLO's build up of conventional forces.

Israel initiated the July 1981 hostilities with vigorous preventive/attrition attacks on PLO bases as part of its strategy of sustained operations. The PLO retaliated with indiscriminate artillery and rocket attacks on Israeli population centers throughout Northern Galilee. Normal life became impossible, and some residents fled the area. The pattern of hostilities was such that any Israeli decision to launch a strike in Lebanon automatically ensured indiscriminate retaliatory PLO attacks on Israeli civilian targets. Unwilling to escalate hostilities at this time, Begin obtained a cease-fire through the mediation of U.S. envoy Philip Habib, thus according the PLO indirect recognition as a belligerent.[26]

By the time Ariel Sharon was named Defense Minister in August 1981, Israel's strategic position had deteriorated. The Syrian missiles remained in Lebanon, and the PLO seemed able to confound Israel's traditional preventive/attrition strategy by inflicting its own unacceptable damage on Israeli population centers. Israel was compelled to take action to restore its counterterror posture by removing the Syrian missiles and neutralizing the PLO's new conventional countervalue capabilities.

Whatever one thinks of the 1982 Lebanon War and its aftermath, the entire operation cannot be explained in terms of Sharon's deceptions and manipulations. Strategic logic required Israel to undertake some kind of initiative to restore its ability to conduct counterterror operations after July 1981. Of course, while the 1982 war did drive the PLO out of Southern Lebanon and Beirut and damaged its power and prestige greatly, it did not defeat the PLO definitively. Moreover, the extended occupation of Lebanon led to the rise of new guerrilla/terrorist enemies among radical Muslim elements.[27]

More recently, the PLO has succeeded in working its way back into areas from which it was driven in 1982, by overcoming the armed opposition of Lebanese factions, notably the Shiite Amal.[28] The IDF has resumed strikes at familiar PLO targets around Sidon, and the Israeli Navy has been active and successful in interdicting the flow of Palestinian reinforcements into South

Lebanon and frustrating PLO attempts to infiltrate Israel by sea.[29]

Intensified PLO terrorist initiatives in 1985 seemed to be aimed at countering King Hussein's peace efforts.[30] They culminated in the murder of three Israeli hostages held in Larnaca, Cyprus, by PLO terrorists demanding release of PLO detainees. This event, in the context of escalating terrorist activity, led to the IAF attack on PLO headquarters in Tunisia where Arafat had been obliged to take refuge when he was driven out of Beirut.[31]

The Tunisian raid reflected once again the Israeli strategy of counterforce attack on PLO bases with the collateral effects of unacceptable damage to the local population and the host state. Tunisia appears to understand this, because PLO terrorism is no longer directed from that country. After the raid of October 1, 1985, a period of intense terror/counterterror interaction ensued that included the seizure of the Italian steamship *Achille Lauro* and the murder of one of its passengers, Leon Klinghoffer; the U.S. interception of the *Achille Lauro* terrorists; the terrorist attacks on El Al airline counters in the airports of Rome and Vienna, on December 27, 1985; the escalating confrontations between the United States and Qadhafi's Libya which culminated in the April 5, 1986, bombing of the *La Belle* discotheque in Berlin, in which many American servicemen were killed or injured; the April 15, 1986, U.S. raid on Libyan military targets related to terrorist operations; and the abortive attempt to plant a bomb on an El Al flight leaving London on April 17, 1986.[32]

The October 1, 1985, IAF raid on PLO headquarters in Tunisia appears to have had a major deterrent effect. For a year and a half afterwards there was relatively little PLO activity, and most of Israel's terrorism problems were caused by radical Muslim forces in Southern Lebanon. This lull in PLO terrorism ended as the Palestinian National Council prepared to meet in Algiers, April 20-25, 1987. The price for renewed unity under Arafat was adoption of a severe hard line against Israel and against Palestinian moderates seeking peace through negotiations. Since the Algiers conference, the PLO has resumed its terrorist tactics, and Israel has responded with its traditional preventive/attrition attacks on PLO bases in Lebanon.[33]

Twenty Years of Israeli Counterterror Strategy in Retrospect

Israeli counterterror strategy, 1967-87, was successful in deterring and defeating PLO terrorist activity emanating from Jordan and Syria. While Syria continues to support the PLO in many ways, it does not permit terror missions to originate in its territory. Moreover, Syrian meddling in PLO affairs is extremely self-serving and disruptive. Israeli counterterror strategy has not been so successful in dealing with Lebanon, the greatest source of PLO terrorism over the last twenty years and presumably for the foreseeable future. On the one hand, there is no viable Lebanese government to coerce: on the other, no Lebanese faction appears to be strong enough to take over the PLO and control it. Moreover, South Lebanon is now a dangerous area for Israeli operations because of the radicalization of Muslim elements there.

This has left Israel in a dilemma. Israel finds it difficult to keep the PLO away from Israel's borders without the IDF occupying Southern Lebanon periodically. But Israeli occupations lead to greater Israeli losses than would be incurred in the usual low-intensity hostilities with the PLO. Ironically, Israel's best hope may lie in a tacit cooperation with Syria which has its own reasons for curbing and controlling the PLO. But tacit cooperation with Syria is ephemeral.

Finally, the Israeli attack on PLO headquarters in Tunisia appears to have been a success, judging by its results: the removal of PLO terrorist operations centers from Tunisia, and minimal terrorist activity for a period of about eighteen months.

Given the dedication of the PLO to its cause of eliminating Israel and establishing a Palestinian state; the PLO's refusal to negotiate in any manner acceptable to Israel; the extreme unlikelihood of Arafat or anyone else making a bold move to break the impasse; and, on the Israeli domestic political scene, the profound opposition to negotiating with the PLO — Israel's war with the PLO may continue indefinitely. There is no reason to expect a change in the basic Israeli counterterror strategy of deterrence and preventive/attrition. That strategy has been pursued for the last twenty years with increasing emphasis on sustained rather than tit-for-tat retaliatory operations. Through its counterterror measures, particularly in September 1970, in the spring and summer of 1974, in March 1978, and in July 1981, Israel has risked escalating the hostilities to conventional international war. In 1982, Israel itself initiated an all-out attack on the PLO that inevitably led to hostilities with Syria.

Thus, PLO terrorism has been contained but not definitively defeated. The price of continued counterterror deterrence and preventive/attrition operations will continue to be collateral damage to Lebanon or any other country imprudent or unfortunate enough to serve as a launching pad for PLO terrorist attacks on Israel. Israel's continuation of this strategy may also risk escalation to conventional international war. But continuation of the strategy is dictated by the exigencies of Israel's war with the PLO. Israeli counterterror operations will continue to mitigate the PLO terrorist threat and may even contribute, through the grim workings of attrition, to changing attitudes in a war that neither side seems able to win or to abandon. ■

NOTES

1. Avner Yaniv, *Dilemmas of Security* (New York: Oxford University Press, 1987), pp. 41-2; Howard M. Sachar, *A History of Israel* (2 vols.: Vol. I, New York: Knopf, 1976; Vol. II, New York: Oxford University Press, 1987), I, 429-71; Nadav Safran, *Israel: The Embattled Ally* (Cambridge, MA: Harvard University Press, 1978), Chapter 1-18, pp. 222-330.

2. Yitzhak Rabin gave classic expression to Israeli strategy in 1966 in explaining a raid into Jordan: "The operation was intended to make it clear to Jordan, and to the population which is collaborating with Fatah, and to Fatah members themselves, that as long as this side of the border will not be quiet, no quiet will prevail on the other side." *Skira Hodsheet* [Monthly Survey], A Journal for IDF Officers (Hebrew), Vol. 13, No. 4, 1966, p. 91, quoted in Hanan Alon, *Countering Palestinian Terrorists in Israel* (Santa Monica, CA: RAND, August 1980), p. 38.

3. Yaniv, *Dilemmas of Security*, p. 39.

4. Alon, *Countering Palestinian Terrorism in Israel*, pp. 49-52.

5. On the Beirut raid and the Security Council reaction see Derek W. Bowett, "Reprisals Involving Recourse to Armed Force," *American Journal of International Law* 66 (1972) 1, 13.

6. Yaniv, *Dilemmas of Security*, pp. 43-5.

7. In a television interview, the Israeli Chief of Staff, Lt. Gen. David Elazar, said that IDF incursions into Lebanon and IAF attacks on PLO targets in Lebanon and Syria were "in retaliation not only for the Munich killing but also for a rising wave of attacks on Israel's borders with Lebanon and Syria." General Elazar stated that, "These actions were part of a continuous war" that should not be regarded as "begun today and finished tomorrow." "Top Israeli General Calls Raids Only 'Part of a Continuous War,'" *New York Times*, September 11, 1972, p. 12, cols. 2-3.

8. "U.S. Casts a Veto in U.N. on Mideast, Citing Terrorism," *New York Times*, September 11, pp. 1, col. 8; 10, cols. 4-6.

9. Sachar, *A History of Israel*, II, 9-11.

10. Yaniv, *Dilemmas of Security*, p. 39.

11. "Israelis Kill 6, Capture 2; New Massacre Plot Seen," *New York Times*, May 24, 1974, p. 3, cols. 1-2; "Israeli Jets Attack Syrians as Fighting Intensifies in Golan," *New York Times*, May 25, 1974, p. 2, col. 3.

12. "Israel Counts on U.S. to Bar U.N. Sanctions," *New York Times*, May 31, 1974, p. 8, cols. 7-8; "Excerpts from Mrs. Meir's Speech to Israeli Parliament on the Accord With Syria," *New York Times*, May 31, 1974, p. 8, cols. 3-8.

13. "Syria Reported in Pledge to Bar Guerrilla Raids," *New York Times*, June 1, 1974, pp. 1, col. 5: 8, cols. 2-4.

14. Walid Khalidi, *Conflict and Violence in Lebanon* (Cambridge, MA: Harvard Studies in International Affairs, no. 38, Harvard Center for International Affairs, 1979), pp. 185-7; Yaniv, *Dilemmas of Security*, pp. 43-6. "Lebanon Annuls PLO Agreement," *Washington Post*, May 22, 1987, p. A 29, cols. 5-6.

15. Yaniv, *Dilemmas of Security*, p. 47.

16. *Ibid.*, pp. 43-6.

17. Mr. Tekoah, Israel, *UN Security Council Official Records*, Provisional Verbatim Record of the Seventeen Hundred and Sixty-Sixth Meeting, 15 April 1974 (S/PV.1766, 15 April 1974), p. 22.

18. *UN Security Council Official Records*, Provisional Verbatim Record of Seventeen Hundred and Sixty-Ninth Meeting, 24 April 1974 (S/PV 1769, 24 April 1974), pp. 21-2, 29-30. See Security Council Resolution 347 of 24 April 1974, *UN Security Council Official Records*, Resolutions and Decisions of the Security Council 1974, Thirty-First Year, pp. 3-4. (S/11274).

19. Yaniv, *Dilemmas of Security*, pp. 60-1.

20. *Ibid.*, pp. 45, 69-70.

21. Sachar, *A History of Israel*, II, 121.

22. *Ibid.*; Yaniv, *Dilemmas of Security*, pp. 71-5.

23. Jillian Becker, *The PLO* (London: Weidenfeld & Nicolson, 1984), p. 204; Richard A. Gabriel, *Operation "Peace for Galilee"*) New York: Hill & Wang, 1984), pp. 50-1, 58; Yaniv, *Dilemmas of Security*, pp. 77-8, 104.

24. *Ibid.*, pp. 78-9.

25. *Ibid.*, pp. 216-45.

26. *Ibid.*, pp. 88-90; Sachar, *A History of Israel*, II, 166-7.

27. *Ibid.*, II, 205-10, Yaniv, *Dilemmas of Security*, pp. 232-45.

28. "The Shiite-Palestinian Battle: Anguish Grows in Torn Land," *New York Times*, December 5, 1986, p. 1, cols. 2-3; John Kifner, "Arafat Tries a Comeback in Lebanon," *New York Times*, Section IV, p. 3, cols. 1-2.

29. Typical Israeli actions are described in: "Israeli Gunboats Shell 2 Palestinian Positions," *New York Times*, December 5, 1986, p. 5, col 1; "Israeli Navy Seizes a Boat Off Lebanon and 50 Palestinians," *New York Times*, February 8, 1987, p. 17, col. 1; "Israeli Jets Raid Target in Lebanon," *New York Times*, March 21, 1987, p. 4, cols. 1-3, "Israeli Warplanes Strike Palestinians," *Washington Post*, May 9, 1987, A 16, cols. 1-3.

30. "Israel Says PLO Behind Terror Surge," *Washington Post*, October 19, 1985, A 16, col. 1.

31. "Israel Calls Bombing A Warning to Terrorists," *New York Times*, October 2, 1985, p. 8, cols. 1-3.

32. For an authoritative account of the background of the U.S. Libyan raid of April 15, 1986, its planning and conduct, see Col. W. Hays Parks, "Crossing the Line," *U.S. Naval Institute Proceedings* 112 (1986) 40-52.

33. A PLO terrorist infiltration was thwarted by the IDF on April 19, 1987 on the eve of the PNC Algiers Conference. "PLO Squad is Crushed Inside Israel," *Washington Post*, April 20, 1987, A 1, col. 4, A 20, cols. 1-5. The Algiers Conference is described in "PLO Acts to Reunite Factions," *Washington Post*, April 21, 1987, A 1, col. 6; A 26, cols. 1-6; and in "Arafat: Still First Among Equals," *Newsweek*, April 27, 1987, p. 42.

[23]

LEBANON: MOTIVATIONS AND INTERESTS IN ISRAEL'S POLICY
Ze'ev Schiff

Israel's recent contortions notwithstanding, policy vis-à-vis Lebanon over the years has followed a set pattern. And the latest turn of events is something of a throwback to the mid-1970s, when the Labor Alignment was in office with Yitzhak Rabin as Prime Minister.

In common with all other Arab countries bordering Israel, Lebanon waged war on the newly proclaimed Jewish State in 1948. Lebanon *per se* has never posed a military threat to Israel. But its very weakness gave rise to fear—the well-founded fear that outsiders would abuse its territory as a base for hostilities against Israel. For the rest, Lebanon with its large Christian community was deemed the Arab country most amenable to a political understanding and favorable to another non-Muslim state in the Middle East. Admittedly too weak to be the first to sign a peace accord with Israel, it was seen as *the* potential second Arab state to join the peace process.

The Israeli attitude was one of restraint—not to push Lebanon into situations liable to upset the delicate domestic balance between its multifarious communities. When terrorist attacks were launched from inside Lebanon, Israel was careful not to hit back at Lebanese government institutions. No such scruples bothered Jerusalem in reprisals against Syria, Jordan and Egypt, where state targets were hard hit as an "inducement" to the authorities to clamp down on terrorists and terrorism. Lebanon was accorded preferential treatment, since manifestly its central government was incapable of restraining terrorist elements within its bounds.

However, Israel did step up reprisals when Fath became operational with telling effect in the mid-1960s. The climax at the time was an incursion of Israeli units into the airport at Beirut, in December 1968, where they blew up planes belonging to Middle East Airlines.

Ze'ev Schiff, on leave from his job as defense editor of the Israeli newspaper, Haaretz, *is a senior associate at the Carnegie Endowment for International Peace.*

In 1970, even before the thousands of armed Palestinians expelled from Jordan had poured into Lebanon, confrontation took an acute turn. Many hundreds of Palestinian guerrillas of various splinter organizations seized control of Lebanese territory bordering on Israel (on the slopes of Mt. Hermon, dubbed by the Israelis "Fatahland") and there set up permanent bases. Israel riposted with large-scale military raids. Previously Israel had contented itself with brief commando hit-and-run strikes. The first large-scale raid was carried out in May 1970, when an Israeli armored force seized large parts of "Fatahland" and stayed there for more than 24 hours. The second major armored incursion took place in 1972, when Israeli forces seized territory up to the Litani River and stayed on a couple of days. Israeli reprisals assumed a grimmer character following the Palestinian massacres of civilians, notably after the slaughter of dozens of school children in Ma'alot and of civilians in Kiryat Shimona (in April and May 1974). At the same time, Israel conducted virtually non-stop "policing operations" in Lebanese territory.

After the Palestinian organizations were ousted from Jordan and had made Lebanon their main springboard, it was glaringly obvious to the Israel government that the deterioration in security along the border with Lebanon called for more vigorous countermeasures. Three objectives dominated Israeli policy vis-à-vis Lebanon during the 1970s: how to cope with PLO terrorism emanating from that country; what attitude to adopt toward the Christian community; and how to react to the Syrian military presence in Lebanon.

Coping then with the PLO in Lebanon meant satisfying immediate security needs. The primary aim was to try to dislodge the PLO from its strongholds in southern Lebanon. To be sure, there was readiness to aid such Lebanese elements as were opposed to the PLO. But at the mid-1970s there was no talk of the political liquidation of the PLO or its total eviction from Lebanon. Solutions were sought largely in the military sphere by a combination of defensive and offensive measures.

To prevent terrorist infiltrations from Lebanese territory, Israel set up a system of fences with electronic devices on its northern border. In Israeli border settlements there was a call for volunteers to join a civil defense guard. Large sums were invested in the construction of underground shelters for the population. Even so, Israel could not afford the stupendous resources needed to build shelters that would be impervious to artillery barrages and could accommodate the entire population for long periods of time. Complementary to its defensive system, Israel dispatched its army into offensive action against Palestinian targets, mainly in southern Lebanon.

Also within this defensive context, in 1976 Israel responded positively to two Lebanese army majors who applied separately for aid to protect Christian villages along the border suffering depredations at the hands of the Palestinians. One of these majors was Sa'd Haddad. (The other was Samir Shidyaq, who left the scene some time ago.) The upshot was the creation of two small, Christian-held wedges in Lebanese territory along the border with Israel. This aid to the Christian villages was part and parcel of what Israel called the "Good Fence."

Relations with the two Lebanese officers and the villages under their care were not the sole link between Israel and the Christian community in Lebanon. Simultaneous ties were developed with the Christians up north.

Whereas security was the underlying factor in ties with the officers and villagers in south Lebanon, more complex motives prompted Israel to establish a link-up with Christian groups in northern Lebanon, particularly those led by Camille Chamoun and Pierre Gemayel. From the outset, the political aspect impinged on strictly military considerations.

At their very first high level encounters with the Israel government in 1976, the northern Christian leaders wanted Israel to wage a full-scale war in Lebanon aimed at ridding the country of both the PLO and the Syrian presence. This Christian demand was rejected by Prime Minister Rabin. The Israeli line was to "help the Christians help themselves"—and, for the rest, as far as possible, to steer clear of Lebanon's domestic problems. Aid took the form of deliveries of light and heavy weapons and munitions, later supplemented by military training. The intention was to help establish a military force in Lebanon capable of standing up to the PLO. The Israel government did not conceal this from Washington, and the US administration neither imposed a veto nor expressed displeasure at Israel's special ties with the Christian militias in Lebanon.

With regard to the Syrian military presence in Lebanon, Israeli policy under the Labor Alignment government was in marked contrast to that eventually adopted after 1977 by the Likud government under Menachem Begin. In 1976 the Syrian army moved into Lebanon to intervene in the civil war there. Until then it had been a hard and fast rule in Jerusalem not to tolerate the dispatch by one Arab country of its army into another Arab country neighboring on, and therefore constituting a potential threat to, Israel. At first Israel was inclined to oppose the Syrian entry into Lebanon, but Prime Minister Rabin, with the backing of the then chief of staff Mordechai Gur, was open to a different line of reasoning. He went along with the unorthodox idea that the Syrian move into Lebanon would not be viewed as an alarm signal; furthermore the Syrian presence was seen to offer certain advantages, such as the dispersion of the Syrian army on the two fronts—Lebanon and the Golan Heights.

Israel did lay down "red lines" as a precondition to its acquiescence to a Syrian military presence in Lebanon. One such "red line" was geographical—the Syrian army was not to occupy territory too close to the Israeli border. Another "red line" placed a taboo on the introduction into Lebanon of certain sophisticated weapons systems, such as ground-to-air missiles. Through American mediation, a tacit agreement on these curbs was reached between Israel and Syria.

After the Likud took office, Israeli policy vis-à-vis Lebanon underwent far-reaching changes, albeit not instantly. On this score, the conduct of the Likud governments falls into several distinct periods bearing the impress of as many different Ministers of Defense.

When Ezer Weizman was Defense Minister from 1977 to 1980, Israeli reprisals against the PLO were beefed up. These came in waves, some of them pre-emptive, without waiting for the PLO in Lebanon to strike first. Even so, under Weizman, there were no intrinsic changes in overall policy. But two events were particularly important. The first was the "Litani" operation in March 1978, launched after the massacre of dozens of Israeli citizens trapped in a bus in Israeli territory. It began with an incursion of up to some ten kilometers and ended with Israeli control of most of the territory up to the Litani River. The escalation was not only in the volume of forces thrown into battle, but also in the Israel army's protracted stay—some four months—in Lebanese territory.

The second notable happening—in consequence of the "Litani" operation—was the setting up of a special force by the United Nations, UNIFIL, which occupied the territory evacuated by the Israel Defense Forces, excluding the enclave along the border controlled by Maj. Haddad which had been expanded into a single enclave running the length of the border and embracing many Shi'i as well as Christian villages.

Israel now had in southern Lebanon two buffer strips held respectively by Maj. Haddad and UNIFIL. Soon, however, it became apparent that these "security" strips could not prevent PLO actions, because Israel had no satisfactory answer to PLO artillery, which could fire at Israeli settlements over the heads of the UNIFIL forces.

When Ezer Weizman left the Defense Ministry, the policy toward Lebanon was well-defined. The guideline was to preserve the politico-strategic status quo in Lebanon, so that it should not be transformed into a hostile country with an offensive infrastructure turned against Israel. Accordingly, aid was to be extended to the Christians who did not want Lebanon to join the ranks of the Arab confrontation states; at the same time, the PLO was to be harassed and denied freedom of action in Lebanon.

Southern Lebanon took pride of place in this Israeli policy. The purpose was to keep the zone clear of PLO and other hostile forces; there must be no military infrastructure there capable of disrupting life in northern Israel. Toward this end, contacts were fostered with the local Lebanese inhabitants, whose conduct—it was thought—might be favorably influenced through a broader understanding with Lebanon all round. It was incumbent on Israel to thwart adverse developments in southern Lebanon pending an overall settlement with Lebanon which would safeguard Israel's vital security interests.

The departure from this policy came after Weizman's resignation from the Cabinet in 1980. The first signs of change became apparent when Prime Minister

Begin took over the Defense Portfolio vacated by Weizman. Initially, these changes were not the fruit of deliberate planning. Rather was it a case of Begin's losing control of events. Gone from the Cabinet was not only Weizman, but also Moshe Dayan, who had resigned from his post as Foreign Minister. Lacking military expertise, and possessing an almost blind confidence in his military entourage, especially in the then chief of staff Rafael Eytan, Begin flunked his test as the politician in charge of policy vis-à-vis Lebanon.

Eytan's stance toward the PLO was ultra-extreme—he favored the liquidation of its strongholds throughout Lebanon. He was also one of the leading advocates of a closer military tie-up with the Christian Phalangists, whose effectiveness was deemed dubious by some of his own advisers. During this period, Israeli military operations were greatly expanded and the army enjoyed a virtually free hand.

The first sharp turnabout in fundamental policy occurred in April 1981, in conjunction with clashes between the Syrian army and the Christian inhabitants of the town of Zahle. Begin was drawn into a ringing declaration that Israel would not allow the annihilation of Christians in Lebanon. Israel was thus proclaimed the protector of the Christian minority in that country. It was a far-reaching commitment, unwarranted by the circumstances. For, as pointed out by intelligence sources in Israel, the troubles with the Syrians in Zahle had been initiated by the Maronites. Henceforth, a provocation on the part of extremist Christian elements might plunge Israel into war with Syria.

Intelligence was unequivocal on this score: these Christian elements were bent on provoking a collision between Jerusalem and Damascus. In the Zahle area two Syrian helicopters were downed by Israeli warplanes in April 1981. The Syrians then deployed ground-to-air missiles in Lebanon. The tacit agreement on "red lines" between Israel and Syria was finished. The status quo, which Israel had been anxious to preserve in Lebanon, was destroyed.

While the Israel government was pondering future action against the Syrian missiles in Lebanon, artillery duels flared up with the PLO in southern Lebanon. These drove the Begin government into a corner. Through American mediation the artillery duels ended in a cease-fire, with Israel entering an agreement to which the PLO was a recognized party. Ironically, the hawkish Begin government had landed itself in a situation where it was according the PLO a formal status. Here, manifestly, was a political and military imbroglio which the government would not and could not long tolerate.

The decisive switch in policy toward Lebanon came with the appointment of Ariel Sharon as Defense Minister in 1981. His approach to the Lebanon challenge differed from that of his predecessors in just about all respects. By and large he found a zealous partner in chief of staff Eytan. Sharon ruled, for instance, that Israel had committed one of its gravest ever security blunders in giving its tacit consent to the entry of the Syrian army in Lebanon. The plain inference was that, at a fitting opportunity, he would have a go at expelling the Syrian army from Lebanon.

He adopted a radical new policy toward the PLO presence in Lebanon. He set himself the optimal target of the political liquidation of the PLO through its total eviction from Lebanon. And to preclude the return of the PLO after the Israelis had driven it out, he wanted his principal Christian partner to be elected President of Lebanon. The man of his choice was Bashir Gemayel, who would sign a peace agreement with Israel on behalf of Lebanon. This sequence of events could not materialize without the Syrian army also being driven out of Lebanon. Otherwise the Syrians would impede the election of Bashir Gemayel as President and would resist the eviction of the PLO.

Whether or to what extent Begin was cognizant of this policy is irrelevant—he is alleged to have been kept in the dark. Also unimportant is whether Sharon's objectives were or were not approved by the Israel Cabinet. What counts is that the Israel Defense Forces were sent to war in Lebanon in 1982 in pursuit of these aims.

Most of Israel's objectives in the Lebanon war were not attained, or only partially attained, and what little was attained was fated to crumble away or prove self-defeating. Bashir Gemayel was indeed elected President of Lebanon, but was assassinated soon after. The Phalangists he commanded were enfeebled after Israel withdrew from the Beirut area. The Syrian army was pushed out of part of the Lebanese Bekaa, but it drove a deep wedge through northern Lebanon, and today controls much of the Damascus-Beirut highway. Its military strength has grown mightily since the war. Moreover, Washington has come round to recognizing that Syria has vital interests in Lebanon and that Damascus can no longer be ignored when a new regime is installed in Lebanon. The outcome is just about the opposite of what Sharon expected the war to achieve.

As for the PLO, Israel did partly accomplish its purpose. The PLO was uprooted from Beirut. Even though it was not expelled from Lebanon as a whole, the aftereffects of the war were such as to cause a deep rift within the PLO, climaxed by a civil war among the Palestinians. The Palestinian leadership which emerged in the second half of the 1960s is in an extremely difficult situation. Palestinians everywhere are demoralized and disoriented. In southern Lebanon, following the destruction of the PLO military infrastructure, the Palestinian social infrastructure is still there—in refugee camps along the border with Israel—saddled with old and new problems.

For Israel, the Lebanon war, far from solving problems, has created new ones. The one positive outcome in the security sphere is the removal of threats to the Israeli townships and villages in Galilee. No longer are they "hostages" to PLO artillery. Even so, Israel's border still cannot be hermetically sealed against terrorist infiltrations. But for the Israel Defense Forces, life has become altogether more difficult. Israeli troops have to face up to guerrilla warfare in

Lebanese territory. Palestinian terrorists have been joined by Lebanese Muslims, among them suicidal fanatics, whose likes the Israelis have never encountered before.

Israel is in a quandary endeavoring to maintain control over hundreds of thousands of Shia in southern Lebanon. And the longer the Israeli occupation lasts, the slimmer are the chances of forging positive ties with the Shia, who are now the largest community in Lebanon.

In regard to the Druze, Israel is also in an embarrassing situation. The clashes between the Druze in Lebanon and Israel's Phalangist friends have greatly perturbed the Druze community in Israel. There is pressure on Israel to choose between veteran allies, the Druze, who perform important functions in Israel's security system, and those relatively new allies, the Phalangists.

Israel's security burden has grown much heavier in the wake of the war. Israeli reservists are called up for many more days' service than in the past, and in a foreign country at that. This is one of the factors causing many Israelis to urge instant withdrawal from strife-ridden Lebanon.

Israel's new Defense Minister, the Likud's fourth, Moshe Arens, has realized that Israel must be more modest in its war aims and confine itself to what is truly essential, that is, the defense of its northern border. This turnabout has not been given an official stamp or publicly proclaimed, but turnabout it is—manifest and unequivocal. In the context of this reversal, Israel no longer poses as the protector of the Amin Gemayel regime. Relations between Israel and the Phalangists are not what they used to be. Down-to-earth realities hold sway.

Israel wants to bring its forces home from Lebanon, but has difficulty in doing so. The notion of forcibly evicting the Syrian army from Lebanon has been dropped. Nevertheless, Israel makes its own pullback from Lebanon contingent on a simultaneous withdrawal by the Syrians. The calculation is that the Israeli military presence in Lebanon will exert pressure on Damascus to engage in a *quid pro quo* deal. Despite Israel's unilateral, partial pullback from the Shuf, Israel and Syria remain locked in a bear's embrace in Lebanon. Israel's complete pullout is conditional on that of the Syrians, who for their part vow not to quit before and unless Israel's meager war gains are wiped out. They have insisted on annulment of the May 17 agreement signed between Israel and Lebanon, but now that Lebanon has taken this step unilaterally, and even were Israel to withdraw, it is by no means clear that the Syrians would also withdraw.

The May 17 agreement was indeed regarded as an Israeli accomplishment. Israel succeeded in getting American diplomacy and Secretary of State Shultz personally involved in one more agreement with an Arab country. But this, unlike the peace accord with Egypt, was more or less imposed on a reluctant Lebanon. Among the Arab confrontation countries. Lebanon is of course the weakest. Two questions arose: Could Lebanon abide by the agreement without thereby further aggravating or even perpetuating its civil war? And could the agreement be implemented without dooming parts of Lebanon to remain in the hands of foreign conquerors? The annullment of the agreement leaves these answers in suspense.

For Israel, however, there is no getting away from the sad truth that dealings with Beirut bear no comparison with doing business with Cairo and that, where Lebanon is concerned, there is no ignoring Syria. In the absence of an arrangement with Damascus, Israel will find itself stuck in southern Lebanon with another million or so Arabs, not only Lebanese, but a substantial minority of Palestinian refugees over whom it will have to exercise dominion. The prospect is disheartening. Among other unpleasant consequences, Israel will have to invest huge funds in what may come to be its alien ''northern bank.'' In sum, Israel's strategic position vis-à-vis Syria has worsened.

The way out of the imbroglio is an understanding between Syria and Israel. They are the two local powers capable of promoting the stability of Lebanon. Israel is apparently coming round to acceptance of a withdrawal from Lebanon in advance of the Syrians—subject to a foolproof undertaking by the Syrians not to stay in Lebanon. There must be the certainty that they in turn will get out.

But this is not all. Israel dare not give its consent to public abrogation of the May 17 agreement with Lebanon. Now that it is abrogated, Jerusalem may have no option but to keep its forces in southern Lebanon indefinitely as a shield for Israel's northern settlements. There is a growing awareness in Israel that Lebanon cannot be forced into whittling down its ties with the Arab world and diluting its own Arab character, but Israel cannot renounce its security interests in the south.

Thus, while there is readiness in Israel to recognize Syria's security interests in the Bekaa close to the Syrian border, in return for Syrian recognition of Israel's own vital security interests, no Israeli Prime Minister of whatever political school can accept a renewal of terrorist activity against the Galilee towns and villages. This is a minimal requirement, backed by Israeli public opinion.

227

Part X
International Responses to Middle East Terrorism

[24]

Economic Sanctions and International Terrorism

*Kenneth W. Abbott**

TABLE OF CONTENTS

I. INTRODUCTION

Economic sanctions have become a prominent part of the American response to foreign state involvement in international terrorism.[1] Since the early 1970s,[2] a series of Congressional statutes[3] has authorized or required the Executive to curtail a broad range of economic relationships with countries the Secretary of State has determined to be supporters of terrorism, a group that now includes Libya, Syria, South Yemen, Iran and Cuba[4] and earlier included Iraq.[5] Under these statutes, the United

---

* Professor of Law, Northwestern University School of Law; Harvard Law School, 1969; B.A., Cornell University, 1966.

1. United States Department of State, Economic Sanctions to Combat International Terrorism, Bureau of Public Affairs Special Report No. 149, July 1986, at 1 [hereinafter State Department Report].

2. For a discussion of the early history of these statutes, see Abbott, *Linking Trade to Political Goals: Foreign Policy Export Controls in the 1970s and 1980s*, 65 MINN. L. REV. 739, 766-71 (1981).

3. For a thorough review of these statutes and others relating to the President's ability to use economic sanctions, see B. CARTER, INTERNATIONAL ECONOMIC SANCTIONS: IMPROVING THE HAPHAZARD U.S. LEGAL REGIME (forthcoming); *see also* State Department Report, *supra* note 1, at 3-5.

4. Export Administration Act, § 6(j)(1), 50 U.S.C. app. § 2405(j)(1) (1982), requires

290   VANDERBILT JOURNAL OF TRANSNATIONAL LAW   [Vol. 20:289

States has restricted all forms of foreign assistance,[6] Eximbank and OPIC financing,[7] arms sales,[8] commercial exports[9] and imports,[10] trade preferences,[11] air transportation[12] and other transactions[13] with one or

---

the Executive branch to notify specific Congressional committees before granting licenses for certain exports to countries that the Secretary of State has determined "repeatedly" provide support for acts of terrorism. The Export Administration Regulations reflect the Secretary's determination. *See* 15 C.F.R. §§ 385.1(b)(1) (Cuba), 385.4(d) (People's Democratic Republic of Yemen, Syria, and Iran), 385.7(b) (Libya) (1987).

5. The Secretary of State removed Iraq from the list of states supporting terrorism, and hence from the related restrictions under the Export Administration Regulations in 1982 because of its "improved record." *See* 47 Fed. Reg. 9201, 9204 (1982).

6. *See* 22 U.S.C. § 2371 (1982), prohibiting the granting of the specified forms of foreign assistance to any country that the President determines (1) grants sanctuary from prosecution to any individual or group that has committed an act of international terrorism, or (2) otherwise supports international terrorism. The restriction applies to all forms of assistance under the Foreign Assistance Act, the Agricultural Trade Development and Assistance Act of 1954, the Arms Export Control Act, the Export-Import Bank Act and the Peace Corps Act. The President can waive the restriction on national security and humanitarian grounds. *See also* Foreign Assistance and Related Programs Appropriations Act of 1986, Pub. L. No. 99-190, § 512, 99 Stat. 1291, 1304 (1985) (prohibits use of appropriated funds for aid to Cuba, Iraq, Libya, South Yemen, and Syria).

7. 22 U.S.C. § 2371 (1982) specifically restricts assistance under the Export-Import Bank Act; the Foreign Assistance Act, *supra* note 6, to which the section also applies, authorizes OPIC activities. As to Eximbank, see also 12 U.S.C. § 635(b)(1)(B) (1982) (authorizing denial of Eximbank financing for specified foreign policy reasons, including support of terrorism).

8. *See infra* notes 150-55 and accompanying text. The Arms Export Control Act prohibits the export of items on the Munitions List to countries supporting international terrorism. *See* State Department Report, *supra* note 1, at 3.

9. *See infra* note 137. *See also* 22 U.S.C. § 2349aa-8(b) (1982) (authorizing President to prohibit export to Libya of any good or technology subject to jurisdiction of the United States or exported by any person subject to jurisdiction of the United States).

10. *See* 22 U.S.C. § 2349aa-9(a) (1982) (authorizing President to ban imports of any good or service from any country that supports terrorism or terrorist organizations or harbors terrorists or terrorist organizations). *See also id.* at § 2349aa-8(a) (authorizing President to prohibit the importation into the United States of any article grown, produced, extracted or manufactured in Libya).

11. *See* 19 U.S.C. § 2462(b)(6) (1982) (prohibiting designation of any nation supporting terrorism as beneficiary developing country under Generalized System of Preferences, with exception for national economic interest of the United States).

12. *See* 49 U.S.C. § 1514 (1982) (authorizing President to suspend air service to any country he determines to be violating Hague air safety convention or supporting any terrorist group that supports the seizure of aircraft, regardless of bilateral air service agreements, and to any third state that maintains air service to such a country); 49 U.S.C. § 1515(e)(2)(D) (1982) (authorizing, and in some cases requiring, President to restrict air service to foreign airports that do not provide adequate security and to third country airports that continue to serve such airports). *See also id.* at § 1515a(b). The

more of the designated states.

The use of such measures has grown apace in recent years. The United States has steadily tightened economic sanctions aimed at Libya in particular over the last decade. This process culminated in President Reagan's national emergency declaration of January 1986[14] which prohibited virtually all economic transactions with Libya and froze Libyan assets subject to United States jurisdiction.[15] The United States also strengthened sanctions against Syria in November 1986 and June 1987, although to a much lesser extent,[16] and tightened controls on exports to

---

State Department takes the position that the Federal Aviation Act also "contains sufficient authority" for the Department of Transportation to prohibit sales in the United States of airline tickets to countries against which the President has imposed aviation sanctions. *See* State Department Report, *supra* note 1, at 4.

13. Under the International Emergency Economic Powers Act, 50 U.S.C. §§ 1701-06 (1982) [hereinafter IEEPA], upon declaring a national emergency based on the existence of "any unusual and extraordinary threat, which has its source in whole or in substantial part outside the United States, to the [United States] national security, foreign policy, or economy," the President may interrupt virtually any economic transaction with foreign persons. *Id.* at § 1701(a). In January 1986, for example, President Reagan imposed economic sanctions on Libya under the IEEPA. Those sanctions included a ban on exports and imports, a prohibition on new private loans and credits, financial controls designed to restrict travel to Libya and the blocking of certain Libyan assets in the control of United States persons. *See infra* notes 14-15.

Statute requires the United States representative to the International Monetary Fund [hereinafter IMF] to oppose IMF assistance to countries harboring terrorists. 22 U.S.C. § 286e-11 (1982).

14. Exec. Order No. 12,543, 51 Fed. Reg. 865 (1986).

15. Libyan Sanctions Regulations, 31 C.F.R. § 550 (Treasury Department regulations prohibiting exports, imports, transportation and travel to and from Libya, performance of contracts supporting projects in Libya and extensions of credit to the government of Libya and blocking assets of the government of Libya within the United States or under the control of United States persons); Exec. Order No. 12,544, 51 Fed. Reg. 1235 (1986) (ordering blocking of assets); 15 C.F.R. §§ 385.7, 390.7 (1987) (Commerce Department regulations revoking export authorizations inconsistent with Libyan Sanctions Regulations); *In re* Suspension of Operations Between United States and Libya, Order 86-2-23, Doc. No. 43,711 (Department of Transportation, 1986), *reprinted in* H.R. Doc. No. 249, 99th Cong., 2d Sess. (1986). For a thorough discussion of the Libyan sanctions, see Bialos & Juster, *The Libyan Sanctions: A Rational Response to State-Sponsored Terrorism*, 26 VA. J. INT'L L. 799 (1986).

Just over two months later, of course, the United States went beyond economic sanctions, using military force against Libya. For a collection of documents relating to the bombing, see DEP'T ST. BULL., June 1986, at 1-23.

16. For a description of the sanctions the United States imposed in 1986, see U.S. Takes Measures Against Syria, White House Statement, Nov. 14, 1986, *reprinted in* DEP'T ST. BULL., Jan. 1987, at 79 [hereinafter White House Statement]. The actions taken included a decision to expand certain export controls, termination of Eximbank

Iran in 1984.[17] For the most part, however, these have been unilateral American measures; international cooperation has been extremely modest.[18]

Understanding and evaluating antiterrorism sanctions is no easy task. Terrorism and state support for terrorism are complex, sometimes ambiguous phenomena. Economic sanctions can also be complex and subtle instruments.[19] Sanctions against terrorism, then, involve complexity com-

---

financing, *see* 51 Fed. Reg. 43,796 (1986), notification of intention to terminate the United States-Syria air service agreement, a prohibition on the sale of tickets in the United States for transportation by Syrian Arab Airlines, advice to United States oil companies that continued Syrian oil operations would be inappropriate, more vigorous visa procedures, a stronger travel advisory relating to Syria and certain diplomatic sanctions. DEP'T ST. BULL., Jan. 1987, at 79.

Congress did not expand the export controls that the White House statement mentioned until June 1987. 52 Fed. Reg. 23,167 (June 18, 1987). At that time, the United States required validated licenses for exports to Syria of all goods and technical data controlled for national security purposes and all aircraft, helicopters and related components regardless of the identity of the purchaser or the size of the transaction. The Commerce Department also made certain outstanding licenses invalid for exports to Syria. *Id.* For a description of the restrictions previously in effect, see *infra* notes 198-214 and accompanying text.

Under the 1987 Regulations, the government will generally deny validated license applications, but it will give favorable consideration, on a case-by-case basis, to several categories of newly controlled transactions including transactions under prior contracts, re-export of certain previously exported goods not originally destined for Syria, exports of foreign-produced goods with a United States-origin content of 20% or less by value and sales of medical equipment. 52 Fed. Reg. 23,167, 23,168 (June 18, 1987), (renumbering 15 C.F.R. § 385.4(d)(4) as § 385.4(d)(5) and adding a new § 385.4(d)(4)).

17. It extended controls on exports of aircraft and helicopters to smaller and less costly models. The government also extended antiterrorism restrictions on items whose export it had restricted for national security reasons to lower value shipments and placed controls on the export of certain outboard marine engines. Under the licensing policy announced at the same time, the United States generally denies licenses for all the controlled items with narrow exceptions for certain preexisting contracts and for foreign-produced goods with low United States content. *See* 15 C.F.R. § 385.4(d) (1987).

18. *See* State Department Report, *supra* note 1, at 2-3. European countries have agreed to participate in narrower sanctions, such as restrictions on arms sales to Libya, and have represented that they would endeavor to prevent their firms from replacing United States firms as suppliers to Libya and other target states. *See* 15 C.F.R. § 385.4(d); Statement of Ministers of Foreign Affairs of the Twelve Meeting in Brussels on Combating International Terrorism, Jan. 27, 1986, *reprinted in* 25 I.L.M. 208, 209 (1986).

19. For a discussion of economic sanctions as both instruments of coercion and devices for symbolically communicating varied messages to multiple audiences, see Abbott, *Coercion and Communication: Frameworks for Evaluation of Economic Sanctions*, N.Y.U. INT'L L. & POL. (forthcoming).

pounded by complexity.

In this Article I hope to take at least a step toward clarifying these matters by presenting a framework for the analysis of antiterrorism sanctions and using that framework to discuss several of the sanctions that the United States currently employs.

Parts Two and Three of this Article set out the elements of the framework. Part Two begins by describing the varying forms or levels of state involvement in terrorism,[20] shown graphically in Figure 1.[21] All forms of state involvement are not alike, at least analytically, and Part Two will discuss the appropriateness of employing sanctions or other measures of influence against different levels of involvement. Part Three will describe in general terms, without reference to the problem of terrorism, the four principal rationales for the use of economic sanctions.[22] Figure 2 depicts these rationales.[23]

Part Four of this Article will then join these two elements together,[24] producing the matrix shown in Figure 3.[25] The levels of state involvement appear on the horizontal axis of this matrix and the rationales for sanctions appear on the vertical axis. Part Four will sketch the application of the four sanctions rationales to state involvement in terrorism—the four rows of the matrix—and illustrate their application with examples from current American sanctions.

II. State Involvement in Terrorism

As Figure 1 shows, one can picture state involvement in terrorism as running along a continuum, from the absence of state support at the left, to the most direct and extensive forms of involvement at the right. For analytical purposes, I have divided this continuum into three discrete sections representing three distinct levels of involvement, although the boundaries between these sections are difficult to draw with precision.

At the first level independent terrorist groups, which Robert Kupperman describes as "self-sustaining organisms,"[26] operate without significant state involvement. They may move from state to state or operate from some jurisdictional no-man's land, such as portions of Lebanon. If

---

20. *See infra* notes 26-37 and accompanying text.
21. *See infra* Appendix p. 326.
22. *See infra* notes 57-79 and accompanying text.
23. *See infra* Appendix p. 327.
24. *See infra* notes 80-220 and accompanying text.
25. *See infra* Appendix p. 328.
26. Kupperman, *Terror, the Strategic Tool: Response and Control*, 463 ANNALS 24, 32-33 (1982).

294   *VANDERBILT JOURNAL OF TRANSNATIONAL LAW*   *[Vol. 20:289*

they operate from a single state, state officials may not know of them or may actively oppose them but be unable to deal with them effectively.

At the second level states provide "support" to otherwise independent terrorist groups. This support can take a wide variety of forms. At the boundary between the first and second levels it may amount to nothing more than toleration of the presence of terrorist groups within a state. Somewhat more affirmatively, it may take the form of moral or verbal support. Support may include sanctuary following a terrorist act. Toward the right-hand boundary, it may consist of more active *ex ante* assistance such as training, the provision of passports, arms, and intelligence information, logistical assistance and similar forms of support.

At the third level states "sponsor" terrorism: they incite groups or individuals to commit terrorist acts, direct acts of terrorism, recruit terrorists for their own programs and carry out terrorist acts through their own agents.

In the real world it will often be difficult to place a state's activities precisely on this scale because of the difficulty of obtaining adequate, reliable information. This problem is common to many areas of international relations but is particularly acute here because of the secrecy with which states customarily clothe their involvement in terrorism.[27] This lack of information forces American officials to speak vaguely of a state's links or connections to terrorism,[28] for example, and even to take action without knowing the precise level of state involvement.[29] In theory, however, the three levels of state involvement in terrorism call for different kinds of analysis and may also call for different measures, at least in degree.

In all three settings it is individuals who carry out acts of terrorism.

---

27. *See* Axelrod & Keohane, *Achieving Cooperation Under Anarchy: Strategies and Institutions,* in COOPERATION UNDER ANARCHY 226, 235 (K. Oye, ed. 1986); Bialos & Juster, *supra* note 15, at 840-41; Wilkinson, *State-Sponsored International Terrorism: The Problems of Response,* 40 WORLD TODAY 292, 294 (1984) (states supporting terrorism act clandestinely and deny responsibility); *Terrorism: Oversight Hearings before the Subcomm. on Civil and Constitutional Rights of the House Comm. on the Judiciary,* 99th Cong., 1st and 2nd Sess. 3, 5 (1986) [hereinafter *Terrorism: Oversight Hearings*] (testimony of Wm. Quandt, Brookings Institute) (any state supporting terrorism will try to "cover its tracks").

28. *See Terrorism: Oversight Hearings, supra* note 27, at 42, 44 (testimony of Prof. Martha Crenshaw, Wesleyan Univ.); Press Conference of John Whitehead, Deputy Secretary of State, Jan. 27, 1986, *reprinted in* 25 I.L.M. 209, 214-18 (1986).

29. At the time of the Libya embargo, the United States government apparently had only general evidence of Libyan support and sanctuary for the terrorists involved in the Rome and Vienna airport shooting incidents. Later, evidence emerged linking Libya more directly with those incidents. *See* Bialos & Juster, *supra* note 15, at 807 n.30.

Whatever the level of state involvement, improving the mechanisms for capturing, trying and punishing individual terrorists, largely in the hope of deterring others, is an important strategy. Most of the legal developments in the fight against terrorism—notably the several multilateral antiterrorism conventions, which require signatory states to take custody of persons accused of specified terrorist acts and either extradite them or submit them to the appropriate authorities for prosecution—are part of this strategy.[30] When terrorist groups are acting independently of state involvement, it is one of the few strategies available.[31]

---

30. International Convention Against the Taking of Hostages, arts. 6, 8, G.A. Res. 146, 34 U.N. GAOR Supp. (No. 39), U.N. Doc. A/C.6/34/L.23 (1970), *reprinted in* 18 I.L.M. 1456 (1979); Convention on the Prevention and Punishment of Crimes Against Internationally Protected Persons, Including Diplomatic Agents, Dec. 14, 1973, 28 U.S.T. 1975, T.I.A.S. No. 8532, G.A. Res. 3166, U.N. GAOR Supp. (No. 30) at 146, U.N. Doc. A/RES/3166 (1974), *reprinted in* 13 I.L.M. 41 (1974), arts. 6-7; Convention for the Suppression of Unlawful Seizure of Aircraft, Dec. 16, 1970, arts. 6-7, 22 U.S.T. 1641, T.I.A.S. No. 7192, *reprinted in* 10 I.L.M. 133 (1971); Convention for the Suppression of Unlawful Acts Against the Safety of Civil Aviation, Sept. 23, 1971, arts. 6-7, 24 U.S.T. 565, T.I.A.S. No. 7570, *reprinted in* 10 I.L.M. 1151 (1971). *See also* Convention on Offences and Certain Other Acts Committed on Board Aircraft, Sept. 14, 1983, art. 16, 20 U.S.T. 2941, T.I.A.S. No. 6768, *reprinted in* 2 I.L.M. 1042 (1963). These conventions also call for cooperation in law enforcement: exchanges of information, coordination of administrative measures and assistance in criminal proceedings. For descriptions of the antiterrorism conventions and other legal developments, see Murphy, *Legal Controls and the Deterrence of Terrorism: Performance and Prospects,* 13 RUTGERS L.J. 465 (1982); Murphy, *Recent International Legal Developments in Controlling Terrorism,* 4 CHINESE Y.B. INT'L L. & AFF. 97 (1984). *See also* General Assembly Resolution on Measures to Prevent International Terrorism, G.A. Res. 61, 40 U.N. GAOR Supp. (No. _____), U.N. Doc. A/RES/40/61 (1986) *reprinted in* 25 I.L.M. 239 (1986); Tokyo Economic Summit Statement on Terrorism, May 5, 1986, *reprinted in* DEP'T ST. BULL. (July 1986), at 5; Venice Economic Summit Statement on Terrorism, N.Y. Times, June 10, 1987, at 6, col. 1.

31. Another strategy is a defensive strategy, based on measures like improving airport security. The multilateral antiterrorism conventions require signatory states to take precautions within their respective territories against the particular forms of terrorism that the conventions address. *See* Murphy, *Recent International Legal Developments in Controlling Terrorism, supra* note 30, at 100-01.

The General Assembly Resolution on Measures to Prevent International Terrorism, *see supra* note 30, at paras. 11-13, calls upon states to take measures that the International Civil Aviation Organization [hereinafter ICAO] has recommended and provided for in the conventions to protect civil aviation and other forms of public transport, urges the ICAO to continue its efforts and requests the International Maritime Organization to study the problem of terrorism on ships with a view to recommending protective measures.

The Tokyo Economic Summit statement commits the "Summit Seven" countries to certain defensive measures, including limiting the size of diplomatic and consular mis-

State sponsored terrorism, at the other extreme, is quite a different matter. If Libya orders its agents to bomb American facilities, for example,[32] it is acting as the principal in the transaction; the individual terrorists planting explosives at its direction are mere agents. The state is initiating terrorist acts that would not otherwise have taken place. Its orders, along with the practical assistance it provides, are the proximate cause of any damage that results. A state in that position is, in short, the primary wrongdoer. The state has acted, moreover, with specific willful intent. It is clearly appropriate for the international community to hold such a state responsible for its actions and to search for strategies that will punish, deter or otherwise change its behavior.

State support, the range of state involvement between mere toleration and extensive involvement just short of outright sponsorship, presents the most interesting situation. At the upper end of the range the boundary between support and sponsorship is indistinct. According to United States sources, for example, from the mid-1970s through 1983, Syria—one of the "charter members" of the State Department's terrorism list—managed numerous terrorist acts directly, using its own personnel. This is a clear case of sponsorship.[33] In 1986 the British trial of Nizar Hindawi again exposed direct Syrian sponsorship[34] and led to strengthened American sanctions.[35] Between those dates, however, Syria turned to a different strategy, one of supporting independent terrorist groups that shared its own aims, like the group led by Abu Nidal, in

---

sions of terrorist-supporting states, tightening visa requirements for persons travelling from such states and denying entry to persons expelled from another state because of conviction for or suspicion of terrorist offenses. *See* Tokyo Economic Summit Statement on Terrorism, *supra* note 30.

The Council of Europe called for similar steps in November 1986, with the support of the United States. *See* DEP'T ST. BULL. 79 (Jan. 1987).

Another possible strategy is to restrict the availability of certain kinds of weapons so that terrorist groups cannot obtain them. The Western nations have cooperated in controlling access to nuclear material pursuant to this strategy. *See* Convention on the Physical Protection of Nuclear Material, Oct. 26, 1979, *reprinted in* 18 I.L.M. 1419, 1422-31 (1979).

32. According to the United States, Libya in 1986 ordered its embassy staffs in several countries to conduct terrorist attacks on American facilities. *See* Address of Robert Oakley, Acting Ambassador at Large for Counter-Terrorism, to U.S. Conference of Mayors, June 16, 1986, *reprinted in* DEP'T ST. BULL., Aug. 1986, at 1, 2.

33. *See Syrian Support for International Terrorism: 1983-86*, DEP'T ST. BULL., Feb. 1987, at 73.

34. *See id.* at 73-74.

35. *See supra* note 16.

order to make its own participation easier to deny.[36] In terms of intent, at least, such support is indistinguishable from outright sponsorship.

In other respects, however, the individual terrorists receiving state support remain the primary wrongdoers, and the involvement of the supporting state is secondary. The supporting state may supply a terrorist group with passports, sanctuary or even arms, but it is not directly involved in the terrorist actions that such a group may perpetrate. In terms of initiative and causation, too, the supporting state may make a lesser contribution than the sponsoring state since the terrorists would be trying to carry out the acts of terrorism even without the supporting state's assistance.

In addition, by contrast to the Syrian example, the supporting state may well have a lesser degree of intent than the sponsoring state. A state may lend its support to a terrorist group out of a desire to gain political favor with other supporting states or out of general sympathy with a cause; it may know the likely consequences of its aid but lack the willful intent of the sponsoring state.[37] A state may also lend its support out of fear. At the lower end of the range, a state may even provide sanctuary to terrorist groups out of simple negligence.

Through most of the range, then, one can characterize the terrorist-supporting state, with its secondary involvement, as a "gatekeeper," a party whose cooperation makes wrongdoing by others possible, or at least easier.[38] Simple domestic analogues include the bartender who serves liquor to an almost-drunken driver and the accountant who provides a clean report on a fraudulent deal.[39] In domestic society we sometimes impose legal restraints and expend scarce enforcement resources on gatekeepers like these as well as on primary wrongdoers. In other situations, however, we disregard the activities of gatekeepers because of the additional costs and practical problems of secondary enforcement or because secondary enforcement seems unlikely to prevent much additional wrongdoing.[40] The economic theory of gatekeeper liability attempts to explain when secondary enforcement is called for and when it is likely to be successful;[41] one can usefully apply this theory to the treatment of terrorist-supporting states.

---

36. *See Syrian Support for International Terrorism, supra* note 33, at 73.

37. Even Syria, it seems, was not aware of all the actions of the Abu Nidal group. *See Syrian Support for International Terrorism, supra* note 33, at 74.

38. *See* Kraakman, *Gatekeepers: The Anatomy of a Third-Party Enforcement Strategy,* 2 J. L., ECON. & ORG. 53, 53-54 (1986).

39. *See id.* at 63-65.

40. *See id.* at 54, 66, 87-88, 93.

41. *See id.*

298   *VANDERBILT JOURNAL OF TRANSNATIONAL LAW*   *[Vol. 20:289*

In general, secondary enforcement is necessary only when direct deterrence of primary wrongdoers—the normal method of controlling wrongdoing—is insufficient to reduce wrongdoing to an acceptable level.[42] Terrorism poses substantial difficulties for primary deterrence. First, because of their tactics, terrorists are often hard to identify and apprehend.[43] Second, the penalties terrorists face, discounted by the odds of capture, may not appear severe.[44] Despite considerable effort, the international community has not yet created an institutional framework—an international criminal court or even a strong network of extradition treaties—guaranteeing that states will prosecute an accused terrorist who they apprehend.[45] Terrorists can discount the nominal penalties even further. Finally, even if prosecution were certain and the penalty were death, the rational calculation of penalties would not deter some fanatic terrorists, like the *fedayeen*, the self-sacrificers.[46] If the international

---

42. *See id.* at 56.

43. *See* Bremer, *Practical Measures for Dealing with Terrorism*, DEP'T ST. BULL., Mar. 1987, at 1, 1-2; Secretary of State Shultz, *Low-Intensity Warfare: The Challenge of Ambiguity*, U.S. Dep't of State Current Policy No. 783, *reprinted in* 25 I.L.M. 204, 205 (1986) ("Despite . . . the widespread recognition that their acts are criminal, few terrorists are caught, and fewer still are punished to the full extent they deserve.")

44. Direct deterrence assumes that a wrongdoer acts as if he were calculating the expected net return of wrongdoing, that is, the expected benefit of the wrongdoing to him less the costs of the wrongdoing and any expected penalty. The expected penalty is the punishment the wrongdoer is likely to incur multiplied by the probability that he will be captured, tried, convicted and subjected to punishment. *See* Kraakman, *supra* note 38, at 56; R. POSNER, ECONOMIC ANALYSIS OF LAW 164-65 (2d ed. 1977). The difficulty of detecting wrongdoing and procuring the conviction and punishment of wrongdoers are common problems in efforts to increase expected penalties and thus strengthen deterrence. *See* Kraakman, *supra* note 38, at 57.

45. Not all states adhere to the multilateral "extradite or submit to prosecution" conventions discussed above, *see supra* note 30, and these conventions cover only certain specific forms of terrorism. For an important regional convention designed to improve the process of extraditing terrorists, *see* European Convention on the Suppression of Terrorism, T.S. 90, *reprinted in* 15 I.L.M. 1272 (1976). *See also* Supplementary Extradition Treaty, U.S.-U.K., Treaty Doc. 99-8, 99th Cong., 1st Sess. 1985, in force 1986. In John Murphy's words, all of the relevant conventions together constitute a "grossly inadequate response to international terrorism." Murphy, *Recent International Legal Developments*, *supra* note 30, at 109. Further, many governments contrive to let accused terrorists go free, with or without trial despite their obligations under the various conventions. *See* Pierre, *Politics of International Terrorism*, 19 ORBIS 1251, 1264-65 (1976); Liskofsky, *The Abu Daoud Case: Law or Politics*, 7 Is. Y.B. H. RGTS. 66 (1977).

46. *See* Pierre, *supra* note 45, at 1254. In the normal analysis of deterrence, the equivalent problem involves persons whose judgment is impaired, so that they cannot make a rational calculation of expected net benefit or cost. *See* Kraakman, *supra* note 38, at 56.

community cannot solve these problems—and they are not easily solved—and if that community still perceives the level of terrorism as unacceptably high,[47] secondary enforcement may be necessary.

We normally turn to secondary enforcement, however, only when private incentives are insufficient to restrain gatekeepers from helping wrongdoers without the investment of additional social resources.[48] Many observers believe, for example, that most lawyers and accountants voluntarily guard against participating in fraudulent acts by their clients in order to protect their own valuable reputations.[49]

For most countries, similarly, the desire to avoid a reputation as a supporter of terrorism—a reputation that might harm their chances of entering into desirable relationships—provides a sufficient incentive.[50] For a few states, however, this incentive is irrelevant, or at least insufficient, and a few states are all it takes to support a significant level of terrorism.

If secondary enforcement were thought desirable, it could, in theory, take the form of positive sanctions such as rewards for withholding support from terrorist groups. It is difficult, however, to determine when a state has in fact withheld its support. It is easier, in spite of the pervasive information problems,[51] to tell when a state has failed to prevent wrongdoing[52] and to respond accordingly.

Based on considerations like these, the international community has moved to impose a form of secondary liability, at least implicitly to be enforced by negative sanctions, on terrorist-supporting states as well as on terrorist-sponsoring states. It has done so most clearly in the Declara-

---

47. Most commentators on terrorism support such a perception and call for stronger measures. A few commentators, however, argue that the present level of terrorism is bearable and that additional measures, especially the use of military force, would be an overreaction. *See, e.g., Terrorism, Oversight Hearings, supra* note 27, at 49-50 (statement of Prof. Martha Crenshaw); Jenkins, *Statements About Terrorism,* 463 ANNALS 11, 12-16 (1982).

48. *See* Kraakman, *supra* note 38, at 54, 60-62.

49. *See id.*

50. Many international relations scholars argue that concern for reputation, especially a reputation for adhering to agreements and conforming to community norms, is a major influence on the conduct of states. Even states that would not conform to a norm for ethical reasons may do so for the self-interested reason that other states may be less likely to enter into agreements or other relations with them in the future if they acquire reputations for flouting community norms. For a discussion of the influence of reputation, see R. KEOHANE, AFTER HEGEMONY: COOPERATION AND DISCORD IN THE WORLD POLITICAL ECONOMY 105-06 (1984).

51. *See supra* note 26.

52. *See* Kraakman, *supra* note 38, at 60.

tion on Friendly Relations,[53] adopted by consensus in the United Nations General Assembly in 1970, as an elaboration on the obligation of states to refrain from the use of force against the territorial integrity or political independence of other states or in any other manner inconsistent with the purposes of the United Nations under its Charter.[54] The Declaration addresses sponsorship by imposing a duty to refrain from organizing, instigating and participating in forceful terrorist acts in another state. It also addresses support by imposing a duty to refrain from assisting such acts. It even reaches to the lower end of the support category by articulating a duty to refrain from acquiescing in the use of a state's territory for organized activities directed toward the commission of terrorist acts abroad.[55]

At least in the case of state support for terrorism, though, these broad duties ignore certain additional questions that the theory of secondary enforcement tells us we should ask. The two most important questions are: (1) to what extent will secondary enforcement be effective in reducing wrongdoing and (2) will any such reduction be worth the additional costs?[56] With the legal obligations already established, states will or should face these questions when they consider imposing economic sanctions.

III.　RATIONALES FOR ECONOMIC SANCTIONS

Figure 2 shows the four most important rationales for the use of economic sanctions arranged from the most broadly coercive—*economic*

---

53. Declaration on Principles of International Law Concerning Friendly Relations and Co-operation Among States in Accordance with the Charter of the United Nations, Oct. 24, 1970, G.A. Res. 2625, 25 U.N. GAOR Supp. (No. 28) at 121, U.N. Doc. A/8028 (1971), *reprinted in* 9 I.L.M. 1292 (1970) [hereinafter Declaration]. *See* Paust, *Responding Lawfully to International Terrorism: The Use of Force Abroad*, 8 WHITTIER L. REV. 711, 714-16 (1986). The Tokyo Economic Summit statement reaffirms the condemnation of terrorism in all its forms and those, including governments, who sponsor and support it. Tokyo Economic Summit Statement on Terrorism, *supra* note 30.

54. U.N. CHARTER art. 2, para. 4.

55. The section of the Declaration that elaborates on the principle of nonintervention in matters within the domestic jurisdiction of other states also provides: "no state shall organize, assist, foment, finance, incite or tolerate subversive, terrorist or armed activities directed towards the violent overthrow of the regime of another State . . . ." Declaration, *supra* note 53, at 1295. It is unclear whether giving sanctuary to terrorists following completion of a terrorist act abroad would alone constitute a violation of the duties stated in the Declaration. For a discussion of state responsibility for terrorist acts, see Lillich & Paxman, *State Responsibility for Injuries to Aliens Occasioned by Terrorist Activities*, 26 AM. U. L. REV. 217 (1977).

56. *See* Kraakman, *supra* note 38, at 61.

warfare and *imposing costs*—to the most selective and subtle—*denial of means* and *symbolic communication.*

Economic warfare is normally a supplement to or a substitute for actual combat; the strategy was highly developed during the two World Wars.[57] This rationale assumes that the "enemy" will need extensive resources for combat, as in a protracted conventional war, and that it will divert any resources that its civilian economy saves by engaging in trade or other international transactions, at least in part, to strengthen its military capacity.[58] The logic of the theory would support a total embargo, since all economic transactions produce gains from trade. More commonly, however, the theory provides the rationale for controls on transactions particularly important to the enemy's economy—bottleneck transactions—whether directly related to its military sector or not.[59]

Imposing costs, or the strategy of leverage,[60] is the most familiar rationale for economic sanctions.[61] Under this theory, the sanctioning state links its trade, foreign assistance, arms sales and other international economic transactions to changes in the target state's behavior: if the target acts in ways the sanctioning state does not approve of—by supporting terrorist activities, for example—the sanctioning state suspends those transactions, imposing costs on the target's economy (as well, of course, as on its own); if the target's behavior improves, the sanctioning state permits such transactions to resume.[62] The theory assumes that the target state will rationally balance the benefits of its current policies against the discounted costs of subsequent retaliation and conclude that a change in policy is in its own interests.[63]

This is essentially the same theory of rational deterrence that underlies many sanctions against individual offenders in domestic society.[64] The aim of imposing costs is not to reduce the target state's capabilities,

---

57. *See* Mastanduno, *Strategies of Economic Containment: U.S. Trade Relations with the Soviet Union*, 37 WORLD POL. 503, 506-10 (1985); Gilpin, *Structural Constraints on Economic Leverage: Market-Type Systems*, in STRATEGIC DIMENSIONS OF ECONOMIC BEHAVIOR at 105-06 (G. McCormick & R. Bissell eds. 1984).

58. *See* Mastanduno, *supra* note 57, at 507-08.

59. *See id.* at 509-10.

60. *See* G. HUFBAUER & J. SCHOTT, ECONOMIC SANCTIONS RECONSIDERED: HISTORY AND CURRENT POLICY 2 (1985); Gilpin, *supra* note 57, at 105-06.

61. *See* Gilpin, *supra* note 57; Abbott, *supra* note 2, at 798-800; G. HUFBAUER & J. SCHOTT, *supra* note 60. For a discussion of the Hufbauer & Schott analysis as an example of the "imposing costs" rationale, see Abbott, *supra* note 19.

62. *See* Mastanduno, *supra* note 57, at 514-15; Abbott, *supra* note 2, at 799-800 (discussing views of Samuel P. Huntington).

63. *See* Abbott, *supra* note 2, at 798-99.

64. *See supra* text accompanying note 40.

302   VANDERBILT JOURNAL OF TRANSNATIONAL LAW   [Vol. 20:289]

as in economic warfare, but to affect its intention or will to engage in particular conduct.[65] If the sanctioning state is unable to force a change in the target state's conduct, it can at least exact a price for defying its demands.[66] The strategy is closely related to the doctrine of countermeasures—retorsion and reprisal—in international law, one of the important ways in which states enforce legal obligations in the decentralized international system.[67]

Denial of means, like economic warfare, is designed to reduce a target state's capabilities, but in a much more limited and selective way. The denial of means rationale typically leads to restrictions on exports or other transactions that directly contribute to a particular disfavored activity.[68] The best example of this technique is the strategic embargo that the United States and other Western nations maintain against the Soviet Union.[69] The embargo is designed to prevent the Soviets from obtaining selected items that would contribute directly and substantially to their military capabilities: arms and a variety of other high technology civilian items with military applications, so-called dual use items.[70] On the same rationale, the United States restricts the export of crime control equipment—which some commentators refer to as "citizen control equipment"[71]—to nations that violate human rights[72] and the export of certain

---

65. *See* Mastanduno, *supra* note 57, at 514-15; Gilpin, *supra* note 57, at 105-06.

66. *See* Knorr, *Economic Relations as an Instrument of National Power,* in STRATEGIC DIMENSIONS OF ECONOMIC BEHAVIOR, *supra* note 57, at 183, 200 (imposing costs may make target state more likely to comply with future demands); D. BALDWIN, ECONOMIC STATECRAFT 132-33 (1985) (imposing costs on target state is form of influence, even if target does not change policy).

67. *See infra* note 103. States employ coercive economic measures in all sorts of interstate relations, not only in response to violations of international norms. Despite efforts to declare such measures unlawful aggression or use of force, the international community appears prepared to accept a considerable amount of economic coercion as inevitable. *See generally* Editorial Comment, *Political and Economic Coercion in Contemporary International Law,* 79 AM. J. INT'L L. 405 (1985).

68. *See* Knorr, *supra* note 66, at 190-94; Mastanduno, *supra* note 57, at 510. Kraakman describes this strategy in general terms as involving "efforts to regulate activities or inputs that are precursors to misconduct." Kraakman, *supra* note 38, at 57.

69. *See* Mastanduno, *supra* note 57, at 524-29; D. BALDWIN, *supra* note 66, at 235-50.

70. Although it may have retarded Soviet military capacity less than a well-designed economic warfare strategy—focusing on bottleneck items in the Soviet economy rather than on items with direct military applications—the selective embargo technique has been the basis on which the United States—which prefers broader controls—and Europe—which prefers less extensive controls—have been able to cooperate in strategic trade controls. *See* D. BALDWIN, *supra* note 66, at 245-46.

71. *See U.S. Export Control Policy and Extension of the Export Administration Act:*

vehicles and machinery for producing military equipment to nations engaged in regional conflicts.[73]

Symbolic communication is a much misunderstood function of economic sanctions. Commentators often suggest that symbolic controls have no instrumental function, that they are simply a way of letting off steam or playing to a domestic political audience.[74] In fact, however, sanctions can perform important functions even when they cannot reduce the target state's capabilities or force it to change its policies.[75]

Sanctions can communicate, more credibly than mere words, the sanctioning state's commitment to a particular position, the seriousness with which it views foreign conduct, its intention to act and its willingness to bear costs. Sanctions can also communicate the threat of harsher action to follow in the future. Messages like these can be important instruments of deterrence.[76] Sanctions can also communicate moderation and restraint, perhaps avoiding unnecessary conflict.[77] They can create a psychological sense of isolation or shame or spur reconsideration of target state policies even if they impose no substantial costs on the target.[78] Sanctions can communicate diverse messages like these to states, groups and individuals other than the immediate target state.[79]

Of the four rationales discussed here, then, two—the first and third—are concerned with affecting capabilities, and two—the second and fourth—with affecting intentions and will. Any given sanction, however, may reflect two or more rationales at the same time. Indeed, almost all sanctions communicate some message regardless of their other effects.

Hearings on S. 737 and S. 999 Before the Subcomm. on International Finance of the Senate Comm. on Banking, Housing and Urban Affairs - Part II, 96th Cong., 1st Sess. 145, 157-58 (1979) (statement of Jerry Goodman) (crime control equipment can be used to monitor and repress dissidents and minorities).

72. *See* 50 U.S.C. app. § 2405(j); 15 C.F.R. § 376.14, 385.4(d)(1)(a). For a discussion of the origin of these controls, see Abbott, *supra* note 2, at 787-90.

73. *See* 15 C.F.R. § 376.16, 385.4(d)(1). For a discussion of the regional stability policy, see Abbott, *supra* note 2, at 761-62.

74. *See* D. BALDWIN, *supra* note 66, at 96-97; Abbott, *supra* note 2, at 822-24.

75. *See* D. BALDWIN, *supra* note 66, at 97-101.

76. *See id.* at 102-14.

77. *See id.* at 104, 185 (United States embargo of Cuba demonstrated restraint when compared with the history of military intervention in Latin America).

78. *See id.* at 61-65.

79. *See id.* at 17-18.

304   VANDERBILT JOURNAL OF TRANSNATIONAL LAW   [Vol. 20:289

IV. THE RATIONALES FOR SANCTIONS APPLIED

We are now ready to consider how the major rationales for economic sanctions apply—in principle and in the practice of the United States—to the different levels of state involvement in terrorism, by examining the matrix in Figure 3.

On most rows of the matrix, the same entries apply to both state supported and state sponsored terrorism, the last two columns. Once the international community has decided on secondary liability for the support of terrorism, in other words,[80] most sanctions strategies are both appropriate and used in practice, subject to considerations of cost and effectiveness, for dealing with both forms of state involvement. The distinctions between sponsorship and support and among degrees of support are reflected primarily in the strength of the sanctions applied.[81] Economic warfare is an exception, however. This rationale seems appropriate, if at all, only for dealing with states that sponsor terrorism or that willfully provide extensive support as a substitute for sponsorship, as a form of hostilities.[82]

Only the denial of means and symbolic communication rationales are relevant to all three columns of the matrix, including the first column, which represents the absence of state involvement. Restrictions on munitions exports, for example, can limit the ability of terrorist groups to obtain sophisticated arms; many kinds of sanctions can convey messages of commitment directly to such groups, although this is rarely their primary purpose. The economic warfare and imposing costs rationales, in contrast, focus exclusively on supporting or sponsoring states.

The remainder of this section will consider individually the four rows of the matrix, each corresponding to one of the rationales for economic sanctions.

A. *Economic Warfare*

Many commentators and policy makers have come to see state sponsorship of terrorism as a form of low intensity warfare against the West.[83] President Reagan has extended this perspective to repeated state

---

80. *See supra* notes 53-55 and accompanying text.
81. *See infra* notes 110-115 and accompanying text.
82. *See infra* note 84 and accompanying text.
83. *See* Jenkins, *New Modes of Conflict,* 28 ORBIS 5, 12 (1976) (some governments see terrorism as a "weapons system," an inexpensive way of waging war); Pierre, *supra* note 45, at 1268-69 (states may see terrorism as "continuation of warfare by other means," inexpensive, covert, and efficient); Kupperman, *supra* note 26, at 25, 32 (support of terrorism is low-cost, low-risk strategy for states); Wilkinson, *Terrorism: The*

support of terrorism. In ordering the embargo of Libya in January 1986, the President said, "By providing material support to terrorist groups which attack U.S. citizens, Libya has engaged in armed aggression . . . just as if [it] had used its own armed forces."[84]

Against this background the economic warfare rationale might appear to support sanctions against states that sponsor or provide extensive support for terrorism. The theory would be that sanctions could reduce the capacity of such states to engage in this form of combat by denying them economic gains from trade that they could use to support terrorism. One could view the United States embargo of Libya[85] as a current application of this rationale.

One must question, however, whether the rationale is appropriate, even for terrorist-sponsoring states. Economic warfare assumes that the enemy needs extensive economic resources for its military sector; its model is a full-scale conventional war.[86] Terrorism, however, requires a much smaller commitment of resources than even a limited war; this is a large part of its appeal.[87] While the authoritarian states that sponsor terrorism could probably divert all the gains from trade realized by their civilian economies to the support of terrorism, they will rarely need to do so.

In terms of the economic warfare rationale alone, then, embargoes of terrorist-supporting states, and even extensive bottleneck controls on transactions of strategic importance to their civilian economies, are probably ill-advised. Such sanctions are unlikely to reduce the economic capacity of the target states sufficiently to limit their sponsorship of terrorism, and the costs incurred by the sanctioning states[88] are accordingly likely to be out of proportion to the benefits.[89]

International Response, 34 WORLD TODAY 5, 6 (1978) (states developing "proxy" terrorists as weapon of coercive diplomacy); Shultz, *supra* note 43, at 205; Tokyo Economic Summit Statement on Terrorism, *supra* note 30 (summit states abhor use of terrorism as blatant instrument of government policy).

84. Economic Sanctions Against Libya, Statement by President Reagan, President's News Conference of Jan. 7, 1986, *reprinted in* 25 I.L.M. 175 (1986).

85. *See supra* notes 14-15, 84 and accompanying text.

86. *See supra* note 85 and accompanying text.

87. Most commentators observe that certain states have turned to the support of terrorism precisely because it is a low-cost strategy, especially when one compares it with more conventional military action. *See supra* note 83.

88. For a discussion of these costs, in the context of the imposing costs rationale, see *infra* notes 138-48 and accompanying text.

89. David Baldwin stresses the need to compare the use of economic sanctions with other courses of action available to governments, including doing nothing, when evaluating the effectiveness of sanctions; he properly points out that most analyses of sanctions

Judging from the statements of American officials, at least, the United States did not intend its embargo of Libya to be an exercise in economic warfare. It based the embargo primarily on two other sanctions rationales: imposing costs[90] and symbolic communication,[91] both of which I will discuss below. In practice, of course, sanctions implementing these two rationales can be all but indistinguishable from economic warfare.

B. *Imposing Costs*

Sanctions designed to impose economic costs are largely irrelevant to terrorism carried on without state support; they are too blunt an instrument to be used in pressuring small groups of terrorists. Sanctions based on this rationale have become one of the major enforcement strategies for dealing with terrorist-supporting and sponsoring states, however, and as such one must consider them at some length.

The United States has expressly based many of its antiterrorism sanctions, at least in part, on the rationale of imposing costs. A 1986 State Department report entitled *Economic Sanctions to Combat International Terrorism* states that "economic sanctions are an integral part of [the] peaceful measures that we can take to deter states from supporting terrorism," and that sanctions "may be used to pressure targeted states to change their policies."[92] Numerous statements by the President and the Department of State demonstrate that imposing costs on Libya in order to deter future support for terrorists or simply to exact a price for non-

---

proceed in a vacuum. *See* D. BALDWIN, *supra* note 66, at 15, 123-28. In the present context, the point is that sanctions based on the economic warfare rationale, are unlikely to reduce significantly the economic capacity of the target state to sponsor terrorism, but will require the sanctioning state to incur economic and other costs. Thus, while some alternatives may be more effective, net of costs, and others less effective, economic warfare will typically be less effective than doing nothing. If one also considers other rationales for economic sanctions, however, the calculus may well change.

90. *See infra* notes 91-148 and accompanying text.

91. A principal goal of the embargo appears to have been to help isolate the government of Colonel Qadhafi from the "civilized world." *See* National Emergency with Respect to Libya, President Reagan's Letter to the Speaker of the House and the President of the Senate, Jan. 7, 1986, *reprinted in* 25 I.L.M. 174, 175 (1986) ("We must demonstrate by firm political and economic sanctions that . . . states that engage in [the support of terrorism] cannot expect to be accepted members of the international community."); Economic Sanctions Against Libya, President Reagan's Statement at News Conference of Jan. 7, 1986, *reprinted in* 25 I.L.M. 175, 176 (1986) ("Qadhafi deserves to be treated as a pariah in the world community. We call on our friends . . . to join with us in isolating him."). For a discussion of a similar rationale in the case of the Syria sanctions, *see infra* note 193 and accompanying text.

92. *See* State Department Report, *supra* note 1, at 1.

compliance with international norms and American demands was a major motivation for the 1986 embargo.[93] Secretary of State Shultz applied the same rationale to the subsequent bombing of Libya: "If you raise the cost, you do something that should eventually act as a deterrent. That is the primary objective. . . ."[94]

The leverage rationale is also apparent in the coverage of more modest antiterrorism sanctions. United States export controls, for example, have focused on commercial aircraft,[95] high technology products,[96] sophisticated oil field equipment,[97] and other items that play important roles in the economies of the target states, but which those states cannot easily produce themselves or obtain from other sources. In 1982 the United States prohibited oil imports from Libya, restricting an important source of foreign exchange.[98] The Bonn Declaration[99]—one of the few multilateral steps toward sanctioning supporters of terrorism, under which the Summit Seven states agreed to halt bilateral air traffic service to countries that refuse to extradite or prosecute airplane hijackers[100]—similarly reflects the imposing costs rationale.[101]

---

93. *See* National Emergency with Respect to Libya, *supra* note 91, at 174 (prior sanctions have not deterred Libya from use of terrorism); Economic Sanctions Against Libay, *supra* note 91, at 175 (sanctions necessary to exact a "high price" from Qadhafi for support of terrorism); Sanctions Against Libya, Statement by Principal Deputy Press Secretary to the President, Jan. 8, 1986, *reprinted in* 25 I.L.M. at 179 (1986) (sanctions necessary to exact "high cost" and "premium," to convince Qadhafi that "terrorism will not be cost-free").

94. *See* Statement of Secretary of State Shultz, DEP'T ST. BULL., June 1986, at 3, 4.

95. For years those concerned with the design of economic sanctions have seen commercial aircraft, which have until recently been produced primarily in the United States, as one of the greatest potential sources of leverage over terrorist-supporting states. *See* Abbott, *supra* note 2, at 769-70.

96. The United States has for several years restricted exports to terrorist-supporting states of all high-technology products and technical data controlled for national security purposes. *See id.* at 770-71; 15 C.F.R. § 385.4(d) (1987).

97. In restricting exports to Libya in 1982, the Department of Commerce announced that it would deny export licenses for oil and gas equipment and related technical data. Expansion of Foreign Policy Export Controls Affecting Libya, 47 Fed. Reg. 11,247 (1982); 15 C.F.R. § 385.7(a) (1987).

98. Proclamation No. 4907, 47 Fed. Reg. 10,507 (1982), continued by Proclamation No. 5141, 48 Fed. Reg. 56,929 (1983).

99. *Reprinted in* 17 I.L.M. 1285 (1978).

100. In a statement on terrorism at the 1987 Venice Economic Summit, the Summit Seven states agreed on measures to extend and strengthen the sanctions they would impose under the Declaration. *See* Venice Statement on Terrorism and Annex thereto, *reprinted in* N.Y. Times, June 10, 1987, at 10, col. 3.

101. *See* Bienen & Gilpin, *Economic Sanctions as a Response to Terrorism*, 3 J. STRATEGIC STUDIES 89, 95 (1980).

In the decentralized international system, economic sanctions like these have a special place, for they are one of the few ways in which states can implement the theory of rational deterrence in support of international norms.[102] Under international law, a state injured by another state's violation of a legal obligation is entitled to respond with countermeasures, or measures of self-help, even if those measures might otherwise be unlawful.[103] International law theory often justifies such countermeasures as restoring symmetry or equality between the states involved.[104] According to the *Revised Restatement of Foreign Relations Law*, international law permits countermeasures only to induce the violating state to terminate or remedy its violation or to prevent further violation.[105] Because countermeasures impose costs on a violating state, however, the threat of their use clearly functions as a deterrent.[106] Since states supporting or sponsoring terrorism violate a legal obligation,[107] antiterrorism sanctions imposed by injured states[108] would normally constitute valid countermea-

---

102. *See supra* notes 56-67 and accompanying text. For a discussion of the problems of decentralized retaliation in maintaining international cooperation, see Axelrod & Keohane, *Achieving Cooperation Under Anarchy, supra* note 27, at 232-47.

103. *See* RESTATEMENT OF FOREIGN RELATIONS LAW OF THE UNITED STATES (REVISED) § 905 (Tent. Draft No. 6, 1987); Case Concerning Air Services Agreement Between France and the United States, Arbitral Award of Dec. 9, 1978, 18 U.N.R.I.A.A. 417 ¶ 81. The injured state is also entitled to take measures of "retorsion," traditionally those countermeasures a state is legally free to take whether or not another state has breached an international legal obligation. "Reprisal," in contrast, is the usual term for counter-measures that would be unlawful were it not for a prior violation of international law. *See* L. HENKIN, R. PUGH, O. SCHACHTER & H. SMIT, INTERNATIONAL LAW 541-42 (2d ed. 1987) [hereinafter L. HENKIN]. Traditionally reprisals were punitive measures, often involving the use of force. *See* RESTATEMENT, *supra*, at § 905, comment f.

104. *See* Case Concerning Air Services Agreement, *supra* note 103, at ¶ 90.

105. RESTATEMENT, *supra* note 103, at § 905(1)(a), comment f.

106. An official comment to the *Revised Restatement* states that the principle of "necessity" would ordinarily preclude countermeasures designed only as retribution for a violation, not as an incentive to terminate the violation or remedy it. *Id.* Section 905 itself, however, provides that a state may use countermeasures to prevent further violation, that is, to deter. *Id.* at § 905(1)(a), and another comment states that the principle of necessity would be satisfied if the violating state refused to negotiate, pay compensation or submit to third-party dispute resolution. *See id.* at § 905(1)(a), comment e.

107. *See supra* notes 53-55 and accompanying text.

108. States not directly injured by a violation of a legal obligation—including obligations relating to the support of terrorism—have sometimes joined in economic sanctions on the theory that the violation affected a community interest. *See* L. HENKIN, *supra* note 103, at 550-51. Action under the Bonn Declaration, *see supra* text accompanying note 99, would appear to fall within this category.

sures under international law.[109]

The principal restriction on the use of countermeasures is that the measures taken must be proportionate or equivalent to the original offense.[110] This principle is in all circumstances difficult to apply,[111] but most of the antiterrorism sanctions the United States has imposed appear to have been roughly proportional.

The United States has generally imposed and strengthened sanctions in response to such factors as the duration and extent of the target state's support for terrorist groups, the target state's sponsorship of or direct participation in terrorist acts, as opposed to more passive support, and the heinousness of the terrorist acts to which the target state's involvement contributed. In imposing the Libya embargo, for example, President Reagan stressed Libya's longstanding "pattern of aggression,"[112] Colonel Qadhafi's use of terrorism as "one of the primary instruments of his foreign policy"[113] and Libya's role in the Rome and Vienna airport killings carried out by the Abu Nidal terrorist group.[114] Similarly, in strengthening sanctions against Syria in 1986, the United States stressed Syria's long pattern of support for terrorism, both as sponsor and supporter, and the evidence of its direct participation, through military and diplomatic personnel, in the attempted bombing of an *El Al* passenger plane by a terrorist recruited for the purpose.[115]

---

109. In the absence of relevant treaty commitments, in fact, the international community would consider most economic sanctions to be retorsions, which states may validly take to respond to violations of international law or unfriendly acts. *See* L. HENKIN, *supra* note 103, at 548-49.

110. *See* RESTATEMENT, *supra* note 103, at § 905(1)(b); Case Concerning Air Services Agreement, *supra* note 103, at ¶ 83. The requirement may also apply to acts of retorsion. *See* L. HENKIN, *supra* note 103, at 550; RESTATEMENT, *supra* note 103, at § 905, comment a (diplomatic relations, communication, and trade are "fundamentals of interstate intercourse and in practice are governed by the conditions of necessity and proportionally and are not seriously disrupted for any but the grossest violation.") It would be difficult to apply the test of "equivalence," *see* Case Concerning Air Services Agreement, *supra* note 103, at ¶ 83, in the case of countermeasures to the support or sponsorship of international terrorism, because "equivalent" measures might be unlawful, and would, in any case, be repugnant to most nations. L. HENKIN, *supra* note 103, at 547.

111. *See* Case Concerning Air Services Agreement, *supra* note 103, at ¶ 83.

112. *See* U.S. Department of State, Libya Under Qadhafi: Pattern of Aggression, *reprinted in* 25 I.L.M. 182 (1986).

113. *See id.*

114. *See* Economic Sanctions Against Libya, *supra* note 84, at 175 ("the latest in a series of atrocities which have shocked the conscience of the world.")

115. *See* White House Statement, *supra* note 16; *Syrian Support for International Terrorism: 1983-86,* DEP'T ST. BULL., Feb. 1987, at 73.

In spite of their seeming appropriateness, however, one must consider whether sanctions designed to impose costs on target states are likely to be effective in reducing undesirable conduct.[116] Unfortunately, most commentators, whether analyzing sanctions in the abstract or looking at past experience, have concluded that sanctions are unlikely to succeed except in unusual circumstances.[117] Well-respected analysts have reached this conclusion explicitly with regard to sanctions aimed at the support of terrorism.[118] Without reviewing the large literature on this point, consider some of the basic problems.

First, successful deterrence may require better knowledge of target state activities than is often available.[119] Failing to respond to state involvement in terrorism because of a lack of information will obviously do nothing to deter such involvement. Responding with economic sanctions when states have *not* been involved in terrorism, or have been involved at a lower level than is believed, will not only entail unnecessary costs for the sanctioning state,[120] but may "spread and [deepen] the conflict without punishing the terrorist groups themselves."[121]

Second, it will often be difficult to implement economic sanctions that impose significant costs on the target states. Most basically, a state can only utilize negative economic sanctions if there are economic links to sever.[122] The United States has few economic links with most of the

---

116. *See* Kraakman, *supra* note 38, at 61; *supra* notes 86-87 and accompanying text.

117. For a number of years, a "striking consensus" on the inefficiency of economic sanctions viewed as instruments of leverage has prevailed among commentators. Abbott, *supra* note 2, at 821. Daoudi and Dajani have compiled pages of quotations demonstrating the overwhelming consensus. M. DAOUDI & M. DAJANI, ECONOMIC SANCTIONS: IDEALS AND EXPERIENCE 43-48, 178-88 (1983). For a recent example, in 1984, the political scientist Klaus Knorr opined that one could best explain most recent uses of economic sanctions, at least those arising during "crises of high diplomacy," as "inept statecraft," or as "degradations of rationality." Knorr, *supra* note 66, at 203. Even Hufbauer and Schott, whose work in some ways rehabilitates the use of economic leverage, *see* G. HUFBAUER & J. SCHOTT, *supra* note 60, at 42 (in "modest policy change cases," states using economic sanctions have often "made some progress in achieving [their] goals"), find success to have been limited and to have come primarily in special circumstances. *See id.* at 42-47, 79-81.

118. *See* Bienen & Gilpin, *supra* note 101, at 89.

119. *See supra* note 27.

120. *See infra* note 138.

121. Axelrod & Keohane, *supra* note 27, at 235.

122. *See* G. HUFBAUER & J. SCHOTT, *supra* note 60, at 84-85. The authors observe that economic sanctions have typically been more effective when directed against friends and trading partners than when aimed at adversaries and states with few economic links. The conclusion to which this observation leads them—"attack your allies, not your adversaries"—is unfortunate, however. *See* Abbott, *supra* note 19.

states involved in terrorism:[123] for example, for some time it has had minimal trade and air traffic with Syria and has given it no foreign aid. In addition, economic sanctions will have little bite if alternate suppliers and markets are readily available.[124] In the modern economy this is usually the case.[125] The fact that other Western states, including many whose economic links to the terrorist-supporting states are more significant than those of the United States, are unwilling to impose strong antiterrorism sanctions, exacerbates the problem[126] and leads to a charge of free-riding on American measures.[127] In terms of rational deterrence theory, a single state will often find it difficult to set a penalty high enough to deter terrorism effectively.[128]

Third, even if a state can impose significant economic sanctions, its actions will only serve to reduce terrorism if the target states respond to the use or threat of sanctions by reducing their support or sponsorship. Some terrorist-supporting states—a radical Islamic state like Iran immediately comes to mind—may weigh the incentives presented by sanctions very differently from the rational state that the theory of deterrence assumes.[129] Against such a state, sanctions may be ineffective or even counterproductive. A similar problem with the deterrence of individual fanatic terrorists, one should note, was one of the principal reasons for considering secondary enforcement against supporting states in the first place.[130]

Finally, secondary liability will only be effective if the gatekeepers can actually prevent the undesirable activities of the primary wrongdoers.[131] Here the distinction between sponsorship and support becomes important. A state that sponsors terrorism and is the primary wrongdoer will presumably be able to call off the terrorists under its command, cease its own participation in terrorist acts and terminate recruitment, incitement

---

123. *See* Bialos & Juster, *supra* note 15, at 842-43, n.141.

124. *See* State Department Report, *supra* note 1, at 1; Abbott, *supra* note 2, at 800-10; Knorr, *supra* note 66, at 191-93.

125. *See* State Department Report, *supra* note 1, at 1; G. HUFBAUER & J. SCHOTT, *supra* note 2, at 80-81.

126. *See supra* note 50.

127. *See* Abbott, *Collective Goods, Mobile Resources, and Extraterritorial Trade Controls*, LAW & CONTEMP. PROB. (forthcoming).

128. *See* R. POSNER, *supra* note 44, at 170-71. It is probably true, however, that economic sanctions often work slowly and cumulatively, so that their effects are difficult to discern. *See* D. BALDWIN, *supra* note 66, at 133-34.

129. *See supra* note 88 and accompanying text.

130. *See supra* note 46 and accompanying text.

131. *See* Kraakman, *supra* note 38, at 61, 63, 66-74.

and similar activities. A terrorist-supporting state, however, may be unable to control the independent terrorist groups it has been assisting even if it withdraws its support.[132]

Once a state terminates its support of terrorism, terrorists can follow several strategies available to any primary wrongdoer. First, they can shop for other states that are still willing to support them, or that are at least unable to evict them.[133] Members of the Abu Nidal group, for example, have moved their operations from Iraq to Syrian-controlled areas of Lebanon, have begun to take sanctuary in Eastern Europe and have begun to receive support from Libya as well as from earlier patrons.[134] Terrorists can turn to illicit markets—operated clandestinely by states or private interests—for arms, passports and other supplies.[135] They can disguise their activities so as to continue using the target state's territory as a base of operations and sanctuary. They can operate with reduced levels of assistance. Terrorist groups can also, of course, attempt to corrupt the original supporting state into continuing some facets of its support surreptitiously,[136] a strategy that exploits the difficulty of obtaining reliable information about state activities.[137]

Along with these weaknesses in the effectiveness of economic sanctions as instruments of influence, one must also consider the costs of employing them.[138] Kraakman suggests three categories of costs associated with secondary enforcement.[139] The first, and most familiar, is administrative cost, the cost of monitoring and penalizing gatekeepers who violate established norms. Domestically, these costs are likely to be relatively minor, although highly visible, because they are marginal costs to a functioning enforcement system that will already be dealing with the primary wrongdoers.[140] Private costs are the costs of compliance that secondary enforcement imposes on gatekeepers, including the costs of the routines

---

132. *See Terrorism: Oversight Hearings, supra* note 27, at 45 (testimony of Prof. Martha Crenshaw).

133. *See* Kraakman, *supra* note 38, at 63, 66-67, 72-74.

134. *See Syrian Support for International Terrorism, supra* note 115, at 73.

135. *See infra* note 81 and accompanying text. *Cf.* Kraakman, *supra* note 38, at 66-69.

136. *See* Kraakman, *supra* note 38, at 63, 69-72.

137. *See supra* note 27 and accompanying text.

138. Effectiveness and cost are the two principal criteria for evaluating the performance of any strategy of enforcement. *See* Kraakman, *supra* note 44, at 61, 74-75. Together, effectiveness and cost determine the utility of a strategy, *see* D. BALDWIN, *supra* note 66, at 119, which one must then compare with the utility of other possible approaches. *See id.* at 120-28.

139. *See* Kraakman, *supra* note 38, at 75.

140. *See id.* at 75 n.61.

necessary to avoid liability and any residual risk of liability. Tertiary costs are those that fall on other parties, such as the innocent customers of gatekeepers who may be caught in the gatekeepers' enforcement routines. Although less visible than administrative costs, these two categories are also important social costs.

In sanctioning states involved in terrorism, the administrative costs will almost certainly be more significant than in domestic law enforcement, for they will not be marginal costs added to an ongoing enforcement system but an entirely different and additional set of costs.[141] Administrative costs in this context will include, among others, the costs of monitoring targets and potential target states[142] and of negotiating with those states[143] and with allies.

The greatest administrative costs, however, will be those resulting from the economic sanctions themselves. These costs include lost gains from trade, indirect economic costs arising out of a reputation for interrupting commercial transactions, additional indirect costs resulting from efforts to minimize the potential impact of extraterritorial application, political costs resulting from friction with targets, potential targets and their allies as well as with the sanctioning state's own allies, and disruption of the open trading system. Although these costs are very difficult to measure[144] or even to estimate,[145] their general nature is fairly well understood,[146] and I will not discuss them in greater detail here.

The private costs incurred by target or potential target states seeking

---

141. Under some circumstances, the costs incurred in imposing sanctions will constitute an advantage. *See infra* text accompanying note 187.

142. This will involve primarily the gathering of intelligence.

143. Section 3(8) of the Export Administration Act, 50 U.S.C. app. § 2402(8) (1982), requires the President to make reasonable efforts to secure the termination of state assistance to terrorists through "international cooperation and agreement" before using export controls for that purpose.

144. *See* D. BALDWIN, *supra* note 66, at 128-30; G. HUFBAUER & J. SCHOTT, *supra* note 60, at 65.

145. *See, e.g.*, G. HUFBAUER & J. SCHOTT, *supra* note 60, at 64-65. The authors note, for example, that cutting foreign assistance as a sanction may actually help the sanctioning state financially, but that the lost contacts may translate into offsetting export losses. One might add to this observation that, if the sanctioning state used the money saved to increase aid to other countries, exports to and investment in those countries might correspondingly increase, although the same firms or industries would probably not be affected.

146. *See, e.g.*, Abbott, *supra* note 2, at 826-57; State Department Report, *supra* note 1, at 2; Moyer & Mabry, *Export Controls as Instruments of Foreign Policy: The History, Legal Issues and Policy Lessons of Three Recent Cases*, 15 LAW & POL'Y INT'L BUS. 1, 149-56 (1983); G. HUFBAUER & J. SCHOTT, *supra* note 60, at 64-66.

314   *VANDERBILT JOURNAL OF TRANSNATIONAL LAW*   *[Vol. 20:289*

to avoid sanctions would not seem severe, at least as compared with the problems arising in domestic economic settings.[147] It should not be difficult for such states to terminate activities directly supportive of terrorism, and doing so might actually bring economic benefits. Exercising due diligence to ensure that terrorist groups are not using state territory might be costly, though, and there might be some risk of residual liability.

Tertiary costs also seem likely to be less troublesome than in domestic law enforcement because there are relatively few transactions between potential target states and innocent persons that the threat of economic sanctions might distort. It is possible, however, that the members of a high-risk group—Palestinians, for example—could become victims of discrimination by a potential target state seeking to avoid all possible risk of sanctions.[148]

Neither private nor tertiary costs, one should note, will be social costs of the sanctioning state, as they are in domestic contexts. In practical terms, then, these costs will not weigh heavily in decisions on the use of economic sanctions.

C. *Denial of Means*

The denial of means strategy calls for restricting sales of selected items that would contribute to a target state's capability to support or engage in a particular form of wrongdoing.[149] In the present context, for example, one might attempt to limit a target state's access to items needed to train, supply, equip and otherwise assist terrorist groups. If effective, this strategy would be a valuable complement to the strategy of leverage since it could help limit the capabilities of terrorist sponsoring and supporting states even when they ignored efforts to deter them. Because of the selective nature of the controls required, moreover, it would be less costly to the sanctioning state than the strategies previously considered.

Restrictions on the sale of arms to states involved in terrorism exemplify the denial of means rationale.[150] In the United States, under the Arms Export Control Act,[151] the President may refuse to make military sales to foreign countries[152] and may prohibit private arms sales[153] for

---

147. *See* Kraakman, *supra* note 38, at 75-77.

148. A domestic analogy is employer discrimination against Hispanics in order to avoid gatekeeper liability under a legal regime aimed at illegal aliens. *See id.* at 77.

149. *See supra* notes 68-73 and accompanying text.

150. These restrictions presumably implement the imposing costs and symbolic communications rationales as well.

151. 22 U.S.C. §§ 2751-2796c (1982 & Supp. I 1983).

152. *Id.* at § 2752(b).

foreign policy reasons. Under this authority, the government prohibits exports of items on the Munitions List to states that the Secretary of State has determined to be supporters of terrorism.[154] In addition, the Act requires the President to terminate arms sales to any country that grants sanctuary to an individual or group that has committed a terrorist act.[155] The Western allies have generally cooperated in the restriction of arms sales,[156] presumably reflecting the widespread concern about the consequences that might ensue if terrorists gained access to sophisticated weapons.[157] These restrictions, by reducing to some extent the availability of weapons on international markets, especially in volatile regions, may have served to hamper even independent terrorist groups.

Under the Export Administration Act (EAA), the United States has explicitly adopted the denial of means rationale for its antiterrorism export controls on goods other than munitions. First, according to the State Department, the licensing requirements in force under the EAA for antiterrorism purposes are "aimed at restricting the export of goods or technology that would contribute significantly to the military potential or enhance the terrorist-support capabilities of [target] countries."[158] In addition, the EAA requires the executive branch to determine whether any proposed export valued at more than $1 million and destined for a terrorist-supporting state would make a significant contribution to the military potential of that state or would "enhance the ability of [that] country to support acts of international terrorism."[159] If so, the Executive

---

153. *Id.* at § 2778.

154. *See* State Department Report, *supra* note 1, at 4.

155. 22 U.S.C. § 2753(f) (1982). An exception exists, however, for situations where the President finds that the national security requires a continuation of sales.

156. *See* State Department Report, *supra* note 1, at 3; Tokyo Economic Summit Statement on Terrorism, *supra* note 30 (Summit Seven countries agree, "within the framework of international law and in our own jurisdictions," to deny arms exports to states clearly involved in the support of terrorism, in order to "deny to international terrorists the . . . means to carry out their aims."); Robert B. Oakley, Acting Ambassador at Large for Counter-Terrorism, statement before Subcomm. on Security and Terrorism of Sen. Judiciary Comm., *reprinted in* DEP'T OF STATE BULL., Aug. 1986, at 5, 7 (describing decision of European Community foreign ministers not to export arms to terrorist-supporting states).

157. *See, e.g.,* Kupperman, *supra* note 38, at 28-29; Jenkins, *supra* note 83, at 11; Pierre, *supra* note 45, at 1256.

158. *See* State Department Report, *supra* note 1, at 4. *See also* White House Statement, *supra* note 16.

159. *See* Export Administration Act, § 6(j), 50 U.S.C. app. § 2405(j) (1982). The threshold value was $7 million for several years; Congress reduced it to $1 million in 1986. Omnibus Diplomatic Security and Antiterrorism Act of 1986, Pub. L. No. 99-399 (amending Export Administration Act, § 6(j)(1)).

branch must notify the designated Congressional committees before licensing the export,[160] a provision clearly designed to discourage the approval of such exports.[161]

The implementation of this policy, however, has been quite unsatisfying. Consider the products that were restricted for export to Syria under the antiterrorism policy of the EAA as of the end of 1986.

First, aircraft and helicopters valued at $3 million or more.[162] These could, however, be sold to scheduled Syrian airlines if assurances against military use were received.[163]

Second, goods and technology subject to national security controls—high technology items with military applications—but only if sold to Syrian military organizations or for Syrian military uses, and only if valued at $7 million or more.[164] Most of these items required a license for export to Syria under the EAA's national security provisions[165]—because of the possibility of diversion to the Soviet Union—long before the United States imposed antiterrorism sanctions.[166]

Third, certain military vehicles and machinery designed to produce military equipment.[167] These items were already controlled for export to many destinations, including Syria, under the "regional stability" policy,[168] a denial of means strategy aimed at limiting military conflicts in

---

The Act also states that it is the policy of the United States to use export controls to "encourage other countries" to cease rendering assistance to terrorists, *id.* § 2402(8), and authorizes the President to restrict exports of goods and technology in order to carry out that policy, *id.* § 2405(a)(1). These provisions appear to be motivated by the leverage and symbolic communication rationales.

160. *Id.* at § 6(j), 50 U.S.C. § 2405(i).

161. *See* Note, *Export Controls and the U.S. Effort to Combat International Terrorism,* 13 LAW & POL'Y INT'L BUS. 521 (1981).

162. 15 C.F.R. § 385.4(d)(2) (1987).

163. *Id.*

164. *Id.* The $7 million floor was consistent with the Congressional notice requirement in effect at the time. *See supra* note 159. As of the end of 1986, the United States considered license applications for the export of such items on a case-by-case basis with reference to both the antiterrorism policy and basic national security considerations. 15 C.F.R. § 385.4(d)(2) (1987).

165. Export Administration Act, § 5, 50 U.S.C. app. § 2404 (1982).

166. Most national security controls cover exports to virtually all destinations, and the government makes decisions on the issuance of licenses in large part with reference to the danger of diversion. *See* Abbott, *supra* note 2, at 752-54; 15 C.F.R. § 385.4(g)(1) (1987).

167. 15 C.F.R. § 385.4(d)(1)(b), 376.16 (1987).

168. *See supra* text accompanying note 4. In addition to special licensing requirements, the regional stability policy has led to the denial of licenses for the export of goods

the Middle East and elsewhere,[169]—limiting Libya's ability to operate in Chad, for example.[170]

Fourth, certain crime control and detection equipment.[171] These items, too, were already controlled for export to many destinations, including Syria, as a denial of means and symbolic communication strategy designed to promote observance of human rights.[172]

And that was all. In June 1987[173] the United States extended controls to all aircraft and removed the exception for sales to scheduled airlines. It extended antiterrorism controls on goods already controlled for national security purposes to transactions under $7 million and to those not involving a military purchase or end use and tightened the policy on licensing such exports. It, however, did not expand any other controls on exports to Syria.[174]

Even as expanded, it appears that most of these controls—especially those based on the national security and regional stability policies, including the controls on aircraft—were designed primarily to limit conventional military capabilities, not the ability to support terrorism.[175]

---

controlled for national security reasons to countries engaged in regional hostilities. *See* Abbott, *supra* note 2, at 761-62.

169. *See* 15 C.F.R. §§ 376.16, 385.4(g)(3) (1987). *See also id.* at § 385.4(e) (controls on export of certain chemicals used in chemical warfare).

170. Libya is subject to separate regional stability controls. *See* 15 C.F.R. §§ 385.4(g)(3), 385.7 (1987).

171. 15 C.F.R. § 385.4(d)(1)(a), 376.14 (1987). *See supra* text accompanying notes 71-72.

172. *See* 15 C.F.R. §§ 376.14; 385.4(g)(2) (1987).

173. *See supra* note 16.

174. *See* 52 Fed. Reg. 23,167 (June 18, 1987). The criteria for favorable consideration of license applications announced as part of the 1987 regulations, *see supra* note 16, only apply to transactions newly controlled by those regulations. *See id.*, adding 15 C.F.R. § 385.4(d)(4)(iii). The extension of controls on national security-controlled items to sales below $7 million parallels a reduction from $7 million to $1 million in the threshold above which exporters must notify Congress of applications to export goods subject to antiterrorism controls. *See supra* note 159. Prior to the announcement of new sanctions against Syria, the government also extended to Syria existing controls on the export of certain chemicals to Iran and Iraq—based on United States opposition to prohibited use of chemical weapons—with an exception for existing contracts. 51 Fed. Reg. 20,467 (June 5, 1986) (to be codified at 15 C.F.R. § 385.4(e)). The government has since subjected additional chemicals to these controls. 52 Fed. Reg. 28,550 (July 31, 1987).

175. Terrorists would find some restricted crime control and detection equipment useful. Examples include certain weapons and protective clothing that the police customarily use and items like leg irons, handcuffs and thumbscrews—controlled as instruments of torture—that terrorists could use in the mistreatment of hostages.

318   *VANDERBILT JOURNAL OF TRANSNATIONAL LAW*   *[Vol. 20:289*

That may be a very desirable goal, but for the most part it is a different goal.[176] The government has largely limited its national security controls, moreover, to high technology products—selected with the strategic forces of the Soviet Union in mind—that are irrelevant to most forms of terrorism whether purchased by civilian or military organizations.[177] In any case, as already noted, most of the antiterrorism controls—sometimes imposed with considerable fanfare—were not actually new controls; the same items were already restricted under another policy.[178] It is hard to avoid the conclusion that the antiterrorism export controls based on the denial of means rationale amount to far less than meets the eye.

It is probably true, however, that it would be fruitless to implement this sanctions strategy much more broadly. Even extensive product controls would have virtually no effect on many forms of support for terrorism such as moral support, financial support,[179] passports, and sanctuary. Even the present controls on arms exports, though they may help restrict the availability of advanced weapons, are likely to have little effect on the volume of ordinary terrorism. Terrorists can, and do, carry out most of their acts using only small arms, ordinary explosives, and similar weapons.[180] These items will continue to be available in licit and

---

176. To the extent such controls denied access to arms that terrorists might use effectively, however, the goal would be the same.

177. *See* Export Administration Act, § 5(d), 50 U.S.C. app. § 2404(d) (1982) (limits controls to the extent possible and consistent with national security purpose, to militarily critical technologies which, if exported, would permit a significant advance in the military system of a controlled country).

178. The Export Administration Regulations provide that the government will administer licensing requirements imposed under multiple policies in accordance with the most restrictive policy. 15 C.F.R. § 388.1.

179. Some economic sanctions do not limit access to specific products, but restrict access to foreign exchange. Examples from United States practice include § 505 of the International Security and Development Corporation Act of 1985, 22 U.S.C. § 2349aa-9 (authorizing the President to ban imports from any country that harbors or otherwise supports terrorists); *id.* at § 504, 22 U.S.C. § 2349aa-8 (authorizing a ban on imports from Libya); Export-Import Bank of Washington Act, § 2(b)(1)(B), 12 U.S.C. § 635(b)(1)(B) (authorizing denial of applications for Eximbank credits if the President determines this would be in the national interest and would clearly and importantly advance American antiterrorism policy); Trade Act of 1974, § 502(b)(7), 19 U.S.C. § 2462(b)(6) (requiring the President not to designate states supporting terrorism as beneficiary developing countries under Generalized System of Preferences). Such sanctions could affect a target country's ability to provide financial support. As with the economic warfare rationale, however, *see supra* note 122 and accompanying text, it is unlikely that this strategy can reduce the economic resources of a target state sufficiently to seriously limit its ability to finance terrorist acts.

180. *See* Jenkins, *Statements About Terrorism*, 463 ANNALS 11, 12-14 (1982); Wil-

illicit private markets and from alternate suppliers, including the Soviet Union.[181]

D. *Symbolic Communication*

Commentators often ignore or denigrate the symbolic uses of economic sanctions,[182] but recent scholarship has emphasized their importance.[183] As noted on the bottom row of the matrix in Figure 3, sanctions can communicate a variety of messages to multiple audiences, including terrorist groups themselves, and can thereby serve important instrumental functions.[184] Examining these symbolic messages may help us understand some antiterrorism measures that other sanctions rationales do not fully explain. To illustrate, the remainder of this section will spell out some of the messages that the United States appears to have communicated by strengthening economic sanctions against Syria in November 1986.

First, the expansion of sanctions against Syria demonstrated to terrorist groups, including those not supported by Syria, that the United States continued to view terrorism as a serious problem. The sanctions suggested a degree of determination to oppose terrorism likely to be reflected not only in economic sanctions and other measures aimed at state support but also in measures designed to prevent terrorist acts and improve the procedures for apprehending, extraditing and prosecuting individual terrorists.[185] To some unmeasurable extent, therefore, sanctions like these may function to deter even independent terrorists.

Second, the expansion of sanctions communicated a variety of messages to Syria itself. Here again, they conveyed determination, commitment to the goal of opposing state supported terrorism and an inten-

---

kinson, *Terrorism: The International Response,* 34 WORLD TODAY 5 (1978).

181. *See* Jenkins, *supra* note 83, at 10; Kutner, *Constructive Notice: A Proposal to End International Terrorism,* 10 COMM. L. LAW 3, at 1, 3. On Soviet supply of weapons—including sophisticated weapons like surface-to-air missiles—see *Libyan-Sponsored Terrorism: A Dilemma for Policymakers, Hearings before Subcomm. on Security and Terrorism of the Sen. Comm. on Judiciary,* 99th Cong., 2d Sess. 77, 92 (1986) (statement of Yonah Alexander).

182. *See supra* text accompanying note 74. *See* Bialos & Juster, *supra* note 15, at 848-49, 852-53.

183. *See* D. BALDWIN, *supra* note 66, at 96-114. For a discussion of Baldwin's work, see Abbott, *supra* note 19.

184. *See* D. BALDWIN, *supra* note 66, at 96-114.

185. For a review of recent United States measures of this type, see Address of Robert B. Oakley, *supra* note 32.

tion to take action in support of that goal.[186] An action like the imposition of sanctions conveys these messages more credibly than mere words because it demonstrates that the United States is willing to bear costs[187] and to accept risks[188] in pursuit of its goals. By imposing sanctions, after all, the United States loses gains from trade, acquires a reputation as an unreliable supplier,[189] and incurs the risk that Syria will cause harm to hostages held by terrorist groups it supports, sabotage the Middle East peace process or use force against Israel or respond in other damaging ways. Sanctions can also communicate a threat of military action. The embargo of Libya was clearly designed to convey such a threat;[190] the sanctions against Syria, in contrast, were not.[191]

Communicating these messages of commitment and action entails clear dangers, of course. One danger is that the United States may have no way of making good on its commitments, so that it comes to look foolish.[192] Another danger is that the United States will feel forced to escalate, perhaps to otherwise undesirable military action, to avoid looking foolish. Both of these dangers are real in the Syrian situation, as they were with Libya.

In fact, however, the Syria sanctions seem to have been designed to minimize the need for further coercive measures by conveying certain psychological messages to Syria. American officials, including the President, went out of their way to characterize the sanctions as demonstrating that the support of terrorism was causing Syria to become isolated,

---

186. *See* D. BALDWIN, *supra* note 66, at 102-08. *See also* State Department Report, *supra* note 1, at 1-2 (economic sanctions "demonstrate our resolve," "demonstrate United States determination to oppose another nation's support of terrorism," and "demonstrate that we support our policies with actions as well as words."). This report is one of the best available summaries of the symbolic uses of sanctions.

187. *See* D. BALDWIN, *supra* note 66, at 107. *See also* State Department Report, *supra* note 1, at 1-2 (sanctions "demonstrate that we . . . are prepared to incur costs in our battle against international terrorism," and "show that we are prepared to accept economic losses, if necessary.")

188. *See* D. BALDWIN, *supra* note 66, at 112.

189. *See supra* notes 141-44 and accompanying text; State Department Report, *supra* note 1, at 2.

190. *See* Bialos & Juster, *supra* note 15, at 848-49, 852-53.

191. *See infra* text accompanying note 201.

192. Baldwin sees a similar effect in the League of Nations sanctions against Mussolini's Italy. One goal of the sanctions was to demonstrate to Hitler the League's ability and will to stand up to aggression. Britain and France, however, were unwilling to go to war even with Italy, and they clearly communicated this lack of resolve by the manner in which they implemented sanctions. As a result, the League sanctions did not deter Hitler, and they have been subject to ridicule ever since. *See* D. BALDWIN, *supra* note 66, at 156-58.

rejected by the "international community of nations" and by the "civilized world."[193] The government explicitly linked the sanctions, in this regard, to recent European diplomatic sanctions. The American sanctions themselves included a reduction in the staff of the American embassy and a suspension of high level diplomatic meetings.[194] Syria, the White House said, could play an important role in a key region of the world, but it could not expect to be accepted "as a responsible power or [treated] as one as long as it continues to use terrorism as an instrument of its foreign policy."[195] The United States designed these sanctions, in short, to apply political and moral pressure as well as economic pressure[196] and to play on the concern for reputation that keeps most states from supporting terrorists in the first place.[197]

As suggested previously, some of the new Syria sanctions were relatively weak. The United States did not order its firms to terminate operations in Syria, for example, as it had earlier done with Libya.[198] Instead, it advised its oil firms that further Syrian oil operations would be "inappropriate."[199] The moderation of the sanctions communicated still other messages to Syria, inconsistent to some degree with the basic messages of opposition and commitment. The use of moderate sanctions seems to have allowed the United States "to make a commitment, but not too much of a commitment," and to "deter and reassure simultaneously," as economic sanctions are peculiarly suited to do.[200]

After the message of restraint that the United States conveyed, albeit not explicitly, was an acknowledgment of Syria's power and influence in the Middle East. By imposing only moderate sanctions, the United States made clear that it did not want to provoke a military or political reaction that might be worse than Syria's support of terrorism.[201] The sanctions also conveyed a desire to maintain some lines of communication

---

193. White House Statement, *supra* note 16.

194. *See id.*

195. *Id.*

196. *See* D. BALDWIN, *supra* note 66, at 134-36. Economic sanctions that convey a threat of military action, similarly, exert influence through the sanctioning state's military power base, not through economic pressure.

197. *See supra* note 78 and accompanying text.

198. *See* Bialos & Juster, *supra* note 15, at 812-14 (discussing ban on contract performance), 824-25 (discussing hardship exceptions).

199. White House Statement, *supra* note 16.

200. *See* D. BALDWIN, *supra* note 66, at 102-05.

201. The Iran hostage crisis was a similar situation. Baldwin believes that the United States designed the sanctions imposed against Iran to communicate moderation as well as resolve, so as to ensure the release of the hostages. *Id.* at 251-52.

or some possibility of cooperation for mutual interests.[202] By limiting itself to economic sanctions and by keeping them moderate, the United States demonstrated that in spite of the Libya bombing a few months earlier,[203] it was not trigger-happy; it would act with restraint, relying on peaceful measures as long as possible.[204] American officials generally went out of their way to distinguish Syria from Libya, which they treated as a special, extreme case.[205] The sanctions and related diplomatic measures conveyed a subtle mix of messages to Syria that may have had the effect the United States desired: as this article was written, Syria had closed the Damascus office of the Abu Nidal terrorist group and had made efforts for the release of Western hostages held in Lebanon; the United States had responded by proposing discussions on a variety of Middle East issues.[206]

Third, the Syria sanctions conveyed messages to other states. The sanctions conveyed the basic message of commitment and determination indirectly to all other terrorist-supporting states, including the Soviet Union, and they sent an implicit message of support to all states working to suppress terrorism.[207] The United States almost certainly imposed only moderate sanctions on Syria to reassure the European allies and

---

202. *See* State Department Report, *supra* note 1, at 3 ("In stark contrast to Libya, we have been able on occasion to use our relationships with [other countries on the terrorism list, including Syria] to the benefit of U.S. interests").

203. *See supra* note 14.

204. The White House statement imposing the sanctions reviewed earlier economic sanctions against Syria and depicted the new sanctions as additional steps in an orderly progression. It also linked them explicitly to European Community sanctions imposed a few days before, which were even more moderate. The statement did, however, say that additional steps would be taken if necessary. *See* White House Statement, *supra* note 16.

205. *See* State Department Report, *supra* note 1, at 3 ("Libya is an exceptional case. There are major qualitative differences between our relationship with Libya and other countries on the terrorism list. We have normal diplomatic relations with Syria. . . ."). The Western allies have also singled out Libya, at the behest of the United States. *See* Tokyo Economic Summit Statement on Terrorism, *supra* note 30.

206. *See* N.Y. Times, June 26, 1987, at 5, col. 5. Several European countries had begun to renew such discussions even earlier; N. Y. TIMES, Mar. 31, 1987, at 2, col. 1.

207. *See* State Department Report, *supra* note 1, at 1 ("Economic sanctions may be used . . . to strengthen the resolve of others, such as neighboring countries or U.S. allies, in dealing with governments that support terrorism."). The sanctions are somewhat analogous to the United States embargo of Cuba, which was designed in part to warn the Soviet Union and its allies of American opposition to Communism in the Western Hemisphere, to reassure and demonstrate support for non-Communist rulers in the hemisphere, and, by analogy to the messages conveyed to terrorist groups, to communicate opposition and determination to Communist revolutionary groups in Latin America. *See* D. BALDWIN, *supra* note 66, at 176-78.

other states concerned by the use of military force against Libya[208] and to demonstrate continued American commitment to the use of peaceful measures and proportionality.[209] Most broadly, the sanctions helped to focus the continued attention of all states, indeed all people, on the problem of terrorism.[210]

Finally, the United States seems to have designed the Syria sanctions to communicate several specific and important messages to its allies in Europe, Japan and elsewhere. First, the sanctions demonstrate continuing American leadership on the issue of terrorism.[211] American officials have long felt that unilateral measures, like these sanctions and the Libya embargo, focus attention on the problem and encourage others to follow the American lead.[212] They view the Tokyo Summit declaration on terrorism[213] and other instances of cooperation as products, at least in part, of American leadership.[214]

More specifically, as the State Department declared, unilateral sanctions serve "to refute criticisms that we ask our allies to make sacrifices

---

208. "Nothing has so vehemently separated America from Europe since 1945." ECONOMIST, April 26, 1986, at 13.

209. *See* State Department Report, *supra* note 1, at 2 ("[The use of economic sanctions] serves to refute criticisms . . . that we are unwilling to try 'peaceful measures' before taking other steps;" "Measures that appear unnecessarily harsh or inappropriate can undermine our credibility with the targeted country as well as with friendly countries whose support we seek.")

210. By analogy, Baldwin observes that the League of Nations sanctions against Italy "began to sensitize the Western democracies to the need to oppose aggression and may have made it easier to arouse public support in subsequent years." *See* D. BALDWIN, *supra* note 66, at 160.

211. The United States made the exercise of leadership much more explicit, however, in imposing the Libyan embargo. *See, e.g.*, National Emergency with Respect to Libya, *supra* note 91 ("The United States . . . calls upon other nations to join with us in isolating the terrorists and their supporters. We must demonstrate . . . that the international community considers such actions intolerable . . . .[E]ach nation must bear its fair share of the vital effort against the politics of terror. I call upon every nation to do so now.").

212. *See* State Department Report, *supra* note 1, at 1 ("[Imposing costly sanctions] helps us to encourage others to follow our example and make the required trade and financial sacrifices.") For an argument that the bombing of Libya also had the aim, and effect, of catalyzing allied action, see Zilian, *The U.S. Raid on Libya—and NATO*, 30 ORBIS 499 (1986).

213. The statement both condemned terrorism and explicitly named Libya as a sponsoring state, a major aim of United States policy. *See* Tokyo Economic Summit Declaration on Terrorism, *supra* note 30.

214. *See* State Department Report, *supra* note 1, at 1, 3 ("[Libyan embargo] may have contributed to our recent success in obtaining multilateral cooperation, albeit limited, on sanctions and other measures.")

while we continue to profit from commercial relations with countries supporting terrorism."[215] The criticisms referred to occurred during the Siberian pipeline episode, when the United States continued to sell grain to the Soviet Union while asking its allies to forego industrial exports.[216]

The United States intended the Syrian sanctions, like the Libya embargo, to demonstrate that it plans to be more restrained in its use of extraterritorial trade controls, another lesson learned from the pipeline case.[217] Finally, the Syrian sanctions sent a powerful message of support to England, which had just convicted Nizar Hindawi of complicity in the attempted *El Al* bombing[218] and persuaded the European Community to adopt diplomatic sanctions against Syria.[219] England, of course, had provided a base for the bombing of Libya;[220] here the United States repaid the favor.

V. CONCLUSION

The foregoing analysis has suggested when economic sanctions may be appropriate measures for dealing with state involvement in international terrorism and has outlined the functions that sanctions can perform in that regard. The difficult questions of effectiveness and cost—in general and in regard to the antiterrorism sanctions actually imposed by the United States—have not been fully answered here.

One could give complete answers to those questions, if at all, only after detailed study of particular cases.[221] It would also be necessary to compare other available measures, including diplomatic responses, covert action, military force and inaction. Often economic sanctions that seem ineffective or unduly costly when examined in isolation appear more reasonable when compared to the other alternatives.[222]

---

215. *Id.* at 1 ("Openly acknowledging that the United States also will suffer from sanctions helps us to encourage others to follow our example . . . .").

216. *See* D. BALDWIN, *supra* note 66, at 280.

217. *See* State Department Report, *supra* note 1, at 2-3 (pipeline sanctions demonstrated that extraterritorial controls cause friction with friendly countries; United States has attempted to moderate extraterritorial reach, where appropriate, as with Libya embargo).

218. *See* N.Y. Times, Oct. 25, 1986, at A4, col. 1.

219. *See* White House Statement, *supra* note 16 (linking American sanctions to European Community action).

220. *See* N.Y. Times, April 16, 1986, at A14, col. 1.

221. For a number of exemplary case studies, see generally D. BALDWIN, *supra* note 66.

222. *See* Bialos & Juster, *supra* note 15, at 849-52 (analyzing options to Libya embargo).

The preliminary analysis in this Article suggests, however, that when one considers all their functions, economic sanctions can play a valuable role, at least at the margin, in a national strategy against international terrorism. At the same time, their effects will frequently be small, especially in the short run, while their costs and risks are likely to be substantial. Economic sanctions alone are no cure for international terrorism.

326   *VANDERBILT JOURNAL OF TRANSNATIONAL LAW*   [Vol. 20:289]

APPENDIX

Economic Sanctions and International Terrorism

Figure 1

STATE INVOLVEMENT IN TERRORISM

No significant state involvement:	State "support" of terrorists:		State "sponsorship" of terrorism:
independent terrorist groups	toleration or acquiescence sanctuary	training passports arms intelligence logistics	incitement, recruitment, organization;
	encouragement		direction of terrorist acts;
			direct participation

Economic Sanctions and International Terrorism

Figure 2

RATIONALES OR STRATEGIES OF ECONOMIC SANCTIONS

A. Economic warfare:

withhold gains from trade: embargo; civilian "bottleneck" items

B. Imposing costs:

deter,
exact price:
restrict transactions giving leverage

C. Denial of means:

deny inputs for wrongdoing:
strategic embargo

D. Symbolic communication:

convey commitment,
willingness to incur costs,
moderation:
restrict appropriate transactions

A & C — designed to influence capabilities

B & D — designed to influence intentions and will

328   VANDERBILT JOURNAL OF TRANSNATIONAL LAW   [Vol. 20:289

Economic Sanctions and International Terrorism

<u>Figure 3</u>

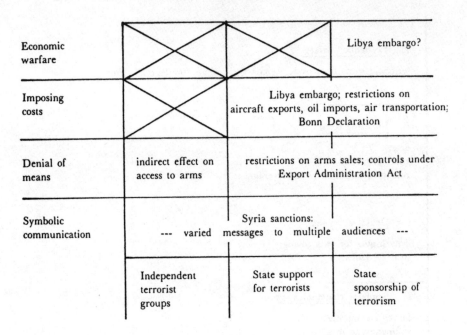

Economic warfare			Libya embargo?
Imposing costs		Libya embargo; restrictions on aircraft exports, oil imports, air transportation; Bonn Declaration	
Denial of means	indirect effect on access to arms	restrictions on arms sales; controls under Export Administration Act	
Symbolic communication	--- varied	Syria sanctions: messages to multiple audiences ---	
	Independent terrorist groups	State support for terrorists	State sponsorship of terrorism

[25]

TERRORIST HIJACKINGS AND THE INADEQUACIES OF INTERNATIONAL LAW

A Case Study of the Kuwait Airways Flight 422 Incident

by Robin E. Hill

This paper outlines developments made during 1988 in the realms of aviation violence. Dealing first with the failure of international law to suppress politically motivated offences, it proceeds to a discussion of the Kuwait Airways hijacking of April and the incident's implications for international co-operation to counter terrorism. This case illustrates the pressing need for urgent measures to be set in place for the genuine suppression of air crime — measures which must now be found through the adoption of new diplomatic, legal and practical initiatives.

WITHOUT doubt, 1988 was not a good year for aviation. With air traffic control difficulties, airport congestion and aircraft maintenance troubles, the year set some most unwelcome precedents for the future operation of this vital industry. However, of far greater significance than these comparatively simple questions of safety and convenience was the issue of aviation security and the threats posed to it by international terrorism. The problems to be overcome in handling the risks of hijacking and sabotage alone affect not only policy makers in government but also carriers and airports in the front line of attack and, not least, individual passengers who must now realise that their personal safety has been called into question by the glaring lapses in security which have become so obvious in recent months.

In terms of the phenomena involved, two incidents from 1988 stand out as key examples of aviation terrorism at its most efficient. First, there was the Kuwait Airways Flight 422 hijacking of April.[1] Then, in December the Lockerbie atrocity took place, calling into question some of the world's most advanced and respected security operations.[2] The former incident is dealt with here, although Pan Am Flight 103 illustrates well another face of the crisis presently encountering aviation.

A useful — indeed a necessary — starting point for a discussion of any terrorist hijacking is to be found in the context of the international legal regime which has sought for two decades to counter threats of violence aboard and upon aircraft. Before the 1960s, international law was correctly viewed as containing a significant jurisdictional lacuna in the entire subject of air crime. No unified attitude prevailed on the role, or even the powers, of states' judiciaries to act against offences committed in the airspace of foreign powers and over the high seas.[3] This, however, was clarified, though not resolved in 1963 by the United Nations' Specialized Agency for aviation — the International Civil Aviation Organization (ICAO). In a treaty which became known as the Tokyo Convention[4] and which was broadly accepted by very many states it was determined that at the very least the state of registration of the aircraft in question enjoyed the powers required

TERRORIST HIJACKINGS   309

to prosecute an offence if it sought to do so.

Only seven years later ICAO convened another conference on the issue because it had become clear that the Tokyo Convention had failed to address the specific and legally divisive subject of international hijacking, which was developing as a serious 'continuing offence', committed between several jurisdictions.[5] This conference resulted in the Hague Convention[6] of 1970 being drafted as a means of regulating the important legal activities involved in extradition and prosecution of suspects on a near universal basis, so as to allow governments to legislate and judiciaries to operate within some broadly internationalised rule system.

The treaty established that the offence of hijacking should be punishable by severe penalties[7] and should be subject to the legal standard expressed in the maxim *aut dedere aut judicare*[8], meaning that an accused person should be subject to prosecution in the state of his or her capture, or else be delivered to a jurisdiction which desired to put the suspect on trial.[9] Furthermore, the Hague Convention set out a range of rules and procedures designed to streamline extradition.[10] It was hoped that as a whole the Convention might, in some sense, suppress the crime of hijacking by means of punitive deterrence.[11]

In the following year, 1971, the 'extradite or prosecute' formula enshrined in the treaty was adopted in another ICAO agreement, called the Montreal Convention,[12] extending the *aut dedere aut judicare* doctrine to acts of sabotage committed against an aircraft in flight. Both Hague and Montreal Conventions proved to be hugely popular agreements, with governments of all political complexions signing and ratifying them in a truly concerted effort to minimise the possibility of offenders finding safe haven as a result of transnational legal incompatibilities. By the late 1980s, the agreements had received almost universal support from governments,[13] thus setting in place a juridictional framework which — on paper — would appear to enable the co-operation required to contain the latent threats from these crimes of hijacking and sabotage. There is, however, a question which is begged by this supposition: Why with three almost universally accepted agreements on crime suppression has aviation terrorism actually evolved and diversified throughout the intervening two decades?

The answer to this question is clear. The phenomena have developed simply because the agreements have proved powerless to restrain their unique development. In the middle of the 1960s, when the theory behind the Hague formula was first being mooted, aviation crime largely consisted in private acts committed for no overtly political motive.[14] Even in the early 1970s the dimensions and effects of terrorism had not been assessed adequately within its new sphere of influence — aviation. Neither the drafters nor the Conventions themselves had been able to deal with the then embryonic threat of political violence, despite attempts to frame treaties of broad application,[15] with the result that the agreements acted only to inhibit offenders who fitted neatly into the character profile tacitly required by the treaties.

This is not to say that the legal regime was without certain benefits.

310   *CONTEMPORARY REVIEW*

There is no question that the new climate of co-operation on extradition must have deterred a number of would-be offenders in the early 1970s, although it is impossible to assess the exact effectiveness of the norms concerned because external factors also played a part in the decline of hijacking at that time. States were taking a stronger domestic line against the crime and airport security was advancing in great leaps, so the window of opportunity was beginning to close on the expedient hijacker in any case.[16] Nevertheless, there is little statistical evidence to suggest that any of these measures contributed to variations in the incidence of aviation crime in the decade. Indeed, throughout the 1970s many forms of offence continued unabated by diplomatic efforts to suppress it.[17]

The continuing inadequacy from the point of view of terrorism suppression stemmed from the fundamental premise of the regime, namely its aim of suppressing air crime by resorting to deterrence. A factor which was consistently overlooked by the agreements was the mindset of the archetypal political terrorist. The Conventions signally failed to take into account the offence category of terrorism, which operated against a background of deeply entrenched political and/or theological aims. The regime failed because the static terms which had been locked into the treaties were forced by changing circumstances to take on board a new politically relevant category of offence type. The Conventions were expected — as they are still expected — to deter a new generation of offenders many of whom would not readily be deterred by the prospect of extradition, prosecution or even severe punishment. Throughout the 1970s and into the 1980s political hijackings have taken place which have captured media attention and forced governments into the most difficult of international crises over a wide range of subjects. From Dawson's Field to Entebbe, Mogadishu to Beirut, the issue of political motivation has ensured that the existence and even the operation of treaty law has sufficed neither to deter certain important categories of offenders nor to suppress the offences concerned.

This was exemplified in 1988 during the Kuwait Airways hijacking which took place from 5th to 20th April. The facts were well reported at the time and centred on the sixteen day ordeal of a largely Kuwaiti set of passengers and crew, hijacked during a flight to the Emirate from Bangkok. Spending three nights at Mashhad Airport in Iran then flying to Larnaca in Cyprus for four days of complex negotiations, the Boeing 747 was eventually sent to Algiers where it remained for a further week. During the course of the hijacking skilful negotiating techniques won the release of over half the hostages on board. Eventually, at the conclusion of the hijacking thirty-one passengers and crew were escorted from the jet while their captors made their escape, probably travelling to the Lebanese capital, Beirut, via Libya.[18]

The philosophy and strategy of the hijackers emulated those which had proved successful three years earlier during the TWA hijack incident.[19] In both cases the terrorists espoused an extremist Shi'ite theology and used the language of martyrdom to reinforce their threats. As with the 1985 incident, the hijackers operated in a large team, the precise size of which

TERRORIST HIJACKINGS   311

was never disclosed but which certainly numbered at least eight persons at the start of the hijacking.[20] Through a calculated process of intimidation, demand and threat they maintained control over the mediators whom they encountered over the radio and occasionally in person at each port of call. On two occasions their warnings were dramatised by murders of Kuwaiti public servants on board,[21] which guaranteed worldwide publicity at the height of the crisis and which forced the already powerless Cypriot negotiators to seek external assistance from the Algerians.

The team almost certainly operated in shifts and appeared to work according to some type of command structure.[22] Within its ranks there were experts in aircraft engineering, piloting skills, crisis psychology and negotiating strategy, acting together as a unit with complete control of their environment, even in the most taxing of conditions.[23] Although their apparent failure to gain any substantive concessions from the Kuwaiti government must be regarded as a defeat for the gang in its foremost aim, there were at least two factors which the hijackers used to great advantage during their two week siege. The first was publicity, often referred to as the life-blood of terrorism. Their warnings were couched in journalistic language, they made their demands very clearly and they produced dramatic images which guaranteed prime-time television coverage, worldwide. Just as had happened with the TWA hijacking, they organised what became known as a 'press conference' to maintain their high media profile when their story looked as though it might slip back to the inside pages.[24] Even the ignominious conclusion of the incident, when the unsuccessful terrorists left the aircraft almost unnoticed,[25] seemed to be timed to minimise adverse publicity in Europe and the Americas, making their command of media techniques all the more impressive.

The second factor which the terrorists used to the benefit of their cause was much more specific, concerning the domestic dimension of the crime in the framework of Iran's internal power struggle. The team's choice of Mashhad as a venue for the hijacking was apparently ideal for their initial purposes, because they must have been aware of the considerable political difficulties which their arrival would cause for the Islamic Republic. As Shia Muslims and natural supporters of the radical Shi'ite terrorist group of the Lebanon and Iraq, the hijackers were assured of large-scale support first from radical clergy in Mashhad, many of whom had been exiled from Kuwait,[26] second, from the militant wing in Teheran, which was seeking new ways of exporting the revolution[27] and third, from extremist public opinion throughout Iran. For these reasons the hijackers would have wanted to play upon the dilemma faced by the ruling pragmatists in finding a solution that would meet with domestic approval.

The principal aim of the incident was, of course, to place pressure on the government of Kuwait, which had been firmly allied with Iraq against the Iranians throughout the course of the Gulf war — then in its final stages.[28] The release of seventeen anti-Iraqi mercenaries imprisoned in Kuwait was demanded very forcefully, but was done from an airport on Iranian territory, making any question of co-operation between the diplomatically distant governments very difficult. Moreover, it is highly unlikely that the hijackers viewed the circumstances of their crime as being sufficient to coerce the Kuwaitis into immediate compromise, as the hijackers would have been well aware that the Emirate had suffered many years of terrorist attacks, yet had not given way to any demands identical to those made from the aircraft.[29] It follows, therefore, that there could have been a subsidiary objective behind the team electing to fly to Iran. Perhaps the gang regarded its chances of escape as being favourable when in an ideologically compatible country, which Iran undoubtedly was.[30] This suggestion is also questionable, as there would have been at least reasonably strong diplomatic and propagandist grounds at that time for Iranian determination to capture the offenders on their surrender and to prosecute them.[31] At any rate, the hijackers could not afford to be confident of receiving Iran's blessing for their revolutionary deed.

However, there is considerable circumstancial evidence in favour of the assertion that the hijack team deliberately placed domestic political pressure on the government of Iran. The authorities would have been sufficiently realistic to understand that the hijackers' very cause, of itself, placed it in a delicate position from the outset. Furthermore, the 747 landed at Mashhad within three days of elections to the *Majlis*, the Iranian Parliament, at which extremists were generally viewed as standing to gain seats from the more moderate pragmatists who had been discredited following Iraqi gains in the war.[32] This evidence suggests that the hijackers correctly identified that their incident could be made to exert much strain on the ruling administration and foment a domestic crisis from which it would be hard for the moderates to recover in the three days before the elections.

In terms of crisis management, there was little Iran could do either to foster diplomatic co-operation between itself and the Emirate or to act against the hijackers. The use of force against those responsible would have risked extremist gains in the elections, but also, on a practical level the aircraft itself was so difficult to storm — even by a highly trained intervention team — that any military venture would have had to be discounted from the start as a final option to be attempted only in the most extreme and pressing of circumstances.[33] In addition to the hijack team being large, with evidence from released passengers suggesting that it was reasonably well armed,[34] there was also the presence on board the aircraft of three members of Kuwait's ruling al-Sabah family, whose safety would have to be maintained if Iran were to escape later adverse propaganda from critics and enemies abroad. With Iranian crisis managers unable to resolve this triangular dispute in which the government had been placed against its will[35] and with the hijackers becoming increasingly prone to violent tendencies[36] there was virtually no choice but to refuel the jet and to permit take-off contrary to Kuwaiti demands that Iran continue to talk with the gang and liaise with the Emirate.[37]

In Cyprus, governmental involvement once more proved inadequate to end the stalemate. The island state had been a landing place of last resort for the aircraft, stricken with dangerously low fuel reserves after hours of

TERRORIST HIJACKINGS   313

circling Beirut Airport waiting for permission to land, which the Syrian-backed authorities wisely refused to grant.[38] Larnaca was accepted as a landing site by the hijackers solely for its proximity to Beirut and not for any particular ability it might have had to resolve the crisis.

This unhappy set of circumstances was reflected in the negotiating stance taken by the Cypriots and their partners in mediation — local Palestine Liberation Organization representatives. During the four days of the airliner's presence on Cypriot territory, negotiators adopted a consistent policy of delaying the terrorists in their demands for fuel and of reassuring them that efforts were on-going to bring about the release of the seventeen convicted prisoners in Kuwait. This tactic soon infuriated the terrorist team and probably contributed towards the two murders being committed, yet the policy was perhaps the most appropriate available to a country of Cyprus's size and diplomatic position, encountering on the one hand violent and unpredictable terrorists armed and equipped for a long siege and on the other a target government which resolutely refused to address the demands facing it.[39] Before long, it had also become clear from released passengers' reports that more terrorists and armaments had somehow appeared after the aircraft had landed at Mashhad,[40] fuelling speculation that the hijackers had received some logistical support from militants within Iran during the 747's visit to Mashhad.

Once again the option of take-off was unavoidable for the Cypriots, because, as with the Iranians, they could not be confident of discouraging the terrorists from turning to violence. On this occasion, however, an important factor in permitting the departure to take place was a suitable airport first being found where a solution acceptable to Kuwait might readily be worked out and implemented.[41] Whereas Iran had simply washed its hands of the 747 and allowed it to fly off with only Beirut as a contemplated landing place for the hijackers, Cyprus first co-operated with outside powers to minimise risks before allowing departure for an appropriate destination. Such a destination had been located in the form of Algeria, the government of which had often acted as a clearing house for similar incidents, including the TWA hijacking three years previously.[42]

Where earlier efforts to negotiate a surrender had failed, Algeria succeeded in winning the confidence of the terrorists, partly because of the nation's revolutionary history coupled with its tradition of mediation and partly on account of Algeria's dogged refusal to sign — and so be bound by — any of the international agreements on judicial action which had been drafted by ICAO. The success of the Algerian policy rested upon an exchange of undertakings with the hijackers and the governments concerned that a peaceful solution would be sought.[43] The terrorists, it seems, were to wait patiently for necessary developments without resorting to violence, while high level bargaining took place to secure the free passage of the hijackers to some state willing to accept them in return for the hostages' freedom.[44] In short, the Algerians did what very few governments would be equipped to do — that is to engineer a face-saving result for both sides where the terrorists gained no substantive concessions and received only minimal publicity. As with any conciliation tribunal, the Algerian mediators depended upon commanding the trust of both camps, achieved in this case through utilising the desperation which had jointly been mounting, first at Mashhad and then at Larnaca.

In earlier years pragmatic ambivalence over similar political hostage crises[45] correctly left Algeria open to accusations of being a safe haven for terrorists, as Palestinian hijackers could reasonably expect to receive favourable treatment upon arrival in the state. Algeria soon became a pariah internationally for its policy of non co-operation, because its isolationism totally undermined the fabric of the Hague Convention. The argument ran that deterrence and suppression depended utterly upon there being no hiding place for the guilty.[46] That contention is highly persuasive at first sight because it is axiomatic that one hundred per cent adherence to the Hague formula is essential if it is to discourage offenders from flying to a jurisdictional 'weak spot'. Nevertheless, it is fair to note that the agreements were not designed to cope with the form of offence so expertly committed by the gang on board Flight 422. Their determination was awesome, their skills were undoubted and their aircraft was impenetrable.

When legal norms are challenged by such practical opposition, it is hardly surprising that they become little more than embarrassing impediments in finding a solution acceptable to the governments concerned. The rule of law is made to suffer every time a hijacker or murderer goes free, but it is only proper to admit, at least, that the rule of law's effectiveness is strictly constrained by the bounds of political feasibility. That being the case, it is for governments to recognise first, that they must find the true limits of co-operation and second, act within them in drafting norms with aims that are both achievable and worthwhile. The bleak reality of modern international relations dictates that sovereign states must be expected, on occasion, to abandon the moral high-ground for a more comfortable position in what might be termed the amoral low-ground. Whether this weakness is put down to international law or to the governments which frame it, the same conclusion is reached. The real world is not a safe place for academic idealism.

Both American and British governments issued immediate condemnations when they learned that double murderers had been released from the grasp of the Algerians when they might have been prosecuted for their crimes.[47] Yet was this supposed to be a realistic option for the Algerians who had carved out this unrivalled and exceptionally useful diplomatic role? The eventual proof that Algeria's position had, in fact, been vindicated within the international community came in the weeks following the incident when no serious calls were made for the government to be punished after freeing the gang. Instead, states were content to see the issue of sanctions imposition gradually fade from the glare of media attention and eventually lapse into public oblivion. No government was prepared to criticise the Algerians in the long term, because it was almost impossible to deny that they had done what circumstances had forced them to do and had done so most effectively for the common good.

The best case that could be made against the Algerian policy is that it served indirectly to further the cause of global terror by showing how weak the international order truly can be, in turn encouraging further possibly more horrifying incidents in future.[48] This argument cannot, however, overcome the truth which, in fact, underpins it, that the world order is palpably weak and positively open to attack at any time. In the circumstances which exist today, the part played by Algeria is analogous to a safety valve acting to diffuse the build-up of diplomatic pressures and to return the international community to its fragile equilibrium. No-one wants the valve to blow, but almost everyone implicity recognises that it plays an important part in the global machine. The obsolescent and unprotected mechanism of law needs this means of support, because as yet it has not been protected in any other way.

The fact remains that until the world admits to itself that its suppression regime cannot of itself be sufficient to win reform, the crimes will continue. After any outrage of aviation terrorism, the first recommendation to emerge from governments is most likely to be for universal adherence to existing standards. Because of this, the Hague formula has acquired a new and highly damaging purpose. It has become a public relations tool by which states seek to prove their concern and to demonstrate their action in the field of aviation terrorism while remaining entirely apathetic to the changing needs of airlines and passengers. In the 1990s, as in this decade, terrorism suppression will not flow from governments merely showing their outrage or declaring their opposition to the crimes.

In conclusion it should be noted that a great deal waits to be achieved in upgrading judicial capacities from their presently inadequate conventional status. The terms of the Hague and Montreal agreements remain excessively vague and totally unenforced, despite several efforts in the 1970s to tie them to sanctions provisions for the event of breach. Enforcement efforts should continue in order to build upon what has gone before, but a new direction is also needed to supplement the existing standards and, more importantly, to protect the integrity of the aviation industry. The reactive approach of deterrence must be superceded by the pre-emptive techniques of practical security, as the principal weapon in the struggle against aviation terrorism, because only by seeking to prevent attacks can the world be reasonably sure that the risks of terrorism will be reduced. In many ways, the political difficulties entailed in improving airport security globally are more daunting than those surrounding judicial co-operation. The benefits, however, merit investing time and resources for upgrading security. Without such action being taken soon, further terrorist acts can be expected, perhaps copying the Kuwait Airways Flight 422 incident or, worse still, emulating the case of Pan Am Flight 103.

NOTES
  1. This incident took place between 5th and 20th April, 1988.
  2. This incident took place on 21st December, 1988.
  3. Shubber, 'Aircraft Hijacking under the Hague Convention 1970 — A New Regime?', *International and Comparative Law Quarterly*, Vol. 22 (1973), p.725.

316   *CONTEMPORARY REVIEW*

4. *Convention on Offences and Certain Other Acts Committed on Board Aircraft*, 1963, ICAO Document 7695.
5. Joyner, *Aerial Hijacking as an International Crime*, (1974), p.114.
6. *Convention for the Suppression of Unlawful Seizure of Aircraft*, 1970, ICAO Document 8920.
7. *Id.*, Article 2.
8. Translated, 'Either deliver or prosecute'
9. *Convention*, supra note 6, Article 7.
10. *Id.*, Article 8.
11. *Id.*, Title and Preamble.
12. *Convention for the Suppression of Unlawful Acts against the Safety of Civil Aviation*, ICAO Document 8966.
13. Dinstein, *Treating Terrorism as a Crime under International Law*, (1989), (unpublished conference paper).
14. US Department of Transportation, *US and Foreign Registered Aircraft Hijackings*, (1986), pp.7-9.
15. Cheng, 'International Legal Instruments to Safeguard International Air Transport', in International Institute of Air and Space Law, *Aviation Security*, (Conference Proceedings), p.33.
16. Wilkinson, *Terrorism and the Liberal State*, (1986), p.252.
17. *Supra* note 14, pp.19-75.
18. *Sunday Times*, Sunday 24th April 1988, p.A13.
19. This incident took place between 14th and 30th June, 1985.
20. A process of deduction arrives at this figure. With 112 passengers and crew embarking at Bangkok, 102 of whom were released throughout the course of the incident and two of whom were murdered, eight persons on the initial passenger list remain unaccounted for and so are probably identifiable as active members of the original hijack gang.
21. The first victim was an army border guard officer and the second was a fire service clerk.
22. *Sunday Times*, Sunday 17th April 1988, p.A12.
23. *Observer*, Sunday 17th April 1988, p.21.
24. *International Herald Tribune*, Monday 18th April 1988, p.1.
25. *Independent*, Thursday 21st April 1988, p.10.
26. *Observer*, Sunday 10th April 1988, p.21.
27. *Independent*, Wednesday 13th April 1988, p.1.
28. *Guardian*, Wednesday 13th April 1988, p.10.
29. *Id.*
30. *Supra* note 27.
31. *Scotsman*, Tuesday 12th April 1988, p.1.
32. *Independent*, Wednesday 6th April 1988, p.1.
33. *Financial Times*, Wednesday 13th April 1988, p.3.
34. *Guardian*, Wednesday 6th April 1988, p.1.
35. *Supra* note 32.
36. *Guardian*, Saturday 9th April 1988, p.1.
37. *Times*, Wednesday 6th April 1988, p.1.
38. *Independent*, Saturday 9th April 1988, p.1.
39. *Sunday Telegraph*, Sunday 17th April 1988, p.9.
40. *Supra* note 28.
41. *Supra* note 27.
42. *Supra* note 28.
43. *Times*, Wednesday 13th April 1988, p.1.
44. *Guardian*, Thursday 14th April 1988, p.8.
45. *Supra* note 14 at p.10.
46. Note the attitude of the International Air Transport Association, *International Herald Tribune*, Thursday 21st April 1988, p.2.
47. *Id.*
48. *Glasgow Herald*, Thursday 21st April 1988, p.4.

[Robin E. Hill is a Researcher in the Department of International Relations in the University of St. Andrews.]

[26]

Journal of Social Issues. Vol. 44. No. 2. 1988. pp. 175–189

Conflict Resolution as the Alternative to Terrorism

Stephen P. Cohen
CRB Foundation

Harriet C. Arnone
City University of New York

We distinguish between the typical sort of short-range conflict management. in which governments must engage, and the long-term processes of conflict resolution, which must include the involvement of entire societies and the replacement of adversarial relations with cooperative ones. How can third parties facilitate conflict resolution? This article discusses five principles that have evolved from attempts to facilitate conflict resolution in the Mideast: enhancement of each adversary's identity. creation of new symbols. enfranchisement of elements within each of the conflict groups. enhancement of indigenous development. and use of indigenous third parties. We argue that this nongovernmental facilitation of conflict resolution (with governmental tacit cooperation) is the real alternative to terrorism.

The findings, generalizations. and assertions stated throughout this article are based on years of research and applied work on conflict resolution and crisis management in the Middle East. In part. the ideas presented in this paper stem from the problem-solving workshops the senior author has organized or participated in during the past 15 years. However, these workshops are only a part of our data base: they offer useful. but not sufficient. information about the generic problems involved in third-party roles. Our conclusions also reflect findings from a multidisciplinary survey research project on conflict images and conflict resolution potentialities in the Middle East. This project, developed and super-

We thank Joseph de Rivera for his helpful editorial assistance.

Correspondence regarding this article should be addressed to Stephen P. Cohen, CRB Foundation, 1170 Peel Street, Montreal, H3B 4P2, Quebec, Canada.

vised by the senior author, has involved research teams composed of Egyptians, Israelis, Palestinians, Lebanese, Americans, and Canadians, who spent three to four years gathering data and analyzing and writing about these matters.

The emerging social science perspective on conflict resolution stresses the satisfaction of basic national needs as the prerequisite for achieving lasting peaceful international relations (Azar, 1979, 1985; Cohen & Azar, 1981). These needs include those for both security and identity. The need for *security* (of both individuals and groups) is most often expressed in physical terms: freedom from bodily harm or injury and from threats of the use of force, and freedom from poverty, underdevelopment, and economic deformities. However, in the national context, this need for security is part of a larger issue that involves the preservation of national *identity* and the acceptance of that identity by other groups and nations. This need for the acceptance of a distinctive identity includes participation in the larger international system, the maintenance and expression of a distinct role in that international system, and the possibility of interaction (social, economic, and otherwise) with other groups—all based on acceptance of that distinctive identity.

Unfortunately, when nations are in conflict, and especially when they are in protracted conflict, they are able to satisfy these needs by pursuing and maintaining the conditions and rationale for their mutual hostility. Moreover, since their identity then involves their combatant status, they tend to see efforts at peace-making as threatening the preservation of their distinctive identity and their significant role in the international system. Hence, if the political leaders and the public of conflicting societies are to become engaged in support of peace, initiatives made to them cannot ask the parties to give up their high-profile roles as adversaries, sources of threat, and objects of negative attention from their opponents in order to become lackluster objects of indifference.[1]

While conflict participants who think of themselves as "moderates" profess that their most profound wish is for the other side to "just leave them alone," we maintain that this is not a real alternative for either side in protracted conflicts. The structure of the situation forces a certain amount of interaction, whether hostile or cooperative. Further, moving from a dominant role in an adversarial system to a negligible role in a quiescent system is not a change that appeals to national leaders or satisfies the need for a national role. It seems too much like submission, and submission seems a synonym for surrender.

The alternative to a dominant *adversarial* role, therefore, must be a prominent *cooperative* role. To resolve conflict, one must not focus on disarmament, but on development. This emphasis on positive identity through national development, on the replacement of an adversarial regional role with a cooperative

---

[1]The data we have gathered in the Images in Conflict Project form the basis of this generalization. However, several publications and a host of speeches, newspaper articles, and editorials from the Near East region support this perspective as well.

one, is a key difference between conflict management (with its emphasis on reducing the negative) and conflict resolution.

Conflict Management and Conflict Resolution

Conflict management initiatives are attempts to *contain* conflict, to avert major breakouts, to bring about cease-fires in already violent confrontations, to negotiate political settlements, to lower the level of mutual blaming and recrimination. On the other hand, conflict resolution initiatives attempt to address underlying inequities and conflicts of values or interests, and to change mutual perceptions, intentions, and behavior. The approaches are similar in that they each work to prevent war, but they differ in the degree to which they build peace.[2]

Peace building takes account of the need to develop a relationship on new terms between old enemies. It creates the conditions for future relations based on equal status and mutually agreed-upon arrangements. *Third parties* helping to resolve the dispute should try to involve broad segments of each society, not just political leaders, in the process of finding a solution. Future peace is built as the parties come to believe their own national concerns can be better served under conditions of peace than of hostility.

It should be said at the outset that *none* of these positive foci are achievable without lowering the level of violence. When conflict is all-pervasive, no act of the adversary can be perceived except as having hostile intent, either open or hidden. No role for the adversary can be accepted as other than a new tactic in the long-term strategy of domination. No interaction with the adversary can seem anything but collaboration, fraternization with the enemy, or acceptance of humiliation. Thus, conflict management and conflict resolution strategies do not differ substantially in their first efforts, which attempt deescalation from the state of high conflict, where zero-sum conceptions dominate both sides. They diverge at the next stage, the period of transition from war to peace, when some cooperative behavior begins to occur and some people can perceive positive interaction when it happens.

Conflict Management: The Contribution of Third-Party Diplomacy

In traditional diplomacy, third-party states attempt to negotiate a political settlement to conflict, to lower the level of violence, and in some cases, to decrease each side's ability to harm the other. Controlling the violence and

---

[2]Some scholars have made other distinctions between "crisis management" and "conflict resolution." For instance, Azar (1986) has argued that conflict management is a broader process that can involve conflict resolution concerns and long-term political and economic development plans and programs, and that this conceptualization distinguishes his work from the more limited preoccupation of crisis management.

lowering the level of threat are essential to building peace. Without them. there is so much suspicion and fear that changing the relationship between enemies is impossible. However. diplomacy. when it succeeds. usually stops at this point—ending the war without creating the conditions necessary for peaceful relations.

The conflict management strategy is to build a wall of separation. It is a strategy of disengagement, of distancing, of separation. of decreasing communication—of seeking quiescence as the alternative to the noise of war. This notion of peace as the absence of war differs markedly from a focus on peaceful relations. which is the goal of conflict resolution. Hence diplomacy in its most traditional form is an approach to conflict management. Among its key features are the following:

1. Diplomacy is an activity of governments.[3] Once some disengagement is achieved. political leaders on both sides begin a process of negotiation. The idea is that each gives up something. compromises with the other. in order to reach a political agreement about future relations between the states. "Selling" the agreement is left to each side's political leadership. Yet agreements that last cannot be made only by those factions within each society who see the value of peace. ignoring the concerns of the opposition. Particularly in Third World conflicts. there often are unempowered opposition and nongovernment actors who. in the name of national interest. can easily undermine leaders' political agreements.

2. Third-party diplomacy uses rewards and punishments as incentives for change. The bargain becomes giving up war in exchange for, say. more foreign aid from the third party or better trading terms. This often works. but while it may improve each side's relationship with the third party, it leaves the main actors' mutual perceptions unchanged. Once the third party's rewards are received or its punishments stopped. the parties themselves are likely to return to their previous state of hostility.

3. Diplomacy legitimizes the existing power balance between the adversaries. It does not aim to achieve equality, but rather to convince the parties that—given present disparities of power—they are better off abandoning the conflict than either pursuing it further or trying to achieve a better bargaining position. This may be sufficient to stop war. but because there is no change in the status relations between the parties. it becomes difficult to develop a settlement in which the needs of *both* sides are met.

---

[3]However. there is a budding literature on informal or private diplomacy. Montville (1987) and McDonald (1987) call it Track II diplomacy. as distinct from Track I (governmental diplomacy). and a number of scholars. including one of the authors. have been heavily involved in this process throughout the Near East region. For a good reference to the work on Track II diplomacy in the Middle East and South America. see Azar (1986).

Building Peace: The Work of Conflict Resolution

The conflict resolution strategy begins with the assumption that a protracted conflict relationship is one of significant structural interdependence. The struggle with the other is an integral part of each side's national identity. If the parties do not find a positive relationship to replace the negative one. if they do not find roles in each other's life system that are nourishing and significant. they will tend to gradually resume the negative interaction and threat roles that they have played so effectively for so long.

Conflict resolution requires parties to transcend typical negotiating postures such as compromising one interest to serve another or adopting positions for bargaining advantage. Instead. they must take an analytic approach, viewing the conflict as a problem for them to solve. Within this framework. the conflict-as-problem is only solved if each adversary can agree that its fundamental requirements have been met. or that the process for meeting them has been established or is being established with the participation of the parties concerned. The balance of power between them is bracketed or made irrelevant to the process by creating contexts of interaction that require consensus of the parties in order for a solution or idea to be acceptable (Kelman & Cohen. in press).

The goal of conflict resolution is to create the necessary conditions for peaceful relations between the parties on the basis of mutual respect and status equality. Unlike diplomacy, conflict resolution cannot be limited to the government system. The approach must involve not just political leaders, but also economic, religious. and cultural leaders. including both proponents and opponents of peace. Those working for conflict resolution must seek *internal* incentives for peace and must work to develop relationships between the conflicting parties. Finally, through an emphasis on economic and social development. conflict resolvers must seek to change the unequal status of the parties (Azar & Burton, 1986).

The endemic nature of conflict in both its destructive and constructive social functions means that the time frame for conflict resolution must be measured in generations. These long-term intervention strategies must take into account the role of standard diplomatic and mediation activity, even as they attempt to advance different. more profound social transformations. In other words. advocating attention to the *roots* of conflict through a human-needs approach or through emphasis on structural victimization should not neglect the importance of reducing physical violence and decreasing the chance of war. Such short-term benefits are indeed significant in and of themselves—even if they can only delay and not prevent the reemergence of conflict violence. However. it is necessary to be alert to the danger that short-term benefits may retard recognition of the need for structural changes based on equal-status peaceful relations.

Principles of Conflict Resolution

The real creative work in conflict resolution is the capacity to establish a linkage between short-term and long-term concerns and perspectives. One needs short-term goals and the search for breakthroughs, and one also needs long-term objectives and plans. Participants in conflict resolution enterprises have to be able to see that if they move from this to that point in the short run, they will also be augmenting the overall move from war to peace in the most comprehensive way possible (see Deutsch, 1973).

In our attempts to work on conflict resolution in the Middle East, we have evolved some principles—some middle-range theory—to guide our interventions. The five principles articulated here are an attempt to bring a needs-based conflict resolution perspective to a political environment in which not only the conflict participants but the primary third parties as well are hard-pressed to believe anything other than the status quo (or worse) is the likely future. In such an environment, visions of synchronizing values or of mutually reinforcing national identities seem more like the stuff of social dreams than new ideas about the deepest problems facing these societies. The following principles are not intended to be comprehensive; rather they make up significant elements in a strategic plan for a conflict resolution approach, useful at a time of uncertainty, where neither peace nor war are imminent but the choice between them hangs in the balance. We shall discuss five such principles, giving an example of how each is relevant to our approach to conflict resolution in the Near East.

Enhance Identity

Third parties in conflict resolution must recognize that for parties in conflict, identity precedes peace as a basic value. Each side is fundamentally concerned with its own position—developing its national culture and goals, and maintaining or advancing its status as a society. Reaching agreement with the adversary is only one of several possible ways of advancing national interests, and it may not be clear that ending hostility and negotiating peace is the best way to do so (cf. Enloe, 1973; Smith, 1983).

The Middle East conflict, for both Arabs and Israelis, has occurred at a critical time in the development of national identity. For each, participation in the conflict has come to symbolize its struggle to become an independent nation, to slough off elements of oppression by others, to emerge in its own right.

In the Jewish case, it has been a struggle to emerge from the historical period of emancipation, an effort to find a Jewish identity that is independent and not subject to the whims of others. On the Arab side, it is an anticolonial struggle, an attempt to define a national culture or a national identity that is not simply a copy—whether a poor or a good copy—of something developed in the

West. These struggles of Jews and Arabs alike have implanted the conflict deeply in their visions of themselves.

The Middle East conflict has made each group's victimization by the other a part of its national history. Each believes its own pain to be unique. And each believes there are nations or groups who want to continue making victims of them—even to destroy them altogether. Israelis fear that their hard-won identity is not simply under a present threat, but will *always* be under threat. Palestinians (who have never achieved sovereignty in their own territory) fear that their own unique heritage will be submerged in Jordanian identity or lost in an assimilation to a general "Arab" identity. In each case the current enemy (be it Israeli, Egyptian, or Palestinian) comes to assume the burden of the group's whole history of victimization.

Identity has another side, however, an aspect that can form the basis for building peace. Each group has things that make it unique, aspects of itself that allow people to imagine a worthwhile future. The terms may differ: a future filled with prosperity, with the fulfillment of cultural or religious ideals, or with progress. Side by side with the image of self as having experienced great pain is the image of self as the creator of great promise. Next to the fear is hope. Too often in the history of peacemaking, the parties—whether the intermediaries or the actors themselves—have failed to understand and make use of this important positive aspect of identity.

Peace-building efforts must not seek to deny national identity. Rather, they must find ways to express and reinforce the creative aspects of each side's national goals. Both parties must come to believe some core element of their unique selves will find better expression through peaceful relations than through maintaining hostility.

Given the prominence of identity concerns, it is not reasonable to expect that major breakthroughs in the conflict resolution process will come about on the basis of internationalist or universalist values. It is common to hear "nationalism" blamed for conflict: i.e., nationalism is the impediment that keeps parties in conflict from adopting more reasonable, compromising, internationally responsible positions. From our point of view, making nationalism the enemy of conflict resolution efforts is a trap. It is more appropriately viewed as the raw material for solution. *Resolving* conflict means finding a way for peace to substitute for war in enhancing national pride and identity (cf. Burton, 1986; Wedge, 1978).

Of course, this is easier said than done. There is a potential contradiction between doing what is necessary to bring whole social systems into the peace process (including their major opposing elements) and trying to give special weight to those more open to contact and communication with the other side. Each goal can undermine the other—and subvert the process in the bargain.

For example, it is evident that resolving the Middle East conflict in ways opposed to the religious impulse of either Jews or Muslims would be unrealistic and inconsistent with basic identity elements. Yet on each side, some religious constituencies maintain ethnocentric themes that make them less than amenable to a conflict resolution approach. As a result, it is hard to imagine how to include them, yet it is clear their exclusion is bound to turn the conflict resolution process into one that generates its own opposition.

Fortunately, most constituencies contain a *variety* of elements, and *some* of these can actually be enhanced by a peacemaking approach. For example, one may be able to work with elements of nonpolitical leadership—e.g., promoting the role of religious leaders by legitimizing their leadership in caring for Jerusalem's holy places. As one example, in 1969, when a religious fundamentalist set fire to the Al Aksa Mosque, the decision to give Muslim religious leaders control over the fire-fighting operation was probably crucial in keeping peaceful relationships and strengthening the legitimacy of the religious leadership.

National identity can be more than simply ethnocentric, and it is important to emphasize positive elements of identity that may enhance peacemaking. Thus one can stress Egypt's pride in being a leader of modernization in the Arab world (rather than its relative dependency on the West), or Iran's role in promoting faith (rather than retarding progress). Needless to say, such enhancement must not (and need not) be at the expense of someone else. Some important identity elements, especially in societies that have been in conflict for many years, are images of self-in-relation-to-the-other. For instance, Party A may see itself as "more modern than Party B." If the third party does not help A find a way to formulate and strengthen its self-image of modernity without implicitly denigrating B, the prospects for sustained positive relations between the two will be weakened.

Create New Symbols and Concepts

The pursuit of conflict creates its own system of language and symbols that have not only conceptual meanings, but strong affective meanings as well. When people use terms like "terrorist" or "the Jewish lobby" in the Middle East conflict, they are not simply describing something, they are also taking sides. When they use these terms, they label themselves, assert their attitudes and political positions, and signal their implicit theories of action and causation in the conflict.

One important function of third parties in conflict resolution is to develop an acceptable symbolic system for expressing new concepts of solutions and peaceful relations—both between the parties and within each party. Symbols must be cognitively appropriate and affectively positive on each side. Moreover, they must make it possible for leaders to communicate the outcomes of the conflict resolution process (new modes of analysis and/or restructuring of relationships) to their domestic audiences. (In regard to the Middle East, Touval, 1982, is particularly informative on this matter and the whole range of mediation activities.)

Thus, when the Israelis refer to the "Yom Kippur War" and the Egyptians refer to the "Ramadan War," third parties may be able to refer to "The War of 1973." Likewise, if the Egyptians want a "settlement" (connoting pragmatic horse-trading) and the Israelis want "peace" (connoting an ideological rapprochement with their own history of Zionism), a third party may be able to encourage references to an "agreement" (with some connotations of both).

Too often in conflict resolution efforts we do not see new symbols emerging. Instead, third parties "cop out" and master the symbolic systems of each adversary. They become conceptually bilingual, using a different "language" with each side and "translating" messages back and forth.

A different mistake, also common, is one involving the within-group dimension. Third parties may adopt the language systems of the so-called moderates on each side, with the result that concepts become internally polarizing in each society. This happens because, in the within-group debate, the moderates tend to demonize those in their society who take a skeptical or hostile view. Moderate Israelis, for instance, do this with the "Right," moderate Palestinians with the "Rejectionists." Analysis of the problem then becomes assigning blame, with the good guys against the bad. It goes like this: "We moderates could resolve our differences with the other side. However, we are kept from doing so because of the hawks, who really don't want peace and keep us from finding a solution." The error is that this analysis denies the reality of between-group differences, thus solidifying internal (within-group) opposition to change.

A nonconfrontational, nonblaming language can only emerge out of interaction—even if at first such interaction is limited or takes place primarily in the mind of the third party. It cannot be born from the language that the parties use to defend their own positions. New language will develop by approximations, but in the process terms may become appropriated by one party or another, and a zone of mutual acceptability is often difficult to protect from appropriation by the conflict management system.

Part of the way to develop the necessary sensitivities for creating new language is to include in the conflict resolution process members of each relevant audience, either through direct communication and interaction or through research about their views. The process of conceptualizing the bases of a peaceful future must include (on both sides) not only empowered elites, but also those outgroups who feel their needs have not been taken into account in the kinds of between-group processes developed so far. In each case (for instance, the Sephardim in Israel, Palestinians from the Gulf, or Western Diaspora Israelis and Arabs), such groups themselves have problematic relationships with their own national communities. By bringing them together with counterparts on the other side. it may be possible to develop fresh. acceptable formulations that better support change.

Enfranchise Elements Within Each of the Conflicting Groups

Within each of the nations in conflict there are population groups who feel little power and influence in the system. When societal leadership develops political agreements with former enemies. these disenfranchised groups (whose needs are not adequately met either in the formulation of the solution or in many domestic issues) form a natural opposition. Sometimes their opposition is as much a protest against being left out as it is a quarrel with the specific agreement that has been forged.

In Egypt. for instance. the intelligentsia have long been concerned about the problem of centralized authority and nonparticipatory government. When Anwar Sadat made peace with Israel. many in this group felt their government was using the peace process as another way of disenfranchising them. They referred to the peace contemptuously as "enforced normalization," but their objection was probably not so much to a forcing of Israel on Egypt as a forcing of the Egyptian government position on them.

If it had been possible to include elements of the intelligentsia in the process by which the peace was created. there might have been a different response. Then the process of finding peace would have advanced their basic need for political participation and a voice in their society, and at least some countervailing forces would have been set into motion against their intellectual and often very pragmatic discomfort with the peace process.

An analysis of the conflict maintenance process can also focus on understanding groups who have vested interests in the conflict. Institutions. bureaucracies. and elements of the economic system have developed with the conflict as a given and. often without awareness. are hostile to processes that reduce their social importance and access to resources. Peaceful relations will begin to create vested interests of institutions. leaders. and economic system elements that see a clear benefit (or at least an equivalent role) in peaceful relations. Again. this is a way in which conflict resolution approaches must be at least as sensitive to the intraparty dynamics as to the interparty ones.

Enhance Indigenous Development

Many people who are genuinely interested in an ethical approach to issues of conflict resolution are stymied by the fact that peace sometimes seems to conflict with justice. Thus. in some situations. peace may be obtained by blessing the status quo and giving legitimacy to morally questionable actors.

For nongovernmental third parties, this basic question cannot be avoided.

Most serious conflicts (other than the Soviet–American one. and some say even that one) are ones in which power disparities are an essential defining element. It is in that context that violence becomes such a serious problem that it can stop the process of conflict resolution on apparent moral grounds.

It is easy to reject and condemn the violence of the strong. It, after all, expresses and reinforces the unacceptable status quo. But what of the violence of the less powerful? Here some conflict resolution theorists and practitioners face a problem they cannot solve.

Within a conflict system, use of violence by the *less* powerful can be the means by which they achieve the confidence and institutional base necessary to change the balance of power. And because some conflict resolvers believe (to a degree, correctly) that when power disparities exist it is not practically possible to achieve and maintain settlements where the basic needs of both sides are met. such conflict resolvers may become legitimators of violent extremism in the defense of virtue.

We disagree with that analysis. We believe it is a responsibility of the third party to help define an alternative, nonviolent form of empowerment through which less powerful parties can affect the status quo and make possible the equal-status contact and communication essential for movement toward peaceful relations.

It is also common for conflict resolution practitioners to take a rather conventional ethical perspective, where one party is ''the victim'' and the other ''the victimizer,'' where one party is ''in the right'' and the other resists accepting that its adversary is right. Third parties are constantly being drawn into a position where advocacy for one of the parties to the conflict is not only demanded by others. but seems demanded by their own assessment of the moral situation.

We believe third parties must maintain a perspective in which the moral legitimacy of *both* parties is an essential element. They must put forward the ethical perspective of peace: that there is a way for basic needs of each side to be met and achieved through peaceful means. Indeed. third parties must understand that there is no way of achieving peaceful relations based on equal status through violent means. without each side's willingness to destroy both the other side and itself. Whether or not the third party accepts the moral legitimacy of both sides. the fact is that each of the sides believes in its own moral legitimacy—thus. if they cannot maintain their legitimacy through peaceful means. they will continue to do so with violent ones.

The necessity of finding an alternative form of empowerment other than violence and the necessity of maintaining the moral legitimacy of the parties in conflict lead to a focus on *development*—economic. social. and cultural—as an essential element in conflict resolution strategy (Azar. 1979; Groom. 1986).

The emphasis on development has two essential aspects. First, it is important to develop *institutions* in the weaker group that have enough internal legitimacy, resilience, and ability to withstand external pressure so that they will be seen both internally and externally as the appropriate and necessary interlocutors in the conflict resolution process. Strong institutions in the nonpolitical sectors of the less powerful society can argue against the notion that talk will inevitably lead to surrender to the more powerful society or acquiescence to an unacceptable status quo. Thus, the strengthening of the universities on the West Bank (which were minor colleges before 1967) has created important institutions that legitimize the voice of the West Bank in the Palestinian council, a voice that may eventually promote a Palestinian–Jordanian accord.

Second, it is important to provide a process through which people can become part of creating positive national identity, cohesiveness, and self-reliance without being dependent on the image of an enemy to be overcome. In settlement strategies, where conflict is seen as a foreign policy problem essentially external to one's own society, the appropriate stance is *neutrality*. Third parties must work to convince each party that they support them—but are not necessarily against the other. This is a difficult accomplishment in a competitive environment.

In conflict resolution, the view that conflicts are within societies as well as between them makes the process, in effect, an intervention in internal affairs. The emphasis on *development* is the key that allows a third party to get in without becoming partisan, to support one side without being against the other.

Involve Indigenous Third Parties

In analyzing the various conflict resolution approaches that have emerged, one cannot fail to notice that many of their principles and ideas were developed in the West, in the comfort and security of states and nations that have often intervened in the international system, particularly in the Third World, in other ways than by resolving conflict. From the perspective of the sociology of knowledge, it is likely that many assumptions of these approaches (both explicit and implicit) resulted from or were consistent with the intellectual environment in which the ideas were developed.

Exogenous third parties, ourselves included, also struggle with the balance between neutrality and engagement as elements in the role. Engagement conveys seriousness of purpose, and imparts the patience and long-term commitment essential for third-party involvement in any deep conflict. Neutrality and balance maintain credibility and assure that third parties, in actuality and as perceived by others, do not become advocates of a particular solution or a particular side.

On both of these counts, indigenous third parties would have an enormous advantage over outsiders. Their engagement and commitment are obvious, and they could learn to develop professional positions of balance. Moreover, they would be able to communicate, using appropriate linguistic and cultural considerations. to wide elements not easily accessible to even the most seasoned outsider. Finally, their involvement would help prevent misinterpretation of the conflict resolution process as an indirect attempt to increase or enhance the Western position in the region. and would help separate *intrinsic* needs for resolving the conflict from *extrinsic* motivations, such as the benefits of developing a relationship with Western powers, especially the United States. It is not that extrinsic motivations cannot sometimes be helpful, but they can overwhelm intrinsic factors.

In our work, two examples of indigenous third parties have emerged. In a pilot study conducted under the auspices of The Institute for Middle East Peace and Development by Basima Ahed and Lynn Ruggiero, it was discovered that a key element in linkage between Israeli Jews and West Bank Palestinians was provided by the Arabs of Israel. The very difficulty of finding an appropriate designation for these people. sometimes called Israeli Arabs, Arabs of 1948. or Palestinians of Israel. among other names, indicates the complexity of their own identity. In West Bank–Israeli relations they have become a critical third party, establishing points of contact and communication in a situation dominated by hostile exchange or purely commercial relations.

On a larger scale, the Israeli–Palestinian relationship, especially as conducted by formal leaders of each group (the Israeli government and PLO leaders) cannot be effectively handled by an exogenous third party such as the United States. Facilitating the conflict resolution process between Israel and the Palestinians requires a level of detailed attention, constancy of involvement, and sustained effort that is simply not possible for the highest levels of the U.S. government. Yet this level of involvement makes sense to regional actors whose fate is directly tied to the outcome of the process. Indigenous third parties. in particular Egypt and Jordan, have a much greater potential here to begin that subtle process of reanalysis of the actual and potential relations between Israelis and Palestinians.

Conclusion: Conflict Resolution Is the Alternative to Terrorism

In the post-World War II international system, it is appropriate for state to speak to state, government to government. while governmental communication with other groups is considered interference in the internal political affairs of another state. This process reinforces the legitimacy of existing political entities and leaders and, by implication. the notion that the state and those leaders are the appropriate political representation of the nation. However, the efforts we have called "conflict resolution" do not occur exclusively within the governmental structure. Rather, they include *nonstate processes* (forms of communication and interaction other than formal bargaining and negotiation, or outside the formal negotiation process), *nonstate actors* (unempowered elements in the society and nonpolitical actors ordinarily considered outside the foreign policy community. such as economic and religious leaders and dissenting ethnic groups), and *non-state third parties* (such as academics. business leaders. and perhaps leaders in the arts and sports).

As one moves out of the northern hemisphere. either to the south or to the Third World and perhaps even to the Eastern bloc. this nonstate emphasis becomes more and more essential because the assumed relationship of correspondence between people. nation. state. and government is more likely to be violated. The typical problem in nondemocratic countries is that there is a wide difference between "government" and "nation"; in the Third World there is also commonly a wide difference between "state" and "nation." The problem in the East is a reflection of the economic and political system: in the Third World it is due to remnants of colonialism and the imperfect processes of national integration. In all societies. East or West. democratic or not. the basic problem is the difficulty of maintaining a form of political participation that. if not democratic. at least gives weight to key political. economic. social. and religious groupings that make up the changing social reality underlying the fixed entity of nation-state.

Because of this. it seems to us that conflict resolution is the peaceful alternative to terrorism. Terrorism is partly an outburst of rage and partly an action based on a strategic analysis by delegitimized groups outside the international system. Terrorism makes the implicit claim that the state monopoly on legitimate use of force in the international system must be challenged in order to attain some balance and redress some grievance. Its purpose is to use violence to place a group and its grievance on the international agenda. The goal is to create a break point at one of two levels: either recognition at the systemic level of a new quasi-state actor (the group for which the terrorists speak). or a challenge to the perception that a given government (or representative) has the legitimate right to speak in the name of the national system. Since conflict resolution maintains engagement while changing the nature of the relationship between the parties. it undercuts the need for terrorism. It. too. is an attempt to empower the unempowered. to support subnational identities. to treat nonstate actors as legitimate. and ultimately to change the underlying balance of power. However. it accomplishes this without violence. simply by respecting identity.

References

Azar. E. (1979). Peace amidst development: A conceptual agenda for conflict and peace research. *International Interactions*. 6. 123-144.

Azar. E. (1985). Protracted international conflicts: Ten propositions. *International Interactions*. 12. 59-70.

Azar. E. (1986). Management of protracted social conflict in the Third World. *Ethnic Studies Report*. 4(2). 59-70.

Azar. E.. & Burton. J. (Eds.). (1986). *International conflict resolution: Theory and practice.* Sussex. England: Wheatsheaf Books.

Burton. J. (1986). The history of conflict resolution. In E. Azar & J. Burton (Eds.). *International conflict resolution: Theory and Practice* (pp. 40-55). Sussex. England: Wheatsheaf Books.

Cohen. S. P.. & Azar. E. (1981). From war to peace. *Journal of Conflict Resolution. 25.* 87-114.

Deutsch. M. (1973). *The resolution of conflict.* New Haven. CT: Yale University Press.

Enloe. C. (1973). *Ethnic conflict and political development.* Boston: Little. Brown.

Groom. A. J. R. (1986). Problem solving in international relations. In E. Azar & J. Burton (Eds.). *International conflict resolution: Theory and practice* (pp. 85-91). Sussex. England: Wheatsheaf Books.

Kelman. H. C.. & Cohen. S. P. (in press). Resolution of international conflict: An interactional approach. In S. Worchel (Ed.). *Intergroup relations.* Chicago: Nelson Hall.

McDonald. J. (Ed.). (1987). *Conflict resolutions: Track two diplomacy.* Washington. DC: Foreign Service Institute. U.S. Department of State.

Montville. J. (1987). The arrow and the olive branch: A case for track two Diplomacy. In J. McDonald (Ed.). *Conflict resolutions: Track two diplomacy* (pp. 5-20). Washington. DC: Foreign Service Institute. U.S. Department of State.

Smith. A. D. (1983). Ethnic identity and world order. *Millenium. 12.* 375-397.

Touval. S. (1982). *The peace brokers: Mediation in the Arab–Israeli conflict. 1948–1979.* Princeton: Princeton University Press.

Wedge. B. (1978). The self system and group violence. *American Journal of Psychoanalysis. 38.* 111-120.

STEPHEN P. COHEN is President of the CRB Foundation in Montreal. Until recently, he was Director of the Institute for Middle East Peace and Development at CUNY Graduate Center. New York, and Associate Professor of Social Psychology there. He received his Ph.D. from Harvard University, and has specialized in group psychology, conflict resolution, and international relations.

HARRIET C. ARNONE was, until recently, Assistant Director for Research at the CUNY Institute for Middle East Peace and Development. She is now at Metronorth, practicing what she has been preaching about conflict resolution. She received her Ph.D. in social psychology at CUNY.

[27]

Effects of Televised Presidential Addresses on Public Opinion: President Reagan and Terrorism in the Middle East

EYTAN GILBOA*
Director
Rothberg School for Overseas Students
The Hebrew University of Jerusalem

Abstract

Presidents employ direct addresses including nationally televised speeches and press conferences to mobilize public support. President Reagan, often regarded as a great communicator, addressed the American public during several crisis situations. This study investigates the effects of Reagan's addresses on public opinion during two major terrorist incidents.

The study is based on rare identical public opinion polls conducted before and immediately after the presidential addresses. A comparative analysis of the polls reveals a substantial increase in Reagan's popularity ratings and greater public support for his principal policies. However, these effects of his addresses were superficial and short-lived; but they might have been sufficient to influence the decisions and behavior of the terrorists.

Introduction

A commonplace notion suggests that for lack of sufficient knowledge about foreign affairs Americans have usually followed presidential leadership in foreign policy.[1] Another widespread commonplace notion is that the public usually unites behind the president during an international crisis. These notions have been tested and found valid only in certain conditions and circumstances.[2] If foreign policy is seen as successful the public supports it, if it is not the public and the media ask questions and demand answers from the president and his officials.

President Ronald Reagan has been one of the most popular presidents in recent American history.[3] Yet, he has been aware of the need to win public support for his major moves on foreign affairs, particularly in crisis situations. Probably due to his early experience on radio and in films he has preferred the use of television and radio to cultivate favorable and supportive public opinion.

The effects of modern television on the presidency are constantly debated. Earlier studies concluded that television has granted a special power to the president by providing him with a direct link to the people.[4] Recent studies, however, suggest that television has undermined presidential authority and leadership.[5] President Reagan is known for his communication skills.[6] However, according to a recent study he received negative coverage on the networks' evening news more than any of his three predecessors.[7]

The same study explains that Reagan has been able to maintain public support despite the negative television coverage by effectively using controlled media, including direct addresses.[8]

A nationally televised speech at prime time is usually a very dramatic move that presidents employ to mobilize public support.[9] Several times during his tenure at the White House, Reagan addressed the American public through a nationally televised speech or press conference. But, what effects, if any, do such appearances have on public opinion? A close examination of public opinion polls using the same questions and polling methodology before and after a nationally televised address, could provide an answer to this question.

Pollsters rarely conduct polls with identical questions before and after a presidential appearance. However, on two occasions, in 1983 and 1985 pollsters conducted such polls before and immediately after significant presidential appearances on U.S. policy toward Middle East terrorism. On October 27, 1983, after the bombing of the Marines' headquarters in Beirut and the invasion of Grenada, Reagan appealed to the public in a special nationally televised speech.[10] On June 18, 1985, several days after the hijacking of a TWA passenger plane to Beirut, he appeared in a special nationally televised press conference.[11] In both cases the addresses dominated the news of the following day. Polls were conducted immediately before and after these appearances, and they examined public evaluations of Reagan's performance and opinions on various policy issues. This study utilizes the polls' results and offers several observations on the possible effects of Reagan's appearances on public opinion.

The American Military Involvement in Lebanon

Following the 1982 Israeli War in Lebanon the United States dispatched a small contingency of about eight hundred Marines to Beirut. With troops from Britain and France, they constituted a peacekeeping force. On the basis of Reagan's statement that the Marines will stay in Lebanon as a peacekeeping force and only for a limited period of time, the Congress approved of this involvement.[12] Various polls however, found that from the outset the public had reservations about the Marines' presence in Beirut. These reservations intensified following several terrorist attacks on Americans and American institutions in Lebanon.[13]

On April 18, 1983 a bomb exploded in the American Embassy in Beirut killing 83 persons, including 17 Americans. President Reagan condemned the attack but said it would not deter the United States from continuing the Marines' mission.[14] In September 1983, Israeli forces withdrew to South Lebanon. Consequently the various Lebanese factions renewed their violent struggles for power and influence. Reagan decided to send an additional two thousand troops and naval units to Lebanon.

Throughout September and October 1983, U.S. troops were constantly subjected to sniper attacks and shelling. On October 23, the Marines suffered a tragic blow. A truck bomb exploded inside their headquarters killing 241 Americans. The high number of casualties, the horrendous terror technique used to inflict the damage and the unclear mission of the Marines in Lebanon contributed to heated public debate in the United States.[15] Congress, the media and the public felt that the high cost was incompatible with the definition of the Marines' mission as peacekeeping.

On October 25th the United States invaded Grenada and two days later Reagan made a nationally televised speech to the public about the events in Lebanon and Grenada. In the speech, which the media described as highly emotional, Reagan linked the two events by suggesting that if the United States had not acted, both areas would have fallen to hostile powers. He described the treacherous nature of the attack on the Marines: a civilian truck smashing into the building where the soldiers were sleeping. Several times he repeated questions asked by the media and the public and answered them. He said "And how many of you are asking: why should our young men be dying in Lebanon? Why is Lebanon important to us?" He then explained the importance of the Middle East to the United States, Europe and Japan. Later he asked again: "So why are we there? Well, the answer is straightforward: to help bring peace to Lebanon and stability to the vital Middle East."

In an obvious reference to his critics Reagan asserted: "Let me ask those who say we should get out of Lebanon: if we were to leave Lebanon now, what message would that send to those who foment instability and terrorism? If Americans were to walk away from Lebanon, what chance would there be for a negotiated settlement producing the unified, democratic Lebanon? If we turned our backs on Lebanon now, what would be the future of Israel?"

Reagan suggested that the Marines' mission in Lebanon had wider goals, including the containment of Communist expansionism, the protection of Israel, and the advancement of peacemaking in the Arab-Israeli conflict. These three themes were probably expected to rally the public behind the president. What then, were the effects of the televised speech on public opinion?

The Effects of President Reagan's Speech

The media sponsored polls routinely examine public evaluations of presidential performance. During crisis situations, of the kind that developed in Beirut, the number and frequency of polls are greatly increased. The polls intensively examined Reagan's performance in three categories: general, handling of foreign affairs and handling the situation in the Middle East. They also presented questions about the presence and mission of the Marines in Lebanon.

Reagan's speech was delivered four days after the attack in Beirut and one day after the invasion of Grenada. Therefore, the ratings in categories (a) and (b) probably reflected evaluations of his performance both in Lebanon and Grenada, but those in category (c) are related only to Lebanon. According to Table 1, the bombing of the Marines' headquarters and the invasion of Grenada had only slight immediate effects on the public rating of Reagan's performance. A month before this tragic event his general rating was positive by a net difference of 10 percent. The rating of his handling of "foreign affairs" was negative by a net difference of 8 percent. Shortly after the bombing his overall rating remained positive by 11 percent and the "foreign affairs" rating remained negative by 6 percent. The October 16 poll also found a negative rating of Reagan's handling of the situation in the Middle East by 12 percent.

TABLE 1

Presidential Approval Rating

Question (a): "Do you approve or disapprove of the way Ronald Reagan is handling *his job as president?*"

Question (b): "Do you approve or disapprove of the way Reagan is handling *foreign affairs?*"

Question (c): "Do you approve or disapprove of the way Reagan is handling the *situation in the Middle East?*"

Date	(a) General		(b) Foreign Affairs		(c) Middle East		(n)
	Approve	Disapprove	Approve	Disapprove	Approve	Disapprove	
U.S. MILITARY INVOLVEMENT IN LEBANON							
Sept. 26, 1983	52%	42%	42%	50%	—	—	
Bombing of Marine Headquarters (Oct. 23)							
Invasion of Grenada (Oct. 25)							
Oct. 26, 1983	54	43	44	50	41	53	(729)
Reagan's Speech (Oct. 27)							
Oct. 28, 1983	63	35	57	39	52	42	(517)
Nov. 7, 1983	63	31	55	37	—	—	
Dec. 13, 1983	59	37	47	45	43	50	(1,506)
TWA HOSTAGE CRISIS							
May 13, 1985	57%	38%	48%	45%	—	—	
TWA Plane Hijacked (June 14)							
June 17, 1985	62	33	46	45	48	32	(508)
Reagan's Press Conference (June 18)							
June 19, 1985	62	33	55	38	68	25	(508)
June 22, 1985	62	34	53	41	69	22	(1,506)
Hostages Released							
July 1, 1985	65	30	—	—	72	21	(1,208)
July 29, 1985	65	31	56	38	—	—	(1,506)

Data Sources: The Washington Post-ABC News Poll, Surveys No. 0196, 1097, 1098, July 1985.

Table 1 indicates however, that immediately after the presidential televised speech the public changed its evaluation of Reagan's performance in all the three categories. The net overall performance rating was up 17 percent, the "foreign affairs" and the "Middle East" ratings turned around from negative to positive, by net differences that went up 24 percent and 22 percent respectively. Ten days later the general and the "foreign affairs" ratings remained almost unchanged. About six weeks after the events in Beirut and Grenada and the televised address the general performance and the foreign affairs ratings dropped by 10 and 16 percent respectively. The approval rate of the "situation in the Middle East" turned negative and fell 17 percent.

In his nationally televised speech Reagan rejected the call for an American withdrawal and explained that "if terrorism and intimidation succeed, it'll be a devastating blow to the peace process and to Israel's search for genuine security." Two polls conducted shortly after the speech indicate a change in the public attitudes towards the withdrawal issue. In August and September 1983 the public disapproved of the dispatching of the Marines to Lebanon, but immediately after the speech, this result reversed. Now 48 percent compared to 42 percent approved of the decision to send the Marines to Beirut.

TABLE 2

Public Opinion Toward American Marines in Lebanon

Question (a): "Do you approve or disapprove of President Reagan's decision to send U.S. Marines to Beirut to help keep the peace and encourage a withdrawal of Israeli, Syrian, and PLO forces from Lebanon?" (Newsweek-Gallup)

Question (b): "U.S. Marines went to Lebanon as part of an international peacekeeping force to try to prevent fighting there. Do you approve or disapprove of the government sending troops to Lebanon for that purpose?" (CBS-New York Times)

Question	Date	Approve	Disapprove	D.K.	(n)
(a)	August 1983	41%	54%	5%	
(b)	September 1983	37	53	11	(1,587)
	Reagan's Speech				
(a)	October 27, 1983	48	42	10	(759)
(b)	October 27, 1983	48	42	10	(545)

Question (c): "Do you think the U.S. forces should be brought back home now, or do you think they should stay and continue their peacekeeping mission?" (Newsweek-Gallup)

Question (d): "Do you think the U.S. should withdraw its troops from Lebanon at the present time or not?" (Gallup)

Question	Date	Withdraw	Stay	D.K.	(n)
(c)	September 1983	53%	38%	9%	
	Reagan's Speech				
(c)	October 1983	42	49	9	(759)
(d)	January 1984	57	34	9	(1,139)
(d)	February 1984	74	17	9	(1,610)

Question (e): "Would you say the U.S. should send more troops to Lebanon, leave the number about the same, or remove the troops that are there now?" (WP-ABC)

Question	Date	Withdraw	Stay	Increase	D.K.	(n)
(e)	October 26, 1983	45%	33%	16%	6%	(729)
	Reagan's Speech					
(e)	October 28, 1983	37	41	17	5	(517)
(e)	January 4, 1984	57	29	8	6	(1,524)

Sources: (a) (c): *Newsweek*, November 7, 1983, p. 19; (b): Mark F. German with Kirk Brown, *Public Opinion Polls on U.S. Policy in Lebanon* (Washington, D.C.: The Library of Congress, February 8, 1984), p. B-6; (d): *Baltimore Sun*, March 1, 1984; (e): *Washington Post*, October 30, December 15, 1983; January 20, 1984.

Responses to question (c) in Table 2 also reveal a reversal in public opinion. Prior to the speech the public supported withdrawal by a plurality of 53 to 38 percent, but after the speech 49 compared to 42 percent said the Marines should stay in Lebanon. When offered three choices, withdrawal, increase of forces or replacement of those who were killed, before the speech 45 percent of the national sample chose the withdrawal option, 49 percent preferred the "increase" and the "replacement" options. After the speech the number of those who favored involvement as against the number of those who opposed it grew to 58 versus 37 percent.

Reagan made an effort to explain the Marines' goals in Beirut. Yet, as Table 3 demonstrates, his success on this issue was more limited. Before the speech a 50 to 37 percent plurality did not think the United States had clear goals for the Marines in Lebanon. After the speech a 48 to 42 percent majority did not think "the govern-

TABLE 3

Goals of Marines in Lebanon

Question: "Do you think that the U.S. government has clear goals for the United States Marines force in Lebanon or not?" (WP-ABC)

Date	Yes	No	D.K.	(n)
October 26, 1983	37%	50%	13%	(729)
Reagan's Speech				
October 28, 1983	42	48	10	(517)
December 1983	33	52	15	(1,506)
January 1984	30	59	11	(1,524)

Sources: Washington Post, October 30, 1983; December 15, 1983; January 20, 1984.

ment had tried hard enough to explain to the American people its reasons for sending the Marines and Navy to Lebanon."[16]

Responses given to questions (d) and (e) in January 1984 reveal a return of the public to the pre-speech views about the American military involvement in Lebanon. The negative views became even firmer. As can be seen in Table 3 the number of Americans who did not think the Marines had any clear goals in Beirut grew substantially. In February 1984, Reagan decided to evacuate the troops from Beirut and as responses to question (d) indicate, a sizeable majority supported this decision.[17]

Public evaluation of Reagan's performance improved considerably after his speech. The approval ratings of his handling of "foreign affairs" and "the situation in the Middle East" changed from negative to positive. The public also reversed its attitudes on specific policy issues and following the speech approved of the military involvement in Lebanon.

The TWA Hostage Crisis

On June 14, 1985, Lebanese-Shiite terrorists hijacked a TWA passenger carrier to Beirut. They murdered U.S. Navy Diver Dean Stethen, took hostage the remaining American passengers and presented various demands to the United States and Israel. They mainly demanded the release of about seven hundred Shiites, Lebanese and Palestinians held by Israel.[18] The hijacking and the terrorists' demands created a major international crisis which lasted almost two weeks. The media played a controversial role in this event.[19] The major networks interviewed the hostages, their families and the terrorists who all called upon the United States government to comply with the hijackers' demands.[20] The battle for public opinion then, became a significant factor in the crisis.

President Reagan confronted three issues. First, whether to negotiate with the terrorists or not; second, whether to ask Israel to release the Lebanese Shiites prisoners in exchange for the hostages as demanded by the terrorists; and third, whether to use military force against the terrorists. According to the initial polls the public favored negotiations with the terrorists, did not think the United States should ask Israel to release the Shiite prisoners, but felt that in order to resolve the crisis Israel should take this action on its own initiative. The public also favored a military reprisal against the terrorists and those who supported them.

The public and the media applied pressure on Reagan to resolve the crisis. On June 18, he appeared in a special nationally televised press conference to explain his stands. In his opening statement he mentioned the murder of Dean Stethen and outlined actions taken to protect passengers travelling with American airline companies. He then warned:

> Let me further make it plain to the assassins in Beirut and their accomplices wherever they may be that America will never make concessions to terrorists. To do so would only invite more terrorism.

In a transparent reference to Israel he added:

> Nor will we ask nor pressure any other government to do so. Once we head down that path, there'll be no end to it. No end to the suffering of innocent people; no end to the bloody ransom all civilized nations must pay.

Reagan's message was clear and tough, but he also appeared very humane and vulnerable: "I am as frustrated as anyone. I've pounded a few walls myself when I'm alone about this. It is frustrating."

The polls reveal enormous awareness of the crisis in American public opinion. According to the June 17 WP-ABC poll no less than 80 percent of the national sample followed the hijacking "very closely" or "fairly closely."[21] By June 22, this number grew to 90 percent. A poll taken by NBC News on June 18 and 19 found that 98 percent of the national sample heard or read about the hijacking of the TWA plane.[22] The three major networks also examined the size of the public that saw, read or heard about Reagan's televised press conference. According to WP-ABC, 55 percent of the public saw, read or heard about the press conference, the figures of NBC and CBS were 46 and 43 percent respectively.

The Effects of Reagan's Press Conference

Table 1 reveals that at the onset of the crisis the American public was divided on its evaluation of Reagan's performance. His general rating improved by 10 percentage points but his rating on the handling of "foreign affairs" fell by 2 percent. His handling of the crisis was approved by a 48 to 32 percent plurality. Following the press conference his overall rating remained unchanged but in the "approve" column of the foreign affairs category he gained 9 percent. This rating held as far as a month after the crisis.

The most dramatic change occurred in the public approval of Reagan's handling of the crisis. After the press conference the ratio in this category jumped 20 percent in the "approve" column and declined 7 percent in the "disapprove" column. Following the safe release of the hostages, this rating further improved to a 72 versus 21 percent approval ratio.

Polls on specific policy issues associated with the hostage crisis reveal moderate changes in the public views. In his press conference, Reagan flatly stated that "America will never make concessions to terrorists." But, he did not rule out negotiations as long as they do not reward the terrorists. Before the conference, the majority of the public favored negotiations by 59 to 32 percent. Immediately after the conference, public opinion still favored negotiations but by a much smaller ratio. Only after the release of the hostages the public completely reversed its stand, and a majority of 51 to 42 percent said that Reagan should not have negotiated with the terrorists.

The second policy issue was whether to officially ask Israel to release Lebanese Shiite prisoners. In his initial statement Reagan said that the United States would not ask or pressure any government to make concessions to the terrorists. In response to a question he specifically rejected Israeli concessions and explained:

> . . . the linkage that has been created makes it impossible for them [Israel] and for us. There was no question but that they were going to [release] in stages . . . but it has now been tied to where such a movement would be in effect giving in to terrorists.

TABLE 4

U.S. Policy on the Hostage Crisis

Question (a): "Which of these two statements do you tend to agree with more: (1) The U.S. *should* be negotiating for the release of the Americans taken hostage even if that means giving in to the terrorists' demands, or (2) The U.S. *should not* be negotiating even if some of the Americans taken hostage are injured or killed?" (WP-ABC)

Question (b): "Which is more important: ensuring the safe return of the American hostages even if it means working out some compromise on terrorists' demands, or discouraging future hostage taking by refusing to deal with terrorists' demands even if it risks the lives of American hostages?" (Newsweek-Gallup)

Question (c): "Do you think Reagan should have negotiated with the terrorists or not?" (WP-ABC)

Question	Date	Should Negotiate	Shouldn't Negotiate	D.K.	(n)
(a)	June 17, 1985	59%	32%	9%	(508)
	Reagan's Press Conference				
(a)	June 19, 1985	53	40	8	(508)
(a)	June 20–21, 1985	57	36	7	(1,506)
(b)	June 20–21, 1985	47	42	11	(1,016)
	Hostages Released				
(c)	July 1, 1985	42	51	7	(1,208)

Question (d): "The terrorists demand that Israel release between 700 and 800 Lebanese Shiite Moslems now being held prisoner. Israeli leaders have said they will consider releasing the Shiites if the U.S. asks them to. What is your view: Should the U.S. ask the Israelis to release the Shiites or not?" (WP-ABC)

Question (e): "Israel is holding over 700 Lebanese prisoners. Should the U.S. government ask Israel to release those prisoners as part of a deal with the Lebanese, or should we not ask Israel to do that?" (CBS)

Question	Date	Should ask Israel	Shouldn't ask Israel	D.K.	(n)
(d)	June 17, 1985	41%	47%	12%	(508)
	Reagan's Press Conference				
(e)	June 18, 1985	35	51	14	(508)
(d)	June 19, 1985	40	51	10	(508)
(d)	June 20–22, 1985	42	48	10	(1,506)
(e)	June 26, 1985	27	61	12	(542)

Sources: (a) (c) (d): *WP-ABC Survey* 0193, 0194, 0195, and 0197 June–July 1985; *Washington Post,* June 26, 1985; (b): *Newsweek,* July 1, 1985, p. 15; (e): *CBS News Poll,* June 19, 27, 1985.

The responses to questions (d) and (e) in Table 4 indicate consistent support for Reagan's stand. This support grew after the press conference but reached a substantially higher level toward the end of the crisis.

A military operation to rescue the hostages was raised at the beginning of the crisis, but due to the dispersion of the hostages in Beirut it was quickly dropped. Yet, during the last phase of the crisis the United States moved warships to the Lebanese shore and after the release of the hostages, considered military retaliation.

In his press conference, Reagan explained:

. . . you have to be able to pinpoint the enemy. You can't just start shooting without having someone in your gun sights. . . . Again I have to say that when you think in terms of, for example, immediate force, you have to say, wait a minute, the people we're dealing with have no hesitation about murder.

Table 5 indicates that public opinion was divided on this issue. Until the release of the hostages about half of the respondents supported U.S. military action. Following the press conference, the public continued to favor a military operation but by a closer ratio. However, polls conducted after the release of the hostages indicate a reversal in public opinion. Now, for the first time since the outbreak of the crisis the majority of the public opposed military action by 56 to 32 percent.

The preceding data and analysis demonstrate that after Reagan's nationally televised press conference his approval ratings rose, especially in the Middle East category. However, the conference failed to alter the public views on the crucial issue of negotiations with the terrorists. Majorities of the samples, although smaller in size, continued to favor negotiations.

TABLE 5

U.S. Military Action

Question (a): "The U.S. should take military action against any Middle Eastern nation that is found to be aiding terrorists against Americans." (WP-ABC)

Question (b): "Even if we cannot identify all those responsible for the current skyjacking, once it is over some people think the U.S. should retaliate militarily against any group with a clear connection to the hijackers to discourage future terrorism. Others oppose this kind of response because it might kill innocent people and trigger more violence against the U.S. Which comes closer to your view?" (Newsweek-Gallup)

Question (c): "Once the hostages are safe, the U.S. should take military action in retaliation for their capture and the killing of one of them." (WP-ABC)

Question	Date	For Military Action	Against Military Action	D.K.	(n)
(a)	June 17, 1985	54%	36%	10%	(508)
	Reagan's Press Conference				
(a)	June 19, 1985	50	41	10	(508)
(a)	June 20–22, 1985	53	36	10	(1,506)
(b)	June 20–21, 1985	50	40	10	(1,016)
	Hostages Released				
(c)	July 1, 1985	32	56	13	(1,208)

Sources: See Table 4.

Conclusions

This study investigates the possible effects of nationally televised presidential addresses on public opinion. The investigation is based on comparisons between polls conducted before and after two significant televised addresses on U.S. policy toward Middle East terrorism. The polls reveal that in both cases the addresses had immediate effects on the public evaluation of Reagan's performance, particularly of his "handling of the situation in the Middle East." In the case of U.S. military involvement in Lebanon, the post speech polls registered a substantial increase in the approval ratings of the president in all the three categories. The approval ratings of his handling of foreign affairs and the situation in the Middle East changed from negative to positive. During the hostage crisis the ratings in the general and the foreign affairs categories improved, those in the handling of the crisis category rose considerably.

A comparative analysis of the polls on specific policy issues also reveal changes in public opinion following the presidential appearances. In the fall of 1983 Reagan escalated the American military involvement in Lebanon. According to the polls the public did not believe the Marines had a clear mission, disapproved of Reagan's policy, and called for the withdrawal of the troops. However, following Reagan's speech the public reversed its stands, approved of the involvement and supported the presence of the Marines in Beirut.

During the 1985 TWA hostage crisis, Reagan refused to negotiate with the terrorists or to ask Israel to comply with their demands. He was also reluctant to use force. According to the polls the public favored negotiations with the terrorists and the use of force, but agreed with the president on his refusal to officially ask Israel to release the Shiite prisoners. The polls reveal that immediately following Reagan's nationally televised press conference, a greater number of Americans supported his policy on all these issues.

The mass media played an important role in the process that started with the presidential addresses and ended with changes in public opinion. In the two cases reported here and in many other cases the media set the agenda—the reservations and the questions that the president had to answer.[23] This role is clearly evident in the context, contents and structure of specific questions and answers that appear in the media's sponsored polls. In his televised addresses Reagan mainly dealt with questions raised by the media, both in reports and public opinion polls. The polls then, were used by the media as another means to set the agenda, and in this way they affected the contents of the presidential addresses.

The president certainly used television to directly communicate a message to the public. But the media intervened in the process. Immediately after the speech reporters summarized it, and later, in the next televised news program they reported and commented on it; the next day the printed media widely reported and analyzed the speech. In the case of the press conference the media was, obviously, a significant participant. The evidence gathered in this study indicates that the special speech to the nation affected public opinion much more than the press conference. This finding is hardly surprising. The president fully controlled his speech, but in the press conference had to answer difficult and even embarassing questions.

Public opinion played a significant role in the cases examined in this study. President Reagan was aware of this role and attempted to win public support through nationally televised addresses. The evidence suggests that these appearances created more favorable opinions toward his perfomance and policy in the immediate post-address period. This effect might be all the president needs to influence decisions and behavior of terrorists.

* *Author's Note: The author acknowledges the support of the Leonard Davis Institute for International Relations at the Hebrew University in the preparation of this article.*

Notes

1. Ralph Levering, *The Public and American Foreign Policy, 1918–1978* (New York: Morrow, 1978): 31.
2. Richard Brody, "International Crises: A Rallying Point for the President?" *Public Opinion* 6 (December-January 1984): 41–43.
3. Everett C. Ladd, "The Foreign Policy Record: Reagan's Sphere of Influence," *Public Opinion* 9 (Summer 1986): 3–5.
4. Newton Minow, John Martin and Lee Mitchell, *Presidential Television* (New York: Basic Books, 1973), and Colin Seymour-Ure, *The Political Impact of the Mass Media* (Beverly Hills, California: Sage, 1974).
5. Don C. Livingston, "The Televised Presidency," *Presidential Studies Quarterly* 26 (Winter 1986): 22–30 and Austin Ranney, *Channels of Power: The Impact of Television on American Politics* (New York: Basic Books, 1983).
6. Steven Hayward, "Voice of America: Ronald Reagan and the American Rhetorical Tradition," *Policy Review* 33 (Summer 1985): 66–69.
7. Fred Smoller, "The Six O'Clock Presidency: Patterns of Network News Coverage of the President," *Presidential Studies Quarterly* 26 (Winter 1986): 31–49.
8. Controlled media is the form of electronic media over which the White House has the most influence, such as presidential addresses and political advertisements. Uncontrolled media includes the evening news, documentaries and other special or regularly scheduled programs on current affairs.
9. See Denis Rutkus, "Presidential Television," *Journal of Communication* 26 (Spring 1976): 73–78.
10. The full text of the speech was published in *The New York Times*, October 28, 1983, p. A10.
11. The full text of the press conference was published in *The New York Times*, June 19, 1985.
12. Reagan's letter to Congress on the Marines in Lebanon was published in *The New York Times*, September 29, 1982, p. 12.
13. Eytan Gilboa, *American Public Opinion Toward Israel and the Arab-Israeli Conflict* (Lexington, Mass.: Lexington Books, 1986): 149–155.
14. *New York Times*, April 19, 1986, p. 12.
15. William Quandt, "Reagan's Lebanon Policy: Trial and Error," *Middle East Journal* 38 (Spring 1984): 237–254.
16. Mark German with Kirk Brown, *Public Opinion Polls on U.S. Policy in Lebanon* (Washington, D.C.: Congressional Research Service, The Library of Congress, 1984): B-7.
17. Reagan's official statement about the withdrawal from Lebanon was published in *The New York Times*, February 8, 1984, p. 9.
18. See Gilboa, American Public Opinion, op. cit., pp. 156–157.
19. William C. Adams, "The Beirut Hostages: ABC and CBS Seize an Opportunity," *Public Opinion* 8 (August-September 1985): 45–48.
20. David Bar-Illan, "Israel, the Hostages and the Networks," *Commentary* 80 (September 1985): 33–37.
21. *ABC News-Washington Post Poll*, Survey No. 0193 and 0194, p. 6.
22. *NBC News Poll Results*, No. 106, July 8, 1985, p. 3.
23. See Anne Saldich, *Electronic Democracy: Television's Impact on the American Political Process* (New York: Praeger, 1979), and David Paletz, and Robert Entman, *Media, Power, Politics* (New York: The Free Press, 1981).

Name Index